ADAM ZAMOYSKI was born in New York but has spent most of his life in England. He was educated at Downside and The Queen's College, Oxford. A freelance historian with a singular command of languages, he has written a bestselling history of Poland, as well as three books of military history and three biographies. His most recent book is *1812: Napoleon's Fatal March on Moscow*. He is married to the artist Emma Sergeant.

Visit www.AuthorTracker.co.uk for exclusive information on your favourite HarperCollins authors.

From the reviews of *Rites of Peace*:

'Zamoyski's account of the labyrinthine twists of diplomacy is both masterly and exhaustive ... I closed this book full of admiration for its author'   MAX HASTINGS, *Sunday Times*

'An exhilarating book ... not since Margaret MacMillan's instant classic on the Treaty of Versailles has there been a book on diplomacy of such richness and readability. Zamoyski advances his case with a story-telling detail that makes his book hard to put down [and] has achieved a rare feat. He has taken the driest of diplomatic archives and turned them into a compelling narrative'
DENIS MACSHANE, *Guardian*

'Magnificent ... both an intellectual and a literary joy to read ... the work of an accomplished raconteur and a formidable scholar. I doubt there will be many more important or rewarding books than this published this year'   ALLAN MALLISON, *The Times*

'Deeply researched, elegantly written, gleaming with the political and sexual depravity of the Congress that decided the fate of Europe, Zamoyski's *Rites of Peace* is outstanding – a delicious, triumphant feast of a book'
SIMON SEBAG MONTEFIORE, *Daily Mail*

By the same author

Chopin: A Biography
The Battle for the Marchlands
Paderewski
The Polish Way
The Last King of Poland
The Forgotten Few
Holy Madness: Romantics, Patriots and Revolutionaries, 1776–1871
1812: Napoleon's Fatal March on Moscow

RITES of PEACE

The Fall of Napoleon &
the Congress of Vienna

ADAM ZAMOYSKI

HARPER PERENNIAL
London, New York, Toronto and Sydney

Harper Perennial
An imprint of HarperCollins*Publishers*
77–85 Fulham Palace Road
Hammersmith
London w6 8jb

www.harperperennial.co.uk

This edition published by Harper Perennial 2008
1

First published in Great Britain by Harper*Press* in 2007

Copyright © Adam Zamoyski 2007

Adam Zamoyski asserts the moral right to be
identified as the author of this work

A catalogue record for this book is
available from the British Library

ISBN 978-0-00-720306-2

Set in Minion by
Rowland Phototypesetting Ltd,
Bury St Edmunds, Suffolk

Printed and bound in Great Britain by
Clays Ltd, St Ives plc

Mixed Sources
Product group from well-managed
forests and other controlled sources
www.fsc.org Cert no. SW-COC-1806
© 1996 Forest Stewardship Council

FSC is a non-profit international organisation established to promote the
responsible management of the world's forests. Products carrying the FSC
label are independently certified to assure consumers that they come
from forests that are managed to meet the social, economic and
ecological needs of present and future generations.

Find out more about HarperCollins and the environment at
www.harpercollins.co.uk/green

Contents

List of Illustrations   vii
List of Maps   xi
Introduction   xiii

1   The Lion at Bay   1
2   The Saviour of Europe   15
3   The Peacemakers   35
4   A War for Peace   49
5   Intimate Congress   64
6   Farce in Prague   82
7   The Play for Germany   98
8   The First Waltzes   118
9   A Finger in the Pie   137
10   Battlefield Diplomacy   151
11   Paris Triumph   169
12   Peace   185
13   The London Round   204
14   Just Settlements   218
15   Setting the Stage   238
16   Points of Order   260
17   Notes and Balls   280
18   Kings' Holiday   296

19 A Festival of Peace   314
20 *Guerre de Plume*   329
21 Political Carrousel   341
22 Explosive Diplomacy   358
23 Dance of War   371
24 War and Peace   385
25 The Saxon Deal   404
26 Unfinished Business   420
27 The Flight of the Eagle   442
28 The Hundred Days   455
29 The Road to Waterloo   470
30 Wellington's Victory   487
31 The Punishment of France   499
32 Last Rites   515
33 Discordant Concert   531
34 The Arrest of Europe   550

Notes   571
Bibliography   599
Index   619

Illustrations

Napoleon in March 1812, shortly before his disastrous Russian campaign. (© *Collection Viollet*)

General Armand de Caulaincourt. (*Musée des Beaux-Arts, Besançon/ Bridgeman Art Library*)

Tsar Alexander I of Russia. (*The Royal Collection © 2007 Her Majesty Queen Elizabeth II, photograph by Rodney Todd-White*)

Alexander's friend and adviser on international affairs, the Polish Prince Adam Czartoryski. (*Private collection*)

Frederick William III of Prussia. (*Berlin, Stiftung Preuss, Kulturbesitz/AKG Images*)

Austria's Foreign Minister Metternich. (*AKG Images*)

Francis I of Austria. (*Wetliche und Geistliche Schatzkammer, Vienna/ Bridgeman Art Library*)

Britain's Foreign Secretary Lord Castlereagh. (*The Royal Collection © 2007 Her Majesty Queen Elizabeth II, photograph by Rodney Todd-White*)

The Prussian chancellor, Baron August von Hardenberg. (*The Royal Collection © 2007 Her Majesty Queen Elizabeth II, photograph by Rodney Todd-White*)

Russia's acting Foreign Minister, Count Charles Nesselrode. (*The Royal Collection © 2007 Her Majesty Queen Elizabeth II, photograph by Rodney Todd-White*)

Friedrich von Gentz, Secretary to the Congress of Vienna. *(AKG Images)*

Karl Heinrich vom Stein. *(LWL-Landesmuseum für Kunst und Kulturgeschichte Münster/Sabine Ahlbrand-Dornseif)*

Wilhelmina, Princess of Sagan. *(Photo RMN/ © Gérard Blot)*

General Charles Murray, Earl Cathcart, British ambassador to the court of Russia. *(National Portrait Gallery, London)*

Sir Charles Stewart, British ambassador to the court of Prussia. *(National Portrait Gallery, London)*

The Prussian linguist, philosopher and ambassador to Vienna, Wilhelm von Humboldt. *(The Royal Collection © 2007 Her Majesty Queen Elizabeth II, photograph by Rodney Todd-White)*

George Gordon, Earl of Aberdeen, Castlereagh's envoy to the Austrian court. *(Reproduced by kind permission of The National Trust for Scotland)*

King Frederick Augustus of Saxony. *(AKG Images)*

Jean-Baptiste Bernadotte, Crown Prince of Sweden. *(The National Museum of Fine Arts, Stockholm, photograph by Erik Cornelius)*

King Maximilian I of Bavaria. *(The Art Archive/Miramare Museum Trieste/Dagli Orti A)*

Frederick I, King of Württemberg. *(AKG Images)*

Tsar Alexander is cheered by the inhabitants of Paris as he passes through the Porte Saint-Denis at the head of his troops on 31 March 1814, with King Frederick William of Prussia at his side. *(Musée de la Ville de Paris/Musée Carnavalet, Paris/Bridgeman Art Library)*

A French view of the capitulation of Paris, 30 March 1814. *(Musée de la Ville de Paris/Musée Carnavalet, Paris/Bridgeman Art Library)*

France's brilliant, pragmatic and versatile Foreign Minister Charles-Maurice de Talleyrand-Périgord. *(Château de Valencay/ Lauros/Giraudon/Bridgeman Art Library)*

Alexander's sister, the Grand Duchess Catherine. *(Photo RMN/ © Droits réservés)*

Alexander and the Grand Duchess take their leave of the Prince Regent at Petworth House on 24 June 1814. (© *NTPL/Derrick E. Witty*)

Metternich's official residence, the Austrian State Chancellery on the Ballhausplatz in Vienna. (*Historisches Museum der Stadt Wien*)

Metternich's study in the State Chancellery. (*Historisches Museum der Stadt Wien*)

Metternich's elegant villa on the Rennweg, just outside Vienna's old town. (*Austrian National Library, Vienna, Picture Archive*)

Since all the silver and gold flatware of the Austrian imperial household had been melted down to pay for the war of 1809, an enormous porcelain service simulating gold was run up for use at the congress. (*Ehemalige Hofsilber und Tafellkammer*)

The notorious Princess Catharine Bagration, 'the naked angel'. (*Photo RMN/© Michèle Bellot*)

Talleyrand's mistress Dorothée, comtesse de Périgord. (*From* Metternich and the Duchess *by Dorothy Giles McGuigan*)

Francis I welcomes Tsar Alexander and Frederick William III outside Vienna on 25 September 1814. (*AKG Images*)

A ball in the indoor riding school of Vienna's imperial palace. (*Historisches Museum der Stadt Wien*)

Lady Emily Castlereagh. Portrait by Lawrence. (*Reproduced by kind permission of the Marquess of Londonderry*)

Frederick VI of Denmark. (*The Museum of National History, Frederiksborg Castle, photograph by Lennart Larsen*)

Frederick VI's mistress in Vienna, Caroline Seufert. (*De Danske Kongres Kronologiske Samling*)

The Pope's envoy to the congress, Cardinal Ercole Consalvi. (*Bridgeman Art Library*)

The 'Festival of Peace' in the Prater in Vienna on 18 October 1814. (*Historisches Museum der Stadt Wien*)

The spectacular medieval Carrousel held at the riding school of Vienna's imperial palace on 23 November 1814. (*Gesellschaft der Musikfreunde, Vienna*)

The Congress of Vienna as imagined by Isabey. *(The Royal Collection © 2007 Her Majesty Queen Elizabeth II, photograph by DB)*

How the outside world saw the congress. *(Musée de la Ville de Paris/ Musée Carnavalet, Paris/Bridgeman Art Library)*

Count Ioannis Capodistrias. *(AKG Images)*

Minutes, taken by Gentz, of a conference of the five great powers on 8 February 1815. *(Author's collection)*

A page from one of Hardenberg's proposals on how to restore Prussia to her former great-power status, showing which areas of Saxony would give her the requisite number of 'souls'. *(Author's collection)*

The imperial sleighing party held on 22 January 1815. *(Historisches Museum der Stadt Wien)*

The Duke of Wellington, who replaced Castlereagh at the congress on 1 February 1815. *(V&A Images/Victoria and Albert Museum)*

Maps

Europe at the end of 1812	8/9
Central Europe at the beginning of 1813	10
The rise and fall of Prussia, 1700–1807	22/23
Habsburg losses, 1792–1810	36
War and diplomacy, June–September 1813	53
The 'historic' and 'natural' borders of France	127
The Netherlands	139
The grand duchy of Warsaw, 1807 and after 1809	161
The Treaty of Paris	198
Europe in 1792 and 1814	223
Denmark	226
Italy – the final settlement	231
The Confederation of the Rhine	242
The Bavarian–Austrian exchange. The eventual deal	267
Russia's western frontier	359
The Saxon and Polish settlements	408
Switzerland	422
The second Treaty of Paris	503
The German Confederation	527
Prussia satisfied	535
Europe in 1815 and 1871	556/557

Introduction

The reconstruction of Europe at the Congress of Vienna is probably the most seminal episode in modern history. Not only did the congress redraw the map entirely. It determined which nations were to have a political existence over the next hundred years and which were not. It imposed an ideology on the whole Continent, derived from the interests of four great powers. It attempted to set in stone the agreement between those powers, with the result that their expansionist urges were deflected into Africa and southern Asia. It entirely transformed the conduct of international affairs. Its consequences, direct and indirect, include all that has taken place in Europe since, including aggressive nationalism, Bolshevism, fascism, the two world wars and, ultimately, the creation of the European Union.

The action was played out in a dramatic series of shifts of fortune, by some of the most fascinating characters of European history. At its heart stood Napoleon, fighting desperately for his throne, yet undermining his chances with every move he made and seeming to court disaster with apparent abandon. On the other side, Tsar Alexander of Russia, by now convinced of a divine calling to save the world, could not see that he posed a threat to it in the eyes of everyone else. The consummate political puppeteer Metternich excelled himself as he cajoled and manipulated in order to mould events to his own vision of a safe world. The vulpine Talleyrand weaved about in a desperate attempt to save something for France, and himself, from the wreckage of Napoleon's empire. The eminently likeable Castlereagh, a thoroughly decent man in every respect, found himself cutting up nations and trading souls as ruthlessly as any practitioner of *realpolitik*. A host of other characters took their places in this great carnival at one time or another, including the Duke of Wellington, who revealed himself to be as good a statesman as he was a general, and a fascinating array of women, who played on the passions and frustrated ambitions of the great men of Europe, leading to moments of high tragedy and low farce. From gore-spattered battlefield and roadside hovel to the gilded boudoirs and ballrooms of Vienna, the scene of the action is eminently worthy of the grandeur and the squalor of the proceedings. And history has passed down an image of courtly elegance and waltzing frivolity familiar to most educated people.

Yet when I typed the words 'Congress of Vienna' into the British Library catalogue, I was rewarded with a list of books on: the First International Meteorological Congress, the Congress on the Biochemical Problems of Lipids, the European Regional Science Association Congress, on congresses statistical, sexual and philatelistic, on the congresses of Applied Chemistry, of Bibliophiles, of Dermatology, of Genealogical and Heraldic Sciences, Varicose Veins, Exfoliative Cytology, Birth Defects, Hepatitis B, Electroencephalography, Clinical Neurophysiology, and many, many more, all held in Vienna over the past century or so. Buried amongst these enticing titles were no more than half a dozen which related to the events of 1814–15.

Further searches revealed that literature on the subject is indeed elusive. It is also extremely one-sided and subjective. The voluminous and dense German studies, mostly produced during the nineteenth-century unification of Germany or during the period of Nazi rule, respond to a demanding agenda. The latest French contribution is entitled '*Le Congrès de Vienne. L'Europe Contre la France*', which sums up a viewpoint characteristic of much French writing on the subject. British studies are marked by an ineffable condescension, based on ignorance of conditions in Europe and a conviction that Britain was a disinterested, and therefore impartial and benign, party. Whatever their provenance, most existing books on the congress are superficial in nature, and the best ones are, ironically, those that honestly set out to cover only the social and sexual side of the proceedings. In short, there is no satisfactory general study of the episode, and as a result most people know little about it, aside from the fact that a great deal of dancing took place.

The reasons for this became clear as I began to grapple with the complexities of the subject. The first is that the Congress of Vienna never actually took place in any formal sense. Just as 'Yalta' stands for negotiations and agreements from 1943 to 1945 and even beyond, 'the Congress of Vienna' is a blanket term for a process that began in the summer of 1812 and did not end until ten years later. As usual in such a long-drawn-out process, it is the minor details left unresolved in the very early stages of the negotiations that come to dominate and distort the proceedings at the crucial final stages. There is therefore no way of producing a comprehensive and comprehensible account of the episode without covering a very long period, which involves a great deal of work and dictates a more complex book than many a historian would wish to embark on.

Another, equally important, factor is the need for anyone intending to approach this subject to have a command of as many European languages as possible. The negotiations of 1812–15 can be likened to a game of poker, and as in poker, the course of the game only becomes comprehensible if one can see what cards each of the players holds and how he plays them. In addition, and this is an aspect that has probably been most difficult for historians brought up in other times to deal with, it is necessary to be able to empathise with the desires and the fears of every player, otherwise their moves and reactions make no sense. The reason it nearly came to war several times during the Congress of Vienna was not that Prussia was being gratuitously aggressive, Russia perverse, or Austria devious, but that each was in dread of being outmanoeuvred by the others.

In writing this book, I set out to give as full an account as possible of the negotiations that led to the peace settlement, in the hope that the succession of events will add up to some explanation of how it was reached. I have tried to present the hopes and fears of each side as dispassionately, but with as much sympathy, as possible, in the firm conviction that there were no 'good' or 'bad' players, merely frightened ones.

The scope of the brief I set myself did not permit me to dwell as long as I would have liked on the politics of the Bourbon restorations, the complex mix of forces attending the resolution of the problem of Italy, let alone the complexities of the German question. One of the most important, if not *the* most important, elements in what we term the Congress of Vienna is the territorial and constitutional reorganisation of Germany, and I have certainly not devoted as much space to this subject as one ought; but I make no apology. It is a story of such layered intricacy that only a seasoned scholar of German history could attempt to do it justice, and only one scarcely less well versed would be able to follow the resulting account. In order to arrive at a comprehensible picture of the congress in its essentials it is necessary to leave aside many contingent issues, however fascinating they might be.

Similarly, in order to make the account easier to follow, I have focused on the principal players and avoided naming some of their second-rank collaborators or antagonists. The numbers of people joining in this great scramble for land, power and influence were so great that many an interesting sub-plot has had to be dropped.

If there is a dearth of good books on the congress, there is no lack of published first-hand evidence, making it virtually unnecessary to delve into archival sources. Not only the acts and treaties, but also the memoranda, *notes verbales*, proclamations, *démarches* and other tools of negotiation have been printed, as have the correspondence of the principal protagonists, their diaries and memoirs. Those of dozens of other participants and onlookers have also been published, as have some of the reports of the Austrian secret police. I did nevertheless make use of some archival sources, partly out of a wish to penetrate closer the workings of the process – there is nothing like holding an original document in one's hand for understanding the form a relationship or a negotiation took. And when I did explore archives I became aware of the fact that some of the printed primary sources are not as reliable as one would wish, and that the decisions taken at a given meeting were not always recorded the same way by all the parties. I therefore resorted to archival sources for some of the more crucial moments in the negotiations.

On the vexed question of place names, consistency is difficult to achieve considering the areas covered by the action. I have tended to use the names which were in current use at the time, with the modern names in brackets after the first mention. I have, therefore, kept to the ubiquitous German spelling when referring to the Treaty of Kalisch, even though the town was then formally in the grand duchy of Warsaw and therefore known as Kalisz. But in the case of capitals and larger cities I have used the modern English form. Thus I refer to Frankfurt in that form, even though the city was universally referred to as Frankfort at the time.

In the interests of readability, I have given no more than one source reference per paragraph, and placed it at the end. The order in which the sources are listed accords with the order of facts or quotations in the text.

I would like to thank Aleksandr Sapozhnikov of the National Library of Russia's manuscript department for his help in providing me with the diaries of Mikhailovskii-Danilevskii, and Galina Babkova for obtaining copies of other documents and articles from Russia. I owe a debt of gratitude to Ole Villumsen Krog, Director of the Royal Silver Room in Copenhagen, for his help and his kindness in making available his invaluable work on the Congress of Vienna, and my researcher in matters Danish, Marie-Louise Møller Lange. Also to Barbara Prout of the Bibliothèque Publique et Universitaire de Genève for sending me copies of manuscripts in that library, and Jennifer

Irwin for her searches at the Public Record Office of Northern Ireland. Angelica von Hase was enormously helpful in penetrating the German literature on the congress and in providing translations of some sources. I am indebted to Barbara de Nicolay for guiding me through the intricacies of the dispute over the duchy of Bouillon. I am grateful to Professor Isabel de Madariaga, Emmanuel de Waresquiel and Dr Philip Mansel for their helpful advice, to Shervie Price for reading the typescript and Richard Foreman for his invaluable advice on titles. I greatly appreciate the reassuring support I received from Richard Johnson, and his forbearance on the subject of deadlines. Robert Lacey has been an exemplary editor and, once again, saved me from making an ass of myself. Perhaps the most noteworthy contribution came from Sophie-Caroline de Margerie, who suggested the subject to me in the first place. And, this time too, my wife Emma has stopped me from going mad, and made life worth living throughout.

Adam Zamoyski
London, January 2007

The Lion at Bay

The clock of the Tuileries had begun striking the last quarter before midnight when a mud-spattered carriage of the ungainly kind known as a *chaise de poste*, drawn at the gallop by four tired horses, swung onto the parade ground in front of the palace. Ignorant of court etiquette, the coachman drove under the central span of the triumphal arch of the Carrousel, reserved exclusively for the Emperor, before the drowsy sentries had time to bar his way. 'That is a good omen,' exclaimed one of the two men sitting inside the carriage, a plump man in a voluminous pelisse with a fur bonnet hiding much of his face.

The vehicle came to a stop at the main doorway, under the clock, and its occupants clambered down. The first, who was the taller of the two, had unbuttoned his greatcoat, revealing a chest covered in gold braid, so the sentries let him and his companion through unchallenged, assuming them to be senior officers bearing urgent despatches.

The two men walked briskly down to the end of the vaulted passage and knocked at a large door. After a while, the concierge appeared in his nightshirt, holding a lantern. The taller of the two men identified himself as the Imperial Master of the Horse, but the concierge and his sleepy wife, who had joined him, took some convincing that the man standing before them was indeed General de Caulaincourt. The uniform was right, but the man's hair was long and unkempt, his face was weatherbeaten and covered with a two-weeks' growth of stubble, and he looked more like a stage bandit than a senior dignitary of the imperial court.

The concierge's wife opened the door, saying that the Empress had just retired for the night, while her husband went off to summon the duty footmen so they could show in the newcomers. Yawning and rubbing her eyes, she shifted her attention to the other man. Although the flickering lantern lit up only a small part of his face, between the high collar of the pelisse and the fur bonnet pressed over his brow, she thought she recognised the Emperor. That seemed impossible. Only two days before, Paris had been stunned by the twenty-ninth *Bulletin de la Grande Armée*, which announced that he was struggling through the snows of Russia with his beleaguered army.

The two men were led down a gallery, open to the gardens on the right, and turned left into the Empress's apartments. They came in just as her ladies-in-waiting were emerging from her private apartment, having attended her to bed. The ladies started with fright at the sight of the bearded man in his dirty greatcoat, but when he announced that he was the bearer of news from the Emperor they recognised Caulaincourt, and one of them went back into the Empress's apartment to announce the Master of the Horse.

Unable to control his impatience, the shorter of the two men brushed past his companion and made for the door to the Empress's apartment. His pelisse had fallen open, revealing the uniform of the Grenadiers of the Old Guard, and as he marched confidently across the room there was no mistaking the Emperor Napoleon. 'Good night, Caulaincourt,' he said over his shoulder. 'You also need rest.'[1]

It was something of an understatement. The General had not slept in a bed for over eight weeks, and had hardly lain down in the past two; he had travelled over 3,000 kilometres in unspeakable conditions, often under fire, all the way from Moscow. Before that he had taken part in the gruelling advance into Russia, which wasted the finest army in Europe, and seen his adored younger brother killed at the battle of Borodino. He had watched Moscow burn. He had borne the hardships and witnessed the horrors of the disastrous retreat, which had brought the death toll to over half a million French and allied soldiers.

Perhaps the most difficult thing to bear for the thirty-nine-year-old General Armand de Caulaincourt, Duke of Vicenza, an accomplished soldier and diplomat, was that he had been obliged to watch all his worst prophecies come true. As Napoleon's ambassador to Russia from 1807 to 1811 he had done everything in his power to keep the two empires from conflict. He had repeatedly begged Napoleon not to make war on Russia, warning him that it was impossible to win against such an opponent. He had continued to make his case as they travelled across Europe to join the army massing against Russia. Once the campaign had begun he had attempted time and again to persuade Napoleon to cut his losses – while remaining utterly loyal, Caulaincourt was never afraid to speak his mind. All to no avail.

On 5 December 1812, as the remnants of his army struggled along the last leg of the retreat, Napoleon had decided to leave it and race back to Paris. He handed over command to his brother-in-law Joachim Murat, King of Naples, with firm instructions to rally the Grande Armée at Vilna (Vilnius) in Lithuania, which was well stocked with supplies and reinforcements, and to hold that at all costs.

He had set off with Caulaincourt in his travelling *coupé*, which was followed by two other carriages bearing three generals and a couple of valets. They were escorted by a squadron of Chasseurs and another of Polish Chevau-Légers of the Old Guard, and briefly by some Neapolitan cavalry. At one point the convoy narrowly missed being intercepted by marauding Russian cossacks. Napoleon had a pair of loaded pistols placed in his *coupé* and instructed his companions to kill him if he failed to do so himself in the event of capture.[2]

Caulaincourt remained constantly at his side, even when they left their escort and companions behind, changing from carriage to improvised sleigh to carriage and to sleigh once again, breaking axles and running half a dozen vehicles into the ground as they flew from

Vilna to Warsaw, Dresden, Leipzig, Weimar, Erfurt, Mainz and eventually to Paris, which they reached in the last minutes of 18 December.

But before he could go home to bed, Caulaincourt had to perform one last duty. He went to the house of the Arch-Chancellor of the Empire, Jean Jacques de Cambacérès, and, after waking him up with the astonishing news of the Emperor's return, instructed him to make the necessary arrangements for the regular imperial *lever* to take place in the morning. Napoleon wanted an immediate resumption of everyday normality.

When on campaign, Napoleon would publish *Bulletins de la Grande Armée* at regular intervals to keep his subjects informed of his actions and to present a heroic picture of his doings. In the twenty-ninth *Bulletin*, published on 16 December, they had for the first time read less than glorious news. It informed them that he had been obliged to abandon Moscow and that his army had suffered terrible losses as a result of the winter weather. Reading between the lines, they could detect a major disaster. But the *Bulletin* ended with the words: 'The Emperor's health has never been better.' His intention was that, two days after hearing the worst, the citizens of France should be able to recover their confidence, with the knowledge that their master was back and in control.

Napoleon's principal reason for abandoning his army and returning to Paris was to muster fresh forces with which to march out and reinforce it in the spring. But there were other motives. One was that he preferred to have his less than reliable Austrian and German allies in front of him rather than at his back. Another, more weighty, was the urgent need he felt to reassert his authority at home. He had been away from his capital for over seven months, and during that time had conducted the affairs of state from his headquarters. This had worked remarkably well, and he had continued to invigilate and order everything from foreign policy to the repertoire of the Paris theatres.

But on the night of 23 October, while he was beginning his retreat from Moscow, an obscure General by the name of Malet and a handful of other officers had attempted to seize power in Paris, claiming that the Emperor was dead. They came very close to success, and although Malet and his accomplices were tried and shot before Napoleon even came to hear of the attempted coup, it had disturbed him profoundly when he did. It revealed to him the frailty of the foundations of his throne, and gave him much food for thought.

On the morning of 19 December the cannon of the Invalides delivered a salute that announced to the astonished citizens of Paris that the Emperor was back in the capital. They were still stunned by the news of his failure in Russia, and eager for further details and some kind of explanation. The sense of anticipation was particularly keen among the officials and courtiers who hurried to the *lever*. But they were disappointed. The Emperor was stern and uncommunicative, and quickly disappeared into his study, to which he summoned his principal ministers.

He was in no mood to give explanations, but rather to demand them, as the representatives of the legislative and administrative bodies discovered when they called on him the following day to pay their respects. He brought up the matter of the Malet conspiracy to show them up as weak, cowardly and ineffectual. What had touched a particularly raw nerve was that the news of his death in Russia, announced by Malet, had led those who believed it to consider a change of regime, instead of making them proclaim the succession of his son, the King of Rome. 'Our forefathers rallied to the cry: "*The King is dead, long live the King!*"' he reminded them, adding that 'These few words encompass the principal advantages of monarchy.' That they had not been uttered on the night of 23 October revealed to him that for all its trappings, the monarchy he had created lacked consistency, and he was still just a general who had seized power, a *parvenu* with no title to rule beyond his ability to hold on to it. He felt this setback personally, and the sense of insecurity it induced would have a profound effect on how he behaved over the next two years, making him more aggressive and less amenable, and leading inexorably to his downfall.[3]

*   *   *

Before he embarked on his fatal Russian campaign, in the summer of 1812, Napoleon had been the undisputed master of Europe, wielding greater power than any Roman Emperor. The French Empire and its direct dependencies included the whole of Belgium, Holland and the North Sea coast up to Hamburg, the Rhineland, the whole of Switzerland, Piedmont and Liguria, Tuscany, the Papal States, Illyria (present-day Slovenia and Croatia) and Catalonia as well as France. All the minor states of Germany, including the kingdoms of Saxony, Westphalia, Bavaria and Württemberg, had been incorporated into the Confederation of the Rhine, the Rheinbund, which was an entirely subservient ally of France, as were the grand duchy of Warsaw, the kingdom of Italy, the kingdom of Naples and Spain. Several of these were ruled by Napoleon's siblings or relatives, or connected to him through dynastic marriages. Denmark and Russia were locked into more or less permanent alliance with France, Austria and Prussia were unlikely allies, and in Continental Europe only Sweden remained outside the Napoleonic system.

While there were many who resented this French stranglehold, others either welcomed or at least accepted it. The only open challenge Napoleon faced was from Britain, but while she was supreme on the seas, her only foothold on the Continent was in Spain, where General Wellington's army was operating alongside Spanish regular and guerrilla forces opposed to the rule of Napoleon's brother Joseph. But Britain was also engaged in a difficult and costly war with the United States of America, which restricted her military potential.

The disasters of the Russian campaign had changed all this, but not as profoundly as one might think. Although he was now at war with Russia and had lost an army trying to cow her into submission, Napoleon's overall position had not altered. His system and his alliances were still in place, and the situation in Spain had actually improved, with the setbacks of the summer reversed and the British and Spanish forces under Wellington repulsed.

The only possible threat to his system at this stage could come from Germany, whose many rulers, beginning with Frederick William of Prussia, found his alliance increasingly onerous, and whose people burned with resentment of their French allies. But Prussia had been reduced to a minor power and bled economically by France over the past few years, while the other monarchs were too weak and too mistrustful of each other to present a credible challenge, and Austria was in no position to make war after her crushing defeat in 1809. Any who still dreamt of throwing off the French hegemony had to take into account the remains of the Grande Armée in Poland and a string of French garrisons in fortresses across Germany.

Napoleon's self-confidence had not been seriously shaken by the events of 1812. He had blundered politically and militarily, and he had lost a fine army. But he knew – and so, despite the Russian propaganda, did most of the experienced commanders of Europe – that he had been victorious in battle throughout. 'My losses are substantial, but the enemy can take no credit for them,' as he put it in a letter to the King of Denmark. And he could always raise a new army.[4]

France was still the most powerful state on the Continent. Russia had no comparable reserves of power or wealth, and had suffered greatly from the devastations of war in the previous year. With the benefit of hindsight Napoleon's reputation and the basis of his power had been damaged beyond repair, but at the time it was clear to all that his position remained unassailable as long as he kept his nerve and consolidated his resources. And that is what he set about doing.

At Warsaw, on his way back to Paris, he had stopped just long enough to assure the Polish ministers that the situation was under control and that he would be back in the spring with a new army. At Dresden a few days later, he reassured his ally the King of Saxony and urged him to raise more troops. From there he also wrote to his father-in-law, the Emperor of Austria, saying that everything was under control and asking him to double the contingent of Austrian troops operating alongside the Grande Armée to 60,000. He also asked him to send an ambassador to Paris, so that they might communicate more easily.[5]

On his return to Paris he set to work at rebuilding his forces. Before

Europe at the end of 1812

St Petersburg

Stockholm

EN

BALTIC
SEA

Moscow

Smolensk

Vilna

RUSSIAN

Danzig

Minsk

EMPIRE

RUSSIA

GRAND DUCHY

Poznan   OF   Warsaw
WARSAW
Zamość

Kiev

Kraków

enna

AUSTRIAN EMPIRE

Odessa

Buda   Pest

Bucharest

Belgrade

ian Provinces

Sofia

O   T   T

NGDOM

Constantinople

OF

M   A   N   E   M   P   I   R   E

NAPLES

Corfu

Key

French Empire
and dependencies

Ionian Islands
(Br.)

French Satellites

Crete

French Allies

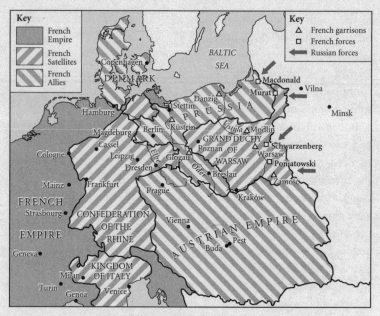

Central Europe at the beginning of 1813

leaving he had given orders for the call-up of the age group which should have been liable to conscription in 1814, and this had yielded 140,000 young men who were already being put through their paces in depots. He also had at his disposal 100,000 men of the National Guard which he had set up as a home defence force before leaving for Russia. Mindful of the political situation in France, he now created a new force, the *Gardes d'Honneur*, made up from the young scions of aristocratic families and those opposed to his rule, drawn from the depths of the most royalist provinces. The improved situation in Spain allowed him to withdraw four Guard regiments, the mounted gendarmerie and some Polish cavalry from the peninsula. And he instructed his other allies in Germany to raise more troops to support him.

According to his calculations he still had 150,000 men holding the eastern wall of his imperium, with at least 60,000 under Murat at Vilna, 25,000 under Macdonald to the north, 30,000 Austrian allies to the south under Schwarzenberg, Poniatowski's Polish corps and the remainder of the Saxon contingent under Reynier covering Warsaw, and over 25,000 men in reserve depots or fortresses from Danzig (Gdańsk) on the Baltic down to Zamość. He was therefore confident that he would be able to take the field in Germany with some 350,000 men in the spring.[6]

But less than a week after his return to Paris, on Christmas Eve, bad news came in from Lithuania. As the remnants of the Grande Armée straggled into what they thought was the safe haven of Vilna, the men's endurance had given way to the need for rest. Murat had failed to organise an adequate defence, and the advancing Russians were able to overrun the city with ease. The confusion and panic had prevented an orderly evacuation even by those units still capable of action, and a couple of days later not many more than 10,000 men crossed the river Niemen out of Russia. Napoleon was devastated by the news. He bitterly regretted having left Murat in charge, and dreaded the propaganda value of the event. But within a day or two he put it behind him, assuring Caulaincourt that it was an unimportant setback.[7]

He was certainly not going to allow it to alter his plans or dent his confidence. The requested ambassador of Emperor Francis of Austria had arrived in Paris. He was General Count Ferdinand Bubna, a distinguished soldier whom Napoleon knew well and liked. In the course of their first interview, on the evening of 31 December, Bubna delivered an offer on the part of Austria to help negotiate a peace between France and Russia. Napoleon dismissed it.

He certainly wanted peace, probably more fervently than any of his enemies. He was forty-three years old. 'I am growing heavy and too fat not to like rest, not to need it, not to regard the displacements and activity demanded by war as a great fatigue,' he confessed to Caulaincourt. His only reason for making war on Russia in 1812 had been to oblige Tsar Alexander to enforce a blockade that he believed would bring Britain to the negotiating table.[8]

With nothing better to do during their long drive from Lithuania to Paris, Napoleon had delivered himself, copiously and unstoppably, of his thoughts, occasionally pinching the cheek or pulling the ear of his travelling companion, as was his wont. Fortunately for posterity, Caulaincourt listened carefully and jotted down these ramblings whenever the Emperor fell into a doze or they stopped to change horses. Napoleon again and again asserted that he longed only for peace and stability in Europe, and that the other Continental powers were blind not to see that their real enemy was Britain, with her monopoly on maritime power and trade. Any peace that did not include Britain was of no value, and Britain was not prepared to envisage a peace on terms acceptable to France. She needed to be forced into compromise.

Three days after dismissing the Austrian offer of mediation Napoleon held a conference with his senior advisers on foreign affairs. The main question discussed was whether it would be better to try to strike a deal directly with Russia, over the heads and possibly at the expense of Austria and Prussia, or to bank on Austria as the principal ally and potential negotiator. The Arch-Chancellor Cambacérès, the former Foreign Minister Talleyrand and Caulaincourt advised the first course of action, the actual Foreign Minister Maret and the others opted for the second. As usual during such conferences, Napoleon listened without committing himself to either course. There would be plenty of time to decide, as he did not intend to negotiate from anything but a position of strength. He would be in that position when he reappeared in Germany at the head of a fresh army, and in the meantime he must concentrate on mustering one.[9]

This was proceeding well. 'Everything is in motion,' he wrote to his chief of staff Marshal Berthier on 9 January 1813. 'There is nothing lacking, neither men, nor money, nor good will.' The only things that were in short supply, he admitted, were officers and a backbone of tried soldiers, but he was confident he would find these among the remains of the Grande Armée, since it was officers and NCOs who generally made up the majority of the survivors. But that very evening, as he returned from a performance at the Théâtre Français, he received an unwelcome piece of news and one with alarming implications.[10]

Prussia had been forced into alliance with France and had contributed an army corps to the invasion of Russia. But popular resentment of France was strong, particularly in northern and eastern parts of the country. It was also strong in the army. On 30 December 1812 General Yorck von Wartemburg, commander of the Prussian corps in the Grande Armée, detached it from the French units and effectively signed his own alliance with Russia. As well as making it impossible to hold the line of defence the French had taken up, forcing them to fall back to the Vistula, this development also raised questions about Prussia's loyalty.

Following fast on this news came the assurance that the King of Prussia, Frederick William III, had denounced the move and issued orders dismissing Yorck from his command. Napoleon's ambassador in Berlin, the comte de Saint-Marsan, sent reassuring reports of Prussia's loyalty, and on 12 January the news that Frederick William was entertaining the thought of marrying his son the Crown Prince to a princess of the Bonaparte family to cement the alliance between the two courts. A few days later, Frederick William's special envoy Prince Hatzfeldt arrived in Paris.[11]

Napoleon was receiving similarly encouraging reports from Vienna. He did not for a moment doubt that his father-in-law the Emperor Francis would stand by him to the end: he was so besotted by his wife Marie-Louise and his son the King of Rome that he assumed Francis must share those feelings for his daughter and grandson. But Francis did not make policy on his own. 'Our alliance with France is so necessary that if you were to break it off today, we would propose to re-establish it tomorrow on the very same conditions,' the Austrian Foreign Minister Metternich had told Napoleon's ambassador in Vienna, Count Otto. Napoleon nevertheless remained on his guard, and decided to replace Otto with someone who could take a fresh look at the situation in Vienna. For this role he chose the comte de Narbonne.[12]

While his recruits were being uniformed and trained, Napoleon attended to the everyday business of government, and relaxed by going hunting at Fontainebleau. He took the opportunity to visit Pope Pius VII, who had been living there as his prisoner following the French occupation of the Papal States in 1809. After some brisk bargaining, Napoleon signed a new concordat with him. This was expedient, as his treatment of the Pope had needlessly antagonised Catholics not only in France, but in the domains of his south German and Austrian allies. But the terms of the agreement were so humiliating that they failed to placate them.

On 14 February he attended the opening of the Legislative Assembly, and made a speech in which he announced that he ardently desired peace. He would do everything to further it, but warned that he would never sign a treaty that would dishonour France. He painted a reassuring picture of the state of international affairs, declaring that the Bonaparte dynasty was secure in Spain, and that there was nothing to fear from the situation in Germany. 'I am satisfied with the conduct of all my allies,' he stated. 'I will not abandon any of them; I shall defend the integrity of their possessions. The Russians will be forced back into their horrible climate.'[13]

The Saviour of Europe

'Gentlemen, you have saved not only Russia, you have saved Europe,' Tsar Alexander had declared to his generals in Vilna on 12 December 1812, shortly after the last French stragglers had left the city. The truth of both assertions is questionable, but it hardly mattered. Thirty-four years old, personable and chivalrous, Alexander was widely perceived as the *beau idéal* of monarchy. His refusal to be cowed by Napoleon and his stalwart defence of his country had inspired universal respect. Although he was almost entirely German, the curious mix of exoticism and spirituality with which European opinion endowed most things Russian lent him an aura of glamour and righteousness, and he was seen as a champion by all those who believed that Europe needed salvation.[1]

But while he felt a consuming urge not to disappoint them, he had no clear idea of how that salvation was to be brought about. His intentions were certainly admirable. 'He wished that all men could help each other like brothers, assisting one another in their mutual needs, and that free commerce could be the underlying bond of society,' according to a young lady to whom he opened his heart at this crucial moment. But he lacked the necessary conviction and determination. 'I sometimes want to hit my head against the wall,' he told her, 'and if I could honourably change my condition, I would willingly do so, for there is none more difficult than mine, and I have no vocation for the throne.'[2]

There was much truth in this. Although kind and generous by temperament, Alexander was quick to take umbrage. Being both weak in character and stubborn, he was easy to influence but difficult to manage. The progressive upbringing to which he had been subjected had destroyed his self-confidence, while his education had been entirely incompatible with his predicament as absolute monarch of the most theocratic and traditionalist power in Europe. They had left him pathetically eager to please, yet determined to prove himself a strong ruler.

'He would willingly have consented to make everyone free, as long as everyone willingly did what he wanted,' in the words of a close friend. He was in thrall to the ideals of the Enlightenment, and liked to project an image of himself as a benefactor of mankind, a tendency that developed with time into a sense of spiritual destiny which would take him very far from those ideals. 'More than ever,' he wrote to his friend Aleksandr Galitzine in January 1813, as he contemplated the salvation of Europe, 'I resign myself to the will of God and submit blindly to His decrees.'[3]

Alexander had ascended the Russian throne in 1801 at the age of twenty-three, following the assassination of his father Paul I, an event in which he had been heavily implicated. He had promptly set up a 'Secret Committee' of close friends who thought like him to assist him in planning the fundamental reform of the Russian state. The one singled out to consider foreign policy was Prince Adam Czartoryski, who funnelled Alexander's utopian urges into a grand project for a future 'system' to govern all international relations.

In common with a number of other European statesmen, Czartoryski believed that the old system of diplomacy, involving a never-ending pursuit of parity based on achieving a necessarily elusive balance of power, was pointless as well as morally unacceptable. He came up with a blueprint for a supranational security system based on federations of smaller states, grouped according to linguistic or cultural affinities, which would lack both the desire for conquest and the cohesion to make war effectively except in self-defence. Alexander was greatly taken with this vision, which appeared to justify a deeply rooted Russian aspiration to extend dominion over all lands inhabited by Slavs.[4]

Neither Alexander nor his advisers saw expansion into Europe as being Russia's destiny – that lay in Constantinople and the east. But Russia's meteoric emergence as a major power over the past hundred years impelled her to take an interest in Europe, if only out of an instinct for self-defence. The powers that needed to be watched were, in the first place, Britain, whose maritime supremacy and eastern dominions were thought to constitute an obvious challenge; France, whose traditional alliance with Ottoman Turkey and interest in Egypt and points further east were a source of unease; and, to a lesser degree, Austria, whose possessions in the Balkans were at the very least an inconvenience. In the 1790s Russia had been drawn into war with France, but it was a conflict in which she had no actual interests at stake beyond the forlorn hope of establishing a maritime base in the western Mediterranean.

Alexander's attitude to Napoleon was an ambiguous one. He could not help admiring his talents and energy, and envied the First Consul's achievements as an efficient modern ruler who had put into effect many of the ideals of the Enlightenment. But he was outraged by his arbitrary brutality, and his distaste for the upstart Frenchman turned to disgust when Napoleon had himself crowned Emperor of the French in December 1804.

In October of that year, as Britain and other powers had contemplated the possibility of war with France, Alexander sent Nikolai Novosiltsov to London with a proposal drawn up by Czartoryski containing his vision of a new order in Europe based on liberal principles and 'the sacred rights of humanity'. The British Prime Minister William Pitt was predictably sceptical, but responded with eagerness. He praised Alexander's 'wise, dignified and generous policy', and singled out three of the points as the main aims of the proposed coalition against France: that France should be stripped of her conquests and reduced to her former limits; that those recovered territories should be safeguarded in such a way that they should never fall to French aggression again; and, most significantly, 'To form, at the restoration of peace, a general agreement and Guarantee for the mutual protection and security of different Powers, and for re-establishing a general system of public law in Europe.'[5]

Nothing came of it, as the coalition which was to usher in this new age was shattered on the fields of Austerlitz, Jena and Friedland. Czartoryski was, reluctantly, dismissed by Alexander in 1806. Taciturn and reserved, he had few friends at court, and was the object of resentment and jealousy on account of his ascendancy over the Tsar. Also, he was a Pole. He had fought against Russia in 1792 in defence of his country, and he had arrived in St Petersburg as a hostage for the good behaviour of his family.

The kingdom of Poland had been wiped off the map in 1795 as a result of a series of agreements between Russia, Prussia and Austria. As well as taking the lion's share of its territory, Alexander's grandmother Catherine the Great had been the prime mover. In common with most enlightened opinion, Alexander condemned this partition of one of the ancient states of Europe, and he also felt a degree of personal guilt. These feelings were intensified by his friendship with Czartoryski, to whom he had vowed that he would restore Poland to freedom when he came to the throne. When the time came he was faced by the impossibility of doing anything quite so contrary to what were perceived as paramount Russian interests. But he never ceased to dream of one day redeeming those vows. This Polish conundrum epitomised the conflict in Alexander's mind between his own ideals and Russian reasons of state, which clashed on many different planes.

Like many Polish patriots, Czartoryski realised that there was no possibility of his country recovering independence in the short term. The best he could hope for was the reunification of its severed portions. He had a vision of Poland as a more or less autonomous province of, possibly even a kingdom within, the Russian Empire, and he served that empire in good faith. But he would never dissipate the suspicions of the court and Russian society in general, which saw in him only a potential enemy. The situation was made no easier by the fact that he had been the lover of Alexander's wife Elizabeth, who had had a child by him. He was a liability and he had to go.

Czartoryski's fall from grace did not affect Alexander's views on international affairs. Nor did it, as the dismissed minister's patriotic Russian opponents had hoped, do away with what they saw as the Tsar's lamentable obsession with Poland.

But it did affect Alexander's attitude to Britain. Czartoryski considered the British to be unreliable and selfish, but nevertheless a necessary ally in the struggle against France. Alexander had his doubts. He was particularly irked by Britain's insistence on the absolute and exclusive nature of what she termed her 'maritime rights', effectively to search every ship at will and to invigilate the high seas. He had accepted her as a necessary ally in 1804, but felt grievously let down in the winter of 1806–07, when he was left alone fighting Napoleon by Britain's failure to support him by sending an expeditionary force into the Baltic.

Faced with the necessity to treat with Napoleon, Alexander not only made peace: he offered the French Emperor a partnership of the kind he had offered Pitt three years before. He fancied that the resulting alliance, sealed during their meetings at Tilsit in the summer of 1807, would permit him to regenerate his empire and add to it by incorporating Constantinople and other parts of the near east while exerting, in partnership with Napoleon, an enlightened and beneficent tutelage over the continent they dominated.

The débâcle of Austerlitz in December 1805, where Alexander had hoped to shine as a military hero only to have to flee the battlefield as his army disintegrated, and his final defeat at Friedland the following year had been personal humiliations. They had also weakened his position in political terms. While he was still widely loved by his people, they suspected him of weakness and feared his reformist tendencies. Ministers such as Czartoryski and the reforming Speransky were seen as conduits of French/Masonic/Polish/Jewish influence which would corrupt the purity of Russia, and he was obliged to dismiss them as well as to abandon cherished programmes. He found himself at odds with an increasingly eloquent public opinion which he could not ignore. While the Tsar of Russia was theoretically an autocrat with no limits on his power, the overwhelming majority of educated Russians concentrated in the army, the administration, at court, in St Petersburg or in Moscow represented the sole agency through which the state could function, and without its good will the autocrat was literally powerless.[6]

While it proved uncomfortable and humiliating in many ways, Alexander's alliance with Napoleon between 1807 and 1812 had allowed him to invade and annex Finland and to acquire a couple of additional slices of Polish territory. He hoped to appropriate yet more, and to move into the Balkans. But none of this was enough. Russia's self-respect demanded that he adopt a more defiant and even provocative policy towards France. This had led inexorably to Napoleon's ill-conceived invasion, and as the Russian army followed the defeated remnants of the Grande Armée out of Russia in the last days of 1812, it was clear to all but the most naïve that Russian rule would be extended further west. The grand duchy of Warsaw was there for the taking, giving Alexander the opportunity to pay his debt of guilt towards the Poles by resurrecting the kingdom of Poland.

The establishment of an independent Polish state would preclude Russia making any territorial gains in the west. Worse, it would probably lead to her having to give back Polish provinces she had seized in the past. Alexander could therefore only contemplate establishing a Polish kingdom within the framework of the Russian Empire, with himself as King. This would, he hoped, allay the fears of Russian opinion. But as it would also extend the frontiers of his empire far to the west, it meant that he would have to have a hand in the arrangement of Germany.

Germany had been more profoundly affected than any other part of Europe by the French Revolution and subsequent interference by Napoleon. In 1789 the German lands had belonged to the Holy Roman Empire, a bewildering patchwork of some three hundred independent sovereignties and thousands of lordships, abbeys and orders, whose forms of government ranged from absolutist monarchy, through ecclesiastical authority, to republican cities. The army of the empire was made up not only of regiments, but companies and even platoons composed of soldiers supplied by different states. The captain of a company might be commissioned by a sovereign count, the lieutenant by a free city and the second lieutenant by an abbess.

All this had been gradually swept away following French incursions into the Rhineland in 1792, and between 1801 and 1809 Napoleon thoroughly rearranged the area. His intention was to reduce and isolate Austria, to enlarge Prussia, which he hoped to keep in the French camp, and to create a number of secondary states such as Bavaria, Baden and Württemberg, whose gratified rulers would be devoted allies. By the Act of Mediatisation in 1803 he suppressed most of the sovereignties, and in 1806 he bound the remainder into the Confederation of the Rhine, the Rheinbund, of which he made himself protector. While he grouped them together in this way, his hold was based on playing them off against each other and keeping them in a state of dependence. And none of them was entirely master in his own house, as Napoleon had left a number of 'mediatised' counts and knights (*Standesherren*) within their realms who were subject not to them but to him.

The winners were not only the Electors of Bavaria, Württemberg and Saxony, who became Kings, or the other rulers who had seen their status raised, but also all those such as merchants liberated from archaic restrictive regulations, artisans who could throw off the shackles of the guilds, the Jews who were able to leave their ghettos, and countless others. The losers were the hundreds of dukes, princes, counts palatine, bishops, margraves, burgraves, landgraves, abbots, abbesses, grand masters and imperial knights who lost lands and prerogatives, as well as the free cities, which saw their independence abolished in the process.

The German state that had gained most was Prussia. By making common cause with France against the other German states in 1795,

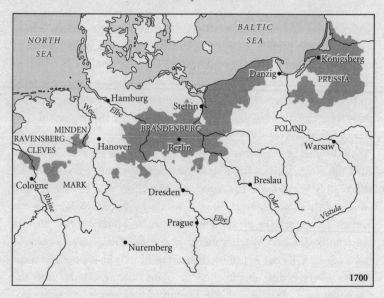

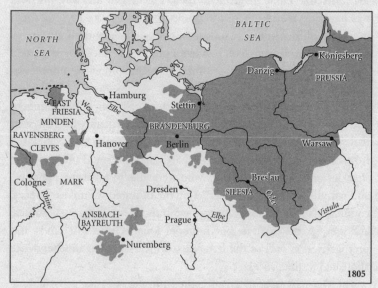

The rise and fall of Prussia, 1700–1807

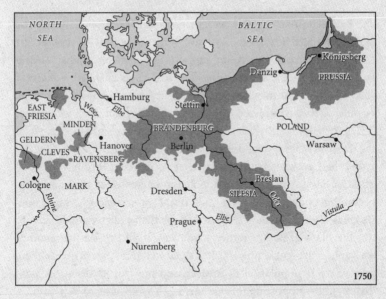

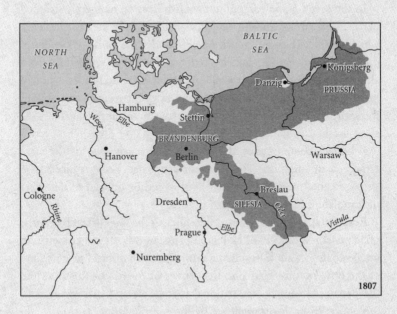

she had acquired valuable territories in the Rhineland, which she later exchanged for more extensive ones in central Germany. She took Hanover as the prize for supporting Napoleon against Austria in 1805. But in the following year Prussia had changed sides, and following his crushing victories over her at Jena and Auerstadt in 1806, Napoleon had considered abolishing the Prussian state altogether.

The kingdom of Prussia had only come into existence in 1701, when the Elector of Brandenburg unilaterally assumed the royal title. By 1750 it had grown territorially by over 50 per cent through the conquest of Silesia. It more than doubled in size between then and 1805, becoming a power of the first rank. But it was a curiously fragile one. Its greatest ruler, Frederick II, used to say that its arms should feature not the black eagle but rather a monkey, as all Prussia was good at was aping the great powers. It fielded six times as many soldiers relative to its population as Austria, and most of its resources were dedicated to supporting this vast army, the sole basis of its power.[7]

In the event, Napoleon did not abolish Prussia; he merely stripped her of most of the Polish provinces acquired over the past decades, which he turned into a French satellite under the name of the grand duchy of Warsaw. He thereby reduced Prussia's population from almost nine to less than five million. What remained of Prussia had to accommodate French troops, who extorted money and fodder through officials who took every opportunity to humiliate the Prussians as they spoliated their country. Given the French Emperor's well-known contempt for the Prussians, the existence of the state remained in question. The Prussian army had been reduced to a paltry 42,000, nearly 30,000 of whom would be obliged to take part in Napoleon's Russian campaign in 1812.

Reaction had set in as soon as the shock of the 1806 defeat had worn off. The large numbers of cashiered Prussian officers joined patriotic intellectuals to wallow in sullen resentment of all things French. Many of the officers took service in the armies of Austria or Russia, while the patriots dreamed of a national resurgence and of revenge, and took heart from the example set by the *guerrilleros* of Spain.

Poets such as Ernst Moritz Arndt, Heinrich von Kleist and Theodor Körner encouraged these feelings with patriotic verse and nationalist catechisms; philosophers and publicists argued about what form Germany should take in an ideal world. Young men came together in the *Tugendbund*, the League of Virtue, to discuss and prepare; others followed Friedrich Jahn in physical preparation for the forthcoming war through athletic exercise.

A number of senior officers devoted themselves to the cause in more practical ways. Gerhard Johann Scharnhorst, Gebhard Blücher, Leopold von Boyen and August Gneisenau worked at restructuring the army and instilling military virtues into the population as a whole. Others, such as Wilhelm von Humboldt, took a hand to the educational system, or sought to reform the state itself. Foremost among these was a civil servant by the name of Karl Heinrich vom Stein, who was, like many of the other reformers, not actually a Prussian.

Stein had been born in Nassau, a *Freiherr* or imperial knight of the Holy Roman Empire. There was nothing in his origins or station that destined him to become a German patriot – indeed his younger brother Ludwig became an officer in the French army. After law studies at the university of Göttingen, he took service in Prussia, originally in the Directorate of Mines, where he made a name for himself as an energetic administrator, builder of roads and digger of canals.

Stein was a man of austere morals and strict principles who disapproved of all excesses, either political as in the case of the French Revolution or moral as in the case of the sexual licence he deplored in others. But he was more elastic when it came to politics.

Though deeply shocked by the treacherous manner in which, by the Treaty of Bâle (Basel) in 1795, Prussia acquired new lands along the Rhine, he nevertheless applied himself to their incorporation into the Prussian state. Any moral qualms he might have had gave way before his overriding instinct to tidy up the messy medieval legacy and rationalise the whole of Germany into one efficient state. In common with many patriots all over Germany, he had come to the conclusion that the only way to place their country and its culture beyond the reach of interference from France or any other power was to create a unified German state strong enough to exclude outside influence and resist military aggression.

The philosopher Johann Gottlieb Fichte was preaching that the nation was a spiritual as well as a physical entity, which embodied something of a higher order than any attachment to a state or a King, and there were many, particularly in the universities, who longed to see a German republic. However much they might have empathised with such views, to patriots such as Stein, Gneisenau and Humboldt it was evident that a united Germany could not be built out of nothing. They therefore served the one German state that appeared to be in a position to gradually engulf the others and bring about the same end – Prussia.

In 1804 Stein was called to a senior post in Berlin. He was horrified at the corruption and inefficiency he encountered there, and dismayed at the mediocrity of the monarch he was serving. He strongly disapproved of Frederick William's alignment with France in 1805 and his consequent seizure of Hanover. Along with others, he persuaded the reluctant Frederick William to switch to the side of the coalition against Napoleon, and when this led to the disasters of Jena and Auerstadt he was dismissed in January 1807, with a string of imprecations from the King.

It was all the more galling for the unfortunate King that a few months later Napoleon, who had reduced Prussia to an entirely subservient condition, having heard that Stein was a good administrator but not that he was a German patriot, instructed Frederick William to nominate him as his principal minister. Stein took the opportunity provided by his new position to introduce an edict of emancipation which transformed Prussia from a feudal monarchy into a modern state, and followed this up with administrative, municipal and military reforms. Barely more than a year later an intercepted letter revealed to the French police the extent of Stein's hatred of the French, and in consequence Napoleon had him dismissed and declared an outlaw. Rendered penniless at a stroke, Stein took refuge in Austrian-ruled Prague.

In 1812 Stein was summoned to Russia by Tsar Alexander. The two had met in Berlin in 1805 and been drawn to each other by the high-minded ideals – and, no doubt, by the priggishness – they shared. As the Grande Armée advanced into Russia, raising doubts as to the competence of Alexander and his generals, the Tsar suffered moments of self-doubt and emotional stress. In these circumstances Stein's unshakeable belief in him as the champion of the universal anti-French cause proved invaluable as both solace and support. His influence over the Tsar grew in proportion.

He took over the direction of a German Committee set up by Alexander to coordinate pro-Russian sentiment throughout German lands, and turned it into an instrument for his own ends. On 18 September 1812, a couple of days after Napoleon had crushed the Russians' last stand at Borodino outside Moscow, Stein produced a memorandum which sketched out his plan to create a unified German state. He was convinced that Russia would prevail in the end, and argued that having defeated the French she must carry the war into Germany and liberate Europe from their yoke.

When, three months later, the remnants of the Grande Armée straggled back across the frontier, the Russian commander Field Marshal Kutuzov and most of his senior officers argued against pursuing them further. Kutuzov would continue to beg Alexander to make peace and go home, and to advise against crossing the Elbe, until his very death, on 28 April 1813 at Bünzlau (Bolesławiec). Even the most ardent Russian patriots, such as his Minister of the Interior Admiral Shishkov and the Archimandrite Filaret, were against Alexander's proposed liberation of Europe. The consensus was that Russia should help herself to East Prussia and much of Poland, providing herself with some territorial gain and a defensible western border, and leave it at that. But Alexander ignored them.[8]

When the Russian armies did advance, Alexander put Stein in

charge of administering German territory in their rear, and he went to work setting up not only organs of local administration, but representative bodies as well. He recruited volunteers, called up reservists, formed a new militia, the *Landwehr*, to be supported by a home defence force, the *Landsturm*, all in the name of the King of Prussia but without his knowledge, let alone his authority.

Although Alexander's behaviour encouraged Stein in the belief that he was going to be able to put into effect his dream of a united Germany, the Tsar stopped short of endorsing it. He wished to be the healer of past ills and the bringer of happiness to the Germans as well as the Poles, and indeed to all the inhabitants of the Continent. But while he enjoyed being the anticipated saviour, he had no fixed programme. He also needed to keep his options open. Nevertheless, the expectations he aroused introduced unaccountable new elements into what was already a volatile situation.

The first obliged to confront these was King Frederick William of Prussia, and he was a worried man in those early months of 1813. 'Make use of the authority granted you by God to break the chains of your people!' Stein exhorted him from St Petersburg at the end of December 1812. 'May its blood no longer be spilt on behalf of the enemy of humanity.' But the Prussian King was not a born hero.[9]

His innate weakness undermined the advantages of a kindly and God-fearing nature, and made him suspicious as he clung to power, while his sense of failure nourished a false pride and a mean streak. He had been forced to give up half of his kingdom only ten years after acceding to it, and had been gratuitously humiliated by Napoleon. The knowledge that everyone compared him with his famous predecessor and great-uncle Frederick the Great only compounded this sense of failure. The one light in his life had been his Queen, the beautiful and universally admired Louise, to whom he had been attached by a true and mutual love. But she had died in 1810. He hung on to the remains of his realm, seeing in a close association with Napoleon the only means of survival.

General Yorck's defection from the French ranks raised the terrifying possibility of French retaliation. Frederick William therefore loudly denounced it as an act of mutiny and made great show of standing by his alliance with Napoleon. But his ally was far away in Paris mustering a new army, the Russians were flooding into his kingdom from the east, and public opinion was against him.

Frederick William should have had every reason to welcome the approach of the Russians. Back in 1805 when they had met for the first time in Berlin, he and Alexander had sworn eternal friendship at midnight over the tomb of Frederick the Great. That friendship had been only slightly marred by Frederick William's forced contribution of troops to Napoleon's invasion of Russia, and the Prussian King knew that he had the sympathy of Alexander. Yet he viewed the approach of the Russian armies with misgivings and even fear.

Alexander's appointment of Stein was, considering their past relationship, almost an insult. Stein's disregard for Frederick William's authority as he set about administering East Prussia was an open affront. It might signify that Alexander was preparing to detach that province from the Prussian kingdom. Stein's calls for a pan-German war of national liberation were even more alarming. He made no secret of his views that all German rulers who had allied with Napoleon were 'cowards who sold the blood of their people in order to prolong their miserable existence'. The prospect of his being let loose on Germany aroused legitimate fears of social upheaval and even revolution, which Frederick William would be in no position to oppose.[10]

He was in an unenviable position. The strong French garrison ensconced in the fortress of Spandau paraded through Berlin daily, reminding him that there were more French than Prussian troops in the country. The probability was that Napoleon would be back in the spring with a fresh army, with which he would crush the Russians. Even if he did not hope for a Russian defeat, Frederick William ardently desired the stability which only such a return could guarantee. What he dreaded above all was the possibility that Alexander and Napoleon might yet reach an accommodation, the principal victim of which would almost certainly be Prussia: an obvious solution would have been for Russia to take East Prussia and all Polish lands up to the Vistula as the price for continued French control of Germany.

Frederick William calculated that if he could negotiate better terms with Napoleon, he would be in a position to reassert his authority, control the hotheads in his dominions and face Russia on more level terms. It was, of necessity, the lesser of two evils. 'By allying with France, the least that could be expected was a further degree of ruin for the kingdom, which would inevitably become the theatre of the war,' wrote the Prussian chancellor, Baron August von Hardenberg, 'but if one were to enter into alliance with Russia, how could one dare to confront once again the implacable vengeance of Napoleon?'[11]

Frederick William therefore sent Prince Hatzfeldt to Paris with the proposal of an active alliance against Russia, on condition that France paid the ninety million francs she owed Prussia and agreed to the restitution of some of her former territory in Poland. The alliance was to be sealed by the marriage of the Prussian Crown Prince to a princess of the house of Bonaparte. Failing to get a response, in February 1813 he made two further such proposals to Napoleon.[12]

But Frederick William could not procrastinate much longer. In the absence of any encouraging signal from Napoleon, and in view of the fact that over two-thirds of his army was by then operating in defiance of him, he made a move. On 22 January 1813 he left Berlin, with its French garrison and swarms of French officials, for Breslau (Wrocław), the capital of his province of Silesia. Although the French ambassador Saint-Marsan accompanied him, the King felt less under surveillance there. While making repeated professions of loyalty to Napoleon, he sanctioned the formation of a volunteer corps of Jägers and the call-up of all men aged between twenty and thirty-four, ostensibly in order to be in a position to offer his ally Napoleon fresh troops in the spring.

On 9 February he sent Colonel Knesebeck to Alexander's head-quarters at Kalisch (Kalisz) to seek assurances that, provided he did not take Napoleon's side in the forthcoming conflict, Prussia was not going to be pushed westwards and turned into some kind of buffer state. Alexander was not best pleased by Frederick William's envoy. Knesebeck asked the Tsar to dismiss Stein and to promise that he would hand over Prussia's old Polish provinces, incorporated into the grand duchy of Warsaw in 1807, which were now under Russian occupation. Alexander took this approach as an expression of a lack of faith in his magnanimity. Ignoring Knesebeck, he despatched Stein to Breslau with a letter to Frederick William and the draft of a treaty of alliance between them. Stein's arrival on 25 February was most unwelcome to the King.

Time was running out, as the Russian armies covered ever greater areas of his kingdom, and the German patriots who marched with them incited his subjects to rise and fight regardless of their King. On 19 February Fichte had ended a lecture he was giving at the university in Berlin with the words: 'This course will be suspended until the close of the campaign, when we will resume it in a free fatherland or reconquer our liberty by death.' Young men from all over Germany flocked to join a *Freikorps* under Adolf von Lützow, dedicated to the liberation of Germany. A wave of excitement rippled across the country. 'German spirit, German courage raised hopes of better days,' wrote the patriotic *salonière* Caroline Pichler, noting that the voices of young men had a fresh, warlike ring.[13]

Frederick William was cornered, and on 27 February he signed the treaty brought by Stein. It was ratified and dated at Kalisch on 1 March. Frederick William set to work raising troops and, as a token of reconciliation with his wayward army, founded the Order of the Iron Cross. Two weeks later Alexander joined Frederick William at Breslau, and on 16 March Prussia declared war on France. Alexander and Frederick William were, for better or worse, allies.

The alliance placed Frederick William in a subservient position. The one promise that he had extracted from Alexander was that in a secret article of the treaty he solemnly undertook 'not to lay down arms as long as Prussia will not be reconstituted in statistical, geo-graphical and financial proportions equal to those she had before'

1806. Since Alexander was already in possession of all the territory Prussia had lost then, Prussia could only wait for him to either give it back, which seemed unlikely, or to use his power to obtain a comparable tranche of land for her from future conquests elsewhere in Germany. The word used, 'equivalents', was harmless enough, but it left unanswered the question of where they were to be found, and who was to be dispossessed in order to provide them – every piece of land belonged to somebody.[14]

While people all over Europe who had grown tired of Napoleonic dominance saw Alexander as a liberator, few appreciated that he had assumed a right to play the decisive role in the future arrangement of Europe. It was not merely a question of his having triumphed over Napoleon. Over the past few years he had come to view his struggle with the French Emperor not only as a personal contest, or as a clash between two empires, but as a veritable Armageddon between good and evil.

The Tsar's idealism coupled with his political disappointments and humiliations on the battlefield had led him towards mysticism. His close friends included followers of Saint-Martin, Swedenborg and Lavater, and he was conversant with the literature of mysticism and with German pietism. As he watched his country being invaded and ravaged in 1812, he had sought solace in resignation to the will of God, and when the fortunes of war swung back in his favour he saw it as a manifestation of that will. From there it was but a short step to seeing himself as its instrument. He interpreted the suffering his country and its people had endured over the previous year as a purifying preparatory ordeal, and saw in it a kind of moral capital that gave him an authority superior to that of any of the other monarchs of Europe.

Like Stein and many German patriots, he had come to see the war as a crusade, not so much against France as against what France stood for – revolution, moral depravity and the usurpation of power. It was this last, Napoleon's almost careless trampling of the ancient rights of other monarchs and his brazen use of force to install and dismiss sovereigns, that offended most. As he prepared to embark on the next stage of his crusade, the liberation of Germany from the usurper, Alexander called on her legitimate princes to join it.

A proclamation issued on his behalf by Field Marshal Kutuzov stressed that the armies of the Emperor of Russia and the King of Prussia were entering Germany with the sole aim of liberating her people and their princes and restoring to them their 'imprescriptible rights'. 'May every German worthy of the name join us with vigour and promptitude,' it continued. 'Let everyone, whether Prince or noble or from the ranks of the people, support with their wealth and their blood, with their body and their life, the liberating intentions of Russia and Prussia.'

The proclamation announced that the two monarchs had decreed the dissolution of the Rheinbund and intended to replace it with something modelled on 'the ancient spirit of the German People'. And it contained a barely veiled threat to any who would not join them. 'Their Majesties therefore demand a faithful and complete cooperation, particularly from each German Prince, and are pleased to hope in advance that there will not be found one among them who, wishing to betray the cause of Germany, will thereby deserve to be destroyed by the force of public opinion and by the power of the arms taken up so justly by them.'[15]

The convention signed by Russia and Prussia at Breslau on 19 March 1813 was more businesslike and precise. It stipulated that all 'liberated' territory would be divided into five districts and placed in the hands of a Central Administrative Council directed by Stein, which would take over the business of collecting taxes, marshalling resources and raising troops. It also restated that all the German rulers would be invited to join the cause, and made it clear that 'any Prince who does not answer this call within a specified period will be threatened with the loss of his state'.[16]

It was a curious way to proclaim a crusade for legitimacy against the usurper, and Frederick William's chancellor, Hardenberg, for one, was afraid that 'this appeal to the passions of the day, even to democratic ideas, so unexpected on the lips of two absolute monarchs, could lead to grave problems in the future'. That was to prove something of an understatement. The two monarchs had in effect adopted the language of the French Revolution and the methods of Napoleon, thereby undermining their own credibility and robbing themselves of the only weapons they would be able to use against the unwonted passions they were arousing.[17]

3

The Peacemakers

Nobody was more alarmed by the new alliance between Russia and Prussia than the Austrian Foreign Minister, Count Klemens Wenceslas Lothar von Metternich, and no power stood to lose more by radical developments in Germany than Austria. She was, in a different way from Prussia, possibly the most vulnerable political unit in Europe.

Her sovereign had been crowned in 1792 as the Holy Roman Emperor Francis II. Besides this prestigious but empty role, he had inherited the huge antiquated realm of the house of Habsburg, an accretion of centuries of conquest, diplomacy and dynastic marriage. It was not long before he had to start ceding outlying provinces of this to Revolutionary France – the Austrian Netherlands (present-day Belgium), Lombardy and the left bank of the Rhine in 1797; Venice and Illyria, as well as the Tyrol, given to France's ally Bavaria, in 1805. The Holy Roman Empire itself was dissolved by Napoleon in 1806, and its sovereign became Emperor Francis I of Austria.

In 1809 an ill-judged attempt to recover some of his provinces while Napoleon was busy fighting in Spain cost him Salzburg, the remains of his possessions along the Adriatic and part of his Polish provinces. He was also forced to seal the ensuing peace by giving Napoleon his favourite daughter Marie-Louise in marriage. He was then obliged to participate in Napoleon's invasion of Russia in 1812

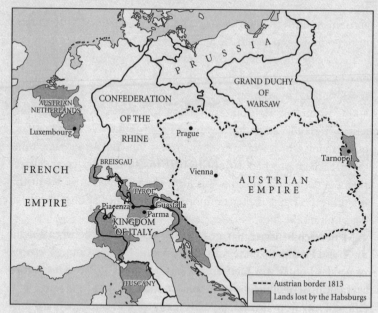

Habsburg losses, 1792–1810

with a 30,000-strong Austrian auxiliary corps under Prince Schwarz-enberg. He was still, at the beginning of 1813, an ally of France.

While both Francis and Metternich were eager to disengage Austria from this alliance and to see French troops and influence excluded from Germany, they also had much to fear from change of any kind. Francis's much-reduced empire was strategically vulnerable, as it was open to attack from every direction. It had no national base, and included large numbers of Slavs, Magyars and other nationalities. The only cement binding this heterogeneous mass together was the monarchy itself, the house of Habsburg. This made it ideologically vulnerable as well. The Enlightenment, the French Revolution and its Napoleonic legacy brought into question everything that made up the monarchy: the execution of the French King Louis XVI in 1793 insulted the divine status of kingship so central to the Habsburg state; the idea of the sovereignty of the people undermined the paternal absolutism on which the monarchy was predicated; and the concept of nationhood put in question its territorial basis.

In the circumstances, the proclamations issuing from Russian headquarters were a cause for alarm in Vienna. They threatened to arouse revolutionary and nationalist passions that could produce reverberations within the Habsburg dominions. More ominously, they suggested Alexander's intention of exerting an influence over the affairs of Germany, which were of vital interest to Austria. At the same time, the proclamations had a similar effect on all the greater and lesser rulers of the region, and this was likely to make them turn to Austria for protection and make common cause with her against Russia in determining the future of Germany.

Metternich believed that a durable peace could only be achieved if the centre of Europe could be rid of the threat of foreign domination and placed under the twin protection of Prussia and Austria. While this required the exclusion of both French and Russian influence from Germany, it also required their preservation as checks on each other's ambitions. Although he and his country were in an extremely dangerous position, he set out to engineer just such a peace. He did not believe the task to be beyond him.

The Austrian Foreign Minister's most striking characteristic was his vanity. In the words of the eminent nineteenth-century historian Albert Sorel, 'Metternich was in his own opinion the light of the world, and he blinded himself with the rays reflected in the mirror he held up continuously before his eyes. There was in him a chronic hypertrophy of the ego which developed relentlessly.' He was in every sense the centre of his own universe. He would write endlessly about what he had thought, written and done, pointing out, sometimes only for his own benefit, how brilliantly these thoughts, writings and doings reflected on him. This egotism was buttressed by a monumental complacency that was proof against all experience.[1]

Metternich was hard-working, honest and cultivated, and not devoid of humour, though of a somewhat ponderous kind. He was very cautious, with plenty of what he used to refer to as 'tact', by which he appeared to mean the ability never to get so far involved in anything as to be unable to pull out. This made him a perfect diplomat and a formidable negotiator. He knew how to make people believe they were getting their own way while he led them, at their own pace, towards the goal chosen by him. If not highly intelligent, he was very perceptive. Above all, he knew what he wanted, and pursued his aims with dogged consistency.

He was physically handsome, innately elegant and distinguished-looking, but slightly spoiled the effect by fussing too much over his hair and his clothes. Possessed of considerable charm, he was amiable and very sociable, which made him popular in any drawing room. He loved music, which often reduced him to tears. Though not exactly raffish, he had an eye for the ladies, and could be seductive when he wanted. During his lifetime he found his way into the bedrooms of some of the greatest beauties of the age. Having triumphed, he as often as not lapsed into the role of sentimental lover. He would pour out his feelings in mawkish letters and flaunt them in curiously adolescent ways – when he was having an affair with Napoleon's sister Caroline Murat in 1810 he ostentatiously wore a bracelet fashioned from her hair.

His career was meteoric. Born in the Rhineland in 1773, he studied at the universities of Strasbourg and Mainz. At Frankfurt in 1792, at the age of nineteen, he witnessed the coronation of Francis II as Holy Roman Emperor, an event that left a lasting impression. After brief trips to Vienna and London he married Leonore Kaunitz, the daughter of Maria-Theresa's renowned chancellor, and in 1801 took up his first diplomatic post, as the Emperor's minister to the Saxon court in Dresden.

From there he was sent as ambassador to Berlin, where he negotiated the treaty between Austria, Russia and Prussia in 1805, the foundation of the Third Coalition. When that had been defeated he was sent, at Napoleon's request, to Paris as Austria's ambassador. When war broke out between the two countries in 1809 he was first held hostage in Paris and then given the task of negotiating the peace, which included arranging the marriage of Marie-Louise to Napoleon. That same year he was made Austrian Foreign Minister, a post which he was to hold for the next thirty-nine years.

Metternich was in every sense a product of the *ancien régime*, believing in a natural order of things, based on established religion, monarchy and a defined hierarchy. He viewed any change as potentially revolutionary, and feared the middle classes, as they tended to nourish aspirations which they could not satisfy without displacing others or changing the rules and destroying existing institutions. The French Revolution he saw as the greatest catastrophe to afflict Europe, and he had a natural tendency to despise Napoleon as its product. Yet he admired him for his achievements and, more importantly, valued the fact that he was an effective source of authority who had contained the forces of chaos in France and might – if only he could be contained himself – be a useful partner in the preservation of the 'natural order' in Europe. Indeed, he rated Napoleon higher on this scale of usefulness than he did many legitimate monarchs.

'The world is lost,' Metternich had written to his friend Friedrich von Gentz back in 1806, after Napoleon had abolished the Holy Roman Empire. He could barely disguise his horror at the Frenchman's doings and his abhorrence of his whole 'system'. At the same time he came to appreciate the usefulness of the Rheinbund, with which Napoleon had replaced the Holy Roman Empire, as a basis for the emergence of a more independent Germany. And he did not subscribe to the view that Napoleon must be got rid of at any cost.[2]

Metternich hoped that the disasters of the Russian campaign would have sobered Napoleon enough for him to realise that his best option was to abandon his dream of a pan-European French Empire and make peace as soon as possible – a peace that Metternich would broker, with attendant advantages to Austria. In order to achieve this, and to keep his options open, he had to somehow extricate Austria from her alliance with France and adopt 'a system of active neutrality'.[3]

Metternich feared the formation of a new coalition against France, as he foresaw that Russia would be its driving force and therefore its leader; and what he feared even more than a restoration of French hegemony over Europe was its replacement by a Russian one. At the same time, he realised that if Russia and France did come to negotiate directly, they might well end up dividing Europe between them, cutting Austria out of the deal.

In December 1812, through Bubna, he offered Napoleon Austria's good services in helping France make peace with Russia. He held out the vision of a strong France retaining many of the gains she had made since 1792, a neutralised Germany watched over jointly by France and Austria, with Russia and Prussia held in check in the east. The future of French conquests in Italy was left vague, as Austria and France could settle that question between themselves at a later date.

Although Napoleon dismissed Bubna's proposals with bluster about his intention to march out in the spring and beat his enemies into submission, Metternich did not despair of bringing him round. At the same time, he began to make preparations for all eventualities. The Treaty of Schönbrunn, which he had brokered himself between France and Austria in 1809, had limited the size of the Austrian army to 150,000. But, assuming that Austria would continue as his ally and expecting to need a larger auxiliary corps soon, Napoleon now encouraged its increase, and Metternich seized the opportunity to order rapid mobilisation of all available forces. He also continued to deepen his dialogue with Russia and other powers.

Metternich knew that Napoleon's ultimate aim was a satisfactory settlement with Britain, and that without one no peace he made with any other powers could be considered final. He shared the opinion, common throughout Europe, that Britain was a self-interested power of marginal importance on the Continent, and he could not disguise a certain exasperation with her apparent arrogance, but he felt she must be brought into the proceedings in the interests of all. In February 1813 he sent an unofficial envoy, Count Wessenberg, to London to sound out the British cabinet on whether it would agree to enter into negotiations under Austrian mediation.[4]

The mission was doomed to failure. Since Marie-Louise's marriage to Napoleon, the view from London was that Austria was a close ally of France and therefore not worth keeping up even unofficial links with. In that year the Foreign Office had stopped paying Friedrich von Gentz, one of its most reliable informants in Austria since 1802. Under the circumstances, the arrival of Wessenberg was seen in London as some kind of intrigue. In matters of foreign policy, the British cabinet was beset by outdated prejudices.[5]

The eighteenth-century view of France as a monstrous and diabolical arch-enemy bent on the destruction of England still prevailed. Another inherited perception was that Britain's natural allies were Russia, Prussia and Sweden. This was based on the notion that Russia was, like Britain, an 'unselfish' power as far as Europe was concerned, and that there were no possible grounds for conflict between the two; that Sweden's interests lay in making common cause with Britain; and that as a northern Protestant power and an erstwhile enemy of France, Prussia must be a sympathetic ally of Britain.

In point of fact, Russia resented Britain's supremacy at sea and foresaw conflict of interest not only over the Balkans and Constantinople, but also in the Mediterranean and, more far-sightedly, over southern Asia. One of the reasons many within the Russian military and political establishment were unwilling to pursue the Grande Armée beyond Russia's frontiers and bring about the total defeat of France was that they suspected Britain would end up as the main beneficiary. These considerations were backed up by economic rivalry and widespread ill-will stemming from a belief that Britain's aggressive trading practices constituted an obstacle to the development of the Russian economy.

So while Britain saw Russia as a natural ally, Russia saw Britain as a rival. Her repeated offers to mediate a peace settlement between Britain and the United States were thinly-disguised attempts to shore up the position of the latter, particularly as a naval power that could act as a counterbalance to Britain on the seas, and in the process put in question Britain's cherished 'maritime rights'. And while Russia opened her ports to all when she broke away from Napoleon's

Continental System, she imposed cripplingly high duties on British traders.[6]

Sweden had not shown herself a reliable ally at any stage in the past two decades, and although her ships and ports did flout the Continental System and continued to trade with Britain, she had, in 1810, opportunistically elected the Napoleonic Marshal Jean-Baptiste Bernadotte as Crown Prince and effective ruler. Prussia too had played a disappointing role. She had fought alongside the French more often than against them, and had perfidiously helped herself to Hanover, a possession of Britain's royal house.

In 1812 Britain acquired a new Foreign Secretary, Viscount Castle-reagh. But he was not the man to take a different view or alter policy drastically. He had been born plain Robert Stewart, the son of an Ulster landowner of Scottish Presbyterian stock. His father had become a member of the Dublin Parliament, married well (twice) and made the most of his connections, becoming Baron Londonderry in 1789, Viscount Castlereagh in 1795, Earl of Londonderry in 1796, and would progress to Marquess of Londonderry in 1816.

Young Robert Stewart, who was born in the same year as Napoleon, was prone to all the enthusiasms of his age. He admired the American rebels who had thrown off English rule, he sympathised with the French Revolution, and entered Irish politics as an enthusiastic patriot, drinking toasts to 'the Gallic Constitution', to 'the People', and even on one occasion to 'the rope that shall hang the King'. But trips to France and Belgium in 1792 and 1793 dampened his enthusiasm for things revolutionary, and as he grew up the dour pragmatism of his paternal forebears began to assert itself over the romantic attitudes derived from his aristocratic mother's.

In 1796 he not only inherited the title of Viscount Castlereagh, he also took command of five hundred men to oppose a threatened French landing at Bantry Bay which meant to liberate Ireland from the English yoke. Two years later, in 1798, he played an active part in suppressing the Irish rebellion, and he was one of the most deter-mined architects of the Union with England of 1801, making liberal use of bribery in order to achieve it. He had betrayed all the fancies of his youth in favour of law and order, which he had come to see as the greatest benefit in public life. This was perhaps not surprising, as by now he had plenty to protect. In 1802 he was nominated President of the Board of Control of the East India Company, and in 1805 he became Secretary of State for War in William Pitt's cabinet. He had arrived at the very heart of the British political establishment.

But it would be wrong to see Castlereagh's change of heart as a self-interested *volte-face*. It stemmed from his acceptance of Pitt's conviction that illegitimate revolution could never bring the kind of stability necessary for the development of civil society, and was reinforced by the common sense that came with age. Nor did it come without a struggle. There can be little doubt that Castlereagh worked hard at reining in the impetuous side of his nature, which occasionally revealed itself in heated words and, most spectacularly, in his challenging George Canning to a duel in 1809 over their political differences.

By his mid-thirties he had become a paragon of middle-class values. He was happily married, abstemious and ordered in his habits, drinking little and rising early, never happier than when he could leave London to spend time on his farm at Cray in Kent, where he indulged his love of gardening and animal husbandry. He enjoyed the company of children. He was kind to servants and generous to the poor. He was industrious and conscientious in his work. He took his ease with books and indulged himself with music, which he loved, playing the cello and singing whenever the opportunity presented itself.

His tenure at the War Office, which came to an end in 1809, had not been deemed a success. His one achievement was to bend rules in order to have General Arthur Wellesley appointed to command the expeditionary force being sent to the Iberian peninsula in 1808. But its benefits did not become apparent until a few years later when, as Lord Wellington, Wellesley won the first decisive British victories over the French. In 1812 Castlereagh became Foreign Secretary, a post altogether better suited to his talents.

Castlereagh was a very able man. He could grasp the complexities of a problem quickly, along with its possible ramifications, and he could write it up in clear, elegant prose. But he was not an original thinker. He knew nothing of European affairs, and lacked the imagination to see what was happening on the Continent. He had imbibed his views on foreign policy from his hero Pitt, and he would remain faithful to them.

When he took over at the Foreign Office Britain was entirely isolated, with no influence on the European mainland. His first actions were therefore aimed at finding allies on the Continent and building up a coalition against Napoleon. Napoleon's invasion of Russia in the summer of 1812 played into his hands, and in July of that year Castlereagh concluded a treaty of alliance with Russia which bound the two countries to help each other in their attempts to bring about the defeat of France.

This was of little comfort to Russia, whose armies were fleeing before the triumphant Grande Armée, and who had to face up to the possibility of other enemies seizing the opportunity to recover lost lands. One such was Turkey, with whom Russia made a hurried peace. Another was Sweden, from which she had taken Finland only three years before, and which would almost certainly wish to recover it. Had Sweden invaded at that moment, Russia's defences would probably have collapsed entirely.

Tsar Alexander opened negotiations with Bernadotte and arranged a personal meeting, at Åbo. In the course of the discussions Alexander managed to convince Bernadotte to let Russia keep Finland, in return for which he would help Sweden take Norway from Denmark, an ally of France. He also undertook to persuade Britain to give Sweden one of the colonies she had taken from France. He did everything to charm the renegade French Marshal, and in order to seal their *entente* he threw out another piece of bait, the prospect of Bernadotte's ascending the throne of France once Napoleon had been defeated.

Shortly after, Castlereagh opened negotiations with Sweden, which culminated in the Treaty of Stockholm, signed on 3 March 1813. The terms were extraordinarily generous to Sweden. Britain undertook to assist her in taking possession of Norway, with military support if the King of Denmark were to prove recalcitrant, to cede her the former French West Indian island of Guadeloupe, and to pay her the sum of £1 million, in return for which Sweden promised to field 30,000 men against Napoleon.[7]

News of the signature of the Treaty of Kalisch between Russia and Prussia on 1 March 1813 was greeted with joy in London, but Castlereagh was less than thrilled. Britain had not been consulted on the subject of the projected treaty, which suggested that Russia felt she could act independently of her British ally. It also meant that Castlereagh had no idea what secret clauses the treaty might contain. And the fact that Britain, Russia, Sweden and Prussia were now aligned against France did not in itself amount to a coalition. Even were that so, experience taught that coalitions were vulnerable to the slightest reversal of fortune.

The first coalition against France had come together in 1793. It combined Austria, Russia, Prussia, Spain and a number of lesser powers. This formidable alliance proved ineffectual when faced with the *élan* of France's revolutionary armies, and it fell apart in 1796. A second coalition, consisting of Britain, Russia, Austria and Turkey, was cobbled together in 1799, but this disintegrated after the French victories of Marengo and Hohenlinden. A third, painstakingly constructed by Castlereagh's mentor William Pitt in 1805, combined Austria, Russia, Sweden and Prussia with Britain, but this too was shattered by Napoleon's victories at Austerlitz, Jena and Friedland. The one allied victory, Trafalgar, had failed to affect the outcome.

By 1807, when he signed a far-reaching alliance with Russia, Napoleon controlled virtually the whole of Continental Europe, making it impossible for Britain to play any part in its affairs, except in Portugal, where a small expeditionary force hung on precariously. Although she was supreme on the seas, much of the advantage this gave her was negated by a tariff war with France. Napoleon's Continental System excluded the British from trading with any part of

Europe, and eventually led to the outbreak of war between Britain and the United States of America.

As he contemplated the possibility of the birth of a new coalition in the spring of 1813, Castlereagh was acutely aware of both the need to direct it and the lack of means at his disposal. Britain's military capabilities were already stretched to breaking point by the double commitment of fighting one war with France in Spain and another with the United States of America across the Atlantic, so all he could contribute was money. And money could not buy sufficient influence to impose unity on a diverse set of allies.

Britain had always been concerned first and foremost with naval matters, and it was only when the armies of Revolutionary France advanced into the Austrian Netherlands in 1792 and threatened to take the estuary of the river Scheldt that a hitherto indifferent Britain felt impelled to go to war. The Scheldt estuary and the port of Antwerp had traditionally been viewed in Whitehall as the ideal base for an invasion of England, and the very thought of their falling into French hands was the stuff of nightmare. Provided the entire Netherlands could be kept in friendly or neutral hands, Britain had no interest in what form of government France saddled herself with. This divided Britain from her allies in the first coalition, who saw it as more of a monarchical crusade against revolution. In time, Britain's views on the subject of France converged with those of her Continental allies, yet significant differences remained. And any coalition was vulnerable to underlying resentments and a distrust based on mutual incomprehension of each other's strategic imperatives.

As an island and a sea power with no land army to speak of, Britain could only participate significantly in the fighting on the Continent through subsidies, which her allies used in order to raise and equip armies. Her naval victories over the French, even when they were on the scale of the battles of the Nile or Trafalgar, made no palpable difference to the situation on the European mainland. It therefore appeared that Britain was not pulling her weight or making the same sacrifices as her allies – the subsidies she contributed were, in their view, more than covered by the wealth of the French and Dutch colonies that fell into British hands and the riches confiscated on the high seas by her navy.

For a Continental power, a battle won brought no such advantages, while a battle lost often entailed the ravaging of its own territory and the necessity to sue for peace on any terms. The British, safe behind their watery defences, could not understand this predicament. They had no experience of foreign invasion and occupation, and bemoaned their allies' lamentable tendency to sue for peace at the first set-back. They tended to look upon any state that had been forced to do so as an enemy. Having no first-hand experience of fighting against Napoleon, the British were inclined to attribute his victories to the failings of their allies' armies and the pusillanimity of their governments. This seemed to be borne out when the one Continental power as strategically invulnerable as Britain, Russia, submitted to Napoleon in 1807.

In the event, Russia had only done so because her Austrian ally had been defeated and forced to sue for peace, her Prussian ally had been shattered and reduced to nothing, and her British one was incapable of sending a single regiment to assist her. But Castlereagh, like Pitt before him, could not imagine what it was like to be left isolated facing a victorious Napoleon across a corpse-strewn battle-field. All he knew was that coalitions tended to fall apart, and he ascribed this principally to their not having a clearly defined purpose and a mechanism to ensure that all parties stuck to it until it was achieved.

As he watched events unfold on the Continent in the spring of 1813, Castlereagh determined that he must somehow ensure that the allies in this incipient coalition would make war together and peace together, on terms agreed mutually and properly defined. That was not going to be easy.

Britain's diplomats had been excluded from a large part of the Continent for the past fifteen years and from the rest of it for the past three or four, so there was a dearth of knowledge in London as to what was going on in various countries and who the important players were. There was a corresponding lack of experienced diplomats, just at the moment when Castlereagh needed them. To Russia he had sent Lord Cathcart, an old soldier with scant diplomatic experience. To Prussian headquarters he now despatched his own half-brother, Sir Charles Stewart, another soldier, and not a particularly distinguished one at that. Stewart was thirty-five years old. He had served on Wellington's staff in the peninsula, where he had displayed impetuous courage but none of the qualities requisite for a command – 'A most gallant fellow, but perfectly mad,' in the words of a brother officer. Stewart would probably have approved of that description. 'My schemes are those of a Hussar at the Outposts,' he wrote to the painter Thomas Lawrence before taking up his first diplomatic post. 'Very short, very decided, and very prompt.'[8]

Castlereagh's instructions to these two dealt mainly with the extent of the subsidies which Britain was to contribute to the allied cause. But they also sketched out the basis of a final settlement towards which they were to work, and expressed the desire to bring about a closer union that would bind the allies to achieving those goals – he did not want this coalition disintegrating like the others, and he did not want the allies making a separate peace once they had achieved their own objectives, leaving Britain out in the cold. He already saw himself in the role of guiding spirit of this budding coalition, and had ambitious plans for it. But he did not as yet contemplate extending it to embrace Austria, and his mistrust of Metternich was so great that he would not even listen to what the Austrian envoy Wessenberg had to say.

4

～✦～

A War for Peace

'I desire peace; the world needs it,' Napoleon declared at the opening session of the Legislative Assembly on 14 February 1813. He desired it probably as ardently as anyone. But he could only make it on terms that were, in his own words, 'honourable and in keeping with the interests and the greatness of my Empire'. He could not contemplate the idea of negotiating from a position of weakness, and his instinctive reaction to his predicament was to win a war first.[1]

His policy of delivering a shattering blow and then dictating the terms of peace had worked well enough in the past, but each of his victories inevitably appeared less dramatic than the last, while repeated drubbings merely tempered the resistance of his enemies. His *modus operandi* was subject to the inexorable law of diminishing returns, but he appears to have been oblivious to this.

Following his failure to rally the remnants of the Grande Armée at Vilna and then at Königsberg in East Prussia, Murat had left his post and gone back to his kingdom of Naples. The man who took command in his stead was Napoleon's stepson Prince Eugène de Beauharnais, Viceroy of Italy. He had managed to stabilise a front along the Vistula in January, and from his headquarters at Posen (Poznań) worked hard at replenishing the ranks of shattered units. On 27 January Napoleon wrote him a long letter reviewing the possibilities for a spring campaign that would take French forces back across the Niemen into Russia in August, and by the beginning of February he was making arrangements to despatch his household there.

The one lesson he had learnt from the Russian campaign was that too many attendants and accoutrements only got in the way. 'I want to have much fewer people, not so many cooks, less plate, no great *nécessaire*,' he wrote. 'On campaign and on the march, tables, even mine, will be served with soup, a boiled dish, a roast and vegetables, with no dessert.' He announced that he would be taking no pages, as 'they are of no use to me', apart from some of his more hardy hunting pages.[2]

By then the French front had been forced back to the line of the Oder, but Napoleon was not unduly worried. On 11 March he wrote again to Prince Eugène, now holding a front along the Elbe, sketching a grandiose plan of attack involving a sweep through Berlin and Danzig into Poland. From Kraków, Poniatowski, supported by the Austrians, was to strike northward and cut the Russian army's lines of communication.[3]

These plans were disrupted, but his confidence was not particularly shaken, when on 27 March the Prussian ambassador in Paris handed in Prussia's declaration of war on France. Napoleon's reaction was to instruct Narbonne in Vienna to offer Austria the Prussian province of Silesia (which the Prussians had captured from Austria in 1745) as a prize if she supported France in the forthcoming war. Metternich did not want Silesia, and he certainly did not want to go to war again at the side of France. In a last-ditch attempt to bring Napoleon to the negotiating table, he sent Prince Schwarzenberg to Paris.[4]

Schwarzenberg's instructions, dated 28 March 1813, stressed that the moment was 'one of the highest importance for the future fate of Europe, of Austria, and of France in particular', adding that it was 'an urgent necessity' that the two courts reach an understanding. He was to make it clear to Napoleon that while Austria would support France sincerely in pursuit of a fair peace, she did not feel herself bound to do so unconditionally. Metternich was particularly anxious to drive home the fact that Napoleon's marriage to Marie-Louise counted for nothing in the present circumstances. 'Policy made the marriage, and policy can unmake it,' Schwarzenberg told Maret. But Napoleon was deaf to these hints.[5]

He spent his days reviewing newly-formed regiments on the Champ de Mars before they left for Germany. In the last week of March and the first two of April he made his final preparations. They included setting up a Regency Council which was to administer France while he was on campaign, and to assume control if anything were to happen to him. Schwarzenberg, who had a long interview with him at Saint-Cloud on 13 April, found him less belligerent than in the past, and genuinely eager to avoid war. 'His language was less peremptory and, like his whole demeanour, less self-assured; he gave the impression of a man who fears losing the prestige which surrounded him, and his eyes seemed to be asking me whether I still saw in him the same man as before.' Thirty-six hours later Napoleon left Saint-Cloud for the army, which he joined at Erfurt on 25 April.[6]

Alexander and Frederick William had already taken the offensive. With the Prussian army under General Gebhard Blücher in the van, they invaded Saxony, denouncing its King as a tool of Napoleon and a traitor to the cause. The King, Frederick Augustus, found himself in much the same position as Frederick William a couple of months earlier, but had even less time to make a decision as to which way to jump. The allies had their reasons for forcing the issue in this way, and they were not creditable ones.

In the secret articles of the Treaty of Kalisch, Russia had promised to restore Prussia to a position of power equal to that she had held before she lost her Polish lands to Napoleon, and to find 'equivalents' for her if necessary. Russia was in possession of those formerly Prussian Polish lands, but made no mention of giving them back, while the use of the word 'equivalents' suggested that Prussia would be rebuilt with German territory. The most desirable block of territory was Saxony. Both Alexander and Frederick William therefore hoped that Frederick Augustus would not declare for the allies and thereby place Saxony in the allied camp.

Frederick Augustus was genuinely attached to Napoleon, to whom he owed his royal crown, and, being endowed with a sense of honour, would have done anything to stand by his ally. But his small army had been annihilated in Russia, and he was now in the front line. He was being urged by Metternich to realign himself, but was both unwilling to do so and afraid of breaking his alliance with Napoleon. He attempted to sidestep the issue by taking refuge in Austria, and on 20 April concluding a treaty with her which guaranteed his continued possession of Saxony. Not long after he left it, his capital Dresden was occupied by Alexander and Frederick William, who marched in at the head of their troops, cheered by the population. But their triumph was to be short-lived.[7]

The allied army, consisting of some 100,000 Russians and Prussians commanded by the Russian General Ferdinand von Winzingerode and the Prussian Gebhard Blücher, marched out to face the French. But Napoleon advanced swiftly and defeated them at Lützen on 2 May. The Russians and Prussians had, according to a British officer attached to allied headquarters, shown bravery and dash, but 'in crowds, without any method'. There had been a general want of direction in the command, and Alexander and Frederick William had only further muddled things by their presence on the battlefield. The retreat was chaotic and bad-tempered, and insults flew between the two allied armies.[8]

The victory demonstrated once again the superiority of French arms, but it was not decisive. Napoleon's shortage of cavalry, a consequence of the previous year's Russian campaign, prevented him from pursuing the enemy and turning their defeat into a rout. Although he trumpeted the news of a great victory for propaganda purposes, he was not satisfied. To Prince Eugène he wrote admitting that in view of the insignificant number of prisoners he had taken it was no victory at all.[9]

Alexander made light of the defeat. 'This retreat was accomplished with admirable calm, tranquillity and order,' he wrote to his sister Catherine, 'and I admit that I would not have thought such a thing

War and diplomacy, June–September 1813

possible except on a parade-ground.' The defeat nevertheless cast a pall over the allied army, and mutual recriminations followed, with Prussians blaming Russians for not holding firm, and vice-versa. The Prussians had suffered painful losses, including that of General Scharnhorst, and morale was correspondingly low. And although the allied retreat fell short of a rout, Alexander and Frederick William had to abandon Dresden and flee to Silesia. The King of Saxony hastily repudiated his alliance with Austria and hurried back to his capital to greet his ally Napoleon, who appeared to be back in control of events.[10]

Metternich was sanguine. He assumed that the defeat of Lützen would have sobered the allies and made them realise how much they needed the support of Austria. At the same time its limited nature would not have given Napoleon enough confidence to make him intransigent. This opened up room for manoeuvre.

Metternich hoped simultaneously to avoid the position of having to make a hasty choice between the two sides and to seize the moral high ground by adopting the role of mediator. This would leave Austria free, if Napoleon refused to cooperate, to join the allies against him – when she was ready, and only after securing favourable terms. It was not going to be easy, and Metternich realised that he might fall between two stools.

He had been in secret communication with the Russian court throughout the past year, with an eye to what might happen if Napoleon's fortunes changed. Although obliged to send an Austrian auxiliary corps into Russia as part of Napoleon's invasion force in 1812, he had instructed its commander, Schwarzenberg, to keep out of any fighting. This Schwarzenberg duly did, through a secret understanding with the Russian commanders facing him. When the Grande Armée began to disintegrate he pulled back into Poland, and on 6 January 1813 started to evacuate the grand duchy of Warsaw, which he was supposed to defend alongside Poniatowski's Polish army. On 30 January he signed a secret convention similar to the one Yorck had concluded with the Russians and withdrew to Galicia, the Austrian province of Poland. This forced Poniatowski to fall back on Kraków, which opened the whole of Poland and the road west to the Russians.[11]

At this juncture Metternich would, circumstances permitting, have preferred to combine with Prussia in mediating a peace settlement between Russia and France, before the Russian army advanced any further west and before Napoleon reappeared on the scene with fresh forces. This would have laid the foundations for a peace that excluded both Russian and French influence from Germany and turned it into a neutral zone under Austrian and Prussian protection. Metternich mistrusted Prussia, which had let Austria down in the past and changed sides more than once out of opportunism. But he liked and respected her tall, distinguished-looking, grey-haired chancellor, Baron Karl August von Hardenberg. And, as it happened, Hardenberg had been thinking along the same lines as Metternich, and made the first tentative contact.

Hardenberg was not in fact a Prussian. Born in Hanover in 1750, he had travelled extensively before entering the service of his sovereign, King George III of England and Elector of Hanover. He had only left his service, reluctantly, after his wife had begun a scandalous and highly public affair with the Prince of Wales. It was then that he had found employment with the King of Prussia, for whom he negotiated the inglorious Treaty of Bâle in 1795, by which Prussia acquired large tranches of the Rhineland in return for ditching her allies and joining France. In 1804 he had become Prussia's Foreign Minister and engineered the annexation of his native Hanover, once again in partnership with France against Austria and Russia, and in 1810 he was rewarded with the post of Prussian Chancellor.

Hardenberg's attempt to negotiate an agreement with Metternich at the beginning of 1813 was overtaken by events; General Yorck's mutiny 'knocked the bottom out of my barrel', to use his own words. With the Russians drawing near and the Prussian army joining them, he could not delay acceding to the alliance Alexander was offering long enough to combine with Metternich in an offer of mediation. Once he saw himself forced to accept the Russian alliance, he tried to persuade Metternich to do likewise, calculating that if Austria and Prussia were to accede together they might do so on better terms. But Metternich was not prepared to take such a chance, and had no desire to swap Austria's subservient alliance with France for a similar one with Russia.[12]

He needed more time to reposition Austria, and for that it was essential to keep both Russia and France at arm's length. Through his secretary Friedrich von Gentz he had secretly assured the Russian acting Foreign Minister, Count Charles Nesselrode, that Austria would break with Napoleon and join the allies, 'for the eternal cause which will assuredly triumph in the end, for that cause which is neither Russian, nor Austrian, which is based on universal and immutable laws', explaining why he could not do so quite yet.[13]

Gentz provided an invaluable conduit for communication with the allies. Born in Prussian Silesia, he had studied in Königsberg under Kant, then worked as a civil servant in Berlin, written for and edited a number of periodicals, and been an agent of the British Foreign

Office before taking service in Austria. He was an old friend of Nesselrode, whom he knew from Berlin, and of Prussia's ambassador in Vienna, Wilhelm von Humboldt. He was a colourful character, sentimental and naïve in his youth, when he had loved deeply and tragically before turning to a rackety life of drinking, gambling and whoring. Along with the poets Friedrich Schlegel and Jean Paul Richter, the two Humboldt brothers, Clemens Brentano, Friedrich Schleiermacher and Georg Wilhelm Friedrich Hegel, he was at the centre of the intellectual circle dominated by the Jewish bluestocking Rahel Lewin, whose members switched lovers and entered into 'intellectual marriages' that did not constrain their freedom. Even after his marriage he carried on an exploitative relationship with Rahel Lewin, sired a child by a mistress, and had a string of affairs with notorious actresses and courtesans.

An extraordinarily hard worker, Gentz continued to study and write throughout. His political development took him from early enthusiasms for the French Revolution, through reactionary monarchism, to more pragmatic views. A clever man, widely travelled and wise in the ways of the world, he was quick to see through people and was an invaluable assistant to Metternich.

Metternich was also in contact with the Russian court through Count Stackelberg, the as yet unofficial Russian envoy in Vienna. And at the beginning of March he had sent his own envoy to allied headquarters at Kalisch. For this mission he had selected Count Louis-Joseph Lebzeltern, a bright young diplomat who had served under him in Paris and in 1810 been sent to St Petersburg to establish a personal link between Alexander and Metternich. Lebzeltern had made himself popular in Russia, which he left only at the outbreak of war in 1812.

When Lebzeltern appeared at Russian headquarters on 5 March he was warmly embraced by Alexander, who expressed the hope that Francis would save Europe by joining the cause. But Lebzeltern detected 'a pronounced mistrust of our intentions'. Alexander's apparent cordiality turned into impatience when he discovered that

Metternich's envoy had brought with him nothing beyond expressions of good will. He demanded immediate commitment, and dismissed the objection that the ground had to be prepared first, declaring that the details could be worked out at a congress to be held later.[14]

This conversation had taken place a full week before Prussia's declaration of war against France, so it is hardly surprising that Metternich had not been ready to commit himself and his country. And there were deeper causes for concern. Russia and Prussia were weak. French might and Napoleon's military talents could easily defeat them in the spring. Both had in the past made opportunistic peaces with France, and might do so again. If Austria were to betray her alliance with France now and expose herself to Napoleon's anger, she would end up paying a heavy price. Metternich's caution was strongly reinforced by his imperial master's aversion to risk.

The Emperor Francis was not a heroic figure. Born in Florence in 1768, he was meant to succeed his father as Grand Duke of Tuscany, but his uncle Joseph II's failure to produce an heir placed his father, Leopold, on the imperial throne, which he himself ascended in 1792. According to his uncle Joseph, Francis was 'of a dull and sullen disposition' and 'intellectually lazy'. Although fairly energetic in his performance of the actions of everyday life, he slowed down markedly whenever thought was required, sometimes literally coming to a standstill. Like his uncle Joseph, he was distrustful of new ideas and almost allergic to enthusiasm and passion in others. Humourless by nature, he was indifferent to most forms of entertainment, and unlike his uncle he was very devout.[15]

He had learnt his lesson painfully in 1809, when, carried away by a wave of patriotic fervour sweeping the country and the optimism of his then chancellor, Count Johann Philipp Stadion, he had embarked on a war to liberate Germany from French domination while Napoleon's back was turned. The ease with which Napoleon, despite being heavily engaged in Spain at the time, had managed to turn about and defeat Austria had left an indelible impression on Francis and Metternich. The only thing that had saved the Austrian state from annihilation had been the politic marriage of Francis's daughter Marie-Louise to the French conqueror. She had been sacrificed to ensure the survival of the Habsburg monarchy. There was no knowing what sacrifices Napoleon might demand if he were provoked again.

Metternich's apparent subservience to Napoleon was unpopular in Austria. He had come to power as a result of the fall of Stadion, and was even accused of having engineered it. While Stadion continued to enjoy public esteem, Metternich was regarded as representing a 'peace party' dedicated to a policy of abasement; there had recently even been plots to assassinate him, hatched by bellicose officers.

While he continued to play for time, his opponents did everything to try to force the issue, obliging him to act in ways that only increased his unpopularity. The Emperor's brother Archduke John was at the head of a conspiracy, fed by British money, to raise a revolt against French rule in Carynthia, Tyrol and Illyria, hoping to launch a *guerrilla* similar to that in Spain throughout French-ruled Italy. This was just the kind of thing that Metternich had no time for – it could achieve little, yet if Napoleon were to hear of Austria's complicity, the retaliation could be draconian. On 25 February he arrested the British courier delivering funds to the conspirators, and a few weeks later a number of other conspirators, including the Archduke himself. The courier was given safe-conduct back to London, and furnished with letters for Castlereagh suggesting the resumption of relations and the despatch of a diplomatic envoy.

At the beginning of April, Hardenberg had sent Metternich a message suggesting a secret meeting between them, in the presence of Nesselrode. Metternich had no desire to discuss German affairs in front of a Russian, nor did he wish to arouse Napoleon's suspicions. Narbonne had alerted Napoleon to the fact that there was 'an underground connection' between Vienna and his enemies, and Metternich knew he was being observed.[16]

He needed to persuade the allies that he was with them in spirit, yet at the same time manoeuvre them away from pursuing the war and towards negotiating a peace. For this purpose he selected his predecessor Stadion, who had served a term as ambassador in St Petersburg, who was known to be anti-French and pro-war, and who would therefore enjoy the confidence of the allies. As he was also known to be a rival of Metternich, the latter could disassociate himself from him if the French were to hear of his presence at Russian headquarters.

Stadion's brief was to propose that the allies sign an armistice with Napoleon and enter into negotiations with him. Shortly after his departure, Metternich had a long interview with Narbonne, whom he tried to convince that Austria wanted to help Napoleon make a favourable peace, with minimal concessions. Narbonne correctly suspected that Metternich was hoping to get Napoleon to agree to negotiations in principle, so as to be able to start upping the terms, thereby forcing him either to accept these or to break off the negotiations, which would allow Austria to declare their alliance null. Sensing that he was getting nowhere with Narbonne, Metternich resolved to address Napoleon through Bubna.[17]

Napoleon had entered Dresden hot on the heels of Alexander and Frederick William. He set about fortifying the city, which he intended to be the base from which he would strike at the allied armies converging on the Elbe. Wishing to be free of court ceremonial and to dispense with etiquette, he had taken up quarters not in the royal palace but in the summer residence of the former minister Marcolini, set in extensive gardens in the northern suburb of Friedrichstadt. Here he could behave as though he were on campaign, working and resting to a rhythm set by the twin exigencies of war and diplomacy. A daily courier from Paris brought news of everything that was going on not merely in the capital but throughout his realm. Agents all over Germany reported on events and morale. Like a great spider at the centre of his web, he watched and waited.

Bubna had his first interview with Napoleon on 16 May. He put forward Metternich's suggested basis for peace: that Napoleon give up the grand duchy of Warsaw, relinquish control over German territory east of the Rhine, and return Illyria to Austria. The interview quickly turned into a harangue as Napoleon accused Austria of duplicity, of arming and of negotiating with France's enemies while pretending to remain loyal to her. He pointed out to Bubna that Schwarzenberg's withdrawal from Poland had been a betrayal of their alliance. He reminded him that during their last interview in Paris, Schwarzenberg had solemnly assured him that the 30,000-strong Austrian auxiliary corps was still at his disposal, but that when the campaign had opened Metternich had withdrawn it.

Napoleon laughed at the basis for negotiation put forward by Bubna, declaring that while it was an affront to him it was certainly too minimal to satisfy his enemies (he was not mistaken, as on the very same day, at allied headquarters at Würschen, Nesselrode was busily adding more conditions, extending the basis to include France's cession of Holland and Spain). Napoleon expressed regret at having married Francis's daughter, and swore that he would not give up a single village.

He was trying to frighten the Austrians into toeing the line. But he was far from confident, and he suspected that a trap was being set for him. After the interview, which lasted four hours, he asked Caulaincourt to question Bubna further in an attempt to penetrate Metternich's real intentions. He realised that if he refused to go along with the proposed negotiations he would be isolating himself, so at a final interview with the Austrian general he declared that he would agree to an armistice and that he was prepared to make peace in principle, on terms to be discussed in due course.[18]

How little Napoleon trusted his Austrian ally by this stage is revealed by the fact that hardly had Bubna left Dresden than he despatched Caulaincourt to the Russian front lines with the request for an immediate ceasefire and for one-to-one talks between France and Russia. If he were going to be forced to give up the grand duchy of Warsaw, he might as well use it to bribe Russia into ditching Prussia and Austria.

This was the nightmare that had been haunting Metternich all along: the possibility of Napoleon and Alexander reaching agreement, necessarily at Austria's as well as Prussia's expense. Metternich knew nothing of Caulaincourt's mission yet, as communications were slow. But the armies were not far apart, war or peace could be made from one day to the next, and all sides lived in suspense. People in Vienna would open their windows at the slightest rumble and listen anxiously for the sound of French guns. These did not remain silent for long.

On 20 May Napoleon struck again. He outflanked the new allied defensive positions behind the river Spree around Bautzen, forcing them to abandon the field and beat a hasty retreat. Although his shortage of cavalry once again prevented him from turning this into a rout and the retreat was relatively orderly, morale on the allied side plummeted as the Russians and Prussians trudged back into Silesia.

The Russian army, some of whose units were down to a quarter of their nominal strength, was in a critical condition, and from the highest to the lowest, the men wanted to return home. The newly-arrived British ambassador Sir Charles Stewart described their mood as 'of a desponding nature' and reported that 'they eagerly looked to their own frontiers'. The rank-and-file, most of whom had been drafted under emergency measures in 1812 to resist the foreign invader, had been promised they could go home once the fatherland had been liberated. Only junior officers, avid for glory and promotion, wanted to take the war into Germany. As far as the rest were concerned, Poland was enough of a prize.[19]

That was precisely what Caulaincourt had been instructed to offer the Tsar. But he had reached the allied outposts on 18 May, two days before the battle, and had been told that Alexander would not receive him. It might have been otherwise if he had arrived four days later. By then the Russians were staring disaster in the face; one more push, or even a vigorous pursuit by the French, and, to quote Stewart, 'the military power of Russia might have been crushed for a generation', a judgement confirmed by the Russian General Langeron.[20]

If Napoleon had continued his advance, the Russians would have been forced to fall back into Poland while the Prussian forces would have had to retreat northwards. The allied army would have split into two forces, easy to defeat separately. Although the French lines of communication would have been extended by such an advance, this would have been more than made up for by the reinforcements Napoleon would have found on the spot in the shape of the garrisons he had left in a string of fortresses from Danzig to Zamość. More to the point, morale in the Russian army would probably have been tipped over the edge and the first flare of a pan-German revolt would have been doused. As it was, the numbers of volunteers coming forward to fight for the liberation of Germany had been disappointing outside East Prussia and Brandenburg.[21]

But Napoleon was worried by the state of his own forces. 'The magnificent spirit that had always inspired our battalions was destroyed,' wrote the commander of the 2nd Tirailleurs of the Guard. 'Ambition had replaced emulation. The army was now commanded by officers who may have been brave to the point of temerity, but who lacked experience and instruction. The soldiers only looked for opportunities to leave their units, to get into hospitals, to keep out of danger.' The marches and counter-marches of the past weeks had not only exhausted the troops, they also gave the impression that their commander was not as sure of his actions as before. Shortage of cavalry restricted reconnaissance and pursuit alike. Paucity of not only cavalry horses but also draught animals meant that the quarter-mastership could not deliver adequate victuals or supplies. To add to the misery, the spring of 1813 was unusually cold and wet. Desertion was rife, particularly in the contingents contributed by Napoleon's German allies, in which whole units would go over to the enemy at night. 'What a war!' Marshal Augereau complained. 'It will do for all of us!'[22]

At a more personal level, Napoleon had been deeply saddened by the death, during the opening shots of the Battle of Lützen, of Marshal Bessières, one of his most loyal and capable commanders. He had been profoundly shaken three weeks later when Marshal Duroc, his sincere friend as well as one of his most trusted collaborators, was hit by a cannonball at Bautzen. Napoleon was at his bedside when Duroc breathed his last.

Instead of pursuing the allies, Napoleon decided to call a halt and wait for reinforcements, so he sent a messenger to allied headquarters with the offer of an armistice of seven weeks. The offer was readily accepted and the armistice concluded at Plesswitz on 4 June.

Napoleon had made a fatal strategic error. The armistice 'saved us and condemned him', as one Russian general put it. Not only did Napoleon save the allies from almost certain defeat, he threw away the initiative, which he would never regain.[23]

5

Intimate Congress

Metternich had received a report of Caulaincourt's mission to Russian headquarters not long before he heard of the allied defeat at Bautzen. The first opened up the terrifying possibility that Napoleon and Alexander might strike a deal over his head, while the second raised the equally alarming one that the allied armies would withdraw into Poland and Prussia respectively, leaving Austria militarily defenceless and at Napoleon's mercy.

The time was fast approaching when Metternich would have to commit Austria to one side or the other, and he was not ready. Schwarzenberg was massing all available Austrian forces at Prague, but would not be ready to take the field before the second week in August at the earliest. Only diplomacy could buy Metternich that time, and when a courier from Dresden brought news of Bautzen at 4 p.m. on the afternoon on 29 May, he sprang into action.

He drove over to the palace of Laxenburg to see the Emperor Francis. He persuaded him to leave Vienna and take up residence at some point midway between Alexander's headquarters and Napoleon's, in order to underline his intention of assuming an autonomous role. The only suitable residence in the area was Wallenstein's former stronghold, the gloomy old castle at Gitschin (Jičin). The move was prepared with the utmost secrecy, but the French ambassador Narbonne got wind of it through his spies at the imperial stables and rushed to Metternich for an explanation. Metternich fobbed him off with evasive answers. The anxious Narbonne immediately set off for Dresden to warn Napoleon, but Metternich had pre-empted him. He had already sent off two couriers, one to Bubna in Dresden instructing him to renew the offer to Napoleon of Austria's good offices as mediator in reaching a peace settlement, the other to allied head-quarters announcing that Francis had left Vienna in order to be closer to his army.

This in itself was hardly likely to convince Alexander of Austria's good faith. He needled Stadion and Lebzeltern about her true inten-tions, and pointed to signs of her treachery. He was furious when he heard that Austria had allowed Poniatowski's Polish corps, which had been isolated in Kraków, to march through Austrian territory in order to rejoin Napoleon's main forces in Saxony. His suspicions were further aroused when news reached him of Bubna's mission to Dresden.[1]

On 1 June, as they were making their way to Gitschin, Francis and Metternich encountered Nesselrode coming the other way. He had been sent by an exasperated Alexander with instructions to pin the Emperor of Austria down to committing himself, on which point he stressed 'that I need a categorical decision, in writing'. The last thing Francis was prepared to do at this stage was to commit himself in writing, but he did give Nesselrode a strong verbal assurance of his intent to join the allies if a satisfactory peace settlement could not be wrenched from Napoleon.[2]

In the circumstances, the armistice of Plesswitz, which came into effect on 4 June, the day after Francis and Metternich reached Gitschin, was a godsend. 'The first great step has been taken, my dearest friend,' Metternich wrote to his wife on 6 June, making out that the signature of the armistice was somehow the consequence of his own deft diplo-macy. In a letter to his daughter written two days later, he complained of the strain of being the prime mover, on whom the eighty million inhabitants of the Continent depended for their salvation. Full of his sense of mission, he set about manipulating events.[3]

His first move was to provide himself with a stage on which he would be able to direct the actors as he wished. One of his reasons for choosing Gitschin was that it lay not far from Ratiborzitz (Ratibořic), the estate of Wilhelmina de Biron, Princess of Sagan. She was one of the four daughters of the late Duke of Courland. Originally an autonomous prince under the suzerainty of Poland, he had foreseen the extinction of that kingdom and of his principality with it, and had purchased substantial estates as insurance for the future. One of these was the principality of Sagan (Żagań) in Silesia, which he had left Wilhelmina on his death in 1800. He had also left her the estate of Ratiborzitz, with a simple but luxurious country house set in the grounds of the ancient castle. As this was conveniently close to Gitschin and to the allied headquarters at Reichenbach (Dzierżoniów), which had already attracted her mother the Duchess of Courland, Metternich suggested that she take up residence there. She could not resist the call to be near the epicentre of events; and, like so many ladies in Europe at the time, she worshipped Alexander, so she agreed.

She was joined there by Gentz, whom Metternich wished to have near at hand, since he had planned to arrange a number of meetings at Ratiborzitz that even Napoleon's spies would not get wind of. 'I live here as in heaven,' Gentz wrote to a friend. He loved the relaxed atmosphere that reigned in the elegant house, and was beginning to fall under the spell of its beautiful châtelaine.[4]

Metternich had met her a few years before and had even begun a mild flirtation with her in 1810, but this had been interrupted by the appearance of the dashing young Prince Alfred von Windischgraetz, an officer in the Austrian army, with whom she fell in love. She still was, but this did not stop her growing close to Metternich during the spring of 1813, when he was feeling politically isolated and under pressure. He would discuss his ideas and policies with her as though she were a colleague. She would now act as his stage manager as he put together one of the great acts of his career.

* * *

Alexander was in no mood for play-acting. Although he had been obliged to accept Napoleon's offer of the armistice, he was still bent on war. It was not in his nature to back down in the face of adversity. At Bautzen, where he had insisted on exercising command at one point, he had, when informed that his right flank had been turned, declared that 'In war the obstinate will always triumph,' and had nearly been cut off as a result. 'I noticed that the idea of breaking off the war without having achieved the grand results he had allowed himself to dream of tormented him like a gnawing parasite,' Gentz reported to Metternich after a meeting with the Tsar.[5]

The allies had established their headquarters in the little town of Reichenbach, to the south of Breslau, but Alexander himself had taken up quarters a few miles away in a derelict country house at Peterswaldau (Pieszyce). He was attended only by Admiral Shishkov and his chief of police, Aleksandr Balashov, as well as a few aides-de-camp. But he ignored their presence, spending hours alone in the overgrown gardens and orchards of the house or walking over to the nearby colony of Herrnhut Moravian Brethren at Gnadenfrei (Piława Górna), with whom he communed.[6]

Partly out of a growing reluctance to relinquish control and partly out of a sense that, since he was the instrument of God, he did not need advice, Alexander delegated less and less. His Foreign Minister, Chancellor Rumiantsev, had suffered a slight stroke and was in no condition to carry out his duties, but rather than replace him Alexander left him in his post back in St Petersburg and took control of foreign affairs himself. Instead of being elevated to ministerial rank, Rumiantsev's natural successor Nesselrode merely became a sort of secretary to the Tsar.

He was perfectly suited for such a role. Born in Lisbon, the son of a minor Westphalian noble in Russian service, Nesselrode had come to Russia in 1796, aged sixteen, and served as a midshipman in the Baltic fleet. He moved on to a commission in the horseguards, and after a spell as aide-de-camp and chamberlain to Tsar Paul, he transferred to the diplomatic service. As a junior diplomat at the embassy in Paris, he established and became the link in a secret communication between Alexander and the then French Foreign Minister Talleyrand. Small and ordinary-looking, he challenged no one. He was a competent bureaucrat, loyal, hard-working and always ready to oblige his superiors. Gentz, with whom he also kept up a clandestine correspondence through war and peace, thought him 'a man of upright character, good judgement, born for work and solid things'. Metternich once said that 'If he were a fish, he would be carried away with the current.' He would probably not have minded, as he saw himself primarily as the Tsar's instrument. 'I am called when I am needed,' he explained to his wife. 'I am completely passive.'[7]

With ministers such as Nesselrode around him, Alexander never needed to fear being contradicted. He also had a number of people in his entourage who had their own programmes and who would support him robustly whenever he needed reassurance. One such was Stein, who could be counted on to argue against all the Russians who were for retrenching on their conquests in Poland. Another was Carl'Andrea Pozzo di Borgo.

Corsican by birth, he was a contemporary and erstwhile close friend of Napoleon, with whom he had made common cause during the early stages of the French Revolution. He had gradually drifted away from and eventually turned against his famous compatriot, becoming an implacable enemy whose hatred was kept warm by burning jealousy. After spending some time in London and Vienna, Pozzo had taken service in Russia, where Alexander had rewarded him with the rank of General and the title of Count. He was more cunning than intelligent, and could certainly be counted on to support Alexander in any venture, however risky, aimed at the destruction of Napoleon.

Strong in the conviction that God meant him to save Europe, buoyed up by the vigorous support of the likes of Stein and Pozzo, Alexander was unlikely to be deflected from his aim. Particularly as every day reinforcements marched into camp from the depths of Russia and newly formed Prussian regiments took their place in the allied ranks.

The situation in the Prussian camp was quite the reverse of that in Alexander's entourage. When news of the armistice became known at allied headquarters 'the Prussian officers were so indignant that they tore off their pelisses and trampled them underfoot', according to Stewart. Their exasperation was shared by Hardenberg, and particularly by Humboldt.[8]

Wilhelm von Humboldt was an ardent patriot, and had put his faith in Prussia as the only agency through which the German lands could be freed. A prominent literary figure and a close friend of Schiller, he had neglected his career as a writer to become a Prussian minister and, in 1810, Prussia's ambassador in Vienna. He was now forty-six years old and somewhat overshadowed by the reputation of his younger brother, the renowned naturalist and traveller Alexander von Humboldt. He was highly intelligent and dedicated, yet many found him difficult to like. He was censorious and at times priggish, which did not prevent him from liberally indulging a seedy taste for preferably fat lower-class girls whom he could treat as objects while writing curiously high-minded letters to his wife Caroline, his 'dearest Li'.

On 13 June he wrote to her from Reichenbach venting his anger at the armistice. Not only was it entirely unnecessary, he felt, it was psychologically damaging to the German cause. The first wave of enthusiasm which had brought volunteers flocking to the Prussian colours had spent itself, partisan activity had fizzled out, and if the allied armies remained behind the Elbe for much longer, it would be impossible to breathe fresh life into the movement for the liberation of Germany. The behaviour of the Russian troops towards the German population was undermining the alliance, while the Russian command was growing increasingly war-weary. Humboldt bemoaned the lack of committed leadership, and feared that in these conditions Metternich, whom he distrusted and disliked, would be able to make an 'Austrian peace' that would leave Prussia in the lurch and cancel out all hope of a Germany free from foreign influence. 'The future looks unbelievably dark and uncertain,' he wrote to her on 22 June.[9]

King Frederick William also thought the future looked bleak, but for different reasons. He did not share his army's spirit of belligerence, and could not make up his mind which threatened him more: the continuation of the war, with its perils and unforeseen consequences, or the conclusion of peace, which would probably take place at the expense of Prussia. His natural inclinations were for the latter course. He would whip himself up into a warlike mood in order to support Alexander, but talk of war raised the spectre of unrest and possible revolution in his mind. 'His Majesty, therefore, cools down rapidly, and sinks back into the same amiable nonentity he has ever been,' noted George Jackson, Stewart's *secrétaire d'ambassade*.[10]

Stewart had come from London a few weeks earlier by a round-about route which had taken him by ship through the Baltic to Prussia, and on to allied headquarters at Reichenbach, where he finally delivered his letters of credence to Frederick William. To his intense disappointment, the atmosphere there was anything but warlike.

There were daily parades as Alexander and Frederick William reviewed newly arrived reinforcements, but there were also banquets, lunch parties and excursions to nearby beauty spots and places of interest. The presence of the sovereigns drew minor German princes eager to pay court to what they assumed would be the new powers in Germany, and ladies who had come to see the chivalrous liber-ator. 'Female society of the most perfect description was within our reach; and its allurements and dissipations often divided the mind of soldier and politician from their more severe duties,' recorded Stewart. Jackson contributed an English flavour. 'We have enlivened our leisure hours by getting up some pony races, which have gone off wonderfully well,' he wrote home. But the British diplomats were far from happy.[11]

Alexander had withdrawn into himself. In between meditations on the doctrines of the Moravian Brethren and his divine destiny, he was penning love notes to Princess Zinaida Volkonskaya, the wife of one of his aides-de-camp, with whom he had enjoyed a dalliance at Kalisch, and who had gone to Bohemia to await his projected arrival there. While pouring out his heart, he stressed the 'purity' of his feelings, and affirmed that he felt no scruples about making her unwitting husband carry the notes between them.[12]

While Alexander believed that the sufferings endured by his people over the previous twelve months entitled Russia to special consideration, Britain had, in the course of the past century, acquired a sense of embattled righteousness which translated effortlessly into an arrogant perception of her needs and her God-given right to them. This was the cause of some resentment, and not only among the Russians.

According to Jackson, Hardenberg seemed to regard Britain 'rather as a thorn in his side, and an obstacle to a peaceful settlement of affairs amongst the three Powers, than as an ally making the greatest efforts and sacrifices to aid in restoring permanent tranquillity in Europe'.[13]

In his instructions to Stadion of 7 May, designed to give as much pleasure as possible to the Russians short of committing Austria to an alliance, Metternich insisted that Britain would have to give up some of her maritime rights, adding that 'England's dominion on [the seas] is no less monstrous than Napoleon's on the continent.'[14]

Lord Cathcart, who had followed Alexander from St Petersburg, and the newly arrived Stewart, who thought highly of himself, felt they were not given enough respect at allied headquarters. But they were both relatively inferior in rank and personal reputation, and they were dealing with ministers and monarchs. Matters were not improved by the fact that they had taken an instant dislike to each other; as a result they did not always see eye to eye or coordinate their actions.

Neither Cathcart nor Stewart was given any information as to what was going on, and their anxiety mounted as they watched couriers come and go. As far as they were concerned, Austria was still an ally of France, and they found the presence of Stadion and Lebzeltern at allied headquarters puzzling. They had no inkling of what Metternich might be up to, and suspected the worst. 'I fear political treachery,' Stewart wrote excitedly to Castlereagh on 6 June. They were taken aback when they were at last informed that an armistice had been signed with Napoleon.[15]

The one thing Cathcart and Stewart did have going for them was money. Russia and Prussia were both desperate to pay and feed their armies and raise the new divisions they would need in order to confront Napoleon. On 14 June Stewart concluded a treaty with Prussia which bound her to put an extra 80,000 men in the field in exchange for an immediate cash subsidy of £666,000. Prussia also agreed to respect British claims to the lands of the houses of Hanover and Brunswick, while in a secret article Britain pledged herself to support Prussia's right to regain a position at least equivalent to that she had held in 1806. The following day Cathcart signed a twin treaty by which Russia was to receive twice as much money in return for an army of 150,000. Britain also agreed to spend £500,000 on refitting the Russian fleet. The two treaties provided for a further advance of £5 million in the form of 'federal paper', which could be issued by the allies to cover the expenses of war. It was backed by British credit and would be redeemed jointly by all three at the conclusion of the war.[16]

Possibly the most important article in the treaties was that which bound the signatories not to enter into any negotiations of any kind with any party without consulting each other. The suspension of hostilities had brought out mistrust between the allies, as each of them considered the possibility that the other might make a separate deal with Napoleon. 'Conjecture was still very busy, and had a wide field of action,' in Stewart's words.[17]

The deepest suspicions were focused on Austria, and on Metternich in particular. On 10 June Hardenberg was sent to Gitschin to obtain firmer commitments from Austria. Amongst other things, he wanted to ensure that the bases for negotiation which were to be submitted to Napoleon should not be too acceptable to him; if Metternich were to offer him terms that he could stomach, Napoleon might seize on the opportunity to make a peace that would satisfy neither Russia nor Prussia, and certainly not their British ally.

The conditions proposed by Hardenberg as the starting-point for negotiations with Napoleon were: 1. The dissolution of the grand duchy of Warsaw and its partition between the three neighbouring powers; 2. The cession to Prussia of Danzig and other areas in northern Germany; 3. The return of Illyria to Austria; 4. The reinstatement of Hanseatic ports such as Hamburg and Lübeck; 5. The dissolution of the Rheinbund; and 6. The reconstruction of Prussia to its pre-1806 status.

When Hardenberg presented these conditions to him, Metternich balked at the inclusion of the last two. He knew they would be unacceptable to Napoleon, and that if they were put to him he would not agree to negotiate at all. This would entail the resumption of hostilities at a moment when Austria was not ready – which in turn would mean that she would have no option but to resume her role as Napoleon's ally. He had also come to the conclusion that it would be politic to preserve the Rheinbund, as this would effectively scotch any plans Alexander and Stein might have for the rearrangement of Germany and any designs Prussia might be nursing with regard to German territory.

Over two days of often heated discussion Metternich managed to make his case that the most important thing was to get Napoleon to agree to negotiations. This would have the twin advantages of buying Austria the time necessary for mobilising her army, and making Napoleon look like the aggressor when the negotiations eventually broke down. That they would break down he had no doubt, because, he explained, the allies would, as soon as the negotiations started, introduce the other two conditions and then include British demands with regard to Spain and the Netherlands. But while he stood by his insistence that Napoleon must be lured into negotiations, he did agree to commit Austria to war when these failed, and a formal convention was to be prepared to that effect.

This went only a little way to dispel mistrust of Metternich at allied headquarters, and the suspicion lingered that he was setting a trap – the awareness of each of the three powers that they could at any moment strike a deal with Napoleon over the heads of the others made them extraordinarily sensitive to the possibility of the others doing so, hence the high degree of mistrust emanating from the notes and letters of those involved in these delicate and secretive talks.

Alexander decided to talk to Metternich himself, and a meeting was arranged for 17 June at Opotschno (Opočno). The two had not seen each other since 1805, and although they had been on cordial terms then, much had happened since to make the Tsar suspicious of the Austrian Foreign Minister. But in a long interview Metternich succeeded in allaying those suspicions by explaining his plan of action. He assured Alexander that if Napoleon agreed to talks, 'the negotiations will demonstrate, beyond any doubt, that he has no intention of behaving wisely or justly', and that war would inevitably follow. Alexander accepted the logic of the plan, and left the meeting in a brighter mood. But that only made the Prussians more suspicious.[18]

Two days later Metternich had a secret conference in the discreet venue of Wilhelmina de Sagan's house at Ratiborzitz, with Hardenberg and Humboldt representing Prussia and Nesselrode Russia, which the latter described as 'one of the most stormy I have ever attended'. In the end Metternich managed to placate them by declaring that while Austria would only bind herself to join Russia and Prussia in war against France if Napoleon did not accept to negotiate on the first four conditions, he nevertheless agreed that a durable peace could not be achieved without excluding France and French influence entirely from Italy, Germany, Spain and the Netherlands. The fruit of these meetings was the Convention of Reichenbach, signed a few days later, on 27 June.

This defined the conditions on which Napoleon was to be invited to negotiate, and stipulated that if he did not agree to them, or if the negotiations did not lead to peace, Austria would automatically become an ally of Russia and Prussia, and declare war on France.[19]

Mistrust nevertheless lingered like an unhealthy fog – with some justification, since the allies had accepted Metternich's assurance that the peace proposals were only a ploy to wrong-foot Napoleon, while he himself was still in favour of making peace provided reasonable terms could be obtained. That seemed infinitely preferable to embarking on a new war as part of a coalition which, in Gentz's words, was 'a weak, rotten, poorly designed structure in which hardly two pieces fit together'. But a satisfactory peace could only be made with the participation of Britain, and Metternich was doing everything possible to make contact with the British cabinet through Wessenberg and various British agents.[20]

The British diplomats had been left out of the secret talks between their allies and Metternich, and seemed to be unaware of them. But Castlereagh was anxious. On 13 June he wrote to Cathcart instructing him to write to Metternich himself and pin him down as to Austria's intentions, and enclosing a letter to the Austrian Foreign Minister in which he insisted on 'without loss of time, be[ing] informed in the most authentic and confidential manner of the views and intentions of the Austrian cabinet'.[21]

Stewart, who regarded himself first and foremost as a soldier and longed to get to grips with the enemy, had gone off to Prussia in order to review the troops concentrating for the next stage of the campaign in northern Germany. It was only when he returned a couple of weeks later that he discovered, entirely by chance, that Russia and Prussia had signed a convention with Austria without consulting their British allies, in stark and insulting contradiction to the engagements made in the subsidy treaties signed with them only ten days before.

The British Prime Minister Lord Liverpool and his Foreign Secretary Lord Castlereagh had already been rattled by the news of their Russian and German allies' signature of the armistice of Plesswitz on 4 June without consulting them. When they were informed of this second breach of faith there was mild panic in London. They had to consider the very real possibility that Austria might succeed in subverting their allies and broker a peace between them and Napoleon which would once again exclude Britain. Faced with this bleak prospect, Castlereagh readjusted his policy.

'You must guard against a Continental peace being made to our exclusion,' he warned Cathcart on 6 July, stressing the weakness of

Britain's position. He hated the prospect of having to take part in a settlement negotiated by Metternich, but there seemed to be no alternative. He had made up his mind to send an envoy to the Austrian court.

'The risk of treating with France is great, but the risk of losing our Continental Allies and the confidence of our own nation is greater,' he argued, instructing Cathcart to inform the allies that Britain would join them in any negotiations they entered into with Napoleon. He listed 'the points on which His Royal Highness can under no circumstances relax', which were that Spain, Portugal and Naples must be returned to their rightful sovereigns, that Hanover be handed back, that an enlarged Holland be restored and that Prussia and Austria be strengthened. A further point concerned Britain's maritime rights, which were not negotiable. To his intense annoyance Russia had recently renewed its offer to mediate in the Anglo-American conflict, which he saw as an attempt to bring these rights up in the international arena.[22]

On his return to Gitschin after his crucial conferences with Alexander and the allied ministers, Metternich had found a letter from the French Foreign Minister Maret asking whether Austria still considered herself to be bound by the treaty of 1812 with France, and if so, whether she would designate a plenipotentiary to renegotiate it so as to accommodate Austria's new role as mediator. Metternich replied with a specious document explaining Austria's behaviour towards France, and then set off for Dresden himself.[23]

He arrived in the Saxon capital on 25 June, and on the following day he presented himself at the Marcolini villa. On his arrival he was struck by the look of weariness and despondency on the faces of the senior officers in the Emperor's ante-rooms. He found Napoleon standing in the middle of a long gallery, his sword at his side and his hat under his arm. The Emperor opened the conversation with cordial enquiries about Francis's health, but his countenance soon grew sombre. Irritated by Austria's tergiversation, and feeling he was being betrayed, Napoleon reacted with his usual truculence. 'So it is war you want: very well, you shall have it,' he challenged Metternich. 'I annihilated the Prussian army at Lützen; I beat the Russians at Bautzen; and now you want to have your turn. I shall meet you at Vienna. Men are incorrigible; the lessons of experience are lost on them.'

When Metternich pressed him to make peace, stressing that this was his last opportunity to do so on favourable terms, Napoleon gave full vent to his irritation. 'I might even consider giving Russia a piece of the duchy of Warsaw,' he ranted, 'but I will not give you anything, because you have not beaten me; and I will give nothing to Prussia, because she has betrayed me.' He declared that he could not give up an inch of territory without dishonouring himself. 'Your sovereigns, born on the throne, can afford to let themselves be beaten twenty times and still return to their capitals; I cannot, because I am a *parvenu* soldier,' he said. 'My authority will not survive the day when I will have ceased to be strong, and therefore, to be feared.'

He suspected that the four conditions for negotiation put forward by Metternich were some kind of trick, as they would not buy peace by themselves (if only because British demands would have to be added), so in agreeing to them Napoleon would be entering an open-ended negotiation. And he saw Metternich as the principal intriguer rather than the honest broker the Austrian minister thought himself.

Realising that he could not force Austria to fight at the side of France, Napoleon attempted to buy her neutrality by offering to return her Illyrian provinces. But Metternich stood firm by his insistence that the only role Austria was prepared to play was that of independent mediator. If Napoleon did not accept this, Francis would consider himself relieved of any obligation to stand by their alliance, and free to act as he saw fit. Napoleon tried to browbeat Metternich, by accusing him of treachery and of being in the pay of Britain, by ridiculing Austria's military potential and by threatening to crush her. He lost his temper more than once, threw his hat into the corner in a rage, only then to resume the conversation on polite, even friendly terms. The meeting lasted more than nine hours, and it was dark outside when the exhausted Metternich left the room.[24]

That evening Metternich returned to the Marcolini villa at Napoleon's invitation to see a play put on by the actors of the Comédie Française, who had been brought over from Paris. He was astonished to find himself watching the famous actress Mademoiselle Georges playing Racine's *Phèdre*. 'I thought I was at St Cloud,' he wrote to his wife before going to bed, 'all the same faces, the same court, the same people.'[25]

Over the next days he had a couple of meetings with Maret and another inconclusive one with Napoleon, who kept invoking Austria's obligations under the treaty of 1812. Metternich did everything he could to persuade Napoleon that he wanted to help him make a satisfactory peace, while Napoleon alternated between bullying and trying to convince Metternich that Austria needed France more than France needed Austria.

Metternich filled in his spare time pleasantly enough. The weather had turned fine and there was a festive atmosphere in the beautiful baroque city, which, in the words of Napoleon's secretary Baron Fain, 'presented the curiously mixed aspect of a capital and a military camp'. The armistice had cheered all those who longed for peace, and there were balls and parties for the French officers and members of Napoleon's court.[26]

Metternich was feeling very pleased with himself. 'I am beginning to believe a little in my star as Napoleon believes in his, when I see that I am now making the whole of Europe turn around a point that I and I alone have determined some months ago,' he wrote to his wife after his second meeting with Napoleon. 'There are crowds of people continually standing under my windows hoping to discover what I think,' he noted with satisfaction, adding that he was frequently stopped in the street and asked whether there would be peace or war. He also took the opportunity to go shopping for presents for his wife and daughter, for which he received touching thanks. But his mind, when it was not occupied with affairs of state, was elsewhere. Metternich had fallen in love.[27]

The object of his affections was Wilhelmina, Princess of Sagan. She had, according to Countess Rozalia Rzewuska, who knew her well, 'noble and regular features, a superb figure, and the bearing of a goddess'; but if she was a goddess, she was a fallen one. 'She sins seven times a day and loves as often as others dine,' Metternich would later write, with some justification. But it was not entirely her fault. 'The consequences of a neglected upbringing and the frightening immorality of her paternal home had the most unfortunate influence on the destiny of the young and charming Wilhelmine,' Rzewuska continues. 'Abandoned to the vivacity of her senses, devoid of any religious principles, her imagination branded by pernicious example, Wilhelmine found herself defenceless against the great dangers which her beauty stored up for her.'

As a young girl she was seduced by her mother's lover, the Swedish adventurer Gustav von Armfeldt, and became pregnant. A hasty marriage was arranged to the Prince de Rohan, who tolerated her continuing depravities as she tolerated his. But their '*entente immorale*' was of short duration. They divorced, and Wilhelmina married the Russian Prince Trubetskoy, who was besotted by her and whom she dismissed 'as they left the altar'. She was similarly curt with her third husband, Count Schulemburg. She was enormously rich and generous with it, and she made up in charm and natural wit what she lacked in upbringing and education.[28]

Metternich had originally regarded her as a friend and confidante, and the passionate feelings she kindled in him took him unawares. In lengthy and somewhat adolescent love letters he expressed his astonishment at the way they had crept up on him. He revelled in the first paroxysms of love, mixing up passionate outpourings with increasingly exalted views on the political situation. 'I am going there like the real man of God, bearing the burden of mankind on my shoulders!' he announced in a note penned hastily as he was leaving for Dresden.[29]

She returned his love, but she did not believe in exclusivity, and continued to receive visits from Windischgraetz whenever he could get leave from the army. She was enjoying life now that her country house had become the nexus of European politics. 'Since the Emperor went to Gitschin at the beginning of June, I established myself here and experienced the most interesting, lively and extraordinary weeks of my life,' Gentz wrote to Wessenberg from Ratiborzitz on 5 July. 'You probably know, my dear friend, that at this strange point in time, when the four foremost sovereigns of the continent, along with their cabinets, ministers, foreign envoys, etc., and with 600,000 men under arms are concentrated in the narrow strip of land between Dresden and Reichenbach, the glamour of the residences and capitals of Europe – that is, as far as interest is concerned – are outshone by three or four Bohemian castles and today, a man of the world no longer speaks of Paris, Vienna, Petersburg, and so on, but of Gitschin, Optoschna and Ratiboržiz. In this last place – on top of everything, a little paradise which the Duchess of Sagan is making into a veritable heaven – one has seen in the last three weeks nothing but crowned heads, prime ministers, diplomatic conferences, couriers, etc.'[30]

As he was getting nowhere in Dresden, Metternich decided to leave on 30 June. He was in his travelling clothes and his coach was waiting below when he received a note summoning him for an interview with Napoleon. He gave orders for the horses to be unharnessed and went to the Marcolini villa, dressed as he was. He found Napoleon in the same mood as before, and was resigning himself to listen to the habitual torrent of bluster and complaint, when the Emperor suddenly ushered him into a study and sat him down at a table at which Maret was poised to take notes. He then asked him to set out Austria's proposals for the mediation. Metternich obliged, and to his surprise Napoleon gave his assent. A note was drawn up to the effect that the belligerent parties would send plenipotentiaries to a congress to be held under Austrian mediation at Vienna or Prague, to begin in the first days of July.

Napoleon suggested including plenipotentiaries from Britain, the

United States of America and Spain, but Metternich demurred. He considered it so unlikely that Britain would agree to take part that he refused to agree to inviting her, as her probable failure to respond might provide Napoleon with an excuse for declaring the congress invalid. It was therefore agreed that only Spain and the United States be invited to send their representatives.

'Never has an important piece of business been expedited so promptly,' Metternich noted with satisfaction. An hour later his carriage was rolling out of Dresden, and on 1 July he was back with Francis at Gitschin. On 4 July he was at Ratiborzitz, conferring with Hardenberg, Humboldt, Nesselrode and Stadion on how to conduct the negotiations in the congress that was to assemble at Prague in a few days' time.[31]

6

Farce in Prague

A few days after Metternich's departure from Dresden, Napoleon received unwelcome news from Spain. Wellington had taken the offensive at the end of May, obliging the French to fall back. Threatened with the possibility of being cut off, Napoleon's brother King Joseph was forced to abandon Madrid. The British caught up with him and the retreating French army and routed it at Vittoria on 21 June. It was a shattering defeat, rendered all the more shameful by the loss of all the army's and the King's baggage.

Berthier and other marshals advised Napoleon to evacuate all his garrisons, pull back his forces from Germany and concentrate a powerful army on the Rhine. It would have been the sensible course. But if he were to pull back he would be abandoning his German allies, and such a sign of weakness would give heart to all his enemies; besides which he found the idea of giving ground hard to stomach. He was also haunted by the notion that his people would not tolerate his making peace on any but victorious terms, that if he failed to come up with something that could be dressed up as a victory, what he called his 'magie' would be dispelled. He therefore held firm, and demonstrated his determination to stand by his allies by signing, on 10 July, a fresh treaty of alliance with Denmark.[1]

Napoleon was still hoping that at some point he might be able to strike a deal with Alexander. 'Russia has the right to an advantageous peace,' he told his secretary Baron Fain. 'She will have bought it with the devastation of her lands, with the loss of her capital and with two years of war. Austria, on the contrary, does not deserve anything. In the present state of affairs, I would not mind a peace that would be glorious for Russia; but I would feel a very real repugnance to see Austria reap the fruit and the honours of a pacification of Europe as the prize for the crime she is committing by betraying our alliance.'[2]

But Alexander was by now the one monarch least likely to make peace with Napoleon on any terms. And even if his own army was not in belligerent mood, he knew that he was strongly supported by the Prussian generals, who were so sanguine that in the course of a military confabulation at Trachenberg (Żmigród) in mid-July, they came to the conclusion that they could defeat Napoleon without the help of Austria.[3]

Napoleon's only hope of peace lay with Metternich, who still favoured a peaceful outcome, for a number of practical reasons. Having inherited a virtually bankrupt state in 1809, he had worked hard to rebuild its finances and was unwilling to see these frittered away on war, the most ruinous activity a state could pursue. War was also notoriously unpredictable, and even if successful could produce unexpected political tremors. Finally, the outbreak of war necessarily relegated diplomatists like himself to a secondary, and therefore unacceptable, role. As he took up residence in his roomy palace in Prague, which had been chosen as the venue for the congress due to open on 10 July, he faced with relish 'the grand and immense task' that faced him, and assured Wilhelmina that 'I will do what I can to save this world.'[4]

He was certainly well placed to manage events, and his choice of Prague as the venue for the congress was no whim. The ancient Czech city lay within the Habsburg dominions, and was embraced by the formidable Austrian intelligence apparatus. As well as running the government of the empire, Metternich's State Chancellery controlled a number of auxiliary services, such as the posts, the archives, and so on. It had a codes office to encrypt and decrypt secret correspondence, and a translation department, since the official language of government for Hungary was Latin, which was also employed in communications with the Vatican and in other state business; the administration of most of the monarchy's German lands was carried on in German; and that of its Italian dominions in Italian, with French remaining the language of diplomacy and the court.

In the last decades of the eighteenth century the sheer quantity of information being processed through this immense machine inspired greater invigilation. With the outbreak of the French Revolution and the supposed threat of Jacobin conspiracy and contagion, the accent was shifted to surveillance. Francis and Metternich shared an almost obsessive fear of conspiracy and revolution, and both believed in being well-informed.

Metternich employed hundreds of spies and battalions of men who were expert at unsealing letters, copying them and resealing them with the speed necessary to avoid arousing suspicion – the letters might be lifted from a post bag while the horses were being changed, or simply removed from a desk in a private house for a few moments. Others would then translate and decrypt the copies. The head of the decryption office once boasted that he had broken eighty-five foreign codes, one of them, used by the Russian diplomatic service, taking him as long as four years to crack. In order to extend the range of his surveillance, Metternich managed, by offering faster communications and cheaper rates, to divert various international postal routes through Austrian dominions, where interesting-looking letters could be examined.[5]

No matter or item was too humble, or for that matter too grand, for the attention of Metternich's spies. The archives of the State Chancellery are to this day full of copies of intercepted letters, some of them of the utmost banality, others of evident diplomatic or political interest, some of them between people of no social or political standing whatever, others quite the opposite. Not only was the public and private correspondence of all foreign diplomats and statesmen to and from Vienna intercepted and scrutinised; even intimate letters between members of the imperial family, including those sent and received by the Emperor Francis himself, were intercepted and copied just like anyone else's.[6]

In the event, the Congress of Prague turned out to be little short of a farce. Napoleon's nomination as his plenipotentiaries of Caulaincourt and Narbonne, both of them negotiators of the highest rank, suggested that his intent was serious. Narbonne, who reached Prague first, was surprised to discover that Frederick William had sent not Hardenberg, but Humboldt, a man of recognised talents but mediocre diplomatic standing, and a declared advocate of war besides. He was downright shocked when he heard that instead of Nesselrode Alexander had sent as his plenipotentiary Jean Anstett, a man of no experience and of poor reputation who, to make matters worse, was Alsatian by birth and therefore theoretically a renegade French subject. It was an astonishing demonstration of contempt for Napoleon and for the congress, and Narbonne informed Metternich that he could not sit down to talks with them, pending the arrival of Caulaincourt with instructions from Napoleon. On hearing the identity of the allied plenipotentiaries, Napoleon held back Caulaincourt, and when he did finally send him he did not furnish him with the requisite credentials.

This boded ill for the congress's chances of success. The armistice had been prolonged, to 10 August, and if terms were not agreed by midnight on that date hostilities would resume, with Austria in the allied camp. This deadline, the nature of the allied plenipotentiaries and Napoleon's sluggishness raise the question of whether anyone was serious about the congress.

'At heart, nobody truly wanted peace,' Nesselrode would later admit, adding that the congress was a 'joke' and that Alexander and Frederick William had been opposed to it from the start. Hardenberg was similarly sceptical, while in his letters from Prague Humboldt repeatedly assured his wife that nobody, least of all himself, was interested in making peace at this stage.

Metternich probably did favour a peaceful solution, though he was growing increasingly sceptical of its chances with each passing day. And while he reassured an anxious Humboldt that there would be war on 11 August whatever happened, he was determined to make it look as though he had been left with no option.[7]

Ironically, the one person who genuinely hoped to gain something from the congress was Napoleon, even though his motives were questionable. Caulaincourt and Narbonne were very much in earnest, though the latter thought peace a forlorn hope, and they set themselves up in a manner befitting a delegation to proper peace talks, much to Hardenberg's amusement. Their brief was to keep negotiations going independently of the armistice. 'After 10 August the armistice works against us,' Napoleon explained: he believed that the Russians and the Prussians would be ready to take the field, while the Austrians would still be unprepared. This would allow him to defeat the Russians and Prussians while continuing to negotiate with Austria. 'This is what we wish, but we must dissimulate and let them believe that we want the armistice to be prolonged indefinitely,' he wrote. It seems that Napoleon still believed that he could make mischief between the allies, and that he would be able to split them at some stage and make a separate peace with Russia.[8]

His calculations were based on two false premises. The first was that the Austrians would not be ready to take the field on 10 August. The second was that a decisive victory over the Russians and the Prussians would tip the balance in his favour. Over dinner on 3 August Metternich explained to Caulaincourt, in whom he recognised a kindred soul, that times had changed in this respect. A battle lost by the allies now would make no material difference, as it could not change their attitude, which was one of exasperation with Napoleon based on the conviction that it was not possible to make a lasting peace with him. A battle lost by Napoleon on the other hand weakened him fundamentally, since it diminished his military prestige.[9]

The congress never did convene properly. Metternich had proposed that rather than sitting down to open verbal negotiations, the plenipotentiaries of the three powers should put their case in verbal notes addressed to him as mediator. Humboldt and Anstett agreed, while Narbonne and Caulaincourt insisted that there must at least be some verbal negotiation. This difference of opinion quickly degenerated into pointless argument, with both sides invoking various eighteenth-century congresses as precedent. 'Nothing could be more amusing than the story of this supposed Congress, which has already lasted more than three weeks without a single question of *form* having been decided, and which will, it appears, be dissolved before it opens,' Gentz wrote to a friend on 30 July.[10]

Gentz was certainly enjoying himself. There was little for him to do, since there were no conferences to minute and no memoranda to draft. The weather was fine, and he would spend the long summer evenings and balmy nights strolling through the beautiful city with Humboldt and Metternich, discussing everything from love to philosophy. Metternich was less happy. Wilhelmina had promised to come to Prague so they could continue their intimacy, but he waited and waited, sending her letter after letter brimming with despair and jealousy. He complained to Humboldt that he had 'lost his *joie de vivre*'.

Humboldt, who was beginning to alter his view of Metternich, assuring his wife that he was intelligent and 'never unreasonable', was in contrastingly high spirits. He was comfortably lodged in a princely palace and filled his spare time with work on his translation of Aeschylus' *Agamemnon*. His superior Hardenberg had recently been distracted by an affair with a woman of whom Humboldt apparently disapproved, and this show of 'depravity' encouraged his speculations that he might be able to take over his post himself.[11]

As the deadline of 10 August approached, Caulaincourt made one last attempt to establish a line of negotiation with Metternich. He explained that Napoleon's suspicions of him were largely based on the fact that the four conditions for negotiation put forward until now were not credible, and invited conjecture as to what others might lurk behind them. If Metternich were to state the allies' full demands at the outset, Napoleon would know what he was up against and respond accordingly.

On 5 August, just five days before the armistice was to expire, Napoleon sent a note to Caulaincourt instructing him to sound out Metternich on his price for abandoning the allies and returning to the French alliance. Metternich's response was contained in a note dated 8 August which confirmed the same four conditions, with the only difference that he now dropped the one that Illyria be returned to Austria and demanded that instead of dissolving the Rheinbund, Napoleon renounce his protectorate over it. He also added the stipulation that the conclusion of a general peace was to be accompanied by an agreement to be enforced by all sides aimed at protecting weaker powers. Caulaincourt said that if it were up to him, he would accept, but expressed doubt as to whether Napoleon would.[12]

'The great moment has arrived at last, my dearest friend,' Metternich wrote to his wife on 10 August. That evening Humboldt, Anstett and all those in favour of war gathered in Metternich's palace. Watches were consulted with impatience, and when the chimes of midnight rang out over the sleeping city Metternich announced that the armistice was over and Austria was now a member of the alliance. He ordered a beacon to be lit which, by a chain reaction, carried the news all the way to the Silesian border and on to allied headquarters at Reichenbach. By the morning Russian and Prussian troops were on the march to join the Austrian army outside Prague. 'Everything is decided, dearest Li,' a delighted Humboldt wrote to his wife.[13]

But in his letter to his wife, Metternich had made it clear that 'the *official* negotiation has finished today *with no result*'. 'There remain 6 days of *unofficial* negotiation; will it lead to anything or not?' he continued. Although he told her he was preparing his campaign baggage, it seems he was not excluding a last-minute negotiated outcome.[14]

On 12 August, just as Caulaincourt and Narbonne were preparing to leave, a courier arrived from Dresden with Napoleon's instructions to make peace at all costs. Caulaincourt called on Metternich without delay, but was told that it was too late. That very day Austria issued her declaration of war, a document full of mournful complaint detailing how she had been wronged by France.[15]

'I am the most unhappy being on earth,' Metternich moaned in a letter to Wilhelmina, who had let him down by not coming to Prague. The probable reason – Alfred Windischgraetz's reappearance at Ratiborzitz – only deepened his despair. 'Adieu! There can be no more happiness for me in this world – may all that remains of it on earth be for you!' he went on, in an interminable letter.[16]

It was not only on account of Wilhelmina that he felt disappointment. He had failed to broker a peace, which would not only have been the best solution for Austria but would also have placed him in the pivotal position he aspired to. Everything was now left to the vagaries of war. Having done all he could to prevent it, and incurred the mistrust and insult not only of the allies but also the war party in Austria, his credibility demanded that he pursue it with enthusiasm.

Napoleon had not given up, and he instructed Caulaincourt to delay his departure from Prague in the hope of being able to obtain an interview with Alexander when the latter arrived a couple of days later. On 18 August, by which time the armies were in the field, Maret wrote to Metternich arguing that no peace congress could possibly be expected to take as little as a month, quoting examples drawn from history and proposing that a fresh congress to include all the powers of Europe, great and small, be convoked to some neutral city. But Metternich dismissed the suggestion. 'The 6 days, my dearest, have passed,' he wrote to his wife on 16 August. 'Hostilities begin tomorrow.' And Napoleon's hopes that an interview between Caulaincourt and Alexander might yield something were very wide of the mark. In his eagerness to pursue the war the Tsar had single-handedly scuppered the only real chance of peace.[17]

Cathcart had received Castlereagh's instructions to the effect that Britain would be prepared to enter into negotiations with France shortly after Caulaincourt reached Prague. He showed them to Alexander, who determined that they must not be passed on to

Metternich. He had never wavered in his determination to pursue the war against Napoleon, and as Nesselrode explained in a letter of 9 August to Russia's ambassador in London, he had only humoured Francis's desire to negotiate in the conviction that nothing would come of it. Having watched Austria gradually come round to the acceptance that there was nothing to be gained from negotiating, he was certainly not going to produce the British proposal to join the negotiations. It would only 'weaken the energetic resolutions taken by the Austrian cabinet' and encourage Napoleon to take the negotiations more seriously.[18]

Had Napoleon known that Britain was willing to participate, he would probably have been prepared to concede a great deal. Britain was his principal enemy. It had been to bring her to the negotiating table that he had invaded Russia. He had wanted Britain included in the Congress of Prague, and hopes had been entertained that she might send a plenipotentiary. The possibility of a general peace with the participation of Britain – involving as it would not only huge economic relief, but also the return of most of the French colonies – could have been dressed up as a victory of sorts and would have allowed Napoleon to claim that he was making peace with honour.[19]

The only victory Napoleon could hope for now was on the battlefield, and that was going to be difficult to achieve. The coalition ranged against him was formidable. Facing him was the main allied army under Schwarzenberg, consisting of 120,000 Austrians, 70,000 Russians under Barclay de Tolly and 60,000 Prussians under General Kleist, a total of 250,000. Behind it stood Blücher's army of Silesia, 40,000 Russians under Langeron, 18,000 under Osten-Sacken, and 38,000 Prussians under Yorck. In the north Bernadotte commanded an army of 150,000 Swedes, Russians and Prussians, bringing the total to well over half a million men. Morale, particularly among the German contingents, was reinforced by a sense that the hour of liberation had struck, fostered by an avalanche of poetry and propaganda, and supported by a nationwide commitment in the form of a 'gold for steel' fund-raising programme and numerous women's welfare committees.

On 19 August Schwarzenberg's combined army paraded before Alexander, Francis and Frederick William. The newly formed units were presented with standards, 'and the three allied sovereigns nailed their respective colours together to the pole, in token of the firmness of their alliance and the intimacy of their union', recorded Jackson. It was, in the words of Jackson's superior, Stewart, 'a most exhilarating moment'. The following day the army took the field.[20]

Napoleon was already on the march. 'I have an army as fine as any and more than 400,000 men,' he boasted to one of his officials. 'That will suffice to re-establish my affairs in the North.' But later in the conversation he complained that he was short of cavalry and needed more men, particularly seasoned troops. His forces were in fact greatly inferior to those of the allies. His garrisons at Danzig, Stettin (Szczecin), Thorn (Toruń), Cüstrin (Kostrzyn), Glogau (Głogów), Modlin and Zamość accounted for almost a quarter of his nominal army of 400,000, and they were effectively left out of the action. They included a large number of seasoned troops and some experienced generals, while the bulk of the 300,000 or so men at his immediate disposal were conscripts with only rudimentary training. Much the same was true of the army of Italy which Prince Eugène had been forming up to threaten Austria's southern flank. By mid-July it had reached a paper strength of over 50,000 men, but there were nothing like as many actually under arms, while their quality and training left a great deal to be desired.[21]

Morale was remarkably good among the troops under Napoleon's immediate command as they marched out of Dresden on 16 August, and they were cheered by the arrival of Joachim Murat, King of Naples, who was to take command of the cavalry. Napoleon's plan was to push back Blücher and then, leaving Marshal Macdonald to cover him, veer south and outflank the main allied army under Schwarzenberg, which was moving on Dresden. The first part of the operation went according to plan, but at Löwenberg (Lwówek Śląski) on 23 August, as Napoleon snatched a hurried lunch standing up, a courier arrived with news from Marshal Gouvion Saint-Cyr at Dresden warning him that the main allied army was already threatening the city, which would not be able to hold out much longer. Napoleon smashed the glass of red wine he was holding against the table as he read the despatch.

He hesitated. A potentially decisive victory was within his grasp. But the fall of Dresden might have grave political repercussions given the current mood in Germany. He changed his plan, ordering General Vandamme with a corps of not much more than 10,000 men to continue with the original aim of attacking the allied rear, while he himself hastened back to Dresden with the main forces.

He arrived outside the city on 26 August, and in the course of the next three days defeated all the allies' attempts to break through, putting them to flight on the third. He was taken violently ill with fits of vomiting at the moment of triumph, and had to go back to Dresden. He was much better by 30 August, but on that day he received three disastrous pieces of news: in the north, Marshal Oudinot had been defeated by the Prussians at Grossbeeren; Macdonald had been pushed back with heavy losses by Blücher on the river Katzbach; and finally Vandamme, who had dutifully cut the main allied army's line of retreat, had himself been surrounded and forced to capitulate with his entire force at Kulm (Chlumec). Although he had triumphed at Dresden, all Napoleon could show for the five days' fighting was a loss of some 100,000 men and a considerable quantity of artillery. If he had persevered in his original intention, he would, in Nesselrode's opinion, have routed the allied army and captured all three allied sovereigns and their ministers. 'That's war,' Napoleon said to Maret that night. 'Up there in the morning, down there in the evening.'[22]

He did not allow himself to be disheartened by this setback. Two days later he moved to push Blücher back once more, and then advanced into Bohemia, harassing the main allied army. But on 6 September Ney, whom Napoleon had sent out to reinforce Oudinot, was himself beaten by the Prussians and Swedes under Bernadotte at Dennewitz.

Napoleon displayed extraordinary energy over the next weeks, taking command of one or other of his corps in order to push back the advancing allies. What saved them was the tactic they had agreed on at the conference held at Trachenberg in July of refusing battle and falling back whenever Napoleon himself took command of the armies facing them, and going over to the attack as soon as he had gone, leaving his troops under the command of one of the marshals.

In any other circumstances Napoleon could have pulled back all his remaining forces and struck at one point with all his might, as he always had in the past. But if he retreated now he would be abandoning his German allies, who would then be forced into alliance with his enemies. He therefore carried on thrusting and parrying, keeping greatly superior allied forces in check. Soon after hostilities began, the weather turned wet and cold. The roads turned into muddy morasses, adding to the difficulty of this highly mobile campaign and reducing the effectives of every unit with each march. He could no longer hold on to his exposed position at Dresden, and on 15 October, having abandoned that, he fell back on the second city of Saxony, Leipzig.

However grim the situation looked from Napoleon's headquarters, the view from the other side of the lines was not correspondingly rosy. The three monarchs, their ministers, their military staffs and the diplomats accredited to their courts were crammed into the little spa town of Toeplitz (Teplice) in Bohemia. This normally delightful place was choked with people, quartered on top of each other in hostelries meant for more gracious conditions. The wounded of Dresden and Kulm lay packed into all the larger spaces available. Among them was Stewart, who despite his ambassadorial role could not resist the lure of the battlefield and had taken a wound at Kulm. The streets were knee-deep in mud, continually churned up by the boots and hooves of couriers on duty and units on the march.

'Toeplitz is now a sad place,' Metternich wrote to his daughter Marie. 'Everywhere is full of wounded; in the redoute hall at the entrance to the gardens they have been amputating arms & legs . . .' She was so moved that, like other patriotic ladies, she tore old linen sheets and garments into strips and sent them to the army for dressing wounds.[23]

The allies' morale was not good. Losses in the fighting at Dresden, Kulm, on the Katzbach and Dennewitz had been heavy. It was proving difficult to raise troops, and desertion was rife, even among officers. The anticipated surge of volunteers inspired by the idea of liberating Germany from the French yoke had not materialised. According to Hardenberg people 'murmured more than they acted'. And the cause was beginning to look less glorious – General von Walmoden's volunteers went about raping and pillaging with abandon those they were supposed to be liberating. The war had taken a further lurch into barbarism, and some of the Russian commanders regularly massacred French prisoners.[24]

The 'harmony, confidence and mutual satisfaction' that Cathcart had reported from Trachenberg, where the commanders of the various armies had agreed their plan of action and mutual support, had been dissipated by mistrust, jealousy and recrimination. A struggle for control of the army was under way.[25]

Alexander had wanted to command the allied army. He had invited General Moreau, the victor of Hohenlinden, who had been in American exile since 1804 when he had been implicated in a royalist plot to overthrow Napoleon, to return to Europe and accept a post on his staff. He assumed that with him and the renegade Swiss General Jomini at his side as advisers, he would be able to realise his dream of proving himself as a commander in the field. The other allies were having none of it, and after acrimonious discussions, which involved Metternich threatening to withdraw Austria from the coalition, Alexander gave way and Schwarzenberg was placed in overall command.

But he was, as Stewart pointed out, in the unprecedented position of having 'two Emperors and a King superintending and controlling not only movements in agitation, but also operations decided on'.

Alexander had interfered during the battle of Dresden, riding about the battlefield issuing orders to individual units without reference to their commanders or the overall plan, and unity of action was further impaired by pronounced hostility and jealousy between the allied commanders. They were mostly mediocre generals, while their troops, a majority of whom were conscripts, reflected all the national and regional prejudices and enmities of their places of origin.

The coalition itself was under constant strain. 'The general desire, whatever may be said to the contrary, is for peace,' noted Jackson, adding that Hardenberg's spirits 'rise and fall, like the weather-glass under atmospheric changes'. Stewart suspected the Austrians of wanting to make a separate peace, while Metternich remarked that he 'had to keep an eye on the allies no less than on the enemy'. There were moments when the only thing that appeared to unite them was the French language in which they communicated with each other.[26]

Metternich nevertheless remained optimistic. 'Everything is going well, beyond expectation,' he wrote to Wilhelmina. 'Everything is beautiful, perfect, and God appears to be protecting his cause.' While acknowledging the contribution of the Almighty, he did not fail to point out that it was actually his own doing. His optimism may have stemmed from the fact that she was now returning his love with passion. '*Mon amie*, you have given me everything you can, you have made me drunk with happiness, I love you, I love you a hundred times more than my life – I only live and will only ever live for you,' he wrote from Toeplitz a few days later. And a couple of days after that he admitted that he found it difficult to distinguish between her and the other great object in his thoughts. '*Mon amie* and Europe, Europe and *mon amie*!'[27]

But when not writing to her, he worked at strengthening the coalition, and on 9 September his efforts bore fruit in the new treaties signed by Austria with Russia and Prussia at Toeplitz. These commit-ted the three powers to continue the war together until a durable peace based on 'a just balance' was achieved. The most significant element was contained in article XI, which bound the contracting parties into a coalition.[28]

The vagueness of the treaties on all other matters, and particularly on territorial arrangements, was intentional. Back in Prague, Metternich had turned his mind to limiting the scope of the war and laying down some ground rules for the eventual peace settlement. 'As far as the allies are concerned, there can be no question of conquest, and, as a result, there must be a return of France, Austria and Prussia to their ancient frontiers,' he wrote. He went on to draw a distinction between '*conquêtes consommées*', by which he meant areas whose cession had been by treaty, and 'territorial incorporations *via facti*, made without the former possessors' formal renunciation of their rights in favour of the conqueror'. Lands falling into the latter category, in which he included Hanover, the mainland possessions of the King of Sardinia, the possessions of the house of Orange, and so on, should be restituted to their rightful owners without discussion. As for '*conquêtes consommées*', as an example of which he gave the lands the Papacy had been forced to cede to Napoleon under the Treaty of Tolentino in 1797, they were to be regarded 'as lands delivered from French domination by the allied powers, as a common acquisition whose disposal should be reserved to the said powers'. The fate of all other liberated areas was to be left to a congress to be held once peace had been made.[29]

Metternich did not at this stage wish to confront the issue of how those 'common acquisitions' should be disposed of. The only lands that had been 'delivered' to date were those of the grand duchy of Warsaw, some of which had belonged to Austria and Prussia before Napoleon's incursion into the region. The common understanding was that all three powers would recover their fair share as a result of a deal to be made privately between them, or '*à l'amiable*', to use the phrase contained in the Convention of Reichenbach. But nothing had been formally agreed. The whole area was under Russian occupation, and Metternich had no doubts that Alexander had his own plans for it, which did not take into account those of either Prussia or Austria.

A seed of discord was gradually germinating, but Metternich was not going to challenge Alexander over the matter. First, because since he held what he wanted while the 'common acquisitions' that were meant to fall to Austria and Prussia had not yet been acquired, Alexander was in a stronger position than both of them. Second, because however alarmed he was by the threat of Alexander holding on to most of Poland, Metternich was far more anxious about Alexander's possible intentions for Germany.

Metternich and Francis were against the recreation of the Holy Roman Empire in any form. But neither did they relish the idea of a Prussian hegemony over the German lands or the plans being hatched by Stein for a unified German state. Alexander was showing a worrying interest in German affairs, and appeared to be looking to place himself in a position of dominance there. He neither encouraged nor restrained Stein, and kept his cards close to his chest, sensing, rightly, that his position was growing stronger every day. There was still everything to play for, and the stakes were high.[30]

The Play for Germany

A lesser man might have been intimidated by the Tsar, but Metter-nich's vanity never allowed him to waver in his belief that he could make him do his will, and he too had come to believe that he was fulfilling 'the decrees of Heaven', as he put it in a letter to his daughter Marie. He had also just acquired a valuable ally, the new British ambassador to the Austrian court, who had reached Toeplitz on 2 September.[1]

Castlereagh had been increasingly alarmed both by the vagueness of the treaties binding the allies and by their omission of matters, such as the future of the Netherlands and the Iberian peninsula, that Britain deemed essential preconditions of a durable peace. Although he persisted in his view of Russia as the principal in the coalition and a natural ally of Britain, and could not shed his mistrust of Metternich, he had come to realise that Britain would have to re-establish direct contact with Vienna.

This was what Metternich had wanted all along, and had gone to some lengths to obtain. At the same time he had been afraid that the British cabinet might send what Gentz described as 'a stock Englishman', who would know nothing and understand nothing. Castlereagh's envoy was no stock Englishman, but he was hardly very qualified.[2]

George Gordon, Earl of Aberdeen, was only twenty-eight years old and had no diplomatic experience. He had a poor command of French, in which all international business was conducted. And he was not a natural negotiator. A classical scholar whose Grand Tour had taken him to Greece and Asia Minor in the early 1800s, he had been unjustly vilified by Byron as an accomplice of Lord Elgin, when his only role had been to recommend that the marbles which the latter had stripped off the Parthenon in Athens and brought to London in 1806 should be acquired for the nation and placed in the British Museum. He was a man of homely tastes and a good landlord, managing to plant over fourteen million trees during his lifetime. He had been deeply in love with his wife Catherine, whose death from tuberculosis in 1812 had left him devastated. He had been drawn into politics by Pitt, whom he admired as much as Castlereagh, and had been offered the embassy to Russia and that to the court of Naples in Sicily, but had declined both as well as the governorship of the Ionian Islands. It was with extreme reluctance that he agreed to undertake this mission, citing, in a letter to his father-in-law the Earl of Abercorn, 'a disinclination' to leave his children 'joined to a feeling approaching contempt for the whole diplomatic profession in general'. But he did not, fortunately, follow his father-in-law's advice that 'An undisguised personal and national haughtiness (with a sweet sauce of studied, unremitting, ceremonious, condescending politeness and attention) is much more advantageous than is supposed or guessed' in an ambassador.

Aberdeen's instructions were vague, and his mission consisted principally of penetrating Metternich's real intentions. His route lay through Sweden, Berlin, Frankfurt an der Oder, Breslau – where he narrowly missed capture by the French – and Prague to Toeplitz. Along the way he had been naïvely delighted by the sight of detachments of Bashkir irregulars following in the wake of the Russian advance. 'They have the Chinese face, and are exactly like the fellows one sees painted on tea-boxes,' he informed his sister-in-law. But his amusement turned to horror when he came upon evidence of their unruliness and brutality. He was similarly dismayed, on reaching

Toeplitz, by the conditions in the overcrowded town, and belatedly realised that he had brought the wrong kit, anticipating that he would be fulfilling the role of an ambassador at court, not at a military headquarters on campaign. 'I never expected to be in such a scrape,' he wrote to Castlereagh on arrival.[3]

Aberdeen presented his credentials on 5 September, four days before the signature of the Treaties of Toeplitz by Russia, Prussia and Austria. He liked the Emperor Francis, and found himself drawn to Metternich, with whom he discussed opera and collecting works of art. He found Alexander 'agreeable and rather clever, but *shewing off* ', and most of his generals despondent and eager to go home. He quickly appreciated that this put Austria in a vulnerable position; he expressed the fear that if Napoleon were to inflict one decisive defeat on it, the coalition would fall apart. And such a defeat appeared more than likely. 'The evils of divided command are everywhere apparent,' he reported to Castlereagh on arrival. 'The vigour of every measure is paralysed, the wisdom of every proposition is almost rendered abortive, by the delay which is necessary to procure the approbation of the different Sovereigns and their advisers.'[4]

Aberdeen did not like Cathcart, who returned the feeling frankly. And although he took an immediate liking to Stewart, he realised that he was not up to his job. He was so appalled by everything he saw and heard that within a few days of his arrival he was actually thinking of resigning his post.[5]

He nevertheless concluded the subsidy treaty which had already been agreed, providing Austria with £1 million, to be paid at a rate of £100,000 per month, and then went on to discuss wider issues with Metternich. As instructed, he expressed his disapproval that Britain's priorities had been ignored in the treaties between the other allies. He also voiced Castlereagh's misgivings about Metternich's policy of trying to detach Murat from Napoleon's camp by the offer of guaranteeing his survival as King of Naples.

The Austrian chancellor explained that the British approach, which was to put all British demands on the table and expect them to be accepted prior to any negotiation, was unhelpful. He stressed the need for a degree of elasticity and warned against statements or actions that forced people or states into the enemy camp. A good example was what had happened with Denmark.

Until 1807 Denmark had been a prosperous power of the second rank, comprising Norway, Schleswig, Holstein, Iceland, Greenland and the Faroe Islands, as well as a string of colonies in the West Indies, India and Africa. She had always embraced neutrality where possible, but maintained an alliance with Russia aimed at protecting her from Sweden. In 1807 her King, Frederick VI, had, like Alexander, been forced into alliance with Napoleonic France, which resulted in the bombardment of Copenhagen by the British fleet, the capture or burning of her own fleet, and the subsequent loss of most of her colonies. In 1808–09 she had been obliged to go to war with Sweden in defence of Norway, and while she had managed to hang on to her province, it was her ally Russia that had gained from the affair, by acquiring Finland from Sweden.

When compounded by the necessity of applying Napoleon's Continental System, all this had brought Denmark to the verge of bankruptcy. Inflation reached such levels that Frederick was obliged to put his own gold plate at the disposal of the bank. In 1812 Alexander proposed an alliance to Frederick, but it was hardly an alluring one. He suggested that Denmark hand over Norway to Sweden (which would compensate Sweden for Finland, lost to Russia in 1809). In return, Frederick would, when Napoleon was finally defeated, be given Hamburg, Lübeck, Bremen and the whole North Sea coast of Germany, and as much of Holland as he wished. Although things were not going well for him in Russia, Napoleon was still the master of Europe, and the idea that Alexander would ever find himself in a position to dispose of swathes of Germany and Holland was absurd. At the same time, Frederick and most Danes regarded Norway, which had been united with Denmark for over four centuries, as an essential part of their country.[6]

Frederick was a straightforward, honest man with a keen sense of duty. It was for these qualities as much as for his unaffected *bonhomie* that he was so much loved by his people. Although his natural sympathies had lain with Britain (he was the son of a princess of the English royal house), and although he had joined the alliance with Napoleon only out of necessity, he was inclined to stand by his ally. But as the magnitude of Napoleon's defeat in Russia became evident at the beginning of 1813, he came under increasing pressure to abandon him. Even his cousin Christian Frederick, who would later rule Denmark as Christian VIII, began to advocate switching alliances and joining Russia, Sweden and Britain.

Frederick's Foreign Minister, Count Niels Rosenkrantz, who had spent a long time in Russia and married a Russian aristocrat, and who had many contacts in Britain, also advocated switching alliances. He sent an envoy to Russian headquarters at Kalisch and made overtures to Britain, offering to join the coalition against Napoleon. His conditions were that Russia guarantee Frederick's continued possession of Norway, and that Britain give back his fleet and some of his colonies, as well as some cash with which to fit out an army.

Alexander encouraged Frederick to turn against Napoleon, but all he offered was a 'deferment' of the decision on Norway. The British cabinet informed Frederick that Norway had already been promised to Sweden, and that he would save everyone a great deal of trouble if he handed it over immediately and joined the allies unconditionally. Metternich did everything he could to make Britain take a more accommodating line, arguing that Denmark would be a useful ally, and should be 'rescued' from its alliance with France, but his arguments fell on deaf ears.[7]

In the face of British and Russian intransigence, Frederick had no choice but to fall back into the arms of the one power which was prepared to stand up for his rights, and on 10 July 1813 he signed a new alliance with Napoleon. Metternich did not give up, and sent a secret envoy to Copenhagen in order to keep a door open for Denmark to join the allies. There was little more he could do while Russia, Sweden and Britain did not support him.

On 3 September Denmark duly declared war on Russia for supporting Sweden's claim to Norway, and on 22 September on Sweden itself. Frederick was motivated in equal measure by his sense of loyalty to Napoleon and by his mistrust of Sweden and Russia. Like many Danes, he suspected that they would not keep to any treaty they signed with him, and were bent on partitioning Denmark and establishing a Russian dependency there (Castlereagh himself would later come to share these fears).[8]

Aberdeen quickly came to see that, viewed from the Continent, some of Britain's attitudes and actions looked a good deal less reasonable than they did from London. One of the first things he realised was that far from being a power to be feared, Austria was in many respects Britain's natural ally. He wrote to Castlereagh explaining this, but the Foreign Secretary remained sceptical and dismissive of Metternich. The conduct of the Tsar also appeared different at close quarters, and did not accord with some of the myths held dear in Downing Street.[9]

Alexander always celebrated the anniversary of his coronation, on 27 September, with pomp, and all those assembled at Toeplitz joined in the festivities. After a service of thanksgiving they rode out to Kulm, where the unfortunate Vandamme had been defeated. There they sat down to a banquet for two hundred in a specially erected pavilion decorated with laurels and ribbons. Back in Toeplitz that evening, a select party assembled in Lord Cathcart's quarters for the ceremony of investing Alexander with the Order of the Garter. 'One could not imagine anything more magnificent and more imposing than this chivalrous ceremony,' recorded one of the Tsar's French aides-de-camp, but Alexander's behaviour 'disgusted every Englishman present', according to Jackson. He arrived late, behaved flippantly, and did not for a moment wipe the 'broad grin' from his face. 'The whole thing was treated, in fact, as a sort of farcical entertainment.' The Tsar compounded this by appearing at dinner the following day with the garter around his thigh.[10]

Alexander's sense of destiny, fanned and flattered wherever he went in Bohemia and Germany by the sycophancy of numerous petitioners and the adulation of even more numerous ladies, had turned him into a problematic ally. Treated by many as the Agamemnon of the coalition, he not surprisingly acted more and more on his own initiative and in pursuit of his personal vision.

A case in point was the ambitions he had encouraged in the Crown Prince of Sweden, the former French Marshal Bernadotte. Bernadotte had been placed in command of the allied forces operating in northern Germany, which included a Russian contingent, Walmoden's German volunteers and a Prussian corps under Blücher as well as his own Swedish troops. It was soon noted that he used the Prussians and Russians to fight the French, while keeping his Swedes ready in Pomerania poised for an attack on Denmark. There were also suspicions, unfounded as it happens, that he might make a separate peace with Napoleon. As well as being perceived as an unreliable ally, Bernadotte was also viewed as an unpleasant upstart, or, to quote Hardenberg, 'as a bastard that circumstances had obliged us to legitimise'.[11]

Alexander, however, did not share these reservations. Back in August 1812, when he had met Bernadotte at Åbo to negotiate their alliance, he had dangled before him the idea that if Napoleon were to be defeated, he, Bernadotte, might replace him as ruler of France. He had brought the matter up more than once since then, and encouraged Bernadotte to prepare the ground.

While Bernadotte adopted the role of king-in-waiting, he did not wish to spoil his chances in the event of a restoration of the exiled Bourbons, so he made contact with them, representing himself as a potential strong arm, a kind of French General Monck. Nor did he neglect to court French revolutionaries who loathed the Emperor in Napoleon and longed for a return to the republic. For their sake he posed as a latter-day Cromwell, and kept up secret contacts with various of the marshals across the battle lines. He released captured French officers on parole, hoping they would provide him with a sympathetic following in France. A natural braggart, he attempted to enhance his appeal by aping Murat in fanciful dressing up, particularly on the battlefield.

Bernadotte's attempts to gain popularity were not crowned with much success. When his forces besieged Stettin, he had tried to win over the commander of the French garrison, but his efforts were met with insults. He was nearly hit by a specifically aimed shell as he inspected his outposts, and sent an angry protest (it was not done to try to kill enemy commanders in such inglorious ways), to which he received the reply that the gunner had spotted a French deserter riding along and had acted in accordance with regulations.

But he was encouraged by the support of Alexander's former tutor, the Swiss philosopher Frédéric César de La Harpe, and by people such as the writer Madame de Staël, who had decided that he would make the ideal ruler for France, a new William of Orange who would introduce constitutional monarchy with a strong hand, and, at her prompting, by Benjamin Constant. 'Remember,' Madame de Staël wrote to Bernadotte from London on 11 October 1813, 'that Europe depends upon *you* for its deliverance.' His head swelled to such a degree that at one stage he actually suggested that he might take the title of Duke of Pomerania, which he had occupied, and as such assume the imperial crown of Germany if for one reason or another it did not go to either Austria or Prussia.[12]

Castlereagh was so alarmed by reports of Bernadotte's waywardness that he instructed Stewart to go to his headquarters to keep an eye on him. Stewart's reports only served to deepen that anxiety. General Pozzo di Borgo, whom Alexander had sent to Bernadotte's headquarters, was shocked by the manner in which he was hedging his bets. When Pozzo had taxed him with this, 'The scene that followed would have warranted calling a doctor,' he reported to Alexander. 'I do not believe that I have ever in my whole life had to make such an effort to remain silent as I listened to so much vulgarity, brutishness and nonsense.'[13]

The reports Castlereagh was receiving from his three envoys at allied headquarters confirmed his worst fears as to the fragile state of the coalition, which raised the possibility that some or all of the allies might make peace with Napoleon without Britain if it suited them. All his efforts had gone into binding them together with obligations not to do so. On 3 October Aberdeen had signed a treaty with Austria whose only specific clause excluded either party entering into any negotiations, talks, armistices, ceasefires or other suspensions of hostilities without mutual agreement. But that was not good enough for Castlereagh, who feared Metternich's propensity for negotiating.[14]

In August Castlereagh had begun work on a project for a comprehensive treaty that would solve the problem once and for all. In a letter to Cathcart on 18 September he wondered whether 'a greater degree of union and consistency may not be given to the Confederacy against France than results from the several Treaties which have been successively signed between the respective Powers'. He attached his 'Project for a Treaty of Alliance Offensive and Defensive against France', which he thenceforth referred to as his 'grand design'.

This set out the principal allied war aims, and suggested inviting powers such as Spain and Portugal into the coalition. It not only proposed to make it illegal for any one of the contracting parties to withdraw from the alliance or enter into any communication with the enemy, but repeated the old recommendation of Czartoryski and Pitt that after the conclusion of peace a perpetual defensive alliance would be maintained for the preservation of that peace.[15]

In a second letter to Cathcart written on the same day, Castlereagh instructed him to show the project to Alexander first, stressing that Russia was Britain's natural partner in such matters. He reminded Cathcart that Britain's maritime rights must be kept out of the discussion, as, were they to become part of the general negotiation, the French would sooner or later seize on them with a view to splitting the coalition.[16]

Conditions were hardly favourable for any kind of diplomatic transactions, and the chances of pinning the allies down to anything as definite as Castlereagh's 'grand design' were slight as the allied armies took the field and the three sovereigns and their ministers set off in their wake.

Metternich had improvised a mobile chancellery, the *Reiseabteilung*, with a number of assistants and secretaries in carriages followed by wagons with desks and chairs, papers, books, maps and even a printing press. The Russians had a similar outfit, but it had come under strain by this stage.

Alexander's First Minister Admiral Shishkov was being bundled around in a carriage with two secretaries and no escort. 'You cannot imagine how sad I am,' he wrote to his wife. 'I am sick, I am terrified, and to cap it all, there is the weather! It is grey, misty and rainy, and the sky is covered from morning till evening with black and purple clouds, as though it were representing the horrors of war.' One moment he would find himself alone on deserted roads fearing capture by the French, then he would run into a jam as he encountered the Tsar's kitchen wagons or a concentration of troops. He often had to beg for a corner of some hut to sleep in. Count Ioannis Capodistrias, a Russian diplomat attached to the general staff and ordered to deal with all diplomatic problems raised by the campaign, found himself sharing roadside hovels with the Russian commander Barclay de Tolly. While the General worked on operational plans, the diplomat wrote out manifestos and memoranda on the same table.[17]

Aberdeen, who had succumbed to 'a severe attack of Cholera morbus', was appalled at the conditions and complained that even in the comparative safety of Toeplitz, which he described as a 'vile hole', they had to pack up everything each morning so as to be ready for a quick getaway in the event of a French attack. He was deeply distressed by the sufferings of the soldiers he saw all around him, but lifted his spirits by admiring the landscape and regaling his correspondents with plentiful dendrological observations.[18]

'We cannot help laughing as we go about from the early morning in full dress, with swords, decorations and all our finery,' noted Humboldt in a letter to his wife after a meeting with Metternich, explaining that if they did not wear full uniform at all times they would be pushed into the ditch by marching columns or trampled by the horses of cavalry. Humboldt was remarkably impervious to the carnage, and enjoyed the opportunity this haphazard existence gave him of indulging his taste for raddled whores and fat lower-class women. Metternich was also surprisingly unaffected by the horrors of war, but complained bitterly of its discomforts. 'What roads, my God!' he wrote to Wilhelmina on 1 November. 'I travelled along with 200 cannon, partly on horseback, partly on foot and partly in a carriage. I left in a carriage because it was pouring with rain. I was spilled, so I gave orders for my horses to follow and mounted the most reliable-looking one, but he collapsed, so I walked, and I fell.' He was always chasing after Alexander, who insisted on playing the soldier rather than remaining at headquarters.[19]

And if conditions were unfavourable to the conclusion of the 'grand alliance', the project itself betrayed Castlereagh's ignorance of what was going on in Europe. Alexander, Metternich and Frederick William had far more important things on their minds than the question of whether or not to include Spain or Britain's maritime rights in their treaties. They were more concerned at this juncture with what was happening in the crucial area of Germany, not in the Iberian peninsula or beyond the seas. It was what happened there that might split the coalition.

In the course of September 1813, as it became increasingly likely that Napoleon would be in no position to defend them, most of the rulers within the Rheinbund began to look about nervously. The allied armies were drawing closer, and the stark choice that had faced Frederick William at the beginning of the year would soon be facing them. The prospects were anything but enticing.

Alexander's public image preceded the westward march of the allies, growing as it went, and all but the most pro-French public opinion hailed him from afar as a chivalrous liberator and divinely inspired righter of wrongs. But his advance was also accompanied by news of Stein's activities, by a wave of subversive muttering and plotting amongst students, junior officers and malcontents of one sort or another, and by a shiver of hopeful truculence on the part of dispossessed imperial nobles who saw the possibility of revenge, all of which made the rulers who had made their accommodation with Napoleon highly apprehensive.

Stein hoped to bring about the establishment of a strong unified German state on the back of a popular uprising fuelled by expectations of social reform as well as national rebirth. His wishful thinking was that a combination of Fichte's lectures, Arndt's poetry and Jahn's gymnastics had produced a nation in the making ready to embrace this dream. His expectations on this score were unrealistic. But his agitation against 'the thirty-six petty despots', as he termed the Rheinbund princes, whom he saw as 'ruinous for the civil liberty and moral fibre of the nation', represented a very real challenge. The convention of 19 March, covering the administration of the occupied territories, had given Stein virtually unlimited powers, and he had established administrative organs answerable only to himself. As soon as he took control of liberated areas of Saxony he doubled the level of requisition imposed by Napoleon, introduced martial law and gave special powers to the police.[20]

Metternich had begun to view the Rheinbund as a useful structure that could be used to preserve Germany from Stein, which is why he dropped its dissolution from his demands to Napoleon during the Congress of Prague. Hardenberg, who viewed Stein's doings with the same distaste as Metternich did, was nevertheless opposed to the preservation of the Rheinbund. He hoped to scoop as many frightened princes as possible into Prussia's protective embrace, and repeatedly suggested to Metternich that they divide Germany along the river Main into a northern and a southern sphere in which they could impose their respective influence. But Metternich wished to preserve the integrity of Germany, and at the same time feared such an extension of Prussian and, by proxy, Russian power over it. As early as 5 April the Prussian minister at the court of Bavaria had tried to bully that power into joining the Russo-Prussian alliance, threatening dire consequences in the event of refusal. Bavaria's immediate reaction had been to turn to Austria for protection, and Metternich had seized on the chance.[21]

He began to negotiate not only with Bavaria. Through Gentz, he orchestrated a campaign in the German press to oppose Stein and to advocate some kind of federation which could accommodate the existing states and their rulers. Pragmatic as ever, he was even prepared to entertain the possibility of the survival as King of Westphalia of Napoleon's brother Jérôme, solely to keep that area out of Stein's ambit.

Alexander had also yielded to pragmatic considerations. After protests from Count Münster, the plenipotentiary of Britain's Prince Regent for Hanover, he softened the original convention on the administration of liberated territories, thereby clipping Stein's wings a little. It had dawned on him that the national revival Stein hoped for might not only create unstable conditions which would be difficult to control, but might even breed hostility to Russian influence in the future. Such influence could best be exerted through pressure applied discreetly to grateful German princes, and Alexander gradually began to see himself superseding Napoleon as their protector. This seemed particularly apt; through his Holstein-Gottorp grandmother, his Württemberg mother and his Baden wife, many of the German princes were close relatives, and he had begun to receive covert requests for protection. They assumed a certain urgency when two of his relatives, the Dukes of the two Mecklemburgs, who had been the first to desert Napoleon openly, confident that they would be welcomed with open arms, had been treated by Stein as conquered enemies, and had in consequence appealed to Metternich for protection. Stein was becoming a liability to Alexander. While he kept him in place as a useful bogeyman, he excluded him from what was developing into a straightforward scramble between Russia, Prussia and Austria for influence in Germany.

These simplified family trees of the rulers of Russia, Austria, Württemberg and Baden only show the more important direct connections, and can therefore give only a very slight idea of the extraordinary degree to which all the rulers of central and eastern Europe were related by blood.

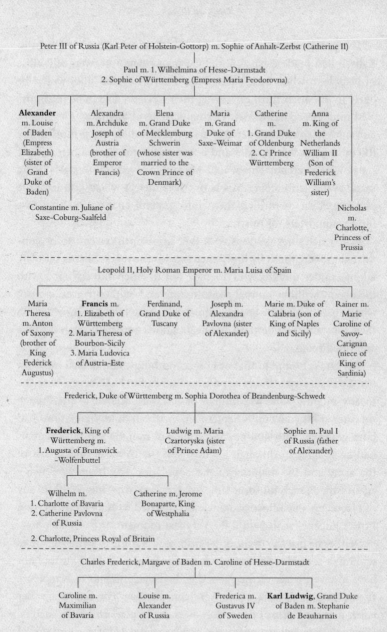

Peter III of Russia (Karl Peter of Holstein-Gottorp) m. Sophie of Anhalt-Zerbst (Catherine II)

Paul m. 1. Wilhelmina of Hesse-Darmstadt
2. Sophie of Württemberg (Empress Maria Feodorovna)

| **Alexander** m. Louise of Baden (Empress Elizabeth) (sister of Grand Duke of Baden) | Alexandra m. Archduke Joseph of Austria (brother of Emperor Francis) | Elena m. Grand Duke of Mecklemburg Schwerin (whose sister was married to the Crown Prince of Denmark) | Maria m. Grand Duke of Saxe-Weimar | Catherine m. 1. Grand Duke of Oldenburg 2. Cr Prince Württemberg | Anna m. King of the Netherlands William II (Son of Frederick William's sister) |

Constantine m. Juliane of Saxe-Coburg-Saalfeld

Nicholas m. Charlotte, Princess of Prussia

Leopold II, Holy Roman Emperor m. Maria Luisa of Spain

| Maria Theresa m. Anton of Saxony (brother of King Federick Augustus) | **Francis** m. 1. Elizabeth of Württemberg 2. Maria Theresa of Bourbon-Sicily 3. Maria Ludovica of Austria-Este | Ferdinand, Grand Duke of Tuscany | Joseph m. Alexandra Pavlovna (sister of Alexander) | Marie m. Duke of Calabria (son of King of Naples and Sicily) | Rainer m. Marie Caroline of Savoy-Carignan (niece of King of Sardinia) |

Frederick, Duke of Württemberg m. Sophia Dorothea of Brandenburg-Schwedt

| **Frederick**, King of Württemberg m. 1. Augusta of Brunswick -Wolfenbuttel | Ludwig m. Maria Czartoryska (sister of Prince Adam) | Sophie m. Paul I of Russia (father of Alexander) |

| Wilhelm m. 1. Charlotte of Bavaria 2. Catherine Pavlovna of Russia | Catherine m. Jerome Bonaparte, King of Westphalia |

2. Charlotte, Princess Royal of Britain

Charles Frederick, Margave of Baden m. Caroline of Hesse-Darmstadt

| Caroline m. Maximilian of Bavaria | Louise m. Alexander of Russia | Frederica m. Gustavus IV of Sweden | **Karl Ludwig**, Grand Duke of Baden m. Stephanie de Beauharnais |

The proclamation issued by Alexander and Frederick William in Kalisch had made clear that any German rulers who were still allies of Napoleon when their states were overrun by the allies would be likely to lose their thrones, leaving their territory free to be incorporated into some kind of new Germanic state of Stein's or Alexander's fancy. Metternich considered it essential to get all the princes of the Rheinbund to change sides and become allies of Austria before their states were overrun. This would not only prevent those states being made available to Stein, Prussia or Alexander, it would also have the pleasing effect of turning them into grateful clients, and therefore future supporters, of Austria.

Metternich's negotiations with the various princes had to be conducted in secret both by him, since they contravened Austria's undertakings under the Treaty of Toeplitz not to enter into any talks with the enemy without mutual consultation, and by the princes, each of whom had a resident French minister looking over his shoulder. As their substance was betrayal, the negotiations were necessarily devious and unedifying.

'My fate is bound to that of France, nothing could detach me from her; I will survive with her or perish with her, but I will never subscribe to any infamy,' King Maximilian of Bavaria declared to the French minister at his court on 15 September, by which time negotiations had been going on with Austria for a couple of months and all essentials had been agreed. Although his own son the Crown Prince, most of the army and the majority of the population had been clamouring against the French for some time, Maximilian, who was a faithful ally of Napoleon and whose daughter was married to Napoleon's stepson Prince Eugène, waited until the very last moment.[22]

Neither he nor any of the other princes was going to switch alliances without a reward, or at the very least a guarantee that they would not have to give up any of the gains they had made thanks to Napoleon. In the case of Bavaria, these were considerable. For one thing, her ruler, a mere Elector of the Holy Roman Empire, had been made a King by Napoleon in 1806. He had benefited from the process of mediatisation, acquiring a great deal of territory, and had done well out of the wars of 1805 and 1809 between France and Austria, relieving the latter of Salzburg, Berchtesgaden, the Inn and Hausrück districts, the Tyrol, Vorarlberg, Brixen, Trent and various smaller enclaves in Swabia.

Metternich needed Bavaria. If Maximilian were to cast himself on the mercy of Alexander or make a deal with Prussia the whole of southern Germany would be wide open to their interference. He therefore agreed to almost all of Bavaria's demands. By the Treaty of Ried, signed on 8 October, Bavaria undertook to leave the Rheinbund and ally herself with Austria, contributing 36,000 men who would operate under Austrian command. In return, Austria pledged her protection and that of her allies, which she had no right to do.

It is the secret articles of the treaty which are significant. One, which was to cause Metternich and indeed all the other statesmen of Europe many sleepless nights in the following year, guaranteed to Bavaria her current territorial extent and, recognising that certain areas would need to be returned to Austria, full compensation to be negotiated later. But by far the most important article was the one stating that 'The two High Contracting Parties regard one of the principal objects of their efforts in the present war to be the dissolution of the Confederation of the Rhine and the total and absolute independence of Bavaria, so that, unfettered and placed beyond all foreign influence, she may enjoy the fullness of sovereignty.'[23]

The Treaty of Ried was a triumph for Metternich, who had managed to enlist an invaluable ally as well as deny one to Alexander. It also overturned Stein's plans for a unified German state. But the struggle for control of Germany was by no means over, and one of its first and greatest victims was King Frederick Augustus of Saxony.

When Napoleon abandoned Dresden the King had been obliged to take refuge in his second city, Leipzig, where Napoleon concentrated his forces, and on which all the allied armies were now converging – even Bernadotte had been browbeaten, by Pozzo di Borgo and Stewart, into joining in the action. The attack opened on 16 October.

The battle for the city, which came to be known as the Battle of the Nations because of the number of nationalities involved, was the largest engagement of the Napoleonic Wars, involving well over half a million men, who were pounded by more than 2,000 pieces of artillery, and lasting three days.

Although heavily outnumbered, Napoleon held his own throughout the first day, delivering some heavy blows at the allies. On the second, the French were gradually obliged to give ground as Blücher appeared in their rear and the full weight of the allied forces was brought to bear. On that day the Saxon contingent in the French army defected and joined the allies, further depleting Napoleon's forces. He lost the initiative, and on the third day his army, which was by then outnumbered by a ratio of two to one, began to lose its cohesion. That evening Napoleon ordered a retreat to the Rhine. Before leaving Leipzig he went to the royal palace and offered Frederick Augustus refuge in France, but the Saxon King declined the offer, stating that he could not abandon his subjects at such a time. Frederick Augustus sent officers to each of the allied monarchs with a request for negotiation, but there was no response.

When Alexander rode into Leipzig he found Bernadotte already in the square before the royal palace, conversing with General Reynier, the French commander of the Saxon army, whom he had just taken prisoner. The King of Saxony was standing at the foot of the stairs with his royal guard. Bernadotte greeted Alexander and offered to present him to Frederick Augustus, but the Tsar snubbed the hapless King and went in to pay his respects to the Queen. A moment later a Russian officer informed the King of Saxony that he was Alexander's prisoner. After some argument as to where the unfortunate Saxon royal couple should be held and by whom, the Prussians took matters into their own hands, and at 4 a.m. on 23 October they were bundled into a carriage and sent under armed escort to captivity in Berlin.[24]

It was not just that the Saxon King had not declared for the allies right at the beginning, nor that he had gone back to Napoleon's side after Lützen. 'The despoliation of the goodly Frederick Augustus had become,' as Hardenberg put it, 'a necessity in the interests of making Prussia strong, and therefore in those of Europe.' More precisely, Saxony was the most suitable compensation Alexander could offer Frederick William in return for Prussia's former Polish provinces, which he was intending to hold on to himself.[25]

The allied victory at Leipzig was decisive. 'I have just returned from the battlefield on which the cause of the world has been won,' Metternich announced in a letter to his wife on 18 October. It was Napoleon's first total defeat, and its scale no less than its psychological impact made it inconceivable that he should ever play a dominant role in Germany again. 'The shame in which he covered us has been washed away by torrents of French blood,' Stein wrote triumphantly to his wife. Humboldt was similarly delighted by his walk over the corpse-strewn battlefield.[26]

'The deliverance of Europe appears to be at hand,' Aberdeen wrote to Castlereagh. But the letter he wrote to his sister-in-law Maria was more muted in tone. 'For three or four miles the ground is covered with bodies of men and horses, many not dead. Wretches wounded unable to crawl, crying for water amidst heaps of putrefying bodies. Their screams are heard at an immense distance, and still ring in my ears. The living as well as the dead are stripped by the barbarous peasantry, who have not sufficient charity to put the miserable wretches out of their pain. Our victory is most complete. It must be owned that a victory is a fine thing, but one should be at a distance.'[27]

Two days after the battle, on 20 October, Metternich was honoured by his sovereign with the title of Prince. For a man who believed in hierarchies as deeply as he did, this was gratifying. 'What a range of sensations I have experienced over the past few days!' he wrote to Wilhelmina that evening. 'The world has been reborn under my very eyes; my most daring dreams have come true – my political standing has doubled; I am at the apogee of my career; it will have been accomplished. Yet everything, sensations, calculations, business – the whole world, are eclipsed by a single thought of *mon amie*; the world, its grandeurs and its miseries are like nothing to me; you, always you – nothing but you!'[28]

After waking him the next morning his valet, Giroux, asked: 'Will Your Serene Highness put on the same suit Your Excellency wore yesterday?' If this did not bring Metternich down to earth, the interview he had with Alexander later that day did.[29]

The Tsar was also in triumphant mood. The great battle, with its apocalyptic overtones, deepened his conviction that he was fulfilling his destiny as God's instrument for the chastisement of Napoleonic godlessness. He too penned a note to his beloved in his moment of triumph. 'I beg you to believe me when I say that I am, more than ever, yours for life in my heart and my soul, and I would add; *Honi [sic] soit qui mal y pense*,' he wrote to Zinaida Volkonskaya, alluding to his recent decoration with the Garter.[30]

Metternich's arrangement with Bavaria had not only shattered Stein's plans; it had also profoundly irritated the Tsar, and it hung like a dark cloud over their meeting. Metternich expressed his disapproval at the activities of the Central Administrative Council, which was treating liberated areas like occupied enemy territory, and indeed at their long-term implications. He demanded that Stein be removed from his post. Alexander dismissed his arguments, declaring that he had made a promise to Stein, and that his authority would be compromised if he were obliged to break that promise.

Metternich could achieve little in the circumstances, and this is reflected in the new convention regarding liberated territories signed by the allied powers the following day. The Council was renamed a Central Executive, and although the rights of those princes who had become allies were to be respected, there was considerable ambiguity in the phrasing, which left Stein with virtually unlimited authority throughout the German lands.[31]

Metternich took the setback philosophically. The behaviour of Stein and of the Russian and Prussian soldiery 'liberating' Germany was beginning to produce a reaction at every level of society, and even many of those who had dreamt of this liberation were having second thoughts. 'I often wonder where our nation is really going,' Humboldt wrote to his wife, lamenting the lack of strong leadership. The poet Johann Wolfgang Goethe was so horrified at the depredations of the supposed liberators in his home city of Weimar that he declared 'The medicine is worse than the illness,' and continued to wear the Légion d'Honneur Napoleon had given him.[32]

Metternich played for time. He intensified secret negotiations with the rulers of the southern states, which gratefully accepted Austria's protective embrace. He was confident that he could outmanoeuvre Stein through *faits accomplis*. Above all, he placed his faith in his ability to manipulate Alexander.

'I argued for at least 3 hrs with your fine Emperor, I told him off as I do my son when he has done wrong,' he wrote to Wilhelmina from Weimar on 25 October. 'The result of my strictures will be that for the next week he will not do anything silly, but then he will start again and I shall have to tell him off again. That has been my role for the past 2 months.' The sense of power this gave him was exhilarating. 'I dashed over to Meiningen to arrange a few minor points in the destiny of the world with the Emp. Alexander and then dashed back here to do the same with my master,' he reported to her six days later.[33]

The feeling that he was fulfilling some grand destiny led him to ponder that of Napoleon. 'What kind of state must that man be in,' Metternich mused in a letter to Wilhelmina, 'he who once stood at the summit of power, and now sees the levers of such an immense construction shatter in his hands!'[34]

8

The First Waltzes

Napoleon struggled back towards the Rhine after his defeat at Leipzig 'in a state of despondency difficult to describe but easy to comprehend', in the words of the Paris Préfet baron Étienne Pasquier. Of the more than 300,000 men under his command three months earlier, only 40 to 50,000 were still with him, and they were for the most part 'no more than a crowd marching without order and incapable of carrying out any vigorous operation'. They nevertheless managed to defeat their erstwhile Bavarian allies under General Wrede, who tried to cut off their retreat at Hanau.[1]

The network of Napoleonic control over Germany that had been built up since 1806 unravelled. Napoleon's brother Jérôme fled from his kingdom of Westphalia as the other rulers of the Rheinbund joined the allies. 'I found him accompanied by his ministers of foreign affairs and war, and still surrounded by all the tattered trappings of royalty,' wrote Beugnot, Napoleon's minister in the grand duchy of Berg, who saw him pass through Düsseldorf. 'The house he was occupying was full of lifeguards, whose theatrical uniforms heavy with gold were wonderfully inapposite to the situation; there were chamberlains on the stairs since there were no ante-chambers, and the whole thing resembled nothing so much as a troupe of players on tour rehearsing a tragedy.'[2]

Private scores were settled as the French regime imploded, and unruly troops bent on rapine added to the misery. The situation was rendered all the more tragic as a typhus epidemic swept through the Rhineland, turning the military hospitals into morgues, striking down exhausted and underfed stragglers and taking with it even healthy men such as the venerable comte de Narbonne, who had survived the retreat from Moscow with such stoicism.

The collapse of Napoleon's power-structure in Germany meant that all the French troops still holding out in fortresses such as Danzig, Magdeburg, Modlin and Zamość were now utterly beyond his reach. They did not even represent a serious inconvenience to the allies, as they were easily contained by small forces of militia. And the retreat of Napoleonic power in Germany was replicated in Italy.

As soon as the armistice had expired in August, Austrian troops had invaded the Illyrian provinces, forcing the weak French garrisons to evacuate. Prince Eugène could do little to halt their advance, and fell back on Milan. In November he was approached on behalf of the allies by his father-in-law King Maximilian of Bavaria, who urged him to safeguard his future by changing sides, but he refused. His wife, Maximilian's daughter, supported him in his resolve. 'Courage, my friend,' she wrote, 'we do not merit our fate, yet our love and our clear conscience will be enough to sustain us, and in a simple cottage we will find the happiness that so many others seek fruitlessly on thrones. I say again to you, let us abandon everything, but never the path of virtue, and God will take care of us and of our poor children.'[3]

Virtue was not much in evidence further south, at Naples, whose King Joachim, Napoleon's brother-in-law Murat, was engaged in secret negotiations with the Austrians in the hope of keeping his throne. Napoleon had ordered his former chief of police Fouché to Naples with instructions to keep an eye on Murat and prevent him from defecting. But while Fouché had little time for Murat, he was even less interested in shoring up the Napoleonic empire, whose fall he was eagerly anticipating for reasons of his own. So he merely observed the game being played out before him, not so much by Murat as by his pushy and scheming wife, Napoleon's beautiful sister

Caroline, who had no intention of giving up the pleasures of royalty at the age of thirty.

Murat disposed of an army of not more than 20 to 25,000 men, magnificently uniformed but undisciplined, barely trained and poorly officered. Metternich, who may have been influenced by fond memories of the short but passionate affair he had enjoyed in Paris a couple of years before with Caroline, seems to have believed that Murat's forces were stronger, and to have been impressed by his overblown military reputation. He therefore thought it prudent to detach Murat from Napoleon by offering him Austria's recognition of his status and promising to obtain Britain's as well. Castlereagh did not approve, but accepted that Metternich must be given freedom of action in this instance, on the understanding that Britain's ally Ferdinand IV of Naples, now holed up in the Sicilian half of his kingdom, would be compensated with land elsewhere in Italy.[4]

Napoleon was back at Saint-Cloud on 10 November. The following day he held a council of state during which he complained that he had been betrayed by everyone, venting particular rage against King Maximilian and vowing vengeance. 'Munich shall be burned!' he ranted repeatedly. He gave orders for the raising of 300,000 soldiers, who were to be found by conscripting ever younger men and taking extra quotas from age groups which had not been heavily levied in the past. But as the area under his control shrank, so did his manpower pool, not to mention the number of uniform and munitions factories. The price of hiring a replacement soldier doubled to 4,000 francs. In Ghent, even a hundred seminarists preparing for the priesthood were packed off to fill the ranks of the artillery. Resistance to conscription increased commensurately. In November 1813 a young man who had been called up shot himself publicly in the main square of Cologne. As it became easier to escape from France and the administration in the country came under strain, the number evading conscription by fleeing or going into hiding rose drastically, and according to some estimates reached 100,000.[5]

On 9 December Napoleon presided over the opening of the Legislative Chambers and lectured them on the need for more men, more money and more determination. He set an example by acting as though nothing were amiss, and court life continued as usual. The receptions were as glittering and crowded as ever.

His remarkable show of confidence failed to inspire any in those around him. 'The master was there as always, but the faces around him, the looks and the words were no longer the same,' recorded one official who attended the imperial *lever* at the Tuileries. 'There was something sad and tired about the very demeanour of the soldiers, and even of the courtiers.' The mood in Paris was one of despondency. 'People were anxious about everything, foreseeing only misfortune on all sides,' wrote Pasquier. 'People no longer had faith in anything, all illusions had been shattered.'[6]

As he contemplated the invasion of France itself, Napoleon did what he could to improve her defences by closing off potential points of entry. One of these was Switzerland, which he had refashioned in accordance with the spirit of the age into a Helvetic Republic, of which he was the Mediator. Following the battle of Leipzig, the head of the government, Landamann Reinhard, had called the Diet to Zürich. The Diet declared the country's neutrality, without going so far as to recall the Swiss troops in Napoleon's ranks. Unable to defend Switzerland and wishing to deny it to the allies, Napoleon withdrew his forces, renounced his role as Mediator and recognised Swiss neutrality.

He also freed King Ferdinand of Spain, a prisoner in France since 1807, on the promise that when he repossessed his throne he would expel Wellington's army from Spanish soil. This would permit Napoleon to withdraw all his troops from Spain and south-western France. Such a ruse might conceivably have worked six months earlier, but was doomed to failure at this stage. Napoleon's only real chance of survival now lay in direct negotiations which might allow him to divide the coalition enough to give him a reasonable peace, or at least buy him much-needed time.

*   *   *

In the first days of November, the allies reached Frankfurt on the Main. The liberation of Germany was complete, and they were now poised on the frontiers of France. For Metternich it was a moment of personal triumph. 'It is I alone who has vanquished everything – hatred, prejudice, petty interest – to unite all the Germans under one and the same banner!' he wrote to Wilhelmina on 5 November. The following evening he rode out to greet his sovereign and escort him into the city in which he had watched him being crowned Holy Roman Emperor twenty-one years earlier. 'What cheering, what holy enthusiasm!' he exclaimed, seeing in it a defining moment in the struggle between good and evil.[7]

For the diplomats and other civilians attending their sovereigns the principal merit of the place was that after having to sleep rough in squalid inns and farmhouses, they could at last set themselves up in some measure of comfort. Metternich informed his wife that he had found 'a charming apartment', and relished being able to give elegant dinners. He also went shopping for silk dress-material to send to her and his daughters.

For the soldiers, Frankfurt offered a welcome rest. There were theatres and other entertainments to take their minds off the war. 'When I went into the Club,' noted Admiral Shishkov, 'I felt as though I were back in St Petersburg, as whichever room I went into was filled with Russian officers.' The city provided those officers with an opportunity to swagger and to reap the gratitude of the liberated citizens.[8]

'We have ladies here at Frankfurt,' Stewart wrote to Castlereagh, assuring him that 'you know me *too well* to think they occupy any portion of my *precious time*'. The consensus was that the nineteen-year-old Priscilla, Lady Burghersh, wife of the British Military Commissioner at Austrian headquarters, was the prettiest. But Alexander, who had begun to lose interest in Zinaida Volkonskaya, was drawn into the plump arms of the comely Dutch-born wife of one of the city's most prominent bankers, Simon Moritz Bethmann. Metternich dismissively likened her to 'a Dutch cow'. It was perhaps just as well, for had Alexander taken a shine to Priscilla Burghersh he might have been disappointed. She was one of the few women in Europe who failed to fall for the charm of the Tsar, who made a disagreeable impression on her when she met him at Frankfurt, and reminded her of her dentist. 'He has certainly fine shoulders, but beyond that he is horribly ill-made,' she wrote to a friend. 'He holds himself bent quite forward, for which reason all his Court imitate him and bend too, and gird their waists like women! His countenance is not bad, and that is all I can say of him.'[9]

There were services of thanksgiving for the liberation of Germany, and balls given by the citizens in honour of the three allied sovereigns and their ministers. Alexander's sisters the Grand Duchesses Catherine and Maria arrived in Frankfurt to grace the proceedings, as did a number of German ladies anxious to safeguard their future prospects. A carnival atmosphere reigned, and the proceedings were not always as decorous as they might have been. At one of the balls lack of familiarity with the waltz and an unevenness in the floor resulted in a collision and a pile-up, with one young lady falling so that 'all her secrets were revealed to everyone', as Metternich informed his daughter Marie.[10]

The city also filled up with princes high and low from all over Germany with more serious things on their minds. Rheinbund rulers were desperate to ensure that they did not lose their realms. The smaller and the more vulnerable their states, the more they sought to reassure all and sundry that they had always detested Napoleon and longed to join the allied cause. Mediatised Standesherren, formerly sovereign princes who had exchanged their ancient bond with the Holy Roman Emperor for one with the Rheinbund ruler into whose realms their estates had been incorporated under the protection of Napoleon, came to denounce those rulers, in the hope of recovering their independence. Imperial knights, prelates and others who had lost their status as a result of Napoleon's rearrangements came to demand reinstatement, brandishing ancient deeds and charters. All had powerful relatives or backers at one or other of the allied courts;

they lined up to put their case to Metternich, Nesselrode and other ministers, and pestered anyone with influence.

In letters to his wife, Stein complained of a 'deluge of princes and sovereigns', a 'princely *canaille* as ridiculous as it is contemptible and despised'. As far as short-term arrangements were concerned, he was the single most important man in Germany. He was in charge of the administration even in those states whose rulers had joined the allies, and they groaned at the numbers of men and horses he was requisitioning, the victuals he was seizing, and the taxes he was levying. Particularly unsettling was his setting-up of Landsturm recruitment districts that totally ignored existing state boundaries. Those who had lost everything thought he might prove sympathetic and take their part against the rulers, but he treated them with similar disdain. They could hardly expect better.[11]

Stein, Metternich and Nesselrode had all three been sovereign nobles of the Holy Roman Empire, and they had lost their status too. They had successfully made new lives for themselves, realising that times had changed. They could not be expected to feel any sympathy for those who had made comfortable compromises with Napoleon or those who had not been able to come to terms with their loss.

Humboldt, who was also besieged by petitioners begging for his protection, found it 'excellent sport' being badgered by princesses who in other circumstances would never have noticed his existence. He developed a formula for dealing with them which consisted of speaking with feigned sympathy of members of the class of petitioner being oppressed by them: a Rheinbund Prince would have to listen to the woes of a mediatised noble, the mediatised noble to the complaints of a deposed prelate, and so on.[12]

Metternich had nevertheless managed to secure Austria's position in southern Germany by signing up the more substantial states as allies. The King of Württemberg, who had been given his crown by Napoleon and grown fat on devouring mediatised states and Church lands, doubling the population of his realm in ten years, had much to lose from any change; he signed a treaty of alliance with Austria that guaranteed his continued sovereignty, within whatever arrangements were finally reached in Germany. He was followed by the Grand Duke of Hesse and the Grand Duke of Baden. The latter had also done well under French rule, marrying Napoleon's adoptive daughter Stephanie de Beauharnais, whom he now repudiated. He tried to obtain outright recognition of his sovereignty by pleading with Alexander, who was his brother-in-law, but Alexander did not like him, and he too was guaranteed sovereignty only within the limits of the eventual German settlement.

When they had planned their campaign in August, the allies had concentrated on forcing Napoleon out of Germany, and their military commanders had only envisaged operations as far as the Rhine. Having reached that natural barrier, which was also the frontier of the French Empire, they hesitated. To carry the war into France would give their enterprise a different character.

Alexander was inclined to continue the advance, but his ministers, particularly the Russian ones, were violently opposed to this course. On 6 November Admiral Shishkov presented him with a long memorandum arguing that Russia had, by defending herself and defeating Napoleon, fulfilled her duty to herself. She had gone on to accomplish Alexander's self-imposed goal of liberating Europe. There could, as a result, be no point or indeed justification for pursuing the war further. Shishkov pointed out that with France pushed back to the Rhine and Germany restored to vigour, Napoleon would never be able to threaten Europe, let alone Russia, again, particularly as she herself would have acquired a new defensible frontier. He also warned that taking the war into France might have the effect of galvanising the French nation in support of their Emperor and their motherland, and inflict defeat on the invaders.[13]

Alexander's generals were of the same view, while his soldiers were keen to go home. The Russian army was down to some 50,000 men, and an anxious Aberdeen reported on 8 November that 'The sentiments of the Russian army are more loudly expressed every day; from the highest to the lowest they are clamorous for peace.' Stewart also warned that they wanted to 'pull up'. The situation in the Prussian army was not much better. Gneisenau painted a dismal picture of its condition: the men were exhausted and short of arms. Most wanted to go into winter quarters at the very least.[14]

But Alexander was supported by people such as Pozzo di Borgo, who would never rest until he saw his enemy Napoleon destroyed; Anstett, who nurtured a similar vendetta; Stein, who wished to see France reduced further; and a number of others in his entourage, mostly non-Russians. They were seconded by Hardenberg and particularly Blücher, who longed to avenge the shame of Jena and the humiliations his country had suffered at the hands of Napoleon. He strongly urged an immediate advance, believing that if they denied Napoleon the opportunity to reorganise his forces, they could defeat him and take Paris within two months. Frederick William was a good deal less bellicose, and frequently expressed the fear that Napoleon's military talents might yet produce a reversal of the situation.[15]

Francis was equally wary, while the Austrian military commanders were similarly respectful of Napoleon's abilities. Metternich was opposed to further advance for other reasons. He did not wish to see France weakened further, as his view of a viable settlement in Europe included a strong France acting as a counterbalance to Russia. He therefore urged making peace proposals to Napoleon, pointing out, to appease Alexander, that they would probably not be accepted, and that this would only enhance the moral standing of the allies.

Conveniently enough, Napoleon's minister at the court of Weimar, the baron de Saint-Aignan, had been captured in the allied advance and brought to Frankfurt. Before sending him on his way back to Paris, on 9 November, Metternich invited him to a meeting with himself and Nesselrode. He told the Frenchman that the allies would be prepared to make peace now. All France would have to do was give up her conquests in Italy, Spain and Germany, returning to her natural frontiers on the Rhine, the Alps and the Pyrenees, thereby keeping Belgium and Savoy as well as the whole left bank of the Rhine. The status of the rest of the Netherlands was left unspecified,

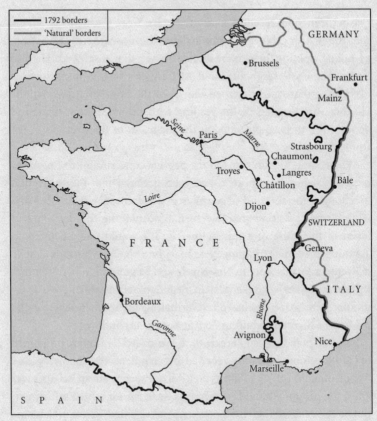

The 'historic' and 'natural' borders of France

and there was talk of negotiation on the subject of colonies and maritime matters.

Metternich suggested that Saint-Aignan write this up in the form of an *aide-mémoire*, which he could present to Napoleon on his return to Paris, and led him into a neighbouring study for the purpose. While they were out of the room Aberdeen arrived, and when they emerged from the study Metternich asked Saint-Aignan to read the document out to the three of them, just to make sure he had listed the terms correctly.

Aberdeen had recently received letters from Castlereagh saying that the British cabinet was not inclined to negotiate with Napoleon, as public opinion in Britain wished to see him destroyed. He also knew that Castlereagh deplored Metternich's 'spirit of catching at everything that can be twisted into even the hope of a negotiation'. He therefore listened to the reading with detached scepticism, and appears not to have protested at the inclusion of the frontier on the Rhine.[16]

When Saint-Aignan came to the passage concerning Britain, Aberdeen asked him to repeat it, and then declared that the expression 'freedom of the seas and of commerce' was too vague. He stated that while Britain was prepared to return almost all the colonies she had taken in the cause of a durable peace, 'she would never consent to anything that might impinge her maritime rights'. The next day he delivered a formal note to Nesselrode and Metternich reiterating that Britain would never take part in negotiations in which these conditions were to be discussed. Nevertheless, his very presence at the reading of the memorandum lent it a spurious authority.[17]

Saint-Aignan reached Paris with the so-called 'Frankfurt proposals' on 14 November, and was received by Napoleon the following day. Napoleon noted at once that, as they did not specify any of Britain's war aims, the proposals could not serve as the basis for a final settlement. But he also realised that they opened up possibilities. Through Caulaincourt, with whom he had replaced Maret as Foreign Minister, he wrote to Metternich accepting the proposals, suggesting Mannheim as the venue for the congress.

He was by now prepared to make peace on the basis of France's 'natural frontiers' and the return of most of her colonies. But this would only be possible if pressure were brought to bear on Britain to agree to France's retention of Belgium, and the only way of bringing the allies to do this was by placing the entire onus for the continuation of the war on Britain. Thus the 'Frankfurt proposals' seemed to offer a chance of introducing a wedge with which to split the coalition.[18]

* * *

'The Coalition is beginning to have the decrepitude of age,' Aberdeen wrote to his father-in-law the Earl of Abercorn, 'and the evils inherent in its very existence are felt daily.' This is not surprising. Russia and Prussia were bound together by treaty, and each of them was bound by other treaties with Austria and with Britain. Austria had also concluded, on 3 October, the vaguest of preliminary treaties with Britain, alongside a treaty of subsidy. Austria had concluded unilateral agreements with Bavaria and a number of other minor powers, while Russia, Prussia and Britain had signed their own treaties with Sweden. All of these treaties were vague, many were contradictory or at least incompatible in spirit, and all of the contracting parties were mistrustful of all the others.[19]

Given the differences of opinion on every question, from whether to continue the advance, to how to dispose of the Polish territories, reorganise Germany and settle a myriad minor matters, and given the deep-rooted antipathies and jealousies running through it at every level, the coalition was at risk of falling apart at any moment. Stewart complained of the continuous 'political chicane, finesse and tracasserie of every kind' that he was being subjected to. 'In short, in proportion as we have success,' he reported to Castlereagh on 23 November, 'separate interests become every day more and more in play, and one cannot look satisfactorily at present to a happy termination, when there is at the head of all this a Machiavellian spirit of political intrigue.'[20]

Castlereagh's 'grand design', to bind all the allies together and commit them to a set of specific goals, had got nowhere. Cathcart had tried again and again to corner Alexander in order to present the project to him, but military matters had always intervened and the audiences had been cancelled. It was not until 26 October that he had managed to have a talk with the Tsar alone. According to Cathcart, Alexander 'did not seem in any shape averse to what is proposed', but he had asked which colonies Britain was prepared to put on the negotiating table, a subject he knew would raise British hackles. It was his way of brushing off Castlereagh's proposal.[21]

Aberdeen, who felt slighted by Castlereagh entrusting the project to Cathcart rather than to him, and who also felt that it had been a mistake not to make the proposal to Metternich first rather than to Alexander, criticised Cathcart's slowness and lack of energy in pressing the matter. In a letter to Castlereagh dated 29 October he suggested that he should himself be put in charge of promoting the project. He backed this up by declaring that Metternich had complete confidence in him, as did Nesselrode, who 'though not very wise himself, has the most perfect contempt for Cathcart, and frequently expresses it'. And for good measure he added that Nesselrode had told him that 'it is impossible to communicate with such an *idiot*'.[22]

Castlereagh's frustration at his three envoys' lack of progress shines through his frequent letters on the subject. But there was little they could do. The conditions of a rapid campaign in foul weather had defeated their efforts until now, and matters did not improve when allied headquarters came to rest in Frankfurt. Castlereagh had attempted to smooth Aberdeen's ruffled feathers by telling him that he was now to play the most important role and to be 'the labouring oar' in the scheme. 'If you succeed in placing the Key Stone in the arch which is to sustain us hereafter, you will not feel that your labour has been thrown away,' he wrote. A couple of days after his arrival, Alexander invited Aberdeen to dine with himself and Nesselrode, but all that came of it was flattery of Aberdeen and complaints against Cathcart: the Russians were evidently trying to play the British ministers off against each other.[23]

On 23 November Stewart wrote to Castlereagh with the news that Prussia would be prepared to sign the 'grand alliance'. Two days later Aberdeen proudly reported back that he had persuaded Metternich, who in turn promised to persuade Alexander of the necessity of adopting Castlereagh's project, and three days after that he assured Castlereagh that 'The Treaty of general Alliance *will positively be made forthwith.*' But on 5 December Stewart wrote saying that Alexander had refused to sign, and four days later Nesselrode and Metternich told Aberdeen that they had not the slightest intention of doing so either.[24]

Failing to see why anyone could possibly object to signing such an alliance, Castlereagh was anxious. All three of his envoys were, in Stewart's words, 'down in the mouth', and two of them wanted to come home. They were on worse terms than ever with each other, and out of their depth in the ocean of intrigue that had engulfed allied headquarters and submerged it deeper with every day it remained in Frankfurt. Their inability to show a united front undermined their position so far that the other ministers were treating them less and less seriously, referring to them dismissively as 'the English Trinity' or 'the Three Englands'.

Castlereagh was being disingenuous in his failure to understand why Metternich and Alexander did not wish to bind themselves by his proposed alliance. He himself was pursuing a policy dictated solely by British interests quite independently of them, in the Netherlands, where he was hoping to create a *fait accompli*. Through Aberdeen, he was paying out cash to assist the Dutch patriots who had raised the banner of revolt against the French on 15 November, and he was exasperated by Bernadotte, who launched a unilateral attack on Denmark instead of marching to their support, for which he had taken British subsidies. He meant the liberation to embrace Belgium, so he could have Antwerp and the Scheldt estuary well in hand.[25]

Not surprisingly, Castlereagh was alarmed at the report, sent in by Aberdeen at the end of November, of intelligence that the Russians were nurturing a plan to marry Alexander's sister the Grand Duchess Catherine to the Emperor Francis's brother Archduke Charles, and to place them on the Dutch throne. He was beginning to see conspiracy everywhere.[26]

Aberdeen tried to reassure him, gently chiding him on his ignorance: 'my dear Castlereagh, with all your wisdom, judgment and experience, which are as great as possible, and which I respect sincerely, I think you have so much of the Englishman as not quite to be aware of the real value of Foreign modes of acting'.[27]

'The successes of the allies are beyond all belief,' Metternich wrote to one of his diplomats on 19 November. 'We are masters of the whole of Germany and of Italy soon as well.' He shed his modesty and the use of the collective noun when writing to Wilhelmina. 'It is all my work,' he declared, 'mine and mine alone.' There was much truth in this assertion, as he had been the helmsman of the coalition over the past months and had prevented it from striking many a shoal.[28]

He had been particularly skilful in handling Alexander. 'Through-out the military operations, I would spend the evenings with His Imperial Majesty,' he later reminisced. 'From 8 or 9 o'clock in the evenings until midnight, we would be quite alone, conversing with the greatest familiarity. We would speak of the most diverse subjects, of private matters as well as of the great moral or political questions of the day. We would exchange ideas on all these things with the greatest abandon, and this absence of any constraint lent a particular charm to this intercourse.' Alexander had come to trust Metternich, as did Nesselrode, and as a result the Austrian Foreign Minister often did not bother to consult Hardenberg or Humboldt. A greater problem was that he began to take his ascendancy for granted. 'The good Empr. is so infatuated with what he calls my way of seeing big that he does nothing without consulting me,' he wrote to his wife on 1 December. Such hubris was alarming, and was about to lead Metternich into a major blunder.[29]

Despite the misgivings about crossing the Rhine and invading France itself, a plan for the next stage of the allied advance had been agreed on 19 November. Devised by Schwarzenberg, it reflected Metternich's caution. The invasion was to be undertaken by three forces: in the north Blücher's Prussians were to cross the Rhine between Mainz and Cologne and sweep into Lorraine; in the south the Austrians were to push Prince Eugène out of Italy, march over the Simplon and advance on Lyon; and in the centre Schwarzenberg with the main Austro-Russian forces was to cross into France between Mannheim and Bâle (Basel), occupy the Vosges and deploy on the plateau of Langres. Once those three objectives had been achieved, the allies would pause and take stock. It seemed unlikely that Napoleon would not have made peace by then – negotiations had been decided upon, and it was only the venue that still needed to be fixed.

In order to shore up their own position in moral terms and further undermine Napoleon's, the allies issued a declaration to the French people, on 1 December, to the effect that they were not making war on France, but only on French 'preponderance'. 'The allied Sovereigns desire that France should be great, strong and contented,' it went on, and held out a powerful bribe, stating that they wanted her to be more extensive territorially than she had been before the Revolution.[30]

The allied plan involved marching through Swiss territory, which posed a nice political problem for the allies, since the Swiss had declared their neutrality. Alexander solemnly promised that the allies would respect this, and backed it up by declaring that he would regard any violation as a declaration of war on himself. Failing to appreciate the depth or the personal nature of this commitment, Metternich was about to do just that.

The Swiss Confederation, as recognised by the Treaty of Westphalia in 1648, had been an association of thirteen cantons and a number of smaller units, ruled variously by either absolute despots, local oligarchies or some form of democratic assembly. Their inherent differences and jealousies were exacerbated by religious divisions and the rival influences of neighbouring powers, particularly Austria and France.

The French had invaded Switzerland in 1798. Geneva became part of France, and the Valtelline was later incorporated into the Napoleonic kingdom of Italy. The remainder became a Helvetic Republic consisting of twenty-three cantons and rationalised in the spirit of the age. Napoleon, who declared himself 'Mediator', suppressed the *baillages*, or feudal tribunals, liberated Vaud and Aargau from the dominance of Berne, and swept away a myriad medieval hangovers. Every citizen was made free and equal before the law. Although this delighted many, it upset local feeling by breaking age-old traditions.

The old and formerly dominant cantons, headed by Berne, resented the new arrangements and longed for a return to the old days, while the newly formed ones, such as Aargau and Vaud, had benefited from French intervention and the protection of Napoleon. The old cantons had historic links with Austria, which had traditionally acted as their protector, and Metternich was hoping to use them to reassert Austrian influence and reintroduce the *ancien régime* into Switzerland as a whole.

One young native of Vaud, Frédéric César de La Harpe, had been persecuted in his youth by the patricians of Berne and been forced to flee. He had gone to Russia, where he had found employment as the tutor of the young Grand Duke Alexander, on whom he had exerted an enormous influence, which he continued to wield now that his pupil was Tsar. La Harpe had later gone to France, and had been instrumental in bringing about the French intervention that had liberated Vaud and Aargau from the domination of Berne and toppled the oligarchs who had ruled that city.

At the beginning of November, Alexander and Metternich had despatched two agents, Capodistrias and Lebzeltern, to Zürich with instructions to persuade the head of the Swiss government, Landamann Reinhard, to declare for the allies, or, failing that, to declare Switzerland's neutrality. In the latter eventuality, they were to negotiate permission for allied troops to march through Swiss territory. The two envoys reached Zürich on 21 November only to find that the Swiss Diet was far from united, and many still felt loyalty to Napoleon. Napoleon's renunciation of his role as Mediator of Switzerland resolved that issue and the Diet duly declared the country's neutrality.

Unbeknown to Alexander, Metternich had also sent an agent to Berne with the aim of encouraging it to undermine the authority of the existing government and to call for a return to the *ancien régime*. The main body of allied troops due to march through Swiss territory were Austrian, which would assure them protection and Metternich a dominant influence in the affairs of Switzerland. By this time allied troops were on the move, and Schwarzenberg's vanguard was about to enter Switzerland between Schaffhausen and Bâle. But, since the Zürich Diet had not produced the necessary authority for them to do so, and realising that this would constitute an infringement of Swiss neutrality, Alexander countermanded their orders.

Metternich could see no reason to disrupt the entire allied plan merely for the sake of Alexander's sensibilities. He persuaded Francis to order Schwarzenberg to go ahead, and at 2 a.m. on 21 December the Austrians entered Bâle, whose garrison had capitulated. When news of this reached Alexander, he flew into a violent rage. 'Metternich has behaved detestably in the Swiss question, and I am indignant about it,' he wrote to his sister. He did not yet realise the full implications of Metternich's actions, which were to be rich in consequence, but he felt personally betrayed and resented his reputation having been damaged. He never forgave him, and the incident poisoned relations between them forever.[31]

Stein was quick to take advantage. 'There is every reason to fear that Count Metternich will bring to the ultimate arrangement of the affairs of Germany the same spirit of frivolity, of vanity, the same lack of respect for truth and principle which has already partly spoiled them and which he has just flourished with such harmful results in Switzerland,' he wrote to Alexander.[32]

Metternich made light of the matter. But he had already come to realise that he would no longer be able to handle Alexander on his own, and neither Hardenberg, Nesselrode nor the 'English Trinity' were of much use. There was also the consideration that as they drew closer to a final settlement decisions would need to be made fast. And while the presence of the three sovereigns at headquarters meant that Russia, Prussia and Austria could agree anything on the spot, the absence of a representative of Britain endowed with decision-making powers meant that the coalition as a whole could not. The British constitution did not permit the head of state to leave the country, so there could be no question of the Prince Regent coming to allied headquarters, but things could not be allowed to go on as they were.

On receiving Napoleon's letter accepting the 'Frankfurt proposals' as a basis for negotiation, on 5 December, Metternich informed Nesselrode and Hardenberg, and they resolved to send Pozzo di Borgo to London to talk to Castlereagh directly. Stewart got wind of this through clandestine access to Metternich's papers, and communicated his sense of outrage to his colleagues. Aberdeen felt he had been tricked and charged Metternich to his face with disloyalty. 'More chicane and manoeuvring have been, and still are, going on concerning this business than on any that has hitherto come within my experience,' commented Jackson.[33]

Metternich, who was mortified to discover that his chancellery had been 'plundered', was not in fact trying to trick anyone. He and his colleagues had merely come to the conclusion that 'the Triumvirate we presently have at our headquarters is not fitted to advancing the cause', and Pozzo di Borgo's mission was to instruct the Russian, Prussian and Austrian ministers in London to ask the British cabinet to nominate one man to speak with authority in its name. They did not mention names, but it was clear whom they had in mind. 'What bliss it would be to have Castlereagh here to put an end to this English Sanhedrin and the silliness of the good Stewart,' Hardenberg noted in his diary on 8 December. Metternich had already written to Caulaincourt deferring the start of the negotiations, anticipating the arrival of Castlereagh.[34]

The British cabinet considered the request at its meeting on 20 December. Foreign Secretaries did not normally travel abroad in the pursuance of their duties. But the circumstances were exceptional. Britain had spent some £700,000,000 fighting the French over the past twenty years, which, according to some historians, represented a greater burden in terms of men and resources than the Great War of 1914–18 would impose. The country could not afford to carry on much longer at this rate, and if a peace settlement unfavourable to her were reached in Europe, she might find herself alone, at war with France and the United States, cut off from European markets, stranded and friendless. The cabinet decided that 'the Government itself should repair to headquarters', in the person of Castlereagh.[35]

'Certainly, that is his only chance of having any finger in the pie,' Lord Grenville wrote on hearing of Castlereagh's departure, adding that if he did not make haste he would probably arrive too late.[36]

9

A Finger in the Pie

A dense fog lay over the streets of London on the afternoon of 26 December 1813 as Castlereagh drove home to No. 18 St James's Square. Although it was Boxing Day, Lord Liverpool's cabinet had forgone their traditional country pursuits and spent the day around the table at No. 10 Downing Street discussing the fine points of his impending mission.

A few hours later, two heavily laden travelling carriages trundled out of the square bearing the Foreign Secretary off on his adventure. Loving husband that he was, Castlereagh could not envisage going anywhere without his wife Emily. She in turn insisted on taking along her young niece Lady Emma Sophia Edgcumbe and little nephew Viscount Valletort, whom she had more or less adopted when, seven years earlier, her sister had died. They set off 'in a fog so intense', according to Emma Sophia, 'that the carriages went at a foot's pace, with men holding flambeaux at the head of the horses'. After covering barely eight miles in this way, they stopped for the night at Romford. They rose early the next morning, paused at Colchester for breakfast, and then drove on to Harwich.

The next day they went aboard HMS *Erebus*, but soon after leaving harbour the vessel was becalmed, and they were obliged to spend the next three days anchored off Harwich. Apart from Lord and Lady Castlereagh, her bulldog Venom, Emma Sophia and her brother, and their tall and gangly cousin Alexander Stewart, the party included Castlereagh's assistant Joseph Planta, his secretaries Frederick Robinson (who in 1827 would become Prime Minister as Lord Goderich) and William Montagu. They had been joined by Pozzo di Borgo, who entertained them with his stock of famously second-hand and oft-repeated anecdotes and *bons mots*.

The dead calm was shattered by a gale. They sailed for Holland in a blizzard, the ship heaving and pitching in the driving snow, with 'the men tumbling about on deck' according to Emma Sophia. When they at last sighted land, the captain informed them that as he did not know the Dutch coast well enough to negotiate it in a storm, they would have to drop anchor and wait for it to subside. So they spent another three days being tossed about on the waves until a pilot who had spotted them came out and guided them into the harbour of Helvoetsluys. The bedraggled and frozen party were met with cheering and gun salutes as they came ashore, and the following day they were speedily conducted to The Hague, to be greeted by the Prince of Orange. While the rest of the party recovered from the crossing, Castlereagh got down to work with the Prince and his ministers, for Holland was to be the linchpin of Britain's rearrangement of Europe.[1]

When the armies of Revolutionary France had occupied the Dutch Republic in 1795, the head of state, the Stadholder William V, fled across the Channel, to spend the last ten years of his life as an exile at Kew. Shortly after his death, his son William, who had taken service in Prussia, was taken prisoner by the French at Auerstadt in 1806. Napoleon recognised his title of Prince of Orange and granted him a pension in order to neutralise him and undermine his standing in England. The French-dominated Dutch Republic, renamed the Batavian Republic in 1795, was turned into the kingdom of Holland in 1806, with Napoleon's brother Louis as King. When Louis proved to be too good a Dutchman, Napoleon deposed him and in 1810 incorporated the kingdom into France.

While the Prince of Orange lived on a French pension, his son,

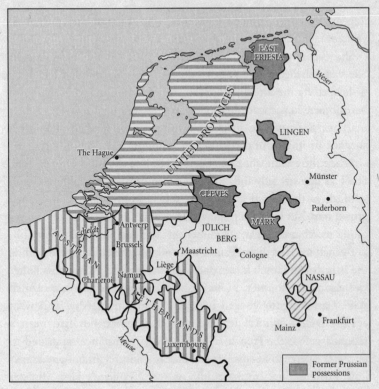

The following labels appear on the map:

EAST FRIESIA

Weser

UNITED PROVINCES

LINGEN

Münster

The Hague

CLEVES

Paderborn

Antwerp

JÜLICH BERG

MARK

Scheldt

AUSTRIAN

Brussels

Maastricht

Cologne

Namur

Liège

NASSAU

Charleroi

NETHERLANDS

Mainz

Frankfurt

Meuse

Luxembourg

Former Prussian possessions

The Netherlands

also named William, studied at Oxford and then went on to serve against the French in the Peninsular War under Wellington. This suited Liverpool and Castlereagh, who envisaged restoring the house of Orange to a strengthened Holland after the defeat of Napoleon. In the spring of 1813 the Prince of Orange, referred to by the British as the Sovereign Prince of the Netherlands, was back in London. That summer Castlereagh began planning a rising in the Netherlands to coincide with the advance of the allied armies, and formed up an Orange Legion, mainly from French prisoners of Dutch nationality. At the same time plans were made for the marriage of the Sovereign Prince's son, known as the Hereditary Prince, to the British Prince

Regent's daughter Princess Charlotte, who was just under eighteen years old.

She was a tall, fresh-looking girl, a little on the massive side. She was intelligent but poorly educated. Her upbringing had been bedevilled by the atrocious morals of her father and the vagaries of her mother, compounded by their quarrels and the break-up of their marriage. She could be unruly and stubborn, and her behaviour often shocked by its lack of decorum and restraint.

When the match was first suggested to her, she was not overjoyed. She had known 'Silly Billy', as she called him, since childhood, and felt little in the way of love for the short, skinny young man he had grown into. But her father managed to convince her of the advantages of the match, and on 12 December 1813 she had given her consent.

By then the Hereditary Prince was in the Netherlands, commanding the British and Dutch forces operating against the French. His father was also in the country. In his desire to strengthen the future Dutch state, Castlereagh envisaged turning it into a monarchy. This went against Dutch political tradition, as the Netherlands had been a republic before the French invasion. But circumstances appeared to favour Castlereagh's plans. 'The Prince is a Sovereign, nobody knows how, but everyone considers him as such,' William's First Minister Gijsbert van Hogendorp wrote to Castlereagh in November 1813, at the same time asking him to resolve the question of his future status. 'It is of course solely up to the Nation to make him a Sovereign, but his title is subject to agreement between the Powers.'[2]

Castlereagh encouraged the Prince to occupy Belgium (formerly the Austrian Netherlands) as the French were forced to abandon it, and discreetly extend his rule over it. Having been assured by the Prince that the Belgians would welcome Dutch rule, Castlereagh, whose knowledge of the area was limited to the study of maps, foresaw no problems. He was however realistic enough to dismiss as outdated the proposal put forward by Hogendorp that Britain take Dunkirk for herself in order to possess a military base on the Continent, as she had before the fall of Calais in 1558.[3]

Castlereagh did not linger in The Hague. He had already wasted enough time on the Channel crossing and he was eager to get on. So, after discharging his business with the Sovereign Prince, he set off again on 9 January 1814. He left most of his party behind in The Hague, despite angry protests from his wife, whose mind was set on accompanying him. His mission would take him through dangerous territory, lately the theatre of war, infested with deserters who had turned bandits and regular troops who were often little better, and roamed by Russian irregular cossacks eager for loot. There could be no question of exposing Lady Castlereagh and her young charges to such dangers.[4]

Castlereagh, Planta, Robinson, Montagu and their various servants clambered into four travelling coaches and set off. Desperate to make up for lost time, they covered the distance of nearly 1,000 kilometres between The Hague and Bâle at breakneck speed, only stopping for the night once. It was a gruelling experience. 'My dearest Em,' Castlereagh wrote from Münster on 13 January, 'We arrived here this morning at 8 o'clock, having travelled without a halt since we parted. The roads for the last forty miles have been dreadfully bad – worse than a ploughed field frozen. The servants' coach broke down, which has given us some hours in bed whilst they were coming up in a country wagon. The last twenty English miles took us 10½ hours and I only marvel at how our English carriages could bear it.'

They made for Paderborn, Cassel and then Frankfurt, where they arrived two days later, and from where Castlereagh complained to his wife that 'our bones are a little sore' and that 'German dirt is beyond the worst parts of Scotland'. He may have been exaggerating the discomfort in order to demonstrate his wisdom at dissuading her from making the trip with him. 'Robinson and I have hardly ever seen any other object than the four glasses of the carriage covered with frost which no sun could dissolve, so that we were in fact imprisoned in an icehouse for days and nights, from which we were occasionally removed into a dirty room with a black stove smelling of tobacco smoke or something worse,' he continued.[5]

Two days later, from Durlach, he was able to report that there had been a thaw, and indeed that he had found time when they passed through Frankfurt to go out and buy her some 'finery'. That night, at a post-house, he met Gentz, who had just come away from head-quarters and was on his way back to Vienna. The next day, 18 January, he reached Bâle, having taken fifty hours to cover the last 350 kilo-metres from Frankfurt in freezing conditions.

His appearance at Bâle caused something of a sensation. He was kitted out in a curious blue tailcoat covered in braid of a kind not seen on the Continent since the 1780s, a pair of bright scarlet breeches and 'jockey boots'. One of his attendants was decked out in what looked like a hussar uniform, and 'appeared to have put his shirt on over his coat', while Planta 'does nothing but flourish about with a long sword and a military cloak', according to one witness. 'Castle-reagh is a pretty man, with a calm, thoughtful and earnest manner,' Humboldt wrote to his wife the following day, greatly amused by the contrast between the Austrian, Prussian and Russian diplomats, all uniformed, booted and dripping with decorations, and Castlereagh, who in his gold-braided blue coat, red waistcoat and breeches, and white silk stockings, 'resembled nothing so much as a footman'.[6]

Alexander had left for headquarters. Before going he had told Cathcart that he wanted to be the first to talk to Castlereagh, and requested that he refrain from holding any discussions with others. Castlereagh had no intention of complying. The next morning at 10 o'clock he called on Metternich, with whom he spent two hours. At midday Metternich had to attend a conference, but the two met again at 4 o'clock over dinner, hosted by Aberdeen and attended by Hardenberg. The latter then took Castlereagh to be presented to Frederick William, but at six he was back with Metternich, with whom he conferred till midnight. 'I spent the day carving up Europe like a piece of cheese,' Metternich wrote to Wilhelmina before going to bed. 'I talked so much that I am quite hoarse, I thought so much that I feel quite stupid. I applied my conscience to so many matters that I am quite spent.'[7]

Metternich began his first meeting with Castlereagh declaring that there was no time for them to sound each other out, and proceeded to give him a summary of his own views and aims. 'If you think as I do, if you wish for the same things, the world is safe – if you do not, it will perish,' he announced. He was overjoyed to discover that they agreed in all essentials. 'From that moment we have been working together like two clerks from the same office. It is as though we had spent our lives together,' he enthused. 'He is cool and collected; his heart is in the right place, he is *a man*, and he keeps his head.' To Schwarzenberg, he put his feelings in only slightly more measured terms. 'He has everything; amiability, wisdom, moderation,' he wrote on 21 January. 'He suits me in every way, and I am convinced that I suit him.' A couple of weeks later he made the most astonishing avowal for a man as vain as him. 'I am equal to Lord C. and he is equal to me, because he is good, excellent, as I assuredly am when it comes to feelings and principles,' he confided to Wilhelmina.[8]

Castlereagh was less forthcoming, and reserved judgement for the while. After meeting Metternich and Hardenberg, and being presented to Francis I and Frederick William, and buying a couple of Swiss dolls for Emily and Emma Sophia and sending them off, he set out to join Alexander at headquarters, which had moved to Langres on French territory.

Castlereagh's official instructions, composed largely by himself in consultation with Liverpool and other senior members of the cabinet, were that France must be excluded from the river Scheldt and the port of Antwerp, Holland must be given the former Austrian Netherlands as a 'barrier' against France, and strengthened by the addition of Jülich and Berg; the Spanish and Portuguese monarchies must be reinstated; and Italy must be so rearranged as to preclude the possibility of future French incursions. Britain would then return all the French colonies she had captured, except for Malta, Mauritius, the Île de Bourbon (Réunion), the Saintes islands and Guadeloupe (promised to Sweden, though Castlereagh was authorised to return

Guadeloupe as well if Sweden could be induced to relinquish her claim and take the Île de Bourbon instead). Britain would also return to Holland all the Dutch colonies she had captured, except for the Cape, for which she would indemnify Holland with £2 million, to be dedicated to building a string of fortifications against the French along the new 'barrier'. A strong Holland incorporating Belgium and defended by such a barrier was Britain's *sine qua non*. Much to his relief, Castlereagh was able to ascertain from his first conversations with them that both Metternich and Hardenberg were amenable to these conditions.[9]

Negotiations, set to take place at Châtillon, were ready to start as soon as Castlereagh arrived. But Caulaincourt, who was waiting at Châtillon, was Napoleon's plenipotentiary, and there was some doubt among the allies as to whether it was with Napoleon that they should be making peace.

Of all the European powers, Britain alone had never recognised Napoleon's title of Emperor of the French, and in all official correspondence he was referred to simply as General Bonaparte. Over the years British public opinion had turned him into a bogeyman, and the majority of the population regarded him with a mixture of horror and disdain. As the war with France dragged on it assumed the character of a fight to the death, and there was a widespread desire to see 'Boney' hanged or at least put behind bars. For his part, the Prince Regent wanted the old French dynasty of the Bourbons reinstated. Its senior living member, Louis XVIII, brother of the guillotined Louis XVI, was living in exile at Hartwell in Buckinghamshire as the guest of the King of England.

Liverpool, Castlereagh and the majority of the cabinet felt that it would be wrong to intervene in the internal affairs of another power, even an enemy one, and impose their choice of ruler on it. They hoped the Bourbons would be reinstated by force of events, but feared that any declaration by the British government in support of Louis XVIII might have the adverse effect of rallying the nation to Napoleon's side.

Alexander on the other hand was determined that Napoleon should pay for his misdeeds with the loss of his throne. But he had a low opinion of the current representatives of the house of Bourbon, and believed that the French nation required a more modern and dashing monarch. His personal favourite was Bernadotte. Rumours of the scheme hatched between them had been circulating for some time, and Bernadotte's posturings had featured in Stewart's reports to Castlereagh in recent months. But the idea was so absurd that nobody had paid it much heed. It was only now that Alexander began to voice it openly, much to Metternich's alarm.

Metternich's legitimist principles should have inclined him to the Bourbon cause. But he did not have much faith in Louis XVIII's ability to keep France stable and strong. And while neither he nor Francis considered the dynastic link with Napoleon of any relevance, his survival would provide a powerful counterbalance to the might of Russia. Francis feared that the restoration of the Bourbons would increase British influence on the Continent to an undesirable degree. If Napoleon did have to go, Metternich envisaged his abdication in favour of his son the King of Rome, with some kind of regency during his infancy.[10]

Castlereagh argued that a regency would be inherently unstable and would embroil Austria in the affairs of France, and that the only viable alternative to Napoleon was a Bourbon restoration. But they were both for making peace as quickly as possible, and agreed that for the time being they should do everything to achieve a satisfactory one with Napoleon, and not press for a change of regime unless his intractability or circumstances made it inevitable. Either way, the idea of putting Bernadotte on the throne had to be knocked out of Alexander's head, and it was one of the first matters Castlereagh broached with him shortly after his arrival at headquarters in Langres.[11]

Castlereagh's intercourse with crowned heads had been limited. The demented George III did not count. The Prince Regent was not a sovereign, and neither the British constitution nor his outrageous conduct and scandalous private life, exposed to the public in print and caricature, demanded that he be treated with more deference than the conduct of affairs and common civility dictated. At Bâle Castlereagh had briefly encountered the anxious and awkward Frederick William and the homely and timid Francis. Nothing had prepared him for Alexander's peculiar combination of autocracy and liberalism, haughtiness and *bonhomie*, priggishness and deviousness.

Castlereagh came quickly to the point, declaring that the Prince Regent would never agree to Bernadotte becoming the ruler of France, and rehearsing all the arguments against it. Alexander professed to agree with him, and 'disclaimed ever having expressed any intention of taking a step to favour the Prince Royal's claims, it being repugnant to his own principles to interfere in the Government of a foreign State'; but Castlereagh was not convinced. He sensed that Alexander would do everything to prevent the Bourbons being reinstated. This alarmed him, for, as he said to Alexander, leaving question marks hanging over a matter such as this introduced a new issue and a possible bone of contention among the allies, inviting intrigue and potentially leading to differences. There were quite enough of these as it was, as he discovered when he arrived at headquarters.[12]

The agreed plan of action was that the Austro-Russian main army under Schwarzenberg was to deploy on the right bank of the Seine, while Blücher's Prussians, reinforced by a Russian contingent, were to operate on the Marne. Each time Napoleon attempted to attack one of these forces, the other was to threaten his rear. In this way the allies, who still feared his military talents, hoped to wear down his forces without risking defeat. Their lines of communication and supply were by now stretched, and they could not provision themselves properly in what had turned out to be a severe winter in a country ground down by years of war exactions and ravaged by the current campaign. The troops were suffering terribly from the cold. The Austrian army alone had 50,000 men lying sick in makeshift hospitals in its rear. The chosen tactic was meant to put maximum pressure on Napoleon to make peace without straining their own resources, exposing them to defeat or committing them to further advance.[13]

Alexander took an entirely different view of the situation: his mind was set on an immediate march on Paris. His warlike ardour was being powerfully fanned by Stein, Pozzo di Borgo and Count Andrei Kirilovich Razumovsky, his former ambassador in Vienna, whom he had called to his side. All three were driven by deep personal hatred of Napoleon. He was also being encouraged by Blücher, Gneisenau and the Prussian military, who wanted to march down the streets of Paris and to blow up the bridges of Jena and Austerlitz and the Vendôme column. Their King, fearful as he was of prolonging the war, could do nothing but support Alexander, on whom his entire future depended.[14]

'I think our greatest danger at present is from the *chevalresque* tone in which the Emperor Alexander is disposed to push the war. He has a *personal* feeling about Paris, distinct from all political or military combinations,' Castlereagh reported to Liverpool on 30 January. 'He seems to seek for the occasion of entering with his magnificent guards the enemy's capital, probably to display, in his clemency and forbearance, a contrast to that desolation to which his own was devoted.' A negotiated peace would certainly rob Alexander of this pleasure. But there was more to it than that.[15]

His sense of mission had moved on from the liberation of Europe to the removal of Napoleon and the inauguration of a new age, and he was not about to make peace with the ogre now. In a letter to a friend written at this time, Alexander describes how in the course of a military conference he was suddenly overcome with the desire to pray, how he got up, went into the next room and fell to his knees, how after a moment of turbulent and emotional prayer he heard the voice of God and arose feeling 'a sweet peace in my thoughts, an all-embracing sense of calm, a hard resolution of will and a kind of blazing clarity of purpose'. He was not going to be easily diverted from his chosen course.[16]

Castlereagh, like Metternich, was apprehensive both of what Alexander might do once he was in Paris and of the possibility that a foreign invasion of the capital, accompanied by a toppling of the throne, might provoke a Jacobin revolution. Aberdeen was not the only one to point out that the position of the allies in France was comparable to that of the French in Spain, 'with the difference of having to deal with a more intelligent and active population'. None of these arguments made any impact on Alexander.[17]

The matter was eventually decided by a categorical declaration from the Austrians that their army would not advance one step unless negotiations were started with Napoleon, and Alexander was forced to give way. Metternich was not slow to congratulate himself, assuring Wilhelmina that he had 'accomplished a task greater perhaps than any achieved by a mortal'. Alexander behaved towards him 'like a mistress who has got into a sulk' for a few days, but he felt he had carried his point.[18]

Castlereagh was nevertheless anxious. From his very first meetings with the sovereigns and their ministers at Bâle, he had been struck by the pervasive miasma of mistrust. 'You may estimate some of the hazards to which affairs are exposed here, when one of the leading monarchs, in his first interview, told me that he had no confidence in his own Minister, and still less in that of his Ally,' he wrote to Liverpool. 'There is much intrigue, and more fear of it. [. . .] Suspicion is the prevailing temper of the Emperor [Alexander], and Metternich's character furnishes constant food for the *intriguants* to work upon.' Not only Alexander, but most of his entourage and his diplomats, remained convinced that Austria could not be counted on and might make a separate peace at any moment.[19]

The only encouraging news that reached allied headquarters at the end of January was that Denmark had abandoned her French ally and joined the coalition. By the Treaty of Kiel, signed on 14 January 1814, Denmark ceded Norway to Sweden. In return, she was to receive what had been Swedish Pomerania and recover the island of Rügen, along with one million thalers. She also had to accept Britain's retention of Heligoland and supply 10,000 men, paid for by Britain, to fight against France.

*   *   *

On his way to the Continent, Castlereagh had expressed the hope that the ministers of the four principal allies might be induced to discuss and settle policy in common rather than in one-to-one meetings amongst themselves. On 28 January he managed to convene the first such meeting, attended by Metternich and Stadion representing Austria, Hardenberg Prussia, and the trio of Nesselrode, Razumovsky and Pozzo di Borgo representing Russia.

Castlereagh opened the proceedings by stating that while they must negotiate with Napoleon as long as the latter was offering to settle, they must also pursue the campaign with vigour. At the same time he urged caution, reminding them of the danger of their situation and the unknown perils that might attend an allied occupation of Paris and a change of regime. He expressed the hope that while there was 'no wish in any of the Allied sovereigns inconsistent with the restoration of the ancient Family, should a change be brought on by the act of the nation itself', they must nevertheless negotiate with the government of France as it stood. Accordingly, they designated plenipotentiaries to assemble at Châtillon by 3 February.

Castlereagh insisted that the 'Frankfurt proposals' were of no relevance, and that they must negotiate on the basis not of France's 'natural' frontiers but rather her 'ancient' frontiers of 1792. Metternich supported him in this, but suggested that France be offered some increases, in areas such as the left bank of the Rhine and Savoy. Castlereagh disagreed, but he also rejected outright the Russian proposal that France should be entirely excluded from any say in the arrangements made with regard to those territories which she would be forced to give up. He then outlined the British cabinet's proposals for a final settlement, which he suggested they accept as the basis for the forthcoming negotiations. In his account of the conference Castlereagh assured Liverpool that he had found the allies 'perfectly sincere and cordial in the exclusion of the maritime question from the negotiations'. Since everything had been kept remarkably vague except for the frontiers of France, the Dutch 'barrier' and maritime rights, the whole exercise had served little purpose beyond that of getting the others to accept in principle the British position. Nor was he going to leave it at that.[20]

The plenipotentiaries assembled on 3 February in the snowbound little town of Châtillon, where Caulaincourt had been kicking his heels for two weeks. Metternich had delegated Stadion, Razumovsky represented Russia, and Humboldt Prussia. Britain was represented by the trio of Aberdeen, Stewart and Cathcart. Castlereagh composed a set of instructions for their benefit, almost a sermon on how they were to behave. 'The power of Great Britain to do good depends not merely on its resources but upon a sense of its impartiality and the reconciling character of its influence,' he lectured them. 'To be authoritative it must be impartial. To be impartial it must not be in exclusive relations with any particular Court.' This did not, apparently, affect the business of getting what Britain wanted, and therein lay the reason for Castlereagh, alone of the ministers, going to Châtillon in person to supervise his three plenipotentiaries.[21]

At the first formal session of the congress on 5 February, he reminded all those assembled that Britain was not prepared to bargain, and would only return French and Dutch colonies if she found the settlement reached satisfactory as a whole. The following day he sketched out his own vision, and insisted on writing into the basis for negotiation not only France's 1792 frontiers, but also the extension of Holland and the creation of the barrier. 'In closing this statement I begged it might be understood, that it was the wish of my Government in peace and in war to connect their interests with those of the Continent – that whilst the state of Europe afforded little hope of a better order of things, Great Britain had no other course left, than to create an independent existence for herself, but that now that she might look forward to a return to ancient principles, she was ready to make the necessary sacrifices on her part, to reconstruct a balance in Europe,' he reported to Liverpool. Having thus staked out Britain's position at Châtillon, Castlereagh hurried back to headquarters, which had now moved on to Troyes, leaving the plenipotentiaries to get on with the business in hand.[22]

Battlefield Diplomacy

'What is the Emperor N. going to do now?' young Marie Leopoldine Metternich wrote to her father from Vienna on 27 January 1814. 'In his place, I would take ship, and I would go to seek fortune in America and I would live there very peacefully in the forests and the deserts. The fruit of the coconut tree would nourish me, and water clearer than crystal would refresh my burning blood and my burnt-out brain. I would hunt monkeys in the woods, I would reflect on my past greatness and would try to console myself for my present misfortune as best I could. That is what I would do if I were the Emperor Napoleon.'[1]

Napoleon had other ideas. Four days before she wrote that letter, on Sunday, 23 January, after attending Mass, he had made his way to the Hall of Marshals in the Tuileries. There he presented his three-year-old son to the assembled officers of the Paris National Guard. He also signed letters patent naming Marie-Louise regent in his absence. The next day he nominated his brother Joseph Lieutenant-General of the Empire, and that evening, after burning his most secret papers, he embraced his wife and son. At 6 a.m. on 25 January he rode out of Paris to join the army.

Although the odds were stacked heavily against him, he was sanguine, believing that he could defeat the allied armies advancing on Paris, and that one decisive victory would reverse the situation. He rebuked those around him who thought the war lost. 'They think they can already see cossacks in the streets,' he had quipped over dinner a few days earlier. 'Well, they're not here yet, and we haven't forgotten our trade.' He assured his wife that he would defeat the allies and dictate peace to her father, whom he referred to teasingly as 'papa François'. 'I'll beat papa François again,' he repeated to Marie-Louise as he hugged her for the last time. 'Don't cry, I'll be back soon.' He would never see her or his son again.[2]

Like the allies, he regarded the congress at Châtillon as unlikely to lead to a quick settlement. But he thought it might prove useful in the event of his winning a significant victory, as he would then be able to wrench a favourable peace from them while they were still in a state of shock. The talks also provided a forum for his attempts to split the coalition, a goal he pursued by every means.

Before leaving Paris he had dictated a letter to his father-in-law the Emperor Francis suggesting he make a separate peace. He pointed out that if the allies were to lose, Austria would lose more than the others, while every allied victory only diminished her standing, since it increased that of the other allies disproportionately. This was true enough, but there was a fundamental flaw in Napoleon's calculations: while the allied generals were still no match for him, the allied statesmen had grown accustomed to defeat, and each new one simply confirmed them in their conviction that no peace with Napoleon would ever endure.[3]

Napoleon took command of the 45,000 men camped at Châlons-sur-Marne on the plateau of Langres facing Schwarzenberg. 'Despite the disasters of the campaign in Saxony, despite the allies' passage of the Rhine, the army was convinced that it would defeat the enemy,' recalled the commander of one of the Tirailleur regiments of the Guard, noting at the same time that the senior commanders were more sceptical.[4]

The French forces were heavily outnumbered. But Napoleon calculated that he only needed to rout the allies and push them back, and he would be able to recover the 90,000 men cut off in fortresses along the Rhine or just beyond the borders of France. He attacked Blücher's positions at Brienne, but after achieving some success he was counter-attacked and defeated at La Rothière on 1 February. The Prussians were jubilant. 'Charles went over yesterday to old Blucher to pay him a visit after his battle,' Castlereagh wrote to Emily. 'He says the old boy invited them all to dine with him at the Palais Royal on the 20th of February with all the *mamselles*.' Such hubris would cost the allies dear.[5]

While Castlereagh had been lecturing the plenipotentiaries at Châtillon, Alexander had taken matters into his own hands at allied headquarters in Troyes. 'The Emperor Alexander has set his heart upon entering Paris,' according to Priscilla Burghersh, 'and is exactly like an eager child about it, swearing to the right and left that he does not mind what they are doing at Châtillon, that he won't sign peace or think of it till they are at Paris.' He was so excited by the Prussian victory at La Rothière that he instructed Razumovsky to suspend negotiations at Châtillon and prepared to set off for Blücher's headquarters himself. Ominously, Bernadotte had suddenly appeared on the scene, and offered to take command of Winzingerode's corps, the most advanced allied unit, at Rheims.[6]

Castlereagh was horrified when he returned to Troyes on 11 February, and forcefully expressed his disapproval over dinner with the Tsar. Alexander seemed embarrassed. He explained that he wanted to get to Paris, and convoke the chambers 'to assemble and declare the national will as to the Crown of France'. He repeated his opposition to reinstating the Bourbons, declaring Louis XVIII to be 'personally incapable', and mentioned the possibility of choosing a King from a junior branch of the family such as the duc d'Orléans.[7]

Castlereagh insisted that the allies should not put themselves in the position of supporting one 'usurper' against another, or even supporting the Bourbons against Napoleon, both of which could end up involving them in a civil war. He pointed out that so far there had been no sign of a revolt against the existing regime in France, and her soldiers were fighting on bravely for their Emperor.[8]

Alexander now tried to embarrass Castlereagh, by producing a letter from his ambassador in London, Count Lieven, who reported a conversation he had had with the Prince Regent in which the latter had declared himself strongly in favour of dethroning Napoleon and installing the Bourbons in his place. Triumphantly, the Tsar suggested that Castlereagh was out of touch with the wishes of his own court. He added that he had already shown the letter to the other allied ministers, an action that could only have been aimed at undermining Castlereagh's standing. Castlereagh responded with controlled fury, later describing the interview as 'painful' and of 'a more controversial character than I would have wished'.[9]

Metternich was even more alarmed than Castlereagh. Over the past months he had grown accustomed to restraining and directing Alexander with relative ease. But his disregard for the Tsar's wishes over Swiss neutrality had wounded the latter profoundly, and lost him the ascendancy. Alexander was now determined to follow his own mind, and would brook no argument.

Metternich assured himself of the support of his new allies Bavaria and Württemberg before going off to confront the Tsar on 14 February, in the company of Castlereagh and Hardenberg. The three ministers made their case in the strongest language, but Alexander ignored their arguments and stood firm. Faced with such obstinacy, Metternich once again played his only remaining card. He stated that if Alexander persisted, Austria would make a separate peace with Napoleon and march her army home. Alexander was obliged to reconsider.

'Yesterday I had the most difficult day of my life,' Metternich wrote to Wilhelmina the next day. 'But I remained true to myself, *mon amie*, and I can say it in the fullness of my heart and my feelings! There is a bunch of madmen here who have taken hold *of your fine friend* [Alexander] who, at the rate they are going, will destroy the world. I took it upon myself to attack them head-on, and I triumphed completely. My friend Castlereagh told me: "You are the greatest minister in the world and I beg your pardon for not having always honoured you with the same confidence."' He added that even Hardenberg had embraced him, and ended with complaints about the strain of being the only person in the world who could be counted on to prevent others from spoiling everything.[10]

It was not so much Metternich's eloquence as the news that arrived from Blücher's headquarters over the next couple of days which dampened Alexander's enthusiasm for a march on Paris and helped the Austrian and British ministers persuade him to authorise the resumption of negotiations at Châtillon.

When Blücher did resume what Castlereagh called 'his march to the *mamselles*', thereby drawing away from Schwarzenberg, Napoleon moved fast, inflicting a series of defeats on his corps one after the other. He routed the advance guard of Olsufiev's Russians at Champaubert on 10 February, trounced Sacken's Russians and Yorck's Prussians at Montmirail on 11 and 12 February, and mauled Blücher himself at Vauchamps on the fourteenth. On 17 February an alarmed Schwarzenberg began to abandon his forward positions at Troyes and sent a request for an armistice, but Napoleon screwed up the piece of paper and threw it on the floor. The following day he attacked and defeated the withdrawing Schwarzenberg's rearguard at Monterau, occupying Troyes on 24 February.

'I would have to write a novel if I were to describe to Your Majesty all the incredible things that have passed,' the Bavarian minister Prince Wrede wrote to his King. Panic set in as the monarchs and their ministers hastily followed headquarters in its retreat from Troyes to Bar-sur-Aube and subsequently to Chaumont. Alexander still blustered about advancing, but his generals and his army were short of supplies and demoralised. He too now suggested they ask Napoleon for an armistice, while Frederick William wailed about impending catastrophe. When Castlereagh tried to rally them he found their spirits 'strongly tinctured with the demoralising Influence of a rapid transition from an advance made under very lofty Pretensions to a Retreat of some Embarrassment, and of much Disappointment and Recrimination'.[11]

There was a similar swing of mood throughout the allied forces, as General Alexander Benkendorff, who commanded a Russian unit in Blücher's corps, noted. 'Everything was going beautifully, we were beating them one after the other, everyone vied with each other as to who would take the keys of Paris, there were intrigues as to who would be governor of Paris, the French were cowards, Napoleon was a fool,' he wrote to a friend, 'but a few blows received and people do not know where to run to, they see ghosts everywhere, every peasant seems to be a demon.' The Austrians were on the verge of a general retreat from France, while Bernadotte was behaving in a manner that raised fears of his defection. 'The criminations and recriminations between the Austrians and the Russians are at their height, and my patience is worn out combating both,' Castlereagh complained to Liverpool.[12]

Napoleon was in triumphant mood. 'They must have been taken aback by my victories; they weren't expecting them,' he exclaimed. 'They thought the lion was dead and it was safe to piss on him.' On 19 February he wrote to Caulaincourt instructing him to settle for nothing less than France's 'natural' frontiers, to hold on to most of Italy and to give as little ground as possible, and above all to refer back to him before agreeing to anything.[13]

There was scant chance of any agreement between the plenipotentiaries assembled at Châtillon. Within two days of his arrival there, Stadion reported to Metternich that 'our work here is taking on the aspect of a bad comedy'. The time had been taken up almost entirely by discussions on matters such as protocol and dress (it was eventually decided that since some of them did not have their full court uniforms, they would dress as they liked).[14]

Alexander had delegated not Nesselrode but the Napoleon-hating Razumovsky, while Frederick William had sent Humboldt. Neither had any desire to see the negotiations succeed, and did their best to obstruct their progress. After attending the first three sessions of the congress, Stadion reported to Metternich that their meetings 'no longer even present the simulacrum of real negotiations', and used the word 'farce' to describe Razumovsky's gratuitously insulting treatment of Caulaincourt, whose despair Humboldt relished.[15]

The British plenipotentiaries had been instructed to seize any possibility of making peace, however much the Prince Regent and public opinion at home might dislike the idea of signing a treaty that left Napoleon in power. 'You scarcely have an idea how *insane* people in this country are on the subject of any peace with Buonaparte,' Liverpool had warned Castlereagh. Jackson was informed by his mother, writing from Bath at the end of February, that she had heard people saying that anyone who made peace with Bonaparte 'deserves to be hanged'. But Castlereagh was not intimidated. 'We shall be stoned when we get back to England, but we must sign,' he wrote to Aberdeen.[16]

The three British ministers felt only sympathy for the likeable Caulaincourt, and Aberdeen was scandalised by the proceedings. 'His diplomatic innocence will kill him if he has to go on witnessing the horror and the outrage of everything that is being done here and the part he is forced to play in it,' wrote an amused Stadion to Metternich. But Stadion was himself distressed by the proceedings, and thought they brought discredit on the coalition.[17]

The first session, on 5 February, was taken up with points of order. At the second, held two days later, the allied plenipotentiaries produced a proposal that France resume her 1792 frontiers and give up her pretensions to all areas outside them, in return for which she would be given back some of her colonies.

Caulaincourt protested that such terms were unacceptable to any but a totally defeated power. They would leave France weaker than she had been in 1792. And as the allies were not proposing a general return to the status quo of 1792, since when Prussia had acquired a sizeable part of Poland and the Rhineland, Russia had swallowed up a large slice of Poland and Finland, Austria had acquired not only her share of Poland but also Venice and other areas in Italy, and Britain had gained a series of strategic colonies, the balance of power in Europe would be fundamentally altered. He referred them to the 'Frankfurt proposals' and to the allied declaration of 1 December 1813, which specifically stated that the allied monarchs wished to see France 'great, strong and contented'.[18]

Caulaincourt would have been prepared to make peace at almost any price, seeing in it the only chance of saving Napoleon from disaster. But his instructions were to propose an entirely unrealistic settlement, with the grand duchy of Warsaw, Eugène's Italy and Murat's Naples as independent states, and with Belgium, along with Antwerp and the Scheldt estuary, as part of France. This was rejected outright by the allied plenipotentiaries, and Caulaincourt had to write to Napoleon requesting fresh instructions.

He also wrote to Metternich begging for an immediate ceasefire, intimating that if this were granted he might be able to persuade Napoleon to accept the 1792 frontiers. Hardly had Caulaincourt despatched his courier to Napoleon than another arrived from Alexander instructing Razumovsky to break off negotiations, and the conference went into a state of suspended animation.[19]

'This little village is quiet and clean compared with Head Quarters,' Castlereagh had written to Emily on arriving there, but even he had found it wanting in distractions, though he only spent three days there. 'Our sojourn here is a kind of hell,' Stadion complained to Metternich. Humboldt was bored, and grumbled at the amount of paperwork he had been lumbered with. Stewart was particularly annoyed, as he would rather have been galloping about the battlefield and feared he was missing out on the action. Caulaincourt tried to enliven the proceedings by arranging a hunting party on 14 February, but they failed to find any game and came home in a state of dejection.[20]

Matters improved when Caulaincourt's household was at last allowed through enemy lines. Even Stewart's spirits rose with the arrival of 'convoys of all the good cheer, in epicurean wines, &c. that Paris could afford; nor was female society wanting to complete the charm, and bannish *ennui*', as he put it. They were cheered by the arrival of the saucy Priscilla Burghersh, who noted that 'the plenipotentiaries spend their lives in giving great dinners to each other, and gorge so effectually that two or three have fallen ill from the effects of their intemperance'. Humboldt left off his paperwork and immersed himself in Plutarch. He was delighted to discover a lover of the classics in Aberdeen, and they spent much time in conversation. Priscilla Burghersh borrowed books from Stewart. 'I am just out of my wits with delight at Lord Byron's new book, "The Corsair",' she wrote home.[21]

The ministers assembled at Châtillon were originally guarded by a contingent of Austrian troops. But after the French victories the region was overrun by the French, and they were protected, in a kind of diplomatic vacuum, by a contingent of French National Guard. The French victories had also caused Alexander to countermand his orders to Razumovsky, and the negotiations resumed on 17 February, in the presence of Castlereagh, who had hurried over to supervise.

Caulaincourt's plea for France's 'natural frontiers' was brushed aside and Stadion read out the text of a treaty proposed by the allies. It did not vary the terms previously offered, but it was more detailed, laying down, for instance, that Germany was to be composed of independent states 'united by a federal bond'. Caulaincourt raised a number of questions which were of particular interest to France, such as whether the kingdom of Italy would continue as a state and whether the King of Saxony's rights would be respected, but received no reply. He agreed to send the proposal to Napoleon, and the negotiations were adjourned.[22]

The congress did not reconvene for ten days, and at the next meeting, on 28 February, the allied plenipotentiaries accused Caulaincourt of playing for time. They set a deadline of 10 March, by which time he was either to accept their terms or produce a counter-project acceptable to the allies. He could not meet this date, as his courier had been intercepted, taken to allied headquarters and kept there for several days. All he could do on that day was again make the case for France's 'natural frontiers', albeit with a few concessions. The two sides continued in this dialogue of the deaf, with the allies using the next session, on 13 March, to state that while they did not wish their project to be viewed as an ultimatum, they would not accept any material changes to it.[23]

On 15 March Caulaincourt finally presented the French proposals, which agreed to the allies' plans for the rest of Europe, provided Saxony and the kingdom of Italy were allowed to remain independent, and that France kept her 'natural frontiers'. The proposals were noted and sent to headquarters, but the rider bearing them crossed one coming the other way, with orders to break off the negotiations. On 18 March the allied plenipotentiaries produced a long justification of their conduct, which concluded that 'the Allied Powers consider the negotiations initiated at Châtillon as *terminated by the French Government*'. The two sides met on the morrow for the last time, to hear Caulaincourt's reply, and the congress was dissolved. A week later, on 25 March, Caulaincourt wrote to Metternich in a desperate final attempt to make peace between Napoleon and the allies. But they had other things on their minds by then.[24]

On 23 February Castlereagh had dined with Hardenberg in the company of a new arrival at allied headquarters, Alexander's erstwhile Foreign Minister Prince Adam Czartoryski. It is unlikely that they got round to discussing the Prince's business, but Castlereagh could guess what his presence at headquarters portended, and he was alarmed. So were Metternich and Hardenberg.

One of the bases for negotiations with Napoleon fixed by the Convention of Reichenbach was the dissolution of the grand duchy of Warsaw 'and the division of the provinces that make it up between Russia, Prussia and Austria' along lines to be decided by the three of them. Although the failure of the negotiations to produce a result rendered the bases irrelevant, the Treaty of Toeplitz contained a secret article which provided for 'an arrangement *à l'amiable* between the three courts of Russia, Austria and Prussia as to the future of the duchy of Warsaw'.[25]

In defiance of these agreements, Alexander continued to nurture his plan of creating a constitutional kingdom of Poland under his own rule. Nesselrode had devoted a lengthy memorandum to discouraging him, while Stein, Capodistrias and Pozzo di Borgo had all argued against the feasibility of his plans, to no avail.[26]

The grand duchy of Warsaw, 1807

The grand duchy of Warsaw after 1809

161

Alexander had worked out that Prussia could be indemnified for the lands he would not be returning to her by the addition of Saxony. This alarmed Metternich, who did not wish to see an enlarged Prussia on Austria's border, and most of the other German princes, who saw in it a dangerous precedent. Metternich regularly made the feelings of his court on this subject known, and it became a bone of contention between Austria and Prussia. This was all the more serious because it prevented them from uniting against Alexander over some of his more alarming schemes.

On 8 January 1814, at a moment when the coalition had reached one of its periodic crises, Metternich had come up with a compromise. Over dinner with Hardenberg that day he told him that Austria would be prepared to allow Prussia to take Saxony, on condition that Prussia supported Austria against Russia on her Polish plans. The proposal was thrown out as bait to lure Prussia away from Russia and bring her to Austria's side. But it turned out to be a hostage to fortune. Even though he was in no position to take it up by supporting Austria, Hardenberg nevertheless kept Metternich's offer in mind and persuaded himself that it stood on its own, not just as part of a *quid pro quo*.[27]

What particularly alarmed Castlereagh and Metternich was that Alexander evidently did not regard what he did in Poland as anyone's business but his own. He felt his prestige to be at stake, a sentiment he expressed forcefully to Stewart on one occasion. 'His Imperial Majesty stated that his moral feeling, honour, and every principle of justice and right, called upon him to use all his power to restore such a constitution to Poland as would secure the happiness of so fine and so great a people,' he reported to his brother. Alexander had gone on to explain that while he could not relinquish his own Polish provinces and create an independent Poland without fear of losing his throne, he could make the Poles happy by granting them national autonomy under his own sceptre. 'His Imperial Majesty *next alluded in rather a menacing manner* to his power of *taking military possession of Poland*, and seemed to be certain of the *facility with which he could obtain his end*, and I doubted much, from the firm and positive manner in which he expressed himself, whether he would ever be diverted from the purpose he now declared.'

The Tsar's aggressive tone struck Stewart disagreeably. He reflected that if Russia were to retain possession of the whole of Poland, she would become a threatening presence at the heart of Europe. Considered in conjunction with what he called 'the successive aggrandisements and incorporations of Russia during the last hundred and fifty years', and the fact that 'her whole system of government is a military despotism', there could hardly be 'a serious and reasonable man in Europe that must not admit that the whole system of European politics ought, in its leading principle and feature, to maintain as an axiom the necessity of setting bounds to this formidable and encroaching power'.[28]

Czartoryski laboured under the illusion that the British were well-disposed towards enslaved nations fighting for their freedom, as the much-vaunted British support for the Spaniards seemed to suggest. He had despatched an agent to London to drum up popular support for the Polish cause, a consequence of which was that the prominent Whig parliamentarian Henry Brougham published an anonymous pamphlet in support of the restoration of an independent Poland which met with much sympathy. But Castlereagh had no time for such sentiments. He saw in Poland only a potential obstacle to harmonious relations between the three Continental allies. He took the opportunity of their first private conversation to inform Czartoryski that his presence at Chaumont was not conducive to allied unity, and urged him to leave. Castlereagh had once again begun to fear for the alliance.[29]

Having recovered from their fright, the allies grew querulous. Alexander was accusing Metternich of treachery, and Frederick William blamed the Austrians for having supposedly failed Blücher. Complaining that his merits were not appreciated, his services made light of and his motives mistrusted, Alexander had withdrawn into detached self-righteousness. Metternich and Schwarzenberg were angry at him for wishing to prolong the war. 'It has become evident that the mutual jealousy of the two imperial courts is beginning to take on an alarming direction,' Count Münster warned the Prince Regent on 25 February.[30]

Fearing that the coalition might come apart, Castlereagh decided to resurrect his 'grand design', and in the unpromising surroundings of Chaumont, 'a dirty and dull town which has nothing to reconcile one to it but a sense of public duty', he set to work on bringing the project into being. 'I have only one small room,' he wrote to his wife, 'in which I sleep and work and the whole chancellerie dines, when we can get anything to eat.' Fortunately, the resourceful Stewart had gone off on a foraging expedition and 'returned in triumph with 3 dozen fowls and 6 dozen of wine'. Sir Charles's enterprises were not all crowned with the same success, but he bore the fortunes of war philosophically.[31]

He seized every opportunity to take the field, as indeed did his fellow ambassador Cathcart, who actually assumed command of a Russian battery at the battle of La Fère Champenoise. It was at the end of that same battle that Stewart met with a severe disappointment. 'I witnessed here a very interesting, but I fear unfortunately too usual an occurrence, that took place in the capture of the convoy and enemy's baggage, &c. at la Feré Champenoise [sic],' he writes. 'Being forward in the *mêlée*, I perceived that some of the Cossacks, most probably from Bashkir, had not only secured a French colonel's *calèche* and baggage, but one of them had seized his wife, whose cries rent the air, and with the aid of two other gallant Tartars was placing her behind him.' Stewart sprang to her defence, and managed to rescue the 'lovely and most interesting Frenchwoman'. He instructed his orderly hussar 'to place her for the moment *en croupe*, and to carry her to my billet at the head-quarters. I was unwilling, and indeed could not at that moment leave the field; but consoled myself with the thought that when I returned at night to my quarters I should receive the gratitude of a beautiful creature, and pictured to myself romance connected with this occurrence. But, alas! How little can we reckon on any future event, and how idly do we all build *des châteaux en Espagne!*

'I fear that my precautions were not so great as I flattered myself they were: the distance between the *champ de bataille* and Feré Champenoise was inconsiderable: the town was in sight; and from the number of officers and troops moving about, I could not imagine my beautiful prisoner would be recaptured; but, sad to relate, either the same Cossacks returned, or others more savage and determined, and perceiving my faithful orderly hussar and prize, fell upon him, and nearly annihilating him, reseized their victim; and although the strictest investigation was made throughout his whole army, by the Emperor of Russia, to whom I immediately repaired, and related the melancholy tale, (and who heard it with all that compassion and interest it could not fail to inspire,) the beautiful and interesting Frenchwoman never reappeared again. I drop a veil over the horrible sequel which imagination might conjure up, and I took much blame for my neglect of a sufficient escort. My hussar crawled to me next morning, half dead from ill usage; and his pathetic tale placed me in a state of mind scarcely less deplorable.'[32]

Such adventures are not normally associated with the conduct of diplomacy, but at this particular juncture in history they were commonplace. Not only did His Britannic Majesty's ambassador to the court of Prussia dash about the battlefield rescuing maidens in distress, and his colleague accredited to the court of Russia personally direct the fire of a field battery; the Austrian diplomat Count Wessenberg fell into the hands of some French peasants who stripped him of all his possessions, the Foreign Minister of His Imperial and Royal Apostolic Majesty the Emperor of Austria was nearly captured by French cavalry, the British Foreign Secretary bumped about rutted tracks scavenging for food, and lesser agents such as the lovely wife of the British Commissioner at allied headquarters also had to put up with undiplomatic hardships. 'My dearest Em,' Castlereagh wrote home on 30 March. 'When I am tried for leaving my wife behind, I shall call Lady Burghersh as my first witness, who was obliged to fly from Chaumont and live in a bivouac with all the heavy baggage of the army, without the possibility of changing her chemise unperceived, except the ceremony was performed in the dark of the night.'[33]

They coped with the situation remarkably well. Metternich, to judge by his letters, was more upset by the mess and destruction left by war, which offended his fastidious nature, than by its human cost, and appeared less worried by the human and animal corpses lying about than by the sullied furniture in the houses he stopped in and the rubbish lying by the roadside. He did not for a moment cease writing to his beloved Wilhelmina, regaling her with tales of his own cleverness and advising her on where to take lodgings in Vienna. He even found time to buy her a dressing gown in Troyes. For his wife he bought some dresses made of a cloth called 'grenatine' which he had never seen before but liked very much.[34]

Shopping for loved ones seems to have been a major preoccupation, and the Britons in particular were bombarded with requests for French lace. 'As to the "rain of veils and cambric" you talk of, I assure you, dear mother, that although I am out in all sorts of weather, and keep, if I may so speak, my weather eye constantly open, yet in none of the places we have been to has anything of the kind yet rained upon me,' wrote a clearly exasperated Jackson from Dijon on 26 March. His complaints were echoed by Castlereagh, who informed Emily that 'I can find nothing pretty for you in this country.' He was having greater success with his diplomatic efforts.[35]

At Chaumont he at last managed to convince the other allies of the necessity of signing a proper common treaty of alliance, and bound into this all Britain's conditions: the 1792 frontiers for France and the enlargement of Holland with a barrier in Belgium, the independence of Spain and Portugal under their rightful dynasties, an independent Switzerland, a return to an as yet undefined grouping of states in Italy free of French influence, and a federal arrangement guaranteeing the independence of the smaller states of Germany. The details of the settlements in Italy and Germany were to be worked out at a congress after the conclusion of peace, to be held in Vienna.

The Treaty of Chaumont bound the allies not to make a separate peace under any circumstances. Each of the four powers was to supply 150,000 men, with Britain contributing an extra £5 million over and above what she was already paying, to be used to raise yet more troops, at the rate of £20 per annum for every foot soldier and £30 for every cavalryman. The treaty was to last for twenty years, and would be renewable at the end of that term. Once peace had been made the allies could scale down their military forces, each keeping 60,000 men available to assist any nation attacked by France.

The inspiration was clearly Pitt's reply to Alexander's proposed new order of 1804, which suggested that after the peace 'the principal Powers of Europe' should 'bind themselves mutually to protect and support each other'. In his covering letter sent to London with the full text of the treaty, Castlereagh apologised to Liverpool for having exceeded his instructions in the matter of subsidies. But he clearly felt no need to justify himself in his letter to Hamilton, the Permanent Under-Secretary at the Foreign Office.[36]

'We four ministers, when signing, happened to be sitting at a whist-table. It was agreed that never were the stakes so high at any former party,' he wrote, adding that he was 'determined not to play a second fiddle. The fact is, that upon the face of the Treaty this year, our engagement is equivalent to theirs united. We give 150,000 men and five millions, equal to as many more – total 300,000. They give 450,000 of which we, however, supply 150,000, leaving their own number 300,000. The fact, however, is that, sick, lame, and lazy, they pay a great number more. On the other hand, we give to the value of 125,000 men beyond the 300,000. What an extraordinary display of power! This, I trust, will put an end to any doubts as to the claim that we have to an opinion on continental matters.' It would indeed.[37]

Gripped by his quintessentially English obsession with the threat posed by France, Castlereagh had in effect constructed a kind of anti-French league designed not only to defeat his country's old enemy but to hold her down after the peace.

The Treaty of Chaumont, signed on 9 March 1814 and dated

1 March, not only distorted the European balance of power in a radical way. It was a completely new departure in the history of international relations. It identified the four signatories, henceforth the Great Powers, as the arbiters of Europe, in effect enshrining the rights of the strongest, in an act which was meant to provide the framework for the conduct of European affairs over the next two decades at least. The four biggest players had taken control of the game, and intended to set the rules from now on.

Paris Triumph

Napoleon was not beaten yet. On 7 March he attacked Blücher's 85,000-strong army at Craonne with no more than 47,000 men, and after one of the bloodiest battles of the Napoleonic Wars drove him back. He pursued him to Laon, but was himself forced to fall back on 10 March after a two-day battle. Three days later he delivered a lightning blow which knocked out an advanced Russian corps at Rheims, killing its commander General Saint-Priest. Hardenberg noted in his diary that 'Cassandra', as he referred to Frederick William, was in a panic, while Burghersh reported that 'Schwarzenberg would almost wish to be back upon the Rhine'. On 20 March, with only 28,000 men, Napoleon took on Schwarzenberg's army of over 80,000. He was in the thick of the action, risking his life as, sword in hand, he rallied his troops.[1]

If he had displayed the same mental agility at any stage in the previous three years, Napoleon would have remained the master of Europe. But now he simply lacked the troops to go on. The sinking morale of his marshals was reflected in their lacklustre performance when operating on their own. On 27 February Soult was beaten by Wellington at Orthez, opening up south-western France. On 17 March Marmont let himself be defeated by Blücher at Fismes; on 22 March Augerau abandoned Lyon without a fight; on 25 March Marmont and Mortier were mauled at La Fère Champenoise.

'Paris is very despondent,' the usually sanguine Maret had reported to Caulaincourt on 8 March. 'The situation is grave, and becomes worse with the passing of every day,' Cambacérès had informed Napoleon on 11 March. 'We are in dire poverty and surrounded by people who are either spent or angry. Elsewhere it is even worse; official reports and private correspondence alike make it clear that we can no longer defend ourselves, that despondency has become general, that signs of discontent are evident in various quarters and that we are about to witness the most sinister events if the strong arm of Your Majesty does not come promptly to our aid.' But Napoleon paid no heed. Like some frantic gambler, he still believed that one throw of the dice could reverse the situation.[2]

The dissolution of the congress at Châtillon had closed the door to a peace with Napoleon, which posed the question of who would rule France after the allied victory. Louis XVIII's brother, the comte d'Artois, was lobbying Liverpool to allow his sons, the duc d'Angoulême and the duc de Berry, to go to France and raise the royalist standard. Liverpool assented, but on condition that they went as private citizens, without any formal backing from Britain. As a result, Angoulême was landed in south-western France, where he caused some difficulty to Wellington, Berry was sent to the traditionally royalist north, while Artois himself went to Switzerland, from where he hoped to join allied headquarters at the appropriate moment.

On 11 March the baron de Vitrolles, an agent sent by a group of supporters of the Bourbon cause in Paris, appeared at allied headquarters, now at Troyes once more. His reception by Metternich was positive, and Castlereagh, who saw in his mission the first evidence of a royalist movement in France, not only received him but advanced him some cash. Alexander was less forthcoming. He asked Vitrolles whether he had ever met the Bourbons, to which the answer was negative. 'Well!' Alexander said, with an expression of disgust mingled with sorrow, 'if you knew them you would realise that the burden of a crown such as this would be too heavy for them.' He told Vitrolles that Napoleon must certainly go, but suggested that he might be replaced by Bernadotte, by Prince Eugène or by a republic.[3]

Vitrolles remained at headquarters and set off with the others for Bar-sur-Seine on 21 March. He was bewildered to find himself travelling in such august company and bizarre conditions. Castlereagh and Metternich were on horseback, the others were crowded into a variety of conveyances. 'Our numerous caravan was rather more domestic than military,' Vitrolles records. 'It presented the singular aspect of an array of coaches and carts of every variety, with a greater number of attributes of the kitchen than of war. At the same time one could see here and there detachments of troops of different nations with curious uniforms.' He watched in astonishment as Metternich, Castlereagh and Hardenberg took lunch, standing about or sitting on bales of straw in the courtyard of a ruined château and having to make do with pâté washed down with a bottle of champagne, for lack of anything else to eat. The sight was no doubt enhanced by the continuing sartorial oddities of Castlereagh, who had acquired a warlike tan. 'He is as brown as a berry with a fine bronzed colour and wears a fur cap with gold,' reported Priscilla Burghersh.[4]

Following Napoleon's latest attack on Schwarzenberg, they were forced to flee in panic once again, abandoning much of their luggage – at one point it was feared that Francis himself might fall into French hands. While Vitrolles made his way to Nancy to meet Artois, the ministers retired to Dijon.[5]

There, on 28 March, they received news that Wellington had entered Bordeaux, which had declared for the Bourbons. Castlereagh felt, as did the rest of the British cabinet, that they need no longer keep up the pretence of impartiality. That night there was a merry dinner at Castlereagh's lodgings, at which Hardenberg and Metternich joined the others in drinking the health of the Bourbons.[6]

Two days later Castlereagh informed Liverpool that they had sent someone to Artois, who had by now followed the allies onto French soil, in order to prepare the ground for a Bourbon restoration. But this was by no means a foregone conclusion. While the allied ministers cowered at Dijon, where they were joined by Francis, Alexander had raced ahead, determined to impose his will on events, and Bernadotte made a dash for Paris, adopting an equivocal pose that left it open for him, if he failed to gain the throne, to become an enabling lieutenant either for a republic or for a Bourbon restoration – either a Cromwell or a Monck. His caution was entirely justifiable, as almost anything could have happened at this stage.[7]

'Never has there been such public inertia in the midst of so much national anxiety, never so many malcontents abstaining from action to such a degree, never so many officials so eager to disavow their master while continuing to serve him with docility,' wrote the historian François Guizot, who was a young man at the time. 'It was a nation of exhausted spectators who had entirely lost the habit of intervening in their own destiny, and who did not know which dénouement they should wish for or fear in this terrible drama of which they themselves were the stake.'[8]

This view is borne out by the entries in George Jackson's diary. At the beginning of February he recorded that every Frenchman he spoke to inveighed against Napoleon. 'Yet it goes no further, it leads to nothing.' A few weeks later he returned to the subject of the universal apathy. 'One prevailing feeling amongst them there certainly is – and but one – it is the desire for peace. For the rest, they are like weather-cocks, to which every wind is welcome.'[9]

Napoleon's overwhelming personality had eclipsed others for the past decade and a half, the nation's revolutionary ardour had been spent long before, and the Bourbons were either a dim memory or entirely meaningless to the majority of the French population. Royalist sentiment was strongest in the south and west of the country, where Catholicism, resentment of central authority and the damage done to the wine trade by Napoleon's Continental System combined to create discontent, and in the north-east, where memories of the royalist risings of the Vendée in the 1790s inspired a numerous poor nobility and regionally-minded peasantry.

As the allied armies moved onto French soil, discontent was voiced, often for opportunistic reasons, but little was done to support either them or any other alternative to Napoleon's rule. When the duc d'Angoulême appeared in south-western France after its liberation by Wellington, he met with scant enthusiasm. The same was true of Artois. Napoleon certainly did not need to fear anything from his subjects.

On 24 March a dispirited Caulaincourt had reached headquarters on his way back from Châtillon and was surprised to find Napoleon in buoyant spirits. Rather than fall back on Paris, which the allies were now marching on, he was determined to inflict a blow on them by striking into their rear, and when he received reports of enemy troops near Valcour he attacked. But he failed to engage the allied forces, which had moved on. On 29 March he finally decided to return to Paris. It was too late, by no more than a day.

None had been preparing for Napoleon's fall more carefully and adroitly than his erstwhile Foreign Minister and current Grand Chamberlain, Talleyrand. Born in 1754 into a prominent noble family, Charles-Maurice de Talleyrand-Périgord was destined for the priesthood rather than the army by a genetic defect in his right foot. Neither limp nor cassock got in the way of a life of dissolute abandon, which continued even after he became a bishop, at the age of thirty-four. He eagerly embraced the Revolution in 1789. It was he who celebrated the great national service on the anniversary of the fall of the Bastille, but he would soon cast off his priestly robes altogether. He avoided the Terror by travelling to England and the United States of America, but was soon back in Paris, and Foreign Minister by 1797. He transferred his loyalties to Bonaparte at the opportune moment and served him well for many years, being richly rewarded for it. In 1804 he became Grand Chamberlain of the Empire, then Arch-Chancellor and Grand Elector, and was given as an apanage the principality of Benevento in what had been the Papal States.

Immensely clever, pragmatic and versatile, Talleyrand was admired and feared in equal measure. Napoleon affected to despise him, but valued his judgement. And despite his physical handicap, and his somewhat androgynous and pasty features, which gave a strong impression of moral corruption, he was still to many a fascinating and seductive figure.

Talleyrand had realised early on that Napoleon's megalomania would drive him into making miscalculations, and he foresaw that sooner or later the Emperor would lead his army and himself to destruction. Talleyrand wished to save France – and himself – from that unpleasant eventuality. In September 1808, during a meeting of the two Emperors at Erfurt in Germany, he had made his position clear to Alexander, and remained in secret contact with him from then on. Having fallen out with Napoleon shortly after and lost the post of Foreign Minister, he was able to stand aside and bide his time.

Following the disastrous Russian campaign, Talleyrand had begun to reflect on the subject of who or what could succeed Napoleon. That the Emperor must go he had no doubt: he could never achieve a lasting state of peace, since his very rule was based on a system of brute force, 'usurpation' in Talleyrand's language, which was self-perpetuating. 'Thus the greatest need for Europe, her greatest interest, lay in banishing the doctrines of usurpation, and bringing back the principle of legitimacy, the only remedy for all the ills that had assailed her, and the only one capable of preventing their return,' he explained in his memoirs. The Bourbons represented legitimacy against usurpation, legality against illegality. Only a return of the dynasty could guarantee future peace and stability, by making France a respectable but not a threatening power. He had begun to prepare the ground accordingly, making contact with people who were in touch with the exiled royals. He kept himself ready and his hands free (declining Napoleon's request that he take over the Foreign Ministry once more at the beginning of 1814).[10]

As Napoleon's future began to look less secure, many of those interested in his downfall or just their own future gravitated to Talleyrand's side. They included a number of convinced royalists such as Vitrolles, and some republicans, but these were outnumbered by people of lesser conviction. A good example was the duc de Dalberg, originally a Baron of the Holy Roman Empire, a man of allegedly republican convictions who hated Napoleon – but not enough to refuse a ducal title from him. Another was the Abbé de Pradt, a man of talent who had been made Archbishop of Malines by Napoleon, whom he nevertheless detested.

Talleyrand meant to reinstate the Bourbons, which would, at a stroke, turn France into the realm of one of the allies' natural associates and save her from their wrath. He hoped thereby to assure for himself safe passage to a key position in the new regime.[11]

He had sent Vitrolles to allied headquarters. But he had no certainty as to how he would be received, and he did not for a moment allow himself to forget that Napoleon was still capable of winning a battle and reversing the situation. As late as 20 March he confided to a friend that Napoleon only had to agree to the allied terms to save his throne, and only needed to be killed in battle to ensure the succession of his son. Talleyrand therefore had to keep all options open.[12]

Before leaving Paris, Napoleon had given orders that if the city were threatened, the Regency Council which he had appointed to administer the Empire while he was on campaign should evacuate the government and take refuge behind the river Loire. From 25 March all contact between him and the capital had been cut by the encircling Prussian and Russian forces. On 28 March his brother Joseph convoked the Regency Council in order to consult it on whether Marie-Louise and the three-year-old King of Rome should remain in Paris. The majority of those present, who included Talleyrand, expressed the view that they should remain where they were, in order to bolster confidence in the defence of the city and guarantee its safety were it to fall. But Joseph read out a letter from Napoleon in which he stressed that his wife and son should under no circumstances be allowed to fall into enemy hands. Fear of the Emperor's wrath if that were to happen persuaded the council to agree to their and its own evacuation. This opened the door to one of the most tortuous and haphazard changes of government and one of the most inglorious restorations in history.

The evacuation began on the following day, 29 March. As the Russian vanguard came in view of Paris, the Empress Marie-Louise and her son set off for Blois, accompanied by the court and members of the Regency Council. After making arrangements for the military capitulation of the city, Joseph followed. As a member of the council, Talleyrand should have gone too, but he delayed his departure.

He realised that as far as the allies were concerned Paris was the goal, and that they would treat with whoever was in control of it. With Napoleon away and the Empress and Regency Council in flight, the city was masterless. Power was, in effect, lying on the streets of Paris, there for the taking. With the air reverberating to the sound of the guns pounding at the northern and eastern defences of the capital, Talleyrand conducted a series of brief negotiations with various interested parties. But there was always the possibility that Napoleon might return and take the city back. Talleyrand therefore made a show of packing up his belongings, and in the evening obediently set off for Blois too. He chose to exit Paris via the gate of Passy, where his friend Charles de Rémusat was the National Guard officer on duty. In accordance with an agreement reached between them earlier, Rémusat refused to let him through on technical grounds, so Talleyrand turned back and went home.

After putting up a fierce but disorganised fight on the outskirts of Paris, Marshals Marmont and Mortier withdrew, leaving only the National Guard to maintain order while the capitulation of the city was negotiated. The guns had fallen silent, but Talleyrand did not sleep. His *hôtel particulier* on the rue Saint-Florentin was a focus of activity through the night, with people coming and going as he sounded out and persuaded all those of mark left in the city. By the morning of 30 March he was ready for the allies. But he could still not exclude the possibility that Napoleon might turn up before they did. What happened next would depend entirely on timing.

Napoleon had set off for Paris at the gallop that morning at dawn, and borrowed carriages along the way as his horses tired. He was determined to take command of the situation, and believed that he could not only mount an effective defence of Paris but use it as a springboard for a counter-thrust that would throw the allies out of France. But as he was approaching the capital that night at about 11 o'clock, he was met by General Belliard, who told him of its capitulation. He sat down by the roadside and took his head in his hands. After a while, he climbed into his carriage and made for Fontainebleau, where the remains of his army began to gather.

A few hours later, on the morning of 31 March, Alexander's aide-de-camp Count Orlov rode into Paris and straight to Talleyrand's house on the rue Saint-Florentin. Talleyrand gave him to understand, in one non-committal sentence, that Alexander had a free hand to do what he liked. It was the first step in what was to be an almost random settlement of one of the most important questions affecting the future of Europe.

By now, various Russian officers were riding into Paris, on their own or with escorts of, at most, a couple of cossacks. Some came on their own initiative, others were sent by Alexander to reconnoitre. There was a complete absence of any sense of threat on either side in what would, under most circumstances, have been a tense and possibly bloody moment. At the very least there was a strong possibility that the Russian rank-and-file, which had already delved deep into the cellars and warehouses full of wine and brandy on the outskirts of the city, would run amok.

One of the reasons for the tranquillity which attended the approach of the Russian troops and their entry into Paris was that many of them were commanded by French émigrés such as Generals Langeron, Damas and Lambert, and attended by dozens of French émigré staff officers. Another was the sense of unreality felt by both victors and vanquished, neither yet accustomed to their new roles. The pro-Bourbon demonstrations mounted by young royalists parading with white flags and cockades were as half-hearted as the manifestations of loyalty to Napoleon. Nobody seemed quite sure of themselves, or of what might happen next.[13]

Not long after Orlov's departure, Nesselrode rode into Paris escorted by a single cossack, and also made straight for the rue Saint-Florentin. Talleyrand was at his *toilette*. This was a remarkable daily performance, often enacted before a series of callers who, in the words of one who witnessed it, could at first 'see only an enormous assemblage of flannel, felt, fustian, percale, a mass of white' being attended by two valets in white aprons under the direction of a third in silk stockings and powdered wig. From the upper reaches of this ragged mass, out of a coil of cravats, jutted a firm chin, a permanently curled lip and a small upturned nose. The valets would begin by removing the woollen stockings and strips of flannel from his legs, which were plunged into a small basin of mineral water. This was the only part of Talleyrand that was ever exposed. 'The remaining parts of his person were covered by drawers, waistcoats, dressing gowns, with various pieces of cloth hanging off every bit of him, and his head wrapped in a kind of tiara of percale, held in place by a pale coloured ribbon,' continues the diarist. 'The two valets would then begin to comb, curl, pomade, powder, while he dabbed at his face with swabs which he dipped into a silver dish held before him for the purpose. Amongst the more remarkable elements in his *toilette* was one, curious enough to overcome the disgust one might have experienced witnessing it, which involved the consumption of one or two large glasses of tepid water which he sucked in through the nostrils and then ejected, more or less like an elephant, through his nose.' Nesselrode does not relate at which point in the process he intruded, but he remembered the moment vividly. 'He leapt up, his hair half-dressed, came towards me, threw his arms around me and covered me in powder,' he writes.[14]

Nesselrode had long seen Talleyrand as one of the most important figures in France, and consequently Talleyrand had little difficulty in convincing him that Alexander must not take up his quarters at the Élysée-Bourbon Palace as planned, on the somewhat far-fetched grounds that this had been mined by parties bent on assassinating him, and should instead come and stay with Talleyrand at the rue Saint-Florentin.

Later that same day, Alexander made his entry into the French capital at the head of his troops, with Frederick William riding at his side. At first the bystanders looked on in shocked amazement, but his appearance and manner were so engaging that this soon gave way to enthusiasm. Having ridden into the centre of the city he too made for the rue Saint-Florentin. As he entered Talleyrand's house, Alexander effectively placed himself at his disposal and in his debt. The post-war political arrangement of France now depended entirely on Talleyrand's ability to convince Alexander, and that was not going to be strained too far in the circumstances.

Talleyrand allowed the Tsar to expatiate on the various possibilities – a regency for the King of Rome, the choice of another Frenchman such as Bernadotte as King, even a republic. He then dismissed all of them, declaring that the problem demanded a more radical solution. He argued that the only institution that could successfully replace the Napoleonic regime was one built on a strong principle that would give it the power to endure. As the rightful King of France, Louis XVIII embodied a principle, the very principle on which the French state had been built. It followed that he was the only possible guarantor of peace, law and order. At the same time France must be given a constitution that enshrined all that was best in the legacy of the Revolution and the Empire.

Talleyrand was, in effect, claiming for the Bourbon cause a new kind of divine right to rule, based not on the old legitimacy of succession, but rather on a more modern and pragmatic kind of legitimacy, founded on principle and mutual acceptance, the very opposite of the usurpation embodied by Napoleon, and therefore a fitting antidote to his rule. Such a new legitimacy, he argued, would benefit not only France. It could act as the mainstay of a new order of peace and stability in Europe.

It was clever psychology. As the bearer of an imperial title less than a hundred years old and, like Napoleon's, unilaterally assumed, Alexander did not like talk of legitimacy in its traditional sense. The idea of a brave new age founded on a fresh concept was appealing.

He agreed to issue a proclamation to the effect that the allies would no longer deal with Napoleon and expected the French people to designate their own ruler. That meant that Napoleon was finished, and all Talleyrand needed to do was deliver a vote in favour of his desired candidate.

Alexander was still unhappy at the prospect of giving the throne to Louis XVIII, and suggested that another member of the house of Bourbon such as the duc d'Orléans be placed on it. Talleyrand objected that the Duke would be 'no less of a usurper for being high-born', and could not provide the required legitimacy. The same argument applied to Alexander's other candidate, the duc de Berry, whom the Tsar was hoping to marry to his sister the Grand Duchess Anna.[15]

Having convinced Alexander, Talleyrand went into action, feverishly rounding up and talking over every member of the existing Legislative Chamber left in Paris. On 2 April a rump of the Napoleonic Senate, sixty-four out of a total of 140, voted the deposition of Napoleon and announced a provisional government under Talleyrand, which promptly released all Frenchmen from their oath of allegiance to their Emperor. On 6 April the Senate passed a decree, ratified by the Legislative Assembly on 9 April, calling Louis XVIII to the throne. The whole exercise was entirely unconstitutional, illegal and therefore not binding on any French citizen. Nor was it binding on the allies, in whose name Alexander had no right whatever to enter into any agreements.

More to the point, Napoleon was still at Fontainebleau in command of some 45,000 men, including the elite Old Guard, not a negligible force even at this stage. A determined attempt to rally the people of Paris in his favour might well have ended in catastrophe for the allies. The option of having him assassinated was considered, but it was not Talleyrand's way of doing things. He suggested that Schwarzenberg propose an armistice to Marshal Marmont, whose 12,000-strong army corps was camped nearest to the capital. When Marmont accepted and moved his camp on 3 April, he appeared to have abandoned

Napoleon. This encouraged others to leave what they assumed was a sinking ship.

Perhaps the most challenging moment for Talleyrand was when Caulaincourt, accompanied by Marshals Ney and Macdonald, arrived at the rue Saint-Florentin with Napoleon's offer to abdicate in favour of his son. Alexander's chivalrous instincts and sentimental nature reacted with sympathy for the fallen Emperor, and he was inclined to accept. Talleyrand and others pointed out that this would be unworkable, as, short of imprisoning Napoleon on another continent, they could not expect him not to assume a dominant role again. Even that argument did not convince the Tsar. It was only when Talleyrand pointed out that going back on the decision to restore the Bourbons at this point would condemn all those, including himself, who had declared in their favour, that Alexander realised it was too late to change his mind. The offer was refused. When the envoys returned to Fontainebleau and informed Napoleon of what had taken place, he wrote out an unconditional abdication.[16]

By all accounts Napoleon remained remarkably composed, and at times even sanguine. He carried on as normal, reviewing troops, working in his study, at first on possible tactical moves as though the war were still on, later on more pressing administrative matters. He affected not to notice as more and more of his entourage disappeared, invoking a variety of unconvincing excuses. He kept in regular touch with Marie-Louise, who was at Rambouillet with their son, and looked forward to being reunited with them. Only on one occasion did his composure falter, and it seems he may have attempted to end his life by taking the poison he had kept with him since the retreat from Moscow.[17]

By contrast, Talleyrand's residence on the rue Saint-Florentin was a hive of activity. 'The Emperor of Russia and his aides had taken over the first floor; his Minister of Foreign Affairs Count Nesselrode and his secretaries occupied the second,' recorded Beugnot, the Minister of the Interior in Talleyrand's provisional government. 'Monsieur de Talleyrand had kept the entresol, where he worked with the members of the Provisional Government. Russian soldiers garnished the staircase, and Cossacks of the imperial guard filled the courtyard and the street. No distinction was made between day and night there; the throng and the bustle were the same. The only tranquillity in evidence were the Cossacks drowsing on the straw.' During those chaotic first days of April the fate of France was decided in Talleyrand's six-room apartment, where he and Alexander dined, worked and received people, Alexander holding court, Talleyrand keeping watch and gently steering him in the desired direction. It was there that Talleyrand, with the sanction of Alexander, turned France into a constitutional monarchy under the Bourbons.[18]

It was also there that the Treaty of Fontainebleau, regulating Napoleon's fate, was prepared. It was characteristic of Alexander in its generosity: Napoleon was treated with respect, and both he and his family richly provided for. He was to be given the Mediterranean island of Elba to rule over. He would keep his imperial title and could take a six-hundred-strong contingent of his Guard with him. He was to be paid a generous pension by France. Alexander had entertained the idea of giving him refuge as a private individual in Russia, then considered Corfu and Corsica before settling on Elba. As Napoleon would only have possession of Elba for his lifetime, his wife was to be given the Italian duchies of Parma, Piacenza and Guastalla to rule over, with the King of Rome, who was to be renamed the Prince of Parma, succeeding her.[19]

Alexander was triumphant. He had broken away from his allies and realised his dream of entering Paris as a conquering hero. From this vantage, he indulged his chivalrous instincts. His generous treatment of Napoleon was only one of many acts. He drove over to la Malmaison to pay his respects to the ex-Empress Josephine, then to Saint-Leu to visit Napoleon's stepdaughter Hortense, erstwhile Queen of Holland. He paid calls on the duchesse d'Abrantès, recently widowed by the death of General Junot. He showed himself in public and went to the opera, where he was cheered to the rafters and reciprocated by smiling and waving at everyone. To Madame de Staël he wrote declaring that he would abolish the Atlantic slave trade. To young Emma Sophia Edgcumbe, who had arrived in Paris with Lady Castlereagh, he gave a lecture on 'moral courage'. But his little holiday was about to come to an end.[20]

Metternich, Castlereagh and Hardenberg were still with the Emperor Francis in Dijon, where they had taken refuge from Napoleon's last attack on Schwarzenberg's army. They did not feel inclined to venture out until the coast was clear, and they were enjoying the comparative luxury of being in a larger town after the hardships of the past weeks. 'This is a delightful town,' Castlereagh wrote to Emily, adding that the people looked 'clean and good-humoured' and that it had been 'formerly fashionable'. More to the point, he was at last able to buy her something – 'a washing gown made here, which I hope you will like'. A few days later he reported that he had 'laid in a stock of silks and old Sèvres china for you'. 'Dijon delights us all,' Metternich wrote to his wife. Another who was enjoying his stay in the city was Humboldt, who according to Metternich had found himself a very accommodating mistress whose delights he listed to Metternich and Hardenberg.[21]

They did not reach Paris until 10 April, and they were not happy with what they found there. All three ministers were outraged to discover that Alexander had concluded the Treaty of Fontainebleau without consulting them. They were unanimous in their assessment that leaving Napoleon on Elba would place him in a position to cause trouble in France and Italy whenever he pleased. They were also indignant that by promising Parma and the other duchies to Marie-Louise, Alexander had pre-empted arrangements to be made as part of a general settlement at a later stage.

The usually placid Hardenberg was furious. 'I permitted myself to reproach the Emp[eror] Alex[ander] on the Convention with Napoleon,' he noted in his diary the day after arriving in Paris. 'He invoked Christianity, which enjoins us to forgive our enemies.' Metternich was beside himself. 'Your fine E[mperor] has done many foolish things and has conducted himself like a schoolboy who has got away from his tutor,' he wrote to Wilhelmina. 'The tutor is at his post once more and things will go better now,' he reassured her. But the tutor could not undo the damage. Along with Castlereagh and Hardenberg, he had no option but to sign the treaty, which they did on 11 April; but he could not forgive 'the biggest baby on earth', as he termed Alexander. 'He has started out by doing a great deal of harm. We have repaired some of it, but we will suffer for some time as a result of the things he got up to in those first moments when he ran away from us!' So would the 120,000 casualties of the Waterloo campaign.[22]

Peace

The Treaty of Fontainebleau settled nothing beyond Napoleon's abdication and future; it would take another two weeks of hard work by all the ministers to sign an armistice, involving as it did large bodies of troops scattered all over Europe, the surrender and evacuation of no fewer than fifty-three fortified positions, the movement of ships, stores and other materiel, the surrender of 12,600 pieces of ordnance and forty ships of the line, the release of prisoners and the repatriation of civilian administrators.

On 16 April Prince Eugène signed an armistice covering the kingdom of Italy, and thousands of French military and civil personnel began their journey home over the Alps, often accompanied by their families and taking with them their moveable property. Two days later Wellington signed an armistice with Marshal Soult which brought peace to south-western France and allowed isolated French garrisons at Lerida, Girona and other fortresses in Spain to start their long trek home. On 23 April the plenipotentiaries of Russia, Prussia, Austria, Britain and Spain signed a full armistice with France, under the terms of which the allied troops were to begin their withdrawal as soon as French garrisons beyond France's 1792 borders, in places such as Antwerp, Danzig, Hamburg, Magdeburg, Mainz and Luxembourg had surrendered and evacuated their positions. Tens of thousands of prisoners of virtually every nationality in Europe, most of whom had given themselves up for a crust of bread or even a place by a fire during the retreat from Moscow, were finally released and sent on their way.[1]

Napoleon too was on his way, into exile. He had left Fontainebleau on 20 April, after a tearful scene in the palace courtyard during which he bade farewell to his faithful Old Guard. He was accompanied by military commissioners delegated by each of the four allies, and as if this were not humiliation enough, he was to owe his safety to them. Outside Lyon, the travelling party encountered Marshal Augereau, who openly insulted Napoleon and had to be restrained by the commissioners. As they passed through Orange the party was greeted with shouts of '*Vive le Roi!*', and further down the road the Emperor was jeered. In one place angry crowds were hanging him in effigy and preparing an ambush. Napoleon was obliged to exchange his uniform for that of one of the commissioners, an Austrian General, and change to a more discreet carriage.

A greater humiliation, and a cause of profound sadness, was that he had not been allowed to take his wife and child with him. Realising how important they were to him and how diminished he would be without them, Metternich had persuaded the Emperor Francis that Marie-Louise and her son the King of Rome should be separated from Napoleon and kept under the control of Austria. A couple of days after reaching Paris, Francis had gone to see his daughter at Rambouillet to persuade her to leave her husband. She protested vehemently, but it did not take long to talk her round. She had already been subjected to spiteful innuendo from some of her ladies-in-waiting to the effect that Napoleon had been unfaithful to her, and similar insinuations had been made more recently by her brother-in-law Joseph, who had compounded his pusillanimity in not holding Paris for Napoleon with breathtaking disloyalty and bad taste by making amorous advances to her.[2]

Marie-Louise was not very clever, and it proved easy to persuade her to abandon her husband to his fate and to set off to take the waters in Italy while her son was taken to Vienna as a hostage.

Knowing that she greatly enjoyed the physical attentions that Napoleon had lavished on her, Metternich had selected a personable Austrian officer in his late thirties with a suitable reputation, Count Adam Adalbert von Neipperg, to accompany her. He wasted little time in becoming her lover and helping her to forget her husband. The only female company Napoleon could console himself with was that of his sister, the beautiful Pauline Borghese, whom he met along the way and who decided to accompany him to Elba.

On the same day Napoleon left Fontainebleau the new ruler of France emerged from his place of exile at Hartwell. He drove to London, where he was greeted by delirious crowds, fêted by the Prince Regent and congratulated by Lord Liverpool, whose government gave him £100,000. On 23 April he set off for Dover. The Prince lent him his yacht, the *Royal Sovereign*, for the crossing, and on 24 April Louis XVIII landed in his kingdom of France.

He had left it at the age of thirty-five, disguised as an English merchant, twenty-three years before, and since then had led a peripatetic existence drifting from court to court, surviving on royal handouts. Following his brother Louis XVI's death by the guillotine in 1793 and his nephew's reported death in prison two years later, he exchanged his title of comte de Provence for that of Louis XVIII, King of France. Cultivated, well-read and intelligent as he was, Louis lacked resolution and physical courage, preferring the quiet life, good food and beautiful things. He soon grew so fat that he could not sit a horse – his movements were described by the English diarist Charles Greville as 'the heavings of a ship'. His pathetic life of exile and his inept attempts to rally French royalists gave him an aura of failure and incompetence, and he was eclipsed by his more active and assertive younger brother, the comte d'Artois.[3]

Although Louis's landing at Calais was triumphal, he was not a happy man. Under Talleyrand's tutelage the French Senate had called Louis Stanislas Xavier de Bourbon to the throne occupied by his late brother, but as King of the French rather than as King of France, and only on condition that he swore to abide by the new constitution they had drawn up. This did not accord with his views on monarchy, which were traditionalist in the extreme.

As far as he was concerned, he had been King of France since 1795, by the grace of God, not through some kind of contract with the people, and he stressed that he was now in the nineteenth year of his reign. He was prepared to countenance a constitution, but it would take the form of a Charter 'granted' by him. Nor did he like the idea that he owed his throne to anyone else, and he made that abundantly clear when Alexander and Talleyrand drove out to Compiègne to greet him. He treated Alexander like a visiting minor monarch, taking precedence, seating him on a stiff-backed chair while he himself took the armchair, and having himself served first at dinner.

The understandably disgusted Alexander returned to Paris at once. 'The Bourbons have learnt nothing and are incorrigible,' he declared for all to hear in Madame de Staël's drawing room. Exiled by Napoleon for her critical opinions on his rule, the renowned writer had spent the past ten years travelling around Europe, and her salon was a major attraction for Parisians and foreigners alike from the moment of her return.[4]

Louis XVIII himself made his entry into the capital on 3 May, to a lukewarm reception, but Alexander did not come to greet him. The Tsar ostentatiously sought the company of people associated with the Napoleonic regime, and on 14 May, while the other sovereigns and the principal ministers were attending a solemn service in Notre Dame in memory of Louis XVI and Marie-Antoinette, he would be lunching with Josephine and Hortense at Saint-Leu. His repeated visits to la Malmaison started something of a fashion, and the ex-Empress was the recipient of calls from the great and the good. But she caught a chill while showing Alexander her rose garden, and died on 29 May. The Tsar was amongst the tens of thousands of mourners who paid their respects.

The capital had become, in Metternich's words, 'a great, vast, beautiful madhouse'. It had filled up not just with the sovereigns, their ministers and their generals, but with their wives, mistresses and other hangers-on. Nesselrode was joined by his young wife, who had followed not far behind headquarters over the whole of the past year, and they settled in at the Élysée-Bourbon, to which Alexander had moved from Talleyrand's house on the rue Saint-Florentin. Emily Castlereagh arrived from The Hague on 18 April, accompanied by her niece and nephew. Metternich's wife wanted to come, but he discouraged her, as he was hoping to lure Wilhelmina to Paris, even though Alfred von Windischgraetz was there with the army.[5]

Wilhelmina did come, on 15 May, with her sister Marie. It turned out to be something of a family reunion, since her mother the Duchess of Courland (Talleyrand's great friend and former mistress) and her younger sister Dorothée were both already in Paris, and the fourth sister, Jeanne, joined them a few days later. They felt just as much at home here, dining with Napoleonic ministers and marshals, as they had in Vienna or Reichenbach. Indeed, there was a remarkable absence of vindictiveness. Talleyrand, who had taken the precaution of sending his secretary into the archives with instructions to remove all documents implicating him in the worst crimes of the past twenty-five years, noted that 'a swarm of adventurers and troublemakers of every sort' besieged the Tuileries claiming to have helped restore the monarchy and demanding recognition of their supposed services. At the same time, it was noted by many that never had a change of regime been accomplished with so little spite or retribution.[6]

Prince Eugène, who had left Italy following Napoleon's abdication and accompanied his wife to the court of his father-in-law at Munich, had been summoned to Paris by his mother, the ex-Empress Josephine, who urged him to see to it that he obtained the fief he had been promised under the Treaty of Fontainebleau. He presented himself at court under his *ancien régime* title of Marquis de Beauharnais, but even the prickly Louis XVIII declared that this was ridiculous and that he must retain his Napoleonic one. He was not given a fief, and did not even manage to get the Austrian army to release his household silver and effects seized in Milan, despite Metternich's repeated promises of help. But he was received with honour everywhere, and

Alexander made great show of friendship and esteem for him in public.[7]

People had taken up their quarters wherever they could, treating officials of the Napoleonic regime as fair game for billeting. Beugnot, formerly Napoleon's minister in the grand duchy of Berg and currently Minister of the Interior in Talleyrand's provisional government, had come back to Paris a couple of days after the entry of the allies. 'I was going to take up residence at home,' he records. 'My apartment was occupied by Lord Burghess [sic], whom I found not remotely disposed to allowing me the smallest part of it. He gave me to understand that he valued it particularly on account of my library.'[8]

Stewart took over the *hôtel particulier* of the Montesquiou family, where he began entertaining lavishly. Accident-prone as ever, he came home one evening in his usual drunken state, tore off his uniform and threw himself onto the bed without bothering to close the french windows into the garden, and woke up to find that not only his richly gold-braided hussar jacket with its diamond-studded decorations, but every single item of clothing had been stolen. He was confined to quarters while a tailor ran up a new uniform, but soon resumed his boisterous life. During a ball Stewart gave one evening, Alexander's brother Grand Duke Constantine asked the orchestra to play a waltz, and had just begun dancing when Stewart walked up to the musicians and told them to play another dance, which he wanted to enjoy with Priscilla Burghersh. Furious at having his waltz interrupted in midstream, Constantine stormed up and protested, to which Stewart retorted that he was the host and the choice of music was his. Constantine left in a fury, threatening revenge.[9]

Cathcart had imposed himself on the hospitality of the once beautiful Laure Junot, duchesse d'Abrantès, recently widowed when her demented husband had thrown himself out of the window. She was the object of fascination for many, including Tsar Alexander, who visited her several times. Metternich, who had enjoyed her favours a few years before, when he had been Austria's ambassador in Paris, and had annoyed her by ditching her in favour of Napoleon's sister

Caroline Murat, now took his lodgings in the residence of General Sebastiani. He was greatly amused by the fact that his imperial master had taken over the residence of Napoleon's other sister, Pauline Borghese, and rested his weary limbs in the very same lavender-coloured bed in which Metternich had slept with the lovely Pauline in his Paris days, during which he had bedded not only both of Napoleon's sisters but his stepdaughter Hortense as well, not to mention the famous actress Mademoiselle Georges.[10]

Frederick William had lodged himself in Prince Eugène's residence, from where he visited the sights under the tutelage of Humboldt's brother Alexander. Hardenberg had, rather masochistically, found billets at No. 1 rue d'Iéna. As his diary attests, he was an assiduous sightseer, and he also worked his way methodically through all the famous restaurants of Paris, beginning with Robert, moving on to Véry in the Palais-Royal, and ending with the Rocher de Cancale.

Others were more interested in what the shops had to offer. Metternich went off in search of fine silks to send Wilhelmina. When she arrived in Paris, she went shopping with him to help him choose dresses for his wife. He also chose furniture, silver and fabrics for his house in Vienna, and, in anticipation of the peace congress due to take place there, booked dancers. The Russian commander Marshal Barclay de Tolly took his wife shopping, but since neither of them trusted their own taste, they asked the urbane General Woldemar de Löwenstern to accompany them, to help them choose.

'Never has so much gold been spent in Paris,' one French officer in Austrian service wrote to a friend in Vienna. 'Millions of ducats circulate every day in this immense [brothel]; the shops are running out of goods; 60,000 c[unt]s, without counting the decent wives of civil and military officers, are in constant service.'[11]

Paris was the greatest metropolis in Europe, its intellectual and cultural centre, the dictator of taste and fashion, and now the political epicentre of the Continent. People were naturally drawn to it, and none more so than the British, a nation of indefatigable tourists who had been cut off from the Continent for two decades, with only a short break during the Peace of Amiens. Excursions to Paris were now all the rage with London society. 'It is raining Englishmen,' Metternich wrote to his wife, claiming that up to six hundred were arriving every day, and adding that the whores of the Palais-Royal were making hay. He also noted the arrival of some English ladies, whose dress appalled him. 'You have to see it to believe it,' he assured her.[12]

Having been cut off from the Continent for so long, British women had lost contact with the mainstream of European fashion and given vent to their own fantasies, with disastrous consequences. A party of English tourists caused more than a stir in Geneva, where the city authorities ordered the ladies to be confined indoors, as an unruly mob gathered whenever they ventured out, giving rise to fears of public disorder. A somewhat unkempt, if dashing, short-skirted look appeared to prevail, even amongst the older women. Schwarzenberg was astonished by Lady Castlereagh's dress sense. 'She is very fat and dresses so *young*, so *tight*, so *naked*,' he wrote.[13]

Not everyone enjoyed their stay in Paris. Lord Burghersh found it full of 'rascals of every sort'. Nesselrode, who had been there before, as secretary at the Russian embassy in 1807, did not like the city, or its inhabitants either. Stein was too disgusted by the 'impure, impudent and immodest race of the French' to derive any pleasure from his stay. And Bernadotte left hurriedly once it had become clear that there was no role for him to play.[14]

One of the greatest attractions of Paris was the Musée Napoléon in the Louvre. This was the product of revolutionary and Napoleonic plunder on a massive scale, organised and given purpose by the remarkable antiquary baron Dominique Vivant Denon. Much of the contents had come from the French royal collections, confiscated châteaux, desecrated churches and dissolved religious institutions. An exceptional collection of antiquities had been brought back from Egypt by the savants who had accompanied Napoleon's expedition there in 1798. But the majority of the works of art had either been looted or extorted under duress, from the Vatican, from royal and ducal palaces, from churches, monasteries and other institutions all over Italy, Belgium, the Netherlands, Spain, Portugal, Germany and Poland.

The museum was a unique creation. Never before had so much of the artistic heritage of Ancient Egypt, Greece, Rome and Europe been brought together, arranged so intelligently or shown so extensively. In areas such as Italian medieval painting, Denon had gathered up from store rooms and attics art that was no longer highly esteemed, and, by showing it to a wider public and writing it up in his catalogues, had validated it and made it fashionable again.

The more cultivated allied diplomats and officers rushed to visit the museum, and painters such as Benjamin Haydon and William Wilkie came over from England expressly to view its treasures. It provided a unique opportunity to see works by artists of whom they had only read. Anxious to ensure the future of his great work, Denon greeted monarchs and lieutenants alike, eager to show them around. He extended opening hours and put on special exhibitions of groups of works in an effort to get as many people into the Louvre as possible. He also volunteered to return all the works which were not on permanent display, some two hundred paintings, several dozen sculptures and hundreds of other works of art.

He need not have worried. All those who visited the Louvre were stunned by the grandeur of the collection. There was a general feeling that the works of art were more accessible, better exhibited and better looked-after here than in the places they had come from. The French led the world in the care of pictures, and had developed the technique for relining them and transferring them from wood to canvas. More important, the visitors understood that the museum itself was a great work of art and a universal institution of enormous cultural importance. The few claims for the return of works were silenced by a consensus, led by Aberdeen and Castlereagh, that the museum, which had been renamed the Musée Royal, must be left untouched.[15]

'This peace, so ardently hoped for by the whole world, will now be made in less than 3 weeks,' Metternich wrote to Wilhelmina on

23 April. 'Then we will convoke a congress, in Vienna perhaps, at which the minor arrangements of the rest of Europe will be treated – and that task will take no more than 3 more weeks.'[16]

His optimism appears breathtaking with the wisdom of hindsight, but was quite justifiable at the time. The ministers of the four principal allies wanted to sign a definitive peace as quickly as possible, and there seemed to be nothing standing in their way. They had already agreed the bases of the settlement in the proposals made to Caulaincourt at Châtillon. France was not likely to prove a difficult partner in these negotiations, as Talleyrand was being statesmanlike and Louis XVIII, who had just been handed another £100,000 in cash by the British government to help him set up house at the Tuileries, was in no position to argue. In the event, he did put forward demands for parts of Belgium, but was quickly called to order by Castlereagh, who sweetened the pill by offering him the enclave of Gex on Lake Geneva and some districts of Savoy. The negotiations nevertheless took a little longer than Metternich had expected, involving as they did a backlog of matters going back twenty years. And the ministers soon found themselves besieged by delegates from a number of aggrieved or hopeful parties, such as the Pope, the republic of Genoa, the city of Geneva, and various groups of Italian and other nationalists. 'The pace of life over the past two months is too much for me,' Talleyrand complained to the Duchess of Courland on 16 May.[17]

On 17 May the Prussian plenipotentiaries almost upset the course of the negotiations by demanding that France repay all the financial demands she had made on Prussia under the treaty of 1812, and produced a bill for 169,785,895 francs. All question of money and reparations had been kept out of the negotiations so far, and Castlereagh was determined that it should remain so. He informed the Prussians that Britain had spent £700,000,000 on the war with France, and was not demanding a penny, and denied their claim outright. The matter was duly buried, after a day of acrimonious discussion. So was the city of Hamburg's demand that France indemnify it for the bullion which Marshal Davout had seized from its banks and paid out as advance salary to his soldiers. The only claims against the French government to be approved under the treaty would be those by private individuals whose property or assets had been confiscated.[18]

Castlereagh, Hardenberg and Metternich had hoped not just to make peace with France, but to settle the outstanding issues of Poland and Germany as well, and they devoted a number of what Castlereagh termed 'tedious and elaborate' conferences to the subject. On 29 April Hardenberg unveiled a plan which he hoped would satisfy all parties. Russia's western boundary in Poland would run down the Soldau and then the Warta rivers and then on to Kraków, giving her a significant increase in territory but not the whole of the grand duchy of Warsaw. Prussia would be indemnified for the Polish provinces she lost thereby with the whole of Saxony, minus a small part which was to go to Alexander's brother-in-law the Duke of Saxe-Weimar. In addition, Prussia was to have Magdeburg, Altmark, Nassau, Berg, Cleves and a strip along the Dutch border, including Mainz. The King of Saxony would be given the provinces of Münster and Paderborn in compensation. The plan also proposed a certain amount of rearrangement of territory in northern Germany, which would have the effect of leaving only Oldenburg, Saxe-Weimar, Saxe-Coburg and Mecklemburg, whose rulers were related to Alexander, and Hanover, which belonged to the royal house of Britain, as independent states in northern Germany. The rest would be, more or less firmly, tied to Prussia. The plan was relatively generous to Austria, which would end up with some 1,644,000 more inhabitants than she had had in 1805, while Prussia gained an extra 602,000. The plan met with the approval, in principle, of Metternich and Castlereagh, though the former insisted that Mainz should go to Bavaria. Stein also approved, although he felt the King of Saxony should be indemnified, if at all, in Italy rather than in Germany.[19]

Hardenberg was eager to get the plan accepted by all four powers before the impending congress, when it might come under scrutiny and criticism from other parties. On 5 May he presented it to Alexander. But the Tsar rejected it outright, declaring that he intended to keep the whole of the grand duchy of Warsaw, including those parts of it which had been Austrian until 1809.

While the allied ministers had busied themselves with the peace, Alexander had been pursuing his own agenda. He had fulfilled his divinely ordained mission of liberating the world, and exorcised Paris to mark the triumph of good over evil by celebrating Mass on Easter Sunday, 10 April, surrounded by his troops, on what is now the place de la Concorde, where Louis XVI had been guillotined. He had prepared for this spiritually since the Monday in Holy Week, which happened to be the day Napoleon signed his abdication. 'The beginning of my devotions was marked, as though by design, by the voluntary abdication of Napoleon, which allowed me to achieve the tranquillity necessary to begin to undertake and to fulfil my duties as a Christian,' he wrote to his friend Aleksandr Galitzine, noting that it had taken an 'Orthodox son of the North' to bring God back into the sinful Babylon of Paris. He confined the Russian troops to barracks, presumably in order to keep them from temptation, which caused much grumbling and led to numerous desertions.[20]

Soon after reaching Paris, Alexander had sought out the ageing Polish national hero Tadeusz Kościuszko, who was living outside the city. Kościuszko appealed to Alexander to create a free kingdom of Poland with an English-style constitution and himself as King, and offered his services. 'Your most cherished hopes will be realised,' Alexander replied, and promised to return all the lands taken from Poland by Russia over the past half-century.

He had already declared to the 8,000 or so Polish troops who had remained loyal to Napoleon that they need fear nothing and that he would take them under his personal protection. He set up a Military Committee consisting of Polish generals under the chairmanship of Grand Duke Constantine, which set about the arrangements for marching them back to Warsaw, where they would be reorganised into a new Polish army; another committee would begin framing a constitution for the kingdom of Poland. He appeared to be furthering his Polish project through *faits accomplis*.[21]

The three allied ministers were horrified. But there was little they could do. Alexander's popularity in Paris was such that he was not susceptible to argument and could not be reined in. His conduct over the Polish issue impelled Prussia to look to her own interests. Prussian troops had occupied the fortress of Mainz, which Austria was intending to award to Bavaria as compensation for the return of the Tyrol and other areas. With Alexander refusing to give an inch on Poland, and Prussia taking up an aggressive stance over Mainz, the climate grew unfavourable to the conclusion of any kind of deal. Castlereagh and Metternich therefore decided to adjourn the settlement of the Polish and German issues.

'Paris is a bad place for business,' Castlereagh complained to the Secretary of State for War, Lord Bathurst. He had persuaded Liverpool to ask the Prince Regent to invite the allied sovereigns to London, in the hope that this would cement good relations and at the same time distract them from the business in hand. Away from his adulators and all the schemers in Paris, Castlereagh thought, Alexander might prove easier to deal with. He and his colleagues therefore decided to conclude the treaty with France as quickly as possible, incorporating into it all those points on which they had agreed, and to leave the rest to be resolved in London. This they did, on 30 May.[22]

'I have completed my treaty with the four great powers,' Talleyrand wrote to the Duchess of Courland that evening. 'It is very good, having been made on an absolutely equal footing, and noble with it.' Given that the allies had invaded France proclaiming that they had only come to deliver the French people from Napoleon's tyranny and had their best interests at heart, they had themselves placed limits on how far they could penalise the country. As a result, the treaty with France that was signed by Russia, Prussia, Austria, Sweden, Britain, Spain and Portugal on 30 May was relatively generous. It was neither vindictive nor punitive, recognising as all the plenipotentiaries did that the best guarantee of peace and stability in Europe lay in the rapid recovery of France from the political evils that had overcome her.[23]

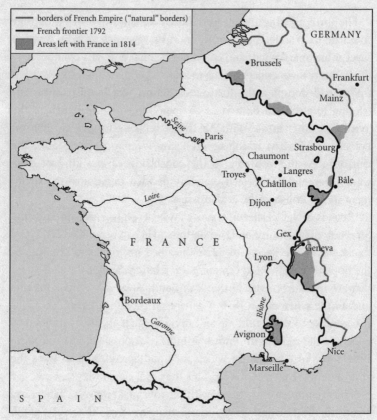

—	borders of French Empire ("natural" borders)
—	French frontier 1792
▓	Areas left with France in 1814

The Treaty of Paris

While France lost her Napoleonic conquests, she recovered all her overseas colonies except for Île de France, Tobago, St Lucia and Mauritius, as well as Saint-Domingue (Haiti), which had expelled the French and declared its independence. And if her empire was smaller than it had been in 1792, she had gained on the European mainland, and in population to the tune of some 450,000 souls. She had been allowed to keep the former Papal enclaves of Avignon and the Comtat Venaissin, and had acquired a large slice of Sardinian territory in Savoy, along with Annecy and Chambéry, the areas around

Philippeville and Mariembourg on the border with Belgium, as well as Sarrelouis (Saarlouis), Landau, Montbéliard and Mulhouse on her eastern frontier, with the result that her territory was more extensive than it had been in 1792 and than it is today.

'We know for certain that France will maintain the rank she has always held,' Talleyrand wrote to his ambassador in London a couple of weeks later. 'Her position will be that of a state which has nothing to fear for itself and which, threatening no one, will have many friends, a position which appears to me far preferable to that where, while dominating everything, it would have secret enemies in the very agents of its power.'[24]

Talleyrand had called the peace 'noble', and it certainly merited that adjective. It contained a number of novel elements which had little to do with the immediate interests of the signatories, including clauses governing navigation on the Rhine and promising that 'in the interests of facilitating communications between nations, and of making them less foreign to each other', other rivers which flowed through or between different countries would benefit from a set of similar rights and rules for those who used them. Talleyrand had even tried to insert a clause which would have created a bilateral disarmament convention.

There were clauses governing the rights of individuals in foreign countries, and clause XVI declared that 'No individual, of whatever class or condition, may be legally pursued, harassed or troubled, in his person or his property, under any pretext, be it his political conduct or opinion, his attachment to one or other of the contracting parties or to governments that have ceased to exist, or for any other reason, except for debts contracted towards individuals or for acts committed after the present Treaty.'

As well as covering the return of colonies, the treaty dealt with complicated questions such as the fishery on the Grand Bank of Newfoundland. It also ensured that the slave trade, abolished in all the French and Dutch colonies while they were in British possession, would not be reintroduced on their return. Castlereagh had pressed for an outright abolition of the trade by all the signatories of the treaty.

His attempts had been blocked by Talleyrand and the representatives of Spain and Portugal, who argued that Britain could afford to abolish the trade, as she had moved more slaves from Africa into her colonies in the past fifty years than the rest of them put together. They went so far as to suggest that Castlereagh's efforts were an attempt to ruin the competition. (The Americans often voiced the similar suspicion that British calls for abolition concealed a plot to control the Atlantic.) 'The English have always been good at making business march alongside honour,' commented the Spanish plenipotentiary. The best Castlereagh could do in the circumstances was to get France to agree to a cessation of the trade within five years.[25]

When, on his return to London, Castlereagh entered the chamber of the House of Commons, everyone stood and cheered, except for William Wilberforce, who later got to his feet to declare that all he could see in the treaty was 'the death-warrant of a multitude of innocent victims'. Over the next weeks eight hundred petitions with nearly a million signatures would pour into Westminster from all over the country demanding that abolition be made one of Britain's demands at the forthcoming congress.[26]

Britain had been the most enthusiastic practitioner of the trade, her ships carrying over half of all slaves traded across the Atlantic, and up to four-fifths of her income deriving from the West Indies, which were entirely dependent on it, by the 1780s. But in that same decade humanitarianism had entered British politics under the influence of John Wesley, the Quakers, James Ramsay, Thomas Clarkson and William Wilberforce. The argument was taken up in Parliament, where it was repeatedly debated and voted on in the last decade of the eighteenth century and the first of the nineteenth, leading to the trade's abolition in 1807. The passion of the abolitionists was as intense as the brutality of the slavers. 'I was not aware until I had been some time here of the degree of frenzy existing here about the Slave trade, and I am unable to describe it to you,' Wellington wrote from London to his brother in Madrid. 'People in general appear to think that it would suit the policy of the nation to go to war to put an end to that *abominable* traffic, and many wish that we should take the field on this new crusade.' The crusade would be fought essentially against France, Spain and Portugal, as Denmark had voted to abolish the trade as early as 1792, while Sweden and Holland had just been forced to agree to abolition.[27]

Wellington was quickly converted, and applied himself in earnest to promoting abolition in France, to which he had been named ambassador. He even tried to bribe the French to drop their five-year deferment with the promise of giving them an extra colony, the island of Trinidad, if they complied. But public opinion in France was largely indifferent to the issue, while her economic interests were heavily dependent on the continuation of the trade.[28]

In all other respects the Treaty of Paris was satisfactory to Castlereagh. His principal goals had been achieved: France had been forced back within her historic frontiers, Holland had been enlarged to include Belgium and the Scheldt estuary, and the Prussian presence on the Rhine had been reinforced, though the details were still to be fixed. And with her acquisition of Malta, the Cape Province, Tobago, St Lucia and Mauritius, Britain had acquired complete strategic control of the Mediterranean and the sea routes to the West and the East Indies. This meant that she would be in the happy position of not having to protect her own vital interests in the ensuing negotiations, which would give Castlereagh greater freedom of manoeuvre and added authority.[29]

Metternich was also pleased with the settlement. 'Peace, *mon amie* – and a good peace,' he wrote to Wilhelmina on 1 June, adding that he had bought her 'some very beautiful things, & not at ridiculous prices'. France was not diminished, which had been one of his principal concerns. The treaty guaranteed Austria possession of Lombardy and Venetia in Italy, and strengthened Sardinia as a barrier to French influence in the peninsula by the addition of the former republic of Genoa. Switzerland, parts of which had been the object of covetous glances on the part of Stein, was to be independent.[30]

Stein was not happy with the treaty. Nor was Hardenberg. His feelings had been so strong when Alexander rejected his project that on that very day Münster wrote to the Prince Regent warning of the possibility of war breaking out. It was true that Prussia had been guaranteed possession of the grand duchy of Berg and the area between the Rhine, the Meuse and the Moselle. But the lack of a final settlement in Germany awarding her the whole of Saxony left her extremely vulnerable. All the other powers were in possession of most if not all of their gains, which suggested the unpleasant possibility that Prussia might end up being left out in the cold.[31]

The Prussian military were disappointed that their triumphs had not been rewarded more fully. They had borne the brunt of the fighting in the later stages of the war, and without their courage and determination Napoleon might well have prevailed. There was much grumbling in Berlin that France had not been stripped of Alsace and made to pay war reparations. Admiral Shishkov was also upset by the leniency shown to the French. It was not just Napoleon who was evil, he argued, and justice demanded the 'extermination' of the whole corrupt and wicked nation. There was also some discontent in London at the generosity of the peace. 'No Murders, No Torture, No Conflagration,' noted one wit, '– how will the pretty women of London bear it?'[32]

A secret article of the Treaty of Paris stipulated that the powers which had been engaged in the recent war would send their plenipotentiaries to Vienna within the space of two months 'in order to settle, in a general congress, the arrangements required to complete the dispositions of the present treaty'. It went on to make it clear that the decision-making would be in the hands of the four great powers. But it was already beginning to dawn on them that, having made peace with France, they could not actually ignore her. A curious anomaly had come into being: while the four were still leagued against France by the Treaty of Chaumont, they were now at peace with her and exchanging ambassadors, so she would have as much right to pass comment and make her influence felt as any of them. This made it all the more urgent, as Metternich, Castlereagh and particularly Hardenberg were concerned, to wrap up the outstanding business between themselves in London, without the interference of Talleyrand. Metternich was not looking forward to London, describing the forthcoming trip as a 'torment' to Wilhelmina, but hoped the whole thing would take no more than six to ten days. He was longing to get back to Vienna to tend his house and the new gardens he was laying out. He still believed there would be 'less to negotiate than to ratify at Vienna', and that the congress would assemble in July and be over by mid-August.[33]

13

The London Round

The visit of the sovereigns and ministers, and particularly of Tsar Alexander, was looked forward to with the greatest enthusiasm by the people of England. They relished the opportunity to see and to express their thanks to the great figures and the warriors whose deeds they had read of in the papers, and a holiday atmosphere reigned throughout the land.

This was only slightly soured by Alexander's sister, the Grand Duchess Catherine, who had preceded him by two months. She had been met at Rotterdam by the Duke of Clarence, the Prince Regent's younger brother and the future King William IV, and crossed the Channel with him. At Sheerness, where she landed, she was met by the Russian ambassador Count Lieven and his wife, the spirited Dorothea, who was quick to foresee trouble. 'The Grand Duchess had an immoderate thirst for authority and a very high, and possibly excessive, opinion of herself,' she noted. 'I never saw a woman so possessed of the need to stir, act, put herself forward and eclipse others.' She was 'seductive in glance and manner' and 'had a dazzling brilliance and freshness of complexion, a bright eye, and the most beautiful hair in the world . . . She expressed herself directly, with eloquence and grace, but she never abandoned the tone of command. Her mind was cultivated, brilliant and daring; her character firm and imperious.'[1]

The Lievens had booked the Pulteney Hotel on Piccadilly overlooking Green Park as Catherine's residence, and on the morning after her arrival there the Prince Regent called on her. She had not finished her *toilette*, and was flustered at having to receive him in this condition. Their meeting was awkward, and after a quarter of an hour the Prince took his leave. 'Your Grand Duchess is no beauty,' he said to Countess Lieven as he passed her on his way out. 'Your Prince is very ill-bred,' the Grand Duchess told her when he had gone. To her brother she confided that she found him 'rather disgusting', and complained of his dirty talk.[2]

Later that day the Grand Duchess was received by the Queen at Buckingham Palace. This was followed by a dinner at Carlton House. Noting that she was dressed in mourning for her late husband, the Duke of Oldenburg, the Prince Regent hinted lewdly at various means of consolation. She glared at him and refused to utter a word. She only spoke to demand that the Italian musicians who were playing at dinner be sent away, as music, she announced, gave her migraines. This annoyed not only the Prince but the Queen as well, and the dinner ended in icy silence.

The Grand Duchess continued as she had begun. She was rude to the Prince's mistress Lady Hertford, and expressed the wish to call on the estranged Princess of Wales, who had been banished from court. More ominously, she applied herself to turning the Prince's daughter Princess Charlotte against the idea of marrying the Hereditary Prince of Orange. The Princess had already changed her mind once, but after a certain amount of persuasion she had relented, and the impending marriage had been announced to the Dutch Legislative Assembly on 30 March 1814. No sooner had that been settled than it was stirred up again, by the Russian minister designate to Spain, Count Tatishchev, who happened to be passing through London on the way to take up his post. He and his wife suggested to Princess Charlotte that she reject the Hereditary Prince and consider marrying one of the Russian Grand Dukes Constantine or Nicholas instead. Liverpool was so incensed by this that he let it be known that the

Grand Dukes would not be welcome during the proposed visit of the sovereigns.[3]

While the Tatishchevs were presumably pursuing Russian state policy, it is unclear whether the recently widowed Grand Duchess's motives for trying to break Princess Charlotte's engagement were similarly inspired. Travelling through Holland on her way to England, the Grand Duchess had been greatly impressed by its wealth. At The Hague, she turned her attention to the Hereditary Prince of Orange as a possible husband for herself.[4]

In a last attempt at saving the marriage, Castlereagh instructed his ambassador in The Hague, Lord Clancarty, to send the Hereditary Prince over to London. The Prince was, in Clancarty's words, 'extremely impatient for the actual possession of his future bride', and keen to reach London. At first the ploy seemed to work. Emma Sophia Edgcumbe noted that the two were 'sitting together, and walking about arm-in-arm, looking perfectly happy and lover-like'. But within a few days Princess Charlotte had once again declared that she could not marry a man who would live outside England, and by the last week of June the engagement was broken off. The Prince sailed back to Holland in low spirits.[5]

That was not the only part of Castlereagh's Dutch plan that was at risk of unravelling. As early as February he had begun to realise that the majority of the population of the former Austrian Netherlands wanted either union with France or a return to Habsburg rule, and not incorporation into Holland. Their feelings were echoed by many Dutchmen, who had no wish to see their country enlarged to include these 'Brabanters', as Castlereagh insisted on referring to them. The French-speaking Catholic Belgians were divided by language and religion from the Protestant Dutch, and they had enjoyed a range of privileges and freedoms under the Habsburgs which they feared losing on incorporation into the new kingdom. Their protests were ignored by the Sovereign Prince, and by Castlereagh, who persuaded the other allies to agree to the formal transfer of the territory to his administration.

Castlereagh's projected frontiers for the new Dutch state, which looked good on the map, also ran into conflict with realities on the ground. Seeing the river Meuse (Maas) above all as a convenient military and therefore a desirable political barrier, he had drawn a line through the middle of a cultural and economic community dating from the sixteenth century. The Meuse had never been a political barrier: it had been an economic and social link, with industries on one bank obtaining their raw materials from the other, and the garden produce of Limburg being exchanged for the grain of Liège.

Matters were not helped by the three Prussian army corps which had moved into Belgium and were treating it as enemy territory. They also occupied areas beyond the Meuse which had been Dutch before 1792, and refused to admit the Dutch administration. The eastern frontier of the Netherlands was overhung by a question mark, as fears mounted that Prussia would not withdraw her troops.

Castlereagh was not particularly bothered by the feelings of the inhabitants, but open discontents could affect the stability of the arrangements. And while he struggled to build up the power of the future Dutch state, Russia was courting both the Sovereign Prince and his son, with the evident intention of preventing it from growing too close to Britain – its naval resources and colonial bases were of great interest to Russia.

Britain was in possession of all of these, having captured them when Holland became a satellite and then a part of France. The list was impressive, including Demerara, Essequibo, Berbice, Surinam, Curaçao, Aruba, Bonnaire, St Eustatius, Saba and St Martin in the West Indies; the Cape of Good Hope and a string of small trading settlements on the coast of Africa; Ceylon, Cochin and a number of trading factories in India; and Sumatra, Malacca, Batavia (Java), Madura, Timor, Macassar, Palembang and other trading posts in south-east Asia. Castlereagh had originally intended to return all the colonies except for the Cape, but there were protests from the City of London and from Liverpool, whose merchants had invested in West Indian colonies such as Demerara, Curaçao and Surinam, and particularly in the settlements of Essequibo and Berbice on the coast of Guiana.

To complicate matters, Sweden, which had been promised the former French colony of Guadeloupe and was now being asked to relinquish her claim so the island could be returned to France, demanded Surinam and Curaçao instead. Castlereagh managed to buy Sweden off with the offer of £1 million in cash. But in order to raise this he had to placate City interests, which he did by retaining Berbice, Essequibo and Demerara, which ultimately became British Guiana. But this upset the Dutch, who felt that the acquisition of Belgium in no way compensated for the loss. They nevertheless agreed to Britain's demand that they abolish the slave trade, which they formally did on 15 June.

Castlereagh also decided to hold on to Cochin, and gave Holland the island of Banka in lieu – mainly because the tin miners of Cornwall feared the competition from the mines of Banka. He had already agreed to pay Holland £2 million, to be dedicated to building a string of fortresses along the frontier with France, in compensation for the Cape and other colonies he would not be returning. In addition, he discussed possible ways of paying off the debt of £6 million Russia had contracted with the firm of Hope in Holland and was in no position to settle.[6]

However much Grand Duchess Catherine might have poisoned the atmosphere, the arrival of her brother and the King of Prussia was nevertheless awaited with unparalleled enthusiasm. People of all classes travelled out of London on the Dover road, joined by others from the surrounding countryside. Some took picnics, others were provided for by stalls that sprang up along the way. Carriages packed with people took up strategic positions on hills or bends in the road that could provide a good view. Small amphitheatres were run up facing the posting stages so people could watch the monarchs as their horses were changed. Exorbitant prices were charged for seats on these and for places at windows overlooking the scene.

On 6 June, Alexander, Frederick William, Hardenberg, Nesselrode and a host of German princes and lesser ministers embarked at Boulogne on HMS *Impregnable*, commanded by the Duke of Clarence in his role as Lord High Admiral. Blücher, who along with Hardenberg had been made a prince the previous day, embarked on the yacht *Royal Charlotte*, and others took passage on one or other of the escorting frigates. Late that afternoon they reached Dover, where a lavish reception awaited them. A freshening wind made it difficult to disembark the carriages, and instead of waiting, Alexander and Frederick William set off for London the following morning, travelling incognito in Count Lieven's chaise. They flew past the waiting crowds unnoticed, and it was the remainder of the party, following in the official carriages, who were acclaimed and fêted at every stage. But the disappointment of the crowds which had wanted to cheer the sovereigns was intense.

The Prince Regent had prepared rooms for them at St James's Palace, but Alexander preferred to move in with his sister at the Pulteney Hotel. This was immediately besieged by a throng clamouring for him to show himself at the window and cheering him madly when he did. The crowd was so great that the Prince Regent would not call on him for fear of suffering some insult or even violence. Alexander therefore drove to Carlton House to see him, but the interview was a short one, and the Tsar emerged from it unimpressed.

He had been followed by the crowd to Carlton House and back. 'Our Londoners seem as if they were crazy, and pursue the foreigners with an eagerness which makes one feel ashamed of one's Countrymen, all trades have been stopped, for nobody would work, and happy those who had gowns and shoes ready made, none could be got to order,' wrote an observer. 'A friend who came from London yesterday, says that nothing can equal the bustle there,' a lady informed her acquaintance. 'No work, no business, nothing attended to but running about the streets, even among the lower classes.' There were illuminations and fireworks, a fair in Hyde Park with a mock naval battle on the Serpentine, and an unrelenting stream of banquets and balls.[7]

The visitors were at first enchanted to be the object of such popularity, and the novelty of having their hands shaken by complete strangers flattered their vanity. The bibulous Blücher, who was attended by Stewart, acting as guide and translator, was delighted at the drink being liberally proffered everywhere. He and the cossack commander General Platov both played to the gallery and were rewarded with the adulation of the mob. But even they began to flag after a few days. When Blücher went to the house of Thomas Lawrence to have his portrait painted for the Prince Regent, the crowd forced their way in and jostled the artist. When Platov came a few days later, he took the precaution of posting a guard of cossacks outside. 'They are all sick to the death of the way they are followed about, and, above all, by the long dinners,' the diarist and politician Thomas Creevey reported to his wife. 'The King of Prussia is as sulky as a bear, and scarcely returns the civilities of the populace.'[8]

The pace was indeed daunting. In his laconic diary, Hardenberg notes that on his arrival, at 4 o'clock in the afternoon of 9 June, he had to shake hands with crowds of people, who virtually carried him into his lodgings in Berkeley Square, then he went to Carlton House for dinner with the Prince Regent, in the course of which Frederick William, Liverpool and Castlereagh were invested as Knights of the Garter, after which he went to the opera with Stewart and on to Lady Graham's with Blücher, not getting home till 3 o'clock in the morning. The next day he drove down to Ascot with Blücher, was 'nearly smothered' as they pushed their way through from their carriage to the Royal Box, and after the races went to dine with the Queen at Frogmore, getting back to London at 1 o'clock in the morning. The following day was taken up with calls, a reception for Frederick William by the Lord Mayor, followed by dinner with Liverpool and supper with Castlereagh, which Hardenberg gave up on and went to bed. 'It is not possible to bear any more of this fatigue,' he noted. He opted out of the royal boat trip to Woolwich on 13 June – to watch

Colonel Congreve give a demonstration of his rockets – and another to Oxford two days later.[9]

It was not just the number of parties that exhausted the visitors. 'The receptions are a fearful crush; people push and shove each other to get in and one finds oneself thrust into small rooms packed with four times as many people as they can hold,' complained Countess Nesselrode in a letter to her sister, adding that the British were socially inept and had no idea of how to host a party. After two decades of isolation from the Continent, not only had British women lost track of Continental fashions, the whole incipient rift between British and Continental society had widened into a chasm. The visitors and the hosts were equally nonplussed at each other's manners and habits. Metternich was astonished at what he saw, and wrote to his wife that London was more alien to the rest of Europe than Peking. 'The women are for the most part of great beauty, but their clothes are a fright,' he added.[10]

Alexander appeared to be enjoying himself. 'A fine waltzer, gallant with the ladies, showing interest only in the young ones and refusing to bestow even a word of politeness on those who were not,' in the words of Countess Lieven. 'He was mobbed, flattered and his conquests were as extensive as his flirtatiousness.' His popularity reflected humiliatingly on the Prince Regent's estrangement from his own people, who regularly pelted his carriage with mud and stones. According to Countess Lieven there were never fewer than 10,000 people gathered outside the Pulteney Hotel, blocking traffic on Piccadilly, while ladies bought tickets to stand on the stairs so they could see the Tsar close by as he went in or out. He occasionally slipped out through the mews at the back in order to avoid having to shake hands with them all.[11]

Alexander went his own way in London. He attended a meeting of the Bible Society and had a long talk with its most prominent members. He met some Quakers and regaled them with his plans for the regeneration of the world. He had a long discussion on the slave trade with Wilberforce, and put it about that he had always been for abolition, and that it had been Castlereagh who had insisted on allowing the French to carry on with the trade. And while he avoided questions about serfdom in Russia, he did take every opportunity to further his plans for Poland.[12]

Within days of reaching London he invited the leading Whig politician Lord Holland to a private audience, and followed this up with invitations to other members of the opposition such as Lord Grey, Lord Grenville and others. Behind these interviews lurked the hope that he might manage to win them over to his plans for Poland. But his efforts do not appear to have borne fruit, as Lord Grey left thinking him 'a vain, silly fellow'. Alexander also called on the philosopher Jeremy Bentham, who was sympathetic to the cause, and would later volunteer his services in drafting a project for a constitution for the kingdom of Poland.[13]

Czartoryski, who had arrived in London in Alexander's suite, had also been busy. He called on Castlereagh, to whom he explained that while the Poles realised they were unlikely to recover full independence, they nevertheless wished to be in a position to continue to live and develop as a nation. He proposed a number of variants which would guarantee this, from a reconstituted Poland under a Russian prince to a partitioned Poland which, though ruled by three different powers, would be recognised as a single state, with its own laws and institutions, an arrangement not dissimilar to the former Holy Roman Empire. Castlereagh listened politely but showed little interest. Czartoryski also talked to Grey and Holland, the legal reformer and Member of Parliament Sir Samuel Romilly and Wilberforce, and while all were enthusiastic in their support of the Polish cause, they could not accept a Poland under Russian rule. At the same time Castlereagh's old rival, now out of office, George Canning, told him that Britain would never go to war to prevent Russian doings in Poland.[14]

The vagaries of the Tsar and the caprices of the Grand Duchess reached new heights at a banquet held by the City of London at the Guildhall on 18 June. The occasion was supposed to have been an all-male one, but the Grand Duchess insisted on attending, so

Countess Lieven and the Duchess of York were also invited for the sake of seemliness. As they entered the Guildhall, passing through a throng of guests, with Frederick William leading the Grand Duchess, followed by the Tsar leading the Duchess of York and the Prince Regent with Countess Lieven, the Tsar insisted on pausing to talk to the chief Whigs he encountered, forcing the Prince Regent to stop and wait behind him.

When the royal party seated themselves at the high table and the musicians struck up the national anthem, the Grand Duchess threatened to have a nervous fit and the musicians were silenced. The astonishment of the several hundred denizens of the City seated at long tables stretching away before the sovereigns quickly turned to anger. The Prince Regent begged the Grand Duchess to permit 'God Save the King' to be played. When she refused, protesting that all music was objectionable to her, the murmurs of discontent turned into a menacing growl, and Countess Lieven was handed a note which read: 'If your Grand Duchess does not permit music, we cannot answer for what will happen to the royal table.' She passed on the information to the Grand Duchess, who relented with 'Let them bray, if they must!' The anthem was duly sung.

The imperial siblings seemed to vie with each other to annoy the Prince and his government. Alexander too snubbed the Prince's mistress Lady Hertford, and expressed the desire to call on the Princess of Wales, from which it took all Lieven's skill to dissuade him. Throughout the sight-seeing trip to Oxford, Blenheim and Stowe arranged by the Prince, Alexander varied his reactions between indifference and mockery, made disparaging remarks about the architecture and showed little interest in his investiture with an honorary doctorate. He was more interested in getting back to London on time to attend the ball given by Lady Jersey, the Prince's ex-mistress. And although he did not reach the capital until 3 o'clock in the morning, he nevertheless hurried to Lady Jersey's where he arrived 'with the sun'. Determined to make his point, he insisted on dancing Scottish reels until 5 o'clock.[15]

'Each succeeding day dispersed the halo of glory with which fancy had exalted the magnanimous Alexander,' Lady Shelley wrote in her diary. 'Reality, and a nearer approach, proves him to be a foolish, good-natured, dancing Dandy. Although he has more good qualities than bad, he is but a weak, vain coxcomb.' She later revised her opinion of his character, but not of his behaviour. Either way, as far as the general public was concerned 'their stay became, at last, a positive nuisance'. Fortunately, the end was in sight. After going to Portsmouth for a review of the fleet, Alexander and his sister took their leave of the Prince Regent at Petworth House, where they paused before travelling to Dover to take ship.[16]

Relieved as he must have felt to see the back of them, Castlereagh was deeply disappointed at the lack of progress made in the negotiations during the royal visit. Far from being easier to control than in Paris, Alexander had bad-temperedly refused to discuss anything that did not suit him, and appeared more determined than ever to pursue his Polish plans.

The ministers had met a few times, but always in a hurry. On 31 May Münster and Hardenberg had a meeting to resolve a number of issues concerning the line of demarcation between Prussian and Hanoverian administrations. On 2 June a full conference resolved the problem of provisioning the occupying troops. On 15 June Castlereagh and Hardenberg agreed that the fortresses of Mainz and Luxembourg should be garrisoned by troops of the future German federation. The following day they concentrated on how to organise the work of the forthcoming congress, and decided that the plenipotentiaries of Britain, Russia, Prussia and Austria, along with those of France, Spain and Sweden, would make up 'a committee which would bring forth the Project for the arrangement of Europe according to the plan previously agreed by the 4 courts, of Austria, Russia, England and Prussia'. The plenipotentiaries of these four courts should therefore meet in Vienna two weeks before the start of the congress in order to agree the project. With the exception of two further conferences dealing with the incorporation of Belgium into Holland and how its revenues were to be used, no other business was transacted.[17]

While Humboldt eschewed most of the entertainments and used his free time to view the Parthenon frieze brought back from Athens by Lord Elgin and other attractions in the British Museum, the only one who derived benefit as well as pleasure from his stay was Metternich. He did not much enjoy the social whirl, finding the manners of the natives too wild. And although Wilhelmina had also come to London, she hated the place and they had little opportunity to indulge their romance. Unlike Alexander, he enjoyed the trip to Oxford. 'One might be in the twelfth century,' he wrote to his wife from St John's College, where he stayed.[18]

He had arrived before the others, leaving Paris at midnight on 4 June, pausing to dine with Hardenberg and Humboldt at Amiens, arriving at Boulogne at 5.30 on the morning of 5 June, and, after a five-hour crossing and an overnight drive from Dover, reaching London in the early hours of the next day. The Emperor Francis had declined the invitation to come to London, pleading urgent duties at home. Unencumbered by his presence, Metternich could move more freely than his colleagues. He took up Aberdeen's invitation and lodged with him at the latter's London residence, Argyll House, off Oxford Street.

The bad behaviour of the others made Metternich appear both civilised and sensible; he harvested all the good will squandered by Alexander and Frederick William. He made himself extremely popular with the Prince Regent, whom he personally decorated with the Order of the Golden Fleece (for which a special dispensation was required, the Prince not being Catholic). He had also persuaded Francis to give the Prince an honorary colonelcy, and the white hussar uniform run up for him was a source of delight to the notoriously dressy Prince. Metternich also talked over all the outstanding matters with Castlereagh, and the two reached agreement on most of them.[19]

While Metternich went out of his way to cultivate Hardenberg and had a few meetings with him to discuss the arrangement of Germany, he was growing anxious at the possible consequences of Prussia's mounting insecurity. Prussia's failure to secure the gains she wanted prompted her to hold on to the various areas where her troops were stationed and to formulate plans for Germany which would give her greater dominance. But Metternich hoped to be able to wean Frederick William away from Alexander and combine with Prussia to resist what he called the Tsar's 'mad schemes' for Poland.

He foresaw tense negotiations ahead, and warned Francis not to begin standing down the army. Austria 'must maintain the most formidable military might until the end of the congress', he wrote. He did not trust Alexander at all by this stage, and thought him capable of making his own arrangements in the areas occupied by his troops in defiance of the other powers. He was nevertheless sanguine. 'We still have a storm to ride out but I am not afraid of it,' he wrote to Francis. 'Once again we are standing at the forefront of the good cause; the principles we proceed along are unassailable and must withstand the onslaught of the mad ideas of the Russian Emperor.'[20]

The date for the opening of the congress had been set in Paris as 1 July, but time was slipping by, and at a conference in London on 15 June the ministers decided to push it back to 15 August. They intended to meet in the first days of that month in order to prepare the plan that they would put to the steering committee of the seven powers. The congress itself, they believed, would not last beyond four to six weeks. But their plans were upset by Alexander, who declared that he must be present, and since he could not waste two months hanging about in western Europe he would go back to Russia. He was not prepared to come back before the end of September, and insisted that the congress should not open till 1 October.

This caused anxiety and raised doubts about his intentions. Metternich voiced fears that he might be planning some kind of *fait accompli*. Before the other powers agreed to the adjournment, Alexander was asked, and agreed, to pledge that he would make no decisions and take no action with regard to the territorial settlement in areas under occupation by his troops. The four ministers drew up and signed an agreement to keep 75,000 men each on a war footing, to be used only under joint decision. In the event, it was not the military threat, but the delay that would cause the greatest problems.[21]

14

~⚬~

Just Settlements

Compromise is usually the fruit of weariness, and comes at the end of a long process, not at the outset. Over the fourteen months leading up to the Treaty of Paris, diplomacy had been conducted on the hoof and the resulting arrangements had an *ad hoc* character. But they were nevertheless part of a continuing dialogue which bound the allies to make allowances and concessions. The postponement of the congress for another three months severed the chain of negotiation, leaving crucial issues unresolved.

Time breeds reflection and, as often as not, a wish to revise and correct. The three months following the London visit provided the allied ministers with the first real opportunity to stand back and take stock of what had been achieved, mull over the implications and reflect on possible corrections. They might have taken a wider view and asked themselves whether, since there was no longer any threat of war and they were all proposing to meet at Vienna in surroundings more conducive to wise reflection, they might not take the opportunity to rethink some of the decisions already taken in order to achieve a more balanced and considered settlement.

They did not. They had been away from home for months, they had neglected their properties and their families, they had not even been in a position to fulfil all the duties attendant on their positions. The sovereigns now had to busy themselves with a myriad matters deferred during their absence from court; the chancellors and Foreign Ministers had to tidy up ministries which had been left masterless for months. And when they did take their leisure, they distracted themselves either like Castlereagh, who revelled in the pleasures of his garden at Cray, or like Metternich, who basked in the company of Wilhelmina. They had no wish to reopen any of the arguments already settled, and hoped they would be able to resolve the outstanding issues in the shortest possible time and to cobble together an arrangement that would stick.

That was not how the dozens of lesser sovereigns, the scores of minor claimants and the hundreds of dispossessed petitioners who were preparing their journey to Vienna saw it. Since a general congress had been called, and since the monarchs of the three major Continental powers were due at Vienna along with their ministers, the assembly would be endowed with unprecedented powers and legitimacy: even the Pope had declared his readiness to attend. It would, in effect, constitute a kind of international supreme court – and a court of appeal. It was therefore not unreasonable to suppose that there was still everything to play for, and even those who had been dispossessed by one or other of the earlier treaties were allowed to hope that this august assembly would not deny them justice.

Their hopes were reflected in public opinion throughout Europe, which, even where no direct interests were involved, embraced the causes of others, such as oppressed nations or the slaves being traded across the Atlantic, longed for universal disarmament or simply hankered after some undefined new moral order. The advent of peace after a long war always brings out millenarian longings. 'Will the Congress of Vienna, this last hope for Europe, rise to the greatness of the moment?' pondered a French pamphleteer. An English publicist believed that it would. 'No, never has a more solemn assembly of men met to discuss greater interests,' he thundered. 'Never has a speechless Europe been seized by such violent and such just anxiety; never has the heart of the world itself been troubled by such expectation . . .' Some fancied that the congress would deliberate in open session in the great indoor riding school of the imperial palace at Vienna, whose galleries would be open to the public. Appropriately, it seemed, Beethoven began work on a choral piece to celebrate its opening.[1]

As they waited for the congress to assemble, people all over Europe reflected on the state of the Continent and discussed the possibilities. The more educated referred back to a long tradition of legal literature, beginning with the Dutch jurist Hugo Grotius, who in his masterful *De Iure Belli et Pacis*, published in 1625, affirmed that there was a divinely ordained general law governing all nations, which implied that no state could ever consider itself in isolation from others. The idea had been taken up and elaborated by Thomas Hobbes, Samuel Pufendorf and the Swiss Emeric de Vattel, and given its modern terminology of 'international law' in Bentham's *Principles of Morals and Legislation* (1789).

A more idealistic canon of literature, originating in the Renaissance, had addressed the problem of achieving perpetual peace. One of its most famous texts was in the memoirs of the duc de Sully, published in 1634. His *Grand Dessein*, allegedly the idea of King Henri IV, divided Europe into fifteen perfectly balanced states bound together in a confederation and governed by a congress. William Penn contributed his own vision in his *Essay towards the Present and Future Peace of Europe* (1693), as did Gottfried Wilhelm Leibniz and the Abbé de St Pierre, whose work of 1712 proposed a confederation of nineteen unequal but mutually supportive states. While they poured scorn on these and other similarly idealistic projects, Voltaire and Rousseau nevertheless wrote of the possibility of achieving lasting peace, and no educated European of 1814 could ignore the existence of the German philosopher Immanuel Kant's work *On Perpetual Peace*, published in 1796. The concept of a just peace to end all wars was by no means a novel one.

The Peace of Westphalia, signed in 1648 at the end of the Thirty Years' War, had set something of a precedent in this respect. It had brought together 109 delegates representing nearly two hundred parties, in negotiations that lasted for five years. It had redrawn the map of Europe, creating new independent states such as the United

Provinces of the Netherlands and the Swiss Confederation, it had created a new understanding of and attitude to state boundaries, and set the tone as well as procedures of diplomacy over the next century and a half. It was in part the breakdown of these procedures towards the end of the eighteenth century that had created the conditions for the Revolutionary and Napoleonic wars.

'What is called the balance was destroyed in 1772,' wrote Talleyrand. 'When we can go back to 1772, then we can start thinking of a balance.' But a straightforward balance of power no longer seemed sufficient to guarantee peace, and many felt that some kind of supranational system of control was needed. Such a view had been propounded by several philosophers in the course of the eighteenth century, but it was during the epic struggles that rent Europe in the first decade of the nineteenth that statesmen and even monarchs began to give voice to it. It was there in Alexander's proposals to Pitt, and clearly stated in the treaty between Russia and Prussia of November 1805, into which Alexander had inserted a clause to the effect that the peace congress which would follow the hostilities must bind all its decisions into a package which was to be placed under the joint guarantee of all the powers.[2]

Writing to the Prince Regent in July 1812, as he contemplated an alliance with Britain, Alexander had expressed the desire for less horse-trading and less formality in foreign affairs, 'and more of those generous and ardent feelings which would permit one to envisage all the nations united for the salvation of their liberty like brothers eager to offer each other succour'. It was selfishness that had brought about the current sorry state of affairs, and he was determined that egoism must be banished from international affairs. Less than a year later, he enshrined his feelings in the preamble of the Treaty of Kalisch. 'The time will come when treaties will no longer be mere truces, when they will once more be observed with that religious faith, that sacred inviolability which underlies the esteem, the power and the preservation of empires,' it ran.[3]

There was, therefore, every reason to suppose that the sovereigns and statesmen who would be taking part in the congress at Vienna were thinking of creating a better world, based no longer on the mutual fear inherent in mere balance but on a sense of collective responsibility for the future peace and well-being of the Continent.

Since the peacemakers were bent on overturning the 'system of usurpations' of the French Revolution and the Napoleonic era, they could have invoked the principle of legitimacy, and many felt that the logical starting point would have been a return to the *status quo ante* of 1792. But invocation of legitimacy against the Revolutionary and Napoleonic 'usurpations' had a sting in the tail.[4]

While most of what had been done since 1792 was indeed at variance with all accepted canons of international law and practice, Revolutionary and Napoleonic France had not been the only state to overthrow dynasties and legal political structures. Various German states had acquiesced in this and gained from it, most notably Prussia, which had been happy to help itself to territories along the Rhine and to Hanover at the prompting of the French. Russia had grabbed Finland from Sweden with Napoleon's blessing. Austria had eagerly taken over Venice and abolished the Most Serene Republic. And all three had sliced up Poland while her anointed monarch was carted off into Russian captivity.

Restitution was hardly a viable option in most cases. Over the preceding two decades states had been overrun and either reorganised or abolished, lost provinces and gained others. Institutions and individuals had suffered the same fate. Justice demanded that states be restored to their rightful rulers, that legitimate institutions be resuscitated and re-endowed, and that individuals be allowed to take possession of the property of which they had been violently and illegally stripped. But new states, new institutions and new owners, not always evil usurpers, had taken the place of the old and created a new status quo. Their rights could not be disregarded entirely. And even if the principle of restitution were to be accepted as the guiding one, there was still the problem of when exactly the legitimate status quo had begun to be overturned.

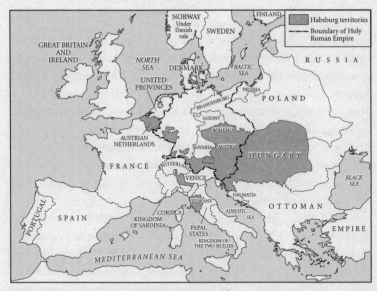

Europe in 1792

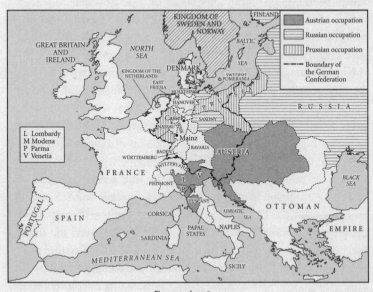

Europe in 1814

If 1792 were chosen, Britain would have to return French, Dutch and Danish colonies, France would have to give up more territory, Russia would have to return Finland to Sweden, hundreds of German sovereignties would have to be restored along with the Holy Roman Empire, Louisiana would have to be bought back from the United States and returned to Spain, and a kingdom of Poland would have to be restored, entailing loss of territory for Russia, Prussia and Austria. Church property would have to be returned on a massive scale throughout the Continent: across Catholic Europe, some 20 per cent of agricultural land had belonged to the Church in 1792, and all but a fraction of it had been confiscated.[5]

But no other date could guarantee any degree of fairness. By the Treaty of Kalisch, Prussia had staked her claim to a return to her status in 1805. But she had acquired much of that between 1792 and 1805, as a direct result of playing the hyena to Revolutionary France. Austria had lost a great deal of land during those same years, so a return to the status quo of 1805 would be less favourable to her.

Talk of carve-ups and compensations naturally raised another question, which had been exercising people's minds a great deal over the past century, namely that of the rights of nations as distinct from those of rulers. The idea that only a nation had the right to decide its own destiny had not been new when the American colonists declared themselves to be one in 1776, and that is why their cause had been so warmly supported throughout Europe. That was also why educated Europeans denounced the partitions of Poland and rejoiced when the Bastille was stormed on 14 July 1789. The heroic *guerrilla* carried on by the Spanish people against the French invaders, the stalwart patriotism shown by the Russian people in 1812 and the enthusiasm of the Germans in throwing off the French yoke in 1813 excited widespread admiration. And while the Poles and the Italians had been on the side of the French, their desire to enjoy freedom alongside their sister nations was self-evident and widely approved. But their aspirations would have to come second to more urgent considerations, of which there were a bewildering and growing number.

During the summer of 1814 a new element had entered the equation: as the first flush of enthusiasm for that paragon of chivalry, Alexander, wore off it began to dawn on people that Russia had gained consistently at every turn in the late wars, and increased her state of possession enormously. This rendered both Austria and Prussia vulnerable, and as those powers were the only ones that could possibly counterbalance Russia, it meant that they would have to be reinforced by the addition of territory, and this strategic need would have to override any considerations of legitimacy. The greater good of the Continent came first. When the Pope's representative asked Metternich before the start of the congress whether he could see his way to evacuating the Legations, a Papal province occupied by Austria, he received the reply that it was 'a European matter'.[6]

But *realpolitik* was not the only light in which the interests of Europe were viewed, and the longer the opening of the congress was deferred, the more the hopes of idealists and dreamers were allowed to expand. By the beginning of the autumn of 1814 much that had appeared entirely settled a few months before was being openly questioned, and with good reason.

A case in point was the situation in Scandinavia. Sweden had joined the coalition against Napoleon in 1812 on the understanding that she would be compensated for Swedish Pomerania, which Napoleon had taken from her, and for Finland, which Russia had annexed, with Norway, then part of the kingdom of Denmark, and Guadeloupe, a French colony in British hands.

Denmark had stood by Napoleon to the last, and when forced to join the coalition against him agreed, by the Treaty of Kiel, to cede Norway to Sweden. Denmark was to receive Swedish Pomerania and the island of Rügen, and be paid one million thalers. It recovered its colonies from Britain, minus Heligoland, which Britain retained, but not its fleet. Britain and Sweden undertook to obtain compensation for Denmark somewhere in Europe for the loss of Norway and Heligoland.

But the Norwegians, who had been under the Danish crown for

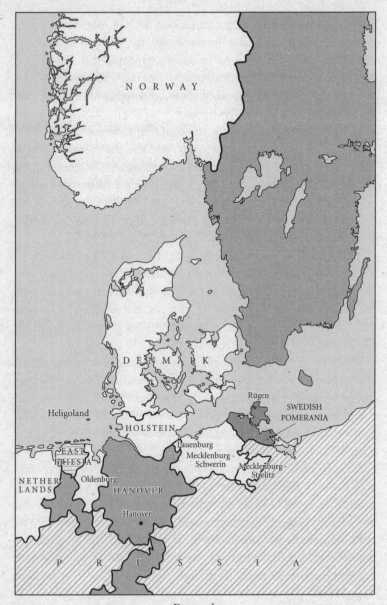

Denmark

five hundred years, balked at becoming Swedish subjects. On 17 May 1814 they proclaimed their independence and elected Prince Christian of Denmark, heir to the Danish throne, as their King. They sent a representative, Carsten Anker, to London to seek British support. Liverpool received Anker coolly. He told him that Britain would not recognise or assist the Norwegians, that Sweden was an ally of Britain, and that for years Norway, as part of Denmark, had waged war on Britain.

The terms of the treaty between Britain and Sweden required the Royal Navy to blockade the rebellious Norwegians, even though by that stage the British government was extremely unwilling to assist Bernadotte in any way. Liverpool despatched a mission to Norway in an attempt to broker a peaceful resolution, but this proved a forlorn hope. As Bernadotte proceeded to apply military force to take possession of Norway, and the Norwegians resisted, public opinion in Britain was greatly exercised, and the government had to ride out some stormy moments whipped up by the opposition.[7]

The result was an ugly stand-off in the region. Bernadotte took the line that since he was being obliged to subdue Norway by force, the provisions of the Treaty of Kiel were invalid. He refused to evacuate the Danish province of Holstein, let alone hand over Swedish Pomerania, Rügen or any cash. He was tacitly supported by Alexander, who had omitted to ratify the Treaty of Kiel and therefore to implement any of its conditions. As soon as Bernadotte's troops had evacuated Holstein in order to take possession of Norway, their place was taken by a force of 60,000 Russians under Bennigsen, who lived off the land and refused to hand over its administration to the Danish authorities. Alexander was, according to one Russian diplomat, hoping that the King of Denmark would not come to the congress, which would leave him with a free hand. The Swedish Foreign Minister, Lars von Engestrom, believed the whole matter should be kept out of the congress, in the hope that Sweden might get to keep the territories she was occupying.[8]

It did not look good. The whole point of defeating Napoleon had been to rescue Europe from the arbitrary exercise of power. Yet here were the victorious forces of legitimacy supporting the ambitions of an upstart Napoleonic marshal against a respectable monarch and the wishes of a nation. What was happening at the mouth of the Baltic was distinctly embarrassing to the statesmen of the great powers. Equally embarrassing was what was happening in Spain.

The country had been Britain's ally for several years, but her King, Ferdinand VII, had been a prisoner in France since 1808, and so the only agency the British government could deal with was the Regency appointed by the Cortes, the assembly of Spanish patriots, entrenched in Cadiz, the only part of Spain not occupied by the French. While entirely dependent on British military assistance in the form of Wellington and his army, the Cortes and the Regency jealously guarded a fiction of control over Spain and overall command of the allied forces in the peninsula. With their country cleared of the French invader, they were even less inclined to play the role of grateful beneficiary, as Wellington and his brother Sir Henry Wellesley, the British minister in Spain, were beginning to discover. Nor indeed was the King of Spain, released from French captivity and eager to resume his throne.

King Ferdinand was a traditionalist who meant to restore the *ancien régime*, and there were many in Spain who welcomed this. But much had changed since he had been deposed in 1808. The liberal ideas brought into the peninsula by the French armies had had an effect, and in 1812 the Cortes themselves had brought in a constitution. The returning King was determined to abolish this and all other traces of liberalism, and asked for British military support for this purpose. Wellington refused. He had a low opinion of the Spanish constitution of 1812, which he described as 'amongst the worst of the modern productions of that nature', but he did not favour the alternative – rule by a camarilla of reactionary clerics and courtiers. He expressed the hope that the King could be prevailed upon to take into account 'the temper of the times', as he put it.[9]

That temper did not suit Ferdinand, and in May he abolished the constitution, splitting the country and the army. Wellington rushed back from France to prevent a civil war. 'I think,' he wrote to Castlereagh from Toulouse, 'I can keep them both quiet.' From Madrid he reported ten days later that the abolition of the constitution had been greeted with demonstrations of loyalty to the King, which had encouraged the latter to start persecuting the *Liberales*, as all those who did not see things his way were known, and to bring back the Inquisition. By the beginning of June, Wellington was becoming exasperated by the intractability of the King and his government. He was also alarmed at their truculence in international matters. His request that they return the district of Olivenza, taken from Portugal and added to Spain by Napoleon, was brushed aside.[10]

Ferdinand sent an ambassador to Paris to negotiate a treaty with France separately from the other allies. He demanded not only that all the Spanish colonies that had declared independence be recognised as Spanish, but that France should buy Louisiana back from the United States in order to restore that. A Bourbon himself, he insisted that all the territories in Italy ruled over by various branches of the Bourbon dynasty in 1792 be restored to them intact. Wellington even feared that Ferdinand might lead Spain into alliance with Bourbon France for this purpose. This fear made Wellesley temper the terms of the new treaty of alliance between Britain and Spain, in order to get it signed – for Castlereagh it was essential that France and Spain be kept apart.

Public opinion in Britain was not impressed by the stories of repression coming from Spain, and the government had to put up with much unpopularity as a result of being seen as weak in dealing with Ferdinand. All Wellington could do was to give the wayward King a kind of written sermon detailing how he should rule. The irony was that Ferdinand was only King by the grace of Napoleon, and had legitimacy really had anything to do with it, he would have been ignored by the allies in favour of his father, Charles IV, who had been forced to abdicate in his favour by Napoleon.[11]

A similar lack of principle was evident in Italy. Britain had been conducting an essentially opportunistic policy there, the object of which was to safeguard her base of Malta by keeping Sicily out of French hands. Ferdinand IV of Naples, who had been forced out of his mainland kingdom, was ensconced in the Sicilian part under the protection of the Royal Navy and a small British military presence.

Ferdinand was no more a natural partner for Britain than his Spanish namesake and cousin, and the alliance was an uneasy one. It was not made any easier by the character of the British minister at Palermo, the thirty-six-year-old Lieutenant-General Lord William Bentinck. Bentinck had fought with distinction at Marengo, in Flanders, Egypt and Spain, and was generally highly thought of, despite having made a mess of things during his governorship of Madras. He was entirely unsuited to the court to which he was accredited: Ferdinand was a lazy, pleasure-loving, weak and false autocrat, governed only by fear of his wife Maria Carolina, an aunt of the Emperor Francis. Bentinck's pronounced liberal views were at variance with their autocratic ones, but, since he was the representative of the only power that stood between Ferdinand and the French, he was in a position to make them felt.

Ferdinand, and particularly his Queen, had made themselves unpopular in Sicily by curtailing the prerogatives of the local nobles, and Bentinck took up their cause on his arrival in 1811. He began a relentless struggle with the Queen which ended in her removal from the island and despatch to the court of her nephew in Vienna in 1813. He also demanded reforms of Ferdinand, which culminated in the adoption in 1812 of a constitution modelled on the British one.

Bentinck, who was enamoured of Italy and believed it should be liberated and united under one crown, had a view of his mission far beyond any entertained in London. His reforms in Sicily were meant as a model which could be exported to the Italian mainland when the time came, and he anticipated that the monarch who would be chosen to rule over this enlarged and liberalised Italian state would not be the one he was accredited to. He was exasperated by the weakness, greed and treacherousness of the royal family, discouraged by the attitudes of those he brought into public life as a counter-

Italy – the final settlement

balance to them, and appalled by the seemingly endemic corruption. At one point he even dreamed of turning Sicily into a British colony as the only means of providing it with decent government.[12]

Bentinck's activities and the various British-inspired attempts at raising anti-Austrian or anti-French guerrilla revolts in other parts of the peninsula suggested to many Italian patriots that the British government was in favour of an Italian state. Nothing could have been further from the truth. Neither Liverpool nor Castlereagh had any knowledge of what was going on in the peninsula or any interest in it, beyond that of ensuring that it was placed beyond the reach of French influence. They were caught out by events in 1813.

The Austrians had had little difficulty in expelling the weak French garrisons from Illyria, but paused on the borders of the kingdom of Italy, which was defended by Prince Eugène and his Franco-Italian army. From Frankfurt in November 1813 Metternich had tried to win Eugène over with the offer, made through his father-in-law the King of Bavaria, of a duchy or even a kingdom in Italy, and the offer was repeated at the beginning of 1814. Prince Eugène refused.[13]

The Austrian commander in Italy, Marshal Bellegarde, then tried to exploit the nationalism of the Italians, calling on the inhabitants of Lombardy to rise against the French. When this failed the clash of arms could no longer be delayed, and the two armies met in a bloody battle on the river Mincio on 8 February 1814, a French victory but an inconclusive one.

The Austrians hoped that Murat would come to their aid by marching up from the south and forcing Prince Eugène to withdraw. Murat had just, on 11 January 1814, concluded an alliance with Austria, which guaranteed him possession of the kingdom of Naples and even promised him additional territory with 400,000 inhabitants at the Pope's expense on condition that he joined the coalition and used his 30,000-strong army against the French. But instead of bringing this force to bear in support of Bellegarde, Murat occupied the Papal territory he coveted, and then paused in Tuscany. From there he began to promote the idea of a united Italy under his own rule, adopting a manner he thought suited to attract the affection of the Italians. 'Murat was seated as a Sultan – Princes and Dukes all standing behind his throne-chair,' noted General Wilson in his diary after seeing him at the opera. 'He is by far the best actor that has appeared in the *royalty theatre*.'[14]

Wilson was the British Commissioner attached to Bellegarde's staff.

He was a Whig, and an ardent supporter of enslaved nations. He could not restrain himself from encouraging every patriotic Italian he met, giving the entirely erroneous impression that Britain was favourable to their cause. The French invasion of Italy had done much to stir up patriotic aspirations in various parts of the peninsula, and French rule had produced a generation of soldiers and administrators ready to give them form. They were naturally encouraged, if somewhat bewildered, to find both the Austrians and Murat apparently backing the idea of Italian independence. Wilson's loose talk raised their hopes even higher, while their sense of confusion increased when Bentinck entered the fray.

Bentinck had been instructed by Castlereagh to reach some kind of agreement with Murat, now Austria's ally and therefore a member of the anti-Napoleonic coalition. This was to be a prelude to the landing of a small British force on the Italian mainland where it could begin operations against the French. As Castlereagh found the Italian scene confusing, he left Bentinck some leeway as to how and on what terms he was to proceed. Bentinck did not like Murat, and even considered him as a kind of rival. For Bentinck had his own vision.

On 9 March 1814, as the allied plenipotentiaries were acting out their charade at Châtillon, Bentinck landed at Leghorn (Livorno) with 6,000 British and a small number of Sicilian troops. As soon as he stepped ashore he issued a proclamation calling on the whole of Italy to rise and resume her place among the nations of Europe. He moved on to Genoa, which he liberated from its French garrison, and then proclaimed the restoration of the Republic. From there he wrote to Wilson encouraging him to exhort the Milanese to rise, giving him and them to understand that Britain would view their actions with favour.

On 16 April, hearing of Napoleon's abdication, Prince Eugène evacuated Milan, leaving the Italian administrators and military personnel in place and withdrawing across the Alps with the remainder of his French troops. This left the Napoleonic kingdom of Italy a focus for the ambitions of every faction. One group of Italian patriots opted for the protection of Britain, suggesting a kingdom of Lombardy with either the Duke of Cambridge or the Duke of Clarence as King, and an envoy was duly sent to London. A larger number wanted the same kingdom under Austrian protection, with Archduke Francis of Austria-Este as King. A deputation was sent to Paris to lobby Metternich, who, with his usual eye for an opportunity, allowed them to hope.[15]

In the meantime, Bellegarde cut the argument short by fomenting a revolution in Milan on 20 April and marching in to re-establish order. Austria took possession of most of northern Italy, disregarding the rights and feelings of all parties. To the envoys of the former republic of Lucca, who had come to plead for the restoration of their independence, the Emperor Francis replied: '*Tutti hanno fame, anch'io voglio mangiare; emmeglio che io vi mangi che se fosse un altro.*' ('Everyone is hungry, and I need to eat too; and it is better that I should eat you than another.')[16]

This suited Castlereagh, who disowned Bentinck's behaviour, which he termed 'most absurd' in a letter to Liverpool. To Bentinck he explained that he did not 'wish that the too extensive experiment already in operation throughout Europe, in the science of government, should be at once augmented by similar creations in Italy'.[17]

'It is impossible not to perceive a great moral change coming on in Europe, and that the principles of freedom are in full operation,' he continued. 'The danger is, that the transition may be too sudden to ripen into anything likely to make the world better or happier. We have new constitutions launched in France, Spain, Holland, and Sicily. Let us see the results before we encourage farther attempts.' He himself had few illusions. Knowing nothing of the countries under discussion, he could only rely on reports from his diplomats, and these were not encouraging. Bentinck's successor at Palermo reported that the locals were 'totally and radically unfit to be trusted with political power', deploring 'their natural depravity at bottom, which will always rise, when the hand of power be removed, to ruin and destroy the fairest projects of philanthropy'.[18]

There was no philanthropy in evidence when the Sardinian King Victor Emmanuel entered Turin on 20 May 1814. The university was closed down the same day. The next day he decreed a return to the laws as they had been in 1770, which meant the reintroduction of torture, flogging, quartering and breaking on the wheel, along with ecclesiastical courts and the royal *lettre de cachet*, and announced that he considered everything that had happened since 1798, when he had been chased out by the French, as 'a long dream' and therefore immaterial. Taking an old court almanac of 1789 he reinstated everyone in their old posts, not pausing to check whether they were still alive. Powdered wigs and the rococo style were brought back into court life, and people whose handwriting reflected a French education lost their jobs. It was said that he even refused to be treated by a physician who had continued to practise under French rule.[19]

All legal transactions, including sales of property, contracts, mortgages and inheritances, that had taken place after 1798 were declared null and void, and this was only reversed when the King was made to understand that his state would cease to function. He nevertheless declared all children born to marriages contracted according to the civil procedure in force over the past sixteen years to be bastards. Everyone of French extraction who had settled in Piedmont was ordered out. 'Frenchmen domiciled there for thirty years, landowners married to Piedmontese women, were expelled from their homes by royal carabineers, conducted to the frontier like criminals, without having been charged with the slightest reproach,' according to one contemporary.[20]

Castlereagh had long ago decided that northern Italy should fall to Austria and a Piedmont enlarged by the absorption of Genoa. These two would defend the smaller independent states to the south, including the Papal dominions, from French influence and from Naples, which, whether it was ruled by Murat or its former King, Ferdinand, might provide a conduit for French designs.

The danger represented by Murat had increased exponentially when Napoleon had been sent to Elba, since the two were in a position to combine at any moment, giving Napoleon a landing ground on the European mainland through which to make a comeback. Castlereagh would have liked to see Murat ousted, but Metternich argued that they could not very well attack him while he was still an ally of Austria, and assured Castlereagh that he would bring about his own downfall sooner or later. But Castlereagh was not convinced, and he and Wellington continued to consider plans for a military expedition against him.[21]

One argument in favour of leaving Murat put for the time being was that it gave Britain some measure of leverage over King Ferdinand of Sicily, who was hell-bent on persecuting the liberals who had worked with the British. Castlereagh realised that as soon as he no longer needed British support, all the Sicilian liberals along with their constitution would be easy prey. On the other hand, Murat was in occupation of some of the Papal provinces, and the Pope counted for something too.

One of the more curious sideshows of the London season that year had been the appearance, for the first time since the reign of Queen Mary, of the red flash of a cardinal's robes. The Pope's envoy, Cardinal Consalvi, made a point of wearing full regalia, down to red stockings and slippers, when he called on the Prince Regent and on Castlereagh. The Prince was delighted by the show and treated him with cordiality, while the crowds in the street followed him about in fascination and with a surprising degree of polite respect. Castlereagh was less interested in the Cardinal's robes than in what support he could get out of him. For if the Pope, who was desperate to recover his dominions at the forthcoming congress, appeared to be the petitioner in this instance, there was much that he could do for Castlereagh.

A Bill for the emancipation of the Catholics in Ireland had been rejected by Parliament by one vote in 1811, and by four in 1814. The Catholics of England and those of Ireland were divided on its provision that Catholic clergy would swear the oath of allegiance, that bishops would be nominated by the British government, and that all their communications with Rome would be vetted. Castlereagh, who represented himself as a friend of the Catholics, wanted the Pope to bring his influence to bear in the matter. He also needed his help on the issue of the slave trade, whose abolition the British public so ardently desired and which was by now being carried on solely by Catholic countries.[22]

Castlereagh was therefore inclined to view the Pope as an ally, notwithstanding that he had celebrated liberation from French rule in much the same way as the King of Sardinia. All those classed as collaborators or freethinkers, which included virtually the entire civil administration and the educational establishment, were dismissed and replaced, where possible, by those who had been in charge before the French had invaded Italy. Old tribunals and feudal rights were reinstated, the Jews were sent back to the ghetto, and the Inquisition was revived, as was the Jesuit Order. In their enthusiasm for reversing everything that the French had done, the new authorities not only abolished the Code Napoléon, disbanded the National Guard and reversed the sale of Church properties, but also turned off the street lighting and forbade vaccination.[23]

But if Italy presented a lamentable spectacle of bigotry, injustice and greed sanctioned by the pragmatism of the great powers, Germany appeared as a land laid waste, strewn with trampled rights and dashed expectations. It was by far the most important element in the impending European settlement, yet few of the statesmen showed any signs of being alive to this. Its minor rulers were at odds with each other and with their people, and neither Metternich nor Hardenberg had formulated a plan, let alone a vision, for the future.

Setting the Stage

Metternich's return to Vienna on 18 July had been marked by a singular show of appreciation. The city authorities organised what amounted to a serenade outside the windows of his office in the State Chancellery, with the musicians and singers of the court and city theatres executing Beethoven's *Prometheus* overture followed by a cantata specially composed for the occasion extolling the Foreign Minister's virtues and saluting his achievements.

He was exhausted, so nobody was surprised that he moved to Baden bei Wien, a fashionable spa town in the Vienna woods two hours' carriage-drive from the city, where he rented a house. When he was at the Chancellery his ante-rooms filled up with petitioners of one kind or another, whereas in Baden nobody could importune him. Over the next two months he would take work out and spend several days on end there, and even when he did need to come into the Chancellery, he would drive out to Baden again after finishing work.

Metternich was good at combining work with pleasure. His wife and children joined him for part of the time, alternating between Baden and his elegant Viennese residence set in extensive gardens on the Rennweg, just outside the old city. Their marriage had from the beginning been one of convenience. His wife was intelligent and socially accomplished, the perfect consort for a man of his standing and ambitions, and she played her part with dedication. He loved her and treated her with the greatest respect, while never letting her existence get in the way of his *amours*.

Baden was a popular resort for those fleeing the summer heat of the city, and another who had taken a house there was Wilhelmina. On Metternich's return from London she had complained that their hearts 'no longer meet at any point'. 'I am beginning to think that we never really knew each other, that we are both of us pursuing an illusion,' she wrote. She felt that he had placed her on too high a pedestal, and that consequently she had fallen too low in his estimation.[1]

It is not clear what had brought about this fall, but it may have been the discovery that she had been having an affair with the young Frederick Lamb, Aberdeen's secretary, who had been in charge while his superior was at allied headquarters. Lamb was combining duty with pleasure, since he was using Wilhelmina to obtain information about Metternich and passing it on to London.[2]

Whatever the problem, the next two months yielded some idyllic moments which made Metternich believe that he and Wilhelmina had become 'inseparable' and were destined to 'share happiness and misfortune' forever. There were nevertheless some violent scenes between the lovers, and the unfortunate Gentz, who was also summering at Baden and taking the renowned waters, had to listen to the blow-by-blow accounts of each.[3]

Metternich nevertheless did manage to give some thought to the lowering problem of Germany. But he could not, even if he had wished to, indulge any fresh radical thoughts, as the territorial arrangements had been agreed in outline by the ministers of the four powers some months before. Prussia would take most of Saxony and extensive areas along the Rhine. Austria was to recover provinces lost to Bavaria in the wars of 1805 and 1809, such as the Tyrol and the Salzburg-Inn district, along with Passau, both strategic imperatives as they covered the Brenner pass and the Danube respectively. The British royal house would repossess Hanover, which was to be elevated to the status of a kingdom, while the other states of the Rheinbund would continue much as they were, with whatever rearrangements were deemed necessary.

But before any of this could be fixed in final form, two fundamental questions needed to be resolved: how much of Poland could be prised away from Alexander, which would clarify how much compensation Prussia would require in Germany, and what indemnities Bavaria would insist on in lieu of Mainz before she relinquished the Tyrol and other areas that were to be returned to Austria.

The first priority was to force Alexander to abandon his plan for a kingdom of Poland and accept a partition of the territory of the grand duchy of Warsaw. In the first place this would reduce the Russian threat and lessen fears of Polish national aspirations in the area. Second, it was only once they knew how much of their old Polish territory they were going to recover that Austria and Prussia could proceed with a division of spoils and influence in Germany. Until Prussia took possession of whatever she was going to obtain in Poland, Saxony and elsewhere in Germany, no single border in Germany could be definitively fixed, any more than the southern and eastern borders of Holland.

What made this all the more pressing for Metternich was that in seeking to accommodate Prussia, he had repeatedly given Hardenberg to understand that he would be able to annex all of Saxony, and in doing so he had over-reached himself. His imperial master, who was closely related by marriage to Frederick Augustus of Saxony, did not like the idea of removing a legitimate ruler from his throne. And public opinion, both in Vienna and throughout most of Germany, particularly Catholic southern Germany, in which Metternich hoped to maintain Austria's influence, was very much against it.

The first foreign plenipotentiary to call on him that summer was the King of Saxony's envoy Count Friedrich von der Schulenburg. Metternich told him that Austria would regard the proposed abolition of the Saxon kingdom as a political crime, that the Emperor Francis was determined that at least part of it should be preserved for its rightful King, and that he himself would do everything in his power to persuade Prussia to drop her claim. But it was only by getting Alexander to give Prussia large tracts of her former Polish possessions that Metternich was going to be able to persuade Hardenberg to relinquish his claims to any part of Saxony.[4]

Until this, and ultimately the Bavarian question, was resolved, the situation would remain fluid – all the more so as most of the states concerned claimed far more than they needed to, insistently demanding provinces which they regarded as entirely expendable in order to have bargaining counters and keep their options open.

One of the worst offenders in this respect was Prussia, whose King and ministers were gripped by insecurity. The Treaty of Chaumont had elevated her to great-power status by placing her on an equal footing with Britain, Russia and Austria, but it was only a piece of paper. Until she came into physical possession of her designated prizes, she would be haunted by the fear of losing that status. That was why Hardenberg insisted that Prussia must end up with at least thirteen million inhabitants, or 'souls', not the nine million that she had in 1805, why Prussian troops had occupied Mainz, and why he would assert vehemently that only the four signatories of that treaty had any say in anything.

Since there was no possibility of finalising the territorial arrangement of Germany at this stage, Metternich encouraged Hardenberg to concentrate on its future constitution. They had agreed in London that they would coordinate their plans in mid-August, in order to have a joint agreement ready before the opening of the congress.[5]

In accordance with the Treaty of Paris all the German states, including Prussia and Austria, were to be bound into a federation stable enough to exclude outside interference and strong enough to defend itself from pressure or even military aggression. Granted that a single state was out of the question, what was required was a replacement for the Holy Roman Empire, a new federation or Bund.

The spirit of the times as well as the circumstances demanded a voluntary coming together of all the parties involved. And while many of the smaller states and minor interests clamoured for a return to

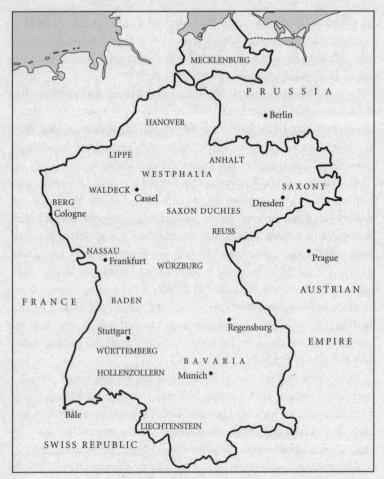

The Confederation of the Rhine

the old Reich under Austrian suzerainty, this was not acceptable to larger states such as Bavaria or Württemberg. It was also undesirable from Austria's point of view – not that Metternich did not wish to play a leading role in Germany. In collaboration with Josef von Pilat, editor of the *Österreichischer Beobachter*, and with the help of Adam Müller and Friedrich Schlegel, Metternich and Gentz projected a vision of Austria as the spiritual leader of a new Germany, drawing her strength and inspiration from a romanticised view of a medieval Catholic past. Such a role would give her influence without responsibility and greater freedom of manoeuvre.

The new Bund would have to be governed by a Diet. But how that Diet was to be elected and what powers it was to enjoy were grounds for radical disagreement. It was clear that neither the Emperor of Austria nor the King of Prussia would willingly abdicate their sovereignty to a federal Diet. Yet they both expected all the other states in the federation to do so. Those who had been elevated to the kingship by Napoleon were unlikely to oblige. The King of Württemberg, a grotesquely fat man as repulsive in character as in body who was such a despot that his own brother begged Stein to find him an alternative estate somewhere in Germany so he did not have to live under his dominion, was determined not to acknowledge any higher power.[6]

Yet neither he nor any of the other rulers was entirely master in his own house. When Napoleon had abolished the Holy Roman Empire and created the Rheinbund, he had preserved the sovereignty of hundreds of minor princes and nobles, replacing their former bond with the Emperor to one with their new King and a right of appeal to himself. It was his way of keeping the whip-hand over the new rulers he had elevated: the King of Württemberg had nineteen princes, twelve counts and some 120 knights within his realm, whose persons, estates and subjects were largely exempt from his authority. These 'mediatised' Standesherren were naturally in conflict with the rulers, as their interests were diametrically opposed. They had clubbed together in various groups, whose representatives lobbied the ministers and monarchs of the great powers for support.[7]

Another element in the equation were those sovereign princes, counts and knights of the Holy Roman Empire who had been stripped of their privileges, and in some cases of their property as well, by Napoleon's reworkings. They included some influential figures and they had a strong case to make. Although their interests were not the same as those of their mediatised cousins, they were also at variance with those of the rulers.

Finally there were those, not so powerful but numerous and voluble, who denounced all these as petty despots standing in the way of a united Germany, and who wanted to see the imposition of a pan-German liberal legal structure that would create one by the back door. If a federal system of justice could be imposed on the whole area, then the local rulers would be effectively neutered and every inhabitant of Germany empowered. Humboldt also favoured the introduction of a kind of bill of rights endowing every German with freedom of movement, of speech and so on.

A number of schemes had been produced, by Stein, Humboldt and others in the course of the previous twelve months, and during the summer of 1814 Hardenberg and Humboldt were both working on new ones, the former in Berlin, the latter in Vienna, where he was accredited as ambassador. In an ideal world Humboldt would, like Stein, have liked to see a united Germany, rid of all the minor rulers. But he was a realist. He also had an idiosyncratic view of the very nature of Germany. 'There is perhaps no other country that deserves more than Germany to be independent and free, because no other is so inclined to use its freedom purely and simply to benefit everybody at home,' he had written to his wife a few months earlier. 'Of all the nations, the Germans have the least destructive and most constructive spirit.'[8]

He believed that Germany's cultural superiority lay in its very diversity, in the rich variety of the communities that made it up, each of them developing organically along its own path. He regarded the preservation of this heritage from outside influence or aggression as the main priority, and therefore saw the principal function of the federation as common defence. Germany did not need to be a great power. As long as Germany could be safeguarded from the evils of invasion, both cultural and military, she would blossom into a dominant civilisation.[9]

Humboldt did not like Metternich, and he regarded Austria as a mongrel power whose interests in Italy and other non-German lands disqualified her from a dominant role in German affairs. He favoured the Standesherren and the dispossessed princes, whom he saw as emanations of German cultural particularism. He also saw in them a useful weapon against Austria's natural allies in southern Germany, Bavaria, Württemberg and Baden. He spent the summer in Vienna, never seeing Metternich as he hated going out into society, working on a project for the German federation.

Unbeknown to him, Hardenberg had also applied himself to the task, and soon produced a project contained in forty-one articles. These more or less summed up the consensus reached in discussions with Metternich over the past year. The project envisaged a governing council composed of the 'directors' of nine *Kreise*, or regional group-ings of states, and a federal Diet with seats for all the sovereign princes and representatives of the mediatised Standesherren. It provided for a federal court of justice, but did not envisage far-reaching harmonis-ation in terms of rights. All the states in the federation were to contribute to its defence and could not go to war without common consent. The only exceptions were Austria and Prussia, which could wage war independently, but would not be entitled to the support of the others in wars not waged in defence of the federation.

Hardenberg's project did not accord with the ideas of either Hum-boldt or Stein, who thought it unwieldy and would have preferred tighter federal ties, with less prominence given to the princes. Ironi-cally, Stein, who had been one of the first and most vocal advocates of a united Germany with a liberal constitution, now found himself sidelined and largely powerless. He was the representative of Alex-ander, which placed him in a false position *vis-à-vis* his German colleagues and severely limited what he could say. Yet Alexander was no longer prepared to be guided by him on German matters, and Stein would often find himself having to promote initiatives he did not agree with. He nevertheless continued to put his case through Joseph von Görres, editor of the nationalist *Rheinische Merkur*.

Hardenberg's project would also upset other parties. At the

beginning of September Metternich received a visit from Baron von Gartner, whose calling card announced that he was the 'Plenipotentiary of 42 Princes and Counts', and who demanded the reestablishment of a Holy Roman Empire under the house of Austria, modified to accommodate the developments of the past twenty years. On 16 September, to Metternich's delight, Count Münster, representing Hanover, called on him and declared that Hardenberg's project, which he had just been shown, was utterly unacceptable.[10]

Metternich was not prepared to commit himself to any project at this stage. His primary concern was to arrive at a territorial settlement that excluded Prussian influence from southern Germany, and since that could not be done immediately, he was playing a waiting game. He courted both the rulers and the Standesherren, intending to apply his influence at the right moment. Above all, he did not want to upset Hardenberg, whom he needed as an ally. The collaboration over the future constitution of Germany was above all a means of creating a rapprochement with him.

In London, Metternich had sealed his alliance with Castlereagh. He had broken his return journey in Paris, where he had a satisfactory meeting with Louis XVIII, who gave him to understand that France would back Austria against Russia. He only needed to bring Hardenberg into the fold in order to create a united front that Alexander would not be able to face up to.[11]

Yet with every day that passed the various parties clamouring for their rights and interests grew louder and more unruly. At one end of the scale, the despotic rulers such as the King of Württemberg had, in Stein's words, taken as their model 'the court of Delhi' and were taking preventive action against possible attempts to erode their power at the congress. In the grip of what Stein called 'a sultanic fever', the King of Württemberg was abolishing rights and clamping down wherever he could in order to create *faits accomplis*. He had intercepted Alexander on his return journey from London, proposing mutual support and hinting that provided Alexander protected him, he would support Russia in anything and everything.[12]

These despots were being aped by the smaller potentates, who were, in the words of the Dutch plenipotentiary Baron von Gagern, suffering from 'an addiction to sovereignty'. Although they had little power or prestige themselves, they acted as magnets for the great mass of discontented in Germany, whether they were nationalists, democrats or dispossessed nobles. 'The mood in Germany is already serious,' Prussia's chief of police Prince Wilhelm Ludwig von Sayn-Wittgenstein warned Hardenberg. 'It will become more so if the German Princes, not powerful in material strength, nevertheless, out of bitterness at their subjugation, sway the Germans by their venerable names and trust, and place themselves at the head of the unruly and the dissidents.'[13]

Vienna gradually filled up with new arrivals as people gathered for the congress. Baden had become extremely lively as a result. One of the chief amusements of any society has always been gossip, and the turn events had taken over the past year or so had greatly expanded the possibilities, as people travelled all over Europe, some meeting new lovers, others retailing news.

One source of fascination was the antics of the Grand Duchess Catherine, who, not content with upsetting the British and helping to break up the projected marriage of Princess Charlotte to the Hereditary Prince of Orange, was now embroiled in a love triangle of pan-European proportions. She had originally set her cap at the Austrian Emperor's brother Archduke Charles, but her mother had put her foot down and declared that this was impossible, as her sister was already married to Charles's brother Joseph. Catherine had transferred her affections first to the Hereditary Prince of Orange, and then to the Prince Royal of Württemberg, who was much taken with her. So much so that he had sent his own wife, Charlotte, back to her parents in Bavaria. Unaware that their marriage had been ruled out by the dowager Tsarina, Archduke Charles was still in hot pursuit of Catherine, who was scandalising and titillating Europe with her brazen displays of affection for the still-married Prince Royal of

Württemberg, who was himself now taking advantage of his solitary state to have other affairs.

All this was doing little to assist the Russian plan to marry Catherine's younger sister the Grand Duchess Anna to the heir to the French throne, Louis XVIII's nephew the duc de Berry. This scheme was being promoted fervently by Pozzo di Borgo, now Russian ambassador in Paris, and Nesselrode, who saw in such a match the possibility of bringing Russia and France together as a counterbalance to Austria and Prussia in the future.[14]

A major obstacle to this match was that the dowager Tsarina insisted on her daughter remaining in the Orthodox Church. Louis XVIII, who had no wish to marry his nephew and heir off to the Grand Duchess, turned this into a stumbling block. More amenable than His Most Christian Majesty Louis XVIII was His Catholic Majesty Ferdinand VII of Spain, who was hoping to obtain the hand of the Grand Duchess for himself.

Unruly princesses and marital problems were very much part of the landscape, and the Princess of Wales had just set off on a scandal-studded grand tour that was to take her as far as Naples. Talleyrand, who would cross her path at Strasbourg on his way to Vienna, was horrified by her demeanour. 'Her conduct at Strasbourg,' he reported to Louis XVIII, 'explains perfectly why the Prince Regent prefers to see her in Italy than in England.'[15]

Another source of fascination and gossip was the fate of the various members of the Bonaparte family. Their fall had been as meteoric as their rise, and it elicited a rich mixture of sympathy and *Schadenfreude*. Napoleon's stepson Prince Eugène de Beauharnais, until recently Viceroy of Italy, was the object of almost universal sympathy. He had an enviable reputation as a chivalrous and gifted soldier, and his loyalty to Napoleon and refusal to feather his own nest at the critical moment were greatly admired, as was the behaviour of his wife Augusta, one of the daughters of the King of Bavaria. 'As for me, I came up by such a humble staircase that I will suffer no harm going back down,' he told General Wilson, who was commiserating with him on his change of fortune. 'I feel sorrow only for my wife, who was born and brought up a Princess.' The recent death of his mother the ex-empress Josephine only increased the general sympathy.[16]

There was sympathy too for Eugène's cousin Stephanie, who had been married off to the Grand Duke of Baden to help cement the Napoleonic hegemony in Germany. She had been cast off by him as soon as this crumbled, and was now living in seclusion, supported by the hope that her brother might find himself in a position to help her.

Much less beloved was Napoleon's brother Jérôme, former King of Westphalia. But he, and particularly his wife, were also to be pitied. She was the daughter of the King of Württemberg, but when she tried to see her brother the Crown Prince in Paris after the fall of Napoleon, she had been informed that neither he nor his father would speak to her until she had divorced her husband. This she refused to do. Alexander had then offered her and Jérôme a retreat in Russia, but they decided on Switzerland, where they proposed to live as private individuals. On her way out of Paris she had been attacked by a royalist adventurer and robbed of all her jewels, in which she had placed her hopes for their future. The jewels had found their way into the possession of Louis XVIII's brother, the comte d'Artois, or *Monsieur*, as he now became, but he showed no inclination to return them. After a spell in Berne, where life was made difficult for them, the couple settled, virtually under house arrest, in Austrian Trieste.

Napoleon's consort the Empress Marie-Louise was another object of universal interest. She had been taken in charge by Count Neipperg, who had been nominated her Chamberlain, and who had accompanied her to the waters at Aix-les-Bains, and then brought her to Vienna. She was forbidden to write to or receive letters from Napoleon. She was lodged, along with her little son the King of Rome, in the imperial summer palace of Schönbrunn just outside the city. Her household included Napoleon's devoted old secretary the baron de Méneval, the former Préfet of the imperial household Bausset, her lady-in-waiting Madame de Brignole and the King of

Rome's governess the comtesse de Montesquiou. They led a quiet life, and would not come into Vienna for any of the ceremonies or festivities of the congress. But they became magnets of curiosity and sympathy, and everyone from Tsar Alexander to the most insignificant envoys and visitors drove out to see the fallen Empress and the little son of the ogre.

The series of bivouac and battlefield negotiations carried on by the coalition from March 1813 to the signature of the Treaty of Paris on 30 May 1814 had been the first instance of foreign policy being conducted directly by monarchs and their ministers – normally, such negotiations were carried on by letter or by third parties in some neutral place. Metternich was a firm believer in personal contact of this sort, likening it to the misunderstandings and explanations of a married couple. 'The tongue is untied, the heart opens and the need to make oneself understood often takes over from the rules of cold and severe calculation,' he once told an ambassador. But this kind of negotiation also had its disadvantages and dangers. It was easier for people to let slip something they would regret or to lose control of their emotions.[17]

Up till now, occasional disagreements among the allies had been drowned out by the roar of cannon, their arguments cut short by the need to move on in pursuit of the French, and their differences dissolved in their common fear of Napoleon. Now they were to resume their negotiations, not only at a direct personal level, but also in the hot-house atmosphere of a small, almost provincial city, under the eager gaze of thousands of interested people, and egged on by some of the ablest troublemakers ever produced by the female sex.

Metternich's main reason for holding the congress in Vienna had been that it would place him in a position of control, but the extent of the advantage to be derived from this would depend entirely on how well-informed he was of his guests' thoughts and activities. Long before his return to Vienna he had realised that he would need to prepare the State Chancellery to deal with the increased volume of work. He would also need to expand his already formidable intelligence-gathering network if it was to be in a position to cover the tens of thousands of new arrivals expected.

The responsibility for this devolved on the *Oberste Polizei und Cenzur Hofstelle*, Baron Hager. This fifty-four-year-old son of a field marshal had had his promising military career cut short by a bad fall from a horse and had transferred to the civil administration, in which he had risen fast. He was a pleasant, polite and tactful individual, generally liked and respected, not the sulphurous, despised but feared creature one might imagine. But he was relentless in the pursuit of his duties.

On 1 July 1814 he wrote to Police Chief Silber informing him of the impending arrival of the crowned heads and other personages and of the necessity 'to take special, more vigorous measures of surveillance' so that he might 'know on a daily basis and in every detail everything about their august persons, their immediate entourage, all individuals who may try to approach them, as well as the plans, projects, enterprises that might arise from the presence of these illustrious guests'. On the same day he wrote to the chief of the police bureau devoted to the surveillance of Jews, instructing him to furnish a list of names of those Jews who might be of use as informers. A close watch would also be kept on the sums of money passing through the hands of the city's Jewish bankers.[18]

The Master of Ceremonies of the Imperial Court, Count Ferdinand von Trautmannsdorff, was asked to instruct all the servants in the imperial palace, the Hofburg, to spy on the royal guests who would be staying there, and to make regular reports on their comings and goings. The imperial servants tried to resist being turned into spies, but were quickly called to order, and with time grew to dislike their guests so much that they would fulfil their new duties with alacrity.[19]

Over the next two months hundreds of agents were recruited throughout the city, mostly among servants, tradesmen, coachmen and landlords, to keep their eyes and ears open and report everything they saw or heard regarding the new arrivals and those they came in contact with. Servants were encouraged to seek employment in embassies and the lodgings of foreign delegations. They were to listen in on conversations, eavesdrop behind closed doors, 'borrow' letters and documents in order to get them copied, translated or decoded at the offices of the 'Manipulation', take keys to desks and strongboxes to the police or make wax impressions on the spot so that copies could be made, and go through pockets, waste-paper baskets and even ashes in fireplaces. They were to record the comings and goings of any person who might be of interest, and to send in regular reports.

Hager found no shortage of volunteers who offered to supply him with information, some of them from the highest echelons of Viennese society. These were particularly useful to him, on account of their intelligence, their knowledge of languages and their familiarity with the issues of the day, while their privileged positions would enable them to get close to the visiting sovereigns and dignitaries.

Finally, there was the postal service, which not only intercepted letters carried by the mail, but also controlled the posting stations, where any courier, even a British King's Messenger, would have to change horses, thus providing opportunities to inspect letters and despatches in transit. The service was expanded to deal with the forthcoming surge. And the decoding offices, located in Vienna and various cities along postal routes, took on extra staff, who were quickly trained up in the skills of code-breaking.

From the great mass of mostly trivial material these activities produced, Hager would compile a daily report, drawing attention to points of interest and enclosing the more pungent documents seized or copied. This report would be delivered to Metternich and to the Emperor Francis himself, who would scribble his own observations and remarks in the margin.

This was but one aspect of the preparations for the congress. Just as important was the planning of ceremonies and entertainments, which was taken in hand by Count Trautmannsdorff. It involved serious forward planning. For instance, since all the silver and gold flatware of the imperial household had been melted down to pay for the war of 1809, and as there was not enough money in the imperial coffers to replace it, an enormous porcelain service simulating gold was run up.[20]

Then there was the question of housing and feeding the distinguished guests. The crowned heads and their entourages, which might include a couple of dozen courtiers and aides-de-camp, were to be put up at the Hofburg, involving various members of the imperial family moving out of their apartments to make room. Each was allotted a complement of servants, their ration of candles, firewood and other necessities. Each would be served dinner and supper in their apartments, at 2 and 10 p.m. respectively, when they were at home. The daily routine of providing them with water for washing, of emptying their chamberpots, dealing with their laundry and other household needs was a logistical nightmare. The very task of marshalling the 1,500 extra servants taken on for the purpose would have been enough of a challenge.

Every sovereign and plenipotentiary of a major power would have sentries posted outside his lodgings, whether in the Hofburg or in town. The sentries would present arms whenever anyone in uniform walked or rode past, with the result that those at the Hofburg did so no fewer than fifty-three times on one morning, while anyone walking around town in the uniform of a senior officer or diplomat would be saluted at every step.

Each sovereign and his party was also to be provided with an adequate complement of carriages, which meant the construction of over a hundred new dark-green vehicles with the Habsburg arms on their doors, the provision of several hundred coachmen and grooms in the yellow imperial livery, and 1,200 white horses – all of which had to be groomed, fed, watered and managed so that they could be at the disposal of any one of the monarchs or their attendants at any time of day or night.[21]

Minor princes and the ministers of the great powers, not to mention lesser mortals, were left to their own devices, and the people of Vienna prepared to make the most out of them. Spare rooms, garrets and even closets were cleared and spruced up, as lodgings would be scarce and high rents could be charged for the smallest space. Prices rose dramatically. Lamb, who had applied himself to the matter of finding lodgings for Castlereagh, wrote complaining that 'there is not one drop of good wine to be had in the whole town'. Always attentive to detail, Metternich had pre-empted him, setting up a great wine warehouse and arranging for vast shipments to arrive before the beginning of the congress. But Alexander would have his Burgundy shipped all the way from St Petersburg.[22]

The Viennese prepared for the congress with eagerness. 'The very first families elbowed each other for positions as ladies-in waiting, chamberlains, or pages,' according to the Viennese nobleman Count Friedrich von Schönholz. 'Those able to sit a horse applied as equerries. Well-off people offered to don servants' garb only to be close to the wondrous events to come. Or else it was the golden snuff-boxes and the monstrous tips that acted as incentives . . .' Families made space in order to accommodate a lodger of importance, as they felt they would be more closely involved in the events.

By custom, the Austrian monarchy allowed the poor to participate in events, and to help themselves afterwards: they were allowed to take down decorations, hangings and other leftovers of the fêtes. After court balls the kitchens would put out great bowls of leftover food, with oranges, pineapples, almonds and other delicacies for the taking. 'The Vienna rabble is a decent sort of mob,' according to Schönholz. They were not impertinent, but felt they had a right to watch what was going on and to feel involved, so they turned out for every occasion and passed comment.

As the congress drew near, people crowded around the Hofburg. 'There a new saddle-cloth was seen: hundreds pleaded for a view of only a corner,' in the words of Schönholz. 'In the royal stables; in the Prater; in front of the palaces of princes, envoys and magnates; before governmental offices and in the courtyards of the Imperial Palace: wherever a scaffold went up, equipment was carried in and out, a glass carriage washed, a rug beaten, the pushing crowd was sure to gather. Every tailor or paperhanger carrying a green roll under his arms swept a veritable avalanche of sightseers along with him.'[23]

As Talleyrand was to point out, a major capital was a bad place for a congress. And this one was getting larger by the minute. Vienna, whose population stood at some 250,000, accommodated 16,000 new arrivals in the course of September alone. Some estimates put the number of visitors during the congress as high as 100,000. This is probably too high, but if not only those who came to the congress, but their servants, their retinues and their troops, as well as the thousands of extra servants drafted in from the surrounding countryside are all taken into account, it may not be too far off the mark.[24]

The crowned heads attending included not only Alexander and Frederick William. There was the awkward albino-like King Frederick VI of Denmark, whose long teeth and constantly moving lips gave him the air of a ruminating goat, according to one observer. There was the King of Württemberg, five feet tall and six in circumference, whose stomach fell in folds onto his knees. King Maximilian of Bavaria, described by Jackson as 'a good, jolly, farmer-like looking fellow, crossed with the heaviness of a German Prince', struck another as resembling a Bavarian brewer. Along with the wives, sons and daughters some of them brought, as well as the grand dukes, dukes and princes of every shape and size, they constituted the greatest gathering of royals Europe had ever seen. Their entourages of ministers, ambassadors, equerries, aides-de-camp, ladies-in-waiting, when added to the Austrian court and the society of Vienna, made up the largest aristocratic gathering there had ever been. And the sheer number of interested parties converging on the city would make this the greatest diplomatic contest of all time.[25]

There were delegations from every state in Europe, as well as from most of those that had been extinguished in the past quarter-century. There were representatives of cities, republics, corporations and even abbeys. There were delegations from families seeking restitution of lands and offices, among them opportunists such as the spurious descendants of the family of Latour d'Auvergne who were hoping to claim the ancient duchy of Bouillon. There was a representative of

Napoleon's marshals hoping to preserve for them the apanages he had given them all over Europe. Marshal Berthier was hoping to be allowed to hold on to the principality of Neuchâtel, which had been ceded to Napoleon and granted to him by treaty in 1806. There were individuals such as Luigi Boncompagni Ludovisi, Prince of Piombino, who demanded to know why he should have been deprived of his island of Elba to accommodate a man who had stripped him of all his possessions. There were others, such as the obsessive of whom one Viennese lady wrote: 'I have no idea what it is he is claiming, but his claim goes back certainly as far as the Seven Years' War.' The full complexity of the problems that lay ahead grew more apparent as each new delegation or envoy arrived.[26]

The King of Sardinia sent the Marchese di San Marzano and Count Rossi. They could depend on Austrian support, and on that of Russia, where the Sardinian ambassador was the renowned writer Joseph de Maistre, who had made a strong case in Russian society for an expanded Sardinia. They would not find it difficult to sideline the envoy of the already condemned republic of Genoa, the Marchese de Brignole-Sale. He in turn could count on the support of Spain, which was jealous of Austrian interests in Italy and wanted a return to the situation as it stood in 1789.

Spain and France did not want Marie-Louise to reign in Parma, as had been specified by the Treaty of Fontainebleau. They wanted the duchy to be given to the Queen of Etruria, one of the daughters of the former King of Spain, Charles IV, and widow of the Prince of Parma. Because her mother had wanted her to be a Queen like her sisters (married to the Kings of Portugal and Naples), Spain had made a complicated deal with Napoleon in 1802 whereby she ceded Parma, Piacenza and Guastalla to France, along with Louisiana in America, in return for Tuscany, which France had captured from Austria and which was renamed the kingdom of Etruria. When Napoleon invaded Spain in 1807 she lost Etruria, which became part of the kingdom of Italy. In the cause of restoring her to her duchies, Spain was prepared to oppose the incorporation of Genoa by Sardinia.

Austria, however, did not wish to see the Queen of Etruria back in Italy, which it saw as its own sphere of influence, so was prepared to uphold the claim of Marie-Louise, who was the Emperor Francis's daughter. But Austria might need to have some pawns to trade, so it held on to the Papal provinces known as the Legations. The Pope's envoy to Vienna, Cardinal Consalvi, could not afford to antagonise Austria too much, as he needed Austrian assistance in order to force Murat out of the Pope's other province of the Marches, and to support him over ecclesiastical matters in Germany.

Murat sent two plenipotentiaries to Vienna, the Duke of Campo Chiaro and Prince Cariati, along with a number of others whom he judged capable of making a promising case on his behalf. Chief among these was Prince Lucio Caracciolo, Duca della Rocca Romana, a man of head-turning beauty who would fascinate the ladies by showing them his left hand, deprived of fingers by frostbite while he escorted Napoleon on the first night of his flight from Russia. But not everyone in Vienna would talk to them, as most of the courts of Europe resolutely refused to recognise Murat and backed the claim of the former King of Naples, Ferdinand IV, who had also sent his representatives.

If Italy was promising to prove difficult to resolve equably, Germany also presented a baffling picture of discord and rivalry. Aside from the claims and reclamations of the existing rulers, which were quite difficult enough to reconcile, the congress would face demands for restitution from hundreds of dispossessed nobles and mediatised rulers. Some Standesherren had got together and elected one of their number in a region, others preferred to go themselves. There were also representatives of the four Hanseatic cities (Hamburg, Lübeck, Bremen and Frankfurt); of the city of Mainz; of the Chamber of Commerce of the city of Mainz; of the Teutonic Order; of the firms of Bonte & Co., Kayser & Co. and Wittersheim & Bock, creditors of the government of Westphalia, which had been abolished; of the Bishop of Liège; of the subjects of Count Solms-Braunfels. One delegation of Catholic clergy demanded full restitution under Papal authority; another, consisting of four delegates led by the Bishop of

Constance, called for the institution of a new German national Catholic Church. The Pope's delegate, Cardinal Consalvi, was there to oppose this. There was also a delegation, consisting of Friedrich Justin Bertuch of Weimar and Johann Georg von Cotta of Stuttgart, publisher of the *Allgemeine Zeitung*, representing eighty-one German publishers and demanding a copyright law as well as freedom of the press. And there were J.J. Gumprecht and Jakob Baruch of Frankfurt and Carl August Buchholz of Lübeck, representing the interests of the Jews. They were one of the few groups eager to preserve changes made by Napoleon, who had granted them full equality, of which the authorities in many German states were now attempting to strip them once more.

There were also those who came to ply their trade, be they actresses, musicians, hairdressers or card sharps, for Vienna had suddenly become the greatest forum for almost any kind of human intercourse. There were those who came to seek a lover, acquire a job, make a killing at the gaming tables, marry a daughter, find a wife. And there were those who came merely out of curiosity.

There were those who just had to be at the centre of events, and one who fell squarely into that category was Wilhelmina, who had moved to Vienna from Ratiborzitz in the spring, renting an apartment in the Palm Palace, not far from the State Chancellery. She knew Vienna and Viennese society well. She enjoyed the best of relations with Alexander and Frederick William, she could count Talleyrand almost as one of the family, and she had Metternich on a string. Her salon would undoubtedly be one of the centres of intrigue, and she would be able to play the part she most enjoyed. But she would find herself pitted against one of the most notorious and most dangerous women in Vienna, Princess Catherine Bagration.

Princess Bagration was the twenty-nine-year-old widow of the Russian General Piotr Ivanovich Bagration, who had died of wounds received at the battle of Borodino in 1812. Her father Paweł Skowroński, a Pole, had been Russia's minister at the court of Naples; her mother, Catherine Engelhardt, was a niece of the notorious Prince

Potyomkin. The Princess had been married off against her wishes, but she had a wilful nature, and followed her whims; she had promptly left her husband and settled in Vienna, where she had bestowed her favours on a string of lovers – including Metternich, by whom she had had a daughter, Clementine. A great beauty, with golden hair and an alabaster complexion, she hated the idea of depriving others of the sight of it, so she wore diaphanous dresses that revealed much and earned her the sobriquet of 'the naked angel'. She was very short-sighted, and this gave her intensely blue eyes a vague, yielding look that few men could resist. She was reported to have a mastery of *recherché* love-making skills. She loathed Wilhelmina and had no intention of being eclipsed by her.[27]

~~~≈≈~~~

Points of Order

'When I arrived in Vienna yesterday I found all Europe assembled in my antechamber,' Metternich wrote to his wife on 19 September. Besides Hardenberg and the Bavarian plenipotentiary Field Marshal Wrede, the room contained four deputies of the Order of Malta, fifteen or so representatives of minor German states and cities, three old ladies with petitions and one pretty young one 'who came to offer me that which is either not worth a cent or which cannot be bought for all the treasure on earth, saying that she was in pressing need of a passport so that she could go and join her *Mummy* in Paris'.[1]

Dealing with the whole of Europe was exactly what Metternich had been hoping to avoid. Before leaving London, the four ministers had agreed to meet in Vienna on 10 September, more than two weeks before Alexander and Frederick William were due to arrive. This would give them plenty of time, as they thought, to settle all the crucial outstanding business between the four of them. They could then present their proposals to the monarchs and to all those attending the congress and obtain universal approval. The entire process would not take longer than six weeks. Metternich had rented accommodation for them in Baden, in the belief that the seclusion and tranquillity of the place would be conducive to harmonious concentration. But things did not work out as he had hoped.[2]

The first to arrive, on 13 September, was Castlereagh. Since Britain had already achieved her goals, he saw his role at the congress as that of mediator. While distrusting the French as much as ever, both he and Liverpool had come to see a defeated France as a potential junior partner in a new *entente* that would strengthen Britain's hand. Wellington, whose position as ambassador in Paris cast him in a pivotal role, and whose views on the French were no warmer, had come to a similar conclusion. 'The situation of affairs in the world will naturally constitute England and France as arbitrators at the Congress, if those Powers *understand* each other,' he had written from Paris in August, adding that Talleyrand would have to be kept on a short rein and that the understanding between the two powers must remain secret so as not to alarm the others.[3]

They had agreed that Castlereagh should pass through Paris on his way to Vienna in order to further such an *entente*, and Wellington welcomed the Foreign Secretary in the new embassy he had bought, Pauline Borghese's former palace on the rue Saint-Honoré. Castlereagh was delighted by his interviews with Talleyrand and Louis XVIII, which revealed that they shared many priorities. But he had no intention of allowing France to play a part at the congress beyond that of support-ing Britain, and was adamant that there could be no question of rewarding her for that with any revision of the Treaty of Paris. Nowhere does he say what he really thought of Talleyrand, but it is clear he found him inscrutable and thought him devious. He did not trust his judgement, and was anxious lest Talleyrand show too much 'exuberance' with respect to their understanding, and thereby excite the jealousy of the other powers.[4]

Castlereagh had asked Aberdeen to stay on as ambassador in Vienna and act as his assistant during the congress, but Aberdeen had de-clined. Instead, Castlereagh nominated his own half-brother Charles, who had been raised to the peerage and took up his post as Lord Stewart. His new title proved a godsend to historians as well as contemporary diplomats, given that a man by the name of Sir Charles Stuart had recently been named Wellington's chargé d'affaires at the British embassy in Paris.

As his second plenipotentiary Castlereagh chose Cathcart, who was still ambassador to the court of Russia, in the hope that he would prove useful in handling Alexander. Although a little slow, Cathcart was no fool. He was devoted to Castlereagh, and diligent in carrying out his wishes. As Britain's fourth plenipotentiary, Castlereagh had chosen Lord Clancarty, the ambassador in The Hague, an intelligent and hard-working man of some experience who understood his intentions. As well as his private secretary Joseph Planta, Castlereagh had brought along the Under-Secretary Edward Cooke, an old friend, and ten young assistants from the Foreign Office.

There could be no question of Castlereagh not taking Emily, and she insisted on bringing her sister. He had written to Frederick Lamb, Aberdeen's embassy secretary, to find him lodgings, and the latter had rented a fourteen-room apartment. Castlereagh did not like it, and soon moved to a larger apartment, of twenty-two rooms, in a building on the Minoritenplatz, just across the square from Stewart's embassy in the Stahremberg Palace and no more than a couple of hundred yards from Metternich's official residence, the State Chancellery on the Ballhausplatz. He had been given the sum of £15,000 to cover the expenses of his stay in Vienna, which must have seemed sufficient, considering that he was not intending to spend more than a couple of months there. But according to one source he was charged £500 a month for lodging himself and his party. He certainly kept his expenses to a minimum, giving only meagre dinners at his Tuesday receptions, and when he gave a ball he cleared Lady Castlereagh's bedroom for the dancing.[5]

During his absence the Foreign Office would be supervised by Lord Bathurst, but the direction of foreign affairs was retained by Liverpool. At the same time Liverpool made it clear to Castlereagh that he could initiate policy and that anything he did would have the full support of the cabinet. Castlereagh did not abuse this confidence, and the two remained in constant contact through almost daily and sometimes several daily exchanges of letters. Nor did he have to consider the reactions of Parliament, which would only be sitting for a short period that autumn, or public opinion, which was not informed enough on the subjects in question. None of the other plenipotentiaries would enjoy such freedom of action.

Certainly not Nesselrode, who reached Vienna the following day, accompanied by his heavily pregnant wife. He had just been nominated State Secretary for Foreign Affairs, but this was an empty title, since the by now inoperative chancellor, Rumiantsev, remained in place, and Alexander would be in Vienna to give Nesselrode orders. The Tsar had issued him with a set of written instructions, and he had no brief to negotiate.[6]

Hardenberg arrived four days after Castlereagh. He took up his quarters humbly in a few rooms on the second floor of a merchant's house on the Graben, the great open space at the heart of the old city. He would later move into the Hofburg with Frederick William. He was to be assisted principally by Humboldt. His freedom of action would be severely limited by his King, who was due to arrive with his two sons, the Crown Princes William and Augustus, in a couple of weeks' time, by a number of Prussian generals who would accompany them, and, not least, by public opinion in Berlin, which was in a state of ferment. There was much disappointment that the heroic surge of the war for the liberation of Germany had yielded such paltry results.

Hardenberg was a devoted servant of his King, prepared to fight ruthlessly for Prussia's interests. But he was a product of the eighteenth century, courteous and kind by nature, and he was ill-suited to be a champion of the new politics of blood and iron. He was being accused of neglecting Prussia's interests and, by not having forced Alexander to give back her Polish provinces, of having brought the country to the position where she was forced to commit an act of cannibalism on Saxony, which Frederick William and most Prussians found no less repugnant than did the rest of German opinion. He was also keenly aware that, in spite of all the verbal agreements and the written treaties, the future of Prussia and her very existence as a power still hung in the balance, since Russian troops were in occupation of all her old Polish provinces and of her promised prize of Saxony.[7]

Having failed to entice the others out to Baden, Metternich joined them in Vienna, where they began holding informal meetings at once. As no minutes were taken, it is not possible to reconstruct with any accuracy the course taken by these first conferences. But the sheaves of rough drafts and scribbled notes preserved in the archives of the Austrian Chancellery, the French Foreign Ministry and the British Foreign Office, taken in conjunction with the diary entries and correspondence of those taking part, give a good idea of their essence. They also reveal that the notes and records made by each party often reflected the wishes of the writer rather than any consensus.

The business of the congress could be broken down into three categories: territorial arrangements not settled by the Treaty of Paris, the new constitution of Germany, and a range of general issues such as the slave trade and navigation of international rivers. Metternich's proposal, which he put to Castlereagh on 14 September, was to delegate the drafting of the German constitution to a body representing the principal states concerned; to leave the general issues to be resolved by the plenipotentiaries of Russia, Prussia, Austria, Britain, France and Spain; but to settle the outstanding territorial questions first between the four principal allies without any outside interference. As a sop to their national pride, the plenipotentiaries of France and Spain could be notified of the decisions taken by the four and invited to comment on them.[8]

Castlereagh did not like the prospect of France and Spain being excluded, partly because it would appear high-handed, but more importantly because it would rob him of the support of France. He produced his own project, which was discussed at the meeting held two days later, on 16 September, probably with the participation of Nesselrode, who had arrived the previous evening.

Castlereagh suggested setting up a Steering Committee representing the six major powers – Russia, Prussia, Austria, Britain, France and Spain – to oversee the congress. This committee would nominate a German Committee to deal with the German question, and other committees to address questions such as the navigation of rivers.

Interested parties who had come to Vienna would be invited to make their case to the Steering Committee, which, after evaluating it, would present its decisions to a general assembly for approval.

'The advantage of this mode of proceeding is that you treat the Plenipotentiaries as a Body, with early and becoming respect,' he explained. 'You keep the powers by Concert and Management in your own hands, but without openly assuming authority to their exclusion. You obtain a sort of sanction from them for what you are determined at all events to do, which they cannot well withhold, and which cannot in the mode it is taken, embarrass your march . . .' This march concerned the crucial question of the territorial settlements in Poland, Germany and Italy, which were to be left in the hands of the four allies.[9]

Castlereagh's form of proceeding met with some approval from the others, but problems emerged during discussions as to which interested parties would be allowed to address themselves to the Steering Committee. It would be difficult, for example, to forbid the plenipotentiary of the King of Saxony to put his case, which would be highly embarrassing for Prussia. Austria, which was still bound by treaty to Murat, would have to demand that his plenipotentiary be admitted, and that would be unacceptable to Britain and France, which recognised not him but Ferdinand IV as King of Naples.[10]

Hardenberg reached Vienna at midday on 17 September, and on the following afternoon the first meeting of the four took place, at Metternich's office. Metternich produced his original proposal with slight modifications reflecting the discussions of the past four days. Invoking the first of the secret articles of the Treaty of Paris, he proposed that they settle amongst themselves all questions regarding the territories ceded by France – i.e. former French territory and that of the French dependencies in Poland, Germany and Italy. Once they had reached agreement, they would communicate their decisions to the plenipotentiaries of France and Spain for their comments, which they would take into consideration before submitting the final version to the whole congress for approbation. France and Spain would also be included in the discussions and decisions regarding wider

European issues. Questions relating to the future German Confederation could be settled by a committee representing Austria, Prussia, Bavaria, Württemberg and Hanover.

Castlereagh voiced his misgivings and repeated his suggestion that France and Spain be allowed to participate in directing the proceedings, but Hardenberg was not about to let Prussia's newly acquired great-power status be diluted by the inclusion of France and Spain. Humboldt, who was at his side, backed him up, reminding the others that this was not a peace congress, since peace had already been made, in Paris. Nor was it, formally speaking, a general European congress. They were gathered in Vienna because it was a convenient place to tie up a whole range of largely unrelated business, which would result in 'particular treaties that have no connection with each other except the general interest of Europe'. He accepted that these treaties should be submitted for final approval to the representatives of all the states of Europe, as this would lend them added legitimacy. But the question of how to apportion the lands liberated from Napoleon and his allies should be decided exclusively by the four powers that had liberated them. He argued against extending the number of decision-makers, observing that only the powers prepared to take responsibility for the security of Europe should be given a say in reordering it. With Nesselrode in agreement, Castlereagh could hardly protest.[11]

The ministers of the four powers held their second meeting the next day. The harmony that had reigned at the first quickly gave way to discord as Nesselrode declared Russia's intention of keeping the whole territory of the grand duchy of Warsaw. Hardenberg insisted that Prussia must recover some of her former Polish lands, and particularly the fortress of Thorn. Metternich claimed Kraków and Zamość with their surrounding areas, reminding those present that Austria had helped to capture the grand duchy. What annoyed both of them most was Nesselrode's repeated use of the word 'Poland', which had been expressly forbidden by a treaty of 1797 between the three partitioning powers when they had abolished that kingdom. Metternich went so far as to threaten war.

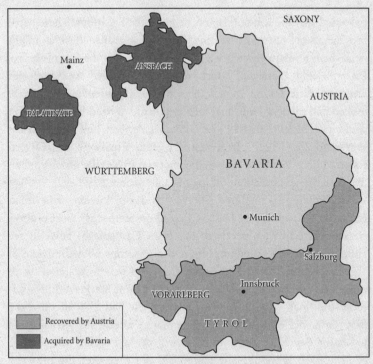

The Bavarian–Austrian exchange. The eventual deal

Tempers did not improve when Hardenberg began staking out Prussia's claims – the whole of Saxony and a number of other areas, including the fortress city of Mainz. Metternich was rattled. By the Treaty of Ried, Bavaria had agreed to return to Austria the Tyrol, the Vorarlberg, Salzburg, the Innviertel and Hausrück. In exchange she was to obtain, through Austria's good offices, the Palatinate, Würzburg, Aschaffenburg, and Mainz and its surrounding area. Prussian troops had occupied Mainz, and showed no signs of handing it over to anyone, certainly not until Prussia's essential demands had been met.

Hardenberg's suggestion that the King of Saxony be compensated with a smaller realm on the Rhine upset British plans for a strong barrier against France, and Castlereagh protested. Hardenberg then proposed that the King of Saxony be given the Legations. These Papal provinces were currently occupied by Austria, and Metternich might need them to compensate the Queen of Etruria for the loss of Parma, Piacenza and Guastalla, which had been awarded to Napoleon's Empress Marie-Louise. In fact, the whole arrangement agreed to date looked in peril of coming apart. The surge of anger and recrimination could not be confined to the council chamber, and the German statesman and Dutch plenipotentiary Hans Christoph von Gagern reported on 21 September that, having been in Vienna no more than five days, he was hearing nothing but talk of war.[12]

Hardenberg was shattered. On his first day in Vienna, rather than rest from his journey he had paid a call on Stein, then on Countess Nesselrode, had then received one from Castlereagh, gone to see Humboldt, at whose lodgings he had discussions with the Duke of Weimar, Gentz, Count Solms and General Knesebeck, going on to call on Count Razumovsky, Count Zichy, Count Stackelberg, Nesselrode, and finally Count Trautmannsdorff. He had then attended the first conference of the four plenipotentiaries, after which he had gone to see the Prince de Ligne and finished off the evening with a *soirée* at Princess Bagration's. The tempo did not ease over the next few days, and, at sixty-four, he was finding it wearing. On the sixth day he took to his bed.[13]

At their next meeting, on 22 September, the plenipotentiaries of the four powers went back to the vexed question of procedure. A redrafted version of Metternich's original proposal was discussed and signed by all except Castlereagh, who registered his disapproval at the exclusion of France and Spain. He did sign it at the next conference, the following day, but only after voicing his reservations, which were duly attached to the minutes. He accepted that all the important decisions were to be taken by the four. 'I consider however the arrangements when so brought forward to be open to free and liberal discussion with the other two Powers, as friendly, and not hostile powers,' he stated. He also declared that he did not 'consent to be absolutely bound by a majority'. Humboldt had attempted to slip in a resolution formally excluding France from any part in the decision-making process, but Castlereagh and Metternich had scuppered it. The only constructive measure that was agreed was the appointment of Gentz as secretary to the congress and minute-taker.[14]

In a letter to Liverpool summing up the first four meetings, Castlereagh expressed disapproval of Prussia's persistence in treating France as an enemy, and his dismay at the only slightly less hostile attitude of the others. 'Whatever may be their differences with each other,' he wrote, 'the three Continental Courts seem to feel equal jealousy of admitting France either to arbitrate between them or to assume any leading influence in the arrangements consequent upon the peace.' As that letter was being written in the early hours of 24 September, the plenipotentiary of France's carriage was rolling into Vienna.[15]

Talleyrand had mixed feelings about going to Vienna. He knew that only he could represent French interests adequately. But he confessed to a colleague that he expected to 'play a very sad role' there, and feared that he would not be able to make his views heard. He also realised that since there was no possibility of his being able to bring back any prizes, he would be open to criticism when he returned. In the end, more personal motives prevailed. His obsessive need to be at the centre of affairs was strongly reinforced by the fact that he was in financial straits, and one of his remaining assets was in jeopardy. His Napoleonic apanage the Principality of Benevento, originally a Papal fief, was now in the kingdom of Naples, and it would almost certainly be returned to its rightful owner if Talleyrand did not take a hand in the matter.[16]

He thought long and hard about what attitude to strike at the congress, granted that he was representing the former common enemy, a defeated power whose boundaries had already been fixed by the Treaty of Paris. He decided to turn this to advantage: since France had nothing to gain from the congress he could take an impartial line in support of legitimacy and international law, which would give him a moral edge over all other plenipotentiaries.

After the signature of the Treaty of Paris, France had only one priority, which was to break out of isolation and resume her place among the great powers in order to exert influence over the settlement in Germany and Italy. The only way she would be able to do this was by dividing the four allies. That would not be difficult, in view of their incipient differences. But Talleyrand would have to move carefully, as the one thing guaranteed to reunite them was any sign that France was attempting to play an active part in European affairs.

Talleyrand's instructions, which reflected his own views as much as they did those of Louis XVIII, made it clear that France was not after any territorial or other advantages for herself. She did have two specific objectives: to remove Murat from the throne of Naples and reinstate Ferdinand IV, and to preserve the King of Saxony on his. The first was dictated by the fear of a Napoleonic threat developing in Italy and the desire to see a Bourbon restored to his throne. The French stand over Saxony was motivated by a long tradition of alliance between the two countries, reinforced by the fact that Louis XVIII's mother had been a Saxon Princess, and the need to acquire allies in Germany in order to be able to exert some pressure on Prussia and Austria. Both of these objectives could credibly be dressed up in the guise of a selfless pursuit of justice for its own sake, along with many a pious utterance about the desirability of restoring an independent Poland.

The tool Talleyrand would use in order to further these aims was the principle of legitimacy and international law, or 'the public law of Europe' as he termed it. This would serve him well, permitting him to embarrass others and occupy the moral high ground. 'We want nothing, absolutely nothing, not a single village,' he would say to all and sundry, 'but we do want to see justice done.'[17]

He was well aware that every time he uttered the word 'legitimacy' he rattled Alexander and Frederick William, whose respective imperial and royal titles had been unilaterally assumed less than a century earlier; and the Kings of Bavaria and Württemberg, the Grand Duke of Baden, and many others who owed theirs to Napoleon. All of them had, moreover, acquired territory in recent years by means that could in no way be described as legitimate.

Talleyrand had decided to give the French delegation to the congress a high profile. He had rented the roomy Kaunitz Palace on the Johannesgasse, and filled it with a large household of servants, including his legendary chef Antonin Carême. A pastry-cook by training but a master in all fields, with a repertoire of over two hundred soups, and the founder of *haute cuisine*, Carême held that 'The culinary art serves as the escort to European diplomacy.' He knew that the best was expected of him, and that he could expect the necessary support – including the despatch of truffles from Paris by diplomatic courier.[18]

Perhaps the most remarkable feature of Talleyrand's household was its hostess. He had not for a moment considered bringing his wife to Vienna with him – his own upbringing under the *ancien régime* meant that he could skate over his revolutionary and Napoleonic past, and take on the grandees of the imperial capital on an equal footing, but she would have dragged him down to the level of a Bonapartist *parvenu*. The daughter of a minor government official and wife of an employee of the East India Company, she had been seduced while still in her teens by Sir Philip Francis in Bengal. Repudiated by her husband, she had returned to Paris, where she survived as a courtesan, and where she later became Talleyrand's mistress. Napoleon had ordered him to marry her just as her charms were beginning to fade, and the vulgarity of her behaviour made her even less suitable. Talleyrand had packed her off to the country, and had no intention of bringing her back into his life. Yet he would need a lady to keep house for him and receive guests. For this role he chose his niece, the comtesse Edmond de Périgord.

Dorothée de Périgord was the daughter of Talleyrand's former mistress the Duchess of Courland, and therefore Wilhelmina's sister – or rather half-sister, since her father had not been Duke Peter of Courland but her mother's lover Count Batowski. She had originally been paired with Prince Adam Czartoryski, but eventually married Talleyrand's nephew Edmond de Périgord, whom she bore two sons and a daughter who had just died. This loss had proved the death blow to a loveless marriage, and Talleyrand, whom she adored, had no difficulty in persuading her to come to Vienna with him.

Dorothée was twenty-one years old, with enchanting looks that mixed childish innocence with dreamy passion to produce an alluring sense of danger. She had, according to the French writer Sainte-Beuve, 'eyes of an infernal brilliance that shone in the night'. She was the product of an unconventional upbringing. 'My religious education was nil; I never said any prayers because I did not know any,' she would later write. She had sought to make up for this by voracious reading, but the library of her tutor contained a great many 'bad' books. She was certainly not shy about the possible implications of her role in the household of the French plenipotentiary. Although Talleyrand's waxen complexion and low-lidded unblinking eyes often gave people the impression that they were looking at a corpse, he had the reputation of a satyr. Despite having been faithful to her husband, and despite her being thirty-nine years younger than Talleyrand, Dorothée and he were probably already lovers.[19]

Talleyrand's delegation was made up of his second plenipotentiary the duc de Dalberg, who was expert on German affairs, the comte de la Tour du Pin, an intelligent aristocrat who had served as a Préfet under Napoleon, and the young comte Alexis de Noailles, an ultra-royalist aide-de-camp to Monsieur of no apparent talents. Talleyrand's justification for choosing him was that since he would almost certainly be spied on by his enemies at court, he might as well choose the spy himself. Talleyrand had also brought the comte de la Besnardi-ère, an able and industrious official of the Foreign Ministry, his private secretary Gabriel Perrey, three Foreign Ministry secretaries and the historian Raxis de Flassan, who was to write up the official history of the congress and the part played in it by the French delegation, for Talleyrand intended to add some glorious pages to his own biography.

Most congresses in the past had adopted a structure and elected a mediator, but Metternich and his colleagues had been so keen to resolve matters informally amongst themselves that they had thrown form to the winds, with lamentable consequences. The tiresome discussions over procedure had achieved nothing beyond wasting precious time, and when the question of territorial arrangements was broached, on 19 September, it became evident that the plenipotentiaries of Russia and Prussia had no power to negotiate or concede anything. In other words, nothing could be done until Alexander and Frederick William arrived.

Metternich had been hoping that the period of reflection between their parting in London and their reassembly at Vienna would have cooled Alexander's ardour, and that his sojourn in St Petersburg would have dampened his enthusiasm on the Polish question. Nesselrode had assured him that public opinion there would oblige the Tsar to change his mind on that score. But he was to be disappointed. Alexander had certainly changed, but not in the way Metternich and Nesselrode had hoped.[20]

Throughout the long march from Russia to Paris in 1813 and 1814 he had been sustained by his sense of mission, by the conviction that he was the divinely ordained tool of God's will. In Paris he had become aware of his immense personal prestige and of the power that went with it, and he had briefly allowed himself to be intoxicated by it. But he had quickly become disenchanted with the French. In London he had been made aware of the limitations of his power and of the transitory nature of his prestige.[21]

He had embarked at Dover on 26 June, and made his way homeward via Calais, Ostend, Antwerp, Amsterdam and Bruchsal, where his wife Elizabeth was sojourning with her mother the Margravine of Baden. She had taken advantage of the opportunity provided by the liberation of Germany from Napoleon to visit her native land after an absence of over twenty years. But she now found Alexander, who had never loved her and had long ago ceased to treat her with even a modicum of tenderness, so altered, moody and unpleasant that she actually contemplated divorcing him and staying there.[22]

Those gathered at Bruchsal included Alexander's old tutor La Harpe and Stein, but his attention was absorbed by Roksandra Sturdza, one of his wife's ladies-in-waiting whose piety he had always admired. A Moldavian born in Constantinople, Roksandra Sturdza had, along with her younger brother Aleksandr, become 'awakened' under the influence of the German pietists. While attending the Empress Elizabeth in Heidelberg the previous year she had met Johann Heinrich Jung Stilling, a former village schoolteacher who had become a renowned spiritual luminary. He preached that Christianity should not be considered as a theological creed, but as a kind of ordeal, a continuous test of submission to the will of God.

On 9 July Jung Stilling arrived in Bruchsal, and on the following day he had a long conversation with Alexander. The Tsar was familiar with his writings, and drank in his exhortations to submit more fully to the divine will and to pray constantly for the strength to fulfil his role of bringing the kingdom of God to earth. On hearing that Jung Stilling and Roksandra Sturdza had contracted a 'mystic marriage' to give each other strength, he begged to be allowed to join it. They gave their assent. The three would now pray for and support each other in the divine cause.[23]

Alexander left Bruchsal greatly comforted and reaffirmed in his purpose. When he reached St Petersburg on 25 July he refused to play the part of the homecoming hero, and cancelled all non-religious celebrations. He declined the title of 'Blessed' that the Holy Synod wished to bestow upon him, taking the opportunity to stress that it had been God who had triumphed, and that his only merit had been to lend himself to the purpose.

All those around Alexander noted the change in him. He was more reflective and withdrawn, more determined, even obstinate, and less inclined to listen to his advisers. He did have to give way in the face of their collective outrage when he raised the possibility of liberating the serfs. But he stood firm when challenged on his Polish plans, which filled all Russians with horror, and was barely more amenable on other matters. When the Prussian ambassador suggested Russia cede some of former Prussian Poland to Prussia, he flew into a rage and threatened to annex the whole of East Prussia and Danzig as well.[24]

In a memorandum dated 7 July and handed to the Tsar in Bruchsal, Pozzo di Borgo and La Harpe warned him not to expect any good will from the statesmen of other powers for the part he had played in the downfall of Napoleon over the past two years. 'The English government is no longer trustful of Your Majesty,' it ran. 'We would go further and say that it has assumed an attitude of alarm, and therefore of coolness, indeed of opposition which is no less declared for being unspoken.' Prussia's loyalty, they suggested, could no longer be counted on, while Austria must be considered as a 'rival'. 'She will look with pleasure on everything which will put distance between Your Majesty and the governance of Europe,' they explained.

Their recommendations were that Austria be outmanoeuvred through intrigue, that a strong German federation be established which would crave Russian protection, that Prussia be flattered and gratified, Britain be allowed its way on the seas and on Belgium, and France cajoled into a dynastic marriage. They concluded by suggesting that Russia should extend her western frontier no further than the line of the Vistula, reinforced with the fortresses of Thorn, Modlin, Sandomierz and Zamość. That would give Russia security and permit her to attend to her pressing internal problems, and 'the power, should she wish to use it, of going to sing the Te Deum in Constantinople'. This memorandum, like Nesselrode's notes on the subject, reveals a remarkable flair on the part of these foreigners for Russia's real interests, and, needless to say, left no room for Alexander's Polish plans.[25]

Alexander was deaf to their reasoning. The 'summary instructions' he wrote out for Nesselrode before the latter left for Vienna made it clear that he wanted to keep the whole grand duchy of Warsaw, though he would be prepared to cede Posen if necessary; that Austria could have what she wanted in Italy, as well as the Tyrol, Innviertel and Salzburg; that Prussia should be given Saxony, with a sliver of it going to Weimar (whose ruler, the Duke of Saxe-Weimar, was his

brother-in-law). 'As far as the other Princes of Germany are concerned, it is necessary to prevent the present state of affairs being
disrupted too much,' he advised, registering his support for the rulers
of Württemberg, Baden, Darmstadt and Oldenburg, and adding that
he wished a principality of some kind to be found for Prince Eugène.[26]

Alexander had left Moscow for Vienna on 14 September. Six days
later he reached Adam Czartoryski's country estate at Puławy on the
Vistula, where he was greeted by a large gathering of prominent Polish
patriots. He spent two days at Puławy, and before leaving pledged
that he would recreate a Polish state of over ten million inhabitants
by adding Polish provinces previously conquered by Russia to the
territory of the grand duchy of Warsaw. He told the assembled Poles
that he had the agreement of Frederick William for this, and believed
that Austria would not object. His greatest problem would be to
weather Russian discontent, but he assured them that he would not
flinch in his purpose, citing the precedent of Finland, to which he had
added previously conquered territories when he took the remainder of
it from Sweden in 1809. 'I shall achieve happiness for myself by
making you happy,' he told the assembled Poles before climbing into
his carriage and leaving for Vienna.[27]

Alexander made his ceremonial entry into Vienna accompanied by
Frederick William at midday on 25 September, a fine sunny day. They
had been met outside the city by Francis, and the three monarchs
rode into Vienna abreast, preceded by the Hungarian noble guard,
resplendent in its lavishly embroidered hussar uniforms and led by
Prince Esterhazy, whose jewelled aigrette and pearl-adorned boots
were the source of universal admiration. They were followed by a
glittering suite of generals, between rows of brilliantly-uniformed
Austrian soldiers, cheered by the people with genuine enthusiasm
and saluted by batteries of ordnance. They rode to the Hofburg,
where they were to stay. Alexander was given the Amalia wing for
himself and his attendants, while Frederick William moved into apartments vacated by the Empress.

There followed a reception during which presentations were made, and at the end of which Alexander summoned Metternich for an interview. 'I have just returned from Court,' Metternich wrote to Wilhelmina that evening. 'Instead of being with my love I had my first skirmish with the Emp. A. He summoned me and I saw that he wanted to see the lie of the land. [. . .] the result is that *he knows nothing* of what *I want* and that *I know exactly* what *he wants*.'[28]

Metternich did not know the half of it. Alexander was intending to spend no more than three weeks in Vienna. He had come not to negotiate, but to state his wishes and lend authority to the settlement by his presence. He was certainly not intending to give an inch on his plans for Poland. 'He has taken the bit between his teeth, and he will either drag the Emperor of Austria along with him or leap over him, but he will not be reined in,' the Tsarina explained to her mother.[29]

The following day it was Castlereagh's turn to be summoned to an audience, which lasted two and a half hours. The Tsar treated him with 'great personal kindness', but did not hide his determination to carry through his plan of creating a kingdom of Poland under Russian dominion. He assured Castlereagh that this had nothing to do with ambition, and 'that it was a sense of moral duty which dictated the measure and that it could not but prove grateful to the British Nation'.

Castlereagh retorted that the people of England would be delighted to see the restoration of an independent Poland, but not a Poland under Russian rule, and challenged the Tsar to make the Poles truly happy by giving them full independence. Alexander admitted that he was not in a position to do this, as public opinion in Russia would not tolerate it. Castlereagh reiterated that his plan was unworkable and would only lead to friction with Austria and Prussia, and that if Alexander were to establish such a kingdom within his empire, it would eventually be abolished by one of his successors.[30]

The next day Nesselrode called on Castlereagh to sound out what he really thought of the Tsar's proposals, and received the same answer. He was also told that if Russia persisted in claiming the whole of the grand duchy 'it would have the colour of an attempt to revive the system we had all united to destroy', by replacing the hegemony of France with that of Russia. Such an attempt would be 'repugnant' to all and would, Castlereagh assured Nesselrode, sooner or later lead to war.[31]

The following morning Castlereagh called on Hardenberg, hoping to enlist his support against Alexander, but he found the Prussian chancellor in low spirits. He had had an audience with his own King the previous day, and had discovered that Frederick William had been persuaded by Alexander to accept his claims on Polish territory. On 28 September Metternich had another conversation with Alexander on the subject of Poland, and found him intractable. The Tsar's manner had changed, and Metternich realised he would not lend himself to being manipulated as before. Also, the tempo of social life was such that it was no easier to pin anyone down in Vienna than it had been during the campaign of the previous year. 'Nothing but visits and return visits; eating, fireworks, illuminations,' Archduke John noted in his diary on 29 September. 'For 8–10 days I haven't been able to get anything done. What a way to live!'[32]

The only ray of light for Metternich in this otherwise desolate landscape came from Baron Hager's daily reports, which showed that the surveillance machine they had put in place had ground into action. One agent had been successfully taken on as a valet at the Russian embassy. The Jewish banking houses had been penetrated, revealing interesting information on the financial circumstances and arrangements of the delegates. An Austrian official in the Chancellery passing information to the Papal Nuncio had been caught out. The British had, annoyingly, hired their own maids, and neither the embassy nor Castlereagh's lodgings had been infiltrated, but various members of the British delegation had been going out whoring, and the Hungarian wine they had taken such a liking to was making them talkative. Some of the reports were trivial in the extreme. One conscientiously noted that the British had been heard complaining that nobody served proper tea in Vienna. Others were more amusing. 'Princess Paul Esterhazy is having an affair that everyone knows about with Prince Charles Liechtenstein (an uhlan officer),' one agent reported. 'The husband, Prince Paul, is as jealous as he is desolate. The Princess's mother, the Princess Taxis, has taken the side of her daughter; all hell has broken loose in the family.'[33]

On 29 September the ministers of the four powers held their first official meeting, with Gentz taking minutes. He noted that the conference was 'very lively' and that there was much 'heated debate'. They nevertheless agreed the text of a declaration setting out their proposed *modus operandi*. It explained the problems likely to arise from a general assembly, and protested that they were guided only by considerations of the general good. 'In order to proceed with order and method,' it argued, 'it was of evident necessity to simplify the work by concentrating it . . .' It then set out the procedure agreed on 23 September.[34]

They resolved to communicate this declaration to the plenipotentiaries of France and Spain on the morrow, one day before it was made public. That evening there were fireworks and the city was illuminated in anticipation of the opening of the congress, due to take place two days later.

17

~~~◦○◦~~~

Notes and Balls

Shortly after 9 o'clock the following morning, 30 September, Talleyrand's ritual *toilette* was interrupted by the delivery of a note from Metternich. It was insultingly brief and made an unpleasant impression on him: it invited the plenipotentiary of France to assist at a conference between the ministers of the four great powers at Metternich's residence on the Rennweg. He was in the process of writing a curt reply when the plenipotentiary of Spain was announced.

Don Pedro Gomez Havela, Marqués de Labrador, was a poet. But there was nothing gentle or retiring in his nature. Nor was he a natural diplomat. 'Raised in Estremadura and educated in Salamanca, he was not destined for export,' in the words of his biographer. He had led an eventful life, as ambassador to two Popes and to the King of Etruria, then as Foreign Minister of the Cortes in Cadiz, interspersed with spells in French gaols. He was a dedicated reactionary and a firm supporter of King Ferdinand's most repressive policies. His priorities at the congress were to restore Ferdinand's sister the Queen of Etruria to the throne of Parma, Piacenza and Guastalla or, failing that, to find her another throne in Italy, perhaps in Genoa (promised to the King of Sardinia under the Treaty of Paris), and to recover Louisiana (incorporated into the United States of America since 1803).[1]

Labrador burst into Talleyrand's dressing room brandishing a note similar to the one the French minister had just received. In his reply, Talleyrand had written that he would gladly join the plenipotentiaries of Russia, Britain, Austria, *Spain* and Prussia, and he recommended that Labrador reply in the same vein, inserting France into his text.[2]

When Talleyrand was ushered in just before the indicated time of 2 o'clock that afternoon, he found himself in a large room with a long table running down the middle, at the head of which sat Castlereagh. Gentz was seated at the other end, pen poised to minute the meeting, while Metternich, Nesselrode, Hardenberg and Humboldt occupied places down the side. Talleyrand limped over to an empty chair between Castlereagh and Metternich, and sat down. He then asked why he had been invited to come alone, without his second plenipotentiary. He was told that all their meetings were held with only the principal plenipotentiaries present. What, in that case, he asked, was Humboldt doing there? The reply was that Hardenberg's infirmity (he was hard of hearing) required the presence of an assistant. Talleyrand rejoined that he too suffered from an infirmity – a fact of which Hardenberg, who regularly referred to him in his diary as '*M. Bocks Fuss*' ('Mr Club-foot'), would no doubt have been aware – and demanded that in future he be allowed to bring an assistant.

Once Labrador had arrived and seated himself, Castlereagh read out a letter from Dom Peter de Sousa-Holstein, Conde de Palmella, the plenipotentiary of Portugal, protesting that he and the plenipotentiary of Sweden had not been invited, and demanding that all decisions be taken in common by all eight signatories of the Treaty of Paris, not just four or six of them. The matter was discussed, but a decision was adjourned.

'The object of today's conference,' Castlereagh told Talleyrand, 'is to inform you of what the four Courts have done since we have been here.' He then turned to Metternich, who handed Talleyrand the declaration regarding procedure which they had so painstakingly agreed on 23 September and officially endorsed the previous day. Talleyrand ran his eyes over the text and frowned. 'In every paragraph of this piece I found the word *allies*,' he reported to Louis XVIII. 'I picked up this word: I said that it obliged me to wonder where we were, whether it was still at Chaumont or at Laon, whether indeed peace had been made, whether there was still a conflict on, and against whom.' Savouring their discomfiture, he then read and reread the text of the declaration carefully, feigning bafflement. 'For me,' he said, 'there are two dates of importance and nothing between them: that of 30 May, on which the convocation of a Congress was stipu-lated, and that of 1 October, when it is meant to convene. Every-thing that has been done in the interval is alien to me and does not concern me.'

Whatever the others had expected of the meeting, it had not been this, and they were bereft of arguments. They withdrew the declar-ation, which became the first of what was to become a heap of discarded effort. They then attempted to persuade Talleyrand and Labrador of the necessity of working through restricted committees, to which all interested parties could address their cases, and whose decisions would be ratified at the end by the first full meeting of the congress.

Talleyrand held to his view that if they wanted to endow their decisions with the approval of Europe, this should be sought at the outset rather than at the end. Castlereagh and Metternich argued that to throw the conference open to all would lead to endless compli-cations and end in chaos. Knowing Talleyrand's aversion to admitting a plenipotentiary of Murat, they explained that they would not be able to exclude one from Naples. But Talleyrand was unshaken. He retorted that he did not know of any King of Naples other than Ferdinand IV, and his plenipotentiary should certainly be admitted.

The firmness he and Labrador showed at this first meeting took the others aback. They had grown used to heeding only each other, and it had not occurred to them that they would be obliged to argue points with the plenipotentiaries of powers they regarded as strictly passive players. 'The intervention of these two persons violently dis-rupted our plans and reduced them to naught,' recorded Gentz in his diary. 'They protested against the form we had adopted, they berated us vigorously for two hours; it is a scene I shall never forget.'[3]

Metternich was so flustered by the end of the meeting that he diverted himself by spending the next couple of hours inspecting the preparations for the ball he would be giving in a few days' time; turning his mind to something frivolous always had a calming effect on him. That evening he went to see Wilhelmina, and spent the night with her. It was not until the following day, when he read the police reports, that he discovered what had been happening in Princess Bagration's apartment across the landing.

Being indisposed that evening, the Princess had told her servants that she was not at home, but late that night she heard someone ringing the doorbell and then a commotion, so she went out onto the landing, undressed as she was, and saw the Tsar climbing the stairs. She welcomed him in, and according to police reports he stayed three hours. He questioned her at length on her affair with Metternich, and would not drop the subject until she had assured him that she had never loved him.[4]

While Metternich and Alexander were indulging themselves in the Palm Palace, Talleyrand was working on a document that would annoy the four ministers even more than his performance of that afternoon. His note was ready the next day, 1 October, when he sent it round to the plenipotentiaries of all eight signatories of the Treaty of Paris. It proposed that while the eight should indeed be the ones in charge of preparing the groundwork and the form the conference was to take, and should appoint committees to deal with specific questions, they had no right to make decisions governing the whole of Europe without the involvement of all the powers concerned.

Having sent off his note, Talleyrand went to an audience with Alexander to which he had been summoned. The Tsar took him by the hand as he came in, but as Talleyrand reported to Louis XVIII, 'his manner was not as affectionate as usual; he spoke in short phrases, his bearing grave and perhaps even a little solemn'. He made a number of enquiries about the political situation in France, and then, taking a more decisive tone, got down to business.

'Now let us talk about our affairs; we must conclude them here,' he said.

'That depends on Your Majesty,' replied Talleyrand. 'They will be concluded promptly and happily if Your Majesty brings to them the same nobility and the same elevation of spirit as He did to those of France.'

'But here everyone must look to his interests.'

'And everyone find his rights.'

'I will keep what I hold.'

'Your Majesty will only wish to keep that which is legitimately His.'

'I have the agreement of the great powers.'

'Does Your Majesty count France among those powers?'

'Yes, assuredly, but if you do not wish everyone to safeguard their interests, what do you propose?'

'I put the law first and interests second.'

'The interests of Europe are the law.'

'That language, Sire, is not yours; it is alien to you and your heart disavows it.'

'No, I repeat, the interests of Europe are the law.'

At no point did they mention Saxony by name, but when Alexander referred obliquely to Frederick Augustus as one of 'those who have betrayed the cause of Europe', he was brought up short by Talleyrand. 'Sire, that is merely a question of dates,' he retorted, reminding Alexander that along with most of the other crowned heads in Vienna he too had at one point made a pact with Napoleon against the others.

As the interview was drawing to a close, Talleyrand asked the Tsar to put the good of Europe first. 'I would rather have war than give up what I occupy,' Alexander replied, and, getting no answer from Talleyrand, repeated: 'Yes, I would rather have war.' Then, throwing up his hands, he exclaimed: 'It's time for the theatre, I have to go, I promised the Emperor, they are expecting me.' He left the room, but returned after a moment, embraced Talleyrand and went out again.[5]

That evening Alexander could be seen dancing and chatting with the most beautiful women at a ball given by Princess Bagration, which he did not leave until 4 o'clock in the morning. It was being whispered around the drawing rooms that Talleyrand had had 'a very sharp and very remarkable interview, in which, on both sides, the most energetic and most threatening demonstrations had not been spared'. The Prussians, fearing that Talleyrand might thwart Alexander's plans on Poland and therefore their own designs on Saxony, were already putting it about that France was trying to provoke a new war.[6]

The next morning, 2 October, Hardenberg conferred with Metternich on what to do about Talleyrand's note. He was furious at this French incursion into the preserve of the four great powers. Metternich for his part was hurt by the Frenchman's refusal to allow him to orchestrate the proceedings. But there were more alarming implications to Talleyrand's actions. The text of the note had been leaked, and this had spurred the plenipotentiaries of thirteen minor German states to gather together and call on larger states such as Bavaria to join them in resisting what they termed the 'usurpation' of the great powers. This gave the conference held at Metternich's that afternoon 'a most unpleasant complexion', in Castlereagh's words. They decided not to lend Talleyrand's note added importance by a formal response, but agreed that they would now have to include Portugal and Sweden in their deliberations at the very least.[7]

That evening there was a great ball at the Hofburg to mark the opening of the congress, attended by several thousand people. It was a magnificent affair, taking in not only the two huge ballrooms but also the indoor riding school, with avenues of orange trees in tubs connecting them. 'The lighting of the great riding house was the grandest thing I ever saw,' Lord Apsley wrote to Lord Bathurst. 'The walls were lighted in every direction with lustres, besides there were in the centre three rows of chandeliers (24 in all) of sixty lights each, the middle row (eight) of seventy.' The Marchese di San Marzano, plenipotentiary of the King of Sardinia, counted 12,000 candles. The publisher Carl Bertuch counted 16,000. The simple act of lighting them had taken a swarm of servants a great deal of time, and the Marchese wondered at the efficiency of the arrangements and the service.[8]

Elise von Bernstorff, a young German married to the Danish ambassador in Vienna, had never seen anything like it. 'In place of the windows there were enormous mirrors which reflected 100,000 sparkling lights,' she wrote. 'The stairs swept down in two arcs to the floor of the riding school, which was covered with parquet and ringed on three sides with rows of seats like an amphitheatre. Blinded and almost dizzy, I paused for a few moments at the top of the stairs, and once I had gone down I could view the dazzling procession as the whole court of Vienna and those of other countries descended.'[9]

'Crush,' Hardenberg jotted down in his diary. He disliked large gatherings and was in a bad mood besides, but even he could not resist adding '– many beautiful women.' Others recorded gossip about who had danced with whom, and some made mocking references to Lady Castlereagh having stayed away on the grounds that it was Sunday – the Sabbath was observed with an Anglican service at the British embassy.[10]

Count Schönholz was most impressed by the quality of the buffets, but agreed with Hardenberg about the crush, for which he blamed the ticket collectors at the doors, who, according to him, resold the tickets they collected, netting a handsome profit. 'Rumour has it that fully a quarter of the 10,000 silver tea spoons, bearing the imperial crest, disappeared among the crowd.'[11]

The opening ball might have been a success, but there was no opening. The next day, 3 October, Castlereagh drafted a declaration postponing the congress, explaining that the plenipotentiaries of the principal powers needed more time to prepare the ground. That same day Talleyrand composed a second note protesting against the adjournment, taking the opportunity to repeat the arguments he had already put before them. And he showed this to a wider group of representatives.[12]

That evening they all met at a ball given by Metternich in honour of the visiting sovereigns. This had been laboriously prepared and minutely choreographed by the chancellor himself. He had constructed a number of buildings around his residence, including a grand entrance with covered staircase leading into a series of chambers, each of which represented a military encampment of one of the allied armies. As the sovereigns passed through these they were greeted by martial music and cheered by troops waving their shakos and bearskins on the ends of their bayonets. From here they passed into the magically illuminated garden, at the end of which they could see a huge buffet prepared 'for the people of lesser distinction'. Turning off the main avenue, the sovereigns found themselves in a small copse arranged as an amphitheatre, where they watched a short play. Going on, they entered a Russian village, complete with dancing and cheering moujiks welcoming their victorious Tsar. Further on they paused to watch some dancers execute a ballet on a lawn garnished with bunches of flowers which, as a finale, they gathered up and laid at the feet of the sovereigns while a group of singers gave voice to their joy and devotion.

After this perambulation, the royal party entered the house, up a covered stairway flanked by orange trees, and into a large hall where a group of soldiers performed their drill, from where they at last reached a newly erected ballroom encircled by a colonnade supporting a gallery from which guests could watch the dancing. As a precaution against fire, there was no fabric used in the decoration of the ballroom, which was festooned instead with garlands of flowers. The sovereigns then watched a fireworks display, at the end of which the ball could at last begin. The people of greater distinction were served supper in the house. An observant guest noted that 'this minister had the plate of a sovereign; more than one hundred and fifty people were served on silver plates, while each table had tureens, urns, salvers, flatware, etc., worked with the taste and mastery reserved normally only for services destined for crowned heads'.[13]

The next morning there was a hunting party for the sovereigns at

Mariabrünn. Over a hundred wild boar were shot, most of them by the hog-like King of Württemberg. After the massacre the royal party adjourned to a nearby castle for dinner, followed by a ball, at which even the usually staid Emperor Francis danced several times with the Tsarina Elizabeth.[14]

On 5 October the four ministers met for what Hardenberg described as a 'very stormy conference about Mr Club-foot's notes'. The upshot was a forceful letter to Talleyrand in which Castlereagh summed up their views. This merely elicited a reply in which Talleyrand protested that while 'nobody likes bringing up difficulties less than I do; nobody wishes more ardently than me to simplify, abbreviate and to conclude', he held to his conviction that denying the whole congress a say in the initiation of the process would be to deny its final decisions popular legitimacy.[15]

Later the same day there was another conference, in which Talleyrand and Labrador took part, described by Gentz as 'long and stormy'. Metternich asked Talleyrand to withdraw his notes, repeating all the reasons why the four should keep control of the proceedings. Talleyrand refused. He stated that if they wished to proceed in that manner, they could do so without him; he would join the others present in Vienna in waiting for the congress to open. This was a barely veiled threat – Talleyrand on the outside, in a position to rally the hundreds of disgruntled petitioners great and small, was not an attractive prospect.

Gentz was in despair. 'I do not dare to say, and nobody would at this point, what will be the precise result of this ill-conceived, miscalculated, poorly prepared congress, which I have no hesitation in regarding as one of the worst projects of this great epoch,' he wrote on 6 October, 'but what I believe to be a certainty is that it will produce none of the advantages which Europe has had the good will to expect of its coming together.'[16]

After agonising over the fate of the congress, Gentz set off, like everyone else in Vienna, for the Augarten park, where a festival had been arranged. The heroes of the occasion were some 4,000 veterans of the late war, who paraded before the sovereigns and then sat down to a banquet with them. Other attractions included pony races, athletic competitions, acrobatic displays, archery contests by Tyrolean crossbowmen and even a hot-air balloon. Gypsies, Hungarian peasants and representatives of other ethnic groups in the Habsburg dominions performed folk dances and a variety of bands and orchestras played as the sovereigns wandered about chatting to the veterans. When night fell the whole scene was illuminated by thousands of lanterns. The secretary to the delegation from Geneva, Jean-Gabriel Eynard, was impressed by the arrangements but struck by the lack of animation of the locals. 'The people walked about without gaiety,' he noted.[17]

Most of them were only there to gawp at the sovereigns. Never in the history of Europe had crowned heads ventured into the crowd with such informality and lack of distance. The fête was well attended as a result, and Countess Bernstorff complained that the crush had been so great 'that many prominent ladies came home with torn dresses and missing some of their gems'.[18]

The next meeting to which Talleyrand and Labrador were invited took place on 8 October. Talleyrand arrived early. Metternich tried to bribe him by offering to expedite the removal of Murat from Naples as a *quid pro quo*. But Talleyrand was not to be caught out that easily. 'Here are paper and pens,' he retorted. 'Please write down that France demands nothing, and would not even accept anything. I am ready to sign that.' Metternich interjected that since France wished to see Murat removed from Naples, that at least was one of her demands. Talleyrand was having none of it. 'It is for me only a matter of principle,' he explained. 'I demand that the one who has the right to be in Naples, be in Naples no more. And that is what everyone should wish as I do. As long as you follow principles, you will find me amenable in everything.'[19]

Talleyrand was a consummate negotiator, and knew how to exasperate as well as how to cajole, when to act and when to keep silent.

'One of the qualities of this statesman,' according to Labrador, 'was an ability to master himself so far that, even in the middle of the most lively discussion, if he could see that he would not carry the advantage, he would resign himself and go to sleep.'[20]

When the others joined them, at 8 o'clock in the evening, Metternich read out the project of a declaration prepared by himself in consultation with Castlereagh, Nesselrode and Hardenberg, adjourning the opening of the congress to 1 November. Asked whether he would sign it with them, Talleyrand declared that he would, provided a phrase was introduced to the effect that the opening of the congress would take place 'in accordance with the public law'. This provoked irritation in most of the ministers, and near apoplexy in Hardenberg, who stood up and began thumping the table with his fist and shouting (as he frequently did, being extremely hard of hearing). 'No, sir, why the public law?' he roared. 'It is unnecessary. Why state that we will act in accordance with the public law? It goes without saying.' To which Talleyrand retorted that if it went without saying, it would go even better if they did say it. 'What has the public law got to do with it?' jeered Humboldt, receiving the reply: 'It is by virtue of it that you are here at all.' There followed what Gentz describes as 'an extremely sharp and infinitely curious discussion'. When the commotion died down a vote was taken, and Talleyrand's point was carried. They had argued for three hours, and it was 11 p.m.[21]

Talleyrand liked to represent his feats during the first two weeks at Vienna as a personal triumph and a victory for France. On the face of it, they achieved little. The four carried on as before, meeting amongst themselves and determined to take all the major decisions without interference from anyone. Alexander sneered that Talleyrand was behaving as though he were the minister of Louis XIV, and Stewart dismissed his behaviour as 'wicked' troublemaking. In a letter to the Duchess of Courland Talleyrand admitted that he was now 'in dispute with all the potentates on earth', and particularly with the Prussians, but comforted himself that 'they are nasty people, and M de Humboldt even more so than the others'.[22]

He had nevertheless achieved his first aim. He had eliminated any possibility of the four former allies doing a deal amongst themselves, and he had won a place for France as one of the players. 'Our words are beginning to carry some weight,' he reported with satisfaction to Louis XVIII. They were certainly picked up where he wanted. 'Is it not very extraordinary,' declared Freiherr von Hake, the plenipotentiary of Baden, ' – for the first time since the beginning of the world the French are talking of principles; and nobody is listening to them?'[23]

Talleyrand's trumpetings on the theme of legitimacy were certainly not free of humbug, for while he denied Murat the royal title bestowed on him by Napoleon, he recognised those the Kings of Saxony, Bavaria and Württemberg had gratefully accepted from the 'usurper'. Nor was he about to give back to the Pope the fiefs of Avignon and the Venaissin. Yet he was not being gratuitously perverse and obstinate. He was genuinely alarmed at the tone being adopted, particularly by Russia and Prussia. The one thing he had hated in Napoleon was his refusal to acknowledge any right but that of the strongest, and he was horrified to see the new masters of Europe slipping into the same habit. 'I recognise in all the cabinets the principles and manner of thought of Bonaparte,' he confided in a letter to the Duchess of Courland on 4 October.[24]

The line he had taken was showing signs of paying off. By casting France in the role of the only one of the major powers that was truly disinterested, he had built up a following among the minor German princes, who saw in his championing of legitimacy their only hope of recovering lost lands and privileges. The refined but relaxed atmosphere of his house, rendered all the more appealing by his witty conversation, its enchanting hostess Dorothée and the culinary masterpieces of Carême, enticed ever more influential personages, giving him privileged access to information (Gentz was a finger-licking regular) and influence in widening circles. He was beginning to enjoy himself.

He operated with seeming effortlessness, keeping to his idiosyncratic routines and behaving as though he were at home. Eynard was struck by this when the delegates of Geneva called on Talleyrand on the morning of 9 October. 'It appeared that this minister was still abed, as attempts were made to prevent us from going up to his apartment, and at the moment when we entered his first salon we saw a young chick hurry out of his rooms, barely dressed,' he noted in his diary. He and his companions were kept waiting, watching valets come and go into and out of the bedroom, and after three-quarters of an hour Talleyrand finally emerged, fully dressed and bedecked with decorations.[25]

Talleyrand's intervention had not only dashed the four ministers' hopes of settling matters rapidly amongst themselves, it had high-lighted a fundamental flaw in their strategy. Metternich and Castle-reagh had planned to form a united front against Alexander made up of Austria, Britain and Prussia, with France in the second rank. But this could never work, however Hardenberg might have wished it.

Frederick William was convinced that he owed his survival on the throne to Alexander, and was personally devoted to him. So, however unhappy he might be at the idea of taking Saxony from her legitimate monarch, he was not going to stand up to the Tsar over Poland. Castlereagh and Metternich were not the only ones to try and fail to persuade him to change his position. His own ambassador in St Petersburg, General Schoeler, voiced a view that many in Prussia had tried to press on their King. 'He seems to be convinced that he owes the rank he has recovered among the sovereigns of Europe solely to the Emperor, without considering that if he had not allied himself to him, the theatre of the war in 1813 would have been the duchy of Warsaw and the position of Russia very precarious,' as he explained. But Frederick William stuck to his own view of the situation. And although Prussian public opinion was increasingly anti-Russian, mainly on account of the behaviour of the Russian troops in their passage through the country, it was avid for territorial gain, which, it seemed, only Russia could guarantee.[26]

On 9 October, in an attempt to rally him, Castlereagh had a long conversation with the Prussian chancellor. Hardenberg produced a formal note he had drawn up, listing all Prussia's territorial demands. Castlereagh had no strong feelings on Saxony, and regarded it as a pawn to be traded in the interests of a satisfactory settlement. Desperate to enlist the support of Prussia, he therefore agreed to the demands, on condition she joined Austria and Britain in confronting Alexander over Poland. He asked his assistant Edward Cooke to produce a *note verbale* on the subject, and the result was a mealy-mouthed document which used specious arguments to prove that by his 'criminal conduct' Frederick Augustus of Saxony had forfeited all rights to his throne, and that consequently his country should be considered to be at the disposal of the allies. 'It is difficult to believe that men with reputations to lose could put their names to such paltry reasoning,' was Gentz's comment. Castlereagh sent this to Hardenberg, effectively sanctioning Prussia's claim and encouraging him to pursue it. Gagern viewed this as a major '*faux pas*', explained only by the ignorance of the 'English islanders'.[27]

Castlereagh then went to see Talleyrand and gave him a dressing-down. He told him that 'it was not for the Bourbons, who had been restored by the Allies, to assume the tone of reprobating or throwing odium upon the arrangements which had kept the confederacy together'. 'I left him in a temper apparently to be of use; but I have lived now long enough with my foreign colleagues not to rely very implicitly upon any appearances,' he admitted to Liverpool.[28]

That evening there was a *bal paré* at court. Once again it was held in the great riding school, in which a platform had been erected for the sovereigns to sit on. 'The sight was stunning, it was as light as at midday with several suns,' according to Anna Eynard, the young wife of the secretary of the Genevan delegation. 'Everything was so brilliant that one could have thought oneself in one of those fairy palaces of which the thousand and one nights have given us such pretty accounts.'[29]

Etiquette required that the men wear full dress uniform with all their decorations, and the women tiaras. On this occasion it had been decided that a number of ladies would create an attraction by dressing up to represent the elements. 'First came Air, enacted by twelve ladies wearing dresses of blue gauze with garlands and Zephyrean wings at their shoulders; then came Fire, consisting of ladies dressed in red dresses, head-dresses of red and gold, gold jewellery and fringes of the same colour round their waist, bearing in their hands flaming torches,' in the words of Anna Eynard. 'Fire was followed by Water: these nymphs were dressed in light green gauze, with many reeds on their heads mixed with rough coral, while some of them had seashells worked into their hair, which cascaded over their shoulders, their breasts covered in coral and pearls, etc., etc. The prettiest of this whole masquerade was without question the Earth, represented by all that it possesses that is most beautiful and most brilliant. [. . .] they wore dresses of silver cloth, their breasts were covered with diamonds, their neatly brushed hair framed their faces in the most modest manner, and this was topped by baskets of diamonds of a delightful shape, which encircled their heads and out of which cascaded quantities of flowers.' Not everyone was as impressed, and San Marzano's diary entry notes 'riches without elegance, mixture of young pretty ones and old and ugly ones'.[30]

After these bizarre apparitions had made their tour of the ballroom and been admired and applauded, the ball began. Formal balls such as this were opened by the Empress and the Tsar, followed by the Emperor and the Tsarina, and so on, dancing the polonaise. This stately dance, a kind of mincing progress around the room, was much appreciated at the first few balls, as it gave everyone a chance to see the royal personages at close quarters. But after a couple of weeks in Vienna, every shopkeeper and street urchin had had ample opportunity to acquaint himself with the faces and figures of the great, so the company was eager to move on to the other dances. These normally included the minuet, the quadrille and the écossaise, which were being supplanted by the more intimate and more lively waltz – though the one danced at the time was slower than that for which Vienna became famous a few decades later.

On this evening, however, the sovereigns continued to parade around the rooms, with the orchestra playing the same polonaise over and over again. The monotony and joylessness of the proceedings soon overwhelmed the company, who assaulted the sumptuous buffet, which offered, according to Anna Eynard, 'a thousand good things to eat, ices, punch, broths, sweets of all sorts, and the finest delicacies'. Stewart contrived to enjoy himself regardless of the monotony of the occasion, and was observed revelling, drunk as a lord in his magnificent hussar's uniform covered in sparkling decorations.[31]

It was not boredom that had made Talleyrand abandon Dorothée at the ball and come home early. 'Things are looking very dark,' he wrote to the Duchess of Courland at 1 a.m. And he was not the only one in gloomy mood. 'You will see we are at sea,' Castlereagh had written to Wellington earlier that day, 'and have only to pray for favourable winds and currents.' It was difficult to see where these would come from.[32]

The activity organised for the next morning was a visit to the battlefields of Aspern-Essling and Wagram. This turned out to be a bad idea. The Russian party, from the Tsar and his brother Grand Duke Constantine down to the most junior subaltern, needled their Austrian counterparts, suggesting that Aspern-Essling had hardly been a victory and defeat had only been averted through luck, and that the defeat of Wagram was a surer measure of their military worth. Hardly the behaviour of allies.[33]

Kings' Holiday

Throughout the previous year the monarchs and their ministers had complained of the conditions in which they were obliged to carry on their negotiations – communicating through messengers galloping the length and breadth of Europe, by boat across the Baltic and the North Sea, meeting on battlefields and in roadside cottages, conferring in provincial inns amid all the uncertainties of a military campaign. They had looked forward to being able to establish a regular congress amid the amenities of a civilised city. But having achieved this, they found that they could hardly talk without being overheard, write a letter that was not read by others, express a view that was not misinterpreted or magnified, or meet anyone without arousing suspicion.

'In the mornings, the Kings, if they are not engaged in playing soldiers, go for strolls on foot; when there are no grand parades or hunts they pay calls; in a word, they lead the lives of young bachelors,' recorded Baroness du Montet, a lady of the court. 'In the evenings they put on full dress uniform, they shine at the truly fairytale parties given for them by the Emperor of Austria.' She felt that 'The Kings are like children who need to play after a period of application,' and saw the proceedings as 'a Kings' holiday'. 'History is taking a rest, the sovereigns are amusing themselves, they are on holiday, and they are enjoying their furlough,' she concluded.[1]

This was certainly true of most of them, but they had all come with some piece of business in mind, and the social distractions were so manifold that they found it hard to concentrate and to make others listen, and so relentless that they soon felt jaded. 'The parties are exhausting me,' Talleyrand complained in a note to the Duchess of Courland after the opening ball. Even Gentz, who was at the centre of everything, confessed that he was meeting so many people, in so many different groups, in different places at different times of the day, that he could no longer follow events, and did not know what was going on.[2]

All those who had come to Vienna in the hope of furthering their interests or redressing some wrong had assumed that they would, at the very least, have access to some international forum which, even if it did not accord them what they wanted, would at least hear them out. They were quickly disenchanted. 'Political affairs are being treated with inconceivable frivolity,' complained the Danish plenipotentiary Count Rosenkrantz. No public body had convened, and the only forum on which they could further their business was that provided by the rituals of court and social life. They vented their anger publicly, but privately resorted to lobbying ministers, princes, people of influence or their mistresses, in the hope of placing their case within the brief of a more important player. This only complicated matters for the more important players, who soon found that whichever way they swung on any question they were bound to upset one client or another.[3]

The sovereigns who had come to the congress, particularly those who had been distinguished by being lodged at the Hofburg, had assumed that they at least would be able to play a part. But it did not take them long to realise that they were to be kept at arm's length. 'We appear to be here for no other purpose but to divert ourselves,' complained Frederick William of Prussia. 'You have no idea how time is being wasted here,' King Frederick of Denmark wrote to his wife on 28 September, shortly after his arrival.[4]

He had only come to Vienna to seek the fulfilment of what was due to Denmark under the Treaty of Kiel, now ten months old. He needed to persuade Alexander to ratify the treaty and withdraw his troops; to obtain possession of Swedish Pomerania and Rügen as well as the million thalers which he was owed in return for giving up Norway; and to obtain payment for the victuals he had supplied the Swedish and Russian armies during their occupation of Danish territory.

Trying to pin down Alexander proved to be a frustrating and humiliating business. The Tsar would assure Frederick that he was on the point of ratifying the treaty and sending the order for his troops to withdraw from Holstein, but did nothing. Whenever the King tried to press him on the matter, he would say that he was late for a parade or a ball, and cut the conversation short. Or that he was waiting for a courier, and that once he had settled a piece of important business he would attend to the ratification. All the treaty required was his signature, but this he continued to withhold.

This may have been because he wanted to show loyalty to Bernadotte, whom he had let down over the French throne. And Bernadotte saw no reason to limit his ambitions to the clauses of the Treaty of Kiel. He was still seeking a grander role for himself, and entertained a number of schemes, one of which was a partition of Denmark between Sweden and Britain, which he assumed would like to increase her dominion of the seas by the addition of Greenland, the Faroes and other colonies.

Castlereagh was not interested in acquiring further colonies and would not have dreamt of reducing Denmark, but he was not particularly supportive of Frederick, who badgered everyone, from Talleyrand to Francis, begging them to intercede with Alexander on his behalf. While most of them were sympathetic, Denmark was low on their lists of priorities. Only Hardenberg, whose daughter-in-law was Danish, was willing to help, but he was in no position to put pressure on Alexander. 'If only the Emperor Alexander were less partial to the Crown Prince [Bernadotte] than he is, everything would be settled easily, as no Russian and no other foreigner is against us,' complained Frederick, 'on the contrary, they are all very much on our side.'[5]

Frederick pursued his purpose tirelessly, making it clear to all that he was not attempting to gain any advantage or even to recover any part of Norway, only to preserve his kingdom from further dissection. He earned universal respect by his gentlemanly and honest behaviour, but nothing more. Others were similarly frustrated.

'Our existence here is very pleasant, but we are told nothing of what is going on or of what will happen to us,' King Maximilian of Bavaria complained. 'The Cabinet of Vienna is treating us as the French used to do.' He and his brother monarchs shored up their sense of importance by exchanging orders and colonelcies in elite regiments of their own armies and receiving the homage of lesser mortals, whom they would occasionally oblige with a decoration. But their pride was on edge. While the sovereigns themselves had resolved the question of precedence by deciding on age as the criterion, there were arguments as the princes and archdukes trumped each other with rank, seniority or age. On one occasion at least it led to an unseemly scuffle between Grand Duchess Catherine and the Queen of Bavaria.[6]

However badly things might go for him, Maximilian did at least have a kingdom to go back to, and in this he was a great deal more fortunate than the hundreds who had come to safeguard, recover or acquire a fief of some kind. 'I am being pushed around, insulted,' complained the Duke of Saxe-Coburg. 'Metternich! . . . that *scoundrel* Metternich! He treats me like a toy! . . . And the Emperor Alexander, who sends me off to his ministers, who send me back to the Emperor! . . . I cannot obtain a strip of land, a single cottage, not one man; and, to add insult to injury, I am sent letters addressed with titles that I am claiming and being denied!'[7]

The position of Prince Eugène was even more frustrating. He was made much of by Alexander, and invited to sit at the royal table at many of the balls and banquets. Metternich repeatedly assured him that he would soon be getting an Italian principality or some other fief, such as the former bishopric of Treves, the duchy of Zweibrücken or even the Ionian islands to rule over. Yet his silver, his wife's jewellery, his personal possessions, even his clothes and his horses, remained in the hands of the Austrian military in Milan.[8]

Just as frustrated, and less hopeful, were the delegation of Geneva, consisting of Edmond Pictet and Sir Francis d'Ivernois, assisted by Jean-Gabriel Eynard. The Treaty of Paris had left Geneva in an impossible position; it was politically integrated into the Swiss Confederation, but physically cut off from it by a wedge of French territory around Gex and Versoix along the north of the lake, and by Sardinia along its southern shore. Pictet had already attempted to remedy this when the allies were in Paris, lobbying Castlereagh and others, with the support of Madame de Staël, to no avail. In Vienna, with the assistance of d'Ivernois, who was regarded in London and had a British knighthood, he again approached Castlereagh, but found him not only uncooperative but also unsympathetic. He did not give them time to present their case, and the best they could do was leave a memorandum with him, which he probably never read. Metternich was more welcoming, and did give them time to put their case. He was duly astonished when they pointed out that in their ignorance of mountain topography he and his colleagues had awarded Sardinia territory around Faucigny and Chablais in the Treaty of Paris which was only accessible through France. But other preoccupations soon pushed their case to the back of Metternich's mind, and all they could do was continue to press their suit with every person they met, in the hope that someone might remember it at some crucial moment.[9]

Much the same went for their countryman Abbot Vorster of the great monastery of St Gallen, a sovereign unit dissolved by the French in 1805, which he was hoping to restore. Although he had the support of Labrador, Consalvi and some of the Swiss delegates, he found most doors closed to him. Alexander brushed him off, and Metternich refused even to accept his memorandum. No more fortunate was the envoy of the republic of Genoa, who was treated in the most peremptory fashion by Castlereagh. The British Foreign Secretary would not let him put his case or even acknowledge the formal note of protest at the illegal extinction of the republic. All the envoy could do was publish it and hand it around.[10]

The Dutch delegates were more fortunate, as their cause was high on Castlereagh's agenda and had the almost undivided attention of Clancarty, but they were not happy at the way they were being treated. 'The English rather order us about,' complained van Spaen, while his colleague van der Capellen felt that things were proceeding 'more or less as if we were not there'.[11]

Those representing minor interests found that, since the great powers occasionally needed to call on the support of those they had taken under their wing in a confrontation over some issue, they wanted to be their exclusive protector, and therefore looked with displeasure on their talking to other great powers. This meant that a cause which was as universally popular as that of Geneva could find no firm backers.[12]

Most had expected to stay in Vienna for no more than a month or so. But while they saw time pass without any result, they could not go home without forfeiting the chance, however slight, of a say in their own fate. So they hung about, increasingly bored and frustrated. Many had come alone, without wives or families, and put up at hotels, expecting to stay no more than a week or two. They were stuck there, dining together night after night. The unforeseen length of their stay and the high prices quickly dealt with their funds.

'The majority of the representatives of the minor courts and the deputies of the cities and corporations are lamenting over the expense of living and have already emptied their pockets,' police chief Baron Hager was reporting as early as 7 October. 'It would nevertheless be good to find means of keeping them here. If they do that they will soon find themselves obliged to seek new resources, and at that moment we will, with little trouble and at the cost of a few favours, be able to untie their tongues.'[13]

The pool of his informers did indeed expand, but the results were disappointing. Many of the agents were complaining of the difficulties involved in purloining keys and letters for long enough to have copies made. Castlereagh's household had, it is true, been penetrated at last, but the agents could not lay their hands on anything of any real interest. 'The agent observes that as the box in Lord Castlereagh's desk contains nothing but private letters, it would be wiser to desist from trying to take cognisance of them, in view of the length and the dangers of such an operation,' Hager wrote on 8 October. Talleyrand's establishment was described by Police Councillor Schmidt as 'nothing less than a kind of fortress garrisoned by people he is sure of'. He had managed to bribe a couple of servants, but these had yielded no more than a few scraps of torn paper. To complicate matters, it appeared that both the Russians and the Prussians had put in place their own networks of secret agents, and that even minor players such as Prince Eugène had bribed various people in order to be kept informed. This raised the possibility that misinformation was being spread.[14]

Much of the information was certainly inconclusive and puzzling. Hager thought he was on to an interesting development when reports began coming in of Alexander's visits to a certain Madame Schwarz, the wife of a St Petersburg banker. There was some evidence that she and another lady from St Petersburg who was also in Vienna, a Madame Schmidt, were lavishing sexual favours on the Tsar – Madame Schmidt had told one informer that he preferred middle-class women to aristocratic ladies when it came to sex. Alexander was seen visiting Madame Schwarz regularly, and even gave her a valuable pearl necklace, but when her husband turned up and reports came in of large amounts of cash being deposited and withdrawn from various Viennese banks, Hager began to suspect that sex was only part of the story, and that there was a plan afoot to undermine the Austrian currency. Fascinating and tantalising as such reports must have been to Metternich, they did not yield anything that could serve a practical purpose.[15]

The vast effort of collecting and collating all this information was almost certainly of less use to Metternich than it has been to historians, whom it has helped to penetrate not only some of the political

RIGHT: This sketch by Anne-Louis Girodet-Trioson, drawn in March 1812, shortly before the Emperor set out on his disastrous Russian campaign, shows an ageing Napoleon who would have preferred to consolidate his gains rather than go to war. Twelve months later he was even more desperate for peace, but only one that would guarantee the continuance of his power. His mounting insecurity rendered him more aggressive, which brought his enemies and his allies together and led to his downfall. It would be they and not him who decided the future shape of Europe and the world.

ABOVE FAR RIGHT: As Napoleon's ambassador to Russia from 1807 to 1811, General Armand de Caulaincourt had done everything in his power to attempt to keep the two empires from conflict, and urged Napoleon to make peace at any price while he still could. Drawing by Jacques-Louis David.

RIGHT: Tsar Alexander I of Russia, personally convinced of his divine calling to save the world, was universally admired and hailed as a liberator. But his imperious behaviour came to be seen as the greatest threat to world peace, while his compulsive philandering turned him into a laughing-stock. Portrait by Sir Thomas Lawrence, 1817.

LEFT: Alexander's friend and adviser on international affairs, the Polish Prince Adam Czartoryski. While the Russian court never ceased to view him as a potential enemy, the other powers saw him as the most dangerous of the Russian negotiators. Portrait by Józef Oleszkiewicz, c.1806.

BELOW: Frederick William III of Prussia, who had been humiliatingly defeated by Napoleon and seen his kingdom reduced to a minor power, threw himself on the mercy of Alexander, whose devoted slave he remained while making aggressive territorial demands which nearly led to war between the allies. Portrait by Antonio Schrader, c.1817, after François Gérard.

LEFT: Austria's Foreign Minister Metternich cajoled and manipulated the other players in order to mould events to his vision of a safe Europe. Blinded by the conviction of his own brilliance, he defeated many of his own purposes, while his amorous pursuits entangled him in intrigue and brought him into conflict with Alexander. Portrait by Lawrence, c.1815.

LEFT: Francis I of Austria. Humourless by nature, he was distrustful of new ideas, indifferent to most forms of entertainment, and very devout. Following the French defeat of Austria in 1809 he had been forced to seal peace by giving his daughter Marie-Louise to Napoleon in marriage, a measure of the lengths he was prepared to go to in order to save the threatened Habsburg monarchy. Portrait by Friedrich von Amerling, c.1832.

ABOVE: Britain's Foreign Secretary Lord Castlereagh played a crucial role in bringing the powers of Europe together for the purpose of defeating France. A thoroughly decent and fair man, he saw his role at the congress as that of mediator, but found himself being drawn into unexpected conflicts and even into contemplating war with those he had seen as Britain's firmest allies. Portrait by Lawrence.

LEFT: The Prussian chancellor, Baron August von Hardenberg. Although prepared to fight ruthlessly for Prussia's interests, he was a product of the eighteenth century, courteous and kind by nature, and ill-suited to the politics of blood and iron being advocated by the Prussian generals at his back. Portrait by Lawrence.

ABOVE FAR LEFT: Russia's acting Foreign Minister, Count Charles Nesselrode. 'I am called when I am needed,' he explained of his role. 'I am completely passive.' Portrait by Lawrence.

ABOVE MIDDLE: Friedrich von Gentz, Secretary to the Congress of Vienna. Clever, widely travelled and wise in the ways of the world, he was an invaluable friend and adviser to Metternich. Engraving by Johannes Lidner, after Friedrich Lieder, c.1824.

ABOVE: The austere German patriot Karl Heinrich vom Stein, who urged the utter destruction of Napoleon, and whose reforms in Prussia laid the groundwork for the eventual unification of Germany. Portrait by Johann Christoph Rincklake, c.1804.

LEFT: Wilhelmina, Princess of Sagan, whose tempestuous affair with Metternich distracted him from the business of the congress and whose amorous adventures with others entertained all of Vienna. 'She sins seven times a day and loves as often as others dine,' Metternich would later write, with much bitterness and only slight exaggeration. Portrait by Gérard, 1800.

ABOVE: General Charles Murray, Earl Cathcart, British ambassador to the court of Russia. An old soldier with little experience of diplomacy, he often found himself bewildered by the intricacies of European affairs, but pursued Castlereagh's aims with diligence and signed the Final Act at Vienna on behalf of Britain. Engraving by Henry Meyer, after John Hoppner, c.1807.

ABOVE: Sir Charles Stewart, British ambassador to the court of Prussia, was no diplomat either, but a soldier who had served on Wellington's staff in the peninsula. 'A most gallant fellow, but perfectly mad,' in the words of a brother officer, he was the source of much entertainment and scandal in Vienna. Portrait by Lawrence.

BELOW: The Prussian linguist, philosopher and ambassador to Vienna, Wilhelm von Humboldt, was not cut out to be a diplomat, and viewed much of the proceedings with scorn. His censoriousness and priggishness did not prevent him from indulging his taste for lower-class girls. Portrait by Lawrence.

BELOW: The twenty-eight-year-old George Gordon, Earl of Aberdeen, Castlereagh's envoy to the Austrian court, was yet another apprentice diplomat, but while he hated everything about the political maelstrom in which he found himself, he was quick to perceive that the British cabinet was out of touch with Continental realities, and tried to correct it. Portrait by Lawrence.

ABOVE: King Frederick Augustus of Saxony, a staunch ally of Napoleon whom the Tsar accused of having 'betrayed the cause of Europe' and attempted to dispossess. Engraving by Johann Rosmäsler, c.1812.

BELOW: King Maximilian I of Bavaria, 'a good, jolly, farmer-like looking fellow, crossed with the heaviness of a German Prince', according to one observer. Although his daughter was married to Napoleon's stepson Prince Eugène, he was the first of the German rulers to change sides, and the price he demanded for it would weigh heavily on the whole congress.

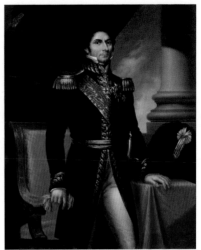

ABOVE: The Napoleonic Marshal Jean-Baptiste Bernadotte, Crown Prince of Sweden, who dreamed of succeeding Napoleon on the throne of France and who blackmailed the allies shamelessly: 'a bastard that circumstances had obliged us to legitimise', in the words of Hardenberg. Portrait by Frederik Westin.

BELOW: Frederick I, King of Württemberg, had such a gross appearance that an employee of the imperial household thought he had seen a pig drive by in one of the court carriages. In the words of one lady, he had 'the spirit of a devil in the body of an elephant'.

ABOVE: Tsar Alexander is cheered by the inhabitants of Paris as he passes through the Porte Saint-Denis at the head of his troops on 31 March 1814, with King Frederick William of Prussia at his side. By Jean Zipper.

BELOW: A French view of the capitulation of Paris, 30 March 1814. Talleyrand appears as a fox, Marshal Marmont as a cat. Prussia (in blue) and Russia (in green) eagerly clutch at the gold offered by England (in red).

LEFT: France's brilliant, pragmatic and versatile Foreign Minister Charles-Maurice de Talleyrand-Périgord, who was determined to save something for France, and himself, from the wreckage of Napoleon's empire, and who came to dominate the proceedings at the congress in his own particular way. Portrait by Pierre-Paul Prud'hon.

BELOW: Alexander's sister, the Grand Duchess Catherine. 'The Grand Duchess had an immoderate thirst for authority and a very high, and possibly excessive, opinion of herself,' noted Dorothea Lieven. 'I never saw a woman so possessed of the need to stir, act, put herself forward and eclipse others.'

BELOW: Alexander and the Grand Duchess take their leave of the Prince Regent at Petworth House on 24 June 1814, before travelling on to Dover to take ship. By Thomas Phillips.

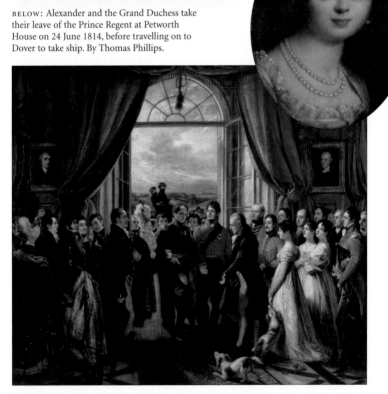

Metternich's official residence, the Austrian State Chancellery on the Ballhausplatz in Vienna. Watercolour by Rudolf Alt.

Metternich's study in the State Chancellery.

Metternich's elegant villa on the Rennweg, just outside Vienna's old town. Lithograph by Eduard Gurk, c.1814.

ABOVE: Since all the silver and gold flatware of the Austrian imperial household had been melted down to pay for the war of 1809, an enormous porcelain service simulating gold was run up for use at the congress.

ABOVE: The notorious Princess Catharine Bagration, 'the naked angel'. Her short-sightedness gave her blue eyes a lost, yielding look that few men could resist. Her many lovers included Tsar Alexander and Metternich, by whom she had a daughter. Portrait by Jean-Baptiste Isabey, c.1812.

LEFT: Talleyrand's mistress Dorothée, comtesse de Périgord. Thirty-nine years his junior, she was the daughter of his former lover the Duchess of Courland.

ABOVE: The meeting of the three monarchs. Francis I of Austria welcomes Tsar Alexander I of Russia and Frederick William III of Prussia just outside Vienna on 25 September 1814.

BELOW: A ball in the indoor riding school of Vienna's imperial palace, by Johann Nepomuk Hochle. 'The lighting of the great riding house was the grandest thing I ever saw,' wrote Lord Apsley.

LEFT: Lady Emily Castlereagh. Having been cut off from the Continent for so long, British women had lost contact with the mainstream of European fashion. Prince Schwarzenberg was astonished by Lady Castlereagh's dress sense: 'She is very fat and dresses so *young*, so *tight*, so *naked*.' Portrait by Lawrence.

BELOW FAR LEFT: Frederick VI of Denmark. His long teeth and constantly moving lips gave him the air of a ruminating goat, according to one observer. He was nevertheless the only one of the attending monarchs to earn universal respect, which did not prevent his efforts at the congress on behalf of his country from ending in almost total failure. Portrait by Christoffer Wilhelm Eckersberg, c.1821.

BELOW MIDDLE: Frederick VI's mistress in Vienna, Caroline Seufert, 'a young woman of the working class, blonde and pink, a pretty grisette'. The two were so faithful to each other that after he returned home she was universally referred to as 'the Danish widow'.

BELOW: The Pope's envoy to the congress, the pragmatic Cardinal Ercole Consalvi, by Jean-Dominique Ingres, c.1814.

ABOVE: The 'Festival of Peace' in the Prater in Vienna on 18 October 1814, the first anniversary of the Battle of Leipzig.

BELOW: The spectacular medieval Carrousel held at the riding school of Vienna's imperial palace on 23 November 1814.

ABOVE: The Congress of Vienna as imagined by Isabey. Standing, left to right: Wellington, Lobo (Portugal), Saldanha (Portugal), Löwenhielm, Noailles, Metternich, Latour Dupin (France), Nesselrode, Razumovsky, Stewart, unknown (leaning), Wacken (Austria), Gentz, Humboldt, Cathcart; seated, left to right: Hardenberg, Palmella, Castlereagh, Dalberg, Wessenberg, Labrador, Talleyrand, Stackelberg.

BELOW: How the outside world saw the congress. Left to right: Talleyrand, Castlereagh, Francis I, Alexander, Frederick William III, King Frederick Augustus of Saxony, the republic of Genoa.

RIGHT: Count Ioannis Capodistrias, a Corfiote nobleman in Russian service. While he could do little for his native Ionian islands at the congress, he earned respect by his hard work and goodwill, and would be rewarded in time by becoming president of a newly-independent Greece. Portrait by Dionysios Tsokos.

BELOW: Minutes, taken by Gentz, of a conference of the five great powers on 8 February 1815. Those present are listed in the left-hand column. Top to bottom: Metternich, Razumovsky, Castlereagh, Wellington, Talleyrand, Hardenberg, Wessenberg, Capodistrias, Humboldt. All the discussions and the official documents were in French.

BELOW RIGHT: A page from one of Hardenberg's proposals on how to restore Prussia to her former great-power status, showing which areas of Saxony would give her the requisite number of 'souls'. Reams of such documents were produced by the various parties in the course of the congress.

ABOVE: The imperial sleighing party held on 22 January 1815. A huge sleigh drawn by six horses and carrying an orchestra opened the procession. It was followed by a second driven by the Emperor Francis, with the Tsarina at his side. Thirty more sleighs, upholstered in green and blue velvet, embroidered with gold, drawn by horses coiffed with ostrich plumes, followed behind.

LEFT: The arrival of the Duke of Wellington to replace Castlereagh on 1 February 1815 was generally welcomed, but the following month he was compelled to leave Vienna because of Napoleon's escape from Elba. His firm and statesmanlike conduct after Waterloo would save France from further emasculation and prevent decisions already reached at Vienna from being called into question. Portrait by Lawrence, c.1815.

and diplomatic manoeuvres, but also the day-to-day activities of many of the participants, and to give an extraordinarily intimate insight into what was really going on in Vienna during those fateful months.

It was indeed a kind of Kings' holiday. While the Emperor Francis maintained his dignity by sticking to his normal routines, only appearing in public at court occasions, the visiting monarchs and ruling princes threw off the etiquette that constrained them within their own courts and revelled in the attractions on offer.

Vienna certainly lent itself to such a holiday, with its theatres, its rich musical life and its many other entertainments. Those attending the congress could see actors and dancers drawn from all over Europe and hear performances of Beethoven's *Fidelio* and Handel's *Samson* with seven hundred musicians under the baton of the court musical director Antonio Salieri. Amongst those who played in Vienna during the congress were Spohr and Hummel. Some of the concerts took place at the Apollosaal, a vast building created for the occasion by the French artist Moreau, containing everything from palatial interiors and gardens with fountains and waterfalls, to Turkish kiosks and peasant cottages.

For the more serious-minded, such as the King of Denmark, who visited them all, there were the imperial library and picture gallery, the Liechtenstein gallery, the Albertina collection, a number of fine churches, monuments and institutions, the palace of Laxenburg with its gardens, and Schönbrunn, with its interesting occupant Marie-Louise.

She was frequently visited by Alexander and his sisters, by some of the other sovereigns and by the merely curious. They were particularly eager to see her little son play with his (French) toy soldiers. She endured all the visits and treated everyone graciously, hoping to gain their support over her proposed acquisition of Parma, which still hung in the balance. But she did not enjoy the attention. 'I am very sad,' she wrote to her friend the widow of Marshal Lannes on 13 October, 'this gathering of sovereigns, this noise, these festivities which I am not obliged to attend but which I nevertheless hear about all afflict me.'[16]

There was certainly no lack of festivities, most of them laid on by the court. They included balls, theatrical and musical performances at court, dinners, visits to the various royal palaces and their gardens, military parades and hunts at one or other of the imperial palaces around Vienna. These were supplemented by balls and *soirées* given by Metternich, by Alexander at the magnificent palace of Count Razumovsky, a former Russian ambassador who had settled in the Austrian capital, by more intimate but much-sought-after dinners held by Talleyrand with the concourse of Carême, by the awkward dancing evenings at Lady Castlereagh's, and by all manner of humbler entertainments laid on by the lesser delegations, down to the tea parties given by the delegates of Geneva. Even Müller d'Arvaangue, the representative of the Swiss Confederation, entertained as best he could, and far more lavishly than his funds permitted, in the belief that it would help further his cause.

There were also a number of Viennese homes open to the visitors. Among these were the salons of the great hostesses, chief among them Countess Molly Zichy, a woman who was not liked but feared and respected. She was so determined to take the lead as the chief *salonière* of Vienna that she overspent disastrously and was obliged to ask Alexander for a loan, which she would never pay back. Both Wilhelmina of Sagan and Princess Bagration, the latter also living way beyond her means, gave dinners and dancing *soirées*. 'To supper at Princess Bagration's,' the laconic San Marzano jotted down in his journal, ' – curious mixture of grand living and bad form.'[17]

Less exalted in social terms but nevertheless well frequented were the houses of the Jewish bankers of Vienna, chief among them that of Baroness Fanny von Arnstein. One of the more interesting salons was that of Caroline Pichler, *egeria* of the German Romantic national movement and inventor of the dirndl. Her salon brought together like-minded German patriots, many of the dispossessed princes, and the publishers Carl Bertuch from Weimar and Johann Friedrich von Cotta, the friend and publisher of Goethe and Schiller.

Another home frequented by the great was that of Gentz, who lived in four rooms on the fourth floor of a house in the Seilergasse with a fine view over the Bastei. 'The approach to his lodgings was frightening,' records Countess Bernstorff. 'The entrance into the courtyard was so rough one could break one's neck; the doorway so low that it nearly destroyed my coiffure; the stairs, steep and dark, gave no hint of the kind of lodgings one was about to enter. In these small rooms was heaped everything that riches, taste and the most refined elegance could find. The senses of sight and smell were delighted, the desire for comfort was sated.'[18]

The luxury was of a particular kind, as the four rooms were devoted above all to the business of the congress, serving as the venue for many a conference and for Gentz's daily work of drafting minutes, memoranda, notes, declarations and letters. The apartment was carpeted throughout with thick, heavy rugs. The furniture was mismatched, old and worn, its arrangement dictated entirely by practicality and comfort. Gentz would read lying down, on an ottoman or a day bed, of which there were several. Each had a writing table beside it of the kind that could be swung across for him to be able to take notes without rising. There were pencils and quills at the ready everywhere. There were no pictures, mirrors or decorative objects, but there were books piled on every flat surface, mainly historical or political works and the classics, most of them with slips of paper tucked into them and annotations in the margins.[19]

His extraordinary workload did not prevent Gentz from attending most of the festivities and many dinners, particularly at Talleyrand's, or indeed from holding dinner parties himself, to which some of the grandest figures attending the congress would come, regardless of the squalid entrance to his lodgings. 'I contributed almost nothing to the conversation,' he recorded after one such evening. 'Metternich and Talleyrand went on in their usual way. Meanwhile I was overcome as never before by the futility of all human endeavour and the foibles of those who hold the world in their hands, as well as by my own superiority; but all this half-unconsciously, and as though lost in a fog that descended on my mind from the empty twaddle of these gentlemen . . .' He had early on taken a dim view of the proceedings, and devoted himself to having a good time and making as much money as he could, as he still liked to gamble and to spend lavishly. He was richly rewarded, as almost all of the participants and petitioners, seeing in him a pivotal figure, gave him large sums of money. 'People accused him of venality, and not without reason,' recalled Nesselrode, 'but he only took money from those who thought as he did.'[20]

The least lavish of the entertainers, but one of the greatest attractions of Vienna, was Charles-Joseph, prince de Ligne, a distinguished soldier who had fought in many of the wars of the eighteenth century. He was an even more distinguished social butterfly, familiar with every court of Europe, the friend of every monarch from Louis XV to Catherine the Great, and above all a renowned wit whose *bons mots* were repeated across the Continent. 'He lives in a kind of shack up a steep and narrow staircase,' recorded Eynard. 'His apartment is made up of three disorderly rooms, in which all manner of things are piled up, and he receives in his bedroom, at the end of which is a large sofa which serves as his bed. One always finds his two daughters, Princess Clary and Countess Palffy and all the most pleasant visitors with him. He always has an excellent fire, a rare thing in Vienna, where one finds only stoves. At midnight, one is served a bad supper which is always the same, be there seven or eight people present or thirty.' Ligne was seventy-nine years old but still bubbling with life, greedy for food, gossip and love. He was never at home if he could be out, and he accepted every invitation proffered, often taking in several dinners a day.[21]

The sheer number of parties, and the rapidity with which they succeeded each other, precluded too much in the way of preparation. This was fortunate for the ladies, most of whom would have been reduced to penury if they had been obliged to produce new dresses for each occasion. 'I do not recall any special expenses, except for the unavoidable one of providing myself with white gloves and shoes, of the hairdresser who came daily, for the two costumes for the Carrousel and the masquerade, on top of the little trousseau which my husband had brought me from Paris, which included several rich dresses and one or two ball dresses,' related Countess Bernstorff. 'In order to give some idea of the simplicity of the fashions at the time I might observe that a small tulle cap with rose-coloured trimmings had to serve me even at the *soirées* where there was dancing. Up to that time caps for young ladies had been unheard of, and the fashion had just come in. The richest ladies of Vienna were distinguished for their simplicity and covered themselves in jewellery only for the great festivities.'[22]

When a new dress was needed in a hurry, a dressmaker and a cloth merchant could be sent out for in the morning, and provided a cloth and a pattern were chosen by 10 o'clock, the dress would be delivered by 5 o'clock the same afternoon, although sometimes the seamstresses would still be at work as the lady was dressing. But on the whole, the same dresses were recycled with much alteration of trimmings and ribbons, which many of the ladies seem to have lent each other willingly.[23]

The range of festivities also precluded too much formality – which would in any case have been difficult to maintain given that most, including many of the court balls, were open to all comers. Some of the great balls in the riding school were attended by over 4,000 people, and some estimates put the numbers as high as 10–12,000. 'Never has an assembly been less ceremonious,' a British traveller noted after attending one. The citizens of Vienna of both sexes could therefore easily mingle with the grandest of the visitors, at court as well as on the Graben, the long open space at the heart of the city which was also a principal artery through which everyone would pass on their way to somewhere else, described by one of the great gossips of the time as 'a kind of open-air club' in which people loitered, promenaded, gathered in groups and met to intercept or simply watch those passing through.[24]

One unwonted effect of all this commingling was that gossip and rumour acquired authority, as anyone could credibly quote an authoritative source. Alexander and Frederick William talked politics to the ladies over dinner or during the dance. The ladies in question could hardly be expected to resist advertising their closeness to a crowned head by passing on what they had been told, with the result that garbled versions of the Tsar's or the King of Prussia's views and intentions circulated round the court and the city.

The intensity of the social life, combined with the sense of frustration felt by the majority of the men present, soon began to have a corrupting effect, in more ways than one. Rivalries came to the surface, mutual antipathies led to confrontations. Several ended in duels, not always in bloody fashion. During a game of blind-man's-buff at a *soirée* given by Princess Turn und Taxis at the beginning of October, the Crown Prince of Bavaria caught the beautiful (and notoriously chaste) Countess Julie Zichy. A gauche youth with a speech defect somewhere between a lisp and a stutter, he could hardly contain his sense of triumph. The Prince Royal of Württemberg, a dashing and popular young man, as different from his grotesque father as he could be, who hated his Bavarian counterpart with a passion, jeered that he had only managed to catch her by cheating and lifting his blindfold. The Bavarian Prince challenged him to retract the accusation, and when he refused, declared that he would meet him the next morning on the Prater with pistols. The Prince Royal of Württemberg, who was a courageous and competent commander, turned up, only to be met by Prince Wrede, the Bavarian minister, with a note of apology.[25]

Women provided the catalyst for much dubious behaviour. Labrador's assistant Don Camillo Gutierrez de los Rios, the son of Don Fernan Nuñez and a ballerina, went around boasting that no woman could spend an hour with him, even if it were in a carriage, without begging to be taken by him. Whether this was true or not, the climate was certainly one of promiscuity. Away from home, freed from the constraints of their own courts, and in most cases uninhibited by the presence of a wife, the men flirted and dallied, indulging in as much sexual activity as social convention permitted. The informality of much of the social intercourse was novel to most of them. 'In every gathering one breathed a scent that aroused the senses,' noted one witness.[26]

Some had brought their mistresses to Vienna. Grand Duke Constantine summoned a certain comtesse Defours, described in a police report as being 'of lowly extraction', whom he showered with jewels and attended frequently, which did not prevent her, as the same report records, from receiving other men at her lodgings. Nor indeed did it prevent him from straying elsewhere. Prince Volkonsky brought Josephine Wolters, a nineteen-year-old who had been disowned by her family of respectable burghers in Cologne when she had run away with a French officer who was subsequently killed at Leipzig. Volkonsky had discovered her in tears after the battle, and after doing his best to console her, sent her to Prague, where she had waited until called. She visited him nightly, dressed as a man, in his quarters at the Hofburg, where he was lodged as part of Alexander's suite. Even the respectable Hardenberg seems to have brought a young actress named Jubille from Paris.[27]

Others found mistresses on the spot. King Frederick of Denmark recruited the twenty-year-old Caroline Petronelle Seufert, described by Baroness du Montet as 'a young woman of the working class, blonde and pink, a pretty grisette'. The two were so faithful to each other that after he left she was universally referred to as 'the Danish widow'.[28]

But most apparently preferred to roam free, and there was no lack of ladies prepared to oblige. A case in point is Princess Bagration. There can be little doubt that she was granting sexual favours to Alexander. But she did not stop there. His brother Constantine was also a persistent visitor, and police reports suggest that he may have been rewarded. By mid-October she was dallying with the younger of the two princes of Bavaria, who would in turn be supplanted by the Prince Royal of Württemberg.[29]

By the middle of November, people were saying that the apartment of Princess Bagration was little better than a brothel. It was reported, *inter alia*, that a respectable young lady who had gone to a *soirée* there with her parents had, while the company was distracted with a party game, been led into a distant room by a Russian officer who locked the door and assaulted her. She had apparently been saved just in time by her father, who beat down the door. The Russians incurred much censure for their morals. 'Agent D . . . reports that the Russians lodged at the [Hof]Burg, not content with treating it like a pigsty, are behaving very badly and constantly bringing in harlots,' ran a police report dated 9 November. But they hardly deserved to be singled out.[30]

There was no need for anyone to go without their pleasure, as the young daughters of the Viennese middle class and minor bureaucrats were available at very reasonable rates, and the city was full of women who had come for the express purpose of furthering their careers in some way. 'It is impossible, when talking of the good and the bad characteristics of the inhabitants of Vienna,' recorded one officer of Alexander's entourage, 'not to mention the unbelievable depravity of the female sex of the lower orders, victims of which one meets at every step in great quantities, among them girls of no more than fourteen years of age, daughters of city employees.'

'Passed an hour with Suzette, a very beautiful woman bequeathed to me by Humboldt,' Gentz noted one day. The police do not appear to have recorded the nocturnal prowlings of Humboldt himself in search of rougher trade, but he never attended any of the balls or court receptions, and more than one of those present in Vienna made reference to his 'repellent morals'. Nor do the police files shed any light on the activities of the porcine King of Württemberg, who was said to be homosexual. For those who were too shy or feared exposure, there were a number of madames and panders prepared to arrange meetings between visitors and whatever they craved.[31]

The renowned French dancer Émilie Bigottini, much favoured by Napoleon, came to Vienna to expand her client base, and immediately attracted the attentions of Grand Duke Constantine and Count Stadion. But she found it more convenient to allow Count Francis Palffy, another admirer, to set her up as his mistress – which did not prevent her from taking other lovers. The French actress

Seraphine Lambert was also something of a favourite of Grand Duke Constantine, and frequently received visits from Prince Eugène.[32]

Prince Eugène also appears to have been intimate with Count Trautmannsdorff's mistress, a dancer known as Madame Petite-Aimée. He too spread his favours wide. A police report of 6 November informs us that 'after leaving the Kaertnerthor theatre, Prince Eugène went to No. 362 Faerbergasse, the house of a certain Madame Suzanne, who has a very pretty daughter'.[33]

Sexual favours were traded for political or other advantage. A young Greek girl who had been seduced at the age of fourteen by the Duke of Saxe-Coburg, then rejected, and came to Vienna to try to obtain custody of their son, whom the Duke had kept, left an account that leaves little room for speculation. While her seducer ranted about Metternich and the unfairness of being left only with his titles, she was gallantly offered support by a variety of protectors, including Alexander, Grand Duke Constantine, and Stewart. 'Alas! I have to say frankly that I found few disinterested men,' she writes. 'Almost all of them, seduced by I know not which aspect of my position and by certain external advantages which have been so disastrous for me, began by pitying me, and wanted to make me accept both their services and their homage [. . .] and only aggravated my misfortune, by placing on the one hand their friendship and my degradation and on the other their disinterest and my distress.'[34]

One who seems to have given himself over to the pursuit of pleasure with abandon was the twenty-eight-year-old Grand Duke of Baden. He had cast off the wife Napoleon had thrust upon him, Prince Eugène's cousin Stephanie de Beauharnais, and clearly felt himself to be on holiday. He began tasting the delights of Vienna as soon as he arrived. He first attracted the attention of the police when he stole another's mistress, the Hungarian-born Parisienne Josephine Morel. She seems to have had some ulterior agenda, and after she brought her husband and children to Vienna, the police decided to expel her. But the Grand Duke called on Count von Trautmannsdorff and made him prevail upon Hager to relent. He was annoyed by her infidelities, but he was nothing if not generous. He had instructed his equerry, Baron Geusau, to take lodgings where he held what seem to have been elegant orgies in which he shared Josephine Morel and a young maid he had seduced in Baron Gaertner's house with a new-found friend, the Hereditary Prince of Hesse-Darmstadt. The latter would reciprocate by sending his own equerry out to pick up girls off the streets to join them. Occasionally the strain would tell, and from time to time the police reported the Grand Duke being in a state of severe indisposition over a couple of days.[35]

At first the Viennese had been proud to see their city singled out as the venue for the congress, and the property-owners among them delighted by the financial benefits. But by the second week of October the police were reporting that people were growing tired, and longed for it all to end. Everything they subsequently saw and heard confirmed them in their growing scepticism as to the efficacy of the congress and their disgust at the antics of its participants.

The greatest casualty was the institution of royalty itself. 'The presence of the Princes is not productive of any advantage,' wrote Karl von Nostitz, a Saxon-born officer in the Tsar's entourage. It was certainly true that their interference made it difficult for their ministers to reach agreement between themselves. But the problem went deeper than that. 'Royalty undoubtedly loses at these assemblies some of the grandeur which attends it,' Talleyrand noted. 'To find three or four Kings and many more Princes at a ball or at tea with ordinary people of Vienna I find very unseemly.' His feelings were echoed by others of a more republican cast of mind. 'How wrong they are, these Potentates, to go out like this without dignity, without anything to distinguish them,' wrote Anna Eynard in her diary, 'for it is then that one sees them as men just like any others, and even as less, for they have been placed in the position of being able to achieve more.' The Genevan plenipotentiary Pictet wrote to his daughter of the 'curious spectacle' of monarchs waltzing away like students. 'If one takes a step back, one risks treading on the toe of an Emperor,' he quipped.[36]

Such proximity was bound to dispel the aura of royalty; it was difficult to maintain the requisite respect when confronted by the poor bearing of one, the waddle of another, the hideous wart on the face of the Elector of Hesse, the nose '*à la Kalmuck*' of Grand Duke Constantine, who according to one observer resembled 'an angry hyena', or the 'bear-like' dancing of Prince Leopold of Sicily. The King of Württemberg had such a gross appearance, with his red snout and the cascading folds of his stomach, that one employee of the imperial household thought he had seen a pig drive by in one of the court carriages. He was also an extremely unpleasant man, with 'the spirit of a devil in the body of an elephant', in the words of one lady. What little respect might have survived the physical scrutiny was in most cases dispelled by their bad manners, and the sheer silliness of most of them.[37]

The Emperor Francis was the exception. He was much loved by his people, and retained their respect by keeping a suitable distance and behaving in a seemly manner. Alexander could be seen publicly flirting like some adolescent with Princess Gabrielle Auersperg, only twenty and already a widow, admittedly a woman of great beauty, but hardly a fitting object for the continuous attentions of the most powerful man in Europe, who was there to reorder the Continent. Hardly less ridiculous was the stiff Frederick William, who had lost his heart to the lovely young Countess Julie Zichy, whom he followed about like a spaniel. When he did address her, it was to tell her about parades and details of the Prussian soldier's uniform. The poor woman was obliged to stand blushing at his side while he droned on, and vainly tried to discourage him by exalted religious discourse.

When Alexander went to the first masked ball he got his just deserts: a lady he walked up to told him he was an oaf. 'Alexander was thunderstruck that anyone should have had the impudence to tell him with frankness what he was,' Anna Eynard recorded in her diary, 'but how could he possibly be offended; he was there, in a milieu which was not his place, and yet it was directly to him, Alexander, Emperor, that the remark had been addressed, for he was not masked!'[38]

19

A Festival of Peace

Although they were obliged to attend all the court festivities, and appeared to enjoy the attractions on offer as much as their imperial and royal masters, the ministers of the great powers had, astonishingly, managed to keep working. Castlereagh had again taken the lead. He determined to tackle Alexander once more on his Polish plans, believing them to be the obstacle preventing progress on every other matter.

He had found his first interview with Alexander, on 26 September, highly unsatisfactory. A mere Foreign Secretary could not pin down a sovereign with as much firmness as he would another minister, and the Tsar had dodged his arguments. His ultimate riposte to everything was to invoke his personal probity and benevolence, which could hardly be gainsaid. Castlereagh had therefore decided to put his case in the form of a memorandum, which Alexander could not ignore. The result, which he transmitted on 4 October, was a long document reminding the Tsar of all the engagements he had entered into at Kalisch, Reichenbach and in subsequent treaties, whose essence was a return to 1805 and therefore to a tripartite partition of Poland.

Castlereagh suggested that if Alexander really did wish to make the Poles happy, he should combine with Prussia and Austria to establish a truly independent Poland. The one thing Britain could not countenance was a Russian-ruled Polish state, as this would not only give

Russia the whole territory of the grand duchy of Warsaw, but also put her in a position to gradually prise back former Polish territory acquired by Prussia and Austria. He was, on the other hand, prepared to see Russia keep the greater part of the grand duchy as part of the Russian Empire, provided Prussia and Austria could be strengthened in order to balance the attendant increase in Russia's power.

On 12 October Castlereagh sent a second memorandum to Alexander, reminding him of all the high-minded ideals he had invoked as his armies advanced into Europe in the spring of 1813, and of the undertakings made in the various treaties of that year. He once again confronted Alexander's own invocation of moral imperatives with respect to Poland. 'If moral duty requires that the situation of the Poles be improved in a manner as decisive as the re-establishment of their kingdom, let that task be undertaken according to a wider and more liberal principle, and by making of it once more an independent nation instead of turning two thirds of it into a most formidable military instrument in the hands of a single power,' he argued, adding that this would be viewed with approval throughout Europe. He ended by warning Alexander that the whole of Europe was opposed to his Polish plans as they stood, and that no arrangement of any sort could be made while he persisted in them.[1]

The following day Alexander paid a social call on Lady Castlereagh, and afterwards closeted himself with her husband for an hour and a half. 'I am sorry to have to report to your lordship,' Castlereagh wrote to Liverpool, 'that the interview ended without any relaxation of opinion on either side.' Alexander stuck to his guns with 'warmth and tenacity', and threatened to use force to achieve his aims. Castlereagh bridled at this. 'It depends exclusively upon the temper in which Your Imperial Majesty shall meet the questions which more immediately concern your own empire, whether the present Congress shall prove to be a blessing to mankind, or only exhibit a scene of discordant intrigue, and a lawless scramble for power,' he admonished the Tsar.[2]

Alexander was also coming under attack from his own side. Pozzo di Borgo, whom he had summoned from Paris to assist him, produced a memorandum undermining his Polish project. He began by pointing out that the frontier he was demanding in the west was so 'aggressive' as to be unacceptable to the other powers. He then poured cold water on the whole concept of an autonomous kingdom of Poland united with the Russian Empire, which would be intolerable to the Russians and unsatisfactory to the Poles. The titles of King of Poland and Emperor of Russia were, in his view, 'two qualifications that cannot be reconciled in any way'. 'The destruction of Poland as a political power virtually defines the modern history of Russia,' he explained. 'The process of aggrandisement at the expense of the Turks has been purely territorial and, I would venture to say, of secondary significance to that which has taken place on the western frontier. The conquest of Poland was carried out principally with the aim of extending the Russian nation's contacts with the rest of Europe and of opening for it a vaster field and a nobler and more prestigious stage on which to exert her power and her talents, and on which to satisfy her pride, her passions and her interests.' To treat the territory of Poland as anything but a conquest would be to strike at the very basis of the Russian state as it had been built up over the past century, he concluded.[3]

Nesselrode agreed with Pozzo di Borgo. He had no sympathy at all for Polish national aspirations. 'If the partition of this country was in principle an illegal measure contrary to public law and the main-tenance of the equilibrium, at least it had the fortunate result of diminishing the germs of discussion and troubles in Europe,' he wrote. Stein concurred, arguing that an autonomous kingdom of Poland would not survive anyway as it had no developed third estate.[4]

But Alexander's resolve was unshakeable. Struggling to live with the contradictions of his upbringing, his character and his position, eter-nally squaring circles in his mind, he had over the years developed a remarkable ability to perform psychological acrobatics that permitted him to believe that he was a liberal while behaving as an autocrat. It was not that difficult for him to convince himself now that he could both recreate a kingdom of Poland and pursue Russian reasons of state.

The only practical result of his advisers' interventions was that Alexander dismissed Pozzo di Borgo, who was sent back to Paris, withdrew Nesselrode from the meetings with the ministers of the other great powers, and sidelined Stein even further. Over the next weeks he would make use of Czartoryski as his principal minister. Castlereagh, Metternich and Hardenberg now had to face up to the fact that they were not going to reach any agreement with the Tsar through persuasion.

Talleyrand suggested that Britain, Austria, Prussia and France issue an ultimatum to Russia on the matter, and on 14 October Castlereagh drew up a memorandum proposing that they lay three options before Alexander: the revival of Poland under an independent monarch, with all three powers returning Polish territory they had taken since 1772; the revival of a similar kingdom within its reduced boundaries of 1791; or a partition of Poland between the three powers, with Russia's western frontier running along the Vistula. If Russia were to accept one of these three options, the congress could be adjourned while the details of this and other arrangements were worked out; but if she rejected all three, they would convoke a full session and lay the matter of Poland before the whole of Europe for discussion and settlement. It was an attempt to blackmail Alexander.[5]

This could only work if Britain, Austria and Prussia stood together. Castlereagh had bought Prussia's support with his promise to back her claim to the whole of Saxony and Mainz, but Metternich was unwilling to follow suit. He and Hardenberg had drifted apart in the course of the past two weeks.

One area of lingering mistrust and rivalry was the plans for the future of Germany. In accordance with decisions taken during their first meetings, the four ministers had nominated a committee consisting of representatives of Austria, Prussia, Bavaria, Hanover and Württemberg to decide the territorial and constitutional arrangement of the German lands.

The German Committee held its first meeting on 14 October. At its second meeting, two days later, the representative of Württemberg protested that he had not been accorded precedence over his colleague from Hanover, which had only been declared a kingdom on 12 October. Württemberg had been a kingdom since 1806 (by the grace of Napoleon), which entitled him to seniority. Six grown men spent the next few hours debating the issue without solving it. Things went no better when they addressed the twelve articles defining the proposed German federation drawn up by Hardenberg. The delegates of Bavaria and Württemberg balked at the extension of constitutional rights to all classes of Germans regardless of which state they lived in. They also bridled at the article which forbade individual states to make war or enter into alliances with other powers. They saw this as an assault on their sovereignty and protested vociferously.

While the German Committee nominated by the four great powers was having its first meeting at the quarters of the Bavarian plenipotentiary Marshal Wrede, a number of representatives of smaller German states were holding a rival session at the house of Baron von Gagern. A third meeting, of minor princes and nobles who favoured a restoration of the old Reich under Austria, was being held at the house of Princess Elizabeth von Fürstenberg.

Hardenberg and Metternich had ostensibly reached agreement on the kind of constitution they wanted to see, and that Austria would assume the presidency of the governing body, with Prussia retaining extensive influence. But this would be defined by the eventual territorial arrangements; and in order to assure themselves votes on various councils and bodies, Austria and Prussia would need to shift boundaries around so as to make this or that client of theirs eligible to sit on them, which involved them in a devious rivalry. Relations between the two powers were also soured by the dispute over the possession of Mainz.

But the real problem was that Metternich had changed his stance over Saxony; public opinion had swung in favour of the King of Saxony, and Metternich's political enemies had begun to play on this. Most of the other German states were also taking an anti-Prussian stand, encouraged by Talleyrand, and Metternich needed their support. Castlereagh confessed to Liverpool that he was 'a little out of patience' with Metternich's failure to stick to their agreed policy. But by this stage Metternich scarcely knew whether he had a policy. The strain of working eighteen hours a day was beginning to tell. Unlike the other Foreign Ministers, he was saddled with the responsibility of playing host and of invigilating events, and he could not allow himself to forget for a moment that there was a coterie of enemies, grouped around Stadion and Schwarzenberg, watching for an opportunity to bring him down. To cap it all, he was going through a personal crisis.[6]

On 1 October Metternich had been able to spend the night with Wilhelmina, confident in her love and support, but this changed in the course of the next few days. Alfred Windischgraetz had appeared in Vienna, and Wilhelmina could not resist resuming her affair with him. 'With friends one counts the days,' she wrote to him. 'With you I count the nights, and I would not want to miss a single one of them.' Metternich was miserable, and did everything to try to regain her exclusive favour. Instead of devoting his thoughts to the problems of Poland and Saxony, he was trying to make himself useful to Wilhelmina. On 9 October, while his three colleagues discussed Hardenberg's note detailing Prussia's demands, one of the most crucial moments of the congress, Metternich sat apart from them in a corner writing a love letter to her.[7]

He was thinking of ways of appealing to Alexander to intercede on her behalf in her case for custody of her daughter by her first lover, Gustav von Armfeldt, who had recently died, leaving the child in the care of her stepmother in Russia. On the evening of 14 October, while Talleyrand and others present were discussing Saxony, Metternich was discussing drawings of the dress Wilhelmina would be wearing at his masked ball, due to take place in four days' time. Later that evening he cornered Gentz and poured out his grief over the fact that he had been superseded by Windischgraetz, a matter that, as Gentz noted in his diary, 'seems to concern him more than the affairs of the world'.[8]

The following morning Metternich received a letter from her effectively ending their affair. This did not stop him from writing pleading and reproachful letters to her, often in the small hours, after he had returned from a dinner or a ball, in a cold study with no fire in the grate and a single candle.[9]

His bitterness was all the greater as Princess Bagration was spreading an unflattering version of her affair with him, probably at Alexander's instigation, or at least to curry favour with him, and the salons of Vienna were being treated to juicy morsels of salacious cattiness. The Princess's apartment was rapidly turning into a centre of Russian political intrigue and opposition to Metternich.[10]

Alexander's attitude to Metternich had hardened. 'The Emperor became accustomed to seeing M. de Metternich as nothing but a permanent obstacle to his intentions, a man relentlessly occupied in thwarting and outwitting him, in fact as a sworn enemy,' wrote Gentz, adding that Metternich's serenity and success in society infuriated the Tsar. By the time of their first clashes in Vienna, these feelings had grown into 'an implacable hatred' which sometimes erupted into 'a kind of frenetic rage'.[11]

'I despise any man who does not wear a military uniform,' Alexander went about declaring, *à propos* of the Austrian chancellor, whom he dismissed as 'a scribe', implying that he was a coward. He also told women that if they valued his friendship they should have nothing to do with Metternich. This only encouraged Princess Bagration and Wilhelmina to make unpleasant comments about him in public and hold him up to ridicule. Their poisoned barbs were soon the talk of the town. 'La Sagan and La Bagration have gone so far that for the sake of decorum of the maintenance of public order and of respect for decency, the police should expel them,' recommended a report that would land on Hager's desk on 1 November.[12]

Metternich appeared to have lost his way. 'He keeps saying that we need only another eight days, then three days, that everything will go well, that we should leave it to him, and then he does nothing,' Talleyrand complained to Gagern. Talleyrand had no time for Metternich's emotional problems, and he himself was not one to let such things upset him. 'Dorothée likes it here and is enjoying herself,' he reported in a letter to her mother the Duchess of Courland. Whether he was already aware of it or not is not clear, but her enjoyment was enhanced by the attentions of a young cavalry officer, Count Clam-Martinitz, who, if he had not already, was about to supersede him as her lover.[13]

On 18 October, the first anniversary of the battle of Leipzig was celebrated with what was termed a Festival of Peace. The Prater, an extensive park on the banks of the Danube, had been decorated with pyramids of captured French cannon and other military trophies. A great mound had been erected beside the Hauptallee, the chestnut avenue running the length of the park, to accommodate an altar at which all the assembled monarchs, regardless of their confession, attended Mass. This was accompanied by a military band and artillery salvoes, which dispelled the autumnal morning mist over the heads of the Vienna garrison drawn up in ranks. The troops then paraded before the sovereigns, and Stein noticed Alexander's displeasure at this display of Austrian martial excellence – he had always taken the line that Austria was a flabby power lacking military prowess.[14]

The parade was followed by lunch for the 20,000 soldiers, at which officers mixed with rankers and sat beside them to enjoy the same food. Lunch was served to a more select group by Count Razumovsky at his magnificent palace, and the festivities continued in the evening at Metternich's residence.[15]

Metternich had again applied himself to provide an elaborate entertainment, and the results would furnish the lovely young Anna Eynard with 'memories for our lifetime'. And this despite a great personal disappointment at the outset. 'At 8 o'clock, while I was dressing my hair, the gown I had ordered for this ball was brought, but it was still in pieces, as the embroidery-work had only just been finished,' she wrote in her diary the next day. 'It was a little late to send it to the seamstress. This gown, embroidered in silver, was remarkably pretty, but I had to content myself with the thought that I would have looked lovely!'[16]

The entrance to the ball was lit up by flaring Bengal torches, and the carriages rolled up a tented drive from which the guests ascended a carpeted and covered staircase lined with footmen whose liveries were so heavily embroidered with gold that it was impossible to tell their colour.

The fête began with a hot-air balloon raising an artificial sun adorned with the arms of the three allied sovereigns, to the accompaniment of a roll of drums and a fanfare of trumpets. The sovereigns were then conducted round the gardens and shown various exhibits and tableaux in specially erected temples of Mars, Apollo and Minerva. Then they came into an amphitheatre with a lawn in the middle, on which stood three temples, one of them dedicated to peace, another to the arts and another to industry. There followed a pantomime accompanied by fireworks. A figure of Discord, attended by infernal divinities and drawn in a chariot pulled by three black horses, drove around the lawn brandishing a torch. People were seen to flee before it in horror, armies clashed in simulated battles and cavalry charges, cities were besieged, attacked and burnt. Women and children took refuge in the temple of peace. Then there was silence, followed by music as peace descended and the people came out of the temple. The finale was a great parade, with each allied nation represented by a General riding in a chariot bedecked with the flags and emblems of his country. They and the survivors gathered round the altar of peace and concord and sang hymns. All this was going on while supper was being served at round tables seating up to a dozen guests. After supper, there was a ball.[17]

'A row of pillars encircling the ballroom formed a number of small chambers off, in which we could refresh ourselves,' noted an appreciative Countess Bernstorff. 'In front of the pillars, facing the dance floor, were rows of comfortable seats for the ladies, while countless lamps made it as bright as day. From these side rooms a heated broad staircase led down to two great halls in which a splendid supper was served.' The guests were deeply appreciative of the fact that there was also a covered and heated staircase leading out of the premises, as when the time came to leave, the jam of carriages was such that some ladies, wrapped only in light cloaks thrown over their ball gowns, had to wait for up to two hours for theirs to be brought forward.[18]

On 21 October Metternich wrote to Wilhelmina accepting that their affair was over. He declared that he did not regret surrendering his heart so completely to her, having 'given my existence itself over to a charm that was only too seductive'. He could not resist admonishing her for having tried to love two men at the same time. He felt he was being punished for having loved too much, but would bear it bravely, as he still loved her. 'You will always remain the being most dear to my heart,' he concluded. Gentz heaved a sigh of relief.[19]

Having sent off his parting letter, Metternich applied himself at last to matters of state and composed his response to Hardenberg's note of 9 October. He had agreed, not very willingly, to join Castlereagh in a last attempt to enlist the support of Prussia by acceding to her demand for the whole of Saxony. This went against the wishes of his Emperor and of public opinion, but there seemed to be no other way out, and he managed to persuade the Emperor Francis to abandon his defence of Saxony.

His note to Hardenberg stated that although 'the hopes of Prussia to incorporate Saxony are a cause of real regret for the Emperor', who hoped that a kernel of it might yet be spared, Austria would be prepared to agree to the annexation under certain conditions. The *sine qua non* was that Prussia should combine with Austria to restrain Russia's ambitions in Poland. He was equally firm in his stance that Mainz must go to Bavaria. That evening he went to the ball at Countess Molly Zichy's, doing his best to avoid Alexander, who was in fine form, dancing with all the prettiest girls. Metternich took the opportunity to show Castlereagh a copy of his note to Hardenberg.[20]

The three of them met the following morning at Castlereagh's in order to concert their actions. Castlereagh found Hardenberg 'extremely warm', a diplomatic way of saying that he was in a rage, over Metternich's refusal to countenance his claim for Mainz. He was also suspicious. Metternich and Castlereagh had both at various times promised to back Prussia's claim to Saxony, but not unconditionally. He could not possibly hope to persuade his sovereign to stand up to Alexander unless he could offer him a cast-iron assurance that he would receive the whole of Saxony and more, possibly Mainz, besides – as well as those parts of the grand duchy of Warsaw which Alexander would be obliged to give up.

Castlereagh nevertheless deemed the meeting 'satisfactory'. They agreed to go ahead with the earlier proposal to offer Alexander three alternatives on Poland and, if he did not agree to one of them, to threaten placing the whole matter before a full congress. Metternich and Hardenberg were to ask their monarchs to talk to Alexander directly in order to try to influence him. Castlereagh took it upon himself to put their arguments on paper and indulge in what Cooke called 'a *guerre de plume*' with Alexander, while Metternich proposed that he would lay their arguments before the Tsar verbally. On 23 October, six weeks after their first meeting in Vienna, they had at last achieved a common front. But it was a fragile one, and it would not withstand the first assault.[21]

That very afternoon, Talleyrand arrived at the Hofburg, summoned by the Tsar. While Castlereagh had been attempting to form a united front against him, Alexander had been doing everything to disrupt his efforts. On 21 October he had sent Czartoryski to see Talleyrand, with the intention of sounding him out on the possibility of a Franco-Russian rapprochement. Sensing that Alexander's Polish plans were to be discussed, Talleyrand opened by stating that France would like to see a fully independent Poland come out of the congress. 'That would be very fine,' Czartoryski replied, 'but it is a dream; the powers would never allow it.' Talleyrand strung the Prince along, pretending to be interested in the veiled suggestions that Russia might be inclined to help France over Murat.[22]

It was not possible for such a visit to go unnoticed and unreported in Vienna, and Castlereagh soon knew of it. He was alarmed, and wrote to Wellington in Paris instructing him to put pressure on Louis XVIII and his government to rein in Talleyrand, whom he suspected of wishing to make trouble. But his fears were groundless.[23]

The Tsar opened the audience on 23 October in the most cordial tone. He gently reproached Talleyrand for having changed his tune since Paris, where he had led him to believe that he favoured the resurrection of Poland. Talleyrand declared that France was warmly in favour of the re-establishment of an independent Poland, but not one under Russian domination, as this would threaten both Prussia and Austria, obliging them to seek enlargements elsewhere, and thereby upset the balance in Europe.

'There is no reason for them to be anxious,' Alexander retorted, immediately undermining this by adding, 'In any case, I have 200,000 men in the duchy of Warsaw, and I would like to see anyone try to drive me out of it. I have given Prussia Saxony, and Austria consents to it.' Talleyrand expressed his doubts as to whether Austria really did consent to this, but kept resolutely to his chosen moral ground. 'But could the consent of Austria make Prussia the rightful possessor of that which really belongs to the King of Saxony?' he enquired. This kind of reasoning exasperated Alexander. 'If the King of Saxony will not abdicate, he will be packed off to Russia; he will die there,' he blustered. 'He will not be the first King to die there,' he added, referring to the last King of Poland, Stanisław Augustus. Talleyrand was shocked. 'Your Majesty will permit me not to believe what he is saying,' he replied. 'The Congress was not assembled to witness a violent assault of this kind.'

Alexander grew angry, and accused Talleyrand of being ungrateful. 'I thought that France owed me something. You are always talking to me about principles, but your public law means nothing to me; I do not know what it is. Do you really think I give much weight to all your parchments and treaties?' he ranted. He had given his word to Frederick William. 'The King of Prussia,' he concluded, 'will be King of Prussia and Saxony, just as I shall be Emperor of Russia and King of Poland. Any good will I receive from France on these two points will be reciprocated with that I will show her on any matter that might interest her.' With this oblique reference to Talleyrand's desire to see Murat thrown out of Naples, Alexander left the room to go to the masked ball being held that evening by Countess Schönborn.[24]

At the ball, to which Hardenberg did not bother to go, Talleyrand cornered Castlereagh and began relating his interview with the Tsar that afternoon; but Alexander saw them, came over and drew Castlereagh away into another room, where he harangued him on the subject of Poland. He was growing impatient at what he saw as the mulish obstinacy of his supposed allies in blocking his plans.

Early next morning, 24 October, it was Metternich's turn. He had a two-hour interview with the Tsar, in the course of which he laid before him the three options agreed jointly with Castlereagh and Hardenberg the previous day. Alexander accused Metternich of insolence, and referred to his meetings with the other ministers as a 'conspiracy'. He declared that he would restore a kingdom of Poland regardless of them, because he had given the Poles his word. Metternich retorted that Austria too was thinking of turning her Polish provinces into an independent Polish state, and the Poles in Warsaw might prefer to join that one rather than be governed by a Russian Tsar. Alexander responded with sarcasm, inviting him to come and inspect the 200,000 men he had under arms in Poland. When Metternich threatened, as the three ministers had agreed, to lay the whole matter before a general congress in full assembly, the Tsar retorted that he did not give a fig for the congress. Losing control of his temper and his manners, he abused the Foreign Minister to his face. Afterwards, Metternich declared to his friends that he would not and could not ever see the Emperor in private again. Later that morning Alexander departed for the Hungarian city of Buda, along with Francis and Frederick William, leaving the stunned Metternich to his reflections. They were not happy ones.[25]

News of the interview between him and the Tsar was soon spreading through Vienna, as were some more personally wounding rumours. There had already been much whispering about his being supplanted by Windischgraetz, maliciously embroidered by his political enemies. But they now had fresh meat for gossip.

On 23 October, on the eve of his interview with Metternich, Alexander had called at the Palm Palace. But instead of going into the apartment of Princess Bagration, who was waiting for him, he turned the other way at the top of the stairs and called on Wilhelmina, with whom he spent some time. This event was known all over Vienna within hours, and was seized on not only by the enemies of Metternich, but by those of Princess Bagration as well; the Tsar's turning right instead of left at the top of the stairs in the Palm Palace was interpreted as his having abandoned his old love and supplanted Metternich in the affections of Wilhelmina.[26]

The ministers were wondering what to do, as 1 November was fast approaching and they were no nearer reaching agreement on the key issues than they had been a month before. If anything, they were even further from it. On the evening of 30 October they had what Hardenberg described as a 'tedious' conference between the representatives of the eight signatories of the Treaty of Paris, in the course of which they read out and discussed a number of projects on the procedure they should adopt for the congress. Talleyrand's proposal for a full session was rejected. Suggestions for a string of committees that would report to the eight were discussed. The problem of whether to admit the plenipotentiaries of Saxony and Naples, and, in the latter case, which ones, was raised. No decisions were reached, and the conference was adjourned to the following day.

The principal attraction that day was a concert in the riding school, with forty pianists seated at twenty pianos playing under the direction of Salieri. That meant that 'there were eighty hands or four hundred fingers playing together', according to the calculations of one member of the audience. No such harmony was evident in the counsels of the plenipotentiaries of the four great powers.[27]

When they next met they went over the same ground yet again, and came to no weightier conclusion than that the opening of the congress would have to be put off once more. In order to keep up some appearance of activity, they decreed that the verification of credentials would begin. As a result, instead of the opening of the congress, 1 November brought no more than an announcement in the court gazette informing plenipotentiaries that they should present their credentials at the State Chancellery for examination by a committee appointed for the purpose. 'The general opinion is that the Congress will now be over quickly,' quipped Pictet in a letter to his daughter. 'All that is needed is the time necessary to recite: "I keep and I take," and to throw dice for the rest.'[28]

20

Guerre de Plume

The sovereigns were back in Vienna. Their trip to Buda had not been a success. Alexander had seized the opportunity of being alone with Francis and Frederick William to attempt to reach an understanding over the heads of their ministers. He warned the King of Prussia against Hardenberg, and suggested to Francis that he dispense with the services of Metternich, arguing that the three monarchs could easily reach agreement between themselves. Francis reportedly replied that he believed these things were better settled by ministers than by monarchs, and that he was entirely satisfied with his. The discussion was described as 'tempestuous'. At one point Alexander declared that he was prepared to go to war in support of his plans, to which the placid Francis had retorted that he would rather fight now and get it over with than in a couple of years' time.[1]

Alexander was not in a good mood on his return. He probably realised that he had blundered up a blind alley. On his arrival in Vienna he had begun by stating his will, assuming that it would be done. When objections were raised, by Castlereagh, then Talleyrand and then Metternich, he had tried to intimidate them. Castlereagh had responded with firmness and two memoranda setting out all the reasons why Alexander's plans were unacceptable. Talleyrand had confronted him with almost disdainful lectures on legitimacy and international law. And Metternich, while appearing to be open to any proposal, had also stood his ground. This had so incensed Alexander that he had lost his temper with him and then demanded that Francis dismiss him. The final humiliation was Francis's refusal.

Metternich's dismissal would have availed Alexander little. If anything, it would have worked against him, as the man waiting in the wings, and the only one who could have replaced Metternich, was Stadion, who was far more aggressive in pursuing Austria's interests. Not only was he adamant that Austria should recover all her Polish possessions lost to Russia in 1809, he was also the champion of the minor German princes, and a supporter of the King of Saxony's cause. If he were in charge, Austria would range herself firmly against Russia. Once his temper had cooled, Alexander realised that he must carry on working with Metternich, but he would try out different means of persuasion.

At the masked ball that followed the 'tedious' meeting on what to do about the opening of the congress, Metternich was approached by a masked man who handed him a piece of paper. It bore a message to the effect that a very highly placed personage who had unfortunately quarrelled with him wished to resume more friendly relations and to persuade him to cease opposing his plans. The highly placed personage was willing to offer £100,000 sterling to be paid out in cash by the most solid bankers in Vienna, and to satisfy another more personal longing of his. The text made it plain that this referred to the favours of Wilhelmina. Taken aback, and failing to recognise the deeper implications, Metternich brushed the man aside. It was only on reflection that he took in what had happened.

Wilhelmina was desperate to get her daughter out of Russia, and would do anything to achieve it. She had begged Metternich to invoke Alexander's help in the matter, which he had done. Alexander had suddenly found himself in a position to make Wilhelmina do his bidding. He had used his power to make her reject Metternich publicly and to treat him with gratuitous spite over the past couple of weeks. And he was now prepared to blackmail her into dismissing

Windischgraetz and resuming her relationship with Metternich if the latter agreed to toe the line over Poland.[2]

Metternich was horrified, not so much by what the incident revealed about Alexander and his methods as by the idea that Wilhelmina might think that he, Metternich, had tried to use such means to get her back. The following morning he dashed off a note to her saying that he would not be attending the ball given that evening by Count Razumovsky, and warning her to avoid talking to the Tsar. 'Never forget that our relations, so pure and so honest on my part, should never have been allowed to lend themselves to complications of the nature of those that the ridiculous conduct of certain persons has led to,' he wrote, adding that he had something astonishing to tell her.[3]

Alexander had not stopped there. He had apparently spread rumours to the effect that the rejected Metternich had tried to find consolation in the affections of the lovely, and exceptionally virtuous, Julie Zichy (who had assiduously rejected all Alexander's passes). He had then informed her that Metternich had boasted to him that he had possessed her carnally. The chaste Countess burst into tears and refused to speak to Metternich again.[4]

'I am not surprised at anything any more when it comes to that man,' Metternich wrote to Wilhelmina the next day. 'I am quite ill, my body has been affected, and my spirit has not been able to defend it for some time. I am still very necessary for a few weeks; they will close the year that has been the most painful of my life, and if they take my life with it, the world will lose nothing but the sad remains of an existence which I do not deserve to prolong.'[5]

Metternich was not the only one to feel despondent. 'People are losing all hope of seeing the Congress finish as they would wish and as they had originally hoped,' reported one of Hager's informers. 'It is being said that the Congress has no principles and that if it does have any, they are extremely bad ones. Far from giving to each that which is his due, it is trying to take from others that which is rightly theirs.'[6]

'I am charmed that our court should, after twenty years of war, be able to shine with a splendour that astonishes everyone, even those nasty Russians,' one Viennese lady wrote to a friend in Paris on 12 November. 'But I would like this performance to end and everyone be able to crawl back into their shell and quietly enjoy the benefits of peace. You must admit that all these crowned heads who have got into the habit of rushing around the world are very inconvenient. I would like a law to be passed in every country after this great migration obliging every sovereign to stay at home.' Jokes were being made to the effect that by drawing out the negotiations, Russia and Prussia were waging a novel kind of war on Austria, aimed at bankrupting her Emperor.[7]

Others voiced less frivolous objections to the congress. 'These sovereigns, who were all brothers when it was a question of annihilating the power of Bonaparte, were apparently only united by necessity, for their own interests and not in the noble aim which they all proclaimed of bringing happiness to the nations,' Eynard wrote in his diary. 'This Coalition, which was dubbed the Holy League, will end in a new war, or at the very least the sovereigns will go their ways in such a mood that they will seize the first favourable opportunity to trouble the world again.' Similar sentiments abounded, and a strong swell of anger was building up, particularly in Germany. 'All the petty passions, all the Machiavellian tricks are every bit as much in evidence as before, and this cause that was proclaimed as a sacred one has become worse than profane,' complained a Viennese clergyman to his brother in Strasbourg.[8]

The recently arrived Russian minister Count Ioannis Capodistrias was appalled by what he found. He quickly assessed that lack of statesmanship had resulted in the leading ministers failing to set down firm principles at the outset. This meant that far from healing wounds, the congress was bound to reopen old ones. Humboldt was of the same opinion, and in a letter to his wife pinpointed the loose wording of the Treaty of Paris as the origin of the mess they were now in. Hardenberg had already, that summer, admitted to Metternich that the root of the problem was their failure to reach agreement back in February 1813.[9]

'They have forgotten that this war was not won by sovereigns but by nations,' Capodistrias went on. 'As soon as Napoleon was overthrown, the interests of nations were forgotten and only the interests of princes were addressed, just as in olden times, and as a result everything has reverted to confusion, to the conflict of interests and to the impossibility of satisfying every country.' In common with the majority of Alexander's entourage, Capodistrias was opposed to his Polish plans, seeing in them an unacceptable extension of Russia into Europe. And while Alexander continued to represent them as a disinterested attempt to benefit the Polish nation, most agreed with Talleyrand's observation that 'His philanthropy has become very invasive.'

Capodistrias was also highly critical of Britain's position, pointing out that there could be no balance when one single power controlled the oceans of the world. Representatives of minor interests, who had instinctively looked to Russia and to Britain as their natural protectors, were coming round to the view that Alexander was beginning to pose a greater threat than Napoleon, while Britain was not concerned with anything beyond her own maritime and overseas interests.[10]

In the past, Kings or their ministers would decide what was best for their states, and all they needed to do was strike an acceptable bargain with the other side. But the past quarter-century had changed that, and public opinion had entered the equation. It was guided by entirely different factors to those governing the decisions of monarchs and ministers, often highly emotional ones, and it was a force, even in an autocracy such as Russia, to be reckoned with. In making their plans for the congress, the ministers of the four great powers had entirely failed to take this into account, and they were beginning to suffer the consequences. 'They've wandered into a bog, and they have no idea how to get out of it,' commented Czartoryski in a letter to his father on 31 October.[11]

* * *

The one most oblivious to these developments was Alexander. Having failed to either browbeat or bribe Metternich, he now set about trying to isolate him. At the court ball on 3 November he accosted Hardenberg and instructed him to present himself at the Hofburg on 5 November, so they could call on Frederick William together. When he had the Prussian King and his minister before him, Alexander brought out his old argument that in view of his great contribution to the cause he should not be denied such a paltry thing as his planned kingdom of Poland. Hardenberg tried to present the case against this, but Alexander would not listen. He asked Frederick William to instruct Hardenberg to act according to his wishes, and to forbid him to cooperate with Austria and Britain. This Frederick William proceeded to do.

Before his departure for Buda, Alexander had commissioned Anstett, who had been out of favour for having voiced doubts about his Polish schemes, to write a reply to Castlereagh's memorandum of 12 October. On his return, on 29 October, he looked through the document produced by Anstett, and on the following day had it delivered to Castlereagh.

Opening with a catalogue of the efforts made and the sufferings borne by Russia in the common cause, it expressed surprise that Castlereagh should have entertained the thought that Russia meant to act in contravention of her treaty obligations. It pointed out that the treaty of 1797 binding the partitioning powers to prevent the resurrection of a Polish state had been superseded by events. It argued, correctly, that the Convention of Reichenbach had been contingent on Napoleon agreeing to negotiate, and had been rendered irrelevant by subsequent agreements reached at Toeplitz and elsewhere. It countered Castlereagh's observations on the recent increase in Russia's power, dismissing the fact that she had been enlarged by the acquisition of Finland with the somewhat specious riposte that she had immediately allowed Sweden to take Norway, and thereby gained a powerful ally for the cause. As to her conquests in the Balkans, they had been necessary for the protection of southern Russia. In fact, everything Russia had done over the past decades had been dictated by the requirements of self-defence.

At the same time the memorandum made it clear that Russia held the grand duchy of Warsaw by right of conquest, maintaining nevertheless that, far from being a threat to Austria and Prussia, this was a liability which rendered Russia herself vulnerable. It concluded by stating that if Britain continued to oppose Alexander over Poland there would be no general peace, and Alexander himself would let the world know who stood in its way. 'The peoples that saw him fight for their freedom and witnessed his moderation will learn the real cause that prevented the re-establishment of that order, of happiness and of tranquillity, for which so much blood has flowed.' His covering letter, brimming over with hurt pride, accused Castlereagh of seeing evil where there was none. 'The purity of my intentions makes me strong,' he wrote. 'If I hold to the order of things that I would like to establish in Poland, it is because in my conscience I have the personal conviction that it would be to act in favour of the general good, rather than for my own interest.'[12]

Castlereagh was stung by this, and annoyed that he had let himself be drawn into an argument. He had meant his memorandum of 12 October as an act of courtesy, he explained to Liverpool, to inform the Tsar of his government's position and of the wishes of Austria and Prussia. It had been received as a challenge and answered in an unnecessarily aggressive memorandum, accompanied by a personal letter from Alexander reproaching him for his alleged impertinence in questioning the Tsar's high-minded motives.

Castlereagh suspected that Alexander was being manipulated by Czartoryski, whom he wrongly believed to be the author of the memorandum. 'Castlereagh is angry with me over Anstett's reply,' Czartoryski noted in his diary. 'All the fury is directed at me. Unbelievable hubbub and hatred.' The unfortunate Prince was not enjoying himself. 'For me, the sojourn in Vienna holds little attraction, as I see few well-disposed faces and hardly ever meet with an amicable welcome,' he wrote to his father on 16 November. One of the few people he did meet with a warm welcome from was his erstwhile fiancée Dorothée de Périgord.[13]

In his answer, dated 4 November, Castlereagh stated that he was convinced that the views expressed in Alexander's letter and memorandum were not his but those of a certain person at his side particularly interested in the matter, at the same time assuring him that the new memorandum which he enclosed was a reply addressed to that person, and not to the Tsar.[14]

The new memorandum refuted Alexander's dismissal of the Convention of Reichenbach, claiming that it had been the crucial act, on which the whole coalition had been based, and could not therefore be superseded by that of Toeplitz, which was not meant to alter the terms on which the allies agreed to cooperate and was more of a confirmation of the earlier act. He argued that the Convention of Reichenbach was still '*en pleine vigueur*', along with the Treaty of Toeplitz, and that Russia had 'no right to annul or alter any of the stipulations or to substitute anything whatever' in them without the consent of the other signatories.

He concluded by stating that the allies had fought the war against Napoleon for their own liberty and that of Europe, not in the hope of extending their dominions, and that the principle of territorial compensation for the costs of the war was inadmissible. 'The peace of the world cannot endure with such doctrines,' it concluded, observing that territorial acquisitions often led to problems and expenses that cancelled out any possible gain. It was a curious argument to find in the mouth of someone who had just presided over Britain's acquisition of a string of new colonies.[15]

As he awaited the answer, on 7 November Castlereagh received a dispirited note from Hardenberg recounting his interview with Alexander and Frederick William. He could see no possibility of further resistance to the Tsar's wishes, and suggested that they allow him to have his way. He argued that possession of the kingdom of Poland would weaken rather than strengthen Russia; the semi-autonomous province would be bound, sooner or later, to try to emancipate itself, and so would grow into a major problem for Russia. It was a counsel of despair; the negotiations had reached an impasse.[16]

'The language of truth and justice is not one Russia understands,' Gentz wrote to the Hospodar of Wallachia on 7 November. 'The most energetic remonstrations, unless they happen to be backed up by serious threats or hostile demonstrations, no longer make the slightest effect on that power; and the conduct of the Emperor Alexander, from the moment of his entry into Paris, and particularly since his arrival in Vienna, has proved abundantly that he will from now on listen only to counsels that nourish his ambition or flatter his favourite ideas.'[17]

The Tsar certainly appeared impervious. 'Alexander enjoyed himself greatly at the Redoute,' one of Hager's agents reported on the morning of 8 November. 'He paid an enormous amount of attention to a masked lady wearing a large hat with a black plume whom we believe to have been Countess Esterhazy-Roisin. From 2 o'clock to 3.30 he was much taken, along with the King of Prussia, by two dominos in black. The beauty of Madame Morel once again produced a great effect. She also spoke to Count Schoenfels and Prince Narishkin. Then it was the turn of the prince de Ligne, who took her under his wing and remained at her side for a long time. The Grand Duke of Baden did not dare show himself with her in the ballroom, but he never ceased circling her and never lost her from sight.'[18]

The next day there was a ball given by Metternich. He might have been in despair over the political situation and his love life, but his masked ball that night was one of the most elegant and enjoyable of the whole season. His villa on the Rennweg had been decorated with a Venetian theme, and the guests were asked to come in national costume or in red-and-white dominos. The place was a riot of dirndls and other peasant dresses, which permitted the ladies to show a little leg, and some had taken the opportunity to dress up as Indians, Persians or Chinese. The Russian ladies spoilt the effect of their peasant dresses by covering them in diamonds, while Lady Castlereagh astonished everyone by wearing her husband's decoration of the Order of the Garter on her head. It was the Danes whose dress was generally praised the most, although the ravishing young Anna Eynard ingenuously noted in her diary that the Swiss had also rated well, as she noticed that all the men came up to her to have a closer look and make compliments.[19]

Alexander's reply to Castlereagh's memorandum of 4 November came in the form of another memorandum, dated 9 November. The covering note, which was unusually curt, expressed the hope that no more such exchanges would take place. The memorandum itself, composed by Capodistrias, asserted that 'the second English memorandum, rather than simplifying questions and facilitating a convergence of the divergent opinions, seems intended to prolong a discussion which, by straying away from the views which motivated it, becomes polemical and can therefore promise no resolution'. Dismissing Castlereagh's reasoning on the Convention of Reichenbach, it launched into a long rehearsal of Alexander's virtues, of how Russia had fought alone, of how, rather than making peace with Napoleon in 1813, which would have left the whole of Europe under his boot, she had instead nobly fought on for its liberation.

There were good reasons for Alexander returning to this theme so assiduously: he had been almost alone in wanting to take the war into Europe, while most of his entourage and his subjects had wished only to improve Russia's defences by rounding them off with a slice of Prussia and Poland and to go home, leaving Europe to sort out its own mess. Having imposed a full extra year of war on his country, he had to show something for it.

Alexander's memorandum also touched on Russia's position as a power and on her interests in Asia, juxtaposing these with Britain's situation and her interests overseas, particularly in India. It suggested that, instead of pleading some woolly 'cause of the principles of the public law of Europe', it would be better to work together towards obtaining for each of the great powers 'the advantages to which they are entitled' and building a peace based 'on the ability of the great states to maintain it', and concluded that Britain was eminently suited to the role of mediator and should apply herself to it.[20]

This curious document was both a rap across Castlereagh's knuckles and an olive branch held out to him. It suggested that Russia and Britain were the two superpowers, with interests of a different order from those of the other states of Europe, and that they should assume the responsibilities inherent in that position. But that did not mean that Alexander was going to start being conciliatory.

On the morning Castlereagh was digesting this latest broadside in the '*guerre de plume*', the sovereigns were wielding real guns at a wild boar shoot organised a few miles outside the city for the relief of their frustrations and the delectation of the hundreds of ministers, courtiers and other onlookers who filled the specially constructed stands. For several days beaters had gone through the extensive forests, gradually funnelling some six hundred wild boar, along with other game, into a holding area adjacent to an open space, effectively a corridor four hundred feet long and 150 wide. 'The sovereigns posted themselves along this space, a few feet apart, and, from time to time five or six beasts were released and forced to pass along the row of sovereigns, who were placed according to rank, so that if the Emperors missed the unfortunate wild boars, the Kings would have the honour of taking aim at them, and if they also missed it was the turn of the Princes, then of the Dukes, then of the Field Marshals, and then of the more lowly,' in the words of the horrified Eynard. 'This hunt, which is nothing more than an assassination of wild boar, lasted all morning, and the monarchs had the glory of killing five hundred of them. The fat King of Wurtemberg, who rather resembles a wild boar himself, killed thirty-five, the Emperor of Austria thirty-three. I have seen nothing more disgusting or more revolting than such a pastime; there is no skill, no risk and no exercise involved, and hunting in this manner is to perform the task of the butcher.'[21]

The Empress of Austria had also distinguished herself at the shoot, killing more than her fair share of the bag, and both she and the Queen of Bavaria were in exceptionally high spirits as the hunting party drove over to Schönbrunn for dinner. After that, they all drove back to Vienna just in time to retire and dress for the masked ball in the Hofburg that evening. The ball was, according to Anna Eynard, 'the height of boredom'. The great rooms were packed with thousands of people of every station, and the crush was so great that the sovereigns had difficulty in opening the ball with the polonaise, and had to be preceded by soldiers pushing back the throng. The heat was so intense that a number of ladies fainted. Many of them were in a state of chronic exhaustion as a consequence of the continuous round of parties, with the inevitable late nights and physical exertions. 'They are all frighteningly thin and sallow,' Marie-Louise informed a friend in Paris.[22]

The following day brought sinister news to Vienna. On the morning of the previous day, 10 November, the Russian troops occupying Saxony had begun to pull out and, by previous arrangement, to hand over to Prussian units which marched in to take their place. These took control and began to prepare for the annexation of the kingdom to Prussia. A proclamation issued by the Russian military governor as he handed over the kingdom stated that he was acting with the knowledge and approval of Britain and Austria.

A couple of days earlier, Alexander's brother the Grand Duke Constantine had left Vienna, to the great relief of all. His bad behaviour had reached new depths when he had struck Alfred Windischgraetz, of whose regiment he had been made Honorary Colonel, with his riding crop during a parade. Windischgraetz had challenged him to a duel, and Constantine had been made to apologise. He departed under a cloud, leaving a mountain of unpaid debts. 'He has behaved like a real Kalmouk,' commented one citizen. But that was not why he had gone. The Tsar had sent him to Warsaw, where he was to take command of the Polish army, formed out of the remains of Napoleon's Polish regiments and the troops of the grand duchy of Warsaw.[23]

Taken together, and in the light of recent threats, these developments could only signify that Alexander had decided to impose his will by force. The Danish plenipotentiary, Baron Rozenkrantz, noted in his diary that he, along with most of those he had spoken to, considered the negotiations to have broken down entirely.[24]

Political Carrousel

Castlereagh had arrived in Vienna on 13 September expecting to broker a satisfactory settlement of the outstanding issues and get back to London within two months. Two months had passed, and precisely nothing had been achieved. Ironically, 13 November did see the eight signatories of the Treaty of Paris, who had called the congress in the first place, officially conclude their first piece of business. But there was nothing edifying about it, and it did not reflect well on Britain.

Much of that day was taken up settling the final details of the incorporation of Genoa into the kingdom of Sardinia. The proud republic had been abolished after invasion by the armies of Revolutionary France and then incorporated into the kingdom of Italy by Napoleon. The Genoese had not ceased to hope for the recovery of their independence, and both the actions of the British agents in southern Europe and the justice of their cause led them to believe that they would do so when the Napoleonic system was overthrown. But the allies had decided early on that the kingdom of Sardinia must assume the role of a barrier against future French designs on Italy, and that it would need to be strengthened by the addition of Genoa.

Labrador made a last-ditch attempt to save the republic. Citing the example of Germany, he suggested that the whole complex question of settling the conflicting claims in the peninsula be handed over to an Italian Committee – which would have removed it from the ambit of the four great powers. But Metternich dismissed the idea, declaring that there was no similarity between Germany, which had been a political entity, and Italy, which was merely a series of states linked by a geographical expression. Castlereagh backed him up, and none of the others objected. Only eight months after Bentinck had marched into the city at the head of a British force and proclaimed the restoration of the republic, *la Superba* was sacrificed to the greater good of preserving peace in Europe, just as *la Serenissima* had been.[1]

Another issue on which the British cabinet's conduct was beginning to look shabby was that of Poland. The Polish cause was gaining in popularity at home, and Liverpool soon found that his preferred solution of a partition of Poland by Russia, Prussia and Austria was out of step with public opinion. Sensing an opportunity to make trouble for the government, the opposition had turned it into 'a question of serious embarrassment' to Liverpool, who deemed it 'very material that we should lose no character by the part we take in it', as he put it in a letter to Castlereagh on 14 October. He urged Castlereagh to disengage from the argument if possible and let the other three powers deal with Poland as they would, but to cover the government against accusations of being weak. 'I think it would be very desirable that there should, if possible, be some record of our having expressed our opinion of how desirable it would be to restore Poland on the principle of 1792, and of our having made some effort for that which we are more entitled to ask, the independence of the duchy of Warsaw under a neutral sovereign,' he wrote.[2]

He was also anxious that with the American war dragging on, Russia might weigh in with another offer of mediation, and use the opportunity to bring up the whole question of Britain's maritime rights. Castlereagh's frequently voiced misgivings about Talleyrand's loyalty only increased these fears, raising the spectre of a Russo-Franco-American line-up against Britain. 'We shall, above all things, I hope, avoid a renewal of the war,' he wrote on 2 November, insisting that Saxony, Poland and Italy were trifles considering the possibility of the resumption of hostilities, which would plunge the whole Continent back into chaos and entail more expense.[3]

But British public opinion had taken up the cause of Saxony as well. The man on the street in London did not like the idea of a respectable old monarch, one much loved by his people, being removed from his throne and dispossessed of his lands, which were to be handed over to a foreign power. The opposition picked up on both issues, and there were stormy debates on the subject in the House of Commons. The government's conduct of foreign policy was looking unprincipled and flabby.

It looked even worse when news got abroad that on 10 November the Russians had handed Saxony over to Prussian occupation, apparently with British approval. Liverpool had no option but to reverse his policy. Only a couple of weeks after affirming that 'the fate of Saxony should be considered subordinate, after the glorious efforts of Prussia in the war, to the effectual reconstruction of that Power', he would be instructing Castlereagh to about-turn and stand up to Prussia over Saxony.[4]

Russia's attempt to create a *fait accompli* in Saxony had shocked Castlereagh and spurred him to action. On 11 November he misinformed Liverpool, reporting that both Prussia and Austria were prepared to back him in blocking Alexander's Polish plans. 'Your Lordship may rest assured that no effort on my part shall be omitted to prevent disunion, and still more, war,' he reassured him, 'but I am confident I speak the universal sentiment, when I declare my perfect conviction, that unless the Emperor of Russia can be brought to a more moderate and sound course of public conduct, the peace, which we have so dearly purchased, will be but of short duration.'[5]

Castlereagh had come to the conclusion that to give way to Alexander at this stage would be fatal. 'You must make up your mind to watch him and resist him if necessary as another Bonaparte,' he warned Liverpool. He rejected any suggestion that they appease him, declaring that 'acquiescence will not keep him back, nor will opposition accelerate his march'. Alexander only listened when confronted with determination, and Castlereagh would not allow 'a Calmuck Prince to overturn Europe'. How he proposed to stop him is not clear. He had no dependable allies, and his own standing had fallen very low.[6]

In his letters to Liverpool, Wellington and others, Castlereagh frequently complained of the self-interest he believed to be guiding most of the Continental powers, and contrasted it with what he saw as Britain's highly moral position. But if anyone in Vienna had ever believed in that, they had become grievously disenchanted.

To begin with, it was only the social graces of the British that were criticised. When Jean-Gabriel Eynard went to a *soirée* at the Castlereaghs' for the first time, he found the hostess gauche and quite ignorant of how to receive people or place them, so that the guests stood around in the groups in which they had come, while Castlereagh himself sat chatting to his English friends. 'Their separation from the Continent over twenty years has turned them into savages,' he noted in his diary on coming home.[7]

'The English ladies are characterised by their sturdy, uncouth way of walking,' observed the publisher Carl Bertuch. 'Everyone is complaining about the lack of breeding of the English and their ladies,' noted Eynard a few weeks later. 'There is no kind of rudeness and gaucherie which they do not commit.' Baron Karl von Nostitz thought the English 'a strange tribe, with their own clothes and manners'. Similar comments abound. A police report dated 9 November informed that 'there is much laughter at Lord and Lady Castlereagh, who are seen everywhere in the streets and the shops, walking arm-in-arm, and who go into every single shop, have everything the establishment contains shown to them, and then leave without purchasing a single item'.[8]

'Lady Castlereagh,' observed Roksandra Sturdza, 'also amused the crowd by her colossal figure, which was rendered even more extraordinary and more gigantic by her dress; she wore ostrich feathers of every colour of the rainbow.' According to Nostitz she 'was always dressed up in ridiculously theatrical ways, colossal and graceless, plump and talkative, the joke of society'. In this she was no different from the many other English women in Vienna. 'The English women stand out by their ridiculous costumes,' recorded Baroness du Montet, who complained of 'the extreme indecency of their dress; their dresses, or rather sheaths, are so tight that their every shape is exactly drawn, while they are open in front down to the stomach'. Eynard was greatly amused by one English aristocrat who 'came into the room in a dress tightly pulled in over her bottom which went down no more than a couple of fingers below the knee', adding that 'this wealthy noble-woman looked like a tightrope walker, or even like one of the ladies of the Palais-Royal'.[9]

The Foreign Secretary's dancing skills also drew comment. 'I still recall the hilarity of a waltz which the first minister of Great Britain executed in the most grotesque manner,' wrote Roksandra Sturdza. But he, and many of the other Britons in Vienna, often preferred various home-grown country dances or Scottish reels, and another onlooker marvelled while watching Castlereagh, his face all serious concentration, at 'that large body, dancing a gig and rhythmically raising its long skinny legs'.[10]

The image of the British delegation was not improved by the behaviour of the ambassador, Lord Stewart, who drank and whored quite openly, touched up young women in public, and who at the end of October had a brawl with a coachman. It had started when Stewart, who liked to drive his own carriage, struck a horse on the head in a struggle for precedence. The incensed coachman lashed out with his whip, whereupon Stewart challenged him to a boxing match. But the Viennese coachman knew nothing of boxing, and set upon His Britannic Majesty's ambassador, who was only saved from injury as well as insult by the intervention of the police.[11]

A remarkable degree of insouciance emanated from the British delegation as a whole. When he called on Castlereagh on 21 October, a minor diplomat was told that His Lordship was not up yet, and when he asked for one of his secretaries he was told that they had gone off hunting.[12]

More damaging to Britain than the comportment of her representatives was the policy they appeared to be pursuing. Britain had traditionally been perceived as a defender of liberty. Yet Castlereagh had not uttered a word in defence of the Poles, had never even considered restoring the republic of Venice, had just condemned the Genoese to Sardinian absolutism, and was now conspiring to dispossess the King of Saxony of his birthright and his subjects of their beloved sovereign. The delegates of Geneva found Castlereagh cold and unhelpful. When Baron Rosenkrantz called on him to ask for his support on behalf of Denmark, he was given to understand that Britain cared for little beyond her desired settlement in Holland and along the French frontier, and wanted the whole business wrapped up as soon as possible so that she could cease paying subsidies to her allies.[13]

Even British calls for the abolition of the slave trade, a cause from the championing of which Castlereagh and his peers derived such a bottomless sense of moral satisfaction, had come to be seen as a prime example of Britain's double standards and brazen self-interest. Castlereagh's note of 8 October on the subject was ignored as a result. 'It is impossible to persuade foreign nations that this sentiment is unmixed with the views of colonial policy,' he explained to Liverpool. He was not likely to change perceptions by his next move, which was to suggest imposing trade sanctions on goods produced in the colonies of those states which refused to abolish the slave trade.[14]

On 21 November Castlereagh wrote Liverpool a despondent and somewhat bitter letter protesting that he had done his best, complaining about Alexander's bullying tactics and the spinelessness of his colleagues. He made out that much ground had been covered, and that the remaining difficulties would be resolved between 'the parties naturally interested'. This was a long way from Pitt's grand vision.[15]

That would not have bothered Liverpool, who was more interested in the situation at home. The opposition was growing aggressive in the Commons, and he needed Castlereagh back to rally the Tory ranks in the House. He planned to adjourn Parliament by the middle of December and to put off the next session until 7 February, in the hope that Castlereagh would manage to settle the more important outstanding business at the congress a couple of weeks before then. He had already found a successor for him in the shape of the Duke of Wellington, now ambassador in Paris.

Wellington, who had been schooled in France, had excellent French. He was also one of very few foreigners, and not that many Frenchmen, who knew how to make a proper '*révérence à la française*', which endeared him to Louis XVIII and the court. He was popular with the upper echelons of French society, whom he entertained lavishly in his magnificent embassy. But he was less popular with ordinary Frenchmen, who had come to see him as a kind of foreign satrap overseeing French affairs. There were even fears for his life. One source of annoyance was his vigorous demands for the abolition of the slave trade. Another was his perceived arrogance, and, not surprisingly, his sporting activities. He had brought over a pack of hounds, and ranged over the French countryside as though he were in the shires, haughtily refusing to pay compensation for damage done to property and livestock. It was only after he was reprimanded at the highest level that he agreed to stop hunting. He gave his hounds to Louis XVIII as a present. But his attitude to the French remained unchanged. 'Lord Wellington has shown a zeal and an attachment for the person of the King which I believe to be very sincere, but which it would be very unwise to confuse with his feelings for this country,' Talleyrand's deputy in Paris, the comte de Jaucourt, warned him.[16]

Liverpool had wanted Wellington to take command of the war in North America, but Wellington saw no opportunity of advancing his career there. 'Though I feel no particular wish to remain here, I don't like to be frightened away,' he wrote on 19 November, making that his excuse for avoiding a transfer to America. In the circumstances, the Vienna posting was an ideal solution, and Wellington could leave Paris without appearing to be running away from anyone. But he would not be taking over for some time, and it was still up to Castlereagh to rebuild Britain's position in Vienna. That was not going to be easy. Stein spoke for many when he described the Foreign

Secretary as lacking in depth and knowledge, and characterised his conduct as '*grandissime médiocrité et timidité*'.[17]

If the Russian handover of Saxony to Prussia had come as a blow to Castlereagh, it was an outright humiliation for Metternich. All his carefully constructed plans had come to naught, and his calculations had proved wrong. Austria was now in a perilous position, in confrontation with Russia and Prussia, supported only by a France whose military assistance could not be called on without raising all sorts of fears throughout Europe, and a Britain which had not only lost its way but had no army on the Continent. His popularity had been dwindling throughout October. The mediatised princes had all but given up on him as a potential champion, and some were now pressing for his replacement by Stadion. Metternich had been unprepared for the growing popularity of the Saxon cause in Austria, as well as throughout Germany, and had only just begun to reposition himself on the issue. The Russian move therefore made him appear as lost and ineffectual as Castlereagh.[18]

Yet, in the event, Alexander's attempt to create a *fait accompli* in Saxony proved to be a blessing for both Castlereagh and Metternich. In their determination to gain the support of Hardenberg in opposing Russian plans in Poland, they had been obliged to commit themselves to supporting Prussian claims on Saxony. This had committed them to pursuing a policy that was unpopular in both their countries. Hardenberg's forced withdrawal from their joint front against Alexander and his acceptance of Saxony at the Tsar's hands effectively released them from their obligation to support his claim to it. And Alexander's strong-arm tactics had gained him nothing.

However much trouble he had caused the others, he had failed to advance any of his own interests significantly. He was, it is true, in physical possession of what he wanted, but his increasing reliance on this rather than on the assent of his allies was making him look like a capricious bully. The transfer of Saxony to Prussian occupation caused outrage throughout Germany. It was more like the kind of arbitrary act associated with Napoleon than what was expected from the supposed liberator Alexander. His international reputation plummeted, while his own subjects were growing impatient.

If Castlereagh's failure could be put down mainly to his somewhat insular approach to the affairs of Europe, Metternich's and Alexander's were in large measure the result of emotional immaturity and the circumstances in which they found themselves. They were caught up in a frenetic round of official receptions and rituals, they had to attend conferences, listen to petitions and read memoranda without end, and they were expected to take their ease at the theatre and in the ballroom, to relax at dinners and receptions. 'The drawing rooms have a pernicious effect on affairs,' Stein remarked in a letter to his wife, 'since they bring together the persons that matter with the intriguers and the gossips.' This made it increasingly difficult for someone like Alexander to keep a clear head.[19]

Metternich was a social creature *par excellence*, and he was never more at his ease than in a drawing room or at a ball. 'When something preoccupies me, I go on working at it while I am doing something quite different,' he explained to a friend. 'The results ripen amongst apparent distractions; my best ideas, my most brilliant moves come to me at table, during conversations or while I am travelling.'[20]

But even he was not proof against prolonged strain and emotional misery. People who called on him in the morning found him yawning and absent-minded. He was also finding it more and more difficult to keep his feelings out of his dealings with Alexander and others, and indeed to separate his private from his public concerns. Gentz was exasperated by the degree to which he had become obsessed with Wilhelmina. Already in the summer, he had found that when he meant to talk to Metternich about world affairs, the conversation would drift onto the subject of his *amours*. He had hoped that this would change under pressure of politics, but found instead that even as the crisis mounted his private conferences with Metternich were 'still more on that cursed woman than on business'.[21]

Alexander not only lacked Metternich's formidable urbanity, he was far less socially experienced than most of those with whom he was mixing, as it was the first time he had spent much time in society. According to one lady he understood neither hyperbole nor irony, which resulted in misunderstandings and occasional offence. His sociability stemmed above all from the desire to be loved. Not only did he never miss a party of any kind if he could help it, he walked about the streets to show himself and spoke graciously to people he met. He mostly dressed in the uniform of Colonel of one of the Russian Guard regiments, which no longer suited him, as he had grown a little plump over the past year, and the tight coat made his arms hang in front of his body like an ape's, while the skin-tight breeches stressed the outline of his fattening bottom. Yet he continued to affect the dash of a young buck. His envy was aroused when Frederick William appeared at one ball in a hussar's uniform, and he decided that he must have one too. 'I found him today trying on eight or nine pairs of hussar's breeches, and inconsolable to find them all too tight or too short,' reported Anstett, adding that a courier was sent off to St Petersburg to fetch his aide-de-camp General Ożarowski's hussar uniform for the Tsar to try.[22]

Alexander's love of uniforms was dictated partly by his lifelong desire to prove himself as a military commander, and it was the same impulse that caused him ostentatiously to go for walks arm-in-arm with Prince Eugène, who enjoyed a reputation as a dashing and brilliant general. 'We soldiers,' he would say to marshals and subalterns alike, clapping them on the shoulder. But while he was happy to exchange a few words with or flatter someone of no consequence, he could be remarkably elusive to those who needed to discuss serious matters.[23]

Alexander had brought his wife the Empress Elizabeth to Vienna. Although no longer young, she had kept her looks and her elegant figure. Her fine blonde hair and a look of melancholy in her eyes completed a picture of loveliness that captivated even the most jaded. But Alexander spent little time with her, and did not encourage her to accompany him to balls and receptions. He was even on occasion insultingly disagreeable to her.

Alexander's mistress, Maria Antonovna Naryshkina, was also in Vienna, with her husband. Alexander told Roksandra Sturdza that she had broken off their liaison that summer, which he assured her 'had broken my heart and still makes it bleed every day'. But this did not prevent him from calling on her regularly until, at the beginning of December, he sent her on her way. This was interpreted as a good sign by Roksandra Sturdza, who was praying fervently for him. 'It seems to me that everything is combining for his spiritual elevation,' she reported to the third member of their mystic marriage, Jung Stilling. 'He is fulfilling his duties as a spouse and as a sovereign; he is determined from now on to avoid any connection that might distract him from his duties, but he is not happy in himself, he is suffering, and the consolations of religion are the only ones he can receive.'[24]

This was not strictly true. Alexander was seeking consolation of some sort with Princess Bagration, as suggested by regular police reports such as that of 3 November, which recorded that he had been seen to enter her house alone on the night of 1 November at 10.30 p.m. and stay there until 2 o'clock in the morning, and by the Princess's declaration that 'She does not love him, she *adores* him.' It is true that another informer reported that Alexander had only actually slept with the Princess a couple of times, and had sinned with a few whores procured for him by his aide-de-camp Chernyshev, but for the most part had only flirted. This was certainly the opinion of Karl von Nostitz, who claimed that the Russians in general had little success in their amorous 'assaults', and that 'their premature shouts of victory have died away in the face of the chastity of the ladies of Vienna', and noted that 'the Tsar is the most easily satisfied; a word and a look suffice to make him happy'.[25]

The flirting was certainly on a massive scale. According to Countess Rzewuska, Alexander had the nature of a coquette. He was desperate to capture the love of every woman he met, in pursuit of which he would tell each one that he loved only her. His attentions in Vienna were focused *inter alia* on Countess Esterhazy-Roisin, Countess Julie Zichy and Princess Gabrielle Auersperg. It may be that it was lack of success, rather than reticence, that limited him to flirtation, as he appears to have been remarkably maladroit in his methods. One of his first lines of approach was to show the lady his handkerchief, which bore an embroidered crown of thorns over his initial, and to complain of the deep personal unhappiness that attended his exalted position.[26]

On one occasion, hearing that Princess Esterhazy's husband was away hunting, he let her know that he would like to come and dine with her. She sent him a list of the ladies she meant to invite, with the request that he cross off the names of any he preferred not to see. He struck out the whole lot, so she sent for her husband, who arrived back just in time to greet the Tsar, who left in a rage after the briefest of intervals and before dinner had been served. On another occasion, his efforts to force his way into the bedroom of Princess Auersperg ended in her barricading the door and calling the police. At Count Francis Palffy's ball, he came up to Countess Szechenyi, whose husband had just gone to dance with another lady. 'Your husband seems to have left you,' said Alexander. 'It would be a great pleasure to occupy his place for a while.' To which the Countess retorted: 'Does Your Majesty take me for a province?'[27]

Nor did Alexander confine himself to courting the great ladies of Vienna. Apart from the whores supplied by Chernyshev, he was said to visit the wives of merchants and other ladies in town. And he did not forget his fleeting love affair in Frankfurt the previous year with Mrs Bethmann, a note from whom reduced him to tears. 'My eyes, deprived of your letters for so long, have had the happiness of contemplating that beloved handwriting, whose very sight proves to me how dear you are to me, how far everything in the world is banished from my sight when I receive something from you,' he wrote back, calling her 'my only love' and expressing the wish of 'flying into your arms to expire of happiness in them'.[28]

The Tsar's spaniel-like attentions to ladies of every station contrasted markedly with the dignified behaviour of his beautiful wife, whose poise and air of melancholy won over the hearts of many in Vienna. They attributed the look of sadness to his ill-treatment of her, but while this was probably part of the reason, there was also another. She and Prince Adam Czartoryski had not seen each other for more than eight years, and it was now about twice as long since they had been lovers. But neither had found happiness since, and his emotions were stirred powerfully when he saw her again in Vienna. He was now forty-five years old, she ten years younger. 'Her face and figure have changed,' he noted in his diary after seeing her for the second time, 'her figure is rounder, her features heavier, her complexion has faded; but taken together, they make for the same charm, and her soul is that of an angel.' They were both careful and discreet, but they wrote to each other and did meet several times in private. 'She is constantly the first and only object of my thoughts,' he confided to his diary a few weeks later, horrified to find himself feeling jealousy of those in close contact with her.[29]

The weather continued fine for most of November, and those gathered in the Austrian capital were able to carry on the round of outdoor as well as indoor entertainments without constraint. On 20 November there was a hot-air balloon demonstration in the Prater, the following night another ball given by Metternich, and on 23 November one of the most stupendous events of the whole congress, the Carrousel, for which preparations had been going on for weeks.

The revival of interest in the Middle Ages, and the desire to stress the spiritual quality of the recent war of liberation, had inspired the staging of a chivalric spectacle, and the upshot was a tournament in which knights chosen from among the war's participants could display their skills. In order to add interest to the occasion, it was decided that each of the twenty-four knights should champion a lady.

While Castlereagh struggled with his memoranda and Metternich wrestled with the problem of Saxony, most of those assembled in

Vienna busied themselves with planning or discussing the details of the forthcoming event. The knights would be dressed in costumes from the time of Francis I, in waisted velvet tunics with long wide sleeves. Over this they would wear a breast-plate, and their costume was complemented by a wide-brimmed plumed cavalier hat, yellow gloves and boots. They were divided into four companies of six, distinguished by the red, green, blue or black of their tunics. Each knight also wore a satin sash, tied at the waist with a swirling bow by his allotted damsel, and was preceded by a groom carrying his banner and followed by a squire holding a shield with his arms.

Their ladies were also divided into four groups of six, distinguished not only by the colour of their dresses, but also by their style: Austrian, French, Hungarian and Polish dress of the early seventeenth century. There was a degree of interpretation of these styles, to allow for maximum use of slashed sleeves, veils, trimmings and jewelled clasps, with velvet, silk and satin being used to dramatic effect. Wilhelmina was in Hungarian green, Dorothée in French black. They had not only worked all their own jewels into their costumes, but, like the other twenty-two, borrowed every piece of jewellery they could. Diamonds and other precious stones were unpicked from their settings and sewn into veils and bodices, and it was said that all the gems in Vienna shimmered into view as the ladies entered. 'Their dresses of velvet and lace were covered in diamonds,' noted an English traveller.[30]

The event took place in the riding school, in which two new stands had been built, one at either end, and whose pillars had been adorned with shields bearing the arms and mottoes of the twenty-four paladins. It looked, according to Anna Eynard, 'more beautiful than ever'. At 8 o'clock a fanfare announced the entrance of the twenty-four 'Queens of Love', each escorted by her champion and conducted to a seat in one of the stands. A second fanfare announced the entrance of the sovereigns, who took their seats in the other stand. The knights then rode in, announced by gaudily dressed heralds and deafening trumpet blasts. They rode around the arena, dipping their lances in salute to the sovereigns and to their ladies, and out again. The tournament began with groups of four knights, one from each company, performing feats of military skill and horsemanship – spearing suspended rings, cutting down and slicing in half suspended apples, and slashing the heads of make-believe Saracens. After this they performed a real joust, charging at each other and attempting to unseat their opponents. At one point Prince Liechtenstein fell and was carried off unconscious, to hysterical screams from the ladies of the court and the 'Queens of Love'. There followed a more pacific round, with all the cavaliers performing a number of figures in unison, a kind of equestrian ballet in time to music.

The knights then led their damsels off to dinner, which had all the appearance of a Renaissance banquet. 'The scent of flowers; the luxury of the dress, whose glittering diamonds harmonised with the flowers' gentler colour tones; the bright candlelight, reflected in the thousands of the chandeliers' prisms, inducing around them an iridescent halo; the golden fruit baskets passed around; a magnificent picture of pomp and circumstance,' noted Carl Bertuch. After dinner there was a ball, and the festivities ended only with the dawn.[31]

Following the event there was a great deal of confusion as people tried to recover the diamonds they had lent the 'Queens of Love'. Wilhelmina had borrowed jewellery from half a dozen ladies and broken up Metternich's jewelled Order of the Golden Fleece in order to prise out the largest stone. She in turn had lent a friend a fine tiara, which the other broke up into various pieces in order to sew onto her own dress, with the result that some dropped out of their settings. 'But she appeared not to care very much, and she was as careless of her own jewels as of those of others,' marvelled the thrifty Swiss Eynard.[32]

Neither exhaustion nor the possible loss of diamonds could dampen spirits. 'Everyone was, to a greater or lesser extent, gripped by a kind of dancing madness, seeming to forget the aim in which they had all assembled at such enormous cost,' according to Roksandra Sturdza. The night after the Carrousel there was a *bal paré* at the

Augarten, the day after that a ball given by Count Stackelberg, the night after that one given by Count Zichy, and the night after that a grand banquet at court. The only reason there was no ball afterwards was that it was the beginning of Advent.

'It has been decided that there will be no dancing in Catholic houses, but that Catholics may dance in the houses of those who do not believe in the Pope,' Metternich quipped to Wilhelmina, adding that it was bad news for him, as he would have to keep receiving. 'And 300 people in one room who do not move in motion are stultifying and stultified.' He himself was in very low spirits. 'Everyone bores me and I cannot see you in private,' he complained. 'I cannot invite you without your lover, and I cannot invite your lover without putting myself through torments.' The following evening, 28 November, after a lengthy late-night interview with Alexander, he confided to her that he was carrying 'a monstrous load' on his shoulders, and that he was like a man wandering in the desert, as nobody gave him a friendly hand, an appreciative glance or a word of sympathy. '1814 is a really loathsome year,' he concluded. 'Good night.'[33]

Alexander had not been to any of the recent balls, or even at the Carrousel, which had to be repeated for him a week later. He had danced himself to a standstill – literally, as while dancing with Lady Castlereagh on 16 November he fainted. He suffered an eruption of erysipelas on his leg, a condition to which he was prone, and had to take to his bed for several days. This enforced period of reflection did nothing to break his determination to keep the promises he had made to Frederick William, to the Poles, and to Prince Eugène.

The rash began to recede after a week, but, as Gagern observed after seeing Alexander on 26 November, 'his temper gained nothing by it'. He was still prickly and obstinate when it came to discussing any matter of substance, although he did begin to go out and enjoy himself again.[34]

On 29 November, at the personal invitation of the composer, he and the other sovereigns attended Beethoven's musical academy in the great Redoutensaal. The programme included his 7th Symphony, his occasional orchestral work commemorating the battle of Vittoria, *Wellington's Victory*, and the cantata *Der glorreiche Augenblick*, specially composed for the occasion, all conducted by the composer himself. The audience particularly liked *Wellington's Victory*, with its simulated cannon-shots and special effects.[35]

'Alexander, who could have played such a fine role, occupies himself only with his pleasures,' Eynard wrote in his diary. 'You see him at every public and private party; he is always the first to arrive, the most eager to dance and the last to retire; you see him occupied only with paying court to ladies while those who have been soliciting audiences for months watch him every evening waste five or six hours which could so valuably be employed elsewhere. The Emperor Alexander, affable as he is, has no dignity; at the various festivities he never sits at the royal table, preferring to flit from table to table like a butterfly; he likes to show himself at public fêtes in a tailcoat and a round hat; at the redoutes in the city, to which all classes are admitted one can see the Emperor Alexander walking about for three or four hours with his aides-de-camp or with the King of Prussia.'[36]

Boundless hopes had been pinned on Alexander. An officer of his entourage records that people came to him with grand philanthropic projects that only a man in his position could undertake. The poet Jean Paul Richter wrote, calling him the 'guardian angel' of Europe and the saviour of the world. A 'Babylonian' trudged wearily into his quarters to present him with a phial of water from an allegedly sacred spring near Ephesus, having followed him on foot as the three wise men did the star of Bethlehem. But on the day after the Beethoven concert, Alexander went to a ball given for children by Prince Schwarzenberg. 'The Emperor Alexander, who appeared to be enjoying himself greatly, danced with all the children,' reported one of Hager's informants. Another had reported ten days earlier that 'the Emperor Alexander and the King of Prussia have become the object of universal contempt'.[37]

22

Explosive Diplomacy

Hardenberg did not like parties, and he was by now certainly too preoccupied to enjoy one anyway. Although Alexander had made Frederick William order him to cut his ties with Metternich and Castlereagh, Hardenberg was still inclined to make common cause with Austria and Britain against Russia. He was deeply convinced that only this could guarantee Prussia security in the long term, and he shared neither his King's admiration for nor his fear of Alexander.

He and Humboldt had actually explored the possibility of making war against Russia in order to reconquer Prussia's old Polish provinces, and thereby dismiss the need to annex Saxony. 'If we really do have to choose between standing with Russia or with Austria and England, in such a case I would be strongly for the latter course,' Humboldt wrote to his wife. There were, it was true, 200,000 Russian troops camped a couple of days' march from Berlin in Poland, and another 60,000 scarcely further away on the other side, in Holstein. On the other hand Prussia would be able to count on the support of most of the states of Germany in such a venture. But Humboldt and Hardenberg could not be sure of Austria, and there was always the possibility of Alexander making a deal with France. They therefore concluded that it would be more prudent to wait a couple of years, by which time Russia would have withdrawn her armies from Europe

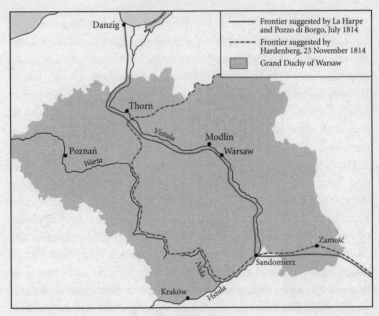

Russia's western frontier

and partly disbanded them, while Germany would have had time to recover from the devastation of the recent war.[1]

In the meantime, Hardenberg and Metternich drew up a proposal setting Russia's western border along the rivers Warta and Nida, which would give Prussia back a sizeable slice of her former Polish territories and Austria a secure frontier, guarded by the strong points of Kraków and Zamość. Hardenberg hoped to take advantage of Alexander's indisposition to present this to him in a persuasive manner.

On the night of the Carrousel, he called on Alexander and laid the proposal before him, adding that if he were to accept this frontier, Austria and Prussia would lay aside their objections to his creating a kingdom of Poland out of the rest of the Polish lands he held. The Tsar appeared disposed to listen, and he struck Metternich, who visited him two days later, as being in a conciliatory mood. But the appearance was deceptive.

Alexander was dimly aware that he had lost some of his popularity, but ascribed this to his stand on the Polish question. As he considered the recreation of a Polish kingdom to be a just and noble aim, he believed himself to be in the right and everyone else in the wrong. He was so set in his purpose that he had come to see himself as carrying on a Manichean struggle against the forces of evil, and to regard all those who tried to dissuade or oppose him as traitors or enemies.[2]

Hardenberg received Alexander's reply, composed by Czartoryski and Stein, on 27 November. It opened with the usual preamble listing the sacrifices borne by Alexander in the fight against Napoleon and a reaffirmation of his determination to bring happiness to the peoples of Europe. It went on to propose that Saxony be ceded to Prussia and Mainz be turned into a fortress of the German Confederation, in which case he would be prepared to allow Kraków and Thorn to become free cities and would dismantle the fortifications of Kalisch and Zamość. But he meant to keep the whole grand duchy of Warsaw.[3]

Hardenberg did not immediately pass Alexander's reply on to Metternich. When he did, on 3 December, he accompanied it with a request that, since she was not going to get any of her old Polish possessions back, Prussia be allowed to take the whole of Saxony. Just for good measure, it was endorsed by a memorandum by Stein pointing out that 'the King of Saxony voluntarily allied himself with the principle of tyranny and of evil, and placed great obstacles in the way of the triumph of the good cause', and had thereby forfeited all his rights. Hardenberg attempted to sweeten the pill by declaring that Prussia was prepared to give Frederick Augustus of Saxony a state carved out of her own possessions around Münster and Paderborn. He pleaded Prussia's strategic and defensive needs and underlined the necessity of a strong Prussia for the survival of peace in Europe.[4]

The proposal was unacceptable to Austria for a variety of reasons. But it did have one positive aspect; since Hardenberg was not going to stand up to Russia at his side, Metternich would be justified in going back on his promise to help Prussia obtain Saxony, which his own Emperor and public opinion were demanding that he defend. Conveniently enough, on 6 December Castlereagh showed Metternich a letter he had just received from Liverpool telling him to preserve at least some part of Saxony for its King, in order to placate British public opinion. Metternich could now reverse his policy on Saxony safe in the knowledge that Britain would do the same.

On 10 December, Metternich made his response to the Russian reply and Hardenberg's note. It did not make pleasant reading for Hardenberg. It rejected the idea of making Thorn and Kraków into free cities, insisting that they must be given to Prussia and Austria respectively, and demanded a more favourable rounding off of the frontier between Russian-held Poland and Austria. It pointed out that Hardenberg's note made no mention of Alexander's intended arrangements in Poland, or of whether he meant to include Russia's Polish provinces in the proposed new kingdom. It went on to stress how necessary a perfect and harmonious union between Austria and Prussia was to the peace and happiness of Europe, before stating categorically that no such union could exist if Prussia were to annex the whole of Saxony. 'All the Prussians and their supporters screamed murder,' according to Metternich. And they would not stop at that.[5]

The wording of all previous agreements between them had made it clear that Prussia would be permitted to take the whole of Saxony provided she supported a *successful* opposition to Russian plans in Poland. Castlereagh had spelled out that 'if the annexation of Saxony by Prussia accords with the safety of Europe, *he guaranteed the consent of England*', even though the destruction of such an old dynasty pained him, but 'his declaration had to be viewed as null in the case where Saxony would be sacrificed to the pretensions of Russia rather than to the interests of Europe'.[6]

But Hardenberg felt that since Britain and Austria had conceded Prussia's right to Saxony in principle, they had no justification for going back on it. The occupation of the kingdom by Prussian troops had appeared to establish it as fact, and the Prussian military and public opinion in Berlin had as good as digested it. In the circumstances, he could only view the change of tack by Britain, and particularly Austria, as a betrayal. His reaction was such that it provoked what Castlereagh described in a letter to Liverpool as 'a diplomatick explosion'.[7]

Hardenberg went straight to Alexander, with the aim of getting his own back on Metternich as well as salvaging Prussia's position. In an attempt to demonstrate to Alexander that Prussia was being penalised by Austria and Britain for having refused to support them against Russia, he showed him all the letters he had received from Metternich on the subject of how best to thwart Russian aims in Poland. It was, in Castlereagh's view, 'a very incorrect act'. It was also a foolish one.

Alexander was incensed when he read the letters. Amongst other things, they exposed him as a liar: back at the beginning of November, in an attempt to talk everyone round to his plans, he had told Metternich one thing and Hardenberg another, misrepresenting their real views, and here, among Hardenberg's papers, was a note by Metternich quoting him in direct contradiction to his assertions to Hardenberg.

Replicating Hardenberg's 'incorrect act', Alexander stormed off to see the Emperor Francis. He was in a 'passionate and violent' mood, according to Gentz. In what was described as 'a violent scene', he flung the papers on the table and ranted about treachery, demanding that Francis dismiss Metternich and declaring that he would challenge him to a duel.[8]

Francis retorted that he knew nothing about the matter, and summoned Metternich. The latter arrived shortly after Alexander's departure and explained himself to Francis, who instructed him to return the following day in order to lay all the justificatory evidence before Alexander. Metternich returned home, only to find Alexander's aide-de-camp General Ożarowski waiting for him. Ożarowski ordered Metternich to write a formal letter to Hardenberg saying that he had misinformed him and misquoted Alexander in his note of 7 November. Alexander was effectively trying to force Metternich to lie in order to cover up his own duplicity. Metternich refused. He realised that he must take to his interview the next day all Hardenberg's letters to him.

Before doing so, he actually called on Hardenberg to warn him, but the latter, astonishingly, said he had no objection to Metternich showing Alexander his papers. Hardenberg's letters to Metternich were, according to Castlereagh, 'the only really objectionable' ones in the case. 'Metternich's are perfectly fair diplomatic papers, avowing in very proper terms the objections of his Court to the Russian views,' he continued. Hardenberg's, on the other hand, revealed a plan to let Alexander have his way over Poland in order to lull him, and to make war on Russia a couple of years down the line, when 'the Allies *might seize an occasion of doing themselves justice*'. In a letter dated 9 November, Hardenberg suggested that it would be easy to raise Alexander's Polish subjects against him.[9]

The interview during which Metternich justified himself before Alexander, supported by Hardenberg's papers, was all the more unpleasant as Metternich had insinuated into the papers a note written by himself detailing Alexander's every disloyal utterance and action towards Prussia. 'This note was, either most ungenerously or most unaccountably, amongst the papers sent, and served not a little to exasperate,' Castlereagh reported. Aides waiting in the next room could hear Alexander stamping his foot with rage.[10]

The mechanisms of diplomacy, devised expressly to guard against such potentially dangerous encounters, had not so much broken down as been dispensed with. Instead of dealing through third parties, who, provided they were professional enough to lay aside their most passionate feelings, acted as neutral buffers, Alexander had insisted on conducting the negotiations himself, and had repeatedly attempted to use his position and personal prestige to force an issue. The inevitable result had been a series of confrontations that could easily have led to war.

Fortunately, he must have realised the moral weakness of his position, as the following day, 14 December, he approached Francis in his most charming and conciliatory manner. He professed his ardent desire to remain on the best of terms with Austria, and declared that while he could not give her Kraków, he was willing as a gesture of good will to hand over the Polish district of Tarnopol with a population of

400,000, taken from Austria in 1809. It was Russia's first material concession, and it defused the crisis, not so much by gratifying Austria as by giving her a pretext to climb down over Poland. 'Austria, having reached the conclusion that she could not save both Saxony and Poland, decided to drop the latter,' in Metternich's words. 'The whole, as you may imagine, made for two days a great sensation,' Castlereagh reported to Liverpool on 17 December, 'but the result perhaps may serve to prove what I have ventured before to allege, that the climate of Russia is often more serene after a good squall.'[11]

Russia and Austria could now be said to have fulfilled the provisions of the various treaties to settle the matter of the duchy of Warsaw '*à l'amiable*', and that permitted Britain to wash her hands of the business. 'I consider the Polish Question as settled,' Castlereagh wrote to Wellington on 18 December. 'The Saxon Question is now the only one that is of much difficulty.'[12]

But if Castlereagh really believed that the 'squall' had dispelled the tensions, he was very much mistaken. The Polish issue might well have been pushed into the background by common consent, but the Saxon conundrum was every bit as intractable. Particularly since, with her former Polish territories now entirely beyond reach, Prussia had to concentrate all her attention on what had become a matter of life and death for her.

Now that Alexander had managed to achieve, in principle at least, a large part of his plan on Poland, he was bound to start losing interest in other aspects of the interminable congress. He still felt in honour bound to support Frederick William because he had promised him Saxony. But his heart was no longer in it, and Hardenberg must have realised this.

On 16 December, just as the smoke of the explosion was being blown away, Hardenberg composed a new note, which he delivered to Czartoryski three days later to be passed to Alexander. It aggressively restated Prussia's demand for the whole of Saxony, claiming that this had always had the approval of the other powers, and concluded with the proposal that Frederick Augustus be compensated for the loss of

Saxony with a new state fashioned out of Prussian possessions on the left bank of the Rhine. This was an act of desperation in more ways than one: Prussia was not only offering to give up territory, she was also reminding Britain, which wanted a strong Prussian presence on the Rhine as a bulwark against France, that she must be supported.[13]

Hardenberg's note was accompanied by much sabre-rattling on the part of the Prussian military, which provoked strong reactions from the Austrians. 'Everything is in a state of tension,' noted Carl Bertuch in his diary on 16 December, 'the talk in the city is only of war.' Stein wrote in his a day later that 'the heads of the Viennese are full of lust for war'. Someone even overheard Alexander saying that blood would have to flow.[14]

There had been talk of war from the moment the allies entered Paris in 1814. People had grown so used to its continuous presence, punctuated with intermittent armed truces, that it had come to seem a first rather than last resort in any situation of conflict. And there were troops standing by all over Europe. The allies had fought each other quite as often as they had fought Napoleon over the past two decades, and there was no shortage of national and regional animosities dividing them. The military of every country had a ledger of scores to settle, and young men who had joined the army in order to further their careers were not happy to see them cut short at some junior rank with the prospect of tedious garrison duty and promotion based only on time served. Civilians resented allied troops as much as they had the French occupiers, particularly in Germany, where the behaviour of not only the Russian army, with its swarms of ill-disciplined cossacks, but the Prussian contingents as well came to be loathed within months of the 'liberation'.[15]

The differences between the allies had been kept in check by the need to make common cause against Napoleon, and with him gone they came to the fore. The euphoria of the days spent in Paris and London veiled them, but by the middle of the summer many commentators could not see how they could be reconciled. 'There are a great many people who are convinced that, however one might try to avoid it, this will all end in a complete rupture between the allied powers,' Gentz wrote at the beginning of July. When the allied sovereigns and their ministers congregated in Vienna the prospect of war receded into the realms of improbability. But by the first days of October things were looking grim, and Gentz was predicting 'either war or a state of affairs worse than war, in which one side will keep what it has and what it proposes to do, while the others will refuse to recognise his rights and to sanction his actions by any kind of authentic act'.[16]

Although none of the major players could face the prospect of war without dread, and certainly none wished to be seen to provoke one, they remained keenly aware of the dangers of too pacific an approach. As trust broke down between them, there was a growing sense that whatever settlement was finally reached, nobody could be counted on to respect it. The question that faced them now was whether it was better to go to war immediately, or to patch up some kind of agreement and live in fear of impending war.

While Russia, Prussia and Austria all had large armies at their disposal, Britain had no troops on the Continent. The regiments which had served under Wellington in Spain over the past seven years were in no state to be redeployed, and virtually all other British forces were engaged across the Atlantic in the war with the United States of America. If it were to come to war, Britain would have to find a proxy on the Continent. At the beginning of October Wellington duly sounded out the French government on whether it would be prepared to go to war over Saxony, and received a positive reply.[17]

The approach did not come as a surprise. On 17 October, the eve of the festival of peace in the Prater, Talleyrand warned Louis XVIII that France must be prepared to fight, and his letter crossed one from the King stating that he was putting the army on a war footing. Within a month the possibility of war had turned into likelihood. 'All the appearances announce a great war,' Cardinal Consalvi warned his deputy in Rome on 18 November. At the root of all these apprehensions lay the continued presence of hundreds of thousands of Russian troops in various parts of central Europe.[18]

In the course of his conversation with Alexander on 14 November, Metternich told him in the most tactful terms that he should withdraw his armies from Europe. 'What has reassured us up to now is the opinion we had formed of your personal character; if we are unfortunate enough to lose it, all hearts will grow cold with fear at the sight of a Russian soldier, and from that moment to the point of universal resistance the interval will be a very short one.'[19]

Thanks to Hager's network of spies, Metternich knew that Alexander was making contingency plans which included a southward Russian thrust into Hungary with the aim of raising a nationalist revolt against Austria. At the same time, Metternich himself was being goaded by Bavaria, which saw in a new war the chance of obtaining not only Mainz but other areas as well.[20]

In his efforts to outflank Austria, Alexander was courting Württemberg, whose Prince Royal was hoping to marry his sister, the Grand Duchess Catherine. He also made a new attempt at rapprochement with France, coming up to Talleyrand during a reception given by Countess Zichy and asking him to come and see him informally, so they might recapture some of their former intimacy. When Talleyrand did call on him, Alexander was 'all calm and sweet', and proposed helping oust Murat from Naples if France would allow Prussia to take Saxony.[21]

Alexander's wooing of Talleyrand alarmed Castlereagh and his colleagues, who feared that Russia might buy the support of France with the promise of a frontier on the Rhine. Alexander could, after all, easily accommodate both France and Prussia, by leaving the King of Saxony on his throne and allowing Prussia to take Hanover instead. Wellington and Castlereagh tried to parry this threat by hinting that they might be willing to allow France an improved frontier, as well as remove Murat from Naples and Napoleon from Elba.[22]

Liverpool felt that even a poor settlement was better than war. An unsatisfactory peace might lead to the outbreak of war in a few years' time, he admitted, yet a war deferred would be a lesser evil. The Austrians were of the opposite opinion. Austria was possibly the most vulnerable of all to a deferred war, as she could be attacked from every side and would be indefensible once she had demobilised. 'It is the deliberate opinion of many of their officers, and, I may add, ministers, that, rather than have the Russians at Cracovie and the Prussians at Dresde [sic], they had better risk a war with such support as they can get,' Castlereagh reported on 21 November. Francis himself felt it would be better to go to war now rather than later. Schwarzenberg had already massed 370,000 men in Hungary and Galicia, and was deploying troops in Bohemia.[23]

The Russian military were also keen to get on with the fighting while they still had a large army in central Europe. Many of them felt that Russia's honour had been slighted by the lack of respect shown to the Tsar's wishes by the sovereigns and plenipotentiaries of the other powers. They were particularly warm on the subject of the British, as the diary of one officer in the Tsar's entourage attests. Asserting that the 'false Englishmen' were actively arming against Russia, he complained that they were accusing Russia of seeking dominion over Europe while they themselves were spreading 'despotic power over every part of Europe and other parts of the world', and that Russia's diplomats had failed to uphold the gains won 'with the blood of our soldiers'. He was convinced that 'war will soon break out between us'. On 26 November Baron Rosenkrantz noted in his diary that 'the Russians are burning with desire to fight the Austrians'.[24]

That same day Liverpool, who was beginning to panic, wrote to Wellington voicing the fear that Britain might be dragged into a war over something that was of scant relevance to her interests. He was also concerned at the drop in the government's popularity. Through his ambassador in London, Count Lieven, Alexander had for some time been feeding the opposition in Parliament and public opinion in the country with information and suggestions that would help it challenge the government and undermine Castlereagh's position.[25]

Bathurst wrote to Castlereagh the following day informing him that the Prince Regent was extremely anxious. 'It is unnecessary for me to point out to you the impossibility of H.R.H. consenting to involve this country in hostilities at this time for any of the objects which have been hitherto under discussion at Vienna,' he warned him. The Prince Regent was being sent alarming reports of impending conflict by Münster, who warned that 'matters have come to a crisis ominous enough for us to have to think seriously of which side to take if war breaks out'. But couriers took ten to twelve days to cover the distance between London and Vienna, and neither the Prince Regent nor Liverpool could hope to direct events there.[26]

On 30 November Alexander sent Nesselrode to see the Bavarian minister Prince Wrede in a last-ditch attempt to persuade him to join Russia in defying Austria. When Wrede replied that he would only join a coalition with the King of Saxony, he received a visit from Hardenberg and Humboldt, who openly threatened him with war.[27]

'It were better to have a new war than that Prussia, after such glorious deeds and so many sacrifices, should come out of the affair badly,' Hardenberg wrote to General Gneisenau on the following day. That very day, 5 December, Castlereagh wrote to Liverpool with the same message. He pointed out that as all the powers were fully mobilised, and anxious to be rid of the expense of maintaining their armies for much longer, they were unlikely to delay using them. This was, according to him, particularly true of Russia and Prussia. 'I think the probability therefore is, that one or both of these Powers, if they do not relax in their pretensions, will provoke rather than procrastinate the war,' he wrote.[28]

Metternich's note to Hardenberg on 10 December raised the temperature. The following day Grand Duke Constantine issued a proclamation to the Polish army urging it to be ready to defend its country. The proclamation was not made public in Warsaw, but only in Vienna, as its purpose was to intimidate. It certainly did. 'The idea of a rupture is, it has to be said, repugnant, but we have to take it into account,' Baron von Gagern reported that day to the Prince of Orange. On 4 December Jean-Gabriel Eynard noted that talk of war had become so general that it appeared imminent. 'Everything is in a state of suspense,' Carl Bertuch noted in his diary on 12 December, 'and the next 4–5 days will reveal whether there is to be war or peace.'[29]

Russia and Prussia had some 350,000 men under arms in Germany and Poland. Austria and France, with Bavaria and their other German allies, could muster many more, but Austria had to keep a fair proportion of them in Italy to guard against a possible stab in the back by Murat. It was being rumoured that Alexander had opened up a channel of communication with him, and even that he might consider bringing Napoleon back on the scene. He was reported to have told Prince Eugène that 'If they force me to, I shall unleash the monster himself on them.'[30]

Castlereagh suggested to Liverpool that the only way of avoiding the outbreak of hostilities was armed mediation on the part of Britain and France. 'The two Powers might truly and powerfully put forward to Europe a coincidence of interests and a similarity of views,' he explained. 'Neither have any direct interest at issue before the congress; both have the strongest and most obvious interest in peace.' But the chances of peace looked slight, and Castlereagh was still in no position to take a lead, having failed to recover his authority.[31]

'The variations in the conduct of the English plenipotentiaries are the key to the whole history of the congress of Vienna,' Gentz wrote on 20 December. 'It is they that explain why, after three months, the congress has not achieved a single result.' Metternich would later blame Castlereagh's initial mistakes for skewing the entire course of the congress. 'Therein, there can be no doubt, lay *the principal cause* of the unsatisfactory result of the Congress,' he wrote in his memoirs. In a letter to Liverpool on 7 December, Cooke himself described Castlereagh as 'in wandering mazes lost', an impression shared by Talleyrand. 'Lord Castlereagh is like a traveller who has lost his way and cannot find it again,' he wrote to Louis XVIII on 20 December, '. . . he does not know which way to turn.'[32]

Dance of War

Castlereagh's position was unexpectedly saved by the intervention of Talleyrand, the one ally he had taken least account of. On 19 December, as threats of war flew all around him, the plenipotentiary of France produced an open letter to Metternich which stopped everyone in their tracks.

In prose that was limpid and elegant, and with devastating logic, he reassessed the situation. He argued that by far the most important and most difficult question facing the congress had been that of Poland. But once it had become clear that the three powers which had partitioned that country were not prepared to give up their shares, the Polish question had been superseded by the Saxon one, which had now become pre-eminent.

He represented this as an exclusively moral issue, claiming that the intention of giving Saxony to Prussia struck at the very basis of all law and custom. 'To recognise such a disposition as legitimate,' he wrote, 'one would have to hold it true that Kings can be judged; that they can be judged by those who wish to and can seize their possessions; that they can be condemned without having been heard, without having been able to defend themselves; that their families and their peoples are necessarily condemned along with them; that the practice of confiscation, which enlightened nations have banished from their code, is in the nineteenth century to be sanctioned by the public law of Europe [...]; that peoples have no rights as distinct from their sovereigns, and can be treated like a dairy herd; that sovereignty can be lost and gained by the single fact of conquest; that the nations of Europe are bound [...] only by the law of nature, and that what is called the public law of Europe does not exist; [...] in a word, that all is legitimate for him who is the strongest.' Having condemned the whole transaction on moral grounds, he then went on to point out that it was quite unnecessary, as Prussia could easily be found the requisite territorial increases elsewhere.[1]

Talleyrand had been assiduously pursuing his own agenda, based on his interpretation of legitimacy and the 'public law of Europe'. He showed sympathy to the dispossessed, and missed no opportunity of accusing the great powers of lack of principle, taunting them that they only had themselves to blame for the sorry state of affairs. He rebuked Castlereagh for his 'spirit of jealousy and strict personal interest', and argued that by refusing to allow a full congress to assemble he and Metternich had allowed Alexander to browbeat them, which he would not have been able to do if he had been confronted by an assembly representing the whole of Europe. He had prepared the ground so well that his letter had the effect of a bombshell.[2]

By raising the standard of legitimacy in defence of Saxony at a moment when the negotiations had all but broken down, Talleyrand effectively turned himself into the rallying point for a new front against the aggressive behaviour of Russia and the territorial greed of Prussia.

This came as a godsend to Castlereagh. Liverpool and his cabinet had been urgently reconsidering their position. In a measured document dated 12 December, Bathurst reviewed Britain's foreign policy in the light of the changes that had taken place since the defeat of Napoleon. Its gist was that the original alliance was dissolved, having been split down the middle by the failure of the negotiations over Poland and Saxony. This meant that Britain had no option but to seek the support of France. While conceding the possible dangers of building up French influence at this stage, he could see no other way of acquiring an ally and at the same time denying one to Russia – the threat of a Russo-French alliance sealed with the promise of Belgium appeared very real in view of the Tsar's continued courting of Talleyrand.[3]

On 23 December Liverpool wrote to Wellington urging him to work at a rapprochement with France. 'The more I hear and see of the different Courts of Europe, the more convinced I am that the King of France is (amongst the great Powers) the only Sovereign in whom we can have any real confidence,' he argued. 'The Emperor of Russia is profligate from vanity and self-sufficiency, if not from principle. The King of Prussia may be a well-meaning man, but he is the dupe of the Emperor of Russia. The Emperor of Austria I believe to be an honest man, but he has a Minister in whom no one can trust; who considers all policy as consisting in *finesse* and trick; and who has got his government and himself into more difficulties by his devices than could have occurred from a plain course of dealing.'[4]

The same day, in reply to Castlereagh's letter of 5 December asking for instructions in case war loomed, Liverpool warned that 'it would be quite impossible to embark this country in a war at present'. But he recognised the need to prepare. 'We agree, therefore, that a *rapprochement* between this country and France is most desirable at the present moment,' he wrote, suggesting that Castlereagh liaise with Wellington to that end.[5]

Matters had by then gone far beyond a mere rapprochement. At the distance he was from Vienna, Liverpool was in no position to direct events. As though in acknowledgement of this, he went off to Bath and his entire cabinet to their country estates for Christmas, leaving only Bathurst to read Castlereagh's incoming letters. The Foreign Secretary might as well have been talking to himself as he wrote out his lengthy missives. He was entirely on his own. But he was beginning to find his way, and he now knew where to look for support against Alexander.

*   *   *

Alexander had recovered from his indisposition and was busily catching up on all the amusements he had missed. 'The time that could be dedicated to affairs is wasted on festivities,' complained Talleyrand on 7 December. 'The Emperor Alexander requests and even commands them, as though he were at home.' The Carrousel was repeated, a second time, for his benefit. He did, admittedly, take the opportunity provided by the event to try to intimidate Francis. But he did not let business get in the way of amusement, and according to a police report he then drove off to Princess Bagration's, where he stayed until 3 o'clock in the morning.[6]

The following day, 6 December, was his sister Catherine's name day, and he gave a ball for her in Razumovsky's palace. 'I have never seen anything more beautiful than his palace,' noted Eynard. 'It is an enchanted place, containing everything that is best in what France and Italy have produced in terms of elegance and good taste.' Fifteen rooms had been transformed into Arabian tents, all richly decorated and each containing a small orchestra which played in unison with the others, so that those dancing the polonaise snaked through all of them without for a moment losing the music. There were performances by Russian dancers, and some of the lustier young Russian officers dressed up as cossacks to execute their native dances, to the delight of the Viennese ladies. Dinner, which consisted of thirty-six courses, was served at twenty tables dressed with the greatest luxury. Of the sovereigns, only Alexander and Maximilian of Bavaria were present; Frederick William was indisposed, while Francis excused himself on the grounds that he did not attend balls in Advent. This detail did not prevent Cardinal Consalvi from being present.[7]

Ever more *recherché* diversions were being dreamed up by master of ceremonies Trautmannsdorff and by various hostesses to distract the assembled company from the business, or apparent lack of business, of the congress. On 9 December the first in a series of new entertainments was held at the Redoutensaal. It consisted of a number of 'tableaux' representing famous events or themes in mythology or history, created by actors in costume under the direction of the painter

Jean-Baptiste Isabey. Hippolytus could be seen defending himself before Theseus against the accusations of Phaedra, Louis XIV courting Mademoiselle de la Vallière, and so on. Some tableaux were still, others developed into '*romances en action*' to the accompaniment of music. A particularly successful one showed the Flemish painter Teniers in his studio leafing through some of his paintings; each time he held one up to the audience, a group of actors in the appropriate costume would bring it to life. Piquancy was added by the fact that all the actors were well-known members of the Viennese or visiting aristocracy.[8]

Isabey himself had taken advantage of the mounting boredom of those assembled in Vienna to promote his own work. He had been assiduously drawing and painting everyone of note, and he now began to stage weekly exhibitions. The idle and the inquisitive flocked to gawp at the likenesses of people whom they saw every day, despite the fact that Isabey flattered all his – mostly female – sitters to the point of caricature. 'There is no woman, however ugly, who, painted by him, does not appear as lovely and ethereal as a sylph,' noted Baroness du Montet after visiting one such show on 19 December. What made the exhibitions even less interesting was the fact that he painted them all in exactly the same manner. 'The Duchess of Weimar, Princess Bagration, and all the Princesses of Europe are swathed, swaddled and veiled in clouds of muslin and obscured by roses.'[9]

The search for new entertainments was relentless. Countess Zichy held a series of chess games, with her guests dressed up as kings, queens, bishops, knights and pawns, standing on a chequered floor. Countess Marie Esterhazy took to holding balls for children, to which Alexander loved to come – here at least he could dance with all the girls and enjoy unmitigated admiration. Alexander's contribution was, one evening at Countess Zichy's, to make everyone sit on the floor in a room lit only by a single candle and tell each other ghost stories.[10]

The one spectacle Alexander did not command was the imposing funeral, on 15 December, of the prince de Ligne. The much-loved wit had been taken ill, but made light of it. To one solicitous visitor he said that he was sure all those assembled in Vienna had become so blasé with all the different entertainments they had been treated to that they must be longing to enliven things with the funeral of an Austrian Field Marshal, but that he was not inclined to oblige them. The following day he was dead, and the public was indeed treated to a magnificent spectacle. His coffin, draped in black and borne by eight grenadiers, was preceded by a black knight riding in effigy and followed by the Prince's charger, fully caparisoned with his empty boots reversed in the stirrups, and escorted by detachments of the imperial guard, marching slowly to the roll of drums draped in black. The procession included several squadrons of cavalry, four batteries of artillery and virtually every dignitary, diplomatic or military, in Vienna.[11]

The most brilliant event of all was the concert and grand gala given at court on 23 December to celebrate Alexander's thirty-fifth birthday. It was distinguished by the last public appearance at the piano of Beethoven, who accompanied the tenor Franz Wild in his lied *Adelaïde*. The composer had over the years benefited from the patronage of Razumovsky, and was present at most of the receptions given by the Russian. In the past weeks he had dedicated a sonata for violin and piano (op. 30) to Alexander and composed a polonaise for piano (op. 89) for Elizabeth.[12]

No amount of frivolity or diversion could affect what appeared to be the Tsar's firm resolve. Writing to the Prince Regent on 17 December, Count Münster complained that Alexander was behaving like a 'dictator'. Even Czartoryski, who knew him well and was close enough to observe him in private every day, noted that he was 'like rock and steel'. But the Tsar may have been bluffing.[13]

On 18 December, the eve of the publication of Talleyrand's letter, Castlereagh received a visit from Czartoryski, 'who although not in any official situation, appears now the actual Russian minister', as he reported to Liverpool. Czartoryski had apparently come to sound him out as to how far he was prepared to go in defence of Saxony;

this suggested that, having achieved much of what he wanted on the Polish issue, Alexander was beginning to look for solutions to the impasse. It was becoming clear to some that he was not prepared to back Prussia to the hilt.[14]

The acclaimed liberator of Europe did not wish to be drawn into the role of a bully in support of an ally whose growing unpopularity threatened to taint him. 'In 1813, Prussia waved the flag of German liberation to gain support,' it was being said in southern Germany. 'In 1814, Prussian greed is in evidence on all fronts. Prussia is a traitor to the European cause and to the balance of power. The storm flags of Europe and of Germany must be raised against Prussia and Russia.' Only Hesse-Cassel and Saxe-Weimar sided openly with Prussia, and Württemberg with Russia, because of the Crown Prince's proposed marriage to the Grand Duchess Catherine.[15]

Ironically, the danger of war increased in inverse proportion to Alexander's willingness to support Prussia. As their interests began to diverge, the Prussians grew desperate to involve Russia and bind her more closely than ever to supporting them over Saxony. The surest way of doing this was to try to force the other side to precipitate a crisis.

On 19 December, the day Talleyrand produced his letter to Metternich, Castlereagh received another visit from Czartoryski, this time accompanied by Hardenberg, Humboldt and Stein. With a mixture of argument and threat, they tried to persuade him to permit Prussia to take the whole of Saxony. Two days later, Alexander presented to Francis Hardenberg's note on this matter. It began by affirming that 'The right of conquest is a legal title for the acquisition of sovereignty over a conquered country,' quoting Grotius and Vattel in support, and bringing up all over again Frederick Augustus's supposedly infamous behaviour in 1813. It went on to demonstrate that Prussia was the only allied power to have lost territory, and demanded the whole of Saxony in compensation. It restated the argument that a strong Prussia was vital to the peace and stability of Europe, that a Prussia extending from the river Niemen in the east to the Meuse in the west could not be strong if it did not have a substantial centre, and that that could only be formed by the addition of Saxony. Frederick Augustus of Saxony could be indemnified, if necessary, with a kingdom of some 700,000 inhabitants cobbled together from areas on the left bank of the Rhine. In a word, Prussia was standing firm, and by delivering the note on her behalf, Alexander was making a show of supporting her.[16]

There seemed to be no way out of the impasse, and tension mounted. Austrian and Prussian commanders exchanged insults, and warlike comments allegedly made by the Tsar or the King of Prussia were repeated and embellished. Rosenkrantz was astonished to be asked by Castlereagh, on 20 December, how many men Denmark could deploy at short notice. 'A second war is necessary,' Humboldt assured his wife that same day, 'and it must take place sooner or later.' Even those who did not believe it would come to war thought the congress would break up in recrimination without resolving anything.[17]

Only one thing was certain, according to Baron Nostitz: that the congress would end 'like those great gambling parties at which the only winners are the servants'. He noted that the two dancers Bigottini and Petite-Aimée had anticipated this. 'They have both left,' he wrote. 'The former took with her 40,000 gulden in Viennese coin and a child, which Franz Palffy acknowledges; he has given the brat 100,000 Viennese gulden and the mother a yearly pension of 6,000 francs. If anyone should think this sum a little low, he could add Bigottini's thirty-six years to it.'[18]

And while some anxiously noted the mounting tension in their diaries, others appeared entirely impervious. 'The Hereditary Prince of Hesse-Darmstadt and the Grand Duke of Baden continue to indulge themselves, sometimes at the lodgings of one, sometimes at the other's, where they hold merry dinners, often in the company of Gaertner's chambermaid,' runs a police report dated 22 December. 'It is still the equerry who provides for the pleasures of the Prince of Hesse, and he often sends for Mlle Lombard or the so-called Countess

Waffenberg, otherwise known as *Lori Toussaint*.' And Frederick William still appeared to some to be more interested in Julie Zichy than in Saxony.[19]

Others, equally impervious to the tensions, pursued more serious goals. A delegation of Serbs led by the minister Mateja Nenadovic appealed to the congress for support in their cause against the Turks. Carl August Buchholz, the representative of the Jews of Hamburg, Bremen and his native Lübeck, chose this moment to make his appeal for full equality for the Jews in the new Germany. He was supported by Humboldt, who also helped the two deputies of the Jewish communities of Prague and Frankfurt. The latter had narrowly missed being expelled by the police on arrival, as Metternich wished to avoid the subject being raised, but powerful interests were brought into play; along with the support of Humboldt and Hardenberg, the Jews also had that of Castlereagh, who had received a letter on the matter from the head of the London branch of the Rothschild family, with a covering note from Liverpool assuring him that 'Mr Rothschild has been a very useful friend,' and adding, by way of postscript: 'I don't know what we should have done without him last year.'[20]

Perhaps the most unlikely piece of business to be transacted against the background noise of sabre-rattling was suggested by Talleyrand at the meeting of the eight signatories of the Treaty of Paris on 10 December. It was that they set up a committee to study the vexed question of precedence, so they might at least eliminate any further unseemly spats over who sat where and who signed before whom. The others agreed, and the committee set to work, holding its meetings at the lodgings of Labrador, who chaired it. But Talleyrand's thoughts were on war.

When Castlereagh apprised him of Hardenberg's note on 23 December, Talleyrand declared that the situation demanded drastic action. His language was 'urgent' and 'his tone was very high and hostile to Prussia', Castlereagh noted. Talleyrand suggested that the two of them combine with Metternich to proclaim publicly that they recognised the rights of the King of Saxony and to pledge to defend them. Castlereagh asked him whether he was thinking in terms of a convention or an alliance. Talleyrand suggested a treaty of alliance. 'I told him that I thought we were already united in opinion, and that to form an alliance prematurely might augment the chances of war rather than of an amicable settlement, which I trusted was the object we all had in view.'[21]

'I think as you do,' replied Talleyrand. 'We must do everything [to maintain peace] except sacrifice honour, justice and the future of Europe.' Castlereagh ventured that a war would be highly unpopular in England, but Talleyrand dismissed this, saying that would depend on how it was represented. 'The war would be popular at home if you gave it a great goal, a truly European one,' he said. When asked what goal he had in mind, Talleyrand replied: 'The re-establishment of Poland.' Such a move would certainly undermine Alexander's credibility and completely outmanoeuvre him.[22]

That evening there was a formal reception at court, after which the Castlereaghs entertained a small party to supper. One of those present was Prince Eugène, whom Castlereagh had come to like, because 'He is the best of the *Buonaparte school*, and has played an honourable and able part.' Another was Jean-Gabriel Eynard, invited everywhere for his ravishing wife, eighteen years younger than him. They made a curious spectacle as they settled down to a simple supper, still in their uniforms and diamonds from the court reception. After supper Prince Eugène and Anna Eynard sang Italian songs, after which Castlereagh launched into a number of English airs. He was in high spirits.[23]

'France is now a principal in the question,' he reported enthusiastically to Liverpool in his next letter, written two days later, on 25 December. It says a great deal about how far hopes of reaching a satisfactory settlement had receded that on Christmas Day Castlereagh should have been celebrating the acquisition of a firm ally and applying himself to drafting a treaty of coalition in preparation for war.

Considering how much effort went into enlivening each day, Christmas seems to have been treated in somewhat perfunctory manner, with little in the way of a build-up and no climactic festivities. The churches were full, but after an unseasonally warm spell in mid-December the weather had turned cold and wet, so there were no processions. On Christmas Eve the Emperor Francis gave a grand dinner at court in honour of Alexander's wife Elizabeth. The next day, there was a concert at court and in the evening a ball given by Princess Bagration. Otherwise, people entertained themselves in small groups.

Hardenberg and most of the Prussians spent Christmas Eve at the house of Fanny von Arnstein, where they were treated to a musical gathering around a fir tree that had been brought into the drawing room, a custom unknown outside certain parts of northern Germany. The Castlereaghs stayed at home, where they were joined for supper by Prince Eugène, the Crown Prince of Bavaria, Cardinal Consalvi, Stewart, the British minister to Switzerland Stratford Canning, Gagern, Münster and a number of Portuguese, Spaniards and Poles. Gentz gave some presents on Christmas Eve, but worked late into the holy night, and through most of Christmas Day as well. On 26 December he and the others went to a ball given by Metternich.[24]

That morning, the King of Württemberg left Vienna. He had decided to boycott the proceedings and take the law into his own hands at home. For all his physical monstrosity and his tyrannical nature, he was not mean, and he knew how to behave like a King. Before leaving, he bestowed half a million florins' worth of presents, mainly in the form of snuff-boxes, rings or cash, to all the officials of the Austrian court, the principal servants who had attended him, and all the plenipotentiaries of the other courts.[25]

The round of entertainments picked up after Christmas, with a court ball on 28 December and a somewhat bizarre picnic in the Augarten the following day. It was the brainchild of Sir Sydney Smith, a man whose reputation preceded him. He had joined the Royal Navy at twelve and commanded a frigate by the time he was nineteen. He had burnt the French fleet at Toulon in 1792, been captured at Le Havre two years later, and escaped from the Temple prison in Paris.

He had appeared at Vienna ostensibly as the representative of the dethroned King Gustavus IV of Sweden, but had also espoused the cause of Christian slaves in Ottoman or Barbary captivity. He wore a reliquary on a chain around his neck which, he claimed, had belonged to Richard the Lionheart, and drove about in a carriage so covered in heraldic devices that, as Baroness du Montet noted, 'That of King Richard, if he had possessed one, could never have displayed more mottos, arms and heroic emblems.' Sir Sydney was undistinguished-looking, as was his wife, and Talleyrand thought that 'There is nothing remarkable about him except his extravagance.' But he had brought with him his daughter-in-law, a girl of such loveliness that Stewart and Prince Augustus of Prussia were soon in hot pursuit.[26]

On 29 January Smith organised a charity picnic in the Augarten to raise funds for the Christian slaves, and in the middle of the proceedings he started a collection. It had evidently slipped his mind that monarchs do not habitually carry money, and when the collecting trays reached Alexander and Frederick William there was much embarrassment.

On 30 December Gentz had made a longer entry than usual in his irregular and often laconic diary. 'The affairs of the world have taken on a lugubrious aspect,' he wrote, looking back over the past year. He put it down to 'the mediocrity and ineptitude' of most of the sovereigns and statesmen. 'However,' he continued, 'since I have nothing to reproach myself with, far from afflicting me, the intimate knowledge I have of this pitiful series of events and of all these petty beings who govern the world serves to amuse me, and I am enjoying this spectacle as though it had been provided for my personal pleasure.'

As far as he himself was concerned, 1814 had been one of the best years in his life. He had made a considerable amount of money, and not only from his writings. The day before, Talleyrand had given him a fortune in cash. Castlereagh had recently made him the generous gift of £600 in gold. 'The year 1815 begins under quite good auspices for me,' he concluded, 'but as for public affairs, I can see that it is pointless to believe that it will ever fulfil the vain hopes entertained by enthusiasts and which I renounce forever.'[27]

His feelings were echoed by the Duchess of Saxe-Coburg-Saalfeld in her diary entry for 31 December. 'This eventful year has now also come to a close,' she wrote. 'The Tyrant has been thrown from his pedestal, and peace reigns from the north to the Mediterranean. And yet I, in common with, I am sure, most thinking Germans, cannot end it with quite the same enthusiasm as the previous one. Greatly and gloriously did the war end at Mont-Martre, but with the calm of peace, alas, all the ugly passions of men have reappeared, and that which even Napoleon could not take from us – Hope – is now dwindling.'[28]

Metternich was also unhappy, for more personal reasons. 'Three months ago you betrayed the lover in me; today the friend will pardon you for everything he can pardon you,' he wrote to Wilhelmina on the afternoon of 31 December, as the snow fell outside. 'All I suffer, all you have made me suffer, all is pardoned with this day that terminates the year that is the most frightful year of my life, because it has been made so by the being to whom I vowed everything the Creator can bestow of good, simple, true feeling in the heart of a man!' Later that day he sent her a bracelet he had ordered in happier days. But he could not stop there. Whether he knew that she was spending New Year's Eve with Alfred von Windischgraetz or not is not known, but three days later he would write again, dwelling on the depth of his love, the shallowness of hers, and the misery she had caused him. He did, however, reflecting over the events of the past year, make one uncharacteristically true observation. 'I was no longer a child,' he admitted. 'Called upon to lead twenty million men, I should have been capable of mastering myself.'[29]

That night, even Providence appeared to stamp disapproval on the dying year. Shortly before midnight the sophisticated modern system of pipes and ducts that heated the magnificent Razumovsky Palace began to pump smoke and then sparks through the building. The fire brigade was roused, but by the time it arrived the entire building was ablaze. It was, according to Friedrich von Schönholz, who had hurried over to watch, 'a spectacle of truly heroic size'. He stood and gazed in wonder.

'Meanwhile, the crowd was swelled by ever new arrivals, more fire equipment kept reporting, more pumps, fresh troops, generals, friends of the Count, guests of the congress on horseback, at last the Princes, too – even the Czar came,' he recorded. The park and surrounding streets were awash with uniforms and plumed hats, helmets, bayonets. 'Soon, there was not a window in the new palace that did not emit smoke or flames, and the copper roof glowed fiery red. This most valuable part of the Count's residence, with its priceless collections, its exclusive library, and all the other treasures, was hopelessly lost and now every effort was bent toward limiting the holocaust to this section of the palace.'

A devoted valet could be seen at a second-floor window throwing out the Count's wardrobe, but the garments landed in the mud and were trampled by the firefighters. Others were throwing out finely bound books, candelabra, vases, silverware, paintings, even clocks, which were either broken as they fell, ruined by the slush or stolen by the mob. A couple of chimneysweeps tried to claim a reward by going down chimneys to rescue some valuables from the Count's study, but were incinerated when the roof buckled and the flames roared up to envelop them.

Razumovsky himself, dressed in a sable dressing gown and a fur cap, sat a little way off under a tree, weeping. Alexander came up and laid a consoling hand on his shoulder.[30]

War and Peace

History does not relate whether the Grand Duke of Baden was among the spectators watching the Razumovsky palace burn, or whether he ushered in the New Year attending to affairs of state or, as is more likely, to one of the ladies of the night he was so fond of.

Fascinating as it might be to know, it is not particularly material, even to his own interests or those of his grand duchy. Perhaps the most striking aspect of the great charade known as the Congress of Vienna is the continuous interplay between the serious and the frivolous, an almost parasitical co-existence of activities which might appear to be mutually exclusive. The rattling of sabres and talk of blood mingled with the strains of the waltz and court gossip, and the most ridiculously trivial pursuits went hand in hand with impressive work.

While he attended every party and dinner he could, and did not miss any of the entertainments provided, Gentz covered reams of paper in clear, well-written prose as he churned out minutes, memoranda, letters and articles for the press. Although there were those, such as Stein and Humboldt, who avoided most of the festivities and preferred to frequent more intellectually stimulating society or to stay at home in the evenings, the former agonising over the Germany that might have been, the latter with his Greek texts, most of the principal actors did not. And this did not affect their capacity for work. Similarly, talk of war did not deflect them from the business of making peace. In fact, the frenetic expansion in the range and variety of futile amusements, and the mounting tensions as war was openly discussed and secretly prepared for in the second half of December, were accompanied by a noticeable growth in the volume and the tempo of work.

The German Committee set up on 14 October had, admittedly, stalled after the representative of Württemberg had stormed out on 16 November. But that did not mean that nothing more was done. Fresh memoranda and notes were produced on all sides, discussed at informal and often secret meetings, argued over and then discarded. 'God knows if anything will ever come of the German business,' Humboldt agonised at the beginning of December, but he and Stein continued to apply themselves to it. Metternich himself was working on a new proposal for a German constitution, which was ready just before Christmas.[1]

A Swiss Committee had been nominated on 12 November, with Stein representing Russia, Wessenberg Austria, Humboldt Prussia, Stewart Great Britain and, later, Dalberg France. Capodistrias and the British minister in Switzerland Stratford Canning sat in on its meetings as advisers. It held two sessions in the last two weeks of November, and no fewer than seven during the tense December days, in the course of which it sorted out the internal boundary and other disputes, and discussed the constitution.

In all the negotiations at the congress the political value of land was calculated not in acres or hectares, but in numbers of inhabitants, commonly referred to as 'souls'. And while some were guided more by quality of land or strategic considerations, Prussia, which had an almost obsessive preoccupation with the military recruitment value of population, admitted only 'souls' into her calculations. One of the problems bedevilling the discussions over how she could be restored to her 1806 status was that the various parties produced conflicting population figures and disputed each other's. Castlereagh therefore suggested setting up a committee which would verify all the figures being bandied about. Foreseeing trouble, he asked Talleyrand not to insist on having a French delegate on the committee, but Talleyrand demurred. As Castlereagh had predicted, Hardenberg refused to allow France a place. After much arm-twisting he was forced to give way, while Talleyrand agreed to nominate only one French delegate while the other four powers would be allowed two.[2]

The Statistical Committee held its first meeting on 24 December, while Talleyrand and Castlereagh were trammelling their new co-alition, and followed this up with a second on Christmas Day and a third on 28 December. The sources at its disposal were poor and often contradictory, and there was obviously no time to carry out any fieldwork. As the main object of the exercise was to arrive at a figure that all could accept regardless of how accurate it was, the committee in many cases simply settled for the mean between the highest and the lowest available. Originally, Castlereagh, Metternich and Talleyrand had wanted the value of the land and the wealth of the inhabitants factored in, but Prussia would have none of it; she was to be indemnified for the loss of the poorest regions of Poland, inhabited by a destitute and backward peasantry.[3]

In vindication of what Talleyrand had been urging from the start, it was becoming apparent that, however incompatible the interests and whatever tensions might come into play, those matters which fell into the ambit of one of the committees were more likely to be resolved than those which depended on the caprice of one or two people. The formality of the proceedings and the resulting sense of collegiate responsibility were in stark contrast to the offhand manner in which some of the weightier matters were being treated.

The unfortunate King of Denmark's continuing attempts to obtain from Alexander the ratification of the Treaty of Kiel were a prime example. He hated calling on the Tsar, referring to his visits as going 'to the guillotine', but he had persevered, finally bringing matters to a head in the second week of November. As Alexander was promising, for a countless time, that he would sign the treaty within the next day or two, Frederick asked him point-blank whether he had anything against him. Taken aback, Alexander protested his good will, but Frederick pursued the matter, asking whether, if he had nothing against him personally, he had anything against him as King of Denmark. Alexander muttered something about whose side Denmark had been on during the war, but he was visibly embarrassed, and must have realised that he could not delay much longer. As he was about to open the court ball on the evening of 14 November by leading the Empress of Austria into the polonaise, he turned to the dejected Frederick and announced that he had that afternoon signed the ratification of the Treaty of Kiel.[4]

But while this ensured the survival of Denmark and paved the way for the withdrawal of Russian troops from Holstein, it had no effect on Sweden, which still refused to honour the terms of the treaty by handing over Swedish Pomerania and paying out one million thalers. Bernadotte was hoping to keep the province and to persuade the other powers to indemnify Denmark by giving it Mecklemburg instead. Neither Frederick nor Rosenkrantz wanted Mecklemburg, and did not wish to see its ruler dispossessed on Denmark's behalf.[5]

A deal more advantageous to Denmark would be worked out later, involving Prussia, which wanted Swedish Pomerania to round off its existing possessions along the Baltic coast. Denmark agreed to relinquish its rights to Swedish Pomerania in favour of Prussia, which reciprocated by offering to cede the principality of Lauenburg to Denmark, along with a million thalers. The advantage of this solution was that it was Prussia that would now put pressure on Bernadotte.

But Bernadotte continued to stall, in the hope that nobody would force him to hand over the province or the cash. His ambassador, Count Charles Axel Löwenhielm, argued that as Denmark had remained an ally of Napoleon even longer than Saxony, she did not deserve to be treated differently. And while Alexander and Hardenberg both promised Frederick that they would put pressure on Bernadotte, they were too busy with the crisis over Saxony and Poland. 'If only I could feel that I will be able to achieve something for my dear country, then I would endure everything with joy,' the hapless King Frederick wrote home in December. In the end, it would be Britain that forced the issue, by informing Bernadotte that Sweden would not get the twenty-four million francs she was due in lieu of the island of Guadeloupe unless she complied with the conditions of the Treaty of Kiel. It was all very unedifying.[6]

'If this goes on, I shall abdicate,' Francis is said to have exclaimed. 'I can't stand this life much longer.' Whether it was this sentiment or more numinous emotions inspired by Christmas that provided the catalyst, a fundamental change did take place. On 26 December Metternich handed Razumovsky a letter from Francis to Alexander which was to alter the whole *modus operandi* of the congress.

On Christmas Eve Alexander had delegated Razumovsky as his plenipotentiary for settling matters between Russia and Austria, and Francis's letter suggested that, putting aside the other problems, they should enter into direct negotiations with the aim of agreeing a common frontier in Poland. On 27 December Metternich and Razumovsky met to discuss the details, and the latter insisted that Prussia be included in the negotiations and Castlereagh be invited to sit in on the conferences. They agreed to meet at 1 o'clock on 29 December at Metternich's office, and, at Metternich's insistence, that minutes be kept.[7]

When invited to attend the meetings, Castlereagh agreed on condition that he be allowed to make a public declaration of his revulsion at the very notion of partitioning Poland, as he did not wish to go down in history as a party to such an act. His second condition was that France was also invited to attend. This last was rejected by the others, on the grounds that the details of their common frontiers in Poland were none of France's business. So when they did meet on 29 December, only Russia, Prussia and Austria were represented. The meeting was conducted with a degree of formality hitherto unknown: Metternich was elected chairman and Gentz secretary. But the matter turned more on Saxony than Poland, with Hardenberg forcefully staking Prussia's claim to the whole of its territory. When Castlereagh declared Britain's opposition, Hardenberg accused him of treachery, referring to the letter he had received from him in October agreeing to Prussia's annexation of it.[8]

In his letter to Liverpool, Castlereagh complained of the 'very warlike' language used by the Prussian delegation. 'They are organising their army for the field, and, I have heard to-day, are employed in fortifying Dresden,' he continued. 'This may be all menace to sustain their negotiation, but they may also meditate some sudden effort, in conjunction with Russia, to coerce Austria, and place themselves in a situation to dictate their own terms on all other points.' In his diary Hardenberg admitted that the conference had been 'quite warm'. The next one, held on 30 December, was even warmer.[9]

Castlereagh insisted that since it was not only Poland that was being discussed at these meetings, they should be lent greater weight by the inclusion of France as well as Britain, both of which were directly interested in the issue of Saxony. The proposal was supported by Metternich, but met with opposition from Razumovksy and Capodistrias, and indignation on the part of Hardenberg and Humboldt.

Hardenberg was at the end of his tether. The fatigues of the congress, combined with a lack of exercise, had, Humboldt noted, made the proverbially courteous chancellor moody. He could not sleep, so he would pace around his rooms or work through the night. 'He is upset beyond measure by everything that is going on, and dismayed that all his hopes have been dashed, and this affects him and his body,' wrote a worried Humboldt, who loved the old man and was afraid of the consequences for Prussia were he to crack under the strain.[10]

Hardenberg was playing a dangerous game. Conversations with his generals had revealed the extent of Prussia's military dependence on Russian support. And during a meeting with Frederick William and Alexander the day before the conference, he was struck by the Tsar's 'ambiguous' response to the question of what Russia would do if it came to war. Alexander, who had got wind of the fact that Castlereagh, Metternich and Talleyrand had reached some kind of agreement, was nervous. Prussia and Russia were still due some British subsidies, so any serious defiance of Britain could entail fiscal problems as well as military uncertainty. He was now as keen to defuse the situation as Hardenberg was to provoke a crisis.[11]

At the meeting of 30 December, Castlereagh again demanded that France be included in the conference, and although now only Prussia was objecting vehemently, it was agreed to 'defer' inviting the French plenipotentiary. The Russian plenipotentiaries declared Alexander's willingness to cede a fraction of the duchy of Warsaw to Prussia, the district of Tarnopol and half of the salt mines of Wieliczka to Austria, and to make Kraków and Thorn free cities. He garnished this climb-down with a preamble which invoked religious principles, 'common political maxims', 'close interests', brotherly love, the efforts they had all borne in carrying on the struggle against tyranny and so on, in an avalanche of meaningless phrases which, as Talleyrand remarked, might have been 'drawn up by a Quaker in a lodge of Freemasons'.[12]

Hardenberg was in no mood to follow suit. He restated Prussia's claim to the whole of Saxony and went on to say that as her troops were in possession, she would regard the refusal of other powers to recognise her rights to it as being tantamount to a declaration of war. Castlereagh protested against this 'most alarming and unheard-of menace'. He pointed out that 'such an insinuation might operate on a Power trembling for its existence, but must have the contrary effect upon all that were alive to their own dignity,' adding that 'If such a temper really prevailed, we were not deliberating in a state of independence, and it were better to break off the Congress,' as he reported to Liverpool. Hardenberg backed down, protesting that he was not trying to bully anyone. But the threat of war hovered over Vienna, and Castlereagh decided to act on Talleyrand's suggestion.

'Under these circumstances I have felt it an act of imperative duty to concert with the French and Austrian Plenipotentiaries a Treaty of Defensive Alliance,' he reported to Liverpool, explaining that it would probably not come to war, but that he would never be able to justify himself if he did not provide for the defence of British interests as well as those held in common with France and Austria. He had prepared the ground with them over the past few days, and indeed had already drawn up the text of the treaty. And he had just received news that gave him all the confidence he needed.[13]

On that very morning of 1 January 1815, news reached Vienna of the signature at Ghent on 24 December of peace between Britain and the United States. 'The news of the American peace came like a shot here,' Lord Apsley wrote to Bathurst. 'Nobody expected it.' As the implications sank in, everyone realised that the balance of power had shifted dramatically, and there was a noticeable degree of gloom among the Prussian delegation. 'We have become more European, and by the Spring we can have a very nice army on the Continent,' mused Castlereagh.[14]

That evening there was a ball at court to welcome in the New Year. Talleyrand was in excellent spirits. His *bon mot* to the effect that the news of the signature of peace with the United States 'sterlings the pronouncements of the British' was being repeated by the guests. It was also noted that when Alexander came up to Talleyrand he looked preoccupied, and that when he walked away after a short talk he looked even more so. He had good reason.[15]

Two days later, on 3 January, Castlereagh, Metternich and Talleyrand signed a secret treaty of alliance between Britain, France and Austria. It was couched in the most anodyne language, and purported to be aimed solely at carrying through the provisions of the Treaty of Paris. But it also stipulated that if any of the three contracting powers were to be attacked or threatened with attack, the other two would immediately come to its assistance with contingents of 150,000 men each. A secret article stated that Hanover, Holland and Bavaria would be invited to accede to the alliance.[16]

'Now, Sire, the coalition is dissolved, and forever,' a jubilant Talleyrand wrote to Louis XVIII on 4 January. 'Not only is France no longer isolated in Europe, but Your Majesty has a federative system which fifty years of negotiations would not have given him. Your Majesty is in concert with two of the greatest Powers, three States of the second rank, and soon all the States which follow principles and maxims which are not revolutionary.' He went on to assure the King that he would soon be 'the head and the soul of this union, formed in defence of principles which he was the first to proclaim'.[17]

Castlereagh was equally jubilant, even if he expressed himself with less exuberance. 'In the present state of the negotiation, I feel myself bound to urge that I should not be withdrawn from hence at least till the important discussions now pending are closed,' he wrote to Liverpool on 4 January. 'With every deference to the Duke of Wellington's ability and great personal authority, he cannot at once replace me in the habits of confidential intercourse which a long residence with the principal actors has established.' He believed that he was in control once more, and that he needed no more than another four weeks in which to tie up all the important business.[18]

Castlereagh had been doing his sums. He calculated that while the Prussian forces of 175,000 supported by their 260,000 Russian allies came to a formidable 435,000, the combined force that Austria, France and Britain could put in the field with the support of their lesser allies came to no fewer than 535,000 men. Brave with this knowledge, he had assured Humboldt privately that 'Great Britain would resist with her whole power and resources, and that every man in Parliament, of whatever party, would support the Government in doing so.'[19]

A few hours after Castlereagh finished his letter to Liverpool, he had a visit from Hardenberg who had come for what he called a 'confidential interview'. In the course of this the Prussian chancellor declared his wish to settle matters amicably, and asked Castlereagh to help broker a settlement. It had all the appearances of a climbdown. 'I have every reason to hope that the alarm of war is over,' Castlereagh wrote to Liverpool the following day.[20]

At 10 o'clock that evening Jean-Gabriel Eynard, who had been invited to supper by Lady Castlereagh along with his wife, found Castlereagh in one of the ante-rooms, entirely absorbed by two blind Italian musicians. He barely nodded in acknowledgement as the Eynards came in, and paid little more attention to the arrival of his other guests, who included the Prince Royal of Bavaria, the Duke of Saxe-Coburg, Talleyrand, Metternich, Cardinal Consalvi and Prince Eugène. At 11 o'clock supper was served, but Castlereagh did not budge from his place. At midnight supper was over, but he had not moved.

'For two long hours he had remained without saying a word to anyone, leaning against the wall beside the two Italians, who did not stop singing, accompanying themselves on a guitar and a violin,' wrote Eynard. 'At last these two unfortunates, exhausted with fatigue, begged for mercy and Lord Castlereagh was persuaded to move to a salon which had been prepared for dancing. He immediately began to waltz, and did so for half an hour. At the moment when we thought he would take a rest, a Scottish reel was played, and he immediately began to dance it, without a woman, with three other Englishmen. Nothing could be more curious than to see that fine face, cold and impassive, atop a body agitated by all the movements that the reel demands; at last, when the three Englishmen grew pale with fatigue, Lord Castlereagh was obliged to stop, and announced: "Oh! I am quite finished too." As it was 1 o'clock, we retired, but I am certain that the minister resumed his dancing.' Castlereagh certainly had much to celebrate.[21]

Hardenberg's informal visit hid a last desperate attempt to prise apart the Austro-Franco-British front. He had tried to persuade Castlereagh to allow Prussia to take Saxony, suggesting that her King be compensated with Luxembourg and a slice of land between the Meuse and the Moselle, which had been earmarked for Prussia. Castlereagh pointed out that this was out of the question, as it would breach the intended barrier against French aggression into Germany. Worse, by placing a King with a grievance and friendly to France on her borders, it would provide France with both a bridgehead and a *casus belli*: she could at any moment embark on a justifiable war to redress the wrong by reconquering Saxony, for which a grateful King would willingly cede Luxembourg. Castlereagh was so alarmed by

Hardenberg's suggestion that he went to see Alexander in order to beg him not to support it. In the event, he need not have bothered.

Hardenberg had also approached Talleyrand, holding out the prospect of France being able to regain Belgium if she went along with his scheme. But Talleyrand told the astonished Prussian that he would refuse to countenance the restitution of Belgium to France even if it were offered. He later explained to Castlereagh that although it could be construed as working against the military interests of France, he would not seek any changes to her frontiers as settled by the Treaty of Paris.[22]

Castlereagh and Metternich had continued to demand the inclusion of France in the formal conferences begun on 29 December. There was still resistance on the part of Russia and Prussia. But Talleyrand declared flatly that if France were not admitted he would have no option but to pack up and go home. Castlereagh stood firmly behind him, and so did Metternich. Alexander was not going to foul his chances of a future alliance with France and dropped his objection, leaving Prussia isolated and therefore powerless.[23]

The first official meeting of the Five took place on 7 January, the second two days later, the third three days after that, on 12 January – the first actually attended by Talleyrand. Many felt that the congress had at last begun, particularly as regular meetings of the eight signatories of the Treaty of Paris were also being held.[24]

Acting on Hardenberg's request that he try to broker an agreement between Prussia and Austria, Castlereagh had on 4 January produced his own proposal. This was an amended version of the Austrian proposal of 10 December, awarding Prussia a little more of Saxony and a little less of Poland, and excluding Luxembourg, which Castlereagh wanted to add to Holland. Compensation for Prussia would need to be found elsewhere, both in Germany and in Poland. The Foreign Secretary asked Alexander for an audience, with the aim of obtaining that and above all to make sure he did not back Hardenberg's plan of relocating the King of Saxony to the Rhine.

When they met on 7 January, Castlereagh had little difficulty in explaining to Alexander why Hardenberg's project was unacceptable, and Alexander agreed to tell Frederick William not to allow him to pursue it further. But then, suddenly changing the subject, the Tsar asked Castlereagh about his new alliance with France and Austria. Taken aback, Castlereagh did not deny it, but he kept his composure enough to state that since they were all in agreement on the fundamental issues, the Tsar had nothing to fear from Britain or either of the other two. But he did point out that Hardenberg's threats and Alexander's apparent support of Prussia had caused the other powers legitimate alarm. He then seamlessly progressed to present and explain his plan for compensating Prussia while leaving the King of Saxony in possession of a considerable portion of his realm. Alexander appeared 'temperate and conciliatory', and conceded that a kernel of Saxony should be preserved. At the conference later that afternoon, Razumovsky declared that 'his august Master had authorised him to approve, in the main, the proposals presented'.[25]

The Prussian proposal was formally considered at the conference of the Five on 12 January. It posited that Prussia, which still needed to acquire 3,411,715 souls in order to reach the level of population she had in 1805, could best make this up with the 2,051,240 inhabitants of Saxony (whose King was to be compensated with Luxembourg and lands between the Meuse and the Moselle), supplemented by the 810,268 Russia had agreed to cede from the duchy of Warsaw, another 299,877 from the duchy of Berg, 3,000 from Königswinter, 131,888 in the duchy of Westphalia, for which Darmstadt would have to be compensated elsewhere, 19,500 from Dortmund and Corvey, 48,628 from part of Fulda and another 729,228 from four former French *départements* along the Rhine, the Ruhr, the Meuse and the Moselle. This would give Prussia a surplus of 681,914 over her population in 1805, which, the proposal argued, was far below the increases made by the other three allied powers. That was certainly untrue for Austria, which had come off much worse as a result of the Napoleonic Wars.[26]

Austria's counter-proposal pointed out the fallacy of this argument, and stressed what Talleyrand had mentioned before: that an educated shopkeeper, artisan or farmer with his own land in a rich part of Saxony or the Rhineland was worth five times as much as a Polish peasant with no education, no land, no skills and not even his own tools, eking out an existence in the wastes of Mazuria. Thus any acquisition Prussia made in Germany would enrich her several times over. It went on to demonstrate, using figures verified by the Statistical Committee, how Prussia could be compensated for the 3,400,065 (not 3,411,715 as the Prussian project claimed) souls she had lost with 3,466,624 while taking only 782,249 from Saxony, leaving some three-fifths of the kingdom to its rightful King. If Prussia still demanded more, then Austria was willing to renounce the 400,000 souls Russia was intending to give back to her with the Tarnopol district, and ask Russia to give an equivalent number of Poles to Prussia.[27]

Gentz could barely contain his disgust at the way things were going. 'The great phrases about "reconstructing the social order", about "a lasting peace founded on a just distribution of force", and so on, and so on, were meant to calm people and to give this solemn gathering an air of dignity and grandeur,' he wrote that very day, 'but the real aim of the Congress *was the dividing up between the victors of the spoils stolen from the vanquished.*' His sentiments were widely shared. 'It is a miserable commerce, this trading in lands and people,' the Austrian Emperor's brother Archduke John wrote in his diary. 'We cursed Napoleon and his system, and justly so, for he degraded mankind, but now the very Princes who fought against it are walking in his footsteps.'[28]

The next formal meeting of the Five did not take place until 28 January, more than two weeks later. Those weeks would test the negotiating skills of Castlereagh to the limit, as he tried to prevent a struggle for power in Germany developing into civil war.

'Nobody is enjoying himself, even the spectators want this business to come to an end,' Baron Nostitz noted on 7 January. 'God only knows how that can be brought about. Every day fresh rumours fly through the city heralding now war now peace.' Although this was not strictly true, and the balls and other entertainments went on, his feelings were shared by many, and thanks to the diligence of his spies and copyists Metternich could read for himself how disillusioned and resentful ordinary people had grown, and how cynically they expressed themselves on the subject of the sovereigns and the ministers.[29]

Respect for the sovereigns had plumbed new depths. Not only did some ladies use the anonymity provided by the mask and the intimacy of the waltz to tell Alexander what they thought of him, but his assets and disadvantages as a dancing partner (that he spat when he talked, that he had clammy hands which he laid on their bare shoulders, etc.) were discussed openly by the young women of Vienna as though he had been just another subaltern. At Metternich's ball on 10 January, Eynard mistook the King of Prussia for a footman and was about to ask him to bring a glass of champagne when he recognised him. The next day Count Palffy had to send messengers begging the sovereigns to delay their arrival at his ball, as the other guests had not yet arrived. Convention demanded, as it still does, that when a member of a reigning house is expected, all the other guests should be present before his or her entrance. This had been punctiliously observed at first, but the aristocracy of Vienna and the visiting diplomats and courtiers had grown so blasé as a result of rubbing shoulders with half a dozen reigning princes on a daily basis that by now they had little inclination to hurry, and preferred to finish their dinners and get dressed in their own time. When the sovereigns did make their delayed entrance at Palffy's ball that evening, only a handful of guests were present. Fewer and fewer people could be bothered to go to the parties at all, and in stark contrast to the crush that attended those in October and November, by January many balls were so sparsely attended that the sovereigns could not even find enough partners to make up a dance. Yet it never occurred to anyone to alter the pattern, and life went on as it had over the past three months, with nightly balls and the usual round of entertainments, some of them quite novel.[30]

As if to underline his increasingly central role, Talleyrand organised a solemn Requiem Mass to be said in the Stephansdom cathedral on 21 January, the anniversary of the death of Louis XVI at the guillotine in 1793. A huge catafalque reaching almost up to the cathedral vault was erected in the middle of the nave, decorated in grandiose but sombre style, with a crown, sceptre and the insignia of the King's orders. The congregation was dressed in black, the ladies with long veils. Salieri conducted the requiem. Talleyrand's own verdict was that 'it was the most beautiful, the most grandiose, the most terrible sight'. But many felt the effect was ruined by the whining voice of the prelate who read out the eulogy he had composed.[31]

Talleyrand used the solemnity of this occasion as a pretext for a number of declarations on the theme of legitimacy and the inalienable rights of monarchs, and to apply this to the case of Saxony. The intention was to cast Alexander and Frederick William in the role of villains. But while Talleyrand was delighted with the event, it is unlikely that it had the desired effect, for that very evening all those who had been mourning Louis XVI were dancing at Countess Zichy's ball, Alexander the first among them.

The next day witnessed one of the most memorable, as well as the most frivolous, entertainments of the whole congress. Heavy snow on 15 January, followed by a strong frost and a cold spell, provided the perfect conditions for Trautmannsdorff to organise a grand sleighing party. Thirty-two sleighs, upholstered in green and blue velvet, embroidered with gold, drawn by horses coiffed with ostrich plumes, assembled in the grand court of the Hofburg. A huge sleigh drawn by six horses and carrying an orchestra opened the procession. It was followed by a second driven by the Emperor Francis himself, with the Tsarina at his side. Then came the others. 'Each sledge was drawn by a single pair of horses, covered with richly embroidered cloths of gold, with plumes upon their heads and necks, and a great mass of silver or gilded bells hanging in the usual manner across their shoulders. A servant in a rich fur cloak stood behind each sledge, and between each, three or four equerries attended, in the uniforms and liveries of the Emperor, or of their respective masters.' The rear was brought up by another large sleigh full of musicians, this time a 'Turkish' band. It was, in the words of Count Otto von Löwenstern, 'a great display of *coquetterie et luxe*'. 'The merry silver bells, the embroideries, the fringes, were all new, and glitteringly bright as the frost-bound snow,' he continues. 'The *cavaliers* for the most part were *beaux*; *les dames*, without exception of course, *très-belles*, and all muffled up in ravishingly becoming velvet and furs.'[32]

The event began with farce. Just as the sleighs were about to move off, Stewart, probably drunk, drove his own coach and four into the courtyard, and stopped, blocking the exit. Lord Pumpernickel, as he had been dubbed, after the character of a cretinous lout in a popular play running at the time, refused to move out of the way, defying orders and threats. It was only after his horses had been seized by their bridles and the carriage had been pulled away that the party could begin.[33]

The procession of sleighs snaked through the streets of the city and out of it all the way to Schönbrunn, where they were drawn up in a rank surrounding the frozen pond, on which a pair of Dutch skaters dressed as milkmaids performed a ballet. They were followed by an Englishman who cut the monograms of the sovereigns into the ice with his skates, after which the company alighted and went into the palace, where they watched a performance of *Cinderella*, then dined and danced before climbing back into their sleighs. The procession then returned to Vienna by torchlight through the falling snow. 'As it approached over the glacis, an open space between the walls of the city and its suburbs, the effect was very striking,' according to one onlooker. 'The ground was covered with deep snow, and the winding course of the procession was marked like a river of fire, by the flames of the moving torches.' Just to round off the evening, there was a masked ball at the Hofburg.[34]

'Tired of balls and fêtes – of which those most eager for them must now have had a surfeit – our *grand monde* frequents the churches,' recorded Count Löwenstern, explaining that they were drawn by the preaching of the former Lutheran dramatist Zacharias Werner, who had become a Catholic priest and made wonderful performances out of his condemnations of the errors of Lutheranism and of the worthlessness of his own plays. On 28 January he delivered himself of a tremendous diatribe against frivolity, which was particularly well attended, but there is no evidence to suggest that it had the slightest impact.[35]

The balls went on, and the Prince Royal of Hesse-Darmstadt had, according to police reports, 'entered into a serious relationship with the so-called Countess Waffenberg, or Lori Toussaint by her real name'. The Grand Duke of Baden continued to enjoy himself, although he had recently received something of a snub. He had paid Madame Lambert what the police informer called a '*visite galante*', and as he was leaving handed her twenty-five florins in paper money. She was so incensed by his low rating of her skills that she promptly pulled fifty of the same out of a wallet, joined them to his twenty-five, and thrust the whole lot into his hand as she pushed him out of her door.[36]

The fun and games could not entirely veil the tensions. It was not only the Prussians who glared at the Austrians and the French. The Russians too were eyeing the British and their secret allies with the greatest suspicion and hostility. Everyone who came to Metternich's ball on 10 January noted the absence of Alexander and his entourage, who also avoided his ball on 23 January. Their relationship had reached a point at which Alexander could hardly bear to look at Metternich, and was reported to have said more than once that if he had not been a monarch he would have fought him with pistols.[37]

Although Castlereagh was engaged in a continuous dialogue with Alexander, Hardenberg and Metternich with the aim of reaching some mutually acceptable compromise, he too prepared for the worst. He regarded the alliance of 3 January as an instrument with which to bring together as many powers as possible into peaceful defiance of Russia, and carried on assiduously collecting new allies. Bavaria signed on 13 January, Hanover six days later, Holland on 23 January, and Württemberg and Sardinia were being groomed.

Talleyrand for his part was exerting pressure on Alexander in his own way – he informed Czartoryski that if France were obliged to go to war, she would announce publicly that she was doing so in the cause of Poland's full independence. Such a trumping of Alexander's promises to the Poles would not only take most of the wind out of his sails, it would undermine the loyalty of his 70,000 Polish troops, many of whom had served under Napoleon over the past two decades.[38]

All this put Hardenberg in an impossible situation. Public opinion in Berlin was demanding the whole of Saxony. Some in the Prussian camp were considering ways of using the Tugendbund, the League of Virtue, to mobilise guerrilla support throughout Germany. A campaign was launched in the press to persuade all Germans that Prussia was their natural protector. There were those, like Humboldt's wife Caroline, who thought a war now would bring about the definitive unification of Germany, even if it did spill much German blood in the process.[39]

'It would be better to lose everything!' Hardenberg was overheard exclaiming as he left a meeting with Metternich on 29 January. He was coming dangerously close to seeing war as the only way out of the impasse, as it would oblige Alexander to stand by his promise to support Prussia. Münster reported to the Prince Regent on 21 January that having previously believed that they would get by without a war, he now found himself fearing it might break out yet. Hardenberg had told him a couple of days before that Prussia would issue an ultimatum 'and she would regard as enemies all who would not join her'. Münster believed that Frederick William did not want war, but feared he might be swept along by events. 'The tone at Berlin is very warlike, and this tone has several times decided similar questions,' he wrote.[40]

Metternich now found himself in a situation not dissimilar to that of Hardenberg, and was being forced to adopt a no less assertive tone. Bolstered by the alliance, he felt a new sense of power and was now more determined to defend Saxony. His unpopularity in Vienna and the taunts of rivals such as Stadion led him to raise his game, and in the first draft of his response to the Prussian proposal of 12 January he introduced a number of additional demands suggested by Schwarzenberg and the military, such as that Saxony be allowed to keep the fortress of Torgau. Even the usually placid Emperor Francis was breathing fire. 'I found him extremely *monté* upon the military question, and his general tone more warlike than on any former occasion,' Castlereagh reported to Liverpool after an interview with him.[41]

'Very few persons give themselves any anxiety about what is passing at Vienna, except as far as it is connected with expense,' Liverpool answered from Bath on 16 January. He himself was only interested in getting Castlereagh back to Westminster. He had sent Wellington to Vienna to relieve him, and delayed the opening of Parliament as long as he could, until 9 February. Bathurst had also been pressing him to return, but on 30 January Castlereagh replied that 'you might as well expect me to have run away from Leipsick (if I had been there) last year', as to leave at such a critical moment.[42]

His presence was indeed crucial, as he and Talleyrand were the only ones standing in the way of an explosion, particularly since Alexander had been swept along by the general mood of sabre-rattling, and while assuring Castlereagh that he wanted to avoid a crisis, could not resist putting on a martial air and bandying threats. He publicly mocked the Austrians and their army. 'We shall see, me and Schwarzenberg, which of us was the greater captain during the last campaigns,' he bragged to a group of Russian generals, assuring them that had he been in command in 1813, the allies would have trounced Napoleon decisively, and adding that he was looking forward to an opportunity of demonstrating his military skills to the world.[43]

The former allies seemed so thoroughly at odds that one of Francis's Chamberlains suggested bringing back Napoleon in order to reunite them.[44]

The Saxon Deal

On the evening of 1 February Wellington's carriage trundled into Vienna and stopped at the door of Stewart's embassy, where the Duke took up his quarters. 'All necessary measures have already been taken for his surveillance,' noted one of Hager's spies the next morning, adding that Stewart had transferred his affections to the actress Seraphine Lambert, whom he had been visiting at night. Hager's sources and Viennese gossips also noted that the Duke had brought with him a Parisian dancer by the name of Mademoiselle Grassini.[1]

The Duke's arrival was welcomed by many who believed that he would prove more decisive than Castlereagh, and that his soldierly energy might finally move things on to some kind of conclusion. It also revived the jaded curiosity of all the inhabitants of Vienna, and there was a fearful crush at the Redoute ball on 2 February, as people swarmed to catch a glimpse of the hero of Vittoria. 'The Duke, wearing plain dress, was not recognised at first, but as soon as his presence was made known he became the object of attention too general and *trop empressée*, and people crowded about him with very little ceremony and politeness,' according to Count Löwenstern, who also observed that Alexander was dancing energetically with a series of ladies whose only claim to distinction was their beauty.[2]

Across the room, the Grand Duke of Baden was paying court to 'Countess Waffenberg', alias Lori Toussaint, and a group of ladies of the town. At 5 o'clock in the morning he was seen climbing into his carriage with one of them. They drove to No. 551 Rumpfgasse, where, having sent back his carriage, the Grand Duke stayed until 7 o'clock. On returning home, he slept until 5 o'clock in the afternoon.[3]

Wellington's introduction to the curious war-dance taking place in Vienna came when, the morning after his arrival, he was graced by a visit from the Tsar of all the Russias. After complimenting him and solicitously enquiring about his journey from Paris, Alexander began to bemoan, with affected anxiety, the fact that from what he had heard France was in poor shape politically, and that its army was riven with dissension and quite unfit for anything. Wellington put him right, briskly affirming that the government of Louis XVIII was strong and that the army was in excellent condition. This news did not, Wellington noted, cheer Alexander, and he left looking more troubled than when he arrived.[4]

On the same day, 3 February, Castlereagh called on Frederick William. The interview lasted a full hour and a half and proved 'the most painful in all respects, that it has been my fate to undergo since I have been upon the Continent', as Castlereagh reported to Liverpool. Sensing that they were not going to be allowed to keep the whole of Saxony, Frederick William and Hardenberg had determined that they must at the very least hold on to a sizeable part of it, including the city of Leipzig, which they had come to see as their prize for the three-day battle. 'It is inconceivable to what a degree His Majesty had been worked upon on the point of Leipsick, the false importance he attached to it, and the deep disappointment, if not resentment, with which he spoke of our espousing the cause of the King of Saxony against him,' Castlereagh added.[5]

The encounter left Frederick William in an ugly mood. He could not hide it during the dinner that night in honour of Wellington, at which Schwarzenberg swaggered and talked openly of war. 'Wellington's arrival is not to the taste of the Prussians, who pretend to make light of the fact with jokes, saying that they will bring Blücher to make up the party,' one of Hager's informants noted.[6]

The following day, 4 February, Castlereagh called on Alexander. Fortunately for him, the Tsar had been considerably softened by the interview he had had the previous morning with Wellington. Chastened by the news that the French were capable of supporting Austria militarily, he was less sanguine than before, and agreed to calm Frederick William. He also responded positively to Castlereagh's argument that they should all make concessions in order to reach a settlement before matters got out of hand. Castlereagh informed Alexander that he would persuade Münster to agree to give up an area with 50,000 souls that Hanover was to acquire, and reduce the increase in territory that Holland was to receive in order to produce another 50,000 for Prussia. He then suggested that Alexander reciprocate by agreeing to give Thorn and the area around it to Prussia. Alexander gave his consent.[7]

Hardenberg had spent that morning working on a fresh note reiterating Prussia's claim to most of Saxony, with Leipzig. He then went off to Talleyrand's for dinner with the Duke of Wellington. It was not until he got home that evening that he saw Castlereagh, who called on him with the news that Alexander had agreed to cede Thorn to Prussia. Hardenberg undertook to persuade Frederick William to relinquish his claim on Leipzig as a *quid pro quo*, but he was wary of making any promises.

It was not until the evening of the next day, 5 February, that he was able to see Alexander to verify that he was indeed prepared to cede Thorn, and then to press Frederick William to drop his claim to Leipzig. 'The King still displeased and outraged by Castlereagh and Austria,' he noted in his diary. He managed to persuade him to concede Leipzig, but only at the price of additional Saxon territory elsewhere. When this was communicated to Castlereagh, he called on Hardenberg that evening, with the offer of more territory from Hanover and Holland. But far from softening him up, this got the Prussian chancellor ranting once more about Leipzig, which had assumed the significance of a trophy of war in the eyes of the Prussian military and public opinion. General Grolmann was declaring openly that the Prussian army would never give up the city without a fight.[8]

'After some effervescence, Prince Hardenberg received my proposition with calmness, and examined the details with attention,' Castlereagh reported. He left him to sleep on the matter and called again in the morning. 'Castlereagh again here. The business was settled at last as well as could be expected, bar the King's approb[ation],' ran the entry in Hardenberg's diary. 'Dined at Stewart's.' When he did call on his King the following day, 7 February, Frederick William began by making difficulties over Leipzig, but eventually gave way. The matter had been settled. Hardenberg then began work on his final note he would submit to the next conference of the Five, to be held the next day.[9]

Hardenberg's note opened with the usual professions of esteem for Austria and Prussia's ardent desire to live in the greatest harmony with her. It went on, somewhat pointlessly, to deny Austria's claim in her last memorandum that she was not gaining much and to argue that she would, according to arrangements made so far, acquire 1,761,340 more souls than she had in 1805. It pointed out the vulnerability of the proposed Prussian state and complained that although the Austrian plan awarded it nearly half of Saxony, it was the worst part, 'poor land, covered in sands, forests and marshes, devoid of commerce, factories, industry, and of all resources'. It went on to state that Leipzig should go to Prussia, which would benefit its inhabitants, before declaring that in spite of all this His Majesty the King of Prussia was prepared to make 'all the sacrifices which are not absolutely incompatible with the interests of his monarchy', and giving way, not without saving face with a few minor demands.

Metternich replied that while he still had to show the Prussian proposals to his imperial and royal master, he felt able to say that he considered them satisfactory. The signature by all those present of the minutes of this meeting was more of a turning point than the official Austrian declaration, made at the meeting of the Five on 10 February, accepting the Prussian proposals or the signature of the articles framing the agreements reached on Poland and Saxony

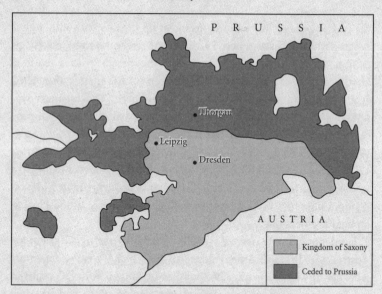

The Saxon Settlement

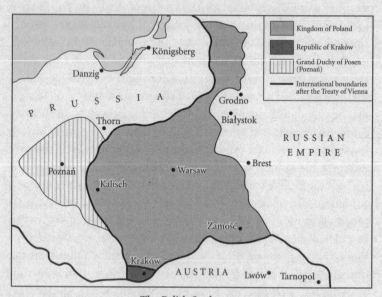

The Polish Settlement

on 11 February. Prussia would get nearly half of Saxony, but King Frederick Augustus would keep two-thirds of his subjects and both of his main cities.[10]

'Saxony is saved,' Talleyrand wrote to the Duchess of Courland, adding his own gloss and registering his merit in the matter. 'This business is well and truly over: the principle of legitimacy is saved: the King of Saxony is free: and Europe owes these great blessings to our King of France who brought all these principles back with him. When he made his appearance on the European stage, everything had to return to its rightful place; beyond that, two or three hundred thousand souls more or less will matter a little to Saxony but not at all to the affairs of Europe or to her interests.'[11]

Talleyrand was getting carried away. On 15 February he would complain, in a letter to Louis XVIII, that 'attachment to the principle of legitimacy counts for very little in the dispositions of Lord Castlereagh, and even of the Duke of Wellington'. Yet that very evening, at Labrador's lodgings, he pressured Cardinal Consalvi to make the Pope accede to the Treaty of Paris and thereby condone France's retention of the ancient Papal fiefs of Avignon and the Comtat Venaissin. Consalvi declared that he would never agree to this, and expressed sorrow that His Most Christian Majesty should wish to despoil the Vicar of Christ. Talleyrand countered by threatening to block the return of the Legations. When Consalvi protested that there were no grounds to deny the Pope what was rightfully his, Talleyrand argued that he had ceded the Legations to Napoleon by treaty, and therefore had no further right to them. Drawing himself up, Consalvi asked how Louis XVIII could acknowledge as legitimate any act of Napoleon's when he considered himself to have been the real ruler of France over the past twenty years, which he had proclaimed from the moment he entered France.[12]

Castlereagh did indeed see things differently from Talleyrand, and did not think legitimacy had had anything to do with it. It was the treaty of 3 January which had been 'productive of all the good consequences', more so than he had ever hoped. While the alliance had, by making Austria too confident, threatened to precipitate a war, it had brought Alexander, who knew of its existence, back to his senses. Britain and Russia were the two powers which had least to gain and most to lose from a war, and as they were the two most powerful players, they had been able to exert decisive pressure in the interests of getting the deal done. Castlereagh was pleased with his work, and reported to Liverpool that 'the leading territorial arrangements have been wound up with a degree of good humour'.[13]

One whose humour could hardly have been described as good was Metternich. The day the Saxon question was finally settled, 8 February, was Wilhelmina's thirty-fourth birthday, and he wrote her a letter not calculated to raise her spirits. 'Heaven has ordered our destinies not as my heart would have desired,' he wrote. 'I had renounced my own life to live only in yours; I had formed dreams of which none came true, I had given you all I possessed – more perhaps than any man has ever given before, more, much more than I had ever believed it in my power to give of love – I have lived in the space of two years through more torment, pain and sorrow than would be found in 20 years of the lives lived by the majority of humans!' He nevertheless wished her happiness and expressed the hope that she would always be surrounded by friends, though he doubted that she would ever find one as devoted as himself. 'I am no longer good for anything, as there is nothing of springtime left in my soul,' he complained.[14]

Another who was in the throes of love and despair was Czartoryski. 'My very soul has wilted,' he noted in his diary on 15 January after an assignation with the Tsarina. She was so unhappy with Alexander that she was sorely tempted to take up her mother's suggestion that she leave him. Czartoryski could hardly believe how his old feelings had revived after twenty years. 'I love her passionately,' he confided to his diary, admitting to being assailed by agonising fits of jealousy. He longed for her to leave Alexander, who had become even more difficult to bear in recent weeks. 'He now uses his generals and diplomats not as advisers, but as instruments of his own will,' noted one of the Tsar's entourage in his diary. 'They fear him like servants their master.' Alexander had become curiously detached, and Roksandra Sturdza reported to Jung Stilling that although 'our beloved seems to me not to have left the good path', he was drifting away from his wife and spending all his spare time with his sisters. 'I need all my reason not to follow with eagerness the plan that you propose,' Elizabeth wrote to her mother on 24 January. 'It is very seductive, and it suits me in every way.' But she had a strong sense of duty, and felt she must sacrifice her personal happiness.[15]

When someone complimented Alexander on his wife's beauty at a ball on 5 February, he took it ill and declared loudly that he found her unintelligent and not at all beautiful. This kind of behaviour gave Czartoryski hope, but it seems to have been dashed in the course of another assignation, in the first days of February, for he was plunged back into despair. 'I am crushed by sorrow and a distaste for the world,' he wrote.[16]

Three days later, the day the Saxon question was finally settled, was Ash Wednesday. The Carnival had been brought to an end the previous day with a grand masquerade, and in the morning the population of the city and most of the visitors flocked to church to have their foreheads marked with the ashes of repentance.

The time had come for Castlereagh to leave. His departure was fixed for 15 February, but he was determined to see all those issues which he regarded as crucial to Britain settled irrevocably before he left. He was equally determined to insure himself against political embarrassment when he reached London, where he would be held to account on those issues that English public opinion held dear. Foremost among these was the abolition of the slave trade.

On 1 January, Castlereagh had a long conversation with Alexander on the subject, and the Tsar seemed willing to back him up. He raised the matter at the meeting of the eight signatories of the Treaty of Paris on 16 January, suggesting that they each nominate a plenipotentiary to a committee which would deal with the question. The Portuguese plenipotentiary Palmella objected strongly to this, saying that only those powers which possessed colonies with slaves should be involved. He was backed by Labrador, who argued that since everyone was agreed on the principle of the desirability of abolition, the only points at issue were how and when to implement the ban. He explained that the Iberian sovereigns were torn in the matter 'between two injustices, one to the inhabitants of Africa, the other to their own subjects'. It was not only the slave-owners in the colonies whose interests would suffer, but all Spanish subjects, as a ban would have a dramatic effect on the economy as a whole. He went on to declare that Spain could not possibly abolish the trade within eight years. The meeting was split between the two Iberian powers and the rest, but the majority was powerless to exert any influence, particularly as Palmella bluntly declared that he did not consider the issue as being subject to international law.[17]

The matter took up the whole of the next meeting of the Eight, four days later on 20 January. Castlereagh appealed to morality and went to great lengths to explain that abolition did not necessarily entail economic suffering for the slave-owners of the colonies. He produced evidence that when the trade had ceased in British and Dutch colonies, the natural growth of the slave population had taken off, thus guaranteeing the continued supply of slaves. He suggested that the conference should at least make a declaration of its intent to abolish the trade, and he was seconded in this by Talleyrand, Nesselrode and the others.

Labrador and Palmella agreed, but only on condition it was made clear that each power could choose when to abolish the trade. Castlereagh then attempted to force Talleyrand to accept the term of three years rather than the five laid down in the Treaty of Paris. He also tried to persuade Labrador to shorten the delay, but the latter pleaded the need to restock Cuba and other colonies. Palmella defended his position by declaring that Brazil lacked the workforce necessary to its economy. He claimed that the Portuguese trade was less cruel in terms of the conditions than the others, and also stipulated a minimum term of eight years.[18]

The truculence of the Spanish and Portuguese annoyed Castlereagh. 'It seems as if the recollection of our services made it impossible for them to do anything without endeavouring most unnecessarily and ungratefully to display their independence,' as he put it. He nevertheless persisted, using every means at his disposal. On 22 January a treaty was signed between Britain and Portugal to the effect that no Portuguese subject would purchase any slaves on the coast of Africa north of the Equator, in return for which Britain cancelled the £600,000 still outstanding on a loan taken out by the Portuguese government in 1809.[19]

At the meeting of the Eight on 28 January, Castlereagh tried a new approach. He explained that since the entire western coast of Africa north of the Equator had fallen under British dominion during the recent wars, the slave trade had been abolished there. He therefore suggested that the ban should remain in force everywhere north of the line. Talleyrand declared that Louis XVIII had already agreed to this, though he proposed drawing the line at Cape Palmas, which would have left a large loophole. Castlereagh pointed this out and insisted on Cape Formoso. With Portugal already signed up, the notion of an immediate ban on this part of the coast was gaining general acceptance, but Labrador continued to defend Spain's interests with obstinacy.[20]

At the meeting of the Eight on 4 February Castlereagh suggested establishing a permanent commission which could further the cause, but Labrador protested that the issue was an internal one for each country and reminded those present that the congress had not been called to decide such matters or discuss morality. Castlereagh raised the possibility of trade sanctions covering goods produced by slave labour, which, reading between the lines of the diplomatic language in which the minutes are couched, provoked some ugly responses. When they next met, on 8 February, all the powers signed a declaration to the effect that the slave trade was repugnant and immoral. They declared the intention of eradicating it and their commitment to work to that end with zeal and perseverance. It was not much of a victory for Castlereagh, but it was the best he could do in the circumstances.[21]

Thanks to the resolution of the Polish and Saxon issues, the question of Prussia's other possessions and frontiers could at last be addressed, which in turn meant that Castlereagh could make the final arrangements with respect to the frontiers of Holland and Hanover. Hanover ceded Lauenburg to Prussia, which would cede it to Denmark in exchange for Swedish Pomerania and the island of Rügen, which Sweden had finally returned to Denmark. The Prince Regent was dismayed by the loss of this hereditary possession, as were the gentry of Lauenburg, who sent an envoy to London to lodge a protest. But Castlereagh was content, as Hanover had acquired instead the formerly Prussian province of East Frisia, which made it more compact, gave it control of the mouth of the river Ems, and brought it into contact along the whole of its western frontier with Holland.

The frontiers of Holland were also now finally fixed. As Prussia required the house of Orange's hereditary province of Nassau for strategic reasons, the Sovereign Prince (who was still waiting to be elevated to the status of King of Holland) swapped this for Luxembourg. He was not pleased when it was explained to him that the actual fortress of Luxembourg would be garrisoned by Prussian troops as a defence against France. He was even less pleased when he realised that as the Duke of Luxembourg he would be obliged to take his seat in the German Diet, and was only placated when the status of Luxembourg was raised to that of a grand duchy. In order to obtain Alexander's sanction of these arrangements, Castlereagh had proposed back in the spring of 1814 that Britain would enlist Holland to join her in paying off half the £6 million Russian debt in that country, but the Tsar had taken advantage of the recent crisis to persuade him to settle half of the Russian share in addition.

On 12 February, Castlereagh and Wellington had a two-hour interview with Alexander during which they discussed all the outstanding matters, such as northern Italy, Naples, the Ionian islands and

Switzerland. Castlereagh also broached the subject of the Balkans and the Ottoman Empire.

Austria, which viewed with anxiety the relentless advance of Russia through the Balkans, had originally hoped that her latest conquests in that quarter might be put on the table and possibly even returned to the Porte. There had been talk of inviting the Sultan to send a plenipotentiary to Vienna. But by the beginning of November it had become clear that Russia was not amenable, and the question was pushed into the background by more pressing matters.

Metternich, Castlereagh and Talleyrand nevertheless hoped to fore-stall further Russian conquest in the region by forcing Alexander to guarantee the Porte's possessions. But Alexander wrecked their plans by coming up with a demand that he be formally recognised as the protector of all Orthodox Christians under Ottoman rule and given the right to intervene on their behalf. Castlereagh refused to entertain such an idea. But he did try, at his last meeting with the Tsar on 12 February, to persuade him to guarantee, in common with the other powers, the Porte's existing possessions. Alexander appeared amenable, and two days later Castlereagh wrote to the British ambassador in Constantinople that he had 'received from His Imperial Majesty the most distinct and satisfactory assurance of his disposition to concur with the other powers in including the Ottoman Porte in the general guarantee to which the present Congress is likely to give occasion'.[22]

But he was to be completely outmanoeuvred by Alexander, who instructed the Russian ambassador in Constantinople to propose the idea himself, knowing that Turkish suspicion of anything issuing from Russia would lead to its rejection. The Sultan did indeed reject any idea of submitting to mediation or being forced to recognise some of the more recent Russian gains as permanent.

Another subject Castlereagh broached with the Tsar was his idea that all the various settlements reached at Vienna be bound together into one final act, which, by making them all part of a whole, would lend each greater weight. He was even contemplating the possibility of all the signatories undertaking to guarantee the entire settlement.

Alexander did not respond favourably, but he did suggest that they formally renew their alliance at the end of the congress, which would have much the same effect. Castlereagh liked the idea, which was close to his original concept of the grand design and to the principle of the Treaty of Chaumont. But he insisted that there could be no such alliance to the exclusion of France, and suggested that they invite all the powers which contributed to the peace to pledge themselves to support it, by force if necessary. Alexander 'entered cordially into this idea', according to Castlereagh. 'Upon the whole the conversation was satisfactory both to the Duke and myself, and left us both not without considerable hope that by adopting a line of conduct conciliatory towards Russia, without, however, relaxing in those precautionary connections to which we owe our existing position, the Emperor may be induced to occupy himself at home, where he has enough to do, and that Europe may be at peace.'[23]

Castlereagh attended two more conferences of the Five, on 12 and 13 February, at which a catalogue of minor matters were agreed. The minutiae relating to the Polish and Saxon questions, defining the complicated swaps and cessions of territory, complete with details of the location of frontier posts and military roads, restrictions on travel and questions of inheritance affected by the demarcation of new borders, were read through, amended and finally adopted.

To the intense disappointment of Czartoryski, and indeed of Alexander himself, the institutions supposed to govern the Poles, who would be living under three different jurisdictions, had not been created. A commission under Czartoryski had come up with a number of recommendations, covering the right of free movement and trade across the new frontiers, the status of '*sujets mixtes*' for Poles whose property would be divided by them, and even a form of pan-Polish citizenship that would allow any Pole to work and indeed stand for public office in all three of the partitions. But these issues had not been addressed by either the Five or the Eight.

Back in December, Liverpool had instructed Castlereagh to demand that if Alexander did keep most of the grand duchy of Warsaw, he should be urged to reunite with it all the Polish lands taken from the former kingdom by Russia after 1791, and to give the new kingdom a constitution (in effect, a stark contradiction of British policy up to that point). He was to make sure that Czartoryski and the other Poles heard of this. He was also to wash Britain's hands of the responsibility for this new partition of Poland by distancing himself from it and challenging the three partitioning powers to respect the feelings of their Polish subjects.[24]

The resulting document, composed by Castlereagh and circulated on 12 January, reaffirmed that the original desire of his government, which he had earnestly striven to fulfil, was 'to see an independent Power, more or less considerable in extent, established in Poland under a distinct Dynasty'. Not having been able to achieve this, he now enjoined those who would rule over Polish populations to bring in 'a congenial and conciliatory system of administration'. 'Experience has proved, that it is not by counteracting all their habits and usages as a people, that either the happiness of the Poles, or the peace of that important portion of Europe, can be preserved. A fruitless attempt, too long persevered in by institutions foreign to their manners and sentiments, to make them forget their existence and even language as a people, has been sufficiently tried and failed. It has only tended to excite a sentiment of discontent and self-degradation, and can never operate otherwise, than to provoke commotion, and to awaken them to a recollection of past misfortunes.' He called on all three monarchs to treat their Polish subjects as Poles and to grant them liberal institutions.[25]

Alexander's response to this, dated 19 January, expressed his happiness that Castlereagh was so concerned for the well-being of the Poles, and assured all and sundry that they could trust him with this. 'What is most astonishing about this piece,' noted Metternich in his memoirs, 'is the clear and forthright manner with which the Poles are informed that all hope of recovering their independence is lost. It is surprising that the sovereign who over the past two years never ceased to flatter them with this hope, should be the very one who today informs them of "the *impossibility* of reviving that ancient political system in Europe of which Poland formed part".[26]

Francis also contributed a declaration, in which he claimed that he had always desired the re-establishment of a free Poland, and had only reluctantly subjected this desire to the superior needs of European security, and undertook to treat his Polish subjects with paternal solicitude. The Prussian declaration was briefer, but included all the same pious expressions. These three declarations would be appended to the minutes of the meeting of the Eight on 21 February.[27]

Castlereagh finally left Vienna at 10 o'clock on the morning of 15 February, after a sleepless night. The diary of the Dutch plenipotentiary von Gagern records that the British delegation were up all night, desperate to complete every piece of business they could before the Foreign Secretary left. 'There were not enough hands for the work,' he wrote, noting that his own staff were just as busy writing out the details of the final arrangements concerning Holland.[28]

Castlereagh's enthusiasm for the concept of a great single act binding all the disparate elements together into one even gave rise to a draft declaration that was to accompany it. This was part apology, acknowledging that the congress had not fulfilled the hopes of many, and part self-congratulation, underlining how hard it had been to deal with the problems involved. But its conclusion was triumphant:

May security, confidence and hope revive everywhere, and with them peaceful labour, progress in industry, and prosperity, both public and private! May sombre anxiety for the future not awaken or bring back the evils whose return the sovereigns would wish to prevent and whose last trace they would like to efface! May religious feeling, respect for established authority, obedience to the law and horror of everything that might disturb public order once again become the indissoluble ties of civil and political society! May fraternal relations, mutually useful and beneficent, be re-established between all lands! May all rivalry, other than that which inspires the noble desire to equal or surpass one's neighbours in the virtues which do honour to the human race, in the arts which elevate it, in the talents that adorn it, disappear from a pacified Europe! And may homage at last be rendered to that eternal principle that there can be for nations as for individuals no real happiness but in the prosperity of all![29]

26

~~~◦~~~

Unfinished Business

Before leaving Vienna, Castlereagh had presented each of the sovereigns with a medal from the Prince Regent, inscribed with the words '*A la Mémoire de la Fin du Congrès*'. The gesture may have been a little premature, but the optimism behind it was not entirely misplaced. Given that the Herculean task of squaring the circle over Poland and Saxony had been completed, the work of the congress must have appeared to be all but done.

Many of the minor but nevertheless important and complicated issues had been addressed in earnest. The various committees set up over the past four months had worked intensively, particularly from the last days of December to the middle of February, reporting back to the conferences of the Eight, which had acquired the prestige and dignity of a full congress.

Perhaps the most exemplary had been the Statistical Committee, set up at Castlereagh's behest on 24 December. It had held a total of six meetings, culminating in that of 19 January. It had ploughed through mountains of often dubious documentation to produce an acceptable set of figures which permitted the final settlement of Prussia's claims.

The Committee on Diplomatic Precedence had been no less efficient. In the course of four sessions, held on 16, 24, 27 and 30 December, it agreed that precedence among diplomats should be dictated by date of accreditation, with no special privileges to be granted to allies or great powers. When it came to treaties, each monarch would sign the copy to be retained by his own chancellery at the top, followed by the others in order of ascending the throne, or, in the case of republics, of election. The same order of precedence was to govern the order of salutes given by ships both in port and at sea. In all cases, the Papal Legate was to have absolute precedence. Lord Cathcart, representing Britain, objected, saying that while his country would be prepared to accord him precedence out of courtesy, it would not do so *de jure*, in which he was backed by the Swedish representative. Both powers were induced to give way.[1]

But when these recommendations came up before the meeting of the Eight on 20 January, the assembled plenipotentiaries were far from happy with the concept of equality they implied. The matter was discussed more fully at the conference of the Eight on 9 February. Palmella and Labrador suggested that all political units be classified into two categories, according to their power status, arguing that it was absurd to treat the ambassador of a tiny principality as if he were on a par with that of Russia or Britain. Nor did they think that republics should enjoy the same consideration as ancient kingdoms. Razumovsky, Talleyrand, Metternich, Löwenhielm and Humboldt argued that there should be three categories. Castlereagh countered with the argument that this would lead to ridiculous and unnecessary complications. After a heated discussion, the matter was sent back to the committee for further scrutiny, along with the rival projects, but in the end the committee's eminently sensible original plan was accepted and set the rules which have governed diplomatic protocol ever since.[2]

The Swiss Committee had been wrestling with more intractable problems. It had been meeting regularly since its inception, on 12 November, with Austria represented by Wessenberg, Britain by Stewart and later the British minister to Switzerland Stratford Canning, Russia by Capodistrias and Stein, and Prussia by Humboldt.

While preparing the allied march through Switzerland in December

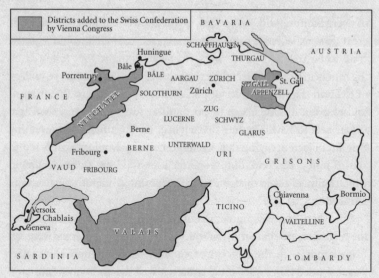

Districts added to the Swiss Confederation by Vienna Congress

BAVARIA

SCHAFFHAUSEN

Huningue

THURGAU

AUSTRIA

Bâle

BÂLE

AARGAU

ZÜRICH

Porrentruy

NEUCHÂTEL

SOLOTHURN

Zürich

ST. GALL

St. Gall

APPENZELL

FRANCE

ZUG

LUCERNE

SCHWYZ

Berne

GLARUS

BERNE

UNTERWALD

URI

Fribourg

GRISONS

VAUD

FRIBOURG

Versoix

Chiavenna

Bormio

Chablais

TICINO

Geneva

VALAIS

VALTELLINE

SARDINIA

LOMBARDY

Switzerland

1813, Metternich had sent in agents to encourage the former ruling aristocracy to come forward with demands for a return to the old regime and seek the protection of Austria. When Austrian troops entered Berne, the former oligarchs seized power and, with Metternich's connivance, began to reconstitute the old order. Other old cantons followed suit, while the new ones rebelled. Faced with the prospect of being reincorporated into Berne, Vaud and Aargau seceded and vowed to defend themselves.

On 3 January 1814 the allies asked the cantons to call a Diet and draw up a constitution. The old aristocratic cantons (Berne, Solothurn, Uri, Untervald, Lucerne, Glarus and Fribourg) set up a Diet at Lucerne, while the democratic ones convoked a rival one at Zürich. Civil war threatened, but the representatives of the allies managed to keep the two sides from coming to blows. Berne and its faction withdrew into a sulky protest, while the Zürich Diet began discussing a baffling number of different schemes for the future organisation of the country amid acrimonious quarrels as the representatives of every canton and interest badgered not only the allied agents on the spot, Capodistrias and Lebzeltern, but even travelled to allied headquarters to put their case.

The allies were by then at Chaumont, and in early March 1814 they announced that they would only recognise a constitution for Switzerland based on liberal principles, promising to add Geneva and Valais to the future confederation. Under pressure from the allies, even the aristocratic cantons participated in the Diet which opened on 6 April (with the reading out of an edifying homily from Alexander). But they continued to disrupt attempts at framing a liberal constitution, confident in the knowledge that they had the support of Metternich.

The Treaty of Paris stipulated that there would be an independent Switzerland with a constitution framed by its own people, but a secret article made it clear that this constitution must be approved by the allied powers. They had also decided to award to Switzerland not only Geneva, but also the former bishopric of Bâle, an ecclesiastical principality of the Holy Roman Empire that had been annexed by Napoleon, the cities of Bienne and Mulhouse, and Neuchâtel, another principality of the Holy Roman Empire, which had been given to Marshal Berthier as an apanage. The details would be decided at the forthcoming congress in Vienna, to which the representatives of Switzerland would only be admitted if they agreed a suitable constitution first.

On 12 September 1814 the Swiss Diet accepted the cantons of Valais, Geneva and Neuchâtel into the Confederation, bringing the total number to twenty-two, and on 20 September it approved a new federal pact. But Berne still threatened to upset everything and destroy the Confederation unless it was allowed to reincorporate Aargau and Vaud. Its citizens felt that they suffered more than the others from the intervention of France – which had even removed its two armorial bears and sent them to the Jardin des Plantes in Paris. The city had lost much land, while its gold reserves, which had been deposited in London, were being retained by the British.[3]

The Swiss delegation to the congress consisted of Jean de Reinhard,

Burgomeister of Zürich; Jean de Montenach, a patrician from Fribourg; and Henri Wieland, Burgomeister of Bâle. Their aims were to secure the recognition of the Swiss Confederation as an independent state and the confirmation of its neutrality; the incorporation of Bâle and Bienne; the acquisition from France of a land link between Geneva and the rest of the Confederation; the recovery of Constance from Württemberg; the return of the Valtelline (currently in Austrian hands); and indemnities for Swiss properties confiscated in Austria and Baden.

Their task was not made easier by the fact that the permanent envoy of Switzerland to the court of Austria, Baron Müller d'Arvaangue, who had been in Vienna for years, was a diehard Bernese reactionary; that almost every canton sent its own delegates; that Bienne had sent a representative to demand the independence of the city; that two envoys from the Jura wanted the restitution of the bishopric of Bâle; that Abbot Vorster wanted the reinstatement of the sovereign abbey of St Gallen; and that most of them seemed to be at odds with each other. 'I accept all the good things you say to me about Geneva,' one of the minor envoys said to an astonished Capodistrias, 'but for us mountain people it is too rich, too clever, too civilised.' Reinhard himself balked at the idea of Geneva acquiring too much territory in Savoy, as it would increase the number of Catholics in the Confederation, a thought that 'terrified him'. The most formidable obstacle to all those of a conservative cast was that the new canton of Vaud had sent to Vienna as its representative none other than Frédéric César de La Harpe.[4]

Not surprisingly, Alexander backed the new cantons and the liberals, while Berne and the conservatives sought the protection of Austria and Prussia. Britain had no stated policy. While Stratford Canning favoured the liberals, Castlereagh's attitude was essentially opportunistic. Talleyrand was keen to defend French interests, and to fulfil a perceived obligation to save the Francophone Catholics of the former bishopric of Bâle from the rule of the German-speaking Protestants of Berne.

At the Swiss Committee's first meeting, on 14 November, Reinhard, representing the Swiss Confederation, addressed the assembled plenipotentiaries and asked for Switzerland's neutrality to be recognised by all and for her frontiers to be tidied up so as to make her more defensible. But the discussion soon turned to the problem of how to make Berne drop its demands for the restitution of Vaud and Aargau. Wessenberg suggested giving Berne part of the old bishopric of Bâle as compensation, and Humboldt backed him up. The matter was discussed at the next meeting, and at the third, on 30 November, the envoy of Berne, Zeerleder, declared that he accepted the independence of Vaud, and only demanded the restitution of Aargau.

At the fifth meeting of the committee, on 10 December, Wessenberg announced that Austria was ready to cede the Valtelline to Switzerland, but then ushered in some representatives of that province who demanded to be allowed to remain part of Austrian Lombardy instead. In the meantime, Talleyrand had managed to have a French plenipotentiary included in the committee, in the shape of Dalberg. Dalberg announced that France would be prepared to cede the strip of land along the northern shore of Lake Geneva at Gex and Versoix with some 10–12,000 souls that the city's envoys Pictet and d'Ivernois were so desperate to obtain, but only if she were indemnified by a smaller slice of Porrentruy, part of the former bishopric of Bâle and the valley of Dappes (part of Vaud). Stewart weighed in with a proposal of surreal complexity involving three cantons, France and Sardinia in a series of exchanges, the upshot of which was to make France withdraw her offer at the next session, on 13 December. By mid-December the arguments were becoming bad-tempered, with insults flying.[5]

The Committee on Swiss Affairs was a perfect example of what was wrong with the whole congress. The 'intervening powers' represented in the committee were ostensibly there to adjudicate impartially on both the internal disputes between the cantons and on a number of minor border adjustments, none of which touched on the vital interests of any but the Swiss. But as each of the five powers had its own clients in Switzerland, and as each of them was engaged in negotiations with the others on entirely different matters, the consequence was that far from being addressed dispassionately, the affairs of Switzerland were dragged into the power struggle over Poland and Saxony.

The attempts at resolving the Swiss question also provide an example of how parties with no connection whatever were brought into conflict. The plenipotentiaries of Geneva, when told that they could not obtain their land link with the rest of the Confederation because France could not be expected to cede more land, suggested that she be compensated with an equivalent strip of territory in Belgium. But as this had already been awarded to Holland, it angered the Dutch plenipotentiary and, by extension, turned Castlereagh against the Genevans, who were threatening his beloved scheme of a strong Dutch barrier against French expansion.[6]

Berne was eventually pacified at the eighth meeting of the committee, on 18 December, by the addition of most of the bishopric of Bâle and of Bienne, and by the promise of the return of the money deposited in London some twenty years before. But Geneva's needs were not met. None of Castlereagh, Metternich, Hardenberg or even Alexander was prepared to support it, and while Talleyrand treated the Genevans with cordiality and often professed his desire to help them, he was determined to deny them their desired land link and even conspired to detach the outlying district of Carouge from the city. In January 1815 Talleyrand came up with a perfidious suggestion that the areas in dispute should be awarded the status of associates of the Confederation rather than integral parts of it, which would have left them open to takeover by France and Austria at some convenient moment in the future.[7]

On 16 January, after discussing the constitutional act framed by the Swiss Diet, the Swiss Committee pronounced it 'imperfect'. It nevertheless decided to approve it, fearing that any attempt at amending it might revive latent disputes. It was indeed an imperfect compromise, a pale shadow of Napoleon's Act of Mediation of 1803, which had been one of the greatest benefits imposed by him anywhere.[8]

With the exception of the Valtelline (whose future Austria insisted must be conditional on the resolution of her claims against Bavaria), most of the issues were settled at the Swiss Committee's twelfth session on 5 March 1815. The same meeting saw a heavy-handed attempt by Alexander to have Berne excluded from any directorial role in the Confederation. He even tried to buy France's vote on the issue by promising Talleyrand to help with the removal of Murat from Naples. The remaining business would be wrapped up at the thirteenth session, on 13 March. The plenipotentiaries of Geneva had achieved nothing. Nor had Abbot Vorster. 'Sad news and true sentence of death for the abbey of St Gallen,' he noted in his diary on 20 March.[9]

Altogether less contentious was the Committee on the Free Navigation of International Rivers, which met for the first time on 2 February 1815 to discuss the arrangements for rivers such as the Rhine, the Meuse, the Neckar, the Main and the Scheldt which flowed through or between different sovereignties. It included representatives of all the riparian powers directly affected as well as delegates of Britain, Austria and France. It held its second session on 8 February, its third twelve days later, its fourth three days after that, and its fifth on 24 February, by which time it had not only covered most of the issues but also decided that a permanent international commission should be established, at either Mainz or Frankfurt, to rule on all disputes and further developments. Its seventh session, on 3 March, filled in details on tolls, levies and duties, and the classification of boats.

The conferences of the Five and the Eight, which were now being held regularly, even found time to address some of the minor business. A committee was nominated to investigate the validity of rival titles to the ancient duchy of Bouillon in the Ardennes. The claims of various individuals to an astonishing variety of lands or rights – such as the Prince of Piombino's demand for the restitution of his island of Elba or the traditional right of the Turn und Taxis family to manage the posts throughout the Holy Roman Empire – were reviewed and, as often as not, thrown out. On 11 February, at Alexander's request, the congress elevated his cousin the Duke of Saxe-Weimar to the status of a Grand Duke.[10]

On 24 February the case of the Order of Malta was considered. The Sovereign Order of the Knights Hospitallers of St John of Jerusalem, based in the holy city in the twelfth century, had been obliged to move its headquarters to the island of Rhodes after the fall of the crusader state. It had been forced out of there by the Turks, and fell back once more, to the island of Malta, donated to the Order in 1530 by the King of Spain, from which its galleys patrolled the Mediterranean and kept the Barbary pirates at bay. In 1798 the knights surrendered to General Bonaparte on his way to Egypt, but in 1800 the island was captured by the British. It was clear to all that, legitimacy notwithstanding, Britain was not going to give up such a pre-eminent naval base as Malta to anyone. The Order had sent two plenipotentiaries, who were prepared to accept virtually any alternative that would provide it with a base for its further survival. Failing that, they tried to obtain compensation from Britain for the fortifications, cannon and equipment of Valetta, amounting to some thirty million francs. Their case was not made any easier by the fact that after the fall of Malta some of the knights had gone to Russia and declared Tsar Paul to be their Grand Master, a move that was both unconstitutional and sacrilegious, since he was neither a Catholic nor a professed knight. Paul accepted the honour, which fitted in not only with his dreams of capturing Constantinople but also of acquiring a naval base in the Mediterranean. This episode had not only undermined the Order's legitimacy but opened the plenipotentiaries to verbal attacks from other members of the Order.

The Swedish plenipotentiary Löwenhielm suggested Spain give the Order the island of Minorca. The indignant Labrador retorted that the Order had proved itself so cowardly that it did not deserve to be given anything. But, he continued, Spain might consider such a gift if Britain were to return Malta itself to its original owner, Spain. He went on to suggest that if Britain was so keen on keeping the island, it should compensate the Order with a plot in Ireland.[11]

The islands of Elba and Corfu were mentioned as possible alternatives, but the lack of consistency of the surviving authorities of the Order, not to mention its recent flirtation with Russia, made it a poor candidate for taking over the Ionian islands or any place of importance. In the end, the Order of Malta did not get 'a single grain of sand', in the words of one of its plenipotentiaries.[12]

The Ionian islands had also been mentioned in connection with Prince Eugène, and even suggested to Marie-Louise, as an alternative to Parma. But they were too important to be awarded lightly. Originally a colony of the republic of Venice, the seven islands had been captured by France and subsequently by Britain, which currently held them. They were the object of Russian and Austrian envy. But as neither France nor Britain was likely to countenance their being awarded to either, local patriots believed there was an opportunity of founding an independent Ionian republic. An ardent proponent was Capodistrias, himself a Corfiote nobleman. His family had been prominent patriots, opposing both Venetian and French rule of the islands, and they had helped to create the Septinsular Republic in 1800. He himself had supported the Russian protectorate over the islands set up under the Treaty of Amiens and helped draw up its constitution in 1803. After the French had once again overrun the islands in 1807 he took service in Russia. Handsome, intelligent and forthright, he had quickly won the affection of Alexander and the esteem of his peers. He hoped that the islands would obtain a measure of autonomy if not outright independence. But their ultimate status would not be determined until a final settlement had been agreed in Italy, as the two questions were closely linked. And Italy was one area where no progress had been made at all.[13]

This was not surprising. Back in October there had been suggestions of appointing an Italian Committee to deal with the outstanding issues on the peninsula, but this had been quickly scotched by Metternich, who was determined that it should become an exclusively Austrian sphere of influence.

The house of Austria had acquired the duchy of Lombardy in 1714, and those of Tuscany and Modena had subsequently come to be ruled by Austrian archdukes. In 1797 General Bonaparte had snatched all these possessions away, but given Austria the republic of Venice in exchange (he took that too in 1805). By 1813 the whole of mainland Italy was under French rule, and the allies accepted that Austria should seek compensation there for her losses in Belgium, Germany and Poland. She had therefore taken possession of most of northern Italy as the French army evacuated it.

The King of Sardinia had recovered his mainland possessions, which had been augmented by the addition of Genoa. Neither Victor Emmanuel nor his brother Charles Felix had male heirs, and as Victor Emmanuel's daughter was married to the Austrian Archduke Francis IV of Modena, Metternich entertained hopes (which would ultimately be dashed) that Austria might scoop that kingdom into its sphere of influence as well.

In the south, Murat was ensconced in Naples, and his troops were in occupation of the Papal province of the Marches, just to remind Metternich that by the treaty of January 1814 he was supposed to be awarded territory that would bring him an additional 400,000 subjects. The Pope was in Rome, clamouring for the expulsion of Murat from the Marches. He was so desperate that he even entered into negotiations with Murat, who was prepared to hand back most of the province, retaining only Ancona and its vicinity, in return for his recognition as King of Naples by the Pope.[14]

The Pope was also calling for the withdrawal of the Austrian troops from his other province, the Legations. But Metternich had no intention of evacuating that or indeed any of the other areas currently occupied by Austrian troops – Tuscany, Parma, Piacenza (an important fortress), Guastalla, and so on. Whoever did keep the Legations in the end, he was determined that at least the strategically important Ferrara should remain with Austria.

Parma and its two dependent duchies had been promised to Marie-Louise by the Treaty of Fontainebleau, and as she was the daughter of the Emperor Francis that meant they would remain within the

Austrian sphere of influence. But there was a question mark over what would happen after her death, as most of the allies were adamant that Napoleon's son should never ascend a throne, however insignificant. Spain wanted the duchies returned to their former ruler, who had become Queen of Etruria and then of nothing. There had been talk of compensating her with the Legations, but, being a devout Catholic, she ruled out any idea of dispossessing the Pope.

It was being whispered that Metternich was maintaining Murat on his throne in Naples out of affection for his former lover Caroline. Surviving letters between them from this period do not bear out any such supposition, and Metternich had better reasons for keeping Murat in Naples for the time being. By toppling him he would be restoring a Bourbon, and therefore providing a conduit for French influence in Italy. And any movement in the current stalemate would give others an occasion to make trouble.

Alexander certainly would if he could. He wanted to find a throne for Prince Eugène. He also wanted to make friends and potential clients in the peninsula, with a view to acquiring a lever of pressure over Austria and possibly even a naval base in the Mediterranean. Towards the end of February he was insisting on setting Prince Eugène up either in the Legations or in Bernadotte's former apanage of Pontecorvo. He was in no hurry to remove Murat, for different reasons from Metternich; he was heard to express the view that there should be an independent power in Italy that was neither Habsburg nor Bourbon.[15]

The only powers committed to removing Murat were France and Britain. But France had to be careful not to appear to be embarking on adventures in Italy, as this would unite the rest of Europe against her. The status quo may also have suited Talleyrand for personal reasons: it is almost certain that he was being paid large sums by King Ferdinand to encourage him in supporting his cause, and seems also to have been in receipt of substantial payments from Murat for the exact opposite purpose.

Britain's reason for wishing to remove Murat was that while

Napoleon was in Elba, Murat could provide a ready-made landing ground for him. Wellington had repeatedly suggested putting together a joint force of French, Spanish, Portuguese and Sicilian troops, supported by a British contingent, to oust Murat. But Liverpool restrained him. There was no stomach in England for military operations, which were equated with high taxes. Also, Murat had been playing to British public opinion and had quite a following in London, fuelled by a stream of returning tourists whom he flattered shamelessly as they passed through Naples.

The interests of Britain and France converged at almost every point in Italy, yet Castlereagh and Liverpool so mistrusted Talleyrand that they conducted their own talks on the subject of Italy with Louis XVIII and his First Minister, the comte de Blacas. They encouraged the latter's jealousy of Talleyrand and achieved nothing but a confusion of the issues, which Castlereagh aggravated by also cutting Talleyrand out of his discussions with Metternich on the subject.[17]

The one who found all the prevarication on Italy most frustrating was the unfortunate Marie-Louise. Although the Treaty of Fontainebleau had awarded her Parma, Piacenza and Guastalla, which were then to pass to her son, she feared she might never take possession of her promised realm. From time to time she would be told that there was a possibility of finding her another fief, in Bohemia, in the Ionian islands or elsewhere. Alexander would call on her, often accompanied by Prince Eugène, and assure her that all was well and that she would soon get her duchies, but nothing happened, and she lived in a constant state of uncertainty.[18]

The other issue that had been left far behind was that of the constitution of Germany. Ironically, the German Committee had been the first to be set up, on 14 October, and there should not have been much need for discussion, given that Metternich had ostensibly accepted Hardenberg's original project, presented to the committee on 16 October.

This envisaged a confederation or Bund of German states from which the bulk of Prussian and Austrian lands (which were not German) were to be excluded. The territorial area of Germany was to be divided into a number of groupings (*Kreise*) of local rulers, with a Diet consisting of three chambers which would meet at Frankfurt under the joint direction of Austria and Prussia.

The project had foundered on the opposition of Württemberg and Bavaria; although the committee held thirteen meetings, Metternich, who was by then at odds with Hardenberg over Saxony, failed to rein them in and merely tried to direct their ire against Prussia. This was to turn against him when the crisis deepened, as Württemberg began to support Russia against Austria.

A voluntary consensus on the subject of a constitution for Germany was unlikely, as the range of options put forward by various parties was bafflingly wide. They included the re-establishment of a German empire, either under the house of Austria as before, or under Prussia; a confederation of equals; a fully federated state; two federal states, dominated by Austria and Prussia respectively; and the total independence of all the units. Having lived under the relatively liberal hegemony of France for the past eight years, many of the rulers did not relish the idea of Austrian or Prussian dominion, while many of the patriots and liberals leaned towards imperial authority in order to curb the ambitions of the medium-sized states, which were by nature more despotic and less pan-German in their outlook.

In this respect, Stein was a good example of how circumstantial complications could distort an original vision. He had always longed for a single united German state, but realised that it would not be possible to create one from scratch. He therefore hoped that Prussia would absorb as much of Germany as it could and dominate the rest. Failing that, he favoured a confederation in which Prussia would be dominant. But by the beginning of 1815 he had been obliged to take a more pragmatic view. Seeing the fiercely independent states such as Württemberg, Bavaria and Baden as the greatest threat to achieving any kind of German unity, he was by the beginning of February arguing for a return to a German empire under the house of Austria.

Conversely, although Metternich was a staunch believer in the *ancien régime* as represented by the Holy Roman Empire, he realised that times had changed, and he now favoured any arrangement that would place Germany under Austrian influence rather than under her domination.[19]

The arguments within the committee were at times acrimonious, with both sides using the press in various parts of Germany to intimidate and ridicule each other. Each party criticised the other's unwillingness to make sacrifices for the sake of the public good, while remaining extremely touchy about its own privileges and pretensions. Württemberg's representative, Count Winzingerode, examined every phrase of every proposal put forward solely from the point of view of his King's interests, and if he felt these were in any way infringed by any part he would reject the whole. Bavaria, whose Foreign Minister Count Mongelas had not even bothered to come to Vienna, was represented on the German Committee by Prince Wrede and Count Rechberg, who indignantly objected to any limitations being placed on the prerogatives of their royal master. The terms of the Treaty of Ried, concluded with Austria in 1813, guaranteed her full sovereignty.

At the thirteenth meeting of the German Committee, on 16 November, the delegates of Württemberg announced flatly that they were withdrawing. That same day twenty-nine smaller German states clubbed together to demand full equality for all states within the Bund under the imperial protection of a restored Austrian Kaiser. By then Prussia and Austria had other things to occupy them. It was not until 24 December that Metternich produced a new proposal, drafted by Wessenberg, which envisaged a loose federation of sovereign states. The moment was hardly propitious, as war seemed imminent.

The King of Württemberg left Vienna on 26 December, in eloquent confirmation of the stance taken by his plenipotentiaries on the German Committee. Nothing could make him warm to the idea of a united Germany, not even Alexander's suggestion that his son the Crown Prince (Alexander's future brother-in-law) should be given command of the German army. He refused to discuss anything that might lead to the abrogation of any of the prerogatives he had acquired from Napoleon. And in order to pre-empt any further such discussion, he had decided to create a *fait accompli*.

Having returned home to Stuttgart, he set about introducing an ostensibly liberal constitution with a representative body in which all the mediatised princes and knights in his dominions would sit on an equal footing with middle-class Deputies of cities and guilds, representatives of the Church and of the university of Tübingen, who would outnumber them. News of the King's presumed liberal move was well received in Vienna, until the howls of protest pouring in from the mediatised brought home the real nature of the measure, which was to bludgeon them into submission and pave the way for absolutist rule. Metternich and Hardenberg reacted with energy. On 31 January 1815 Russia issued a strong declaration on the subject. But there was no disguising that the great powers had lost control of the situation in Germany.

On 2 February, thirty-two by now furious German princes and cities issued a declaration complaining that months had passed since they had been asked to present their credentials, and that they had not yet been allowed to put their case. They called for the immediate establishment of a German Congress in which they should all be represented and which could address the question of a constitution for Germany.

No such congress was called, but on 10 February Prussia produced a revised project for a constitution, drawn up by Humboldt. It was presented in two versions, one with and one without governing *Kreise*. The Prussian note recommended the one which did include five *Kreise*, each of them under the chairmanship of one of the major states – Austria, Prussia, Bavaria, Württemberg and Hanover.

The following day, Stein came up with a counter-proposal, backed by Alexander, for a return to the old empire under the house of Austria. Hardenberg protested, arguing that the Austrian dynasty and government were too flabby both intellectually and politically to provide the leadership for a future German state. Stein argued that Austria would grow less 'un-German' if she were invested with an imperial role in Germany.[20]

Such a degree of indecision and evident lack of unity only served to encourage confusion, which was a breeding ground for private ambitions and a cause of distress and paralysis for those subordinate interests which needed to know what the great powers were planning in order to tailor their own demands. The result was that, for instance, the Pope's plenipotentiary Cardinal Consalvi and the other representatives of the Catholic Church in Germany could not begin to formulate coherent solutions to the problems confronting the Church and its relations with the present and future temporal authorities.

The Catholic Church had over the past half-century presented an easy target for all rulers in need of funds. In 1750 there were well over 15,000 monasteries and 10,000 nunneries in Europe, along with tens of thousands of churches, vicarages and prebends, hundreds of bishops' palaces and countless other estates, not to mention priceless collections of gold, silver and jewelled liturgical vessels and works of art of every kind. The Church owned some 20 per cent of the land across Catholic Europe and up to 25 per cent of the surface of many a city – the abbey of St Germain-des-Prés covered two modern *arrondissements* of Paris. Such wealth was difficult to justify in the increasingly secular post-Enlightenment world, and in the decades before the French Revolution Catholic rulers such as the Holy Roman Emperor Joseph II were able to close down hundreds of monasteries and confiscate their wealth with impunity. The French Revolution initiated the theft of all the Church's property in France, and over the next decades a combination of French reforms and opportunistic confiscations by Catholic rulers in Bavaria, Württemberg and elsewhere in southern Germany meant that by 1814 virtually no religious houses survived in France, Germany, Belgium, Switzerland, Spain or Italy, and only four hundred in the kingdom of Naples.[21]

On his return to Spain, King Ferdinand reinstated the monasteries suppressed by the French, but however much they affected a return to the *status quo ante* in most things, not one of his brother monarchs followed suit. And although the Pope did not fail to set out his claims to all confiscated Church property, he did not entertain great hopes. The restitution of most of the property was either impossible or politically unfeasible. As this meant that the Church was left without any means of subsistence, the only solution was to negotiate its funding by the state, as had been done under the concordat signed with France in 1801 and subsequent replicas enacted in other parts of Napoleonic Europe. And until the Pope knew who would rule where, Consalvi could not begin to negotiate fresh agreements.

Funding was only one of the problems confronting the Church. Two decades of revolution and war had disrupted its normal functioning to such an extent that it was now entirely dislocated, with bishoprics and other offices vacant, some of them for a considerable time, and in a state of utter confusion as to the workings of ecclesiastical authority and its relation to local secular authorities. The Pope had to busy himself *inter alia* with the consecration of a new Bishop of Louisiana, which had been cut off from Rome for over a decade, the reorganisation of the status of Belgian Catholics, formerly embraced in the concordat with France within their new Protestant kingdom of Holland, and the formulation of a method for the appointing of Irish bishops. He nominated the Bishop of Chioggia as administrator of the Venetian patriarchate, which was vacant, but this irritated the Emperor Francis, who had acquired Venice and intended to introduce Joseph II's reforms there as well as in his other Italian provinces. Meanwhile, Alexander had decided to create the office of Metropolitan Bishop of Vilna with the power to nominate bishops in his province, which was quite unacceptable to the Pope. In France and other countries subjected to French revolutionary government, there were sharp conflicts between those bishops and priests who had accepted the new authorities and those who had protested against them, while in dioceses which had been vacant for many years liturgical and theological conflicts had sprung up in the vacuum of authority.[22]

The situation was at its worst in Germany. 'The churches of Germany are in a state of disorder and decadence which brings out the greatest anxiety in the souls of good Catholics,' Consalvi wrote to Metternich on 14 November 1814, shortly after reaching Vienna. The long period of isolation from Papal authority had given rise to a number of different orientations among the Catholic bishops, priests and congregations of Germany, reflecting the ideas of the Enlightenment, the French Revolution, the new nationalism and Protestant pietist influences, to name but a few. A strong party, headed by Carl Theodor von Dalberg, formerly Archbishop Elector of Mainz and Arch-Chancellor of the Holy Roman Empire, now Archbishop and ruler of Ratisbon (Regensburg) by the grace of Napoleon, wanted a national Catholic Church of Germany only loosely connected to Rome. Another party, whose most prominent spokesmen, the 'Orators' Baron Franz von Wambold, Cathedral Deacon of Worms, and Joseph Helfferich, Cathedral Prebendary of Speyer, stood for spiritual renewal and closer ties with the Vatican, while insisting on the ancient rights of cathedral chapters in the nomination of bishops. These two parties reflected divisions in Rome itself.[23]

Cardinal Consalvi belonged to that party in the College of Cardinals known as the *liberali*, who were pragmatic and forward-looking, and shared the ideas of the Pope on larger issues. They were opposed by the *zelanti*, who included Consalvi's deputy in Rome, Cardinal Pacca, and indeed the Nuncio in Vienna, Monsignor Severoli, at whose nunciature Consalvi was lodged. Vienna thus became the scene of a struggle for power between Dalberg, who was trying to get Consalvi removed, and Consalvi, who was trying to assert his position as the only plenipotentiary in matters concerning the Catholic Church who should be recognised by the congress.

He was hoping to overrule all local Church differences by having the relations between Church and state as well as Church and Rome defined in the proposed German constitution, as this would oblige all the rulers to abide by it and accept Papal authority. But many of the rulers, particularly those of Württemberg and Bavaria, wanted to sign individual concordats with Rome. Until Metternich and Hardenberg could agree and enforce a constitution, Consalvi was condemned to a state of anguished appeasement.

But progress on the constitution had become hopelessly enmeshed in the wrangles over the territorial settlement. With the problem of Saxony and Prussia's 'equivalents' out of the way, that of Bavaria had taken centre stage. According to the Treaty of Ried, Austria was to repossess her old provinces of the Tyrol and the Inn with Salzburg, and Bavaria would be compensated with the Palatinate and Mainz. But Britain and Russia did not wish to see Mainz, which was of crucial strategic importance, go to Bavaria. There was a lingering fear that France might one day enter into alliance with Bavaria and Austria, thereby creating a formidable axis; this could only be prevented by the existence of a strong German fortress at Mainz. After the application of much pressure, and some horse-trading, Bavaria was induced to give up her claim to Mainz, which was to become a fortress of the Bund, manned by a mixed German garrison under Prussian command. But Bavaria wanted compensation.

She wanted the Palatinate and other areas which were currently in Württemberg, the Hesses and Baden. The Grand Duke of Baden had no wish to give up any territory, and on 2 March 1815 delivered a strong memorandum on the subject. Although Alexander was his brother-in-law, he did not like the frivolous and hedonistic Grand Duke. Stein had no time for him either, and in any case believed that the interests of rulers such as him should take second place to those of Germany. On 4 March, in an effort to reach a bargain over the Palatinate, he sent for the Grand Duke of Baden so the matter could be settled directly, but the Grand Duke was unable to come, being severely indisposed as a result of strenuous nocturnal activities. Four days later he was well enough to spend the evening in dalliance with Madame Morel, accompanied by the Princes of Hesse-Cassel and Hesse-Homburg.[24]

If Stein's somewhat priggish nature was offended by the profligate Grand Duke's behaviour, his intelligence cannot fail to have been affronted by the sheer silliness of his imperial master. The arrival of Lent put a stop to balls and more festive assemblies, but instead of prompting people to meditate on the transience of earthly pleasures, it led them to seek out ever more recherché ones.

On 15 February, at Countess Zichy's, Alexander and Countess Wrbna-Kageneck got into an argument about whether men or women took longer to dress, and decided to test the issue. Bets were laid as each retired to a nearby room with a witness and undressed, and when time was called they both dressed again and reappeared, the Countess winning the bet. Alexander got his own back by showing off his whistling skills, to the accompaniment of Sophie Zichy at the piano.[25]

A party game that had been popular at the court of Louis XIV was revived with much success. It involved everyone bringing trinkets and presents which were jumbled together, and for which lots were drawn by all, with the winners presenting their prizes to the person of the opposite sex of their choice. At one such 'lottery' held by Princess Esterhazy on 1 March, Alexander flew into a rage when not only did the magnificent gift he had brought go to Marie, the daughter of Metternich, with whom he was no longer on speaking terms, but also the lot brought by Gabrielle Auersperg went not to him but to a Prussian officer, who refused all the Tsar's blandishments to hand it over.[26]

This kind of behaviour, widely reported in increasingly disaffected, if not shocked, tones, offended sensibilities all over Europe. It struck German patriots as little short of blasphemous, and acted as an irritant on public opinion, particularly in Prussia. The failure of Frederick William and Hardenberg to obtain the whole of Saxony, or at least Leipzig, had gone down badly in Berlin. They had published exaggerated accounts in the Berlin press of how much they had managed to hold on to, but these had failed to impress, and the windows of Hardenberg's house in Berlin were smashed by an angry mob. The manner in which the congress was seen to be reaching its decisions also suggested that since these were not sanctioned by any justification or purpose higher than that of gratifying the greed of individual rulers, none of them need be regarded as final.[27]

Humboldt tried to appease his wife, who was echoing the indignation of the German patriots, and particularly of a war party gathering around Blücher. He admitted that not enough had been achieved, but argued that expectations, which had been based on Prussia's military input into the war of 1813–14 rather than on political realities, had been too high. It was not so much that Prussia had not acquired enough territory, but that other 'wicked' parties had. 'Prussia is now the greatest power in Germany, with some eight million Germans, which means a military power in Germany of 240,000 men,' he explained on 23 February, and went on to assure her that 'In the course of the next war, which will break out, Prussia will fill out all the gaps and grow larger in Germany.' He actually looked forward to a war with Bavaria, which would prove her undoing and strengthen Prussia. 'The battle against wickedness has not been fought to the end, and will have to be renewed, at some time,' he was convinced.[28]

But the sovereigns and plenipotentiaries at Vienna were oblivious to such discontents. They carried on with their vacuous entertainments, untroubled by any forebodings; on 21 February, fifty-six battalions of Landwehr troops were demobilised. The end was in sight.

On 6 March, at its eleventh session, the conference of the Five discussed how to get the King of Saxony to accept the arrangements made; it was decided that Talleyrand, Metternich and Wellington would go to Pressburg (Bratislava), where he was waiting to re-enter his reduced dominions, in order to obtain his assent. It then turned its attention to the matter of how to combine the many individual agreements reached into one coherent final act; after what seemed like an interminable discussion a Drafting Committee was nominated, under the direction of La Besnardière, Anstett and Gentz. The meeting then adjourned. It was 3 a.m.

The Flight of the Eagle

At the ungodly hour of 6 o'clock on that same morning, 7 March 1815, Metternich was shaken awake by his valet Giroux. A courier had arrived at the door with a despatch marked 'urgent', so Giroux had decided to wake his master, in spite of having been told to let him sleep late. Metternich took one look at the envelope, which was marked: 'From the I[mperial] & R[oyal] Consulate General in Genoa'. He laid it on his bedside table and turned over to go back to sleep.

But, having been disturbed, he slept fitfully, and at 7.30 he reached over and opened the envelope. It contained the briefest of notes:

> *The English commissioner Campbell has just sailed into the harbour to enquire whether there has been any sighting of Napoleon, given that he has disappeared from the Island of Elba. The answer being negative, the English frigate put to sea without delay.*

Metternich sprang out of bed, dressed quickly, hurried across the open space separating the Chancellery from the Hofburg and was at the door of the Emperor's bedroom by 8 o'clock. Francis took the news with his usual calm, not to say placidity. 'Napoleon seems to wish to try his luck in a new adventure, that is his business,' he said. 'Ours is to assure to the world that peace which he has disturbed for so many years.' Metternich next called on Alexander and then on

Frederick William, and by 10 o'clock he was sitting down to a meeting with the plenipotentiaries of the other four powers, while couriers headed off in all directions.[1]

A few hours later, Wellington received a despatch from Burghersh, now British minister at Florence, giving more details of the escape, but it was still not clear where Napoleon was headed, or what he intended to do. Even counting the volunteers who had joined him on Elba, he only had about a thousand men with him, so he did not represent much of a military threat as such. He might be bound for Naples, where he would find Murat with an army ready and waiting for him, or for France, where his reception was more doubtful.

The entertainment scheduled at court for that night was a panto-mime entitled *Le Calife de Bagdad*, and it went ahead as though nothing had happened. But the atmosphere was anything but light-hearted. 'It would be difficult to give an account of the various expressions of astonishment, fear, hope, of all the real or simulated feelings which the great personages present at this occasion allowed to escape,' in the words of one observer. Clancarty reported to Castle-reagh that 'Though there was every attempt to conceal apprehension under the mask of unconcern, it was not difficult to perceive that fear was predominant in all the Imperial and Royal personages there assembled; and, however much their principal officers endeavoured to make light of this event, the task of disguise was too heavy for them.' The King of Bavaria 'lost his appetite from fear', in the words of a Russian officer, while Alexander himself was visibly shaken, according to Archduke John. Even Metternich, who gave the impression that the news had no effect on him whatever, was visibly less composed when he returned home.[2]

The implications were indeed alarming. If Napoleon were to land at Naples, as most people surmised, he might, with the use of Murat's army, be able to raise the whole of Italy and threaten Austria. Austria's freedom of action against him would be severely limited by con-siderations of the position Russia and Prussia might take. Although tension had eased in recent weeks, there was still a military alliance in existence binding Austria, France, Britain, Holland, Bavaria and Hanover against Russia and Prussia. On 5 March, two days before he received news of Napoleon's escape from Elba, Louis XVIII was writing to Talleyrand with instructions on what to do in the event of war breaking out. It was not beyond the realms of possibility that Alexander might seize the chance of breaking up the alliance by reaching an agreement with Napoleon.[3]

News that Napoleon had landed not in Italy but on the south coast of France reached Vienna late on 10 March. The sovereigns and their ministers are often said to have been informed of it during a ball given by Metternich. 'The news spread through the rooms with the rapidity of an electric spark,' according to one memoirist. 'The waltz was interrupted, and while the orchestra played on in vain people looked at each other in bewilderment.' It is also said that the Emperor Francis declared that he had had enough and that there would be no more festivities. In fact there was no ball that night, and there had been none for some time, since it was Lent. The only distractions during this period were dinners, concerts and the occasional play.[4]

Napoleon's landing in France rather than Italy took the pressure off Austria, but opened up other possibilities. His reappearance in France would put the Bourbon regime to the test, and with it the wisdom of those who had installed it. Alexander, who had been against the restoration from the start, might be tempted to revisit his old projects. The only groups who had shown not just pleasure, but outright joy at the news of Napoleon's escape were disappointed German patriots and the Prussian military. It was not difficult to guess that what delighted them was a perceived opportunity to use the forthcoming war against Napoleon as an excuse to reopen the German question, and indeed to expand Prussia territorially. At the same time, a new war might have some untoward consequences for entirely different reasons.

Count Münster was not alone in believing that the conduct of the allies over the past year had undermined their credibility and that they stood on shaky moral ground. 'On all sides it has been evident that war was made rather against the success of Bonaparte than against his principles,' he wrote to the Prince Regent on 18 March. 'No justice has been rendered to the feeble. The oppression of many of the provinces of Germany has been continued, and the burdens laid on the people have in many places been augmented by the abuses of the Provisional Governments.' He expressed grave doubts as to whether German soldiers could be made to fight again. His misgivings were given substance within days, as various of the northern German contingents declared that they would refuse to serve alongside Prussian troops, let alone under Prussian command.[5]

In southern Germany and Westphalia there was even some cheering of Napoleon when news broke of his escape. 'Weary of war in 1813, the people greeted the allies with joy,' Baron Hainau reported on 28 April 1815, 'but that joy did not last; the peasant was treated with the cane and, the allied army having permitted itself to commit the greatest disorders, people began to ardently desire the return of the French, or rather of a general peace.' The officers of the Prince's guard at Darmstadt went so far as to drink the health of Napoleon.[6]

There was a fear that there would be risings in support of Napoleon in Switzerland, particularly in Aargau and Vaud, and that states neighbouring France, such as Bavaria, might find it expedient to break ranks. 'If Buonaparte could turn the tide, there is no calculating upon his *élan*,' Castlereagh warned Wellington from London, 'and we must always recollect that Poland, Saxony, and much Jacobinism are in our rear.'[7]

There was also the unpleasant probability that if Napoleon did manage to seize Paris, he might find, in the archives of the French Foreign Ministry, a copy of the secret Anglo-Franco-Austrian treaty against Russia and Prussia, which he would certainly not fail to make public. While he expressed the belief that Alexander would not react violently if this came to pass, Castlereagh warned Wellington of this possibility.

Although there had been an attempt to contain the news of Napoleon's escape, it had quickly leaked out. 'These terrifying tidings produced terrible confusion,' according to Baroness du Montet. 'People ran about, stopping each other, enquiring, forming little groups in every street.' More to the point, Austrian paper money fell from a rate of eleven to gold coin to twenty-one in the space of a week.[8]

The uncertainties bred a welter of rumours – that Napoleon had been beaten and forced to re-embark, that he had been victorious and taken Lyon, that he had been defeated by Monsieur outside Dijon, that he had been joined by Soult, that he had been routed by Ney, that he had taken Louis XVIII prisoner, and so on. Conjecture of every kind fed on the rumours, and the correspondence of individuals and officials alike swarms with the most improbable stories. Conspiracy theories abounded. According to some the congress had been permeated by spies, while the more paranoid represented Napoleon as manipulating events through a sinister web of agents. Only the Grand Duke of Baden remained aloof. According to a police report of 15 March, he had acquired a new object for his attentions, the daughter of the owner of the Leopoldstadt Theatre, and was dining and dallying with her nightly.[9]

Public opinion was quick to blame the British, who in the common perception were deemed to be Napoleon's guardians. Alexander wrote to his brother Constantine that the British had shown 'an ineptitude and a really criminal insouciance' in letting the ogre escape. Some thought that they had actually facilitated his flight, either so as to be able to recapture him and then deal harshly with him, or in order to frighten the other powers. 'Bonaparte's evasion has caused a strong sensation, and we are accused as the authors of it,' a British diplomat reported from St Petersburg.[10]

But Britain had no role in the exile of Napoleon beyond that of having provided the ship in which to take him to Elba, and was only seen as his gaoler because she was universally viewed as the policeman of the seas. If anyone was to blame it was Alexander, who had, acting entirely on his own initiative, designated Elba as the place of Napoleon's exile and allowed him to take a contingent of troops. The

French blamed Alexander's 'sentimental' politics for placing Napoleon on Elba, but also censured Metternich's reluctance to chase Murat out of Naples.

They, and particularly Talleyrand, had every reason to be anxious. Both as a former servant of Napoleon and the chief engineer of the Bourbon restoration, he was deeply implicated. And his position at Vienna as the plenipotentiary of France depended on whether the King he represented could maintain himself on the throne.

It was reported that he heard the news of Napoleon's escape from the lips of Dorothée, who would perch on the end of his bed in the mornings and read out his letters. As the story goes, she expressed dismay at the possibility of the rehearsal for a play in which she was to perform being cancelled, and he reassured her, saying that everything would go ahead as usual. Talleyrand was certainly a past master at hiding his emotions. Hardenberg would write that the news of Napoleon's escape from Elba had 'made M. de Talleyrand move from an insulting hauteur to the most shameful pusillanimity', but there is no contemporary confirmation of this. Rosenkrantz noted that, far from being downcast like the others, Talleyrand appeared sanguine. To a fellow Frenchman who asked him what he would do, Talleyrand shrugged his shoulders and answered, 'I don't know, I shall wait and see.'[11]

Talleyrand assured everyone that Napoleon had no following in France, and that nobody would welcome him if he were to land there. 'If, as I hope, we act in this circumstance with prudence and firmness, by quelling the evil at its source and not allowing it time to make any progress, this event cannot have any unpleasant consequences, and could indeed have some useful ones,' he wrote to his deputy Jaucourt in Paris on the day he heard the news, pointing out that it would at last force the Austrians to act against Murat and provide an opportunity of removing Napoleon from the scene entirely. 'I am convinced that Buonaparte's undertaking will have no evil consequences, and that there will be no necessity to have recourse to foreign powers,' he wrote a couple of days later. This did not stop him from instructing Jaucourt to go through the files at the ministry and remove all papers that might prove embarrassing if they were to fall into Napoleon's hands.[12]

The whole affair raised some nice questions of international law. Talleyrand was the first to appreciate that if Napoleon were to topple the Bourbons and represent himself as the *de facto* ruler of France, and then accept the terms of the Treaty of Paris, the other signatories of that treaty would, legally speaking, have no grounds for not recognising him, and certainly no justification for hostilities against him. The only way of avoiding this was to disqualify Napoleon himself, and that is what Talleyrand promptly set out to do.

He persuaded the ministers of the other powers that they must issue a joint declaration, and produced a draft. This argued that by leaving the island of Elba Napoleon had broken his only legal right to exist, and that he was therefore an outlaw and fair game for anyone to kill. When they met to discuss this on 13 March, some of the other plenipotentiaries protested against such extreme language, on legal grounds. Metternich objected because he did not want the door closed entirely on some form of negotiated settlement with Napoleon if that were to prove possible or necessary. After some discussion and a great deal of shouting, the text was amended. While it kept to the same argument and declared Napoleon to have placed himself outside the law, the final declaration did not actually sanction his murder. At the same time, it proclaimed the determination of all eight of the signatories of the Treaty of Paris to support Louis XVIII in defence of his throne. It was a somewhat specious argument, but it let them off the hook.[13]

'Bony's conduct is very extraordinary,' Wellington wrote to Burghersh on 13 March, adding that he thought his decision to land in France worthy of one 'fit for Bedlam'. But there was nothing extraordinary about Napoleon's move, given the impossible situation in which he had been placed by his vanquishers. And his venture was not as lunatic as Wellington thought.[14]

Alexander's irresponsible generosity towards the beaten Napoleon in 1814 had resulted in the Treaty of Fontainebleau, by Clause III of which the island of Elba 'will constitute, during his lifetime, a distinct principality which will be held by him in free possession and peaceful enjoyment in full sovereignty'. Elba was granted a flag (white with a diagonal crimson band decorated with Napoleon's armorial three bees), which was saluted by British and French warships as they entered and left the harbour of Portoferraio. According to accepted international law her ruler was entitled to have diplomatic representatives in every European capital and to send a plenipotentiary to the congress at Vienna. Instead, he was being treated not just as a pariah but as a prisoner, and was watched carefully by the Royal Navy and the spies and agents of half a dozen powers. Even his letters to his wife were intercepted.[15]

His own agents and well-wishers all over Europe supplied him with a stream of information to the effect that the rulers of Europe were planning to remove him from Elba and imprison him in a more remote place, or simply to have him assassinated. While much of this information was based on rumour and conjecture, it was not groundless.

As early as September 1814 the Emperor Francis had assured the ambassador of the King of Sardinia that he would seize the first opportunity to remove Napoleon from Elba and confine him in a more distant island, and Metternich confirmed this. At one of their first meetings, the plenipotentiaries of the four allies had agreed 'to apply themselves to the means of removing Napoleon from the island of Elba' and transferring him to a Spanish or Portuguese island or colony in South America. The Azores and other islands in the Atlantic were mentioned, and on 8 November Eynard was told by the King of Bavaria that the British island of St Helena in the South Atlantic had been chosen. 'The matter is being dealt with as I speak,' he assured him.[16]

News of these discussions did trickle out. When Lord Holland heard from a correspondent at Vienna that there was talk of moving the Emperor from Elba to St Helena, he raised the matter in the House of Lords, where the government spokesman would neither confirm nor deny the allegation. This was printed in the London papers, which Napoleon received regularly. He might also have heard of a plan being hatched in Turin in October 1814 by France, Spain and Sardinia to combine in an operation to remove and imprison him.[17]

The rumours of plots to assassinate Napoleon were not groundless either. There were several unofficial projects hatched in extreme royalist circles in France, and Louis XVIII's ministry did nothing to discourage them. If anything, it was keen to force the issue. In doing so, it actually gave Napoleon a perfectly viable excuse for military action against France.[18]

While the Treaty of Fontainebleau also affirmed that all the signatory powers would guarantee Napoleon's rights and, for instance, protect his shipping against the Barbary pirates, his only official relations with any power were defined by the same Clause III, which stipulated that in return for his giving up all claim to property and effects in France, that country would pay him an annual pension of two million francs. France was not among the signatories of the treaty, but on 31 May 1814, under pressure from Alexander, she had formally undertaken to respect its provisions.

Talleyrand was repeatedly pressed by Castlereagh, Metternich and Alexander to fulfil France's obligations, and piously passed on the request, but nothing was done. The government of Louis XVIII considered that, like Murat, Napoleon must go, and the sooner the better. And whether assassination or invasion were the chosen option, it would be made a great deal easier if lack of funds obliged him to disband his guards. Alternatively, it might provoke him into making a rash move that would bring the whole of Europe out against him, the assumption being that this time he would be given no quarter when finally cornered. The Bourbon ministry calculated, correctly, that this was the surest way to engineer the monster's final downfall, but miscalculated dramatically on the price to be paid for it.[19]

Napoleon knew that he was taking an enormous gamble by breaking out of Elba. But he had every reason to believe that if an assassin did not get him first he would awake one morning to find the island blockaded by the Royal Navy and invaded by Austrian troops from the Italian mainland. He realised that he was too dangerous for his enemies to leave where he was. He believed he had no choice. He sensed that time was running out. He reckoned that he had a good chance of succeeding, and he was right. It was timing, the factor in the equation over which he had no control, that would prove his undoing.

By 14 February 1815 Napoleon had decided to act. Over the next days he reviewed his troops, who were issued with an additional pair of boots, had the horses of his Polish cavalry brought in from pasture, and gave orders for his one brig the *Inconstant* and a couple of transport ships to be prepared, and supplies moved down to the harbour of Porto Longone. At nightfall on 22 February the *Inconstant* began loading.

On 24 February the Royal Navy frigate that had taken the British Commissioner Colonel Campbell off to the Italian mainland returned with a group of six English tourists whom the Emperor gratified by receiving. The following day was spent drafting proclamations to be read to the French people. That evening he told his mother of his plans. The next day, Sunday 26 February, Napoleon attended Mass at 9 o'clock. At four that afternoon the troops ate their dinner on the quayside. An hour later the drums began to roll and they started to embark, followed by their Emperor. When darkness fell, the small flotilla weighed anchor. On 1 March the *Inconstant* sailed into the Golfe Juan, and Napoleon stepped onto French soil.

Bourbon rule in France had not been a success. The marquis de Lafayette had taken a dim view of the restoration, commenting that 'Never has a triumph been attended by so little glory,' but glory was not what the French people had wanted in 1814. They had been eager for peace, and were prepared to accept with relief and even enthusiasm any regime that could provide it. They had also grown tired of the increasingly despotic and intrusive machinery of the Napoleonic state, which swallowed up their sons by conscription and their wealth through taxes.[20]

In many ways, Louis XVIII was the ideal successor to Napoleon. He was in no sense a competitor. His legitimacy, which had nothing to do with military prowess or other talents, guaranteed a stability both external and internal that the other could never provide. 'He knew perfectly how to speak as a King,' in the words of one observer, and was well fashioned to play the role of an unthreatening and kindly father to a nation in need of repose and healing. That he was obese, hardly capable of sitting a horse and utterly devoid of any dash or charisma should have been endearing contrasts to the martial giant who had held them in thrall for so long and ultimately let them down.[21]

But Louis was predictably out of touch with the nation he had been called to reign over, and he made a series of grave errors of judgement at the outset. His insistence on counting 1814 as the nineteenth year of his reign amounted to a rejection of all that had happened in the course of those years. So did his refusal to adopt the tricolour flag. His act of 'granting' a charter, having previously refused to countenance the constitution drawn up by Talleyrand and approved by the chamber that had voted his restoration, was a calculated insult to the concept of the sovereignty of the people, which even Louis XVI had been forced to acknowledge.

In the comte de Blacas, Louis appointed a Prime Minister who was not up to the situation. A minor noble from Provence, intelligent and cultivated, he was politically inept and personally charmless. He was also powerless. The King's brother, Monsieur, exerted a nefarious influence from the Pavillon de Marsan next to the Tuileries where he resided, and which became a symbol of the coterie of diehard former émigrés who wanted to turn the clock back, repossess their lands, and extirpate all those who had taken part in the Revolution or held office under Napoleon.

The King was not strong enough, even if he had really wished it, to bring Frenchmen together and heal the wounds of the past twenty-five years. These were in evidence before his very eyes, at court, where virtually every regime and faction that had held power in France since 1789 was represented. The old aristocracy and particularly the returned émigrés went out of their way to ostracise, ridicule and insult those who had come to the fore since 1789, and the women were the worst. 'They would make charming jokes about their ways, their names, their manners and their dress,' records a lady belonging to the old aristocracy. 'If they wore diamonds, those around them would say that they came from the chalices and ciboriums of the churches of Spain and Italy.' Such behaviour at court set the tone. Not only returning émigrés and wronged former servants of the *ancien régime*, but all those who had been out of favour under Napoleon for one reason or another and had scores to settle picked it up.[22]

The new regime's treatment of the military was particularly wrong-headed as well as unjust. The appointment as Minister of War of the despised General Dupont, who had capitulated to the British at Bailén in 1808, was one of many public insults to the army. Marshal Davout, the most distinguished and respectable of Napoleon's lieutenants, was exiled from Paris. The inevitable redundancies resulting from the reduction of the size of the army were bound to be unpopular. That the Imperial Guard and those who had distinguished themselves over the past decades were specifically targeted only made things worse. Heroes were insulted and cast aside while émigrés in their seventies who had been junior officers in 1789 were given high ranks commensurate with the seniority they would have achieved if they had served in the intervening twenty-five years. As well as turning most of the active men of France against the new regime, this deprived it of an effective army. The institution of a new royal guard and of aristocratic Compagnies Rouges of the King's household could not make up for this, and the throne was left all but defenceless.

The discontent of the cashiered officers was shared by those in service, and plots were hatched to overthrow the regime and bring back Napoleon. Signs of trouble were visible everywhere, but Paris seemed calm enough during the first months of 1815, and it was easy to ignore them. As recently as 4 December 1814 Louis XVIII had dismissed rumours of plots against him as alarmist and assured Talleyrand that 'My sleep is as tranquil as in my youth.' He was not alone in his complacency.[23]

'Everyone was dancing!' recalled the duchesse de Maillé. 'It is of course true that people always danced in Paris: those who were not having their heads cut off in 1793 danced, those who were not being killed on the battlefield during the Empire danced, and as nobody was being killed during the Restoration, everybody danced.'[24]

28

~∽o੮~

The Hundred Days

Napoleon came ashore on the beach of Golfe Juan at 5 o'clock on the afternoon of 1 March. A tent was pitched for him in a clearing surrounded by olive groves and he sat down by a bivouac fire while General Cambronne rode over to nearby Cannes with a small detachment to procure horses and victuals. Cambronne was rebuffed and returned empty-handed, so Napoleon decided to move as fast as he could directly on to Grenoble.

Over the next two days his small force made its way with difficulty along rutted roads and mountain tracks, their Emperor often dismounting to scramble up the steep inclines, falling several times, watched from behind rocks and stone walls by suspicious peasants. On 4 March, at Digne, he addressed a small crowd that gathered in the square, and was cheered. The following day at Sisteron and then Gap he met with muted enthusiasm. At Laffrey on 7 March he found his road barred by a battalion of the 5th of the Line. Napoleon rode out in front of his own column and, a pistol-shot away from the ranks of infantry drawn up across the road with their muskets at the ready, he dismounted and walked forward. 'Soldiers of the 5th of the Line, look at me,' he shouted. 'If there is one among you who would shoot his General, his Emperor, let him do it; here I am!' The front rank lowered its muskets, and then a cheer went up as the men surged forward to surround their former commander. That night, at

455

9 o'clock, he entered Grenoble in triumph. General Labedoyère and the troops that had been deployed to apprehend him also rallied to his side.[1]

The next day he entered Lyon amid delirious manifestations of joy and took up his quarters in rooms vacated that morning by Monsieur, who had been sent out by Louis XVIII to oversee his defeat and capture. The local authorities, civil and military, and the population as a whole made it abundantly clear to Napoleon that his reading of the situation had been right, and that his gamble had been justified.

He continued his march through Villefranche, Mâcon, Tournus, Châlons and Autun. At Avallon on 16 March, two more regiments sent out against him went over to his side. At Auxerre two days later Marshal Ney, who had been despatched at the head of a large force and had promised to Louis XVIII that he would bring the ogre back in a cage, presented himself humbly before the Emperor and was warmly embraced.

On the morning of 20 March Napoleon drove into the Cour du Cheval Blanc of the château of Fontainebleau, where he had bidden a tearful farewell to his troops exactly eleven months before. He left Fontainebleau at 2 o'clock that afternoon for Paris. Along the road the 1st, 4th and 6th Chasseurs à Cheval and the 6th Lancers presented arms to him, and at half past ten that night his carriage rolled under the arch of the Carrousel and up to the Tuileries.

As the crowd gathering outside hailed its Emperor, the erstwhile Préfet of the palace, Saint-Didier, marched in at the head of the imperial household. 'Lackeys, officers of the table, cooks, kitchen boys, each of whom had unearthed his old livery, triumphantly took possession of the disordered apartments, the unmade beds, the still smoking stoves, and chased out with their brooms and their spits what was left of the royal household,' in the words of one contemporary.[2]

Louis XVIII had left the palace in the early hours of that very morning. 'I hope that France will no longer have need of your swords,' he had declared to Napoleon's marshals when they rallied to him less than a year before, expressing the hope that they would become the pillars of his throne, 'but, by God! Gentlemen, if the need to draw them should arise once more, I will, gout-ridden as I am, march at your side!' But in the event he had cowered in the Tuileries, sending off one force after another, handing out cash to the troops in an attempt to buy their loyalty.[3]

On 18 March, when Napoleon was nearing Paris, the King sent a trusted valet off with the crown jewels and four million francs in gold, with instructions to make for Lille and then England. When it became clear that Paris could not be held, some of his advisers suggested he fall back on royalist Bordeaux or the Vendée where he could rally the people to his cause. But he was afraid of falling into Napoleon's hands.

Just after midnight on the morning of 20 March he left the Tuileries by a back staircase. His carriage trundled out of Paris in the pouring rain, making for England. His household troops, the Maison Militaire, trudged half-heartedly after him through the mud of Picardy, dwindling with every step as deserters peeled away to join Napoleon. Fearing to remain in France a moment longer, Louis crossed into Belgium at the nearest point instead of making for Calais. He wanted to take ship at Ostend, but Monsieur persuaded him to pause at Ghent. In doing so, he managed to rescue from the ignominious débâcle a shred of dignity and hope for the future.

Napoleon's resumption of power had been seamless. The morning after his return to the Tuileries, the entire imperial court, headed by the former Queens of Spain and Holland and the wives of the marshals, gathered in the throne room to greet him. 'Fleurs-de-lys had banished the bees everywhere, yet looking at the immense carpet of the throne room in which they waited, one of these ladies noticed that one of the fleurs-de-lys had become detached,' writes General de Lavalette. 'She pulled it off, to reveal a bee underneath. All these ladies then set to work, and in the space of less than half an hour, to the bursts of merriment of the entire assembly, the carpet became imperial once more.'[4]

When he called at the Tuileries that evening, Lavalette found Napoleon in his old uniform surrounded by ministers, and for a moment thought himself ten years back in time. 'The subject and the tone of the conversation, the presence of all those persons who had worked under him for so long, contributed to efface entirely from my memory both the Bourbons and their reign of nearly a year.' And this despite the busts of the royal family still adorning the room.[5]

Unlike the Bourbons, Napoleon had learnt a great deal from the events of the past two years, and he was not about to repeat their mistakes. He did not attempt to resume his absolutist rule, and instead sought strength and political legitimacy in the Revolutionary tradition. As soon as he had reached Lyon, he dissolved the Chambers of Peers and Deputies, abolished 'feudal titles', expelled a few returned émigrés and sequestrated lands they had recovered. He also issued a decree summoning the representatives of the entire nation to come to Paris in May, in a repeat of the National Federation of 1790. He couched his statements in rhetoric about 'nobles and priests', and even talked of stringing them up from lamp-posts.[6]

Napoleon hoped to install a constitutional system that would marry the best traditions of the Revolution to a liberal monarchy. One of the first things he did was to summon the political thinker Benjamin Constant in order to enlist his support. Constant did not like Napoleon. He nevertheless believed that in his present mood he represented the best chance of providing France with a favourable form of government. Another whom Napoleon needed to have at his side was the man who would have taken Talleyrand's role in March 1814 if he had been in Paris at the time – Joseph Fouché, duc d'Otrante.[7]

It is difficult in the space of a few lines to give an adequate idea of this extraordinary product of the Oratorian Order's spiritual education who went on to join virtually every faction in the course of the French Revolution, always one step ahead, ruthlessly repressing and putting to death former colleagues and friends as he went. He helped the rise to power of General Bonaparte, whose chief of police he became, and was rewarded by the Emperor Napoleon with the duchy of Otranto in Italy. He remained chief of police until 1810, when he was replaced by Savary following the discovery of his dealings with the exiled Bourbons.

Always looking for the next regime in his determination to remain at the helm, Fouché had opened communications with them when he saw Napoleon's star begin to wane. In 1813 Napoleon had sent him to take over as Governor of Illyria and thence to Naples, mainly in order to keep him out of Paris at such a critical time. Fouché was aware of this, and watched helplessly from afar as the empire crumbled. He raced to Paris as soon as he could, but he was too late, and Talleyrand had assumed control of the situation.

In spite of his Revolutionary past and the taint of having voted for the death of Louis XVI, Fouché managed to gain favour with Monsieur and a position of influence. But he did not believe the Bourbon regime would last, and he plotted with General Drouet d'Erlon to raise the garrison of Lille for Napoleon in the event of a comeback by the Emperor. His ultimate wish was to provide France with a regime which would be capable of preserving some of the legacy of the Revolutionary and Napoleonic periods, and his preferred option was to bring about a regency for the King of Rome in which he could hold the reins of power. That was why he wrote to Napoleon advising him to exchange his realm of Elba for private exile in the United States – with Napoleon out of the way across the Atlantic, the allies might be more amenable to the idea of a regency for his son.[8]

When Fouché heard of Napoleon's landing at Antibes he activated the d'Erlon conspiracy, but this misfired. At the same time he was asked by Louis XVIII to enter the government. He stalled for as long as he could, and was saved from having to commit himself to the crumbling Bourbon cause by Napoleon's entry into Paris. Napoleon did not trust him, but, just like Louis XVIII, he needed him. He made him chief of police again, as only he could keep republican elements under control. Fouché played along. 'Well, here he is again,' he commented to a colleague about Napoleon's return. 'It's not him we wanted, but one cannot remove him like a pawn from a chessboard. We shall see what we can do to keep him.'[9]

Napoleon did all he could to represent his return to power as an internal French matter, and therefore of no concern to other European powers. From Lyon he wrote to Marie-Louise, requesting that she join him with their son. As his Foreign Minister he appointed the universally respected Caulaincourt, who wrote to Metternich with assurances of France's peaceful intentions. Napoleon proclaimed his acceptance of the terms of the Treaty of Paris, and wrote to Alexander assuring him that he would abide by it. At his behest Queen Hortense wrote to the Tsar to persuade him to accept the situation. In an attempt to endear himself to Britain, he abolished the slave trade outright.[10]

While serving Napoleon as chief of police, Fouché also supplemented Caulaincourt as a kind of unofficial Foreign Minister. He sent an old republican friend of La Harpe to Switzerland with a letter for Alexander, in which Napoleon declared his peaceful intentions and his readiness to accept any arrangement acceptable to the allies. He also opened up channels of communication with Metternich.

Metternich was unnerved by the developments, and anxious not to be caught out. Should Napoleon manage to strike a deal with one of the allies, he was determined to be in on it. He sent a letter to Fouché, written in invisible ink and transmitted by an employee of the Viennese bank of Arnstein & Eskeles on routine business in Paris. But Napoleon's spies spotted him delivering the letter. Napoleon sent his own man to meet Metternich's agent, in Bâle. The negotiation ended in inconclusive verbiage, as Metternich did not wish to commit himself.[11]

While he worked with energy at building up an effective army, Napoleon was hoping to avoid, or at least delay, conflict. He was counting on the universal war-weariness and the differences that had emerged between the allies ranged against him. In the hope of aggravating these, he ordered Caulaincourt to hand to the departing Russian chargé d'affaires in Paris, Pavel Butyagin, a copy of the

Anglo-Franco-Austrian treaty of 3 January against Russia and Prussia, which had duly been discovered in the archives of the French Foreign Ministry. He was to be disappointed.

Within hours of hearing the news of Napoleon's escape from Elba, and long before they had any idea of where he was headed, the plenipotentiaries of the Five began mustering their forces against him. By 12 March Wellington was able to report to Castlereagh that they planned to deploy three large corps: an Austrian one in Italy of 150,000 men; another composed of 200,000 Austrians, Bavarians, Badenese and Württembergers on the upper Rhine; and a third consisting of an Austrian contingent and the Dutch, British and Prussian troops in Flanders, of which he was to take command. A Russian army of 200,000 would assemble in their rear at Würzburg. Liverpool began transferring units from Ireland to Holland, to reinforce the 4,000 British troops there.

The Austrians grew nervous when it became clear that while all available Austrian troops would be concentrating on the borders of France, a vast Russian army would be massing in their rear. 'However great might be the danger threatening us from Paris, it is not as great as that menacing us from Warsaw,' one of the Austrian archdukes was overheard saying by a member of Alexander's entourage. Metternich took measures to limit the risk by making elaborate arrangements for the Russian troops to march along narrow corridors both well provisioned and policed.

Alexander volunteered to take overall command as 'Dictator', with Frederick William, Schwarzenberg and Wellington as advisers, but the latter protested vehemently, confiding to Castlereagh that he would 'prefer to carry a musket' than participate in such an arrangement. He took a far less exalted view of the Tsar than most of his contemporaries, and was less in thrall to the Russians, who, as he put it to his brother, 'have neither wealth nor commerce, nor anything that is desirable to anybody excepting 400,000 men, about whom they make more noise than they deserve'.[13]

As the allies argued over command it became apparent that they must create a basis for what was in effect a new coalition. On 16 March Castlereagh suggested to Wellington that the Treaty of Chaumont was the only basis on which they could safely proceed, and Wellington began working towards that end. But imposing unity on the allies was not easy.

On 17 March a council of war held at Wellington's lodgings turned into a contest between Austria and Prussia as each vied to take command of the contingents furnished by the smaller German states, in a repeat of their political scramble for Germany. Austria snatched Hesse-Darmstadt's 8,000 men from under Prussia's nose, and Prussia responded by demanding to command the contingents of all the north German states, bar Hanover. Wellington refused. Hardenberg tried to bribe him with a contingent of Prussian troops if he would let Blücher command all the others. General Knesebeck insisted that only if they were placed under Prussian command would the smaller contingents feel they were fighting for Germany. But at a meeting of the Five on 1 April Prussia was forced to relinquish command of the contingents of Brunswick, Oldenburg, Nassau and the Hanseatic cities, leaving it only with that of Hesse-Cassel and half that of Saxony.[14]

In a great show of patriotism, Bavaria and Württemberg offered twice the number of troops required from them, but Metternich was not fooled, realising that they were hoping to guarantee themselves a greater say in the peace settlement at the end of the campaign. When Bavaria was invited to accede, along with all the lesser states, to the renewed alliance between the four original allies, Wrede demurred, insisting that she would only sign her own alliances with the allies, as a principal, not as one of the acceding minor powers. After much wrangling, all the Kings were allowed to sign full separate treaties. There was also the question of money.[15]

While he bragged to Talleyrand that he would himself face Napoleon in battle, Alexander also flatly announced to Wellington that he could not make a move until British cash began to flow, and the plenipotentiaries of all the other powers which had volunteered troops took the same line. Wellington assured them that money would be found, and set about haggling with his government in London, which finally agreed to pay up to £5 million and another £2 million in lieu of its share of 150,000 extra men.[16]

At this stage the allies still assumed that Louis XVIII would manage to contain the problem on his own. It seemed inconceivable that a man with barely a thousand soldiers could take over a kingdom with an army of 150,000 men at its disposal. But the man was Napoleon, and every one of the people sitting around the tables in Vienna, with the exception of Wellington and those of the British delegation who had not spent any time on the Continent in his heyday, had at one time or another known what it was to be gripped by the terror of his approach.

They had ample opportunity to pray to the Almighty to be delivered of the evil, as Easter was upon them. On 23 March, Maundy Thursday, the entire court assembled in the great hall in which balls were normally held, for the traditional ritual enacting Christ's washing of his disciples' feet. Two long tables set with twelve places each, at which twelve Viennese paupers of each sex were seated, had been set up on two raised platforms. The Emperor and Empress made their entrance, attended by the archdukes and archduchesses and followed by a detachment of the Hungarian noble guard. They then proceeded to serve the paupers a three-course dinner, waiting on them like servants. 'The tables were then removed, and the Empress and her daughters the Archduchesses, dressed in black, with pages bearing their trains, approached,' records an English traveller. 'Silver bowls were placed beneath the feet of the aged women. The Grand Chamberlain, in a humble posture, poured water upon the feet of each in succession, from a golden urn, and the Empress wiped them with a fine napkin she held in her hand. The Emperor performed the same ceremony on the feet of the men, and the rite concluded amidst the sounds of sacred music.' The rites of Easter continued the next day with the Stations of the Cross, and came to a climax on Easter

Sunday with a solemn Mass attended by all the sovereigns and ministers as well as the court. The ministers had briefly returned to practical matters on Holy Saturday to sign a treaty similar to that of Chaumont, but including France and the second-rank powers as well. It was a timely move.[17]

On Tuesday, 28 March, news reached Vienna that Napoleon was in Paris. That meant that they were, in some respects, back where they had been in 1813. Among the first reactions of some of the statesmen was the fear that all they had worked for for so long and achieved at the cost of so many hours of discussion and argument might be lost. From London, Castlereagh wrote to Wellington suggesting that they sign a treaty as soon as possible enshrining at least that which had been agreed so far, so as to place it 'out of the reach of doubt'.

His letter crossed one from Wellington which assured him that the prevailing feeling in Vienna was 'a determination to unite their efforts to support the system established by the peace of Paris' and that all were conscious of the importance of the situation. 'All are desirous of bringing to an early conclusion the business of the congress, in order that the whole and undivided attention and exertion of all may be directed against the common enemy [...] Upon the whole, I assure your Lordship that I am perfectly satisfied with the spirit which prevails here upon this occasion,' he concluded.[18]

Alexander and Francis conferred about the letters they had received from Napoleon and agreed not to reply to them. This was reassuring, as Russia and Austria were the two powers that might conceivably come to terms with a Napoleonic France. In another show of solidarity, the allies publicly brushed aside Napoleon's declaration to the effect that nobody had the right to choose a ruler for France but the French people with a riposte that certain requirements of international law transcended a nation's right to choose its ruler. It was the first time in international affairs that a group of states effectively arrogated the right to intervene in the internal affairs of another country in the name of the greater good of Europe.[19]

When Butyagin reached Vienna and, on 8 April, handed Alexander the copy of the treaty of alliance against him that Caulaincourt had given him, the Tsar, who had suspected its existence for some time, took it calmly. He brandished it before Metternich in public, only to declare that he never wished to hear it referred to again. He cut short the King of Bavaria, who had come to proffer his excuses, saying that they must concentrate on defeating Napoleon. But both Nesselrode and Stein could see how angry he was.[20]

Alexander not only reproved the British for letting Napoleon escape, he also attempted to shift blame onto Metternich and Talleyrand by accusing them of having drawn out the congress unnecessarily. On one occasion he even declared that it was God's punishment for their having been quarrelling amongst themselves over trifles. The whole affair only served to confirm him in his conviction that he was a lone warrior for good surrounded by conniving moral pygmies.[21]

When Metternich had come to him with the news of Napoleon's escape, the two men found themselves alone together for the first time since their interview of 24 October 1814, and Alexander had taken the opportunity to declare that since they were both Christians they should forgive each other and embrace, which they did.[22]

To Louis XVIII, Alexander wrote that 'the first effect that this event has had on the sovereigns assembled at Vienna was to tighten the bonds to which Europe owes the peace and France the tranquillity which it was beginning to enjoy under its legitimate King'. He treated Talleyrand with greater cordiality than ever, and called to assure him that he had cast all their past disagreements out of his mind. 'The incident of Buonaparte's appearance in France, so disagreeable in other respects, will at least have that advantage that it will hasten the conclusion of affairs here,' Talleyrand wrote to Louis XVIII on 12 March. 'It has doubled the zeal and activity of everyone.' A couple of weeks later he reported that the work of the congress would probably be finished by mid-April.

There were only three major questions remaining to be settled: the indemnities that would convince Bavaria to hand the Tyrol back to

Austria, the German constitution and the question of what to do about Murat.[23]

The last of these now proceeded to settle itself, as Napoleon's escape from Elba had prompted Murat to act. His first move was to offer his services to the allies. The proposal was taken seriously, and Castlereagh, who had on 12 March written to Wellington suggesting they join with Austria in removing Murat from Naples, wrote less than two weeks later authorising him to sign an alliance with Murat if he thought the King of Naples was acting in good faith.[24]

But long before Wellington received the second of these letters, Murat had changed his mind and marched out at the head of his army. From Rimini on 30 March he issued a proclamation to the people of Italy that was not so much a gesture of support for Napoleon as a declaration of war on Austria. 'Providence, at last, calls you to freedom,' it ran. 'One cry can be heard from the Alps to the gorges of Scylla, and that cry is: *the independence of Italy*. Eighty thousand Neapolitans, led by their brave King, have left their home to liberate you . . .'[25]

'Murat must be destroyed early, or he will hang heavily upon us,' an alarmed Wellington wrote on 8 May from Brussels, where he had made his headquarters. He need not have worried, as Castlereagh had, quite illegally, declared war on Murat, and Metternich had already sprung into action. Murat was declared an outlaw, like Napoleon, and the Austrian forces in Italy moved quickly. They defeated him without much trouble at Tolentino and his vaudeville army melted away. Murat himself took ship for France to offer his services to Napoleon, and Ferdinand IV returned from Sicily to resume his throne. The first thing he did was to sign, on 29 April, a convention with Austria pledging himself, in return for full military assistance, 'to allow no change which could not be reconciled with the ancient monarchical institutions, or with the principles adopted by His Imperial Majesty [Francis] for the internal government of his Italian provinces'. Metternich had managed to ensure that, although a Bourbon had returned to the Italian mainland, he was to be entirely beholden to and controlled by Austria.[26]

The arrangement of the rest of Italy now fell into place. Parma was granted to Marie-Louise as stipulated in the Treaty of Fontainebleau, but only for her lifetime. Her son would receive an establishment in Austria. On her death, the three duchies would pass to Maria Luisa of Spain, erstwhile Queen of Etruria, and by descent to her children. In the interim, the Queen of Etruria would have the former republic of Lucca, which would, when she progressed to Parma, be added to Tuscany, which was awarded to Archduke Ferdinand. Modena went to Archduke Francis. The Pope was given back the Legations (although Austria retained the right to garrison Ravenna), the Marches, previously occupied by Murat, as well as the duchies of Pontecorvo and Benevento – for supposedly facilitating which Talleyrand would be richly rewarded.

At first, it looked as though the resolution of the German question would also be expedited as a consequence of Napoleon's reappearance on the scene and the sense of renewed solidarity it engendered. But it was not to be, mainly on account of Bavaria, which was still locked in dispute with Austria over compensation. In fact, Bavaria sought to exploit the crisis, and Marshal Wrede began to make increased demands for the compensation she was to receive for retroceding Salzburg and the Tyrol. He demanded more of Hanau, Isenburg and Fulda; and territory from Württemberg, from Hesse-Darmstadt and from Baden. The Bavarians had adopted the technique previously used by the Prussians, of 'discounting' mediatised souls – that is to say not counting those inhabitants of a given area who were subjects of a local semi-autonomous lord, on the grounds that they did not represent the same taxable potential as the others. This meant that claims could be inflated beyond measure. They had, in Talleyrand's words, earned themselves the title of 'Prussians of the south' by their greed and obstinacy.[27]

Metternich was so desperate by this stage that although the negotiations were supposedly between Austria and Bavaria alone, he laid the whole matter before the meeting of the Five on 3 April. The first thing to be settled was that Mainz was to go to Hesse-Darmstadt, while the fortress was to be a federal stronghold, garrisoned by troops drawn from the two Hesses, Nassau and Prussia, under Prussian command. After a heated discussion Archduke Charles was placed in command of the combined garrison. Furious at having definitively lost Mainz, the Bavarians upped their demands to include Mannheim and Heidelberg, but after a forceful intervention by Alexander on 5 April it was agreed that Bavaria would obtain those areas on the death of their ruler, who was the last of his line.

If this resolved the fate of Mainz it did nothing to solve the underlying problem, and the conflicting claims of Bavaria, Baden and the two Hesses on the banks of the upper Rhine remained unresolved. Meanwhile Bavaria was still in occupation of Salzburg and the Tyrol, which should have reverted to Austria. Metternich's options for finding land with which to indemnify Bavaria were shrinking fast. In January he had been persuaded by Castlereagh to give Prussia some territory to the south of the Moselle which he had earmarked for Bavaria. Ever more arcane combinations of swaps were required in order to induce minor rulers to give up the necessary territory. The Landgrave of Hesse-Homburg was heard to complain that he had been given 'a district in China' when he was awarded the faraway region of Meisenheim am Glan. And as the pool of available land shrank, all those who had been left out, and particularly those who had been promised something by Alexander, gathered round expectantly.

Alexander had given Prince Eugène his word that he would find him a fief somewhere in Europe, and was determined to stand by his promise. He had tried to find him one in Italy, but Metternich's prevarication and Talleyrand's opposition had prevented that. He now sought to find him one in Germany. This outraged many. Humboldt declared that if Prince Eugène were given a principality in Germany, he would leave the congress. But Alexander was adamant that he would not leave Vienna without awarding him something. Others whom he had promised to help were the Duke of Saxe-Coburg, his brother-in-law the Duke of Saxe-Weimar and his cousin the Duke of Oldenburg.[28]

Alexander pressed Münster to cede some border areas of Hanover to Oldenburg, for which he promised to obtain from Prussia an equivalent that could be added to Hanover on the other side, for which Prussia in turn would be compensated with some strips of territory along the Rhine formerly belonging to Oldenburg. This initiated a new bout of haggling and soul-counting.[29]

Having recovered from their shock at Napoleon's escape, the various interested parties had shifted attention back to their former concerns and carried on much as before, with the difference that now they seemed to be positioning themselves for a fresh contest. Hardenberg had been drawing out the negotiations for some time now, employing a variety of tricks. Clancarty complained to Castlereagh that he was tardy in delivering documents, and showed maps of proposed border settlements to him late at night, when it was difficult to distinguish the colours on the shaded areas. The Prussians also kept trying to 'crib' slices of French territory along the border. Hardenberg also began to stall on the question of wrapping all the agreements reached into a single treaty and signing it as soon as possible.[30]

All this terrified Talleyrand, who detected in it a desire to keep questions open in the hope that a new war would require a new peace. And a new peace would not be as favourable to France as the Treaty of Paris. It was clear to him that the knives were out for a fresh carve-up.[31]

~~~◦~~~

The Road to Waterloo

Wellington was also anxious. He had left Vienna on 29 March, the day after news had come that Napoleon had reached Paris, leaving Cathcart to take over as Britain's plenipotentiary at the congress. He meant to take command of the allied contingents in the Netherlands, but on arrival in Brussels, which he had chosen as his headquarters, he discovered that there were hardly any troops there. He worked hard over the next weeks, badgering Liverpool to send him more and trying to knock into shape those already there. They were mostly militia units and many of the men had never seen active service of any kind. 'I have got a detestable army, very weak and ill equipped, and a very inexperienced staff,' he complained to Stewart at the beginning of May.[1]

And he was not greatly reassured by his allies. The Dutch troops under his command showed little appetite for war, while the Prussians under Blücher, who was supposed to act in close support, were a problem in themselves. As they marched through the Netherlands they took everything they required in victuals, horses and equipment, saying that the British would settle the bill, despite their having been paid a generous subsidy by Britain. Their behaviour and treatment of the local population also left much to be desired.

Their conduct towards the Saxon contingent assigned to Blücher's command was so insulting that the Saxons mutinied and attacked the

Prussian headquarters. Blücher, who had been forced to flee by the back door with Gneisenau, took harsh reprisals, and Saxon soldiers were executed by Prussian firing squads. It was hardly a promising start to a combined campaign against the greatest general in Europe.[2]

From Wellington's perspective, it did not look as though the alliance was capable of delivering concerted action, and a real sense of threat is evident in his letters. He was worried that the Austrians in Italy would get bogged down fighting Murat, while Sardinia did not appear to be doing anything to threaten or even check France in the south. Schwarzenberg, who was supposed to cross the Rhine between Strasbourg and Bâle, and make for Langres at the head of 150,000 Austrians, Bavarians, Württembergers and other Germans, did not appear to be in any hurry to move.

'With the force which is assembling in all quarters, it appears to me impossible that with common prudence and arrangement, we should fail in our military operations,' Wellington wrote to Metternich from Brussels on 20 May. But he felt exposed, as it was most likely that Napoleon would attempt to defeat each of the allied corps separately, and would probably start with him. He was alive to the psychological importance of the forthcoming contest. 'The only real misfortune that could affect us in the present circumstances would be a setback, even temporary, to any of the major allied units,' he wrote to the duc de Berry.[3]

Wellington also found himself in a pivotal position politically, since Louis XVIII had established himself with his entourage in nearby Ghent. In theory the King of France was, following France's accession to the renewed Treaty of Chaumont, one of the allies, but the situation was far from clear-cut. 'We are *indivisible* as to war against [*Napoleon*],' Stewart wrote to Lord Burghersh from Vienna on 15 April. 'But as to the restoration of the King great intrigue exists. The Emperor of Russia hates all the Bourbons, and is convinced they cannot reign in France. A strong party exists for the Duke of Orleans . . . In short, I see much devilment ahead.'[4]

The poor show put on by Louis XVIII and his supporters could not fail to open up the whole question once again, so much so that Castlereagh advised against bringing any Swedish troops into play lest it revive Bernadotte's plans. But not even Alexander was thinking of Bernadotte any more.[5]

Alexander had been personally wounded by the treatment he had received at the hands of Louis XVIII, and the French King had done nothing since to assuage his hurt pride. In a long conversation with Cathcart at the beginning of May the Tsar explained that he doubted whether the Bourbons were capable of holding on to their throne. He declared that he was against leaving Napoleon in place in any guise, and that he no longer entertained the idea of replacing him with Bernadotte or any of the marshals. But while he would not let his personal feelings stand in the way of a second restoration, he considered the duc d'Orléans the best candidate for the throne. Many, both inside France and outside it, were of the same mind, and Orléans neither encouraged nor discouraged them. In Château-briand's felicitous phrase, he 'did not conspire in fact, but by consent'.[6]

The position of the British government was, as it had been in 1814, that the Bourbons represented the best prospect of peace and stability, but that it would be wrong and unwise to support them openly. A significant section of British public opinion was opposed to becoming involved in another conflict, and if the government were to try to take the country to war in the name of restoring the Bourbons, it would be playing into their hands. So while Castlereagh sent Louis XVIII money and despatched an envoy to his headquarters at Ghent, he affected a lack of interest in the matter. The motion brought in the Commons against going to war was duly defeated.[7]

Castlereagh urged Wellington to restrain the allies from issuing any premature declaration 'till the character of the contest is more precisely established; for although interference on the part of the great Powers of Europe would, in the judgment of His Majesty's government, be both wise and necessary if sustained by an adequate national support, yet, consistent with the principles on which the Allies have hitherto acted, it would be a very different question to march into

France for the purpose of restoring a Sovereign who had been betrayed and abandoned by his own troops and subjects'.[8]

Hardenberg was of the same view, and in his instructions to Count Goltz, the Prussian minister at the court of Louis XVIII, he warned that 'despite the desire of the allied powers to see them re-established on the throne of their ancestors, it would be dangerous to try and explain this in a too precise manner in the present crisis'. This position was entirely illogical, as both their common proclamation of 13 March declaring Napoleon to be an outlaw and the renewed Treaty of Chaumont obliged the allies to come to the aid of Louis XVIII.[9]

Wellington was by now in touch with Fouché, who had approached him secretly with the aim of sounding out whether Britain would be inclined to accept Napoleon under any conditions, and at the same time in order to guarantee himself asylum in England if he needed to flee Napoleon's vengeance. Fouché had also established contact with Talleyrand, Metternich and indirectly Alexander. Once he was convinced that the allies would never accept a regency and that only Alexander was in favour of Orléans, he opened secret negotiations with Louis XVIII in Ghent. He had become the man of the moment, and would play much the same role as Talleyrand had a year earlier.[10]

Talleyrand was in something of a predicament. His loyalty to Louis XVIII was unshaken. But he feared that once Napoleon was defeated the King would be in no position to stand up to the royalist *ultras*, who would impose a reactionary government and unleash a wave of reprisal across the country, something with which Talleyrand not only did not wish to be associated but also feared personally. If Louis could not be saved from these people, then Talleyrand might have to look elsewhere for a ruler of France. Nor did he wish to find himself on the wrong side if Metternich and Francis were to convince Alexander to make some kind of deal with Napoleon on a regency for his son the King of Rome, which he could not rule out.

Talleyrand's position in the Austrian capital was unenviable. When Louis XVIII left Paris, the institutions of government ceased to function and his source of finance dried up. Napoleon confiscated all his property in France, which meant that he could not draw on that or even raise a loan against it. He found himself with no money, and began letting staff go. Wellington came to the rescue and advanced him £10,000.

The Duchess of Courland had fled from Paris at the approach of Napoleon and now turned up in Vienna, where she moved in with Talleyrand. Whether he found it amusing to have his mistress and ex-mistress, mother and daughter, under the same roof is doubtful, particularly as by now Dorothée was in the throes of her affair with Clam-Martinitz. To complicate matters, his old friend Casimir de Montrond turned up in Vienna and also moved into Talleyrand's lodgings.

Through secret channels Talleyrand received an offer from Napoleon to restore his property if he agreed to work in his interest in brokering a peace. Another envoy from Napoleon, whose principal mission was an attempt to bribe Metternich, delivered a threat to Talleyrand that he would be tried for treason if he did not cooperate.

Not surprisingly, Talleyrand was the focus of universal suspicion. Although the order of the forces ranged against him was such that Napoleon's chances of survival were slim, residual fear of him was so great that a degree of paranoia gripped Vienna. Every new arrival was seen as a spy, and everyone with a French connection as a potential plotter. This was very much in evidence in the treatment of Marie-Louise and her entourage. As soon as Napoleon's escape from Elba was known, Metternich made her sign a letter to her father the Emperor to the effect that she never wished to go back to Napoleon or to France. His aim was to have a document to show nervous allies who might suspect Austria of being open to proposition by Napoleon. He also made her change her liveries and remove the French imperial arms from her carriages.

Napoleon's letters to Marie-Louise were intercepted and read by Francis and Metternich, who dictated her replies, which were tender but evasive, complaining of the difficulties of writing. What her real feelings were is hard to assess, as she appeared to those around her to be equally anxious about Napoleon's safety and her own prospects of obtaining Parma. Every few days she was summoned to Vienna for an interview with her father as though she were intending to flee, and a plot for her escape was actually invented.

The young Anatole de Montesquiou-Fézensac, an erstwhile aide-de-camp to Napoleon, arrived in Vienna from Paris to visit his mother, who was one of Marie-Louise's ladies of the bedchamber and the governess of the King of Rome. Metternich had been looking for an excuse to get rid of Madame de Montesquiou. She was adored by her charge, who always referred to her as '*Maman Quiou-quiou*', and was deemed to be an unnecessarily patriotic French influence on the boy.

Her son's arrival provided the perfect pretext. Marie-Louise was summoned to the Hofburg and told to bring the King of Rome, who would henceforth be lodged under the eyes of the Emperor, and to dismiss Madame de Montesquiou. The reason given was that a plot had been discovered to kidnap her and her son and to take them to Paris, and the Montesquious, mother and son, were implicated. They were ordered to leave, but this order was countermanded, and they were forced to stay in Vienna where they could be kept under surveillance.[11]

News of this 'plot' flew round Vienna, greatly facilitating Hager's task of tightening security. 'The level of surveillance became unbearably irksome,' according to Napoleon's former secretary Méneval, currently in Marie-Louise's entourage. 'The police would home in on one like wasps, follow one everywhere, managing to gain entrance into one's very home under a million pretexts.' Prince Eugène, who had considered himself beyond suspicion given his close ties with the Tsar and the other principal players, was also unpleasantly surprised to discover that the number of spies around him had been doubled.[12]

He was not the only one of the Bonaparte family who was being watched as though they were highly dangerous. Jérôme, ex-King of Westphalia, was being followed by police, while his wife, who now went under the name of Countess Hartz, was the object of attempts by her father the King of Württemberg to force her to come back to Stuttgart, where she could be cut off from her Napoleonic entourage. 'Nothing will ever be able to separate me from the interests of Jérôme, or of those of the family which I am proud to belong to,' she wrote to her sister-in-law Elisa, now going under the name of Countess Compignano, but she had to take precautions against being kidnapped.[13]

In one report Hager explained to Francis – and one can almost hear the complaint in his tone – that one of his agents had picked up in Chernyshev's quarters a letter written in invisible ink addressed to a Miss Itzstein in Frankfurt, but actually from Alexander to Louise Bethmann. 'In accordance with the orders issued by Your Majesty, the Ministry of Foreign Affairs decided not to submit this letter to chemical manipulation, and to allow it to be sent after replacing it. As this operation and consultation had taken some time, Chernyshev noticed the disappearance of the letter, and demanded it back from his Russian valet, whom he gave a sound hiding to. The latter, knowing nothing of the seizure of the letter, could do nothing, and our agent was adroit enough when he came back from *the Manipulation* to slip the letter between the desk and another piece of furniture, where it was naturally found in the course of the search Chernyshev ordered to be carried out under his own eyes.'[14]

Much of the surveillance was as prurient as ever, and hard to reconcile with any possible threat from France. Agents reported regularly on the amorous escapades of the Grand Duke of Baden and his partner in dalliance the Prince of Hesse-Darmstadt. Their merry dinners with girls at the lodgings of the Grand Duke's equerry were now even more frequent, in the absence of balls and other entertainments. As they intended to leave soon, they were making the most of their last days, and the Prince was taking intensive tender leave of 'Countess Waffenberg'. He finally left on 12 April, having spent his last night in her arms. The Grand Duke, who had meant to leave on the eleventh, changed his mind and stayed on for another month, possibly because he had discovered a new 'flame' in the person of Josepha Kronsteiner, the daughter of a lemon and orange seller.[15]

Police reports also inform that Count Löwenhielm was paying assiduous court to his Frau Werzer, while Frederick Lamb had apparently resumed his former liaison with Wilhelmina, and was spending the nights at her apartment. Across the landing, her arch-enemy was rejoicing in the arms of the Crown Prince of Württemberg, who appears to have forgotten that he was courting the Grand Duchess Catherine and had fallen for the charms of la Bagration. When he left Vienna on 11 April, she accompanied him in his carriage some fifteen miles, and the adieus were so tender according to the police informer that he thought they might result in a third bastard for the Princess. He noted that she was distraught when she drove back into the city.

She certainly had reason to be. She had finally run out of money, and her cook had been digging into his own pocket to keep her table going. He too had now run out of money, and declared that he could not cook another dinner until she paid him. With her rich patrons departing, she was in peril of ending up penniless. She might have been cheered had she known that Wilhelmina was also feeling the pinch and selling off some of her jewellery.[16]

'We are completing the sad business of the congress which, by its results, is the most mean-spirited piece of work ever seen,' Dalberg wrote to his wife on 11 April. His jaded tone may have had something to do with the '*maladie galante*' which, according to reports reaching the police, he was suffering from. But while the work went on relentlessly, matters were being settled in increasingly random ways, or simply dismissed after a nod of acknowledgement. That was certainly the case on 14 April, when the congress paused to consider the petition of Carl Bertuch on the protection of literary copyright.[17]

A total lack of principle was also manifest in the way the Swiss question was dealt with. It had assumed some urgency, as it was feared Napoleon might try to rally parts of Switzerland to his cause or find some way of exploiting its internal differences and turn it against the allies. The Swiss Committee's resolutions were hastily approved by the Eight on 20 March. Two days later all the deputies of the various cantons and other Swiss interests listened as Metternich read out the decisions reached. The package was then referred for ratification to the Swiss Diet. Such peremptory treatment was the norm.

Having solemnly proclaimed the desirability of Switzerland's neutrality, the powers proceeded, at the beginning of May, to badger the Confederation to join the alliance against Napoleon. Metternich sent officers described as 'observers' to Switzerland to keep an eye on the situation, and finally, in June, the allies demanded that their troops be allowed to march through its territory, which the Swiss Diet could not readily refuse.

Napoleon's return had also made it imperative to agree a political constitution for Germany before the coalition went to war. The passions dividing Germany were such that anything might happen in the event of a reversal of fortunes. Only on 27 April Prince Wilhelm von Sayn-Wittgenstein led a large array of Standesherren in an appeal to Frederick William which was an attempt to put Prussia in the position of protector of Germany – and therefore of all the minor princes, including those in Bavaria, Württemberg and Baden. Nobody doubted that the rulers of those three states, and indeed some of their lesser colleagues, would, if forced to choose, prefer to enter into alliance with Napoleon rather than submit to any such restriction of their prerogatives.[18]

Hardenberg and Humboldt were as alarmed by this initiative as Metternich, and by a combination of bullying and sleight of hand the latter managed to wrest a series of concessions from them, and agreement on the final form of the constitution was reached by mid-May. All questions that might provoke discussion but were not essential were set aside in the rush to attain this consensus, among them Prussia's attempt to include a clause governing the future status of the Catholic Church in Germany.

The long-awaited German Congress met on 23 May. It was little more than an expanded German Committee, with Austria, Prussia, Hanover, Württemberg (which did not deign to send a representative) and Bavaria joined by Saxony, Hesse-Darmstadt, Baden, a Danish plenipotentiary for Holstein and a Dutch one for Luxembourg, and the delegates of the minor princes and the four free cities.

This congress would hold ten sessions, but its role in shaping the German constitution was minimal. Metternich managed the first meeting with his usual skill, reading out the project he had agreed with Hardenberg, then handing out copies to all those present and telling them to reconvene three days later. The only effects the discussions of the German Congress were to have were purely negative ones, as in the case of the clause guaranteeing rights to the Jews, inserted at Humboldt's insistence. When Metternich began reading this out, the plenipotentiary of Bavaria, Count Rechberg, started to laugh out loud, and the others followed suit. Metternich wanted to strike it out in order to facilitate the acceptance of the rest, but Humboldt fought tooth and claw to keep it. As a result the clause was amended to a pious hope and the issue was referred, like so many others, to the future German Diet, which was to meet at Frankfurt on 1 September.

The broadened session of 29 May brought together no fewer than thirty-seven representatives, and the result was a shouting match, with minor rulers demanding that they be categorised as 'sovereign', others quibbling over when the Bund should go to war and over what, and all of them protesting against the idea of a federal court. Metternich kept making concessions just to get agreement on points of principle, and more and more issues were referred to the future Diet for settlement. Even so, the plenipotentiary of Bavaria walked out of the session of 3 June, and a number of others registered their protests at the next, on 5 June. At the end of this, Metternich announced that the signing of the Final Act of the congress had been set for 9 June, and that they must agree a constitution by 8 June, so it could be included. It was an ultimatum, and it restored a semblance of order. After a few minor concessions, Bavaria agreed to return to the fold. So, at the last minute, did Württemberg, though its consent did not reach Vienna until the morning of 9 June.

The upshot of all this was the Federal Act, signed on 8 June, which set up a perpetual union of thirty-four sovereign princes and four free cities, to be governed by a Federal Diet sitting at Frankfurt. Austria was awarded the presidency of the Diet and of an inner council of seventeen, which comprised Austria, Prussia, Hanover, Bavaria, Saxony, Württemberg, Baden, Hesse-Cassel, Hesse-Darmstadt, Holstein, Luxembourg, a deputy of Saxe-Weimar and Saxe-Gotha, one of Brunswick and Nassau, one of Mecklemburg-Schwerin and Mecklemburg-Strelitz, one of Oldenburg, Anhalt and Schwarzburg, one of Hohenzollern, Lichtenstein, Reuss, Schaumburg-Lippe, Lippe and Waldeck, and one of the four free cities (Lübeck, Bremen, Hamburg and Frankfurt). The Diet had the theoretical power to declare and make war, raise an army and regulate all disputes between the component states, but as it had no executive to speak of and no federal court, it was in no position to do any of these things. It was no more than a skeleton constitution to be fleshed out when time permitted.

'It is thus that the hope of the people of Germany will be disappointed, for it is obvious that what has not been settled in Vienna will not be accomplished at Frankfort,' Münster reflected in a letter to the Prince Regent on 15 May. The Diet did not begin work till November 1816, and the recommended additional work on the constitution would not be completed until five years later.[19]

While Metternich and Hardenberg struggled to tie up the loose ends that might yet lead to the unravelling of the settlements they had reached in Germany, others began to make their farewells, pack up and leave. Tradesmen and creditors swarmed at the doors of those rumoured to be preparing to go, minor players in the congress waited on the sovereigns, who distributed orders and decorations, snuffboxes and other gifts.

Humboldt, who would receive at least seven jewelled snuff-boxes, suggested in a letter to his wife that he might unpick the stones and make up some jewellery for her, but she did not like the idea of wearing diamonds, and proposed they use the proceeds to pay off their debts. He was also given a minor order by Alexander, which he had no intention of ever wearing, but the diamonds were so small that it was hardly worth unpicking. At the same time he was overwhelmed when, on 4 June, an elderly deputy of the Jews of Prague came to him with three emerald and diamond rings as a token of thanks for all he had done on their behalf. Humboldt refused, so the Jew offered him 4,000 ducats in their place. This Humboldt refused too, but he later learnt, through Gentz, that he would be sent a silver dinner service instead. Gentz told him he should accept the gifts, as he himself happily did, but Humboldt declared that when one felt as passionately as he did about the issue of equal rights for Jews, one could not take money, and the two old friends quarrelled.[20]

The gifts handed out bore little relation to any actual service rendered, as the case of the King of Denmark demonstrates. Frederick VI left Vienna on 16 May 1815 in dejected mood, having failed to achieve anything. 'All the work that has been put in to furthering this most righteous cause has been in vain,' he complained. 'I wish all my efforts here had been equal to the task, but these are people who can be swayed only through fear, and I have no means of applying this.' Not only had Denmark come away from the congress territorially reduced; the King's attempts at rebuilding her shattered economy had fared little better. He had tried to obtain from Metternich some French ships captured in the Adriatic, he had tried to make Britain pay a consideration for having been able to exploit Denmark's West Indian colonies over the years, and he had even tried to sell her West African colonies, which had originated as slave emporia and were now redundant. All to no avail. Yet he gave snuff-boxes to all concerned, and lavish tips to the servants at the Hofburg who had waited on him. The cost of the Danish attendance at the congress, amounting to 460,000 thalers, was still being paid off in 1817. Frederick was nevertheless cheered by his subjects when he drove into Copenhagen on

1 June, and his reign, which lasted until his death in 1839, was remembered long afterwards as 'the good old days'. Only a very small part of the overall cost of his attendance at the congress, the pension of five hundred ducats a month he left to his mistress during his stay in Vienna, Caroline Petronelle Seufert, could be said to have been well spent. She lived on until 1873, when she was run over by a carriage on the streets of Vienna.[21]

Prince Leopold of Sicily gave his Viennese mistress, the daughter of a Frau Fisher who owned a wine shop, the sum of 10,000 florins in cash and settled a pension of five hundred florins a month on her. He also promised to revisit her. Frederick William, who gave the usual selection of gifts and orders, also tipped every servant of Julie Zichy's household, weeping copiously as he took his leave.[22]

There were no more balls, only *soirées*, dinners and smaller gatherings, and the visitors made the best of the fine summer weather to seize a few last carefree moments before they returned to the restrictions that governed their normal lives.

Stewart was now having an affair with Wilhelmina, at whose lodgings in the Palm Palace he was spending almost every night. 'They have chosen an inn near Laxenburg which they have transformed into a f—ing-shop,' reported one informant. He went on to say that since the departure of Castlereagh, the British plenipotentiary's house as well as Stewart's embassy in the Stahremberg Palace had been turned into 'a brothel and a pothouse' in which 'actresses from the suburbs and chambermaids' could be seen plying their skills, and disreputable types of various kinds joined in the gambling in Clancarty's office.[23]

Although he would stay on as ambassador for a while longer, Stewart too would be leaving with the Emperor Francis when the latter repaired to headquarters. In the interests of slimming down his establishment, he was trying to sell his pack of hounds, but could find no buyers, as they were good only for hunting foxes, which nobody did in Austria. Meanwhile he continued to amuse the inhabitants of Vienna with his eccentricities. On 11 May he was seen riding through the Graben evidently drunk, clutching a bunch of lily of the valley, with which his horse's head was liberally bedecked.

On 16 May Countess Molly Zichy and Countess Flora Wrbna gave a dinner for Alexander and a select few at Griefenstein on the Danube, twenty kilometres upstream from Vienna. The fun and games were so wild that the whole neighbourhood was talking about them for days. 'I love Gabrielle Auersperg so much that if I were not married I would certainly marry her,' Alexander was heard to exclaim.[24]

His wife had left already, on 8 March. On the morning of her departure Czartoryski had asked her to divorce Alexander and marry him. She had promised to give it her consideration, although her sense of duty called her to remain with her husband. Later the same day Alexander had made it clear to Czartoryski that he would never grant her a divorce.[25]

However crushed he might have felt, Czartoryski also had reason to be pleased. On 15 May Frederick William had issued a proclamation constituting his Polish lands into the grand duchy of Posen, with its own constitution and a Pole, Prince Antoni Radziwiłł, as Lieutenant. On 21 May Alexander formally announced the creation of a kingdom of Poland, and before leaving Vienna pledged to grant it a constitution enshrining all the old Polish freedoms, as well as new ones such as free education for all classes and extensive privileges for cities, emancipation of the Jews and enfranchisement of peasants. 'Strange soul,' Czartoryski mused, conceding Alexander 'greatness' but remarking that 'there is something in it that is small, low, limited'. The Tsar left Vienna on 25 May, making for headquarters at Heilbronn, followed, eventually, by most of the other players of the congress. Diplomacy was moving back to the battlefield.[26]

No one was more alarmed by this than Talleyrand, who realised that the Treaty of Paris and all his subsequent gains for France would probably be challenged under pressure from the military. His triumph in bringing France out of isolation and into the circle of the Five had turned to ashes with the reappearance of Napoleon. This had been compounded by personal sadness. On the day following the news of

Napoleon's escape, 8 March, he had set off, with Wellington and Metternich, for Pressburg to obtain the King of Saxony's acceptance of the partition of his kingdom. With befitting dignity, Frederick Augustus had refused. But that was not why Talleyrand was sad. He had taken the opportunity to visit Madame de Brionne, an old flame of his youth who had emigrated in 1789 and was now living in Pressburg. They had not seen each other since those days, but had corresponded and remained close. She was ill and close to death, and he was so moved by their meeting that he had taken a long walk on the banks of the Danube afterwards. Shortly after his return to Vienna, he heard of her death.

Nor was that his only cause for sadness. He was about to part with Dorothée, whom he had lost to Clam-Martinitz but whom he nevertheless adored having beside him, and he would soon be saying goodbye to her mother, whom he loved with an enduring affection and friendship. 'Adieu, I am leaving you with extreme sorrow,' he wrote to her, '. . . your memory, your tenderness will support me in my troubles. I love you with all my soul, and for the whole of the life that heaven still preserves for me. Adieu.' He was feeling ill and apprehensive of what the future held.[27]

No less apprehensive was Princess Bagration, who had made herself extremely unpopular in many quarters, and had even lost the favour of the Tsar. She was penniless and besieged by angry creditors. At the beginning of June her belongings were impounded and she was placed under house arrest by the city magistrates for debts that amounted to over 300,000 francs. Various friends had agreed to stand surety for her, on her assurance that her father-in-law in Russia would pay her debts, but he stoutly refused to do so, and, faced with having to go to gaol, she too followed Alexander, or rather fled to Heilbronn.[28]

Gentz had originally been supposed to share the task of writing all the treaties concluded into a single Final Act with Anstett and La Besnardière. But Anstett was suffering from a prolonged and acute attack of gout, probably aggravated by his notorious fondness for the bottle, while La Besnardière was so overwrought by what was happening in France that he fell ill and decided to return home. So the work fell to Gentz alone, and he applied himself to it furiously, producing a document of 121 articles embracing in one coherent whole all the decisions and agreements made over the past nine months.

It was reviewed and approved as he went along at the now frequent meetings of the Five – 7 June saw their forty-seventh meeting since 7 January. These meetings also concluded various outstanding pieces of business so they could be written into the Final Act. The deal involving Lauenburg and Swedish Pomerania was finalised, settling all the differences between Prussia, Sweden and Denmark. And every effort was being made to resolve the continuing wrangles over Mainz, for the armies were on the march, and that area might well become the theatre of war at any moment.

There had been some talk of inserting into the Final Act a general guarantee of the state of possession of every party concerned, but Clancarty, who had taken over from Wellington as Britain's plenipotentiary, blocked this on the grounds that it would in effect oblige the signatory powers to go to war over every infringement of the Final Act. Alexander also rejected the idea, as the possessions of the Porte would have been embraced by the guarantee, and this would have effectively blocked Russian plans for expansion in the Balkans.

The Final Act was ready on 8 June. It was to be signed by the eight signatories of the Treaty of Paris and subsequently acceded to by all the other parties concerned. The plenipotentiaries of the Eight gathered for the purpose on the evening of Friday, 9 June in the great reception hall of the Hofburg, in the presence of all the contracting parties. It was the first and only time the congress had assembled in full, and its only corporate action was to listen as the text of the Final Act was read out.

Cardinal Consalvi would not sign it, and instead delivered himself of a denunciation of the congress for having failed to return to the Pope his French fiefs of Avignon and the Comtat Venaissin and the city of Ferrara. Labrador also refused to endorse the proceedings, in protest at the arrangements reached in Italy. Nesselrode professed his eagerness to sign, but warned his colleagues that he could not do so until Alexander had read the document himself. He therefore raced off post haste to headquarters while the others appended their signatures and their seals, and the document was not finally signed by all until 26 June. By that time a war had been lost and won.

30

~~⌇◦⌇~~

Wellington's Victory

At 11 o'clock on the night of 21 June a dirty travelling-coach rolled into St James's Square and came to a halt outside No. 18. Passers-by stopped and stared with curiosity at two military colours, their staffs topped with gilded Napoleonic eagles, which protruded from one of the coach windows. Its occupant, Major Henry Percy, one of Wellington's aides-de-camp, alighted and bounded up the steps of Castlereagh's house. On being informed that the Foreign Secretary was dining with Mr Edmund Boehm at No. 16, along with the Prince Regent and Lord Liverpool, Percy seized the two French colours and went to find him there. A moment later he burst into the dining room, threw the colours at the feet of the Prince Regent and announced that Wellington had won a great victory over Napoleon, who had fled the field followed by the remnants of his shattered army. Before he had finished telling the assembled company the glorious news a crowd had gathered outside, and the Prince Regent came out onto the balcony. Percy unfurled the captured French colours while the throng below sang 'God Save the King'.

Napoleon had staked everything on a quick victory. It was only if he could knock out the forces mustering against him one by one that he could avoid being hopelessly outnumbered. So, on 4 June he presented his new army with its colours, and a week later set off to war.

With the 123,000 men under his command he marched out against

Wellington, who had 112,000 British, Dutch and German troops, and Blücher, with another 116,000 Prussians and north Germans, who were cooperating closely. Napoleon's only hope was to drive a wedge between them and defeat one after the other. At Ligny on 16 June he took on Blücher and his Prussians, and drove them back in some disorder while Marshal Ney held off the British at Quatre Bras. The following day he handed over the pursuit of the Prussians to General Grouchy, while he himself set out to defeat Wellington.[1]

The two armies met on the morning of 18 June near the village of Waterloo. Wellington had taken up defensive positions and played safe. Napoleon launched a series of attacks which ground to a standstill in some of the most tenacious and vicious fighting of the Napoleonic Wars. The fate of the battle hung in the balance until the middle of the afternoon.

Blücher had not been as badly beaten as Napoleon had thought, and he had managed to dodge Grouchy's pursuit. At 4 o'clock he appeared on Napoleon's flank, and the fate of the French army was sealed. As the allied armies surged forward from two sides, the Grande Armée crumpled and broke, and while the Old Guard and some other units made a heroic and suicidal last stand, the rest fled in disorder.

Napoleon raced back to Paris and walked into the Élysée-Bourbon Palace early on the morning of 21 June. 'The blow I have been dealt is a mortal one,' he confided to Caulaincourt before getting into a hot bath, as he often did when he needed to collect his thoughts. He spent the next four days in a state of indecision. He eventually decided to abdicate in favour of his son, and left Paris for la Malmaison, where he spent a few days with his stepdaughter and sister-in-law Hortense de Beauharnais, ex-Queen of Holland. There he reviewed his options before making for the west coast with the intention of taking ship for America.[2]

Along with the captured French colours, Percy had brought the Prince Regent a despatch from Wellington. The Waterloo Despatch, as it became known, was immediately made public. It is a fascinating document when considered in relation to the known events, as it clearly sets out to falsify the record by marginalising the Prussian role in the victory. Wellington may have been guided by personal vanity, patriotism or reasons of state. The fact remains that by making Waterloo appear as an essentially British victory he put himself in much the same position when he advanced on Paris as Alexander had been in the previous year. And this made him master of the situation in political terms.

The immediate beneficiary of this was to be Louis XVIII. Wellington advised him to make for Paris with all speed, independently of the British army, while he himself entered into communication with Fouché, and wrote to Talleyrand urging him to make haste and join the King. But Talleyrand was in no hurry. He did not want to leave Vienna before the Final Act was signed by all parties, and he was loath to leave Dorothée alone with Clam-Martinitz. He sent Louis XVIII a long memorandum listing all the King's mistakes, recommending that he dismiss Blacas, and that he detach himself from the British and make for one of the major French cities under his own banner.

Not surprisingly, when Talleyrand did join the King, at Mons, he was given a frosty reception. Louis had fallen under the influence of his brother and his coterie of *ultras*, who bridled at Talleyrand's suggestion that the King appoint a liberal government and issue a public proclamation admitting his errors. Talleyrand was dismissed by Louis, who signed a proclamation threatening all those who had shown themselves to be 'unfaithful' to his cause.

Wellington was having none of it, and forced Louis to ask Talleyrand to form a provisional government with, at his own insistence, Fouché as Minister of Police. The *ultra* royalists were appalled. When he saw Talleyrand enter the room leaning on Fouché's arm, Châteaubriand could see only 'Crime leading Vice'. Without reference to any of the other allies, Wellington in effect reinstalled Louis XVIII on the throne with a liberal government. 'He is an admirable man,' Talleyrand wrote to the Duchess of Courland. 'His character is fine and straight.'[3]

But the situation was utterly unlike that in 1814, when the Parisians had greeted the allies with exhausted equanimity if not enthusiasm and the invading armies had behaved like generous liberators. From the moment the Prussians entered Paris on 6 July it was clear that they regarded themselves as conquerors entitled to wreak their revenge on a prostrate enemy. Blücher issued a demand to the city authorities for an immediate payment of 100 million francs and a complete set of uniforms and boots for his 110,000 men.

On 7 July a Mr Ribbentropp called on Vivant Denon, the Director of the Musée Royal, with the demand that all works of art removed from Berlin be returned. Denon invoked the convention drawn up at the capitulation of Paris four days previously, which guaranteed the safety of all public and private property. But three days later Prussian troops turned up and started taking pictures down from the walls. Having removed those that had been taken from Prussia, they then began reclaiming objects on behalf of rulers whose territory had been absorbed into Prussia by the Congress of Vienna, and finally on behalf of other German rulers.[4]

Blücher decided that the Pont d'Iéna, named in commemoration of Napoleon's victory over the Prussians in 1806, was an insult to Prussian arms, and his troops set about mining the bridge in order to blow it up. At Talleyrand's suggestion, Louis XVIII, who had entered Paris two days after the Prussians, announced that he would seat himself on the bridge and defy them to blow him up with it. He also signed an edict to the effect that all streets, squares and bridges in the capital would reassume the names they bore in 1790. More to the point, Wellington wrote to Blücher in protest and sent a company of British soldiers to guard the bridge.

The following day Wellington set off for Saint-Cloud, where Blücher had taken up his quarters, accompanied by Castlereagh, who had hastened over from London. The Prussian ignored them. Metternich, who had likewise hurried to Paris in the vanguard of the Russian army, also tried his luck, but fared no better. 'He inhabits this beautiful château as might a General of hussars,' he wrote to his daughter Marie after his visit to Blücher on 13 July. 'He and his aides-de-camp smoke in those places where I had seen the court in full dress; I dined with him in the room in which I had spent so many hours in conversation with Napoleon. His army's tailors have set themselves up where one used to go to the theatre, and the band of a jäger regiment are fishing out the goldfish in the great ornamental pool under the windows of the château.'[5]

What Blücher thought of the Waterloo Despatch would probably be unprintable; he believed his role in the destruction of Napoleon to have been decisive both in 1814 and at Waterloo, and he was not about to defer to anyone. 'The Prussians are very insolent, and hardly less offensive to the English than to the French,' John Croker, Secretary to the Admiralty, wrote to his wife on 13 July. 'The Duke says that they actually forget that there is a British army in Paris.'[6]

The arrival of Alexander on 10 July should have restored a sense of order, if not unity, among the allies. 'The Prussians are conducting themselves in an inconceivable manner,' a shocked Nesselrode wrote to his wife shortly after entering the capital with the Tsar. Alexander was horrified too, and urged restraint on the Prussians. But he refrained from imposing his authority. His spiritual, not to say mental, condition had undergone a further transformation in the past few months, and his mind was now taken up with other things.[7]

On the evening of his arrival at headquarters in Heilbronn on 4 June, a woman had forced her way into his quarters, brushing aside coachmen, servants and aides. She was Baroness Julie de Krüdener, the fifty-year-old widow of a Russian diplomat. She had achieved fame after the publication in 1803 of her sentimental novel *Valérie*, in which a young man tormented by illicit passion for his best friend's wife takes an inordinately long time to die of love. But shortly afterwards she had undergone a spiritual crisis and set out on a quest for solace that led her first to the Moravian Brethren and then to Jung Stilling, whose disciple she became. In 1814 she had become convinced that Alexander was a man singled out by God to redeem the world, and she had been in correspondence with Roksandra Sturdza during the congress to check on his spiritual progress.

Marching into his lodgings at Heilbronn, she announced to him that she had been sent by God to inform His 'Elect' that he had not undergone the purification necessary for him to fulfil His will. She brought him round to the view that all his ambitions had hitherto been founded not on virtue but on vanity. 'You have not yet humiliated yourself before Jesus,' she hectored, admitting that she herself had been a sinner and had only found relief in penance. She ordered Alexander to his knees and spent the night in tearful prayer with him.

From Heilbronn she followed him to Heidelberg, where Alexander had taken up his quarters on the banks of the river Neckar in the house of an English expatriate by the name of Pickford. The Baroness installed herself in a nearby cottage, and Alexander would join her and her daughter at night for marathon prayer sessions. He revelled in confessing his sins, dwelling in particular on the disgusting nature of the sexual ones.

On hearing the news of Waterloo, he hurried over to join them in prayer. 'Oh, how happy I am, my Saviour is with me!' he exclaimed as he rose from his knees. 'I am a great sinner; yet he has deigned to make use of me to procure peace for the nations. Oh! If only all those nations would understand the ways of Providence, if only they would obey the Gospel, how happy they would be!' Eager not to be left out, he set off for Paris at once, with Nesselrode, Capodistrias, Cathcart and a small escort, leaving his army to catch up with him later.[8]

Alexander's entourage had noticed a change in his mood, and his soldiers found him an increasingly difficult task-master, as he began applying to them the harsh standards he was inflicting on himself. He had become a strict disciplinarian, punishing officers severely for the slightest faults. He flew into a rage when a company of his troops lost step on parade in Paris and ordered the commanders of three regiments to be placed under arrest – in a British guardhouse, to add to the humiliation.[9]

As if to underline how valuable his personal authority would have proved at this juncture, Louis XVIII called on Alexander less than two hours after his arrival in Paris and bestowed on him the Order of the Holy Spirit. But Alexander remained curiously aloof from the realities of the situation. On one occasion he lectured a group of Prussian officers, reminding them that they were Christians and that they should banish from their hearts the spirit of revenge, which was foreign to the teachings of Christ. But he seemed reluctant to take any action.

'We continue to have considerable difficulty with the Prussians,' Castlereagh reported to Liverpool on 12 July. '. . . There is a republican spirit in that army, which is very little amenable even to its own government.' Intoxicated by their victory over the French at Waterloo, the Prussian military revelled in the spirit of national revival and the dreams of 1813, which had been so frustrated by the diplomats in 1814. Many regarded their British allies as little better than traitors to the cause, suspecting that they would once again show leniency to the defeated French. An assertive, even revolutionary mood prevailed, and Hardenberg admitted to Castlereagh that he felt as though he were surrounded by 'Praetorian bands'.[10]

Hardenberg arrived in Paris with Humboldt on 15 July, and took up quarters in the *hôtel particulier* of the late Marshal Lannes on the rue de Varenne. He had been threatened by Gneisenau and others, who accused him of having wasted German lives by not standing up for Prussia at the negotiating table after her soldiers had died on the battlefield for the good of the cause. The majority of the troops at Waterloo had been German, and public opinion in Prussia demanded blood and revenge. Not only were Hardenberg and Humboldt in no position to rein in Blücher, they were under pressure to draw blood themselves.

Soon after reaching Paris, Humboldt submitted a memorandum to the other allies which argued that the surest way of restricting France's ability to threaten the peace of Europe in the future was to reduce her territorially. He also asserted that the allies had every right to exact indemnities to cover the expenses of the war they had been obliged to fight. He suggested that France be stripped of Flanders, Alsace-Lorraine and the Franche-Comté, along with the towns of

Dunkirk, Lille, Strasbourg, Metz, Mulhouse and Belfort, the lion's share of which would go to Prussia.[11]

Fights between Prussian soldiers and French civilians on the streets of Paris were assuming alarming proportions, with deaths on both sides, and on 14 July Wellington warned Liverpool that if they did not manage to restrain the Prussians they might find themselves in the same situation the French had in Spain, with a national *guerrilla* flaring up. 'I assure your Lordship that all the information I receive tends to prove that we are getting into a very critical state,' he wrote, 'and you may depend upon it that, if one shot is fired in Paris, the whole country will rise in arms against us.'[12]

The situation was certainly dangerous, judging by Fouché's secret police dossier. Paris was in a volatile state, with crowds gathering at the slightest hint of trouble, ready to pick fights with allied soldiers. Many who had not stood up for the Bourbons or emigrated with Louis had gone into hiding. Dedicated revolutionaries, republicans and followers of Napoleon felt they had no more to lose and yearned to make one last attempt to impose their agenda, by whatever means.

Royalists who had considered the 1814 restoration to have been too benign now clamoured for blood. The duchesse de Maillé, who drove out to greet Louis XVIII as he approached Paris, found him tired and saddened, but Monsieur and his entourage were breathing fire. 'They wanted to kill everyone,' she recorded. 'Everyone was a traitor, everyone deserved death. They talked only of shooting one lot and of hanging the others.'[13]

Fouché also noted that 'a rage to proscribe overtook every faction of the royalist party', and that denunciations poured into his office by the thousand. 'Everyone had had a fright, and there is nothing more cruel than fear,' commented the comtesse de Boigne. There were demands for the return of *ancien régime* tortures and penalties in what she called an 'epidemic of revenge'. Royalists in the Chamber of Deputies behaved just like the *conventionnels* during the Terror of 1793, demanding a policy of cleansing, or '*épuration*'.[14]

The same pattern was replicated throughout the country, with local variations, and if passions ran high in Paris, they were often out of control in the provinces. When news of Waterloo had reached Marseille, royalist bands entered the city bent on revenge, and in the space of two days at least fifty people and possibly as many as 250 lost their lives, with another two hundred suffering injuries, even though over a hundred of the most actively Bonapartist families had already fled. After the capitulation of Toulon, which had been held for Napoleon by Marshal Brune, self-appointed royalist commissions carried out an *épuration* as a result of which over a thousand people fled the city, while eight hundred men and fifty-five women were arrested. Brune himself was set upon and murdered at Avignon. His body was defiled and tossed into the Rhône. A couple of days later General Ramel was murdered at Toulouse, as the area around that city was terrorised by self-styled 'Legions'.

Purportedly royalist gangs went on the rampage in many cities, particularly in the Midi, looting houses and shops, molesting anyone they saw fit to and attempting to break into prisons in order to lynch supporters of Napoleon. Much of this activity was criminal rather than ideological; the range of targets was wide, and motivation was often based on local and arcane discontents.

Fouché gradually brought the situation under control. But there would be isolated incidents in the provinces for months, and the process of weeding out those deemed too sympathetic to Napoleon, between 50,000 and 80,000 civil servants, would be a long one. At the same time, Wellington struggled to impose a system of billeting and victualling that would not be too onerous for France, and to bring some of the worst excesses of the troops under control.[15]

This was far from easy. Instead of being stood down, newly formed allied contingents kept pouring into France, not only increasing the burden but causing fresh problems. Men who had not been allowed the chance of a fight smarted for an opportunity to bully any Frenchman or indeed woman they could, and the lately-arrived Bavarians surpassed the Prussians in aggression.

The Prussian and Bavarian commanders in the provinces refused to heed calls to hand over the administration of the occupied regions to the French, preferring to collect taxes and dues themselves. Aside from the fact that this allowed them to extort whatever they wanted from the locality with impunity, it prevented the functioning of any local authority. They felt entirely justified, as, according to Humboldt, they were doing exactly what the French had done in Prussia.[16]

Neither Wellington nor any of his colleagues had any idea where Napoleon might be, and this added to the tensions of the situation. More than anything else they feared that he might escape to the New World, where he would remain an uncomfortable presence. 'We wish that the King of France would hang or shoot Bonaparte, as the best termination of the business,' was Liverpool's opinion. Failing that, the British should be given charge of him. Not only because they had a supply of remote places in which to incarcerate him, but also because if one of the Continental powers were to take him, there was always the danger that they might decide to use him as a political pawn one day.[17]

The fear of Napoleon was such that the allies treated the problem almost as though it were a question of containing a contagious virus. On 17 July, when it was still thought Napoleon might have managed to escape to America, Castlereagh wrote to Liverpool suggesting that the allied powers address themselves to President James Madison of the United States requesting him to send the fugitive back into their custody. He also urged that they should make the provisions of the treaty of 25 March proclaiming Napoleon an outlaw part of the binding law of Europe and extend it to his entire family.[18]

By this stage, unbeknown to Castlereagh, Liverpool or Wellington, Napoleon was pacing the deck of HMS *Bellerophon* en route for England. He had meant to sail for America, but wasted much time attempting to negotiate a safe passage with British naval captains blockading the French ports. On 15 July, fearing capture by French forces loyal to the Bourbons, he went aboard the *Bellerophon*, Captain Maitland, off Rochefort, and threw himself on the mercy of the Prince Regent.

As it happens, the allies had agreed that when they caught him they would send him to Britain, where he would be imprisoned, probably at Fort St George in Scotland. But the idea of holding him on the British mainland appeared less attractive soon after the *Bellerophon* dropped anchor in Plymouth Sound. Thousands sailed or rowed out to catch a glimpse of the fallen ogre, and local boatmen made fortunes rowing visitors from as far afield as London round the man-of-war. Napoleon would observe them through his eyeglass and raise his hat to the ladies, to their intense delight. Tired of being hailed and asked what he was doing when not on deck, the crew took to hanging out a board on which they would chalk 'At Breakfast', 'In Cabin with Captain', 'Writing with his Officers', and so on.[19]

Liverpool was desperate to get Napoleon away, to Malta, Gibraltar, St Helena, the Cape of Good Hope, or anywhere else. He was anxious lest the English tendency to make a hero out of a fallen man take on political dimensions. A group of sympathisers had already hired an eminent QC, who obtained a subpoena for Napoleon to appear at the Court of King's Bench the following November, but the boat trying to serve it on the Emperor was threatened by Captain Maitland with being blown out of the water if it came any closer. The government itself was taking legal advice as to the propriety of its treatment of the captive, and realised that if he were to step ashore it would 'pose very nice legal questions'.[20]

The final choice was the South Atlantic island of St Helena, whose climate was deemed by Liverpool to be 'particularly healthy'. 'At such a distance and in such a place,' he wrote to Castlereagh on 21 July, 'all intrigue would be impossible; and, being withdrawn so far from the European world, he would very soon be forgotten.'[21]

On 28 July it was announced that Napoleon was to be sent to St Helena, where he would be guarded by the British, with each of the other allies, including France, sending a commissioner to supervise. The *Bellerophon* weighed anchor on 4 August, and on 7 August, off Torbay, Napoleon was transferred to HMS *Northumberland*, which was to take him to his place of exile.

Wellington and Castlereagh were also of the opinion that Louis XVIII should show a degree of ruthlessness to those soldiers and officials who had betrayed him by going over to Napoleon even before he had left Paris. They lamented the French King's apparent flabbiness, and insisted on the execution of Marshal Ney, General de Labedoyère and General de Lavalette. Ironically, it was thanks to a British officer that the latter was sprung from gaol and spirited away to safety. But the others were duly executed, an act whose legality appeared dubious and whose memory was to blacken the Bourbon regime in the eyes of many and yield martyrs to its opponents.[22]

❦

The Punishment of France

The congress had reconvened in Paris, and if there were no balls or carrousels to distract the sovereigns and their ministers from the work in hand, it was hardly an ideal place for sober reflection. The city was full of British, German and Russian soldiery, camped in gardens and squares as well as barracks. It also quickly filled up with the minor players of the congress, wives, mistresses and other camp followers, and with tourists, mostly British.

The monumental nature of Waterloo and its symbolic stature as Napoleon's final nemesis had stirred the imagination of many. Walter Scott and Lord Byron were among the legion of sentimental visitors who would turn the battlefield into a place of pilgrimage. And, as in the previous year, hordes of English tourists made straight for Paris. While the main draws then had been sightseeing and shopping, the main pursuit now appears to have been a hunt for trophies to take back home. Lord Apsley reported on a veritable scramble for anything from a marshal's baton to a tricolour flag, complaining that the Duke of Wellington, who had already procured for himself the famous Canova statue of Napoleon, had virtually cornered the market. 'I am going to buy a bust of Boney,' Apsley concluded. Humboldt complained that the British had bought everything there was to buy in Paris, with the exception of china. 'Berlin will be swamped with Sèvres china,' he warned his wife, regretting that he had failed to get his hands on any himself.[1]

'We are here thanks to the victory of 18 June and to God, who wishes us well, but we have done nothing good,' Stein wrote to Capodistrias from Paris on 28 July. 'And I fear that as usual we will make a bad business of the diplomacy.' They would.[2]

In a letter to Castlereagh, Talleyrand argued that since the war of 1813–14 had been fought against France, it had required a treaty to end it, but as the recent campaign had been declared pointedly against a single man, peace could be deemed to have returned once he had been defeated and apprehended. There was therefore no need and no justification for any new treaty or peace settlement.[3]

The logic was faultless, but it had little currency in the prevailing mood. The seeming ease with which Napoleon had collected the reins of power and raised a formidable new army had frightened all those who had been merrily dancing on his grave at Vienna. Even the most reasonable sought some guarantee that it would not happen again, and within days of their arrival in Paris the principal allies began a debate amongst themselves on the subject.

The root of the problem, according to Count Münster, was that the allies had not defined whom they were fighting and why: they had declared that they were making war only on Napoleon, but were now proposing to penalise his enemy Louis XVIII, whom they had restored to his throne; they were proposing to make peace with France, with which, according to their own proclamations, they had not been at war; and to add insult to injury, they had forced the King of France to take notorious Jacobins and regicides into his government, after having spent the past quarter of a century waging war on everything they stood for.[4]

Capodistrias submitted a memorandum on behalf of Alexander which pointed out that the aim of the allies had been to deliver France from Napoleon and the forces of revolution, to enforce the conditions of the Treaty of Paris and to ensure that all the decisions made at the congress in Vienna be respected. Since they had defeated Napoleon and he was now their captive, and since their armies were in occupation of France, the first two aims had been achieved, while the second two could best be served by supporting Louis XVIII. So the allies should do no more than restrict the military potential of France through the destruction of one or two of her fortresses and demand financial recompense for the costs they had been forced to bear in assisting Louis XVIII to regain his throne.[5]

Wellington was broadly of the same view. He was adamant that as they had not made war on France, only on Napoleon, 'the Allies have no just right to make any material inroad on the Treaty of Paris'. He took a practical view of the matter, warning that if they were to appropriate territory that was indisputably French, even a monarch as pacific as Louis XVIII would be obliged, sooner or later, to join his people in revindicating it, and if he did not, some new revolutionary dictator would. Nothing united a country as much as a grievance, and this one would be more than justifiable grounds for war. 'Revolutionary France is more likely to distress the world than France, however strong in her frontier, under a regular Government,' he wrote to Castlereagh, 'and that is the situation in which we ought to endeavour to place her.' According to him, the best guarantee of peace in the short term lay in the dismantling of some French defences and the occupation by allied troops of strategic points for a few years.[6]

The Prussians were having none of it. Hardenberg and Humboldt were heard talking of partitioning and even 'exterminating' France, and on 4 August the former produced a note which began by stating that Europe had generously forgiven France and let her off lightly in the previous year, but that in view of the French people's treachery another such show of leniency would be unpardonable. He suggested that while some cash indemnity would undoubtedly come in useful, it could not compensate the losses suffered by the allies or provide the same guarantees of security as cession of territory.

He backed up his proposals with astoundingly specious arguments based on his own assessment of the French national character. 'A nation which has more egoism than patriotism will find it less hard to cede provinces than to pay money, since the onus of a contribution falls on each one, while the cession of a few departments falls only on the whole and on the government,' he explained. He went on to say that as military occupation would be more aggravating to such a people than the outright loss of a few frontier areas, it would be wiser to take territory than to impose a temporary occupation. Finally, he expounded a theory that every nation had its natural limits, within which it could defend itself but which did not threaten others. France had been in such a position at the accession of Louis XIV, but since then had expanded to engulf the natural defences of neighbouring states, and turned herself into a permanent threat. It would therefore be for the good of France as well as Europe to seize this chance of cutting her down to size. How this theory accorded with Prussia's astonishing expansion over the same period he did not say.[7]

The Prussian position was supported by the Dutch, who saw an opportunity of making territorial gains. Their plenipotentiary, Gagern, had reached an agreement with Hardenberg whereby Holland would relinquish her claim to Luxembourg in favour of Prussia if Prussia backed Holland's demand for areas of France bordering with Belgium such as Dunkirk and Lille. Bavaria and Württemberg also saw an opportunity to round off their domains with French territory. Sardinia demanded more of Savoy.

'It is curious to observe the insatiable spirit of getting something without a thought of how it is to be preserved,' Clancarty reported to Castlereagh from Brussels on 4 September. 'There is not a Power, however feeble, that borders France from the Channel to the Mediterranean, that is not pushing some acquisition under the plea of security and ratification of frontier. They seem to have no dread of a kick from the lion, when his toils are removed, and are foolish enough to suppose that the great Powers of Europe are to be in readiness always to protect them in the enjoyment of their petty spoils.'[8]

Clancarty's judgement was unfair only in relation to the Swiss. Pictet had turned up in the hope of at last obtaining a land link between Geneva and Switzerland, but the atmosphere was not propitious; Castlereagh was unhelpful, while the French resented the part (supposedly neutral) Swiss troops had played in the allied invasion

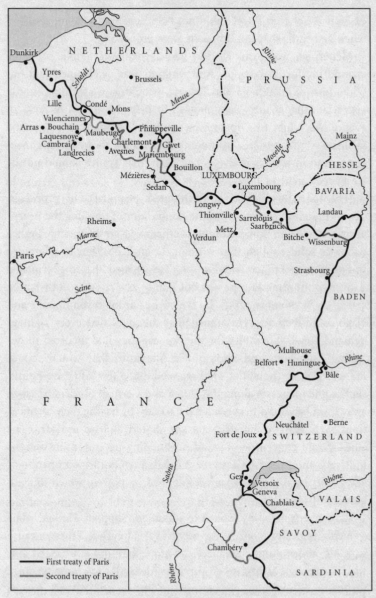

The second Treaty of Paris

of France. Yet even Pictet could not help exclaiming '*Pauvre France!*' when he heard what the Prussians were proposing.[9]

Metternich was torn. He too had a vociferous public at home clamouring for reparations. And while he was determined that nobody, least of all Prussia and Bavaria, should gain anything, he did appreciate that if they were allowed to help themselves to areas of France this might free up some territory in Germany, which would facilitate a final settlement of competing claims there. But his main consideration was, as it always had been, that France should not be weakened further.

'The war of 1815 is not a war of conquest,' he prefaced his proposals. 'It was undertaken solely with the double aim of toppling the usurpation of Napoleon Bonaparte and of affirming a government in France on bases solid enough that it might be in a position to guarantee tranquillity to France and Europe.' He stressed that the principal danger confronting Europe was not France as a country but what he called '*le jacobinisme armé*', by which he meant revolutionary and Napoleonic methods. He argued that the allies had every right to demand a cash indemnity for the expense they had incurred in defeating Napoleon, and also to take measures that would reduce France's military potential. He suggested that a few 'offensive points' such as the fortresses along the Dutch and German borders be taken away from her and others rendered harmless by having their fortifications razed. But he insisted that she should lose no territory. The allies should concentrate instead on building up sound institutions in France and preserve the peace through a temporary occupation of key points by 100–150,000 men, supplied by powers which did not border with her.[10]

Hardenberg naturally looked to Russia for support. He had summoned a reluctant Stein all the way to Paris to argue Prussia's cause with Alexander, but the Tsar received him coolly and reproached him with the behaviour of his compatriots. Alexander saw no advantage for Russia in enriching powers such as Prussia and Bavaria. France no longer represented any threat to Russia, and might in the future prove a useful ally. By posing as her defender now he could gain influence at no cost. And while the recent marriage of his youngest sister Anna, rebuffed by the duc de Berry, to the Prince of Orange brought Holland into Russia's sphere of influence, Alexander need not support Holland against France at this point, for he knew that all three other principals would be in favour of awarding it some gains from France.

Castlereagh found himself in an awkward position. He took the same view as Wellington, Alexander and Metternich. But British public opinion, which had condemned the first Treaty of Paris as too lenient, now called for harsher measures, and the British press became as strident as the German in its demands for revenge and compensation. The Prince Regent caught the mood, and so did Liverpool. 'The prevailing idea in this country is, that we are fairly entitled to avail ourselves of the present moment to take back from France the principal conquests of Louis XIV,' he wrote to Castlereagh on 15 July, using arguments very similar to those of Hardenberg and Humboldt. He dismissed Alexander's generous attitude as self-interested humbug, and favoured the Prussian proposals.[11]

In response, Castlereagh pointed out that Louis XVIII was an ally and that they could not in all decency strip him of any part of his patrimony. 'It is not our business to collect trophies, but to try if we can to bring back the world to peaceful habits,' he argued. In his desire to show respect for arrangements previously reached with the King, he even went so far as to disregard Napoleon's abolition of the slave trade.[12]

He recommended long-term military occupation rather than territorial reduction, on the grounds that this would keep the allies united by the necessity to cooperate in the surveillance of France. If each were allowed to take his prize and go home, they would go back to their individual interests and prove difficult to reunite when the need arose. A prolonged military occupation would give substance to his beloved concept of a continuing alliance.[13]

He accepted Metternich's view that France should lose some of her 'offensive points', and believed public opinion at home could be placated by stripping her of some of the gains she had been left with in 1814. But while he could not argue with Liverpool's contention that Britain must support Prussia, which had been the cornerstone of his own policy, he warned of the danger of being wrong-footed by Russia.

Castlereagh had over the past year adopted the view that France ought to be Britain's natural ally. It was therefore essential that Britain should not appear in the ranks of those who wished to dismember her while Russia posed as her protector. The best way to achieve this in his view was to rein in Prussia's greed and at the same time force Alexander to agree to some cessions of French territory. On 17 August Castlereagh reported to Liverpool that he had persuaded Alexander that Landau should be awarded to Germany, and that various areas of Belgium and Savoy which had been left to France by the Treaty of Paris be given to Holland and Sardinia respectively.[14]

Castlereagh was in a hurry to conclude a new treaty and to get home. Liverpool was urging him to make haste, as public opinion and the opposition were complaining about the continuing expense of the war, which was difficult to justify now that Napoleon was in custody. Castlereagh had moved into the British embassy as the guest of the ambassador, Sir Charles Stuart, where most of the meetings between the allied ministers were held. He was soon joined by Lady Emily and her niece Emma Sophia Edgcumbe. But he was not enjoying himself, and the mood in the French capital had nothing of the festive atmosphere of the previous year.

Wellington, on the other hand, was beginning to enjoy his stay very much. He had managed to rein in the Prussians a little, and with Napoleon safely aboard a British man-of-war he no longer feared any serious trouble. He had taken over an *hôtel particulier*, where he gave dinners and balls, mainly for the huge numbers of Britons who flocked to the French capital. He was the hero of the hour, and some of the ladies had come over specifically to show their appreciation in the most personal manner.

Metternich too was in no great hurry. Not because he was enjoying his stay – quite the contrary. Complaining about the endless discussions between the allies, he confided in a letter to his wife that 'Personally, I would think myself in heaven if I could only get away from the horrible business of this eternal coalition.' His mood would hardly have been improved by the presence of the old dross of his life, including Princess Bagration, who was fleeing from her creditors, and Wilhelmina, who was sitting for a portrait by Gérard.[15]

Metternich had recovered his usual composure by retreating behind a façade of superiority and self-congratulation. 'The D. of Sagan is here, apparently entirely in the arms of Stewart,' he informed his wife. 'She has broken with Windischgraetz, she weeps when she speaks of Lamb, and she says that she is weary of Stewart and that is why she is seeing only him. I hardly ever see her, and I am only too happy that she is not weary of me, for then she would love me, and that she does not love me, because then I would be weary of her.' He reminded his faithful spouse that thanks to his extraordinary skill and exertions his Emperor and the monarchy were stronger than they had been at any time since the days of Charles V; he did not wait for her to congratulate him, seeing to that himself. He told her he was looking forward to their planned trip to Italy, sent her dresses and presents he had bought in Paris, and urged her to look after herself and the child she was expecting – which had been conceived in the intervals between his despairing letters to Wilhelmina at the beginning of January.[16]

Metternich had summoned Gentz to Paris to assist him. The unfortunate secretary had been so exhausted by the task of composing the Final Act that he had retired to a villa in the country outside Vienna as soon as it had been signed. But he answered the summons with eagerness, as he had missed out on Paris the previous year and wanted to make up for it. He traipsed around the sights, went to the theatres and tried out all the restaurants. 'One must be a resolute pavement-trotter, and strong and healthy besides, in order to enjoy this monstrous city,' he wrote to a friend. But he was enjoying himself greatly, and even appears to have made friends with some 'English ladies'.[17]

The delay suited Metternich, as it did Hardenberg, for entirely extraneous reasons: with public opinion at home baying for retribution, neither was in a hurry to publish the news of another generous peace with France, and they hoped that the passage of time might cool tempers in Berlin and Vienna. The knowledge that German and Austrian troops were ravaging France soothed the most vindictive, and any suggestion of withdrawing them caused uproar. Hardenberg also had to reckon with Blücher, who was so inflamed against what he called 'the despotism of the diplomats' that he actually resigned his command at one point.[18]

'So long as they can feed, clothe, and pay their armies at the expense of France, and put English subsidies into their pockets besides,' Castlereagh explained to Liverpool, 'you cannot suppose that they will be *in a great hurry* to come to a final settlement. [. . .] The Prussians have not only brought an entire new *corps d'armée* of 40,000 men forward, much to the annoyance of the King of the Netherlands, on whom they have been feeding by the way, but have reinforcements to an equal amount in full march to fill up their other corps, making their force in France, according to their own returns, 280,000, for which they draw rations.' The Bavarians were also sending wagonloads of troops, and at the end of August, by which time there could be no possible need for them, Spain announced that she intended to move in 80,000 men. According to Prussian estimates there were by then some 900,000 allied troops in France, costing that country a fortune to feed.[19]

Castlereagh could not challenge the Prussian proposals until he had convinced his own cabinet of the necessity of reaching a relatively generous settlement with France. He and Wellington put their arguments forcefully and repeatedly in despatches to Liverpool, and at the end of August Castlereagh sent Stewart to London to explain the situation to the cabinet and the Prince Regent. Having at last obtained their grudging approval, on 2 September Castlereagh set out his view of the terms that should be offered to France. These were that she should cede to Sardinia and to Switzerland those areas left to her by the first Treaty of Paris, that the suzerainty over Monaco should pass from France to Sardinia, the areas of Mariembourg and Philippeville to the Netherlands, the district of Landau to Germany, that a couple of other fortresses should be dismantled, that France should pay an indemnity of 600 million francs, and finally that an allied force of 100,000 should be left in occupation of strategic points for five years.

There followed more than two weeks of argument, much of it bad-tempered, with Hardenberg and Humboldt. While Castlereagh had based his calculation of the reparations due by France on her violation of the Treaty of Paris in the previous year, the Prussians came up with voluminous computations of every penny France had cost them since 1789 (conveniently forgetting that it was thanks to France that they had acquired the Rhineland in 1795 and Hanover in 1805). They therefore held out for a cash indemnity of 1,200 million francs, double that proposed by Castlereagh. They also insisted that Prussia must be strengthened, through the cession of Sarrelouis by France and of Luxembourg by the Netherlands. Lastly, they demanded that the occupation last for not five but seven years.

On 7 September, while walking in the Champs-Élysées, Castlereagh was kicked by a horse and had to take to his bed for over a week, which delayed matters. It did at least spare him having to attend one of the more extraordinary events of the entire proceedings, organised by the Tsar for the edification of all.

Alexander had asked Baroness Krüdener to follow him to Paris, and she had arrived on 14 July. He was installed at the Élysée-Bourbon, and he lodged her in a house further along the rue Saint-Honoré which could be reached through the gardens of both. He called on her almost daily, sneaking through the garden out of uniform, and she took him through a laborious process of purification and preparation. A gaggle of her devotees and other mystics, 'highflyers in religion', as Castlereagh termed them, had gathered around her, and Alexander would listen to and discuss with them.[20]

Unlike the previous year, when he had given of himself generously, Alexander now avoided social gatherings. 'He has become an entirely different man from the one of last year in Paris and of the Congress of Vienna, when one could see how much pleasure he found in society,' noted Major Aleksandr Mikhailovsky-Danilevsky in his diary, adding that the Tsar had become secretive and suspicious, displaying all the characteristics of a misanthrope, often asking to be left alone.[21]

His name day fell on 11 September, and he decided to celebrate it with a ceremony devised by himself and the Baroness. As the site, he chose the Plaine de Vertus, between Épernay, Brienne and Châlons, a conveniently flat open space dominated by a single hill, called the Mont-Aimé. He marched his army there, and on 10 September 150,000 men paraded before him and a large number of guests, who included not only the other sovereigns, their ministers, military commanders and their entourages, but also a number of Parisians and visitors from London.

It was an extraordinary display of discipline and precision, a minutely choreographed military ballet. After the parade, Alexander entertained three hundred guests to a dinner by Carême, whom Talleyrand had obligingly lent the Tsar during his stay in Paris. They began with oysters, followed by a choice of three soups, including the Russian peasant's staple cabbage soup (*shchi*), a choice of twenty-eight hors d'oeuvres, twenty-eight cold entrées and twenty-eight '*grandes pièces*', then a choice of: turbot fillets in anchovy butter, tête de veau in turtle and Madeira sauce, fricassee of chicken and vol-au-vent *à la Toulouse*; followed by roasts (quails, chickens and loin of beef), with *entremêts* of vegetables, and tailed off with meringues, jellies and other puddings.[22]

The following day, 11 September, the feast of St Alexander Nevsky, patron saint of Russia, the troops mustered in seven corps which gathered round seven specially built altars. Baroness Krüdener, in long black gown, moved from altar to altar, leading a bareheaded Alexander. The Mass was celebrated with all the pomp the Orthodox Rite could furnish, with the soldiers making up the choir. The company then sat down to another Herculean dinner by Carême. 'This

day has been the most beautiful of my life, I shall never forget it!'
Alexander exclaimed to the Baroness that evening, saying that he had
prayed for all his enemies, and for the salvation of France. On the next
day he inspected the corps individually and handed out decorations.
Barclay de Tolly was given the title of Prince.[23]

Alexander was already working on his own recipe for perpetual
peace, and took little interest in the squabbles over the settlement to
be reached with France, which he left to his plenipotentiaries Nesselrode, Capodistrias and Razumovsky. Castlereagh could therefore not
count on his support against Prussia. By the same token, Hardenberg
could not rely on Russian support either, which made him more
amenable.

By way of compromise, Castlereagh agreed to the Prussian claim
over Sarrelouis and let it be understood that he would favour some
kind of arrangement over Luxembourg more favourable to Prussia,
but he insisted that the indemnity be fixed at no more than 600
million francs. After a further bout of haggling he suggested that
another 200 million could be demanded from France and dedicated
to building fortresses along her border.[24]

With that, the allies had finally agreed on the terms to be offered
to France, and they were a good deal more favourable than they
might have been. But if Castlereagh could feel some satisfaction at
having saved France from the vindictiveness of the Germans, he was
to be less successful in dealing with another problem which had
surfaced.

The way the Prussians had helped themselves to what they believed
to be rightfully theirs in the Louvre could not fail to awaken other
interested parties to the possibilities. On 5 August Austria put in a
demand for the return of all works of art plundered from its
dominions, which now included Venice and most of northern Italy.
The Pope sent the sculptor Antonio Canova to plead for the return
of works taken from the Vatican collections. The Prince Regent had
woken up to the idea that he might acquire some choice pieces for
himself, including the Apollo Belvedere, originally from the Vatican.

'The men of taste and *virtu* encourage this idea,' Liverpool informed Castlereagh on 3 August. He was inclined to indulge it as well. He could understand the French not wishing to lose provinces or pay indemnities. 'But I confess I have no regard whatever for their feelings with respect to the plunder they have taken from other countries,' he wrote. 'The feeling is altogether one of vanity, and of the worst description; and by permitting it we are only encouraging a sentiment which will hereafter prove hostile to the just rights of other countries.'[25]

Castlereagh was not greatly concerned over the museum, but he disagreed with Liverpool, as he did not wish to punish France unduly. He therefore wrote back making the case against the stripping of the Louvre, in which he was supported by Wellington. He should have been able to count on the support of Russia, which had nothing to gain by restitution. But Alexander was not prepared to stick his neck out. He had himself done very well, furtively buying up the late Empress Josephine's entire picture collection, notwithstanding that much of it had been plundered from Hesse-Cassel, whose ruling Prince was making awkward noises on the subject.[26]

On 10 September Castlereagh submitted a memorandum in which he made great play of the fact that, though sorely tempted, the Prince Regent had decided not to take or even buy anything under pressure, as that would be to emulate Napoleonic practices. But he went on to say that no just peace could leave the robber in possession of the property of the innocent or tolerate the survival of revolutionary spoliations. What had made him change his mind is unclear. Humboldt believed that he was hoping to win over the Belgians, the Dutch and various minor German princes to his territorial and constitutional plans with the return of their works of art. Whether this was the case or not, Castlereagh tried to maintain a detached attitude. 'In taking, therefore, the disinterested line, we have, in fact, made no real sacrifice, whilst we shall escape odium and misrepresentation,' he wrote to Liverpool the next day. He could hardly have been more wrong.[27]

On 20 September the allies agreed that plundered works of art should be returned, and that France be obliged to comply. Talleyrand countered by pointing out that the Treaty of Paris had left the Louvre intact and therefore recognised its contents as the property of the French nation, and that there were no grounds to question this. Denon was sending away Dutch and other raiding parties quoting Article 11 of the convention governing the capitulation of Paris on 3 July, which specifically guaranteed the safety of all public and private property. But Wellington sent British troops into the Louvre to remove the works destined for Belgium and posted guards around the building.[28]

In a rambling letter of 23 September Wellington tried to finesse his way around the article of the armistice, which he had himself signed, by saying that in the verbal exchange which preceded its signature there had been an understanding that the Louvre would be excluded. He convinced nobody. His and Castlereagh's role in the matter, as well as the appointment of the connoisseur diplomat William Hamilton to oversee the restitution, meant that Britain was seen as the villain of the piece.[29]

Hamilton did not improve matters by taunting Denon that the French were unfit to look after such works of art, proof of which being the fact that the whores of the Palais-Royal were permitted to ply their trade under the windows of the Louvre. He strongly backed Canova, who had arrived in Paris at the end of August to further the Pope's claim. This was flimsy, since the objects taken from the Vatican had been ceded to France under the Treaty of Tolentino, so technically did not qualify for restitution. Hamilton managed to persuade Castlereagh, who in turn convinced the other ministers to allow the Pope to reclaim his property.[30]

Denon's great work was gradually destroyed, as 2,065 paintings, 130 statues, 289 bronzes and 2,619 other works of art were removed. Even English tourists were appalled. 'The Louvre is truly doleful to look at now, all the best statues are gone, and half the rest, the place is full of dust, ropes, triangles and pulleys, with boards, rollers, etc.,' observed one. The inhabitants of Paris flocked to the museum to gaze on the works for the last time, and wept openly as they were taken away. Humboldt, who had visited the Louvre every day, finding in it 'incredible delight, and my only joy here', termed it an act of 'iconoclasm'. 'That Paris is losing one of its greatest glories cannot be denied,' he wrote to his wife on 27 September.[31]

The worst moment, and one that would blacken the reputation of the British more than any other, came on 27 September, as Austrian troops were ordered to clear not only the great parade ground in front of the Tuileries but also the adjacent streets of the jeering and raging crowds as British engineers removed the four horses of St Mark's from the top of the triumphal arch of the Carrousel. The soldiers larked about in the chariot as they carried out their business and left the arch itself in a pitiful state, with bas-reliefs and statues lying in pieces at its base.* When Wellington appeared in the royal box at the theatre a few days later he was booed so vehemently that he had to leave. It was ironic that, while being the only one of the occupying powers to take nothing, Britain was seen as the chief vandal.[32]

---

* Copies of the horses were made in the 1820s, and the whole quadriga was recreated on the arch, where it remains to this day.

32

Last Rites

Talleyrand was in a black mood. All that he had achieved over the past eighteen months had been destroyed: the bloodless and amiable return of the Bourbons in 1814 was being travestied by the vindictive and mean-minded second restoration; the favourable conditions obtained for France by the Treaty of Paris were to be revised; and the equal status he had worked so hard to attain for her in Vienna was no more. And if there was one thing he hated above all others it was being left out of important transactions, and he was entirely excluded from the conferences of the Four as they argued over what terms to offer France. He could only guess at what they were planning.

He was also excluded from more personal transactions at home. Dorothée had arrived in Paris and moved in with him at the rue Saint-Florentin rather than with her husband Edmond. But her intimacy with Talleyrand was blighted by the presence of Clam-Martinitz, who had arrived with the Austrian army, whom she was seeing daily. Edmond de Périgord challenged him to a duel, but came off badly, with a sabre cut across his face, and retired from the scene. As soon as he was given leave, Clam-Martinitz left Paris for Vienna, taking Dorothée with him.

This was a source of great sorrow for Talleyrand. Whether or not his feelings for Dorothée had developed into the senile obsession that some contemporaries describe, he had become immensely attached to her, and valued her companionship and her intelligence highly. His mood would not have been lightened by the news that one of his properties, which had been confiscated by Napoleon during the Hundred Days, was now being put up for sale by the Prussian military authorities occupying the area.

But Talleyrand was not one to give up. He had managed to put together a reasonably efficient government, and was introducing various liberal measures in the hope of foisting a liberal constitution on the country by means of *faits accomplis*. He fought daily battles with the King as he forced him to make new peers and packed the upper house with liberals. At the same time, he pared down the list of 'traitors' to be punished, removing people such as Caulaincourt and his own natural son the comte de Flahaut from it. But his every action enraged Monsieur and the *ultras*, who were only waiting for the opportunity to topple him. They canvassed against him energetically, and the results of the elections held in September were very unfavourable to him. This only served to weaken his position *vis-à-vis* the allies.

On 19 September they nominated their plenipotentiaries for the negotiations with France. Wellington and Castlereagh were to represent Britain, Razumovsky and Capodistrias Russia, Metternich and Schwarzenberg Austria, and Hardenberg and Humboldt Prussia. They invited Talleyrand, Dalberg and baron Louis, the three plenipotentiaries of France, to a conference on the following day. But there would be no negotiations.

Talleyrand might have been kept in the dark, but he had managed to find out that France was going to be offered humiliating terms, in the form of a non-negotiable ultimatum. It was therefore with no illusions that he went to the conference on 20 September.

This was opened by Castlereagh, with a short admonition addressed to the Prussian plenipotentiaries to the effect that there were to be no more arguments. He then laid before the French plenipotentiaries the terms agreed by the allies. In their final form, these involved

France giving up about two-thirds of the territory acquired between 1790 and 1792 which had been left to her by the Treaty of Paris. Along with all the territory in Savoy and along the lake of Geneva, it included the area around the fortresses of Condé, Philippeville, Mariembourg, Givet and Charlemont, which were to go to the Netherlands; the enclave of Sarrelouis which was to go to Prussia; and the wedge of land around Landau and the two forts of l'Écluse and Joux, which was placed at the disposal of Austria. The fort of Huningue was to be dismantled. France was to pay 600 million francs in war reparations and a further 200 million for the construction of enemy forts along her border. An allied force of 150,000 men was to be left for seven years in occupation of the forts of Valenciennes, Rocroi, Bouchain, Cambrai, Maubeuge, Landrecies, Laquesnoye, Avesnes, Longwy, Thionville, Bitche and the bridgehead of Fort-Louis, to be provisioned at the expense of France.[1]

The proposed terms were not as drastic as the Prussians would have wished, but they were nevertheless humiliating for France, and personally unacceptable to Talleyrand. Humboldt noted that they made 'a deep impression' on the French plenipotentiaries. 'I felt profound indignation as I received this communication, which was perhaps even more insolent in its form than in the iniquitous demands it contained,' wrote Talleyrand. The following day, 21 September, he delivered his reply.[2]

Since there had been no war between France and the other powers, there could be no question of conquest, he argued, and since Louis XVIII was their ally, they could not extort money from him. By their declaration of 13 March they had recognised him as an ally and branded Napoleon as an outlaw. If they were to decide that he was not their ally after all, it followed that they recognised Napoleon as the ruler of France during the Hundred Days. Since his allies had incurred considerable expense in helping Louis recover his throne, it was only right that they should be indemnified for it, but since they had not paid with territory they could not expect to be indemnified with territory. He pointed out that since they were all agreed that the rule of Louis XVIII should be upheld, they ought not to be undermining him. In conclusion, he stated that the King would nevertheless be prepared to cede some of the territory left to France under the Treaty of Paris and to pay some measure of indemnity. He was even prepared to allow the allies to occupy a few fortresses, though certainly not for as long as seven years. The precise terms would have to be negotiated, and the form of an ultimatum was unacceptable.[3]

The response, delivered the following day, curtly restated the terms laid out in the ultimatum of 20 September. It was accompanied by a declaration to the effect that the allies had never meant to conquer, and that their territorial demands were based entirely on considerations of their own security. What had satisfied them in 1814 in this respect could not satisfy them now.[4]

Having read this, Talleyrand went to see Louis XVIII and laid before him a last-ditch plan of defence. He suggested that the King issue a personal appeal to the allies, as a monarch to his brother monarchs, stating that giving in to such terms would rob him of all credibility with his own people, and that if they insisted on them he would refuse to continue on the throne. It was a clever strategy, given that if the future regime of France were to come up for discussion once again the allies would be in disarray and France would probably erupt into a civil war which would engulf their armies.

Louis refused to go along with the plan. He suggested accepting the allied demands in principle and trying to negotiate a few concessions. Talleyrand could not agree to this. 'For my part, it would have been a renunciation of everything I had done at Vienna and would have annulled the precautions I had taken to make sure that the alliance that had been formed against Bonaparte should not be turned against us,' he explained. He stated that if the King did not issue the appeal, he would be obliged to hand in his resignation. Louis held firm, and on the following day, 23 September, Talleyrand duly tendered his resignation, followed by his entire cabinet. Louis accepted it with, according to Talleyrand, 'the air of a man much relieved'.[5]

Louis's refusal to issue the appeal had a motive, and that motive could be traced back to Alexander. The Tsar had always been against punishing France. He had little sympathy for the greedy Prussians, Bavarians and Dutch, had had enough of Talleyrand and, finally, wanted to regain some of his moral ascendancy in France. Through Pozzo di Borgo he had let the King know that he would like to see Talleyrand dismissed, and that if this were to happen and Louis were to appeal directly to him, he would help France against the other allies. Alexander was not concerned with guarantees against French aggression, partly because his empire did not share a frontier with France, and partly because he had found his own formula for keeping the country under control: he would put his own man in Talleyrand's place.

That man was Armand Émmanuel du Plessis, duc de Richelieu. Born in Paris in 1766, he had emigrated at the beginning of the Revolution and taken service in Russia, along with his friend the prince de Ligne. He had distinguished himself in action at the siege of Ismail and been rewarded by Catherine the Great and later by Tsar Paul, attaining the rank of general. In 1803 he had been made Governor of Odessa, and two years later of the whole of the Crimea and the surrounding area, known as New Russia. An intelligent and enlightened man, he had over the next eleven years turned the squalid little port into a fine modern city with a thriving economy. Alexander liked and admired the cultivated Frenchman, and kept him at his side during the allied invasion of France in 1814.

Richelieu had left Paris with Louis XVIII at Napoleon's approach. Talleyrand had offered him a post in his government following Waterloo, but he had declined, on the grounds that he had been away so long that he knew hardly anyone in and very little about modern France. He was similarly reluctant to assume office now, but when he realised that his doing so would earn France the firm support of Russia, he agreed.

Louis was amenable. He badly needed an ally to stand up for him against the others, and if he had been less than enthusiastic about

Alexander in the past, he could not be choosy now. He had never liked Talleyrand, and resented being dependent on him and Fouché. Both of these 'indispensable' men of the moment were now dispensable. On 23 September he wrote the appeal Talleyrand had asked him to issue the day before, with the difference that it was addressed only to Alexander. On 26 September the duc de Richelieu was installed as head of the government of France, while Talleyrand was put out to grass, with the title of Grand Chamberlain.[6]

'I left power without great regret,' Talleyrand noted in his memoirs. In fact, he was furious. He also left it with a sense of foreboding, judging by a monologue which he delivered himself one evening to Madame de Rémusat. 'There is no government, there is only the will of the Emperor of Russia,' he lamented. 'I was obliged to take the part of France against him, and I lost. But what madness! To take up the cause of France when one has only the Duke of Wellington on one's side, and not even the support of France itself, which understands nothing. France is no longer, that is what I should have realised.' He was horrified that the Tsar of Russia should have been allowed to assume a position from which he could dictate his will to Europe and nominate governments in France.[7]

Alexander was also giving his other allies cause for concern. A couple of days after the religious ceremony on the Plaine de Vertus, he invited Metternich to dine with him and Baroness Krüdener. Metternich was surprised to see, when they sat down to dinner, that there was an unoccupied fourth place at the table. To his polite enquiry he received the reply that it was laid for Jesus Christ.[8]

At about the same time, Alexander composed the text of a 'Holy Alliance' he hoped to persuade the other sovereigns to join. The document proclaimed that the sovereigns had 'acquired the conviction that it is necessary to base the direction of policy adopted by the Powers in their mutual relations on the sublime truths taught by the eternal religion of God the redeemer'. As a result they would 'solemnly declare that the present act has no object other than to manifest to the universe their unshakable determination to take as the rule of their conduct, both in the administration of their respective states as in their political relations with all other governments, only the precepts of that holy faith, the precepts of justice, charity and peace, which, far from being applicable only to private life, should on the contrary have a direct influence on the decisions of Princes and guide all their actions, being the only way to consolidate human institutions and to remedy their imperfections'.

In consequence, taking the divine command to treat all men as brothers, the monarchs vowed to remain united by a fraternal bond and would behave as brothers should. They would also regard themselves as being co-rulers of a great Christian family, and would strive not only to treat each other and their own subjects as Christians should, but to care for their spiritual development.[9]

Capodistrias, to whom Alexander showed the project, did everything he could to discourage the Tsar. Failing to get him to drop it, he suggested that he issue it in the form of a proclamation of personal belief rather than that of a treaty. But Alexander was not to be put off, and showed his project to Francis.

Francis was sceptical. He consulted Metternich, who thought the document absurd but harmless, and sent him to sound out Frederick William, who thought it ridiculous. The two monarchs asked Metternich to try to reason with Alexander, but told him not to upset the Tsar. He had been conciliatory of late, and they were prepared to put up with his quirks. So, after insisting on a few minor modifications, they agreed to sign it, which they did on 26 September.[10]

Alexander then showed the document to Castlereagh, asking him to obtain the Prince Regent's signature. Castlereagh forwarded it to Liverpool on 28 September, delicately explaining in a covering note that Alexander had acquired a bad dose of religious mania. 'The Duke of Wellington happened to be with me when the Emperor called, and it was not without difficulty that we went through the interview with becoming gravity,' he related. He realised that it would be laughed out of court in London. 'Foreseeing the awkwardness of this piece of sublime mysticism and nonsense, especially to a British Sovereign, I examined with Prince Metternich every practical expedient to stop it,' he assured Liverpool. 'When it reached me, in fact, the deed was done, and no other course remained than to do homage to the sentiment upon which it was founded, and to the advantages Europe might hope to derive from three such powerful Sovereigns directing all their influence to the preservation of peace.'

'The fact is, that the Emperor's mind is not completely sound,' he wrote. 'Last year there was but too much reason to fear that its impulse would be to conquest and dominion. The general belief now is, that he is disposed to found his own glory upon a principle of *peace* and *benevolence*.' As he handed him the document, Alexander had dwelt on the intense pleasure it had given him to sign it in the most irreligious capital in Europe. Castlereagh had assured Alexander that the Prince Regent 'would unite, [*de*] *coeur et d'ame*, with his august Allies', and suggested that Liverpool obtain the Prince's signature, arguing that the document could be treated as a formal communication between one sovereign and another, rather than as a transaction of state.

'It is quite impossible, however, to advise the Prince to sign the Act of Accession which has been transmitted to him,' Liverpool replied after putting Castlereagh's argument to the cabinet. 'Such a step would be inconsistent with all the forms and principles of our government and would subject those who had advised it to a very serious responsibility.' A treaty was necessarily an act of state if signed by the head of state, and the only way out was for the Prince Regent to write Alexander a private letter containing the same wording. That is what he eventually did.[11]

Two days after the signature of the Holy Alliance, Alexander left Paris. On the eve of his departure he called on Baroness Krüdener and announced that he would devote the rest of his life to bringing the reign of Jesus to Russia, and invited her and her associates to come to St Petersburg to help him. A couple of weeks later he wrote to his sister Catherine of his relief at having got away from Paris. 'I could see all around me only the desire to make hay at the expense of France, and the wish to submit to that passion for revenge which I hold in supreme contempt,' he wrote.[12]

Having reviewed the situation under pressure from Alexander, the allied ministers decided, at a conference on 2 October, to soften their terms by leaving Givet, Charlemont, Condé and the forts of Joux and l'Écluse to France, knocking 100 million francs off the indemnity and limiting the occupation to a period of five years, with the possibility of reducing it after the first three. The new French ministry of the duc de Richelieu accepted these terms in principle, but there followed weeks of discussion over details, particularly on the indemnity and on certain demands put forward by Alexander, who wanted to ensure that France would not slide into royalist reaction.

Castlereagh did his best to neutralise the Tsar's efforts. 'I have endeavoured to keep the internal affairs of France in the background, and to make the colour of our political attitude and our contingent interference as European as possible,' he informed Liverpool on 15 October – which did not prevent him from putting pressure on Louis XVIII to agree to the immediate abolition of the slave trade. 'I have at the same time, in order to soften the aspect of a treaty which is necessarily directed against France, recognised sufficiently the principles of concert with the legitimate sovereign, so as to mark, that it is not against the government or the nation, but against an eventual faction in France, that our precautions are directed.'[13]

Whatever he might say, the allies were dictating to France how she was to be governed. Gentz believed that the conditions imposed by the allies were 'against nature, in direct opposition to the principles, the sentiments and the wishes of nineteen twentieths of the nation, and in direct opposition to the eternal laws of social progress'. And if Castlereagh felt he had helped to spare the country the worst on that score, he was less inclined to favour it when it came to financial matters.[14]

Gentz was also highly critical of the line taken by the British on this question. While they were not as grasping as the Prussians, who kept demanding more in reparations and indemnities, the British plenipotentiaries nevertheless squeezed France, and Wellington later admitted that they had overdone it. 'I think one of our great mistakes was to demand too much money from these people,' he confessed to Gentz at the end of November. 'If we had been content with 400 million, we would have got them without much difficulty; while now we will ruin France without gaining anything from it, for I am afraid that things are going to go very badly.'[15]

The second Treaty of Paris was not signed until the evening of 20 November. The intervening period was taken up not only with discussing its details and drafting conventions on various connected matters, such as the rations that every officer and ranker was to receive while in occupation of France, the methods of dealing with deserters, running hospitals and applying customs regulations. It was also spent in negotiations aimed at tying up as many of the loose ends left by the Final Act as possible, so they could be bound into the new treaty.

One such was the preparation of a formal act guaranteeing Swiss neutrality. Another was the future of the Ionian islands, which touched on a number of delicate points for the countries concerned. Russia would have liked to possess them, but in view of the certain protests from Turkey and Britain, both of which would see this as another stage in the creeping advance of Russian power down the Balkans, Alexander refrained from staking a claim. Castlereagh would have preferred to award them to Austria, as they fitted with her Venetian acquisitions and her influence would have guaranteed an element of stability in the area. But Russia would not hear of this, and Alexander preferred Britain to keep them if he could not acquire them himself.

Castlereagh was reluctant to lumber Britain with the responsibility and expense of exercising a protectorate over the islands, but he could see no alternative. Russia's plenipotentiary in this matter was Capodistrias, who would have liked Russia to acquire the islands and permit the gradual evolution of an autonomous nation state.

Alexander convinced him of the impossibility of this, and suggested that he work with Castlereagh to bring about a similar end under a British protectorate.

Castlereagh liked Capodistrias, whom he thought 'a very intelligent, pleasing and reasonable man', but he had no time for the Corfiote's plans. 'Capo d'Istria gives us a great deal of trouble with his metaphysics, and it is difficult to bring him to a clear point, or to be sure that there is not some secret meaning in what he writes, but upon the whole, when close to him, we get on tolerably well, but when he can fire these long memoirs upon us from the North Pole, there is no possibility of getting to the bottom of his meaning,' he confided in Lord Bathurst on 22 October. In the end, the islands were constituted as the United States of the Ionian Islands, to be governed by a British High Commissioner under a constitution to be drawn up by an assembly elected locally.[16]

Capodistrias also played an active part in settling the issue of the border between France and Switzerland. The Swiss Diet had sent Pictet to Paris in an attempt to secure a land link between Geneva and the rest of the Confederation. Castlereagh, who had been markedly unsympathetic in Vienna, now softened – perhaps because he and Pictet discovered a common interest in merino sheep. But it was Capodistrias who helped Pictet obtain not only the land link through Versoix and Gex (only about two kilometres wide at one point) linking Geneva to the Confederation along the north shore of the lake, but also an '*arrondissement*' linking two other pieces of Genevan territory, and the destruction of the fortress of Huningue, which threatened Bâle.

In a letter to the city authorities of Geneva on 11 November, Pictet wrote that if Capodistrias were ever to pass through the city they must ring all the bells in recognition of what he had done for them. But Pictet himself, and above all his colleague d'Ivernois, achieved a spectacular success on their own. They managed to convince the King of Sardinia to allow two of his provinces, Faucigny and Chablais, to be embraced by Swiss neutrality in exchange for free passage of people

and goods; while the King would enjoy all the revenue from the two
provinces without having to pay for their defence, Geneva acquired
a land link with the rest of Switzerland along the south shore of the
lake – which also neutralised the Val d'Aosta, a favourite French route
into Italy. As both parties wished to avoid any interference by France,
the deal involved secret negotiations which were concluded in Turin
the following year.[17]

These were by no means the only collateral negotiations going on
in Paris at the time, or indeed the only ones that would drag on into
the following year. Amongst the liveliest was the scramble for the 700
million francs to be paid by France, with Sardinia, Switzerland and
Denmark joining the eight signatories of the Treaty of Paris in the
competition. Those over the compensation of Bavaria for the territory
she was to return to Austria were anything but lively: while an agreement was finally reached, it could only take the form of an intention,
which Britain, Russia and Prussia pledged themselves to encourage
the two parties concerned, Austria and Bavaria, to honour, and which
was to come into being at a conference to be held in Munich in the
next year.[18]

All manner of other negotiations were going on concurrently as
various states and parties took advantage of the presence of the
plenipotentiaries and ministers in Paris. They ranged from the final
details of the settlement of Russia's Dutch debt to complicated exchanges of territory between Prussia and Hesse-Cassel, taking in some
more private matters along the way. Gentz was lucratively engaged in
collecting 'expressions of satisfaction and gratitude' from various
parties, including a magnificent one from Richelieu.[19]

On 19 October the still disconsolate Talleyrand, who had retired to
his country seat at Valençay, wrote to Metternich suggesting that since
they both had private business to settle in Naples they might use the
same agent, as this would save them money, proposing a M. Domurey,
the French Consul at Ancona. The nature of Metternich's business is not
known, but was probably not very different from that of Talleyrand's.[20]

The German Confederation

Talleyrand's Napoleonic apanage the principality of Benevento had originally belonged to the Pope, so he had no legitimate grounds for trying to keep it and would never have succeeded anyway. He was nevertheless determined to negotiate the highest possible price for giving it up. The principality lay within Murat's kingdom of Naples, and he had offered Talleyrand the sum of five million francs, payable at the end of the congress, if he furthered his cause. But the rightful King of Naples, Ferdinand, had also been keen to enlist Talleyrand's support at the congress. After Murat's defeat Talleyrand made himself indispensable in Ferdinand's negotiations with Consalvi, who was trying to recover the province for the Pope. It was indeed returned to him in the Final Act, but a secret treaty bound the Pope to indemnify Ferdinand financially and to pay the revenues of the principality to Talleyrand, retaining only a commission for himself. Another agreement, between Ferdinand and Talleyrand, awarded the latter the Neapolitan duchy of Dino with its revenues, along with a lump sum of 1.5 million francs.[21]

The greatest loser in all this was Murat himself. After his defeat by the Austrians in June, he had landed at Cannes and written to Napoleon offering his services. Annoyed by his betrayal in 1814 and possibly even more by his enthusiastic support in 1815, which put paid to his own attempts at presenting himself to the world as a peace-loving monarch, Napoleon was predictably cool. He instructed his wayward brother-in-law to stay where he was and to do nothing. Murat took a house outside Toulon and waited, but when the Midi was swept by anti-Napoleonic terror following Waterloo, he was forced to go into hiding and then to flee to Corsica. At the end of September he marched on Ajaccio at the head of a motley band of five hundred men and captured it.

It was at Ajaccio that he received a letter from Metternich informing him that his wife Caroline had been brought safely to Trieste aboard a British warship, and offering them the choice of any town in Bohemia, Moravia or Upper Austria in which to retire as private individuals under the name of the Count and Countess of Lipona. Fiery and foolish as ever, Murat rejected this.

He embarked for Naples with a force of 250 men. His flotilla was dispersed by bad weather and he found himself at sea alone, with only a couple of dozen companions. He was probably now intending to sail on round Italy to Trieste, to accept Metternich's terms, but he was forced to put in to the little port of Pizzo in Calabria. He came ashore, announcing to the astonished locals that he was their King. He was promptly set upon, and would have been hacked to pieces had it not been for the intervention of a local nobleman, who gave him shelter. But he also notified the authorities, who arrested Murat.

The hero of a dozen battlefields was given a summary trial and executed by firing squad on 13 October 1815. Caroline consoled herself in the arms of General Macdonald, a French officer of the Neapolitan army, and later with a string of other lovers.

The second Treaty of Paris, signed on the evening of 20 November, made reference to the first treaty and to the Final Act, with the deliberate intention of linking all the agreements reached over the past eighteen months into an interdependent package. It was also accompanied by the signature of a fresh treaty that went far beyond the matter in hand, and one particularly close to Castlereagh's heart.

A couple of days after his arrival in Paris on the tail of Wellington's army, he had begun to lobby for the creation of a permanent coalition that would be activated as an 'immediate consequence of Bonaparte's succession or that of any of his race to power in France', and would bring about an automatic 'European invasion' of it. He had managed to convince his colleagues, and on 20 November the plenipotentiaries of Russia, Prussia, Austria and Britain signed the Quadruple Alliance, which was remarkably similar to the Treaty of Chaumont.[22]

It bound the four allies to act jointly in the preservation of the arrangements they had made, and to prevent any member of the Bonaparte family ever coming to power in France again. They undertook to field 60,000 men each to reinforce the existing army of occupation in the event of such a threat. It also bound them to hold congresses of Foreign Ministers regularly in order to review the situation in Europe and coordinate the measures necessary for the preservation of peace. It was an open-ended commitment, in effect creating a kind of security council dedicated to the preservation of the status quo and turning the four great powers into the policemen of Europe. It stood in stark contradiction to the treaty they had signed at Vienna on 25 March, by which all the European powers, including France, undertook to act jointly against the Napoleonic threat; the

Quadruple Alliance was directed primarily against France herself, which it singled out as a dangerous delinquent. A curious new departure in European affairs.

Discordant Concert

Alexander made his way home in leisurely manner via Switzerland, where he would climb out of his carriage to walk or go into roadside cottages and engage their astonished inhabitants in conversation. Continuing his journey through Bohemia, he paused for five days at Schwarzenberg's residence of Frauenburg, apparently because Gabrielle Auersperg was staying there. He then went to Warsaw, where on 27 November 1815 he signed the constitution of the new kingdom of Poland, drawn up by Czartoryski. Based on the Polish constitution of 1791, it ordained a bicameral parliament and guaranteed the freedom of the individual and of the press. While Poland was 'indissolubly' bound to Russia through the person of its King (Alexander I of Russia became King Alexander II of Poland), it had its own flag and its own army.

Instead of Czartoryski, whom everyone had expected him to nominate as his lieutenant in Poland, Alexander chose a former Jacobin and Napoleonic General, Józef Zajączek. In the course of putting in place the institutions of the new state, Czartoryski had come into conflict with Grand Duke Constantine, who was based in Warsaw as the commander-in-chief of the Polish army, and who behaved like a demented satrap. Czartoryski left public life and devoted himself to intellectual pursuits.

Along with Francis and Frederick William, Alexander also

guaranteed the constitution of the new republic of Kraków. This tiny state of 1,150 square kilometres, with a population of no more than 90,000, was endowed with an army and a constitution also largely written by Czartoryski. But while he attended solicitously to the well-being of the Poles, Alexander failed to address the problems facing his own people.

Russia's economy had been in a parlous condition since the start of the century. This was made worse by heavy military expenditure since 1807; the ruinous effects of the Continental System from 1807 to 1812; the French invasion, which led to the devastation of the west of the country and the destruction of Moscow; and finally the vast expense of carrying the war into Europe and all the way to Paris. The very structure of the Russian state was in poor shape, as Alexander had first brought in reforms aimed at creating and empowering ministries to deal with various areas of governance, and then undermined these by taking back control himself. The huge army, which stood at well over 400,000 men, was a drain on the economy of gigantic proportions, but instead of reducing it, Alexander actually began recruiting more qualified officers from various European countries. In an effort to make the army pay for itself, he implemented a plan devised by General Arakcheyev whereby military units were assigned land on which they were to set up 'military colonies' providing not only for their own upkeep, but an excess to be sold. The colonies were regarded by the soldiers as penal camps, and the enterprise ended in fiasco.

Alexander himself drifted away from his earlier liberalism into increasingly morose reaction. He grew more and more moody, often treating those around him, even senior officers, like miscreant children. Censorship was tightened, and the secret police kept a close watch on any who could be described as freethinkers or liberals. It was not long before he began to grow irritated at the Poles' enjoyment of the freedoms he had granted them, and started curtailing them.

For the most part, Russian society embraced the Tsar's view that the events of 1812–14 had demonstrated that God had singled out Russia as His agent on earth, precisely because the Russian people had rejected the Enlightenment and remained faithful to their old ways. In 1816 Alexander's friend the historian Nikolay Mikhailovich Karamzin published the first part of his twelve-volume *History of the Russian State*, which projected a vision of a divinely ordained people whose duty it was to reject corrupting outside influences. Minds closed, and everything foreign was regarded as suspicious. The German philosopher and theologian Franz von Baader was denied entry to the country, the Bible Society was denounced by Admiral Shishkov as a conspiracy against the Russian state, and Alexander's old friend Aleksandr Galitzine was removed from the Ministry of Education for propagating 'the creed of Satan'.

This contrasted starkly with the mood of the young officers who had fought in defence of Russia and had liberated Europe from Napoleon. Colonel Maievsky had been overjoyed when he received orders to march his brigade back to Russia. 'How many delights and joys suddenly sprang up before us,' he wrote. 'Each of us gave free rein to our imagination: each one of us expected either Suvorovian honours or dreamt of some enchanting Dulcinea who would reward him with a kiss for all his efforts, his bravery and his triumph.' They were in fact rewarded with stricter discipline and suspicion. Those amongst them who talked admiringly of what they had seen in western Europe and of how Russia could be modernised soon learnt to meet only in secret. On hearing of Alexander's death of typhus at the age of forty-seven on 19 November 1825, many of them would rise up in revolt in the hope of bringing constitutional rule to Russia, and be subsequently executed or sentenced to harsh penalties.[1]

A similar pattern of retreat into reaction on one hand and a sense of betrayed hope on the other affected Germany, where the mass influx of English manufactured goods undermined the economy, and a catastrophic harvest in 1816 brought hunger and mass emigration to America. Many areas were traumatised by the political and territorial changes of the past decade, which had cut through religious and political loyalties as well as economic and social communities, upset traditional trading practices and altered the legal status and rights of individuals. Almost 60 per cent of the population of Germany had changed rulers, often more than once, in the period between 1789 and 1815. Expectations of the congress had been high, yet it had led only to further dislocation, and the disappointment was consequently deep.[2]

One of those who had more reason to be pleased than anyone else was Frederick William. Although he had been thwarted over Saxony, he had survived the storm and Prussia had emerged as the dominant power in Germany. In the east, she had managed to hold on not only to East Prussia and Danzig, but also to a strip of her former Polish territory, renamed the Grand Duchy of Posen, which linked Prussia with her province of Silesia. In the north, she had consolidated her position along the Baltic through the acquisition of Swedish Pomerania. In the west, she had held on to Cleves and acquired lands on both banks of the Rhine, including Westphalia, the old duchies of Jülich and Berg, the valley of the Moselle, and the cities of Cologne, Bonn and Treves.

These western provinces did hold problems for Prussia. The inhabitants of the Rhineland were overwhelmingly Catholic and Francophile, and they had shown little enthusiasm when German and Austrian troops marched in to liberate them. In some areas peasants had conducted a regular *guerrilla* against the allied troops, murdering stray soldiers and small details, triggering severe reprisals. Even many of those who were glad to have become part of Germany once more were not happy to have become Prussians. Cities such as Cologne and Aachen clamoured for the restoration of old rights and privileges, and the whole area remained highly vulnerable in the event of France resuming a policy of expansion. The western provinces were also separated from the rest of the Prussian state by Hanover and Hesse-Cassel. But, as Humboldt put it in a letter to his wife, 'With the first war that comes, Prussia will fill in the gaps.'[3]

Prussia was now not only the largest German state; having exchanged most of her former Polish subjects for German ones, she could challenge Austria for leadership in Germany on the grounds of

NORTH
SEA

BALTIC
SEA

Königsberg

Danzig

Hamburg

Stettin

Hanover

Berlin

Warsaw

Cologne

Breslau

Dresden

Prague

Nuremberg

Vienna

Losses in Poland

Gains in Germany

Prussia satisfied

being a more thoroughly German power. And, although this was not appreciated at the time, possession of the Ruhr and the Saar basin, with its vast coal deposits, would give her control of the powerhouse of industrial and economic growth in Germany.

Much to the dismay of people such as Stein and Humboldt, Frederick William quickly set about abolishing some of the reforms they had brought in after 1807 and muzzling dissent. Most of his subjects were content enough to go back to sleep, as the poet Heinrich Heine put it, and Prussia slipped into reaction. Blücher and Gneisenau continued to bluster and grumble about the paltry results of their victory over France; they became heroes of the secret students' societies, and, after his death in 1819 the old Marshal assumed the status of a national icon. But Frederick William reigned on, doing his best to stay out of trouble, until his death in 1840.

Other German monarchs took the same attitude, in the hope that tranquillity would restore a kind of *ancien régime* normality. Neither Maximilian of Bavaria nor Frederick Augustus of Saxony wished for anything but peace and quiet. The more restless Grand Duke of Baden died in 1818 – whether it was from his exertions at Vienna or the boredom consequent on having to give them up is not clear. Even the liberal-minded Wilhelm I, who succeeded his corpulent father as King of Württemberg in October 1816, trod carefully and defended his prerogatives and the particularism of his kingdom. Lesser princes associated in a league of aristocracy which vowed to reverse all the 'morbid political theories' of the past quarter-century.

Stein retired from public life in disgust, inveighing against the petty tyrants who had destroyed his dream of a united Germany. In 1819 he established a society for the study of German history which published documents relating to 'Germanic' peoples, covering Visigothic Spain, Lombard Italy, Carolingian France, Belgium and Holland, as well as Eastern Europe, a cultural claim to supremacy on the Continent that no doubt consoled him for the failure.

That same year Humboldt had finally been given a ministerial post by Hardenberg; after the signature of the second Treaty of Paris he had been assigned to the Territorial Commission at Frankfurt, then represented Prussia in the Diet of the Bund, the Bundestag, and then been posted as minister to London. But he was out of favour with Frederick William, who delayed until 1817 the rewarding of his services with the gift of an estate, and he continued to hover on the edge of public affairs in Prussia. Having failed to obtain Hardenberg's post even after the latter's death in 1822, he devoted himself to his studies, publishing on the origins of the Basque language, and later on the ancient Kawi language of Java.

Resistance to the new status quo was restricted to students, junior officers and a handful of intellectuals, and it was largely passive in nature, except in the Rhineland. But it did have a voice. The German nationalist Joseph Görres used his influential *Rheinische Merkur* to denounce the Vienna settlement, representing it as a betrayal. As far as he was concerned the congress had done little more than sanction the usurpations of the minor German monarchs, who got to keep what they had stolen under Napoleon and used the opportunity to increase their prerogatives at the cost of the people of Germany. Similar views were expressed in prose and verse by the Romantic poets of the day such as Arndt and Uhland, and all those who had hoped that the signature of the Final Act had somehow put the genie of 1789 back in the bottle were in a state of alarm. The *Rheinische Merkur* was closed down by the Prussian government in 1816, but that had little effect beyond exalting the nationalist cause further.[4]

On 18 October 1817, over four hundred members of the students' organisation the Burschenschaft, from twelve universities, met at the medieval castle of Wartburg, where Luther had translated the Bible, to celebrate the tercentenary of this and the fourth anniversary of the battle of Leipzig. After listening to recitations, speeches and exhortations, they sang hymns, swore oaths, took 'communion' and embraced each other. They then marched off to a nearby hill where they lit a great bonfire into which they began to cast all the objects of their hatred. One of the first into the flames was a text of the Final Act of the Congress of Vienna. Such apparently harmless antics had a disproportionate effect on anxious conservatives all over Europe, and particularly on Metternich.

Only a couple of months earlier, he had written to Nesselrode that the world was suffering from 'a specific malady' which he called '*mysticism*'. He had become obsessed with the idea that a new kind of heresy was working through a variety of 'sects' to undermine the whole European system, and saw its influence and its threat everywhere. He even feared that Alexander had fallen victim to it. 'Since 1815, he has dropped jacobinism in order to embrace mysticism,' he wrote to Francis in August 1817. 'Nevertheless, as his tendency is always revolutionary, his religious sentiments are as well.' Gentz too wrote frantic letters, to Metternich, Nesselrode and others, warning of the 'fermentation' taking place in restless minds all over Europe, and generating a mood of hysterical paranoia which caused them to see revolution in everything. Reading the correspondence of these upholders of the status quo, one cannot help questioning the balance of their own minds as they develop ever more far-fetched and lurid conspiracy theories and identify yet more 'pestilential doctrines'.[5]

Metternich considered Baroness Krüdener, who had taken to wandering around Switzerland preaching Christian virtue and giving alms to the poor, as 'more dangerous than any other'. When he heard that she was intending to enter Austrian dominions, he had the border closed and gave orders for all boats on the Swiss shore of the Bodensee to be removed lest she make a secret raid. 'Madame von Krüdener, fantastical and extravagant in her devotion, but well-meaning, affectionate, and humane in her conduct,' wrote Joseph Görres, 'had been calumniated by priests, insulted by the different police, and at length conveyed by a succession of brigades of *gens d'armerie* to the frontiers of Russia, merely because she not only prayed with the people, and announced the day of judgement to them, but also clothed the naked and fed the hungry.'[6]

Metternich had left Paris for Italy on 26 November 1815, quite content with the way the final negotiations had gone and with the terms of the second Treaty of Paris. By 4 December he was in Venice. He had been looking forward to this trip for some time, as had his wife and children, who had travelled from Vienna to join him. But while he hoped they would have ample time to see the sights, this was not a family holiday. Metternich was accompanying Francis on an imperial progress through his Italian possessions and dominions. He spent the next four months travelling around northern Italy, and although he managed to avoid encountering Wilhelmina, who had set off on a more amorous trip to the peninsula with Stewart, or Dorothée, who was doing the same with Clam-Martinitz, he did not like what he saw.

The Vienna settlement had given Austria unquestioned hegemony over Italy. Not only did she now rule the whole of Lombardy-Venetia and Illyria directly: she controlled or dominated all the minor states to the south; she had a convention in place with Naples which prevented anything from changing in that kingdom without Austrian approval;

and she had created a barrier against French influence by building up Sardinia, which should reciprocate by maintaining a friendly attitude to Austria. But the settlement had a fundamental weakness. While it gave Austria a huge stake in Italy, it did not give her outright control. She had become the guardian of the whole peninsula, but she did not have enough power to fulfil that role unless all the other states supported her unconditionally.

There were early signs that they would not. Sardinia, henceforth referred to more often as Piedmont, was the most organised and efficient state on the peninsula. It felt both threatened by and resentful of Austria, and quickly came to see in her a rival for influence in the rest of Italy. These feelings were ably exploited by Alexander, whose diplomatic and secret agents in Turin and other Italian courts did everything to counter Austrian influence and represented the Tsar as their natural protector.

Although this alarmed Metternich, what really filled him with dread was what he would call '*la prétention italienne*'. He had always brushed aside any idea that the Italians might be allowed their own state, on the grounds that they were incapable. 'No country is less fit than Italy to be given over to government by its people,' he would write as late as 1833, 'as the Italians lack the first precondition for the existence of such a government; they have neither the character, nor the gravity nor the conduct necessary for it; in a word, they are not *a people*.' He and Francis would, over the next decades, contribute powerfully to making them one.

Illyria and northern Italy were by 1813 weary of French rule, which was characterised by high taxation, punishing levels of conscription and a galling arrogance on the part of every official. The inhabitants were consequently well-disposed to liberation by the Austrians. While many did aspire to some form of Italian independence, a benign Austrian regime was appealing to the majority in 1814. But this changed within months of the clumsy, centralised Austrian administration taking control. Taxation remained as high as it had been under the French, and levels of conscription were not reduced. And if the

French had been arrogant, the Austrians were contemptuous. While Napoleon had encouraged Italians to play a part in the administration of the kingdom of Italy, the Austrians did not. Against the advice of Marshal Bellegarde, Francis insisted on disbanding the Italian army and assigning Italian conscripts to Austrian regiments, which resulted in mutinies and fights between soldiers of the two nationalities.

Almost every measure taken by Metternich with regard to Italy over the next decades had the effect of a red rag to a bull, building up resentment which in turn inspired subversion and rebellion. He did not temper his policy, as he had convinced himself that he had no other option. The Austrian realm he had reconstructed through the Congress of Vienna needed a period of calm in which to consolidate and recuperate from the upheavals of the past twenty-five years, and he was determined to pre-empt any turbulence through decisive action. 'What use is it for Europe to have seen that system of physical conquest collapse under its own weight,' he wrote to Baron Vincent in Paris at the end of 1819, 'if that system is to be replaced by that of a moral subversion far more difficult to combat, and without doubt, more menacing for society as a whole than could be the ephemeral existence of a mere conqueror?'[7]

On 23 March 1819 the German writer and playwright August von Kotzebue, who also happened to be in the service of the Tsar, was murdered in Mannheim by an exalted theology student by the name of Karl Sand. The act shocked conservative opinion throughout Europe, and gave Metternich his chance to stamp out what he saw as a set of undesirable developments in Germany. He arranged a meeting with Frederick William at Toeplitz to gain his support for a far-reaching anti-revolutionary programme, and then summoned the ministers of the leading German states to Karlsbad (Karlovy Vary). They proceeded to adopt a series of resolutions regarding what would now be called security, which they framed in the draconian 'Karlsbad Decrees'. In September these were presented to the Bundestag at Frankfurt, which passed them into law, turning the German Bund into a highly repressive state. Freedom of movement was curtailed, the police were given extra powers, censorship was carried to ludicrous levels, every university was given an inspector and every classroom its spies. Even church sermons were to be noted down in shorthand by policemen.

Metternich also used the opportunity provided by the scare over Kotzebue's murder to foist his own vision on the ultimate shape of the German constitution, which was still being finalised by the Bundestag. In the course of a series of ministerial meetings held in Vienna between November 1819 and May 1820, he produced a Final Act consisting of sixty-five articles. This was a profoundly illiberal constitution, restricting both the possibility of evolution and the capacity for effective action by the Bund. But it was passed obediently by the Bundestag on 15 May 1820.

Metternich's actions elicited a sharp protest from Castlereagh. The Austrian chancellor had acted almost single-handedly, bullying Frederick William and other German monarchs into going along with him, consulting neither Britain nor Russia, let alone France, and demonstrating a shocking disregard for the concept of solidarity they had pledged themselves to at Vienna. And Castlereagh was dismayed not only by Metternich's high-handedness, but by the growing disparity it revealed between the various allies' views of the aims and scope of the Quadruple Alliance.

From the moment of his return from Paris in 1815, Castlereagh's policy had been the object of criticism, even from members of his own cabinet; some felt that he had committed Britain too deeply in European affairs, others that the Quadruple Alliance was a repressive measure that threatened the liberties of Europe. The treaties were ratified in the Commons, by 240 votes to seventy-seven, but Castlereagh knew that even if he had wanted to, he would not be able to involve Britain in the affairs of the Continent very far in the future.

The country was exhausted by a quarter-century of war, and the level of government borrowing over that time meant that while spending on the army and navy was cut back drastically, taxes remained high. Britain had acquired a string of new colonies, including Malta and the Ionian islands in the Mediterranean, and Gambia, Ascension Island, the Cape of Good Hope, Mauritius, the Seychelles and Ceylon along her route to India, which transformed the nature of her overseas possessions as a whole, and would require attention and investment. Even if there had been any appetite for 'foreign entanglements', as Castlereagh's European policy had been referred to by some, the means to pursue them were lacking.

Yet Castlereagh remained anxious about the state of affairs on the Continent. Within months of his return home, before the end of 1815, he was receiving alarming reports from his diplomats all over Europe: Prussia was sabre-rattling and threatening to annex more of Saxony and other territories; Russia was not reducing her army but recruiting foreign officers, claiming to be in peril of aggression by Prussia; Bavaria was refusing to respect agreements reached in Paris; Austria was threatening her with war; and even Hesse-Darmstadt was making threatening noises.

'I take advantage of a bad day to spare the pheasants and to send you a despatch,' a worried Castlereagh wrote from the depths of the country to his minister in Berlin on 28 December, urging him to do all he could to calm tempers. 'The existing state of European relations may possibly not endure beyond the danger which originally gave them birth, and which has recently confirmed them,' he continued, 'but it is our duty, as well as interest, to retard, if we cannot avert, the return of a more contentious order of things: and our insular situation places us sufficiently out of the reach of danger to admit of our pursuing a more generous and confiding policy.' He was hoping that the Quadruple Alliance would act as a guarantee of stability and prevent the allies coming to blows. But things were not to turn out quite as he hoped.[8]

Article VI of the Alliance stipulated that the four great powers should keep in touch through regular conferences. A conference of ambassadors was duly set up in Paris to deal with minor issues and to monitor compliance with the agreements reached at Vienna. Among the first matters that came up before it was the dispute between Spain and Portugal over their respective colonies. Weightier issues were to be dealt with by congresses of Foreign Ministers and, in some cases, monarchs.

In September 1818 a full-blown congress assembled at Aix-la-Chapelle (Aachen). Alexander was present in person, flanked by Nesselrode and Capodistrias; Francis came with Metternich; and Frederick William was accompanied by Hardenberg and Count Bernstorff. Castlereagh and Wellington represented Britain, and Richelieu was allowed to attend as the representative of France.

The congress had a whiff of its predecessor at Vienna, as a number of minor princes turned up, accompanied and joined, almost inevitably, by various *grandes dames*. One such was Countess Lieven, wife of the Russian ambassador in London, who took the opportunity to renew what, in a letter to her brother, she called her 'tender passages' with Grand Duke Constantine. She also started an affair with Metternich, which was to last for some time and give rise to another fascinating correspondence. Metternich had recovered from the emotional bruises of 1814–15, and was even on amicable terms with Wilhelmina, whom he saw regularly in Vienna, and he plunged into this new romance with his usual sentimental abandon. Among the less exalted people drawn to Aix-la-Chapelle was Sir Thomas Lawrence, who took the opportunity to paint full-length portraits of Alexander and Francis for the Prince Regent.[9]

The principal business of the congress, which was to consider the necessity of keeping allied troops in France, had been discussed and settled beforehand, and was despatched quickly. The allies had already withdrawn 30,000 men of the occupation force in the previous year, and they now agreed to withdraw the rest; the last allied troops left French soil on 30 November 1818. In the same spirit, the unpaid balance of the indemnity which had been demanded of France was written off. But Richelieu's request that she be admitted to the Alliance met with stiff opposition.

After some discussion, however, Castlereagh and then Metternich came round to the view that it would be safer to include France than to leave her out, and she was admitted. But this raised questions as to the purpose of the Alliance, which had been primarily directed against France and the Napoleonic threat. Alexander had for some time been suggesting that the Alliance should form the basis of a comprehensive 'system', and in a memorandum dated 8 November he proposed that the allies should bind themselves into a closer union, and pledge themselves to defend the system they had brought into being. He suggested the creation of a common European armed force, and offered the services of the Russian army. While Metternich and Frederick William were not averse to such a reinforcement of the status quo, seeing in it not only a guarantee of their own state of possession but also an obstacle to further Russian expansion, Castlereagh opposed the idea. He did not like the Tsar's invocation of sublime principles, and mistrusted the intentions hidden behind it. Alexander's evident interest in southward expansion into the Balkans and Turkey, his diplomatic machinations in Spain and his surreptitious involvement in the Ionian islands worried Castlereagh; his repeated suggestions that the allies conduct a grand campaign against the Barbary pirates suggested yet another ploy to secure a naval base for Russia in the western Mediterranean.

On 15 November 1818 the plenipotentiaries assembled at Aix-la-Chapelle signed a declaration setting out what they had decided during the congress and expressing their satisfaction that tranquillity had returned to Europe. They reaffirmed the need for the continuation of the Alliance, but ruled out changing its character. 'The object of this union is as simple as it is great and salutary,' the declaration affirmed. 'It tends towards no new political arrangement, to no alteration of the relations sanctioned by existing treaties. Calm and constant in its functioning, it has no other aim than the maintenance of peace and the guarantee of the transactions which created and consolidated it.'[10]

A profound gulf had nevertheless opened up between the allies as to the real purpose of their alliance. While Castlereagh stuck to his view that it was there to guarantee stable relations between the powers and thereby peace to Europe, Alexander increasingly saw it as a means of bringing into being a new age, and, incidentally, of allowing Russia to play a grand role far beyond her frontiers. Metternich, on the other hand, saw in it a means of uniting the great powers in a kind of counter-Reformation against the liberal ideas that had invaded Europe in the late eighteenth and early nineteenth century, and indeed against anything he did not like the look of.

As a result, while the Tsar's often erratic behaviour made him an unreliable ally for Austria, Alexander and Metternich were essentially united by their aims. Their incipient *entente* was fortified by the differences between the two of them and Castlereagh. This became apparent when, on hearing that the liberals had made some significant gains in the French elections of 1819, Metternich and Alexander proposed that the allies should intervene militarily. Castlereagh protested vehemently, stating that correcting the 'internal eccentricities' of France did not lie within the ambit of the Alliance.[11]

But restraining Alexander and Metternich would prove more difficult the following year, which turned out to be an eventful one. In January 1820 a military mutiny or *pronunciamiento* in Spain obliged King Ferdinand to accept the constitution of 1812 which he had abolished. The news had the effect of a whiplash on Alexander: more than one Tsar had been toppled and/or murdered by army mutinies. The news which arrived a couple of weeks later, that on 13 February the heir to the French throne, the duc de Berry, had been assassinated only deepened his sense of horror.

Alexander called on the allies to make a joint protest and threaten military intervention if the Spanish constitution were not revoked. Austria, France and Britain rejected this, the first two principally because they feared it might lead to Russian armies marching through their territory. In July the kingdom of Naples was shaken by revolution, and the King was forced to accept the same Spanish constitution of 1812. In doing so he had contravened the secret treaty between Austria and Naples of 12 June 1815, by which Ferdinand was not to make any changes in his kingdom without the permission of

Austria. Metternich therefore had a perfect pretext for intervention, one that not even Castlereagh could argue with. But he was not entirely sure that the Neapolitan revolt had not been fomented by Alexander in the first place, and was loath to march his armies down to Naples, leaving his back uncovered and vulnerable to attack from Russia. He therefore attempted to involve Russia in the act of putting down the revolt.

Alexander saw an opportunity to push through his idea of a 'general system', and called for a new congress to deal with the Spanish and Neapolitan questions. Metternich suggested that they leave the matter to a conference of ministers in Vienna, but Alexander insisted on a full congress of monarchs, and Metternich was obliged to agree. He proposed they meet at Troppau (Opava) in Bohemia on 20 October in order to frame a set of rules governing when the allies should intervene in the affairs of other countries and when they should not. Castlereagh could not accept the idea, and resolved to boycott the congress, to which he sent Stewart as an observer.

Castlereagh's opposition was not based on any liberal principles, and the government of which he was a member presided over an increasingly reactionary regime itself. The end of the Napoleonic Wars had seen a collapse of prices in British agriculture and industry, resulting in high unemployment and terrible poverty. Strikes and demonstrations turned into riots more than once, and troops were used against them. In 1817 *Habeas Corpus* was suspended. In August 1819 a political meeting on St Peter's Fields outside Manchester was put down with unnecessary brutality. This 'Peterloo Massacre' led to the passing of the 'Six Acts', as repressive a body of legislation as much of what was being passed on the Continent, and reactions were no less revolutionary. In February 1820 the police uncovered the Cato Street conspiracy, which meant to blow up the entire cabinet.

At Troppau, Alexander, Frederick William and Francis drew up a protocol setting out the bases on which they felt military intervention in the affairs of other countries was justified – when the change originated from below. The Tsar's sense of purpose was only strengthened when news reached him of a minor act of insubordination by some of his Semeonovsky Guards in St Petersburg, which he interpreted as a full-blown mutiny and ordered to be suppressed with extreme severity.

The monarchs also summoned Ferdinand of Naples to attend them, at a congress to be held at Laibach (Ljubljana) in January 1821, to explain himself for having failed in his treaty obligations to Austria. This congress too Castlereagh refused to attend. Once again he sent Stewart, who read out Britain's rejection of the allies' arguments in favour of intervention and her protest at any such action, declaring it to be inconsistent with the principles embraced jointly in 1815. But the allies ignored him. King Ferdinand, who had obediently come to Laibach, was instructed by Metternich to ask the allies for help, and Austrian troops duly marched into Naples. When, later the same year, a similar rising was staged by the military in Piedmont, Austria intervened once more, with Russian support.

The three autocratic powers were acting in defiance of Britain and France, justifying their actions with self-serving proclamations. But just as it was beginning to look as though the gulf between them and the two constitutional powers was unbridgeable, two things occurred which completely changed the situation. One was the outbreak, in the spring of 1821, of an uprising in Greece against Turkish domination; the other was the fall, in December of the same year, of Richelieu's government and its replacement by an *ultra* royalist administration.

The cause of Greek independence was close to Alexander's heart, and very popular in Russia. It called out to her sense of destiny and fitted neatly with long-term plans to extend her influence through the Balkans and capture Constantinople. The man who had precipitated the rising, Count Alexandros Ypsilantis, had been one of the Tsar's aides-de-camp, and there were plenty of others in Russia waiting to emulate him. The implications of this brought Castlereagh and Metternich together in their suspicion of Russia and their desire to preserve the Ottoman Empire from Russian expansion. At the same time, the new government in France declared that it intended to intervene militarily in Spain, which brought France closer to the Russian position. Alexander himself was now torn between his reactionary urge to stamp out any sign of liberalism in Europe and his wish to support a popular uprising in Greece.

The Alliance was in disarray, and it was agreed that a new congress should be held in Vienna to agree a course on Greece, to be followed by one at Verona, in September 1822, to consider all the great questions of the day and agree a common course of action. The matters to be discussed were not only Spain and Italy, but the situation of Turkey, the independence of the Spanish colonies in South America and the slave trade. This time Castlereagh, now Marquess of Londonderry, was intending to attend. But in the course of the summer he fell ill from the strain of defending his policies in Parliament. He went to his country home at Cray in Kent to rest, but his condition deteriorated rapidly, and he began to show signs of derangement. His doctor took the precaution of removing his razors, but on 12 August he found a penknife, cut his throat and bled to death.

Castlereagh had already drawn up detailed instructions on the line Britain was to follow at the forthcoming congress in Vienna, and these were handed to Wellington, who was to represent Britain. Castlereagh's successor as Foreign Secretary, his old rival George Canning, was not greatly interested in European affairs, did not share his European colleagues' paranoia about revolution, and did not like the concept of a joint hegemony by the great powers, which he referred to as 'the European police system'. Wellington was therefore not in a strong position at Verona, to which the congress had moved.[12]

This congress did not draw many people, with the notable exception of Countess Lieven, who dismissed the only other lady of note in Verona, Madame Récamier, as a 'nobody' and quickly assumed a dominant role. 'Every evening the Congress assembles *chez moi*,' she wrote to her brother in St Petersburg. 'Both Count Nesselrode and Prince Metternich urged me to allow this as a resource for them, and I find every advantage in such an arrangement.'[13]

That the affairs of the world were being discussed and decided by a handful of men in the drawing room of the pushy, meddlesome and self-interested mistress of one of them, is highly apposite – the 'congress system' was not a system of any recognisable form, while the 'Concert of Europe' was no more than a series of arguments between individuals, whose convictions were entirely personal. Countess Lieven employed all her feminine charms to change Wellington's mind and bring him round to her imperial master's way of thinking, and whether Britain would become involved in a crusade against the Spanish constitutionalists or not depended on his ability to resist them.

Alexander was only prepared to curb his desire to intervene on behalf of the Greek rising on condition that the Alliance would intervene in Spain. Neither France nor Austria wished to see Russian troops marching across Europe, while Britain feared the repercussions an allied invasion of Spain might have in the Spanish colonies and therefore on trade. They therefore stood firm against him, and he was obliged to join in a declaration condemning the Greek rising without getting his way on Spain. By default, France was allowed to intervene in Spain on her own, while Britain delivered itself of pious protests. That was, to all intents and purposes, the end of the experimental 'congress system', and the end of British involvement in the affairs of Europe for decades.

34

～○◦～

The Arrest of Europe

Back in the summer of 1815, as he was relaxing in his villa outside Vienna a couple of weeks after the signature of the Final Act, Gentz had noted down some of his reflections on the events of the past nine months. 'Never have the expectations of the general public been as excited as they were before the opening of this solemn assembly,' he wrote. 'People were confident of a general reform of the political system of Europe, of a guarantee of eternal peace, even of the return of the golden age. Yet it produced only restitutions decided beforehand by force of arms, arrangements between the great powers unfavourable to the future balance and the maintenance of peace in Europe, and some quite arbitrary rearrangements in the possessions of the lesser states, but not one act of a more elevated character, not one great measure of public order or security which might compensate humanity for any part of its long sufferings or reassure it as to the future.'

He had no doubts as to the reasons for this. In the first place, he blamed the failure to agree proper rules. 'As the congress was never defined, and the powers of its members were never determined according to any fixed and recognised principle, it drifted to the very last moment on a sea of uncertainties and contradictions,' he explained. This drift favoured the great powers. 'It is evident that in such a state of affairs only might could be right, and that the weak had no other resource beyond that of protection and intrigue.' But the resulting conviction that they could do as they wished only brought out the differences between the great powers, inhibiting their ability to agree on any of the important issues. 'They only agreed, in fact, when it was a question of laying down the law to others.'[1]

Stein's verdict was hardly less withering: the congress was not only a missed opportunity, it had ended in 'a farce'. He blamed 'the distractedness and shallowness' of Alexander, the 'obtuseness and coldness' of Hardenberg, Nesselrode's 'feeble-mindedness, meanness and dependence on Metternich', and 'the frivolity of all' for the failure to achieve anything for Germany.[2]

Their judgements may appear harsh, but they were shared by many. 'Of all the plenipotentiaries who were called to this congress, there is but a very small number who have left satisfied,' the Saxon minister Georg von Griesinger reported to his monarch. Foremost among the disappointed parties were those who had been denied justice – the representatives of Genoa, of the Order of Malta, of the republic of Lucca, of various principalities and monasteries. Many of them were still publishing pamphlets of protest in the 1820s, inveighing against the injustice of the settlement. The Bernese patrician Baron Müller d'Arvaangue continued to bombard ministers and monarchs with petitions and pamphlets, complaining that '*illegitimate* peasants' had been given powers in the Council of Berne, and declaring that 'the real Swiss relish the mediation of the Congress of Vienna no more than they did that of Bonaparte'. He lamented the loss to Berne of Vaud and Aargau, arguing that the piece of the old bishopric of Bâle the city had received in compensation was of no value, being entirely foreign in spirit.[3]

In this at least he was right. The inhabitants of the district in question never accepted their new condition, and on 20 May 1965, the 150th anniversary of the Swiss settlement at Vienna in 1815, there were huge demonstrations, with flags flying at half-mast throughout the province. There was no lack of such local discontents. And next to these minor interests came the private individuals whose suits were crushed between the jarring interests of heavier contestants.[4]

Having been promised the earth, Prince Eugène was, at Alexander's behest, eventually offered Bernadotte's old apanage the duchy of Pontecorvo, without the means of actually taking possession of it. But he did manage to negotiate an indemnity of five million francs from the King of Naples for giving up his claims to it. All his private properties in the Legations and the Marches were confiscated by the Pope, but in the end his father-in-law King Maximilian of Bavaria relented, giving him an estate and the title of Duke of Leuchtenberg.

His uncle Jérôme fared less well. At the beginning of the Hundred Days he had escaped from Trieste by boat, joined his brother in Paris and commanded a division at Waterloo. His first thought after the débâcle was to go to America, but he feared that if he were to do that he would never again see his wife, whose father the King of Württemberg was putting pressure on her to disown him. Jérôme went to Württemberg, only to be placed under arrest by his father-in-law, who tried to bully him into signing over all his property, threatening to keep him in gaol until he did. After some time he was reunited with his wife and child, in a fortress where they were under constant guard. It was only after they had been stripped of everything they owned that they were released. They went to Austria, where Francis permitted them to live privately under the name of the prince and princesse de Monfort. Following numerous appeals to Alexander they eventually obtained permission to settle in Rome, which they did in 1823.

It was not just the family and henchmen of Napoleon who were penalised. Throughout the lands of the old Holy Roman Empire hundreds of princes and lesser nobles who had been stripped of their lands and their prerogatives by Napoleon failed to receive satisfaction from the congress, and were more or less destitute. Beyond that, thousands of individuals, some great, some humble, had seen their fortunes overturned by the changes of regime and administration.

The unfortunate Camillo Borghese, Prince Aldobrandini, had,

under duress, sold the gallery of antiquities at the Villa Borghese in Rome to the French government, in exchange for some land in the valley of the Po and a share in the salt mines of Kreuznach. In 1814 the returning King of Sardinia had seized his lands, and only after pressure had been applied on him by the ministers of the great powers did he return them, in 1816. But the salt mines were on territory which was transferred first to Prussia, then to Bavaria, both of which refused to honour his title. The matter was brought up by his son at Vienna, then at Aix-la-Chapelle in 1818, at Troppau, Laibach, and at Verona, where he was no closer to getting justice than he had been in 1814. There were hundreds of such cases, some involving grandees, some minor nobles, some the humblest of property-owners.[5]

It is in the nature of things that great events leave victims in their wake, and one should not let their voice colour judgement on the merits of the settlement as a whole. But even among contemporary historians and commentators, there were very few defenders, and many outright critics, of the congress, which became a byword for injustice, incompetence and above all disreputable practice and intrigue. In his diatribe against Castlereagh in *Don Juan*, Byron uses words such as 'botching', 'patching' and 'cobbling' to describe his work at Vienna.[6]

A century later, on 28 January 1919, as he prepared his team of negotiators for the Paris Peace Conference which was to forge a new settlement following the First World War, the US President Woodrow Wilson expressed the hope that 'no odour of Vienna' would be brought into the proceedings.[7]

It was only some time later, towards the middle of the twentieth century, that the settlement reached at Vienna began to be viewed in a more favourable light. One of its most enthusiastic apologists was Henry Kissinger, whose doctoral thesis, published in 1957, some years before he became Secretary of State to President Richard Nixon, provides the most vigorous defence. He argues that in international affairs there is an inescapable priority to pursue order and stability over justice or any other consideration. Diplomacy can only operate within a system that all parties accept and therefore regard as legitimate, since only such a universally recognised framework can provide the terms of reference for negotiation and the sense of security that give it credibility. Such a system he defines as 'legitimacy'. He goes on to state that the French Revolution and the Napoleonic Wars had destroyed the old legitimacy and failed to create a new one, with the result that all parties, including Napoleon, felt continuously threatened and insecure. According to him, the Congress of Vienna succeeded in forging a new 'legitimacy', which lasted a hundred years and was therefore of great benefit to humanity. 'Not for a century was Europe to know a major war,' he declared, echoing a by then accepted view that the congress had guaranteed a hundred years of peace.[8]

More recently, in his magisterial *The Transformation of European Politics, 1763–1848* (1994), Paul W. Schroeder developed the theory that the congress saw the change from an old conflictual system to one of concert and political equilibrium, from a scramble for a nebulous balance of power to a system of negotiation based on the mutual acceptance of each other's vital interests. 'What happened, in the last analysis, was a general recognition by the states of Europe that they could not pursue the old politics any longer and had to try something new and different,' he writes. He endorses the 'century of peace' view by calculating that the ratio of battlefield deaths to the population of Europe was seven times greater over the eighteenth century than the nineteenth, though he does not mention whether he makes allowances for improved medical care, whether he takes into account the colonial wars of the nineteenth century as well as those of the eighteenth, or whether he includes the dead of the barricades, street fights, national uprisings and Siberian chain gangs in his nineteenth-century 'battlefield' figures. Either way, it is not a particularly significant indicator.[9]

There was, in fact, no 'hundred-year peace'. There was certainly no general European war for four decades – but then there had not been one for the three decades before 1793. And even in the absence of a general war, there was plenty of fighting going on. The decade following the signature of the Final Act saw wars break out in Spain, Italy and Greece, involving the intervention of France, Austria and Russia, and ultimately Britain and Turkey. Two major wars broke out in 1830, one in Belgium, between France and Holland, one between Poland and Russia. The 1830s witnessed two protracted and vicious civil wars in Spain and Portugal, as well as a wave of popular risings in Switzerland which nearly turned into civil war in 1847. Between 1846 and 1848 there were full-scale wars involving Russia, Prussia, Sardinia and Austria, fought in Poland, Hungary, parts of Germany and Italy. In 1854 Britain, France and Sardinia went to war on Russia in the Crimea. In 1859–60 there was war between France, Sardinia and Austria which was so bloody that it inspired the foundation of the Red Cross, and in 1866 one between Prussia, Austria and Denmark. Nor should one ignore the wars fought by Britain and Russia over central Asia, in Afghanistan, Georgia, Chechnya and elsewhere, just a fraction of the seventy-two separate British campaigns fought during the reign of Queen Victoria. Nor the bitter conflicts that engulfed Spain's former American colonies. Nor indeed the dozens of revolts and insurrections that took place across Europe between 1820 and the Polish Insurrection of 1863–64. They were all put down with military force and they all cost lives. The Franco-Prussian war of 1870 caused carnage on a scale hitherto unknown, and led to the internecine bloodbath of the Paris Commune. And that covers just the first half of the 'century of peace'.

The second problem with the Kissinger view is that the Vienna settlement itself was never entirely consummated, and that it broke down very quickly. The concert of the great powers, such as it was, did not survive the Congress of Verona in 1822. And the new status quo was overturned in 1830, barely fifteen years after the signature of the Final Act.

In July of that year, revolution broke out in Paris, and after three days of street fighting the Bourbons were swept from power and replaced with the duc d'Orléans, who became Louis Philippe, King

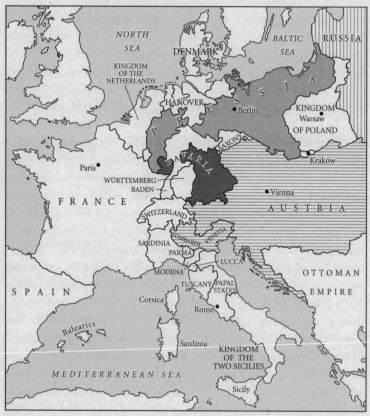

Europe in 1815

of the French. The following month witnessed revolution in Brussels against Dutch rule. Tsar Nicholas mobilised his army to intervene, but in November revolution broke out in Warsaw and Alexander's pet kingdom of Poland declared its secession from Russia, with Czartoryski at the head of the government. The Belgian rebels were thus saved from Russian intervention and a new kingdom of Belgium was recognised, with a redundant German Prince as King. But their Polish brothers were less fortunate. After a ten-month campaign they were overpowered by Russian armies, the kingdom of Poland was

Europe in 1871

abolished and its territory incorporated into the Russian Empire. Czartoryski, who had escaped to Paris, was hanged in effigy by the Russians. In the space of a few months two of the most hard-fought issues of the congress had been blown away – Britain's cherished 'barrier' against France and Alexander's autonomous kingdom of Poland.

Further linchpins of the Vienna settlement were knocked out in 1846, when the free city of Kraków was annexed by Austria, and in 1848, when a national rising in the grand duchy of Posen ultimately obliged Frederick William's successor to abolish its autonomy, and risings elsewhere in Germany galvanised the Bundestag into action and nearly brought into being the unified German state dreamed of by the liberals in 1814. That same year saw further revolts all over Italy and in France, which demolished more elements of the Vienna settlement, Austria's hegemony in Italy among them. And in 1849 a fatal blow was delivered to the heart of the settlement with the election of Louis Napoleon Bonaparte, the ogre's nephew, as President of France, which he would follow up by becoming Emperor two years later. The very thing the Quadruple Alliance had been designed to prevent had occurred. Less than two decades later he was toppled by the Prussians, and a German empire came into being. By then the political map of Europe bore little relation to that so sententiously sanctified only half a century before.

These events point to the third flaw in Kissinger's argument, namely that the Congress of Vienna did not in fact establish a new 'legitimacy' at all. The plenipotentiaries of the great powers had indeed tried 'something new and different'. But it was not something that could be dignified with such a word. They had merely decided to reorganise and run Europe by accord between themselves, without reference to the minor powers, let alone public opinion.

Perhaps the most significant document in this respect is the Troppau protocol. This likened change imposed from below to a disease which undermined a state and cut it off from healthy European powers, whose duty it was to intervene in order to restore it to health and bring it back into the fold. By effectively proscribing all change from below without placing any restraints on the powers of rulers, such a system arrested normal development and created a situation in which, since absolutist rulers were unlikely agents of social, economic or political development, change could only be brought about by violent revolution.

'As it was, the peace of 1815 was constructed without the slightest effort to secure its perpetuity by something stronger than conventions and protocols – by uniting mankind in a bond of common interests,' wrote Harriet Martineau in her *History of the Thirty Years' Peace* in 1846 (no believer in the 'century of peace', she). In fact, the peacemakers of Vienna had attempted to reconstruct a European community in total disregard of the direction in which the Continent was moving. As a result, their new system excluded not only those, such as the liberals and revolutionaries, whom they saw as enemies: it was so thoroughly out of sympathy with the *zeitgeist* of the times that it alienated most educated people in Europe.[10]

The generation which had seen in the fall of the Bastille in 1789 a harbinger of better days might have been disillusioned by much of what had followed. But while the process begun by the Revolution and continued under Napoleon was still running its course, many felt that there was still hope. That is why on hearing the news of Waterloo the English radical William Hazlitt mourned instead of celebrating, drowning his sorrow at the end of all promise in the bottle.

Even conservatives, be they political thinkers like de Maistre or poets like Novalis, dreamed of something more spiritual, and harked back to the Middle Ages in search of a sense of Christian unity with which to confront the forces of revolution, rather than just rely on the bayonets of the army and the spies of the police.

Yet Metternich and his peers preferred those weapons. Police chief Hager had fallen ill at the end of 1815 and died in July of the following year, but the Austrian police machine continued to grow and to extend its tentacles all over Europe, even to the extent of being in a position to intercept and steam open letters at the post office in London. The others were not far behind, and Cathcart complained to Castlereagh from St Petersburg that 'every letter is opened and read, with no other distinction than in the degree of care in the making them up for delivery or transmission after perusal'. As often happens in such circumstances, the instigators of the surveillance fell victim to their own invention. A letter from Countess Lieven to Metternich, dated 19 September 1819, was sent to him with every conceivable precaution: it travelled to Paris in the diplomatic bag addressed to Sir Charles Stuart, encased in four envelopes, the first of which was addressed to the Austrian embassy secretary in Paris, Baron Binder, the second of which bore the instruction to place it in the diplomatic bag to Vienna, the third of which was addressed to Metternich's secretary Floret in Vienna, and the fourth with no superscription at all, since Floret knew what he was supposed to do with it. This did not prevent a neatly written copy of it ending up in the police archives in Paris.[11]

Metternich's methods did not stop at invigilation. As they began to smell dissent or disaffection in every quarter, his police arrested and interrogated young men all over Italy and other Austrian dominions. The methods they used were not gentle, and many suffered cruelly. The Prussian and Russian machinery of repression replicated this, and the state prison and the penal colonies of Siberia began to figure in the European imagination to no less a degree than the infamous *lettre de cachet* and the Bastille had done in the writings of Voltaire and his peers. This state terror continued unchecked in Austria until her defeat in 1866, and in Russia for decades after that, alienating further generations from the new 'legitimacy' of 1815. It could hardly have been otherwise, when in 1846 Metternich decided to uphold that legitimacy by calling on the peasants of Galicia to rise up and massacre their landowners, whom he suspected of preparing a national rising, promising a bounty for every head brought in.

The attempt by Metternich and his colleagues to reimpose the *ancien régime* by force was condemned to failure. While in the eighteenth century it had been challenged by the likes of Voltaire and a handful of free-thinkers, its latter-day reincarnation was rejected by most of society. And that was no longer something statesmen could ignore, as the intervening twenty-five years had awakened and empowered a new force in politics – public opinion.

A good example of this is provided by the position of the Jews. They were, on the whole, very poorly treated by returning monarchs. Despite the valiant efforts of Humboldt and Hardenberg, the status of the Jews in Germany had been left to the Bundestag to decide, and this allowed local rulers to do largely as they pleased – which resulted for the most part in their disenfranchisement or even expulsion. But while only a few lone voices had called for their emancipation before 1789, Napoleon's reforms, which liberated them throughout Europe and accorded them equal rights in all areas under his rule, had altered popular perceptions, and the reimposition of draconian restrictions and medieval exclusions in 1814 offended all progressive opinion.

'A violent conflict is dividing Europe,' the former Napoleonic diplomat baron Édouard Bignon wrote in 1822. 'The intellectual powers of the peoples are directed towards the improvement of the social order. The cabinets, on the other hand, are deploying all their powers, intellectual as well as physical, to arrest this march of the peoples, and even to make them retrace their steps.' This vision of European civilisation being led by its policemen was not limited to Napoleonic sympathisers: Gentz had foreseen it in Paris in 1815, while Harriet Martineau wrote of Castlereagh having repressed 'the better impulses of Europe' and saw him as 'the screw by which England had riveted the chains of nations'. It informed and largely moulded the development of the Romantic movement in the arts throughout the Continent, which was far more political in hue there than it was in Britain. It associated itself naturally with and embraced the cause of revolution and of the downtrodden or the excluded – even to the extent of turning Napoleon into a hero.[12]

The news of his death, which occurred on 5 May 1821, was reported in London on 4 July, but it was overshadowed by the British public's interest in what would happen at the forthcoming coronation, from which the new King, George IV, had banned his unruly Queen. It was said that when the messenger announced the fallen Emperor's death with the words: 'Sire! I have to tell you that your greatest enemy is dead!' the King replied: 'No! By God! Is she?' But on the Continent the news stirred deep emotions, some of which would grow into an almost religious cult, one whose demons were the architects of the Vienna settlement and the Holy Alliance.[13]

One thing that had offended many, even among the more privileged observers at the congress, was the way in which 'souls' were counted, bundled into units and traded across the negotiating table like cattle. This was widely regarded as 'a violation of the dignity of man and of the rights of nations', in the words of Dominique de Pradt, one of the architects of the Bourbon restoration, writing in 1815, and it tainted the work of the congress as a whole in the eyes of many. It was also a great political mistake.

Such treatment of subjects cut through the bonds of loyalty that made them accept the rule of a sovereign without question. The shunting around of populations undermined traditional social networks of control and discipline. The result was not only a marked increase in discontent among the lower orders of society, but also a new spirit of mutinous resistance to authority which would make every state in Europe more difficult to govern. 'The Congress of Vienna has demonstrated that it is easier to be awarded souls than to conquer hearts,' wrote Pradt, 'yet the former are worth little without the latter.' The mistake was compounded where not just bundles of souls but whole nations were involved, and the most obvious failure of the congress was its refusal to address the problem of stateless nations such as the Germans, the Poles and the Italians.[14]

Apologists for the Vienna settlement have argued that the statesmen of 1815 should not be blamed for failing to take account of the force of nationalism, since they could not be expected to have known how powerful it would grow. Being men of their time, the argument goes, they were not aware of the phenomenon of modern nationalism, and could therefore not possibly foresee its potential force.

This is absurd. Huge shifts in perception had taken place over the two or three decades before 1815, and even the most old-fashioned had come to regard states as more than just the patrimony of their ruler. The outcry over the partitions of Poland and later of Saxony, regarded as crimes by Alexander himself, was rooted in the fact that a state had come to be seen as a moral entity with a right to a life of its own.

It is true that the numbers of those who embraced the nationalist gospel were very small. But their influence was nevertheless profound, as the statesmen of the time were well aware. The longing of the Germans for a separate German state filled the writings of their poets and pamphleteers since the 1780s, became a fact of political life after 1806, was given form in organisations such as the Tugendbund, was used by Austria in 1809 to galvanise military support, was acknowledged by Napoleon and his officials, invoked by Stein and the Prussian military, and universally feared by all the crowned heads of Germany in 1813. To pretend that Hardenberg, Alexander and Metternich could somehow have been unaware of its force is ridiculous. Even the British, in trying to raise popular revolts against France's Bavarian allies in the Tyrol, were aware of it.

Much the same goes for Italy, which many of those present at the congress actually wished to see united, and which Metternich himself considered to be the single greatest threat to the Habsburg monarchy. And as for the Poles, they were a byword for national feeling. Between 1797 and 1815 Revolutionary France and then Napoleon enlisted the enthusiastic support of more than 100,000 of them on the promise of furthering the resurrection of Poland. Alexander used Polish national feeling as a threat against Prussia in 1805 and tried to enlist it against France in 1811. And one of the most fundamental problems at the heart of the negotiations in Vienna was the fear that any kind of independent Poland would constitute a vital threat to Russia, Prussia and Austria. Even Castlereagh was aware of the strength of national feeling closer to home, having first ridden its waves and then fought to put it down in Ireland.[15]

There was doubt, frequently expressed, as to the ability of these nations to create a viable state – though why the Italians should be deemed capable of creating a viable state when ruled by the near imbecile Victor Emmanuel and not when allowed to rule themselves remains unclear. But there was certainly no lack of awareness of the strength of national feeling in Germany, Poland and Italy, and by failing to take it into account in their arrangements the architects of the settlement defeated their own purpose and sowed the seeds of untold problems in the future.

At a purely practical level, a striking aspect of the Congress of Vienna is how backward-looking some of the participants were when trying to forge a secure future. Castlereagh's almost obsessive preoccupation with securing Belgium and the Scheldt estuary, which he shared with most of his cabinet, derived from a three-hundred-year-old fear of invasion which had grown entirely out of date. Peace could have been made months earlier, at less cost, if he had been willing to leave the area to France, but he saw it as possibly his greatest priority and devoted a significant proportion of his bargaining resources to obtaining it. In the event, his precious barrier in Belgium was blown away in 1830. Britain was obliged to recognise an independent Belgium, in defence of whose neutrality she would have to go to war twice in the twentieth century; Castlereagh's attempts to create a barrier against French expansion into Germany ended up giving Germany a back door into France, which Britain had to try to close in 1914 and 1940, at immense cost in lives and resources.

Metternich's similarly obsessive desire to dominate Italy in order to deny it to France was rooted in the sixteenth-century wars between Francis I and Charles V, and it was to be the greatest drain on resources for the Habsburg monarchy over the next half-century. He too, in building up the Sardinian kingdom as a barrier to French influence, created the power that would drive Austria out of Italy. And Metternich should not have required the wisdom of hindsight to see this. In 1816 the representative of Genoa at the congress, the Marchese de Brignole, published a pamphlet in which he pointed out that far from creating a barrier against France, Austria had set Sardinia on a course of expansion, which she would pursue by playing France and Austria off against each other. 'Encouraged by an increase of such importance [the acquisition of Genoa], this power will pursue a policy of trading its alliance, as it always has in the past, in order to gradually, with the help of France, take over the whole of Italy,' he wrote.[16]

Similar blind spots resulting from historic or atavistic obsessions affected most of the negotiators, and produced some equally damaging effects. Poland would become a terrible liability to Russia and sap its strength throughout the next century; the Rhineland was to goad Prussia into expansion and ultimately war with France; Sweden would not profit by Norway, which it eventually had to give up, and so on.

The inability to take a fresh view of things and learn from mistakes characterised the policies of the great powers in many areas over the decades following the Congress of Vienna. Metternich typified this attitude, seeking out challenges to his system and attempting to stamp them out before they could take shape in a continuous, frantic, self-perpetuating round of repression. It was utterly in character that when in 1825, he heard that a new university was to be founded in London, he wrote to George IV warning against permitting such a germ of sedition. He viewed what he saw as the laxity of the London cabinet with the concerned condescension of someone who knows better, and he did not significantly alter this view even when, in 1848, revolution in Vienna obliged him to take refuge in London, the only European capital not to be shaken by civil upheaval.

From there he contemplated the wreck of his life's work, with no kindred spirit in whom to confide. Wilhelmina had died in 1839, having managed to add a few more lovers and a fourth husband to the list. It was said that she had died at her dressing table, making herself up for a *soirée*. 'She died at her post, like a brave soldier in his trench,' quipped one unkind soul. Metternich did see his old flame Princess Bagration, who had married an English General, Lord Howden, and moved to London. He came across her in Richmond, and was astonished to find that she was still wearing the diaphanous dresses that had earned her the sobriquet of 'naked angel' forty years before. She would live on till 1857, by which time most of the players of Vienna had long been dead.[17]

The first to go had been Castlereagh, in 1822. The next was Hardenberg, who exerted himself with a new mistress during the Congress of Verona and succumbed to pneumonia shortly after. Alexander ended his days in Taganrog in 1825. Capodistrias, who had become President of the newly independent Greece, was assassinated in 1831. Gentz died in 1832, in the middle of a last fling with a ballerina.

Francis I followed him three years later, Frederick William in 1840. Nesselrode outlived Metternich by three years, living until 1862, but he too never varied from the attitude of vigilant policeman. The only one of them who did develop and go on to a new life, in tune with the times, was Talleyrand.

Talleyrand had been galled by his dismissal in 1815, and while he affected to withdraw from politics he could not resist making trouble for Louis XVIII and his new government, even resorting to opportunistic alliances with *ultra* royalists to do so. His witty jibes earned him disgrace at court, but he was triumphant. He had done well financially out of the congress, and in 1817 he sold a sizeable batch of the French Foreign Ministry's archives, which he had somehow managed to remove, to Metternich for 500,000 francs and the promise that he would be given asylum in Austria should the situation in France prove dangerous for him. Dorothée had tired of Clam-Martinitz, and moved in with Talleyrand, now as his official mistress. He seized the opportunity provided by the revolution of 1830, and was sent to London by the new King, Louis-Philippe, to procure British acceptance of the new status quo in France and later the formation of an independent Belgium. He enjoyed a last period of glory as French ambassador in London, with Dorothée at his side, before retiring to his country seat of Valençay, where he died in 1838. Dorothée died at Sagan in 1862.

If there is much to criticise in the work of the peacemakers of 1815, it has to be admitted that they did face a formidable task, one that defied any ideal solution. Just because certain arrangements they made turned out to have evil consequences, it does not follow that the opposite course would have yielded more benign results. And they did achieve their principal aim, which was to bring about peace after a quarter of a century of war. The congress does stand as a watershed in the affairs of the world, if only by virtue of what was said and discussed. Even by its stumbling progress, it suggested a different approach to the conduct of international relations, and it initiated a series of processes which were to become part of the furniture of world affairs.

Despite the collapse of the congress system after Verona in 1822, the idea and practice of consulting and cooperation survived. Some form of conference or congress would henceforth be held to deal with every major crisis, and conferences of ministers and ambassadors were called to deal with specific problems, suggesting a growing sense of solidarity between the powers.

But it remained a frail solidarity, undermined by mutual suspicion and fear, for the settlement had not created any kind of balance of power. Britain had emerged vastly stronger and virtually invulnerable, except perhaps through Russian attempts to subvert her rule in India. Russia had gained a protective buffer in the west, leaving her free to pursue dreams of conquest in the Balkans and in Asia. Austria on the other hand had come out of the peacemaking process as a highly vulnerable state, entirely dependent on the good will of her neighbours. Prussia, while gaining in size and power, had also exposed herself to attack from all sides. So while Britain and Russia were free to indulge their appetites outside Europe without fear of attack from it, Austria could only hope for the continuance of the status quo, while Prussia could only wish for war, which was the one way she would be able to 'fill in the gaps', as Humboldt had put it. The Prussian state remained a work in progress until 1870. But by then it had set itself up as a direct threat to France, and also to Russia, posing new challenges that could only be resolved through war.

The Vienna settlement, and the Quadruple Alliance, placed France in a position which her people could only consider humiliating. The perceived necessity of righting this wrong led inexorably to the sabre-rattling of 1840, the war of 1870, to 1914 and beyond.

The way in which the Congress of Vienna excluded all the second-rank states and concentrated power in the hands of the great powers led to the decline of formerly powerful states such as Sweden, Denmark, Holland and Naples, with a consequent narrowing of the range of possible alliances, further reducing the possibility of an equilibrium of forces. It also bred more arrogant attitudes among the great powers. When, in 1863, the Prussian chancellor Otto von Bismarck was warned by a British diplomat that he ran the risk of incurring the disapproval of Europe, he barked back: 'Who is Europe?'[18]

The Congress of Vienna was also a watershed in that the rights of people and nations had entered into the councils of monarchs and ministers. Much attention had been devoted by the peacemakers in Paris in 1814 to safeguarding the immunity and interests of individuals, and much ink to the rights of nations. More remarkably, the fate of the Jews, hitherto regarded as pariahs not worthy of the same consideration as other men, had actually made it onto the agenda. Even more astonishingly, the predicament of black slaves had been the subject of lengthy discussion and legislation.

Yet neither the Jews nor the slaves, any more than the nations without states, saw much immediate improvement in their condition – Jewish disabilities remained in place for decades in many places, while the slave trade was only gradually stamped out, and the institution itself not abolished till 1838 in the British colonies, almost thirty years later in the United States, and not until the end of the century in Brazil.

In some ways, this new consciousness of the wrongs inflicted on individuals and communities, be they racial, religious or national, only aggravated their sense of exclusion and consequent alienation. The Germans, disappointed in their hopes of a German homeland, abandoned the pursuit of their cause for a pursuit of culture, taking comfort in the concept of German exceptionalism based on an inward-looking hurt pride, a dangerous retreat that cut them off from the rest of the world. The Danes too, traumatised by the loss of Norway and their former glory, sought solace in a new patriotic literature. The French, forced to abandon many of the social gains and the glories of the Revolutionary and Napoleonic period, were all but condemned to a pointless and often bloody cycle of revolution and reaction that left one or other part of the nation in a state of psychological emigration for most of the century. The Italians, like the Germans, achieved national unification in 1870, but during the years preceding that, they, like the Poles, were condemned to an unnatural, repressed, clandestine existence that bred subversion and ultimately aggression. This affected only a fraction of the population, but they were the most restless elements, and they would provide the legends on which the masses would be nourished in future; it would not be a wholesome diet.

While the Congress of Vienna failed to guarantee a century of peace, it did bring into being a simulacrum of stability, a kind of *pax Europaea*, identified with law and order, fine public institutions, scientific progress, prosperity for an expanding middle class, railways, electric lighting, opera and many of the components of civilised life. But this was bought at immense cost, levied both in Europe and overseas, particularly in Africa, and it sowed the seeds of its own destruction.

The Vienna settlement imposed an orthodoxy which not only denied political existence to many nations; it enshrined a particularly stultified form of monarchical government; institutionalised social hierarchies as rigid as any that had existed under the *ancien régime*; and preserved archaic disabilities – serfdom was not abolished in Russia until half a century after the congress. By excluding whole classes and nations from a share in its benefits, this system nurtured envy and resentment, which flourished into socialism and aggressive nationalism. And when, after the 'Concert of Europe' had fought itself to extinction in the Great War, those forces were at last unleashed, they visited on Europe events more horrific than the worst fears Metternich or any of his colleagues could have entertained.

It would be idle to propose that the arrangements made in 1815 caused the terrible cataclysms of the twentieth century. But anyone who attempted to argue that what happened in Russia after 1917, in Italy and Germany in the 1920s, 1930s and 1940s, and in many other parts of central and southern Europe at various other moments of the last century had no connection with them would be exposing themselves to ridicule.

Notes

Abbreviations
AE – Ministère des Affaires Étrangères, Paris
BC – Biblioteka Książąt Czartoryskich, Kraków
BL – British Library, London
BPU – Bibliothèque Publique et Universitaire, Genève
HHSA – Haus-, Hof- und StaatsArchiv, Vienna
NA – National Archives, Kew
ON – Österreichische Nationalbibliothek, Vienna
PRONI – Public Record Office of Northern Ireland, Belfast
SUA – Státní Ústřední Archiv, Prague

In the notes I give the author under which the source is listed, followed by the date of publication, if there are more than two titles listed under the same name.

Chapter 1: The Lion at Bay

1. Caulaincourt, II/349–51; Bourgoing, 1862, 98–101. There are discrepancies between the various accounts of Napoleon's homecoming. I have chosen Caulaincourt's, on the basis that he was physically as well as mentally closest to the Emperor throughout.
2. Bourgoing, 1862, 21, 29
3. Napoleon, XXIV/342–3; see also Caulaincourt, II/339–40
4. Napoleon, XXIV/369
5. Napoleon, XXIV/340
6. Driault, 59; Thiers, 195
7. Caulaincourt, II/389–90, 393–4

8. Caulaincourt, II/315
9. Cambacérès, 1999, II/429
10. Napoleon, XXIV/380–1
11. Fain, 1824, I/210
12. Fain, 1824, I/238–41, 296–9, 301–3, 306–7; Abrantès, XI/90–1; Castellane, I/222; Broglie, I/214, 218, 220
13. Fain, 1824, I/222

Chapter 2: The Saviour of Europe

1. Shilder, III/134
2. Choiseul-Gouffier, 166
3. Czartoryski, 1887, I/345; Ley, 1975, 62
4. Kukiel, 30–1; see also Skowronek
5. Webster, 1931, 388–94
6. Martin, 9
7. Schroeder, 1994, 24; Grunewald, 61
8. Shishkov, I/167, 244; Zorin, 251, 264
9. Stein, IV/188
10. Kraehe, I/151
11. Hardenberg, 1828, XII/17
12. Hardenberg, 1828, XII/13–15; Fain, 1824, I/231–7
13. Kügelgen, 136; Bruun, 173; Pichler, II/224
14. Angeberg, I/1–2; Martens, F., VII/74
15. Angeberg, I/7–8
16. Angeberg, I/5–7
17. Hardenberg, 1828, XII/42

Chapter 3: The Peacemakers

1. Sorel, 1894, 5
2. Kraehe, I/43
3. Gentz, 1876, I/8
4. Gentz, 1876, I/13; Oncken, I/416–20
5. Buckland, 1933, 459ff, 491ff; Fain, 1824, I/296–9
6. Wilson, 1860, 234; Stanislavskaia, 66ff; Maistre, 1851, I/324
7. Angeberg, I/2–4; Martens, G.F., I/558
8. Chamberlain, 1983, 106; Levey, 182

Chapter 4: A War for Peace

1. Napoleon, XXIV/521
2. Napoleon, XXIV/464, 468, 500, 539
3. Napoleon, XXV/61–3; Driault, 76

4. Fain, 1824, I/247–75; Driault, 76
5. Oncken, I/439; Méneval, III/129
6. Oncken, II/624
7. Bonnefons, 377; Koch, X/200–3
8. BL, Bunbury Papers I, 12; Londonderry, 32–3
9. Beauharnais, IX/94
10. Alexander, 1910, 150; Rochechouart, 217, 219–20; BL, Bunbury Papers I, 18; Londonderry, 25–6, 31
11. Driault, 51
12. Kraehe, I/154
13. Nesselrode, V/3, 14, 20, 38–9, 50, 65, 69, 75
14. Oncken, I/421ff; Driault, 74; Nicholas Mikhailovich, 1912, II/138ff, 166
15. Bibl, 1936, 13
16. Oncken, I/446; Kraehe, I/172; Driault, 91
17. Oncken, II/673–8
18. Angeberg, I/13; Metternich, 1880, I/250; Fain, 1824, 390
19. Broglie, I/223; Müffling, 45–50; BL, Bunbury Papers I, 25; Hardenberg, 1828, XII/83–4; Londonderry, 33; Müffling, 31
20. Londonderry, 34; AE, Russie 25, 142
21. Löwenstern, II/131–2; Müffling, 45
22. Vionnet, 81–3; Fain, 1824, I/430; Otrante, 1945, II/388–9
23. Fain, 1824, I/426–7; AE, Russie 25, 130

Chapter 5: Intimate Congress

1. Broglie, I/224–5; Metternich, 1880, I/139–40; Nicholas Mikhailovich, 1912, II/167, 175, etc.
2. Nesselrode, V/103
3. SUA, Acta Clementina 12, 33/4, 7/9
4. Gentz, 1868, I/8
5. Maevskii, 256; Metternich, 1868, I/251
6. Shishkov, I/206–7
7. Grimsted, 198, 207
8. Wilson, 1861, II/45–6; Webster, 1921, 69
9. Kraehe, II/4; Sweet, 1941; Humboldt, IV/26–30, 32–3, 42; see also Benkendorff, 331
10. Jackson, II/204
11. Jackson, II/149
12. Aroutunova, 99, 101
13. Jackson, II/204
14. Oncken, II/640–1
15. Castlereagh, IX/22

16. Angeberg, I/9–12
17. Londonderry, 68
18. Sorel, 1904, VIII/136–8; Nicholas Mikhailovich, 1912, II/184; Driault, 118
19. Nesselrode, I/99; Martens, F., III/107
20. Gentz, 1876, I/20–1; SUA, Acta Clementina 12, 33/8; Gentz, 1868, I/12–13; SUA, Acta Clementina 5, 2/19–80; Klinkowström, C., 79–83
21. BL, Aberdeen Papers XXXV, 52
22. BL, Aberdeen Papers XXXV, 56, 60; Webster, 1931, 144–5, 148–9; Webster, 1921, 8, 9, 14–15; Castlereagh, IX/22, 30–2
23. Angeberg, I/13–17
24. SUA, Acta Clementina 12, 33/9; Metternich, 1880, I/147–53, II/461–2; Nesselrode, V/108–15; Fain, 1824, II/36–44
25. SUA, Acta Clementina 12, 33/9
26. Fain, 1824, II/57
27. SUA, Acta Clementina 12, 33/9; Acta Clementina 14a, 5/19
28. Metternich, 1909, 111–12; Rzewuska, I/261
29. Metternich, 1966, 24–8
30. Klinkowström, C., 79
31. Angeberg, I/18–19; Klinkowström, C., 81; Metternich, 1880, I/154–7; Fain, 1824, II/45ff

Chapter 6: Farce in Prague

1. Otrante, 1824, II/196–7; Fain, 1824, II/66–7; Otrante, 1945, II/404
2. Fain, 1824, II/79–80
3. Londonderry, 372–3; Humboldt, IV/78
4. Metternich, 1966, 32
5. Bertier, 1959, 106, 116–17; Bibl, 1927, 257–329
6. HHSA, St K. Interiora Archiv, Intercepte 1, 7 passim
7. Nesselrode, I/99–100; Humboldt, IV/52, 76; Hardenberg, 1828, XII/207; Klinkowström, C., 81; SUA, Acta Clementina 12, 33/12ff; Metternich, 1881, I/255–6; Sorel, 1904, VIII/173; HHSA, St K. Interiora 78, 3
8. Humboldt, IV/69; AE, France 666, 219; Sorel, 1904, VIII/158–9
9. AE, France 667, 75; SUA, Acta Clementina 12, 33/20
10. Broglie, I/235–9; HHSA, St K. Interiora 78, 3
11. Gentz, 1868, 40; Humboldt, IV/62–3, 79; Sweet, 1978, II/138
12. Kraehe, I/182–3; Jackson, II/206–8
13. SUA, Acta Clementina 12, 33/21; Humboldt, IV/92
14. SUA, Acta Clementina 12, 33/20
15. Fain, 1824, II/205–17; SUA, Acta Clementina 12, 33/1
16. Metternich, 1966, 38–9
17. PRONI, D.3030/P, 74; Angeberg, I/47; SUA, Acta Clementina 12, 33/22

18. BL, Aberdeen Papers XXXVI, 161–3
19. Webster, 1931, 157; PRONI, D.3030/P, 72; Otrante, 1824, II/159; Talleyrand, 1935, 176
20. Jackson, II/218; PRONI, D.3030/P, 75
21. Beugnot, II/4–6; Beauharnais, IX/108, 117
22. Nesselrode, I/103; Garros, 424
23. SUA, Acta Clementina 12, 7/12
24. Hardenberg, 1828, XII/51–4; Benkendorff, 331; Löwenstern, II/101–3
25. Angeberg, I/25–6; BL, Bunbury Papers I, 84; Londonderry, 101–2
26. Metternich, 1880, I/161–3; Jackson, II/293; Londonderry, 132; PRONI, D.3030/P, 79, 76; Metternich, 1880, I/166; see also Wilson, 1861, II/109
27. Metternich, 1966, 54, 59, 80
28. Angeberg, I/50–2
29. Metternich, 1880, I/160
30. Metternich, 1880, I/161, 168–9

Chapter 7: The Play for Germany

1. Metternich, 1881, I/258
2. Klinkowström, C., 64
3. Balfour, I/69, 71; Chamberlain, 1983, 126
4. BL, Aberdeen Papers XXXV, 293; Chamberlain, 1983, 128, 130
5. BL, Aberdeen Papers XXXVI, 1, 3, 9; PRONI, D.3030/P, 82, 84
6. Flamand, 331–2; Nørregard, 30; Langslet, 20, 66, 70
7. BL, Aberdeen Papers XXXVI, 200
8. Langslet, 76–80; Hardenberg, 1828, XII/97–8; Castlereagh, X/77
9. Webster, 1921, 97
10. Rochechouart, 243; Jackson, II/286, 289; PRONI, D.3030/P, 88
11. Londonderry, 77; see also Wilson, 1861, II/74, 145; Méneval, III/213–15; Hardenberg, 1828, XIII/180
12. Scott, 468; Rochechouart, 251; Londonderry, 233; Driault, 160; Rain, 29–30; Staël, 1970, 446, 460; Stein, IV/239
13. PRONI, D.3030/P, 90, 91; Ordioni, 110
14. PRONI, D.3030/P, 88; Angeberg, I/56; BL, Aberdeen Papers XXXVI, 15
15. Webster, 1921, 19, 24–5
16. Webster, 1921, 31–2
17. Capodistrias, 175; Shishkov, I/349–50
18. Balfour, I/96, 99
19. Humboldt, IV/114; Sweet, 1978, II/150–1; Metternich, 1966, 93–4
20. Kraehe, I/151, 193
21. Klinkowström, C., 56
22. Driault, 183

23. Angeberg, I/56–60
24. Bonnefons, 457–8, 463; Rochechouart, 267; Angeberg, I/197
25. Hardenberg, 1828, XII/258
26. SUA, Acta Clementina 12, 33/39; Stein, IV/439
27. Chamberlain, 1983, 134
28. Metternich, 1966, 82
29. McGuigan, 163
30. Ley, 1975, 72; Aroutunova, 111
31. Metternich, 1880, I/168–9; Angeberg, I/60–3
32. Humboldt, IV/115, 155–6
33. Metternich, 1966, 87, 90
34. Metternich, 1966, 88

Chapter 8: The First Waltzes

1. Pasquier, II/96–7
2. Beugnot, II/38
3. Beauharnais, IX/299ff, 284–5, 295
4. Martineau, G., 7; Otrante, 1824, II/437; Sorel, 1904, VIII/194, 237; Webster, 1921, 95
5. Pasquier, II/99; Cambacérès, 1999, II/491, 495: Rowe, 217–18; Pradt, 1814, 18; Cambacérès, 1973, II/1099, 1112
6. Beugnot, II/54; Pasquier, II/100
7. Metternich, 1966, 98–9, 99–100
8. Shishkov, I/373
9. SUA, Acta Clementina 12, 33/48; PRONI, D.3030/P, 114; Metternich, 1966, 105; McGuigan, 171; Burghersh, 1893, 82–3
10. SUA, Acta Clementina 12, 7/20
11. Jackson, II/340–1; Stein, IV/469, 476
12. Humboldt, IV/178
13. Metternich, 1880, I/163; Shishkov, I/238–42
14. BL, Aberdeen Papers XXXVII, 114, 146; PRONI, D.3030/P, 115; Londonderry, 387–8; Müffling, 395–7
15. Müffling, 92; Weil, 1891, I/1–2
16. Webster, 1921, 98, 111, 103, 102
17. AE, France 669, 7ff; Angeberg, I/74–8
18. Angeberg, I/77–8; Sorel, 1904, VIII/220–1; Fain, 1825, 5, 20, 49–56
19. Chamberlain, 1983, 162; see also BL, Aberdeen Papers XXXVII, 317
20. PRONI, D.3030/P, 108
21. Webster, 1921, 25; BL, Aberdeen Papers XXXVI, 307
22. Chamberlain, 1983, 139, 141
23. BL, Aberdeen Papers XXXVI, 12

24. PRONI, D.3030/P, 108, 113; BL, Aberdeen Papers XXXVII, 205; Chamberlain, 1983, 155; Webster, 1931, 175
25. Chamberlain, 1983, 150; Webster, 1931, 181, 184–5, 198
26. BL, Aberdeen Papers XXXVII, 217
27. PRONI, D.3030/P, 112–15; BL, Aberdeen Papers XXXVII, 166, 203
28. ON, 6/86, 3; Metternich, 1966, 134, 140, 147
29. Metternich, 1880, I/323; Humboldt, IV/128; SUA, Acta Clementina 12, 33/53
30. Angeberg, I/78–9
31. Lebzeltern; Capodistrias, 178ff; Rappard, 92; Chapuisat; Alexander, 1910, 160
32. Stein, IV/508
33. PRONI, D.3030/P, 115; Jackson, II/383; BL, Aberdeen Papers XXXVII, 317
34. Chamberlain, 1983, 160; Hardenberg, 2000, 755; Angeberg, I/79
35. Castlereagh, IX/454; Schroeder, 1994, 486; Chamberlain, 1983, 162; Webster, 1921, 62–3
36. Buckingham, II/45–6

Chapter 9: A Finger in the Pie

1. Brownlow, 29
2. Fraser, 236–7; Hogendorp, IV/222–35, 262–5, 269, 271
3. Renier, 214
4. Hogendorp, V/228–9; Löwenstern, II/101–3
5. PRONI, D.3030/T/MC3, 292
6. Metternich, 1966, 181; Webster, 1931, 200; Humboldt, IV/226
7. Webster, 1921, 131; Metternich, 1966, 180
8. Metternich, 1966, 179, 183, 202; Metternich, 1880, I/181; Klinkowström, A.F., 797, 800; see also Fournier, 1900, 251
9. Webster, 1921, 123–8
10. Metternich, 1880, II/182; Fournier, 1900, 349; Gentz, 1876, I/51; Weil, 1891, I/69
11. Webster, 1921, 133, 136–8
12. Webster, 1921, 138–44
13. Fournier, 1900, 299; Hardenberg, 1828, XII/378; Mikhailovskii-Danilevskii, 28; NA, FO 92, 3; Nesselrode, V/152; Londonderry, 245–6
14. Grunewald, 259–61; Gentz, 1876, I/60–1; Hardenberg, 2000, 770; Weil, 1891, I/351–8, II/68, 70
15. Webster, 1921, 144
16. Nicholas Mikhailovich, 1912, I/132–3; Zorin, 278
17. Chamberlain, 1983, 165
18. Metternich, 1966, 198–201
19. Webster, 1921, 145; Webster, 1931, 201; SUA, Acta Clementina 5, Gentziana III, 15

20. Webster, 1921, 141–4
21. Webster, 1931, 209
22. Webster, 1921, 146

Chapter 10: Battlefield Diplomacy
 1. SUA, Acta Clementina 14a, 5/250–1
 2. Caulaincourt, III/13; Hortense, III/174, 177
 3. Fain, 1825, 64–6, 72–5
 4. Vionnet, 105
 5. PRONI, D.3030/T/MC3, 292
 6. Burghersh, 1893, 172; Hardenberg, 2000, 771–2; Webster, 1921, 147–8
 7. Webster, 1921, 149
 8. Webster, 1921, 150–1, 154–5
 9. Castlereagh, IX/266–73, 312
10. Fournier, 1900, 289, 291, 293; Hardenberg, 2000, 772; see also Metternich, 1880, I/185–6; Metternich, 1966, 207
11. Hardenberg, 2000, 773; Brunov, 377ff; Hardenberg, 2000, 773–4; NA, FO 92, 1, 3 (26 February 1814); Weil, 1891, II/314, 349, 397
12. Benkendorff, 349; NA, FO 92, 3; see also Metternich, 1880, I/190
13. Caulaincourt, III/15–16; Montbas, 805–6; Fain, 1825, 75–8, 284–5
14. Fournier, 1900, 308, 369–73
15. Fournier, 1900, 316, 308, 311–13, 318; Caulaincourt, III/33
16. Gash, 108; Jackson, II/411; Chamberlain, 1983, 169
17. Londonderry, 275; Fournier, 1900, 318
18. Angeberg, I/105–7; AE, France 669, 62–80
19. Alison, II/272ff; Caulaincourt, III/15–24; Fournier, 1900, 310; see also Gentz, 1876, I/62–70; Fain, 1825, 255–7, 289–94; Montbas, June, 815–18; AE, France 668, 179–82, 205
20. Webster, 1931, 505–6; Fournier, 1900, 315; BL, Bunbury Papers I, 179
21. Londonderry, 278; Burghersh, 1893, 181; Humboldt, IV/259
22. Angeberg, I/111–15; AE, France 668, 250, France 669, 95
23. Angeberg, I/120–9; AE, France 669, 136–77
24. AE, France 669, 178–98, France 670 passim, France 668, 321–2, 328, 455–8; Angeberg, I/130–41; Hardenberg, 2000, 781; Montbas, June; AE, France 668, 461
25. Martens, F., III/107, 123
26. Brunov, 301; Grunewald, 225; Edling, 208
27. Hardenberg, 2000, 767
28. Londonderry, 275–7; Alison, II/240–2
29. BC, 5239/IV, 3; Webster, 1921, 163
30. Hardenberg, 2000, 777; Klinkowström, A.F., 819; Fournier, 1900, 303

31. PRONI, D.3030/T/MC3, 292
32. Londonderry, 288–90
33. PRONI, D.3030/T/MC3, 292
34. SUA, Acta Clementina 12, 34/24
35. Jackson, II/418; Webster, 1931, 506
36. Webster, 1931, 388–94; Webster, 1921, 157, 165
37. Webster, 1921, 166

Chapter 11: Paris Triumph

1. Hardenberg, 2000, 782; Castlereagh, IX/336–7; BL, Bunbury Papers I, 181
2. AE, France 669, 78; Cambacérès, 1973, II/1131
3. Webster, 1921, 168–71; Vitrolles, 216–17; see also Rochechouart, 285–91
4. Vitrolles, 226; see also Waresquiel, 2003, 437; Webster, 1931, 243
5. Weil, 1891, III/34–5, 505, 512, 553
6. Webster, 1921, 171–2; Hardenberg, 2000, 784
7. Webster, 1921, 173–4; Scott, 467; Beugnot, II/78–80; NA, FO 92, 4 (3 May 1814)
8. Guizot, I/24–5
9. Jackson, II/400, 405; see also Humboldt, IV/231
10. Talleyrand, 1957, II/265ff, 306; Waresquiel, 2003, 424
11. Talleyrand, 1957, II/307–8
12. Sorel, 1904, VIII/311–12; Talleyrand, 1891, 170; Coigny, 240ff
13. Boigne, I/328; Maevskii, 383–4; Rochechouart, 325; Boigne, I/330–1
14. Rémusat, I/270–1; Nesselrode, I/114
15. Talleyrand, 1957, II/314; see also Beugnot, II/103; Rochechouart, 346ff; Bourienne, X/37–42; Pasquier, II/246; Boigne, I/332–3; Choiseul-Gouffier, i; Gentz, 1876, I/77
16. Rain, 79; Pasquier, II/313, 327; Waresquiel, 2003, 446–7; on Maubreuil Affair, see: Vitrolles, I/422ff; Pasquier, II/366ff
17. Fain, 1825, 398ff
18. Beugnot, II/100
19. Caulaincourt, III/156–7; Broglie, II/263; Webster, 1921, 176; Webster, 1931, 250
20. Berry, 24; Brownlow, 76
21. PRONI, D.3030/T/MC3, 292; SUA, Acta Clementina 12, 7/27; Metternich, 1966, 241
22. Hardenberg, 2000, 786; Metternich, 1966, 244, 248

Chapter 12: Peace

1. Angeberg, I/157–60; Bonnal, I/3
2. Pasquier, II/237–8
3. Mansel, 1981, 147

4. Boigne, I/383–4; Shilder, III/227–8, 231
5. Metternich, 1966, 243
6. Talleyrand, 1957, II/320; Waresquiel, 2003, 737–8
7. Beauharnais, X/255, 288, 291–2
8. Beugnot, II/99
9. Londonderry, 328–30; Boigne, I/401–2
10. Metternich, 1966, 243; Otrante, 1824, II/180; Coigny, 245–6; SUA, Acta Clementina 12, 34/28
11. Hardenberg, 2000, 786ff; Löwenstern, II/424; Montet, 122
12. SUA, Acta Clementina 12, 34/32
13. Chapuisat, 34; McGuigan, 274
14. Burghersh, 1912, 58; Nesselrode, I/63; Stein, IV/627; Bourienne, IX/146
15. Löwenstern, II/431; Chatelain, 218–21; Chamberlain, 1983, 168; AE, France 671, 217
16. Metternich, 1966, 252
17. Talleyrand, 1891, 259
18. AE, France 673, 91ff; Webster, 1931, 273; Sorel, 1904, VIII/349; Münster, 176–7
19. NA, FO 92, 4 (5 May 1814), 105–6; Stein, IV/642–3
20. Shilder, III/223, 232–3; Nicholas Mikhailovich, 1912, 135
21. Kukiel, 115; Zawadzki, 226; Shilder, III/235–7; Potocka, 361
22. Castlereagh, IX/511
23. Talleyrand, 1891, 281
24. Talleyrand, 1880, I/167
25. Thomas, 235, 573; AE, France 673, 51, 57–8; Angeberg, I/173; *Considérations importantes . . .* ; Labrador, 36; Webster, 1931, 576
26. Webster, 1931; Pollock, 204
27. Wellington, 1845, VII/534
28. Wellington, 1845, VII/545, 557–9, 574
29. NA, FO 92, 4 (30 May 1814)
30. AE, France 673, 326 (wrongly described as being to Princess Lieven)
31. Münster, 163; Martens, III/168
32. Hardenberg, 1828, XIII/445; Zorin, 250–1; Creevey, I/191
33. Angeberg, I/170; AE, France 673, 326; SUA, Acta Clementina 12, 34/33; McGuigan, 298

Chapter 13: The London Round

1. Alexander, 1910, 227–8
2. Alexander, 1910, 229, 179–80
3. Webster, 1931, 299, 451; see also Renier, 181
4. Alexander, 1910, 169–76
5. Castlereagh, X/53; Brownlow, 107; Castlereagh, X/61; Hogendorp, V/401

6. Renier, 200, 225–6; Castlereagh, IX/255, 307, 317, 340–1, 354–5; *Mémoire adressé . . .*; Castlereagh, X/23; Renier, 268, 234–5, 275; Webster, 1931, 304–5; Castlereagh, X/41, 54; Renier, 324–33
7. Festing, 192; Jackson, II/435–6, 441; see also Shelley, 58–9; Brownlow, 108
8. Creevey, I/196
9. Hardenberg, 2000, 790–1
10. Nesselrode, V/195–6; SUA, Acta Clementina 12, 34/38
11. Alexander, 1910, 238–9
12. Pollock, 243; Webster, 1931, 413ff
13. Creevey, I/195; Nicholas Mikhailovich, 1912, I/150
14. Kukiel, 116; Zawadzki, 229; Fournier, 1918, 209
15. Alexander, 1910, 242–4
16. Shelley, 62, 157–8, 63
17. NA, FO 92, 5/2, 3, 4, 6, 14, 16
18. Humboldt, IV/348; SUA, Acta Clementina 12, 34/39
19. Gentz, 1876, I/89–93
20. Fournier, 1918, I/206–8, 209–10, 212, II/24–5, 30–1
21. Angeberg, I/183; NA, FO 92, 8, 9, 13

Chapter 14: Just Settlements

1. Senancourt, 7; Croft, 8; Metternich, 1880, I/203
2. Talleyrand, 1976, 114; Martens, II/486
3. Shilder, III/499; Martens, G.F., III/234
4. Bartlett, 145; Alison, II/241 (note)
5. Beales, 3
6. Rinieri, 1904, 129
7. Angeberg, I/91–104; Webster, 1931, 306, 542, 308–9
8. Weil, 1917, I/243–4; Dolgorukov, 272
9. Webster, 1921, 182
10. Wellington, 1845, VII/486; Castlereagh, X/27
11. Webster, 1931, 310–13; Wellington, 1845, VII/503, 504–7
12. Webster, 1931, 255–6
13. Beauharnais, IX/299ff; Hortense, II/178
14. Wilson, 1861, II/344
15. Rath, 1950, 309–10; Bianchi, I/48, 339–43; Verga, 318; Haas, 27
16. Eynard, J.E., I/173
17. Castlereagh, X/10
18. Castlereagh, X/18; Webster, 1931, 314
19. Gallenga, III/311–14; Boigne, II/75
20. Boigne, II/82
21. Castlereagh, X/114–15

22. Rinieri, 1904, 126, 131, 152–6; Buschkuhl, 51
23. O'Dwyer, 135

Chapter 15: Setting the Stage

1. Metternich, 1966, 258
2. McGuigan, 318–19
3. Metternich, 1966, 262; Gentz, 1861, 286
4. Kraehe, II/80
5. Fournier, 1918, 28
6. Kraehe, II/19
7. Kraehe, II/321
8. Humboldt, IV/165
9. Sweet, 1978, II/140ff
10. Kraehe, II/120
11. Fournier, 1918, 32
12. Kraehe, II/76–7; Stein, V/9, 11–13
13. Gagern, II/44, 46; Kraehe, II/183–4
14. Nesselrode, V/196–7; Pozzo, 15, 16, 49, etc.
15. Talleyrand, 1881, 1
16. Wilson, 1861, II/338
17. Metternich, 1964, 52
18. Weil, 1917, I/10–11
19. Weil, 1917, I/xxiii, 123–4
20. HHSA, Zeremoniell Protokoll, 47; Krog, 224
21. Eynard, J.E., I/4–5; Méneval, III/267
22. Castlereagh, X/57; Kraehe, II/85; Mikhailovskii-Danilevskii, 186
23. Spiel, 78–80
24. Kraehe, II/118; La Garde, 3
25. Jackson, II/353; Eynard, J.E., I/46
26. AE, France 673, 37; Montet, 115; Boncompagni, 27; AE, France 688; Kraehe, II/189
27. Nicholas Mikhailovich, 1905, I/49

Chapter 16: Points of Order

1. McGuigan, 325; Metternich, 1966, 263–4
2. Fournier, 1918, 27–8, 211, 215; Gentz, 1868, I/152; Fournier, 1913, 109–16
3. Castlereagh, X/93
4. Castlereagh, X/76, 92; Webster, 1921, 191–2
5. Webster, 1931, 332; Ivanov, II/22; BPU, 38
6. Shilder, III/271
7. Castlereagh, X/95–7

8. HHSA, St K. Kongresakten 2, 1
9. HHSA, St K. Kongresakten 1, 46, 54–5
10. HHSA, St K. Kongresakten 1, 68, 71
11. Sweet, 1978, II/178–9; Webster, 1934, 175–83; Webster, 1921, 194–5
12. Gentz, 1876, I/106; Sorel, 1904, VIII/383
13. Hardenberg, 2000, 796, 798
14. HHSA, St K. Kongresakten 2, 7–10; Talleyrand, 1881, 340–6; HHSA, St K. Kongresakten 1, 1; Gentz, 1861, 288
15. Webster, 1921, 195
16. Pasquier, III/67, 69
17. Talleyrand, 1881, 38–9; Sorel, 1904, VIII/393
18. *Les Classiques de la table*, 368
19. Dino, 137–9; Noel, 111
20. Gentz, 1876, I/100; Fournier, 1918, 213
21. Shilder, III/242
22. Nicholas Mikhailovich, 1909, II/504–5
23. Ley, 1975, 86; Zorin, 279
24. Shilder, III/246, 231, 254, 256–7, 272; Kraehe, II/131–2
25. Shilder, III/534–6
26. Shilder, III/537–40
27. Askenazy, 127, 369–73; Kukiel, 119; Zawadzki, 1993, 231–3; Shilder, III/264–8
28. Metternich, 1966, 265
29. Nicholas Mikhailovich, 1909, II/582; Pozzo, 82
30. Webster, 1921, 197
31. Webster, 1921, 199
32. Hardenberg, 2000, 798; John, 174
33. Weil, 1917, I/14, 28–9, 65, 92, 99, 101, 111, 127
34. Gentz, 1861, 290–1; Angeberg, I/252–3

Chapter 17: Notes and Balls

1. Villa-Urrutia, 123
2. AE, France 682, 4; HHSA, St K. Kongresakten 1, 250; Labrador, 35
3. In his memoirs (Talleyrand, 1957, II/396), Talleyrand states that he sat between Metternich and Hardenberg; HHSA, St K. Kongresakten 1, 4; Talleyrand, 1881, 10–18; AE, France 672, 17–48, France 682, 10; Talleyrand, 1957, II/395–8; Gentz, 1861, 289, 320; for this and subsequent meetings see also: NA, FO 92, 7
4. Weil, 1917, I/191, 193, 205
5. Talleyrand, 1881, 18–21
6. Weil, 1917, I/200; Hardenberg, 2000, 799; Gentz, 1876, I/113; Talleyrand, 1881, 26
7. Webster, 1921, 202–3; HHSA, St K. Kongresakten 2, 14

8. Historical Manuscripts Commission, 297; Rinieri, 1903, lviii; Bertuch, 21; Perth, 45
9. Bernstorff, I/155
10. Hardenberg, 2000, 799
11. Spiel, 93
12. Angeberg, I/264
13. HHSA, St K. Kongresakten 1, 352; Eynard, J.E., 256
14. Perth, 47
15. Hardenberg, 2000, 800; Angeberg, I/270–2
16. Gentz, 1876, I/107; Gentz, 1861, 322; Gentz, 1876, I/115–16
17. La Garde, 78; Eynard, J.E., I/6
18. Bernstorff, I/156
19. Talleyrand, 1881, 33
20. Labrador, 45
21. Talleyrand, 1881, 35–6; Gentz, 1861, 324
22. Jackson, II/449; Talleyrand, 1976, 52, 55
23. Talleyrand, 1881, 46–7; Gagern, II/70
24. Talleyrand, 1976, 43
25. Eynard, J.E., 8–10
26. Weil, 1917, I/11–12, 171–2, 185–6; Webster, 1921, 201–2
27. Angeberg, I/276–8; Webster, 1931, 344; Gagern, II/62, 96
28. BPU, 203–5
29. BPU, 11
30. Rinieri, 1902, lviii; BPU, 14–15
31. BPU, 16; Bertuch, 51; Pichler, III/49–50
32. Talleyrand, 1976, 48; Castlereagh, X/162
33. Shilder, I/288; Weil, 1917, I/261

Chapter 18: Kings' Holiday

1. Montet, 112, 114
2. Talleyrand, 1976, 40; Gentz, 1861, 321
3. Rosenkrantz, 38, 50
4. Rinieri, 1902, lix; Weil, 1917, I/139, 364–5, 442, 475
5. Nørregard, 49–50, 25–6, 31–2, 62, 102
6. Weil, 1917, I/139, 364–5, 422, 475; Rosenkrantz, 38, 50; Beauharnais, X/304
7. Panam, 187
8. Beauharnais, X/305, 312, 322
9. Pictet, E., 169
10. Vogler, 8; Brignole, 10, 20ff
11. Renier, 291
12. Eynard, J.E., I/194

13. Weil, 1917, I/239
14. Weil, 1917, II/17 passim, 8, I/237, 326, 557, 422–3, 247
15. Weil, 1917, II/45, 63, 89, 102–3, 106, 109, 111, etc.
16. Gachot, II/113
17. HHSA, Zeremoniell Protokoll, 47; Rinieri, 1902, lv
18. Rzewuska, 263; Bernstorff, 164
19. Gräffer, 1–4
20. Mann, 212, 213–14; Nesselrode, I/35
21. Eynard, J.E., I/180, 119
22. Bernstorff, I/173
23. BPU, 148–9
24. Bright, 10; La Garde, 187
25. Rosenkrantz, 134; Rinieri, 1902, lx; Weil, 1917, I/259, 268
26. Villa-Urrutia, 123; La Garde, 251
27. Weil, 1917, I/351, 272, 759
28. Montet, 116
29. Weil, 1917, I/317, 364, 576–7
30. Weil, 1917, I/560, 498
31. Mikhailovskii-Danilevskii, 195; Spiel, 277–8; Mann, 214; Dolgorukov, 2754
32. Weil, 1917, I/282, 316, 317
33. Weil, 1917, I/650, 478
34. Panam, 199–200
35. Weil, 1917, I/495, 506, 650, 665
36. Weil, 1917, I/207, 257; Pichler, III/43; Nostitz, 131; BPU, 60–1; Talleyrand, 1881, 103; Pictet, C., I/xxi
37. Thürheim, 91–2, 99; Eynard, J.E., I/15; Bernstorff, 150, 154; Perth, 75
38. BPU, 62

Chapter 19: A Festival of Peace

1. Angeberg, I/280–8
2. Webster, 1921, 206–8
3. BC, 5238/IV, 15–21
4. Grimsted, 200; Stein, V/180
5. Angeberg, I/291–3
6. Webster, 1931, 345
7. Bertier, 148
8. Gentz, 1861, 327
9. Metternich, 1966, 267; McGuigan, 362, 367
10. Weil, 1917, I/316
11. Metternich, 1881, II/475–7
12. Stein, V/183; Bertuch, 55–6; Weil, 1917, I/442

13. Gagern, I/81–2; Talleyrand, 1976, 60; Gentz, 1961, 335
14. Stein, V/179
15. Pichler, III/33–5; La Garde, 23–5; Eynard, J.E., I/40
16. BPU, 25, 30
17. BPU, 31–2; Eynard, J.E., I/42; Thürheim, 108; Metternich, 1880, I/268
18. Bernstorff, I/158–9
19. Metternich, 1966, 267–9; Gentz, 1861, 330
20. Angeberg, I/316–20
21. Webster, 1921, 212–15; McGuigan, 372; Hardenberg, 2000, 802; Wellington, 1861, IX/374ff
22. Talleyrand, 1881, 74
23. Webster, 1921, 212–13, 217–19; Talleyrand, 1881, 61–3
24. Talleyrand, 1881, 75–7; for Talleyrand's real views on Poland, see: AE, France 672, 41–4
25. Kraehe, II/209, 229; Webster, 1934, 70; Metternich, 1880, I/483; Webster, 1921, 229; Dolgorukov, 273
26. Weil, 1917, I/351–2
27. Eynard, J.E., I/78
28. HHSA, St K. Kongresakten 1, 38–41; Angeberg, I/358–62; Pictet, C., 197

Chapter 20: Guerre de Plume

1. Talleyrand, 1881, 87–8; Webster, 1921, 229; Weil, 1917, I/495; Stein, V/185; Thürheim, 93
2. Wellington, 1861, IX/473; Weil, 1917, I/443
3. Metternich, 1966, 269
4. Weil, 1917, I/316, 444
5. Metternich, 1966, 270
6. Weil, 1917, I/423–4
7. Chuquet, 453; BC, 6032, 109
8. Eynard, J.E., I/75; Chuquet, 461
9. Weil, 1917, I/275ff; Humboldt, IV/400
10. Weil, 1917, I/276; Eynard, J.E., I/147; Talleyrand, 1976, 56, 70
11. BC, 6032, 104
12. BL, Liverpool Papers LXXI, 49; Angeberg, I/352–8
13. Webster, 1921, 222–4; BC, 6164, 38, BC, 6032, 110; Handelsman, I/104
14. Angeberg, I/393
15. Angeberg, I/394–401
16. Hardenberg, 2000, 803–4; Angeberg, I/406–8; Hardenberg, 1828, XII/457–8
17. Gentz, 1876, I/120
18. Weil, 1917, I/483–4
19. BPU, 65–7

20. Angeberg, I/450–6
21. Eynard, J.E., I/116–17; Bright, 18–19
22. BPU, 70–1; Gachot, II/133
23. McGuigan, 396; Chuquet, 453; Weil, 1917, I/521–2
24. Rosenkrantz, 74

Chapter 21: Political Carrousel

1. Angeberg, I/424–7
2. Webster, 1921, 210–11, 219–20; BL, Liverpool Papers LXXI, 242; Gash, 112
3. Webster, 1921, 221
4. Webster, 1921, 217
5. Webster, 1921, 231–3
6. Webster, 1931, 352; Rosenkrantz, 45
7. Eynard, J.E., I/39–40
8. Bertuch, 51; Nostitz, 147; Eynard, J.E., I/136; Pictet, E., 176; Weil, 1917, I/498
9. Edling, 178; Nostitz, 143; Montet, 137; Eynard, J.E., I/181
10. Edling, 178; La Garde, 192; Nicholas Mikhailovich, 1909, II/585
11. Weil, 1917, I/434; Eynard, J.E., I/89–90, 97; La Garde, 191
12. Eynard, J.E., I/52
13. Eynard, J.E., I/8–10; Rosenkrantz, 48
14. Webster, 1921, 215–16
15. Webster, 1921, 236–40
16. Jaucourt, 36, 90, 103
17. Castlereagh, X/202; Wellington, 1861, IX/424–6; Stein, V/103
18. Metternich, 1881, II/481;Weil, 1917, I/446
19. Stein, V/104
20. Bertier, 104
21. Gentz, 1861, 300, 332, 336, 337
22. Rzewuska, I/257; Weil, 1917, I/266–7
23. Thürheim, 93
24. Edling, 199; Ley, 1975, 97
25. Weil, 1917, I/282, 460–2, 318; Nostitz, 143–4
26. Rzewuska, I/259
27. Weil, 1917, I/282, 317, 665, 569; Thürheim, II/94–5
28. Rosenkrantz, 37; Weil, 1917, I/591
29. BC, 6164, 38, 40
30. Bright, 14
31. Bertuch, 58–9; BPU, 83; Thürheim, 11–12; Eynard, J.E., I/161
32. Eynard, J.E., I/161–2
33. Metternich, 1966, 273, 274
34. Gagern, II/79

35. Krog, 182; Weil, 1917, I/619
36. Eynard, J.E., I/329
37. Mikhailovskii-Danilevskii, 171–2, 128; Weil, 1917, I/644, 422, 557

Chapter 22: Explosive Diplomacy
 1. Stein, V/82; Humboldt, IV/418
 2. Stein, V/187, 190–1
 3. Kraehe, II/257
 4. BC, 5238/IV, 177; Angeberg, I/485–91
 5. Angeberg, I/505–9
 6. Metternich, 1880, II/490; Alison, II/508
 7. BL, Liverpool Papers LXXI, 336
 8. Weil, 1917, I/669; Gentz, 1861, 347; Stein, V/158
 9. Kraehe, II/241–2, 269
10. Eynard, J.E., I/207
11. Metternich, 1880, I/486; BL, Liverpool Papers LXXI, 336; Webster, 1921, 257ff, wrongly dated by Webster as 7 November; Gentz, 1876, I/124; Metternich, 1880, I/326–7; Hardenberg, 2000, 807
12. BL, Liverpool Papers LXXI, 396
13. Angeberg, I/531–5
14. Bertuch, 71; Stein,V/199; Eynard, J.E., I/214; see also Weil, 1917, I/689
15. Weil, 1917, I/172
16. Gentz, 1876, I/87, 113–15
17. Castlereagh, X/160–1, 173–5
18. Talleyrand, 1881, 58, 71; Jaucourt, 53; Weil, 1917, I/464; Webster, 1921, 227; Rinieri, 1902, 135
19. Gentz, 1876, I/122–3
20. Weil, 1917, I/512
21. Talleyrand, 1881, 119–27
22. Webster, 1931, 356, 558
23. Webster, 1921, 244, 240; Webster, 1931, 551–5; Kraehe, II/241
24. Mikhailovskii-Danilevskii, 126; Rosenkrantz, 90
25. Webster, 1921, 246; Stein, V/102–4
26. Webster, 1921, 247; Webster, 1931, 555
27. Webster, 1931, 357; Weil, 1917, I/648
28. Sweet, 1978, II/191; Webster, 1921, 251–4
29. Gagern, II/85; Eynard, J.E., I/182; Bertuch, 67
30. Rosenkrantz, 90, 113; Sorel, 1904, VIII/403
31. Webster, 1921, 252–4
32. Gentz, 1876, I/127; Metternich, 1880, I/479–80; Wellington, 1861, IX/473–4; Talleyrand, 1881, 191

Chapter 23: Dance of War

1. Angeberg, I/540–4
2. Talleyrand, 1881, 78–9, 99–102
3. Historical Manuscripts Commission, 314–15; Talleyrand, 1881, 157
4. Webster, 1921, 267–8
5. Webster, 1921, 266
6. Talleyrand, 1881, 172–3, 167–8; Weil, 1917, I/647
7. Eynard, J.E., I/187–8; La Garde, 200
8. La Garde, 133–4; BPU, 145–8
9. Montet, 133
10. La Garde, 94; Montet, 115; La Garde, 394–6; McGuigan, 419
11. Eynard, J.E., I/194; La Garde, 239; Jackson, II/465; Mansel, 2003, 261
12. Krog, 184
13. Münster, 205; BC, 6164, 38
14. Webster, 1921, 268–70
15. Spiel, 27–8
16. Angeberg, I/553–6
17. Eynard, J.E., I/214; Rosenkrantz, 114; Humboldt, IV/441
18. Humboldt, IV/441; Nostitz, 140
19. Weil, 1917, I/709, 751
20. Webster, 1931, 543; Kohler, 45–6
21. Webster, 1921, 272–3
22. Talleyrand, 1881, 198
23. Castlereagh, X/509; BPU, 148–56
24. Weil, 1917, I/735–6; Gentz, 1861, 350
25. Weil, 1917, I/752
26. Montet, 136; Jaucourt, 218; Weil, 1917, I/443
27. Gentz, 1861, 332, 351–2
28. Augusta, 147
29. McGuigan, 426–7; Metternich, 1966, 276
30. Spiel, 131–5

Chapter 24: War and Peace

1. Humboldt, IV/434
2. NA, FO 92, 9/203
3. AE, France 686 passim
4. Nørregard, 60
5. Nørregard, 71–2
6. Nørregard, 74–5, 104, 150–1; Thorsøe, 65
7. Spiel, 82; Angeberg, II/1858; NA, FO 92, 10/18, 20, 21, 23, 37
8. NA, FO 92, 10/13

9. NA, FO 92, 10/58

10. Humboldt, IV/436, 448

11. Hardenberg, 2000, 810–11

12. NA, FO 92, 10/58; Angeberg, I/579–82; Rosenkrantz, 121

13. NA, FO 92, 10/58

14. Historical Manuscripts Commission, 319; Wellington, 1861, IX/521; Webster, 1931, 371

15. Gagern, II/95; Eynard, J.E., I/236–7

16. Angeberg, I/589–92

17. Talleyrand, 1881, 209

18. Webster, 1921, 281

19. Webster, 1931, 372

20. Hardenberg, 2000, 810–11; Alison, II/556; Webster, 1921, 282–3

21. Eynard, J.E., I/241–2

22. Webster, 1921, 282–4; Hardenberg, 2000, 811

23. NA, FO 92, 10/98

24. There is some uncertainty as to when the meetings of the Four turned into meetings of the Five. According to Angeberg, I/594, 597 & II/1881–3, the first meeting of the Five took place on the seventh, the second on the ninth and the third on 12 January. But the minutes of the meeting of the Four on 9 January contain Castlereagh's formal demand for the admission of France, and there are no extant minutes of the first two meetings of the Five. HHSA, St K. Kongresakten 3, 3 starts with the third meeting, as does Angeberg, II/1883. From all this and FO 92, 10/13, 58, 98, 103, British and Foreign State Papers, 597–601, and Klinkowström, A.F., 487, it would appear that the discrepancy stems from the fact that while France's right to attend had been conceded early on, and agreed at the fourth conference of the Four on 7 January, Talleyrand's actual admission was delayed until 12 January.

25. NA, FO 92, 10, 103; HHSA, St K. Kongresakten 2, 42

26. Angeberg, I/602–4; AE, France 682, 69; HHSA, St K. Kongresakten 3, 3

27. Angeberg, I/677–83

28. Metternich, 1880, II/474; John, 185

29. Nostitz, 141; HHSA, St K. Interiora Archiv 7

30. Weil, 1917, II/217; Eynard, J.E., I/251; BPU, 255

31. Talleyrand, 1976, 106; Bright, 37; Montet, 133–4

32. Bright, 34–5; Jackson, II/467

33. Spiel, 221

34. Bright, 34–5; McGuigan, 435; La Garde, 304ff; Eynard, J.E., I/291–3; BPU, 230–9

35. Jackson, II/465

36. Weil, 1917, II/113, 108

37. Rosenkrantz, 122–3

38. Alison, II/556; BC, 6164, 40
39. Weil, 1917, II/14, 116
40. Weil, 1917, II/107; Munster, 223
41. Webster, 1921, 294–6
42. Webster, 1921, 299
43. Weil, 1917, II/2–3
44. Weil, 1917, II/57

Chapter 25: The Saxon Deal

1. Spiel, 233, 236; Weil, 1917, II/121, 127
2. Rosenkrantz, 135; Hardenberg, 2000, 814; Jackson, II/469
3. Weil, 1917, II/152
4. Talleyrand, 1881, 260–2
5. Webster, 1921, 297, 299–302
6. Rosenkrantz, 140; Weil, 1917, II/127
7. Webster, 1921, 299–301; Webster, 1931, 384
8. Rosenkrantz, 143
9. Hardenberg, 2000, 815; Webster, 1921, 302
10. HHSA, St K. Kongresakten 3, 32; Angeberg, I/706–24
11. Talleyrand, 1976, 114
12. Talleyrand, 1881, 281; Rinieri, 1902, 279; Gallavresi, 7
13. Webster, 1921, 304
14. Metternich, 1966, 277
15. BC, 6164, 40; HHSA, St K. Interiora Archiv, Intercepte 7, 212
16. BC, 6164, 38, 40, 41; Mikhailovskii-Danilevskii, 149; Ley, 1975, 98; Weil, 1917, II/166
17. Webster, 1921, 274–5; Angeberg, I/612–14
18. Angeberg, I/660–760
19. Webster, 1921, 412; Angeberg, I/670–2
20. Angeberg, I/684–7
21. Angeberg, I/697–703, 724–7; AE, France 685, 259ff
22. Gentz, 1876, I/145–7; Webster, 1912, 69, 73
23. Webster, 1931, 429; Webster, 1934, 79; Webster, 1921, 303–4
24. Webster, 1921, 263–4
25. HHSA, St K. Kongresakten 3, 85–8; Webster, 1921, 287–8
26. HHSA, St K. Kongresakten 3, 94ff; Metternich, 1880, II/487
27. HHSA, St K. Kongresakten 3, 100ff, 104
28. Gagern, II/133
29. Angeberg, I/866

Chapter 26: Unfinished Business

1. Angeberg, I/503; HHSA, St K. Kongresakten 1, 29ff; Rinieri, 1902, 193
2. Angeberg, I/735
3. Rappard, 111–18; Müller, 1815; *Colloque Patriotisme*
4. Chapuisat, 30; Pictet, E., 180
5. Angeberg, I/521, 513–15; Pictet, E., 187
6. Gagern, II/78
7. Pictet, E., 193, 154–7, 178, 182–3
8. Rappard, 123
9. Talleyrand, 1881, 310; Vogler, 10
10. Angeberg, II/1890; AE, France 688
11. Labrador, 37–8
12. Flassan, 11, 12, 19–21
13. Grimsted, 226–9; Valsamachi
14. Consalvi, 1899, 58–9
15. Talleyrand, 1881, 145–6; SUA, Acta Clementina 1, 29; Jaucourt, 213–14; Rinieri, 1903, 619
16. Noel, 109
17. Webster, 1934, 126–7
18. Méneval, III/374–5, 398
19. Stein, V/214
20. Kraehe, II/321; Angeberg, I/688, 737; Stein, V/214; Humboldt, IV/483–4
21. Beales, 2–3, 8, 86, 286–7
22. Consalvi, 1899, 33–40, 45; Ruck, 85; Rinieri, 1904; Buschkuhl, 48–9, 55
23. Ruck, 116
24. Stein, V/219; Stein, V/220; Weil, 1917, II/302
25. Weil, 1917, II/211, 217; Thürheim, II/117–18; Mikhailovskii-Danilevskii, 150; Humboldt, IV/485
26. Talleyrand, 1881, 312
27. Jaucourt, 218–19; Rosenkrantz, 181; Weil, 1917, II/247, 251, 259; Humboldt, IV/481
28. Humboldt, IV/481–2, 485

Chapter 27: The Flight of the Eagle

1. Metternich, 1880, I/204
2. Hardenberg, 2000, 818; Méneval, III/412; Castlereagh, X/264; Mikhailovskii-Danilevskii, 173; Weil, 1917, II/297
3. Talleyrand, 1881, 314
4. La Garde, 436
5. Münster, 227, 232; Müffling, 204
6. Driault, 346–7; Weil, 1917, II/513
7. Pictet, E., 213, 235; Wellington, 1861, IX/623

8. Webster, 1921, 318; Montet, 137; Mikhailovskii-Danilevskii, 173

9. Méneval, III/415; HHSA, St K. Interiora Archiv, Intercepte 7 passim; Weil, 1917, II/354

10. Weil, 1917, II/297–8; Castlereagh, X/287; Shilder, III/548

11. La Garde, 434; Hardenberg, 1828, XII/475; Rosenkrantz, 176; Méneval, III/439; SUA, Acta Clementina 3, 36, 58ff

12. Jaucourt, 222–3, 232, 242; Weil, 1921, II/312

13. Kraehe, II/330; Talleyrand, 1881, 326; Angeberg, II/912–13; HHSA, St K. Kongresakten 2, 94; Humboldt, IV/494

14. Wellington, 1861, XIV/539

15. Angeberg, II/147–55

16. Bianchi, I/12; Münster, 186; Webster, 1931, 438; HHSA, St K. Kongresakten 1, 70; Eynard, J.E., I/97; see also Talleyrand, 1881, 43

17. Holland, 196; Bianchi, I/395

18. Sorel, 1904, VIII/415; Bonnal, I/47–65; Weil, 1917, I/404–5

19. Talleyrand, 1881, 42, 285, 288–9

20. Lafayette, V/301

21. Maillé, 12

22. Maillé, 19

23. Talleyrand, 1881, 159

24. Maillé, 23

Chapter 28: The Hundred Days

1. Garros, 460

2. Garros, 459–62; Broglie, I/297

3. Reiset, 504

4. Mansel, 1981, 226; Romberg & Malet, 55; Lavalette, 344

5. Lavalette, 345–6

6. Alexander, 1991, 2; Castellane, I/283–5

7. Constant, 17, 132

8. Otrante, 1824, II/286–9

9. Méneval, III/525

10. SUA, Acta Clementina 1, 23, 198; Shilder, III/549–50

11. Talleyrand, 1881, 380ff; Jaucourt, 273–4; Metternich, 1880, I/208; Madelin, 242–3

12. Mikhailovskii-Danilevskii, 184; Kraehe, II/329

13. Wellington, 1845, VIII/2–3, IX/606

14. Webster, 1921, 313, 316–17; Kraehe, II/332–3, 335–6

15. Kraehe, II/340–1

16. Talleyrand, 1881, 365; Wellington, 1845, VIII/3, 55, 99, 101

17. Bright, 38–9

18. Wellington, 1861, IX/590–1; Wellington, 1845, VIII/1
19. Webster, 1921, 331
20. Pozzo, 143; Stein, V/231; Shilder, III/308
21. Weil, 1917, II/344–5; Ley, 1975, 100
22. Metternich, 1880, I/328
23. Romberg, 9; Talleyrand, 1881, 365, 328, 368
24. Webster, 1921, 310, 314–15
25. Straus, 102
26. Wellington, 1845, VIII/68; Chodźko, 203
27. Gagern, II/138, 166
28. Straus, 33; Beauharnais, X/324–5
29. Münster, 247
30. Castlereagh, X/262
31. Bourgoing, 1965, 71

Chapter 29: The Road to Waterloo

1. Wellington, 1845, VIII/66
2. Wellington, 1845, VIII/84–5, 106; Flockerzie, 668; Kraehe, II/354; Müffling, 208ff
3. Wellington, 1845, VIII/98–9, 71, 72–4, 117–18
4. Burghersh, 1912, 175
5. Webster, 1931, 452
6. Castlereagh, X/350; Pozzo, 142–9, 165ff; Sorel, 1904, VIII/428–9; Rain, 126–7, 133–52; Châteaubriand, 1951, I/947; Webster, 1921, 330–1, 357–73
7. Webster, 1931, 443–6, 452
8. Webster, 1921, 313
9. Weil, 1917, II/605
10. Madelin, 330–1; Pozzo, 93–4; Sorel, 1904, VIII/432–3
11. Noel, 106; McGuigan, 461–2; SUA, Acta Clementina 1, 23, 198ff; Méneval, III/412, 415, 446, 422–3, 428–9; Montesquiou, 365ff, 414
12. Méneval, III/413; Beauharnais, X/330
13. Weil, 1917, II/509, 515
14. Weil, 1917, II/561
15. Weil, 1917, II/398, 419, 427, 442, 462, 466
16. Weil, 1917, II/259, 427, 450 (for a different take on this scene, see Thürheim, 101), 220
17. Weil, 1917, II/470, 648
18. Angeberg, I/618–38, II/934; Chapuisat, 64; Kraehe, II/355–6
19. Münster, 264
20. Humboldt, IV/450–6, 565
21. Nørregard, 137; Flamand, 412; Weil, 1917, II/588; Nørregard, 197

22. Weil, 1917, II/549, 600
23. Weil, 1917, II/517, 571, 598, 613–14, 620, 642, 555, 623
24. Weil, 1917, II/588, 427, 435, 505, 722
25. Kukiel, 132; BC, 6164, 41
26. Handelsman, I/113
27. Talleyrand, 1976, 199
28. Weil, 1917, II/626, 644–5, 651, 663, 666, 686, 716

Chapter 30: Wellington's Victory
 1. Oman, 338; Roberts, 20–1; Garros, 466–7
 2. Garros, 470
 3. Talleyrand, 1957, II/457–64; see also Waresquiel, 2003, 495–505
 4. Chatelain, 227–34; Gentz, 1868, 173
 5. Webster, 1921, 341; Wellington, 1861, XI/3, 20; SUA, Acta Clementina 12, 8, 4
 6. Croker, I/62
 7. Weil, 1917, II/691; BC, 5444/IV, 407
 8. Ley, 1975, 111; Empaytaz, 12–27; Edling, 232–5
 9. Mikhailovskii-Danilevskii, 250
10. Empaytaz, 34; Webster, 1921, 342; Hardenberg, 2000, 825; Webster, 1921, 370–1
11. Sweet, 1978, II/211; AE, France 672, 83–91
12. Wellington, 1845, VIII/207–8; see also Pozzo, 242–3
13. Maillé, 38
14. Boigne, II/133, 155–6; see also: Castellane, I/309; Otrante, 1824, II/381; Broglie, I/319; Boigne, II/122; Resnick, 9, 11, 17, 52, etc.
15. Mansel, 1981, 327
16. Humboldt, V/17
17. Gash, 121; Castlereagh, X/416, 430
18. Webster, 1921, 347–9
19. ON, 6/86, 10
20. Gash, 121; Oman, 346; Castlereagh, X/434; Historical Manuscripts Commission, 376ff; Webster, 1921, 342, 350
21. Castlereagh, X/434
22. Webster, 1921, 339–41, 344, 345–7

Chapter 31: The Punishment of France
 1. Historical Manuscripts Commission, 372–3; Humboldt, V/17
 2. Stein, V/257
 3. Talleyrand, 1957, II/475
 4. Webster, 1931, 562–9
 5. AE, France 672, 75ff
 6. Wellington, 1845, VIII/235–9; Webster, 1921, 357

7. Angeberg, II/1479–82
8. Webster, 1921, 375
9. Pictet, E., 259, 268
10. Gentz, 1876, I/174; AE, France 672, 98
11. Castlereagh, X/445
12. Angeberg, II/1469
13. Webster, 1917, 361–2
14. Webster, 1921, 362–6; Castlereagh, X/485; Webster, 1931, 469
15. Castlereagh, X/476; SUA, Acta Clementina 12, 35/9, 20
16. SUA, Acta Clementina 12, 35/15, 20, 22, Acta Clementina 14a, 373–4
17. Mann, 233; Gentz, 1868, 183
18. Sweet, 1978, II/212
19. Castlereagh, X/485–90
20. Gentz, 1868, 179; Ley, 1975, 130; Edling, 241; Webster, 1921, 382; Mikhailovskii-Danilevskii, 284
21. Hortense, III; Nesselrode, V/215, 221; Mikhailovskii-Danilevskii, 281
22. Carême, II/126–31
23. Empaytaz, 40; Mikhailovskii-Danilevskii, 264–6; Shilder, III/341–2
24. Castlereagh, X/497–8; Webster, 1921, 378
25. Freeman, 208; Castlereagh, X/453, XI/27
26. Castlereagh, X/435; Freeman, 208; Mikhailovskii-Danilevskii, 279
27. Angeberg, II/1510–14; Humboldt, V/78; Castlereagh, XI/12
28. Angeberg, II/1520–2; Humboldt, V/74
29. Angeberg, II/1543–6
30. Freeman, 209, 214
31. Chatelain, 250; Freeman, 210; Humboldt, V/17, 78, 82, 84
32. Freeman, 220; Brownlow, 171; Pictet, E., 289; Humboldt, V/74, 78

Chapter 32: Last Rites

1. Angeberg, II/1523–6, 1528
2. Humboldt, V/74
3. Talleyrand, 1957, II/479; Angeberg, II/1531–3; AE, France 672, 126
4. Angeberg, II/1535–7
5. Talleyrand, 1957, II/481–3; Waresquiel, 2003, 522–3, writes that Talleyrand's interview with Louis and his resignation took place on 19 September, and that Talleyrand was therefore no longer in office when he attended the conference of 20 September. I have preferred to follow the sequence of events given by Talleyrand in his memoirs, as it accords better with other sources and seems more probable – I find it difficult to believe that Talleyrand would have attended the two meetings, on 20 and 21 September, and continued to argue the case for France if he had no longer been in office.

6. Pozzo, 209–11

7. Talleyrand, 1957, II/483; Rémusat, I/237

8. McGuigan, 492

9. Empaytaz, 41; Angeberg, II/1547–9; Zorin, 299–335

10. Capodistrias, 201; Metternich, 1880, I/210–12

11. Webster, 1921, 382–4

12. Empaytaz, 48; Alexander, 1910, 203

13. Webster, 1921, 338

14. Nesselrode, V/236

15. HHSA, St K. Interiora 78, 11; Nesselrode, V/234

16. Historical Manuscripts Commission, 389–90, 391

17. Pictet, E., 330

18. HHSA, St K. Interiora 79; Angeberg, II/1557, 1570

19. HHSA, St K. Interiora 78, 7, 11

20. Bourgoing, 1965, 74

21. Waresquiel, 2003, 488–9; Rinieri, 1904, 555–76

22. Webster, 1934, 142

Chapter 33: Discordant Concert

1. Maevskii, 289

2. Breuilly, 50

3. Humboldt, IV/246

4. Sweet, 1978, II/194; Ramm; Rowe; Perth, 108; Schenk, 86–7; Görres, xvi, 14

5. Metternich, 1880, II/59, III/51–4; Schenk, 117–18; Nesselrode, VI/29–37

6. Görres, 170–1; Reinerman; Bianchi, 437–48; Webster, 1912, 82–3; Metternich, 1880, II/90; Bertier, 172

7. Haas; Rath; Wawrzkowicz; Bianchi, 442–55; Perth, 109; Metternich, 1964, 73

8. Nicholas Mikhailovich, 1913, 1–5; Castlereagh, XI/99, 114, 119, 137 passim, 104–6

9. Angeberg, II/1638; Lieven, 1902, 37

10. Angeberg, II/1760

11. Ward & Gooch, II/32

12. Green; Ward & Gooch, 57

13. Lieven, 1902, 60

Chapter 34: The Arrest of Europe

1. Gentz, 1876, I/153–7

2. Grunewald, 296; Stein, V/220

3. Flockerzie, 670; Müller, 1815, 1816

4. Heraud & Beguelin, 18, 33

5. Aldobrandini

6. Pradt, 1815, 1819, 1821; Capefigue; Martineau, H.; Bignon, 1821, 1822, 1864; Derry, 4

7. Webster, 1923, 3

8. Kissinger, 315

9. Schroeder, 1994, vii–viii

10. Martineau, H., I/11

11. Castlereagh, XI/102; Bertier, 116–17

12. Bignon, 1822, 3; Derry, 2

13. Oman, 352

14. Pradt, 1815, I/55, II/108–17; Pradt, 1819, 11

15. Weil, 1917, I/286; Pradt, 1815, II/25ff

16. Brignole, 56

17. Rzewuska, I/263

18. Barraclough, 33

Bibliography

Primary Sources

Archival

Biblioteka Książąt Czartoryskich, Kraków:
Adam Czartoryski papers: 5214/V, 26; 5219/V, 1, 9; 5220/IV; 5227/IV, 3, 4; 5238/IV (Pozzo di Borgo, Stein memoranda & notes); 5239/IV (memoranda & notes), 2, 3, 4, 7; 5242/IV (drafts & memoranda); 5444/IV (letters from Capodistrias, etc.); 5516/IV; 6029/IV; 6032/IV (letters to father); 6092/IV (letters to mother); 6164/IV (Adam Czartoryski's diary).

Bibliothèque Publique et Universitaire, Genève:
Journal d'Anna Eynard, Ms. Suppl. 1959

British Library, London:
Liverpool Papers, LXXI, Add. 38260
Bunbury Papers, I, Add. 37051
Beauvale Papers, I, Add. 60399
Aberdeen Papers, XXXV, XXXVI, XXXVII, Add. 43073–5
Lamb Papers, I, V, Add. 45546, 45550

Haus-, Hof- und StaatsArchiv, Vienna:
St. K. Interiora, 67, Metternich-Hudelist Correspondence; 75, Metternich-Gentz Correspondence; 78, Gentz Correspondence; 79, Wessenberg Correspondence.
St. K. Interiora Archiv, Intercepte 1, 7
St. K. Kongresakten, 1, 2, 3
Zeremoniell Protokoll 47

Ministère des Affaires Étrangères, Paris:
Mémoires et Documents
France: 666–7, Congrès de Prague; 668–71, Congrès de Châtillon; 672, Prince de
Talleyrand; 673–4, Conventions et traité de Paris 1814; 681, Congrès de Vienne,
Correspondance; 682–3, Congrès de Vienne, Protocoles de Conférences; 684,
Congrès de Vienne, Naples, Russie et Pologne, Savoie, Gênes, etc.; 685, Con-
grès de Vienne, Navigation des rivières et traite des nègres; 686, Commission
de statistique & Affaires d'Allemagne; 688, Congrès de Vienne, Protestations
et Réclamations; 689, Histoire et Apologie du Congrès de Vienne depuis son
ouverture jusqu'aux traités du 20 novembre 1815 inclusivement, par M. de
Flassan; 692, Traité du 20 novembre 1815.
Russie: 25, Langeron, Campagnes au Service de la Russie.

National Archives, Kew:
FO 92: 1. Castlereagh to Liverpool, 3. Castlereagh to Liverpool & Bathurst, 4.
Castlereagh to Liverpool, 5. Protocols of Conferences in London, 9. Castlereagh to Liverpool, Talleyrand, Congress Documents, Protocols of conferences, 10. Castlereagh to Liverpool, Conferences of 4, conferences of 5.

Österreichische Nationalbibliothek, Vienna (ON):
Metternich correspondence: Ms. 6/86.

Public Record Office of Northern Ireland, Belfast:
Castlereagh Papers: D.3030/T/MC3/291 & 292 Castlereagh to his wife; D.3030/G/
1–16; D.3030/P Charles Stewart's Correspondence.

Státní Ústřední Archiv, Prague:
Rodinný Archiv Metternišský:
Acta Clementina 1: 23, Marie Louise; 29, Caroline Bonaparte; Acta Clementina
3: 36 Talleyrand; Acta Clementina 5: Gentziana II, III; Acta Clementina 12:
.7 Metternich; 8, Marie Metternich; 33, 34, 35, Eléonore Metternich; Acta
Clementina 14a: 4, 5, Marie Metternich.

Printed

Abrantès, Laure Junot, duchesse d', *Mémoires de madame la duchesse d'Abrantès*,
12 vols, Paris 1835
Adresse au Congrès de Vienne, par M. de St.-L., Paris 1815
*Adresse au Congrès de Vienne, envoyée à tous les Peuples du Nord, de l'Italie, de
l'Espagne et du Portugal, Concernant les véritables dispositions des puissances
alliées envers la France*, n.p., n.d.
Aldobrandini, Francesco Borghese, prince, *Requête de François Borghese, prince
Aldobrandini, au Roi, demandant l'intervention du Gouvernement français pour*

lui faire restituer la propriété des salines de Creuznach et de Durkeim, attribuée au grand-duc de Hesse et au roi de Bavière par l'acte final du Congrès de Vienne. Paris 2 mars 1822

Alexander I, *Correspondance de l'Empereur Alexandre Ier avec sa soeur la Grande Duchesse Catherine*, St Petersburg 1910

— *Pisma Imperatora Aleksandra Petrovicha k R. S. Sturdze (grafine Edling)*, in *Russkii Arkhiv*, no. 11, Moscow 1888

Angeberg, Comte d' (Leonard Chodźko), *Le Congrès de Vienne et les Traités de 1815: précédé et suivi des actes diplomatiques qui s'y rattachent, avec une introduction historique par M. Capefigue*, 2 vols, Paris 1864

Antidote au Congrès de Vienne, ou l'Europe telle qu'elle doit être sous le rapport de la politique, de la religion, et de l'équilibre des États, Vol. I, *en Belgique* 1816

Arblay, Fanny, *Diary and Letters*, Vol. VI, London 1905

Aroutunova, Bayara, *Lives in Letters. Princess Zinaida Volkonskaya and her Correspondence*, Columbus, Oh, 1994

Augusta, Duchess of Saxe-Coburg-Saalfeld, *In Napoleonic Days*, London 1941

Balfour, Lady Frances, *The Life of George Fourth Earl of Aberdeen, K.G., K.T.*, Vol. I, London 1923

Barante, Baron de, *Souvenirs*, 2 vols, Paris 1892

Beauharnais, Eugène de, *Mémoires et correspondance politique et militaire du Prince Eugène, annotés et mis en ordre par A. Du Casse*, 10 vols, Paris 1858–60

— *Protestation de Son Altesse le prince Eugène de Beauharnais contre tout ce qui a été résolu, décidé et arrêté par le congrès de Vienne*, Paris, n.d.

Benkendorf, Alexander, *Zapiski Benkendorfa, Mémoires du comte Alexandre Benkendorf Général de Cavalerie, Aide-de-camp de S.M.E. l'Empereur de Russie*, Moscow 2001

Bernstorff, Gräfin Elise von, *Ein Bild aus der Zeit von 1789 bis 1835 Aus ihren Aufzeichnungen*, Vol. I, Berlin 1896

Berry, Mary, *Extracts from the Journals and Correspondence of Miss Berry*, Vol. III, London 1866

Bertuch, Carl, *Tagebuch vom Wiener Kongress*, Berlin 1916

Beugnot, Comte, *Mémoires du Comte Beugnot, Ancien Ministre, 1783–1850*, Vol. II, Paris 1868

Bignan, Anne, *L'Abolition de la Traite des Noirs. Épître aux Souverains de l'Europe rassemblés au Congrès de Vienne, qui a obtenu la première mention honorable au jugement de l'Académie Française, à la séance publique du 25 aout 1823*, Paris 1823

Bignon, Louis-Pierre-Édouard Baron, *Précis de la Situation Politique de la France depuis le mois de mars 1814 jusqu'au mois de juin 1815*, Paris 1815

— *Du Congrès de Troppau*, Paris 1821

— *Les Cabinets et les Peuples*, Paris 1822

— *Souvenirs d'un Diplomate*, Paris 1864

Boigne, Adèle, comtesse de, *Récits d'une Tante. Mémoires de la Comtesse de Boigne*, 3 vols, Paris 1907

Boncompagni Ludovisi, Luigi, Prince of Piombino, *Mémoire présenté par D.Louis Boncompagni Ludovisi, Prince de Piombino et de l'Isle d'Elbe, au Congrès de Vienne*, 1815

Boulart, Général Baron, *Mémoires Militaires*, Paris n.d.

Bourgoing, Paul Charles Amable, Baron de, *Itinéraire de Napoléon Ier de Smorgoni à Paris*, Paris 1862

— *Souvenirs d'histoire contemporaine*, Paris 1864

Bourrienne, Louis Antoine de, *Mémoires de M. de Bourrienne, Ministre d'État, sur Napoléon, le Directoire, le Consulat, l'Empire et la Restauration*, Vols IX & X, Paris 1829

Bright, Richard, *Travels from Vienna through Lower Hungary, with some remarks on the state of Vienna during the Congress, in the year 1814*, Edinburgh 1818

Brignole, Antoine de, *Quelques erreurs réfutées, ou Exposé de la conduite du marquis Antoine Brignole, lors de sa mission auprès du Congrès de Vienne, en qualité d'envoyé du Gouvernement de Gênes*, 1816

British and Foreign State Papers, Vol. II, London 1839

Broglie, A.L.V.C., duc de, *Souvenirs*, Vol. I, Paris 1886

Brownlow, Emma Sophia, Countess, *Slight Reminiscences of a Septuagenarian*, London 1867

Brunov, F.I., *Aperçu des principales transactions du Cabinet de Russie sous les règnes de Catherine II, Paul I et Alexandre I*, in *Sbornik Imperatorskovo Russkovo Istoricheskovo Obshchestva*, Vol. XXXI, St Petersburg 1880

Buckingham, Duke of, *Memoirs of the Court of England during the Regency*, 2 vols, London 1856

Burghersh, John Fane Lord, *Correspondence*, London 1912

Burghersh, Priscilla Lady, *The Letters of Lady Burghersh*, London 1893

— *Correspondence of Lady Burghersh with the Duke of Wellington*, London 1903

Cambacérès, J.J. de, *Lettres inédites à Napoléon, 1802–1814*, 2 vols, Paris 1973

— *Mémoires inédits*, 2 vols, Paris 1999

Capodistrias, Count Ioannis, *Zapiski grafa Ioana Kapodistria o evo sluzhebnoi deatelnosti*, in *Sbornik Imperatorskovo Russkovo Isotricheskovo Obshchestva*, Vol. III, St Petersburg 1868

Carême, Antonin, *Le Maître d'Hôtel Français*, 2 vols, Paris 1842

Carnot, *Mémoire adressé au Roi en juillet 1814 par M. Carnot*, Paris 1815

Castellane, Boniface de, *Journal du Maréchal de Castellane*, Vol. I, Paris 1895

Castlereagh, Robert Stewart, Viscount, *Correspondence, Despatches and other Papers*, 12 vols, London 1853

Caulaincourt, Armand Augustin Louis, duc de Vicence, *Mémoires*, 3 vols, Paris 1933

Châteaubriand, François René de, *De Bonaparte et des Bourbons*, Paris 1814

— *Congrès de Verone. Guerre d'Espagne*, 2 vols, Paris 1838

— *Mémoires d'Outre-Tombe*, 2 vols, Paris 1951

Chodźko, Léonard, *Receuil des Traités, Conventions et Actes Diplomatiques concernant l'Autriche et l'Italie*, Paris 1859

Choiseul-Gouffier, comtesse de, *Reminiscences sur L'Empereur Alexandre Ier et sur L'Empereur Napoléon Ier*, Paris 1862

Les Classiques de la table, à l'usage des praticiens et des gens du monde, Paris 1843

Clausewitz, Carl von, *Historical and Political Writings*, trs. Peter Paret & Daniel Moran, Princeton 1992

Coigny, Aimée Franquetot de, *Mémoires*, Paris 1902

— *Journal*, Paris 1981

Colletta, Pietro, *Pochi Fatti su Gioacchino Murat*, Naples 1820

Conclusion du Congrès de Vienne, et situation presente des puissances étrangères, n.p., n.d.

Congrès de Vienne. Extrait du procès-verbal des conférences des puissances signataires du traité de Paris. Conférence du 12 mai 1815, n.p., n.d.

Consalvi, Ercole Cardinal, *Mémoires*, 2 vols, Paris 1864–66

— *Correspondance du Cardinal Hercule Consalvi avec le Prince Clément de Metternich*, ed. Charles van Duern, Louvain 1899

Considérations importantes sur l'abolition générale de la traite des nègres, adressées aux négociateurs des puissances continentales qui doivent assister au Congrès de Vienne. Par un Portuguais, Paris 1814

Constant de Rebeque, Benjamin, *Mémoires sur les Cent-Jours*, Paris 1961

Correspondance diplomatique des Ambassadeurs et Ministres de Russie en France et de France en Russie avec leurs gouvernements, de 1814 à 1830, ed. A.A. Polovtsov, 3 vols, St Petersburg 1902–07

Le coup de Jarnac du prince Talleyrand-Périgord, avant la fin du congrès de Vienne, où il venait de jouer un si beau role, n.p., n.d.

Creevey, Thomas, *The Creevey Papers*, Vol. I, London 1903

Croft, Sir Herbert, *Réflexions soumises à la sagesse des membres du Congrès de Vienne et à tous ceux pour le bonheur desquels ils se sont rassemblés*, Paris 1814

Croker, John Wilson, *The Croker Papers*, Vol. I, London 1884

Czartoryski, Adam Jerzy, Prince, *Essai sur la Diplomatie*, Paris 1864

— *Alexandre Ier et le Prince Czartoryski. Correspondance Particulière et Conversations 1801–1823*, Paris 1865

— *Mémoires du Prince Adam Czartoryski et Correspondance avec l'Empereur Alexandre Ier*, 2 vols, Paris 1887

Déclaration de l'Empereur de Russie aux souverains réunis au Congrès de Vienne, du 1er–15 mai 1815, sur les affaires politiques, amenées en France par le retour de Napoléon Bonaparte; avec des notes critiques et politiques, par J.-T. Brugière, Paris 1815

Despinay Saint-Denis, Colonel Marquis, *Observations sur l'ordre de S.-Jean-de-Jérusalem et de Malte, avec l'exposition des motifs qui doivent engager la sainte-alliance à rendre à cet ordre, en exécution du congrès de Vienne, sa souveraineté légitime, et a l'établir dans la Grèce ou dans quelqu'une de ses parties, pour terminer la guerre du Levant*, Paris 1825

Dino, Dorothée de Talleyrand-Perigord, duchesse de, *Souvenirs*, Paris 1908

Divov, N.A., *Chastnoe pismo na drugoi den' po vstuplenii v Parizh*, in *Russkii Arkhiv*, no. 11, Moscow 1888

Dolgorukov, Prince Nikolai Vasilievich, *Iz zapisok kniazya Nikolaya Vasilievicha Dolgorukova*, in *Russkii Arkhiv*, no. 11, Moscow 1892

Edling, comtesse, *née* Stourdza, *Mémoires*, Moscow 1888

Espagnac, Jean-Frédéric-Guillaume d'Amarzit, comte d', *Défense relative à la propriété du domaine de Sassolo dont le fisc de S.A.R. le Duc de Modène François IV cherche a s'emparer au détriment des finances de S. M. Très-Chrétienne*, n.d., n.p.

Eynard, Charles, *Vie de Madame de Krudener*, 2 vols, Paris 1849

Eynard, J.E., *Au Congrès de Vienne. Journal de Jean Gabriel Eynard*, 2 vols, Paris 1914–24

Fain, Agathon Jean François Baron, *Manuscrit de Mil Huit Cent Treize*, 2 vols, Paris 1824

— *Manuscrit de Mil Huit Cent Quatorze*, Paris 1825

Flassan, Raxis de, *Lettre de M de Flassan, en réponse à la lettre de M. le commandeur Berlinghieri, l'un des ministres plénipotentiaires de l'Ordre de Malte au congrès de Vienne. 20 Novembre 1829*, Paris 1829

Fleury, A.M., *Réponse au Mémoire de M. Carnot*, Paris 1815

Forgues, Eugène, *Le dossier secret de Fouché (juillet–septembre 1815)*, Paris 1908

Fournier, August, *Der Congress von Châtillon. Die Politik im Kriege von 1814*, Vienna 1900

— *Die Geheimpolizei auf dem Wiener Kongress*, Vienna 1913

— *Londoner Präludien zum Wiener Kongress*, in *Deutsche Revue*, 43, Berlin 1918

Franceschetti, General Dominique César, *Mémoire sur les Évènements qui ont précédé la Mort de Joachim Ier, roi de Naples*, Paris 1826

Gachot, Édouard, *Marie-Louise Intime*, 2 vols, Paris 1911

Gagern, H.C.E. von, *Mein Antheil an der Politik*, Vol. II, Stuttgart 1826

Gentz, Friedrich von, *Tagebücher*, Leipzig 1861

— *Briefe an Pilat*, Vol. I, Leipzig 1868

— *Dépeches Inédites aux Hospodars de Valachie*, Vol. I, Paris 1876

The German Sausages; or, the Devil to pay at Congress; a poem. By Peter Pindar Esq, London 1815

Goldsmith, Lewis, *Observations on the appointment of the Right Hon G. Canning to the Foreign department; and its effects on the state of Society in England and* on European politics; comprehending a review of the political state of Europe since the Congress of Vienna in 1815, London 1822

Görres, Joseph, *Germany and the Revolution*, trs. John Black, London 1820

Gräffer, Franz, *Kleiner Wiener Memoiren*, Vienna 1845

Gruner, Karl Justus von, *Déclaration du Congrès en réponse à la supplique que lui ont adressée les nobles émigrés français, rédigée par Tu-Jus Gruner*, Brussels 1815

Guizot, F.P., duc de, *Mémoires pour servir à l'histoire de mon temps*, 8 vols, Paris 1858

Hardenberg, Karl August von, *Mémoires tirés des papiers d'un homme d'état*, 12 vols, Paris 1828–38

— *Tagebücher und autobiographische Aufzeichnung*, ed. Thomas Stamm-Kuhlmann, Munich 2000

Haydon, Benjamin Robert, *Correspondence and Table Talk*, Vol. I, London 1876

Hertslet, Edward, *The Map of Europe by Treaty*, Vol. I, London 1875

Historical Manuscripts Commission, *Report on the Manuscripts of Earl Bathurst preserved at Cirencester Park*, London 1923

Hogendorp, Gijsbert Karel van, *Brieven en Gedenkschriften*, vols 3–5, The Hague 1876

Holland, Henry Richard Lord, *Foreign Reminiscences*, London 1850

Hortense, Queen of Holland, *Mémoires de la Reine Hortense*, 3 vols, Paris 1927

Humboldt, Wilhelm von, *Wilhelm und Caroline von Humboldt in ihren Briefen*, vols IV & V, Berlin 1910–12

Hyde de Neuville, Baron, *Mémoires et Souvenirs*, Paris 1890

Ivanov, V.M., *Zapiski vedenia vo vremia puteshestvia Imperatritsy Elizavety Alekseievny po Germanii v 1813, 1814 i 1815 godakh*, St Petersburg 1833

Jackson, Sir George, *A Further Selection from the Diaries and Letters of Sir George Jackson, K.C.H. from 1809 to 1816*, 2 vols, London 1873

Jaucourt, Arnail François, comte de, *Correspondance avec le Prince de Talleyrand pendant le Congrès de Vienne*, Paris 1905

Jérôme, King of Westphalia, *Mémoires et Correspondance du Roi Jérôme et de la Reine Catherine*, 8 vols, Paris 1865

John, Archduke of Austria, *Aus dem Tagebüche des Erzherzogs Johanns von Österreich 1810–1815*, Innsbruck 1891

Klinkowström, A.F. von, *Österreichs Theilnahme an den Befreiungskriegen*, Vienna 1887

Klinkowström, Clemens von (ed.), *Aus der alten Registratur de Staatskanzlei. Briefe politischen Inhals von un an Friedrich von Gentz*, Vienna 1870

Klüber, J.L., *Acten des Wiener Congresses in den Jahren 1814–1815*, 9 vols, Erlangen 1815–19

Koch, G.G. de, *Histoire Abrégée des Traités de Paix, etc.*, Vol. X, Paris 1818

Krüdener, B.J. von, *Valérie, ou Lettres de Gustave de Linar à Ernest de G...*, 2 vols, London 1804

Kügelgen, Wilhelm von, *Jugenderinnerungen eines alten Mannes*, Berlin 1870

Labrador, Pedro Gomez Havela, Marqués de, *Mélanges sur la vie Privée et Publique du Marquis de Labrador*, Paris 1849

Lafayette, Marie-Joseph Motier, marquis de, *Mémoires, Correspondance et Manuscrits du Général Lafayette*, Vol. V, Paris 1838

La Garde-Chambonas, Auguste Louis Charles de Messence, comte de, *Fêtes et Souvenirs du Congrès de Vienne, tableau des salons, scènes anecdotiques et portraits, 1814–1815*, Paris 1901

Laignel, P.G., *De la nécessité d'employer quelque marin auprès des négociateurs français lorsqu'ils ont à traiter avec l'Angleterre, et principalement dans la circonstance actuelle du Congrès assemblé à Vienne*, Paris 1814

Langeron, L.A., comte de, *Mémoires de Langeron, Général d'Infanterie dans l'Armée Russe*, Paris 1902

Las Cases, Émmanuel Auguste Dieudonné de, *Mémorial de Sainte-Hélène. Journal de la vie privée et des conversations de l'Empereur Napoléon à Sainte-Hélène*, 4 vols, London 1823

Lavalette, Antoine Marie Chamans, comte de, *Mémoires et Souvenirs*, Paris 1905

Lebzeltern, Louis-Joseph, Count, *Mémoires et Papiers*, Paris 1949

Lettre à un Saxon sur la réintegration de la Saxe et de son Souverain, publiée à l'occasion du Congrès de Vienne, 1814

Lettre du commandeur Berlinghieri, ancien ministre plénipotentiaire de l'Ordre souverain de St-Jean de Jérusalem au Congrès de Vienne, à M. de Flassan, Paris 1829

Lieven, Dorothea, *Letters of Dorothea Princess Lieven, during her Residence in London, 1812–1834*, London 1902

— *The Unpublished Diary and Political Sketches of Princess Lieven, together with some of her Letters*, ed. Harold Temperley, London 1925

Ligne, Charles Joseph Lamoral, prince de, *Oeuvres Posthumes Inédites*, ed. F. Leuridant, Paris 1921

Londonderry, Charles William Vane, Marquess of, *Narrative of the War in Germany and France in 1813 and 1814*, London 1830

Louis XVIII, *Les Devoirs d'un roi*, in *Feuilles d'Histoire*, 1 Sept 1909

Löwenstern, Woldemar Hermann, Baron von, *Mémoires du Général-Major Russe Baron de Löwenstern*, 2 vols, Paris 1903

Maevskii, D., *Moi vek, ili istoriya generala Maevskavo*, in *Russkaia Starina*, 1873, nos 7–8

Maillé, Blanche Josephine, duchesse de, *Souvenirs des deux Restaurations*, Paris 1984

Maistre, Joseph de, *Lettres et Opuscules Inédits*, Vol. I, Paris 1851

— *Correspondance Diplomatique*, 2 vols, Paris 1860

Martens, F., *Sobranie Traktatov i Konventsii zakliuchenykh c inostrannymi dierzhavami*, vols III & VII, St Petersburg 1876–85

Martens, G.F., *Nouveau Receuil de Traités d'Alliance, de Trève, de Neutralité, de Commerce, de Limites, d'Échanges, etc . . .*, vols I & III, Göttingen 1817

Martineau, Harriet, *A History of the Thirty Years' Peace*, 4 vols, London 1877

Maubreuil, Marie Armand de Guerry de, marquis d'Orvault, *Adresse au Congrès, à toutes les puissances de l'Europe*, London 1819

Mémoire adressé le 8 octobre 1814 aux hautes puissances, assemblées dans le Congrès de Vienne, Par MM. les Vicaires-généraux du Diocèse de Gand, dans l'absence et suivant l'intention expresse de Monseigneur le Prince de Broglie, Évêque de Gand

Mémoire présenté au Congrès de Vienne, le 17 décembre 1814, au nom de S.A.S. Le Prince Philippe d'Auvergne, duc régnant de Bouillon, Sedan 1814

Mémoire présenté par les Ministres plénipotentiaires de l'Ordre Souverain de St Jean de Jérusalem au Congrès Général à Vienne, Vienna 1814

Méneval, Baron Claude-François de, *Mémoires pour servir à l'Histoire de Napoléon Ier depuis 1802 jusqu'à 1815*, 3 vols, Paris 1894

Metternich, Prince Clemens Wenzel Lothar von, *Mémoires, Documents et Écrits divers laissés par le Prince de Metternich*, ed. A. de Klinkowstroem, vols I–III, Paris 1880

— *Aus Metternichs nachgelassenen Papieren*, ed. Richard von Metternich-Winneburg, vols 1–4, Vienna 1880–81

— *Lettres à la Comtesse de Lieven*, Paris 1909

— *Aus Diplomatie und Leben. Maximen des Fürsten Metternich*, ed. Arthur Breycha-Vauthier, Vienna 1964

— *Clemens Metternich-Wilhelmina von Sagan: ein briefwechsel 1813–1815*, Graz 1966

Mikhailovskii-Danilevskii, Aleksandr Ivanovich, *Zapiski 1814 i 1815 godov*, St Petersburg 1836

— *Memuary 1814–1815*, St Petersburg 2001

Montesquiou-Fézensac, comte Anatole de, *Souvenirs sur la Révolution, l'Empire, la Réstauration et le règne de Louis-Philippe*, Paris 1961

Montet, baroness Alexandrine de la Boutelière de Saint-Mars du, *Souvenirs*, Paris 1904

Müffling, Carl, Baron von, *The Memoirs of Baron von Müffling*, London 1997

Müller d'Arvaangue, Louis Rodolphe Baron, *Respectueuse adresse à Son Altesse Royale le Prince Régent de l'Empire Britannique*, Paris 1815

— *Aux Vrais Suisses*, Paris 1816

— *Réponse à l'Auteur du Congrès de Vienne, en ce qui concerne la Suisse*, Paris 1816

Münster, Ernst, Count von, *Political Sketches of the State of Europe 1814–1867, Containing Count Ernst Münster's Despatches to the Prince Regent, from the Congress of Vienna*, Edinburgh 1868

Nada, N. (ed.), *Le relazioni diplomatiche fra l'Austria e il regno di Sardegna*, Vol. I, Rome 1964

Napoleon I, *Correspondance de Napoléon Ier*, vols XXIV & XXV, Paris 1868

Nesselrode, A. de (ed.), *Lettres et Papiers du Chancelier Comte de Nesselrode 1760–1850*, 6 vols, Paris n.d.

Nicholas Mikhailovich, Grand Duke, *Russkie Portrety XVIII I XIX stoletii*, 5 vols, St Petersburg 1905–09

— *L'Impératrice Élisabeth, Épouse d'Alexandre Ier*, 3 vols, St Petersburg 1909

— *L'Empereur Alexandre Ier*, 2 vols, St Petersburg 1912

— (ed.) *Doniesienia abstriiskovo poslannika pri russkom dvore Lebzelterna za 1816–1828 gody*, St Petersburg 1913

Nostitz, Baron Karl von, *Leben und Briefwechsel*, Dresden 1848

Observations sur une déclaration du Congrès de Vienne, Paris 1815

Oncken, Wilhelm, *Österreich und Preussen im Befreiungskriege*, 2 vols, Berlin 1876–79

Orléans, Louis-Philippe d', *Mon Journal. Événements de 1815*, 2 vols, Paris 1849

Otrante, Joseph Fouché, Duc d', *Mémoires*, 2 vols, Paris 1824

— *Mémoires*, 2 vols, Paris 1945

Panam, Pauline, *Mémoires d'une Jeune Grecque*, London 1823

Pasquier, Étienne Denis, *Mémoires du Chancelier Pasquier*, 3 vols, Paris 1893

Perth, Matthias Franz, *Wienerkongresstagebüch 1814–1815*, Vienna 1981

Pichler, Caroline, *Denkwürdigkeiten aus meinem Leben*, 3 vols, Vienna 1844

Pictet, Edmond, *Biographie, travaux et correspondance diplomatique de C. Pictet de Rochemont, Député de Genève auprès du Congrès de Vienne, 1814, envoyé extraordinaire et ministre plénipotentiaire de la Suisse à Paris et à Turin, 1815 et 1816*, Geneva 1892

Pictet de Rochemont, Charles, *Correspondance Diplomatique de Charles Pictet de Rochemont et de François d'Yvernois 1814–1816*, Geneva 1914

Ponce, Nicolas, *Considérations politiques sur les opérations du Congrès de Vienne et sur la paix de l'Europe*, Paris 1815

Potocka, Anna, *Mémoires de la Comtesse Potocka*, Paris 1897

Pozzo di Borgo, Carl'Andrea, *Correspondance Diplomatique du Comte Pozzo di Borgo*, Paris 1890

Pradt, Dominique Dufour, abbé de, *Récit historique sur la restauration de la royauté en France*, Paris 1814

— *Du Congrès de Vienne, par l'auteur de l'Antidote au Congrès de Rastadt, etc.*, 2 vols, Paris 1815

— *L'Europe après le Congrès d'Aix-la-Chapelle*, Paris 1819

— *Congrès de Carlsbad*, Paris 1819

— *Rappel de quelques prédictions sur l'Italie, extraites du Congrès de Vienne, 1815 par M. de Pradt*, Paris 1821

Projet de pacte fédératif des Français et de tous les peuples de l'Europe, contre les Anglais et les soi-disants souverains, assemblés en congrès à Vienne, Paris 1815

Protestation de l'Impératrice Marie-Louise adressée au Congrès de Vienne contre l'occupation du trône de France par les Bourbons, 19 février 1815

Réflexions sur le Congrès de Vienne, année 1814

Reiset, Marie-Antoine, Général vicomte de, *Souvenirs*, vols II & III, Paris 1900–02

Rémusat, Charles de, *Mémoires de ma vie*, Vol. I, Paris 1958

Rinieri, Ilario, *Corrispondenza inedita dei cardinali Consalvi e Pacca nel tempo del Congresso di Vienna*, Turin 1903

Rochechouart, Léon Comte de, *Souvenirs sur la Révolution, l'Empire et la Réstauration*, Paris 1889

Romberg, E. & Malet, A., *Louis XVIII et les Cent Jours à Gand. Receuil de documents inédits*, Paris 1898

R—l Loggerheads! Or the Congress of State Tinkers! A poem by Peter Pindar Esq, London 1815

Rosenkrantz, Niels, *Journal du Congrès de Vienne, 1814–1815*, Copenhagen 1953

Ruck, Erwin, *Die Romische Kurie und die Deutsche Kirchenfrage auf dem Wiener Kongress*, Basel 1917

Rzewuska, Rozalia, *Mémoires de la Comtesse Rosalie Rzewuska (1788–1865)*, 3 vols, Rome 1939

Saint-Marsan, Antoine-Marie-Philippe, Marquis de, *Le journal du marquis de Saint-Marsan (28 juin 1814–7 juin 1815)*, Revue Napoléonienne, no. 4, 1904–05

Sarrazin, Jean, *Défense des Bourbons de Naples contre les panégyristes de l'usurpateur Murat, ou avis au Congrès de Vienne*, Paris 1815

Senancourt, Étienne de, *Simples observations, soumises au Congrès à Vienne et au Gouvernement fraņçais par un habitant des Vosges*, Paris 1814

Shelley, Frances Lady, *The Diary of Frances Lady Shelley 1787–1817*, London 1912

Shishkov, A.S., *Zapiski, Mnenia i Perepiska*, 2 vols, Berlin 1870

Spiel, Hilde, *The Congress of Vienna: an eyewitness account*, trs. R.H. Weber, Chilton, Phil., 1968

Staël-Holstein, Germaine de, *Madame de Staël et le Duc de Wellington. Correspondance Inédite 1815–1817*, ed. Victor de Pange, Paris 1962

— *Madame de Staël, ses amis et ses correspondants. Choix de lettres*, ed. G. Solovieff, Paris 1970

Stein, Freiherr vom, *Briefwechsel, Denkschriften und Aufzeichnungen*, vols IV & V, Berlin 1933

Talleyrand, Charles-Maurice de Talleyrand-Périgord, prince de, *Correspondance Inédite du Prince de Talleyrand et du roi Louis XVIII pendant le Congrès de Vienne*, Paris 1881

— *Lettres de M. de Talleyrand à Madame de Staël*, in *Revue d'Histoire Diplomatique*, 1890, I/78

— *Talleyrand Intime, d'après sa correspondance avec la Duchesse de Courlande*, Paris 1891
— *Talleyrand et les Archives de Vienne*, ed. C. Benedek & O. Ernst, in *Revue de Paris*, 15 December 1933
— *Lettres de Talleyrand à Caulaincourt, Revue des deux mondes*, no. 30, 1 November 1935
— *Mémoires*, 2 vols, Paris 1957
— *Lettres de Talleyrand à Metternich*, ed. Jean de Bourgoing, *Revue de l'Institut Napoléon*, no. 95, April 1965
— *Le Miroir de Talleyrand. Lettres Inédites à la duchesse de Courlande pendant le Congrès de Vienne*, ed. Gaston Palewski, Paris 1976
Thürheim, Gräfin Lulu, *Mein Leben*, Vol. II, Munich 1913
Turgenev, Nikolai Ivanovich, *Dnevniki*, Vol. VII, Moscow 1913
Traité de Paix entre le roi et les Puissances alliées, conclu à Paris, le 30 mai 1814; suivi des actes du Congrès de Vienne, signés le 9 juin de l'an de grâce 1815 par les plénipotentiaires des puissances alliées, publiés d'après la Gazette officielle du 19 juillet même année, Paris 1815
Valsamachi, Demetrio, Count, *Note sur la République des Sept-Iles, Présentée au Congrès de Vienne*, Vienna 1815
Vionnet de Maringoné, Louis Joseph, *Souvenirs*, Paris 1913
Vitrolles, baron de, *Mémoires*, 2 vols, Paris 1950
Webster, C.K., *British Diplomacy 1813–1815. Select Documents Dealing with the Reconstruction of Europe*, London 1921
Weil, M. H., *La Campagne de 1814 d'Après les documents des Archives impériales et royales de la guerre à Vienne*, 4 vols, Paris 1891–96
— *Les Dessous du Congrès de Vienne, d'après les documents originaux des archives du Ministère Impérial et Royal de l'Intérieur à Vienne*, 2 vols, Paris 1917
Wellington, Arthur Wellesley, Duke of, *The Dispatches of Field Marshal the Duke of Wellington during his various campaigns*, Vol. XI, London 1838
— *The Dispatches of Field Marshal the Duke of Wellington during his various campaigns*, vols VII & VIII, London 1845–47
— *Supplementary Despatches, Correspondence and Memoranda*, vols 8–15, London 1861–1872
Wilson, Sir Robert, *Narrative of Events during the Invasion of Russia*, London 1860
— *Private Diary of Travels, Personal Services, and Public Events, during Mission and Employment with the European Armies in the Campaigns of 1812, 1813, 1814*, Vol. II, London 1861

Bibliography

Studies

Actes du colloque: patriotisme et nationalisme en Europe à l'époque de la révolution française et de Napoléon, Paris 1973

Alexander, R.S., *Bonapartism and revolutionary tradition in France. The fédérés of 1815*, Cambridge 1991

Alison, Sir Archibald, *The Lives of Lord Castlereagh and Sir Charles Stewart*, 3 vols, London 1861

Arsh, G.L., *I Kapodistria i grecheskoe natsionalno-osvoboditelnoe dvizhenie 1809–1822*, Moscow 1976

Artaud de Montor, Alexis-François, *Histoire de la vie et des travaux politiques du comte d'Hauterive, comprenant une partie des actes de la diplomatie française*, Paris 1839

Artz, Frederick B., *Reaction and Revolution 1814–1832*, New York 1934

Askenazy, Szymon, *Szkice i Portrety*, Warsaw 1937

Baillou, Jean & Pelletier, Pierre, *Les Affaires Étrangères*, Paris 1962

Barraclough, G., *European Unity in Thought and Action*, Oxford 1963

Bartlett, C.J., *Castlereagh*, London 1966

Beales, Derek, *Prosperity and Plunder. European Catholic Monasteries in the Age of Revolution, 1650–1815*, Cambridge 2003

Bertier de Sauvigny, Guillaume de, *La Restauration*, Paris 1955

— *Metternich et son temps*, Paris 1959

— *Metternich et la France après le Congrès de Vienne*, 2 vols, Paris 1968

Bianchi, Nicomede, *Storia Documentata della Diplomaziia Europea in Italia*, Vol. I, Turin 1865

Bibl, Viktor, *Die Wiener Polizei. Eine Kulturhistorische studie*, Leipzig 1927

— *Kaiser Franz der Letzte Römisch-Deutsche Kaiser*, Leipzig 1936

Black, J.L., *Nicholas Karamzin's 'Opinion' on Poland, International History Review*, III, 1981

Blinn, Harold E., *New Light on Talleyrand at the Congress of Vienna, Pacific Historical Review*, no. 4, 1935

Bojasiński, J., *Rządy Tymczasowe w Królestwie Polskiem. Maj-grudzień 1815*, Warsaw 1902

Bonnal, E., *Les Royalistes contre l'Armée (1815–1820). D'après les archives du Ministère de la Guerre*, 2 vols, Paris 1906

Bonneau, François, *Talleyrand à table*, Châteauroux 1988

Bonnefons, André, *Un allié de Napoléon. Frédéric Auguste premier Roi de Saxe et Grand Duc de Varsovie*, Paris 1902

Bourgoing, Jean de, *Vom Wiener Kongress*, Vienna 1964

Breuilly, John, *The State of Germany. The National Idea in the Making, Unmaking and Remaking of a modern Nation-State*, London 1992

Brunov, F.I., *Aperçu des principales transactions du Cabinet de Russie sous les règnes de Catherine II, Paul I et Alexandre I*, in *Sbornik Imperatorskovo Russkovo Istoricheskovo Obshchestva*, Vol. XXXI, St Petersburg 1880

Bruun, Geoffrey, *Europe and the French Imperium 1799–1814*, New York 1938

Buckland, C.S.B., *Metternich and the British Government from 1809 to 1813*, London 1932

— *Friedrich von Gentz' relations with the British Government during the Marquis of Wellesley's Foreign Secretaryship of State*, London 1933

Buschkuhl, Matthias, *Great Britain and the Holy See, 1746–1870*, Dublin 1982

Buxbaum, Gerda, *Der Wiener Kongress. Eine Dokumentation mit einem Nachwort*, Dortmund 1983

Capefigue, M., *Le Congrès de Vienne dans ses rapports avec la Circonscription actuelle de l'Europe*, Paris 1847

Carrié, René Albrecht, *A Diplomatic History of Europe since the Congress of Vienna*, New York 1958

Chamberlain, M.E., *Lord Aberdeen: A Political Biography*, London 1983

— *'Pax Britannica'? British Foreign Policy 1789–1914*, London 1989

Chapman, Tim, *The Congress of Vienna. Origins, processes and results*, London 1998

Chapuisat, Édouard, *La Suisse et les Traités de 1815*, Geneva 1914

Chatelain, Jean, *Dominique Vivant Denon et le Louvre de Napoléon*, Paris 1973

Chuquet, Arthur, *L'Année 1814*, Paris 1914

Cole, H., *Fouché. The Unprincipled Patriot*, London 1971

Colloque Patriotisme et nationalisme en Europe a l'époque de la révolution française et de Napoléon, Moscou 1970, Paris 1973

Coupland, R., *The British Anti-Slavery Movement*, London 1933

Daudet, Ernest, *À travers trois siècles*, Paris 1911

Daudet, Léon, *Une Vie d'Ambassadrice au Siècle Dernier. La Princesse de Lieven*, Paris 1903

Derry, John W., *Castlereagh*, London 1976

Driault, E., *Napoléon et l'Europe. La chute de l'Empire. La Légende de Napoléon*, Paris 1927

Dupuis, C., *Le Ministère de Talleyrand en 1814*, 2 vols, Paris 1919–20

Empaytaz, H.L., *Notice sur Alexandre, Empereur de Russie*, Paris 1840

Escoffier, Maurice, *Un procédé diplomatique de Talleyrand (affaires de Pologne 1814)*, *Revue des Sciences Politiques*, no. 29, 1913

Ferrero, Guglielmo, *The Reconstruction of Europe. Talleyrand and the Congress of Vienna 1814–1815*, trs. Theodore R. Jaeckel, New York 1941

Festing, Gabrielle, *John Hookham Frere and his Friends*, London 1899

Fitzpatrick, B., *Catholic Royalism in the Department of the Gard, 1814–1852*, London 1983

Flamand, L., *Frederik den Sjettes Hof*, Copenhagen 1855

Flassan, G. de Raxis de, *Histoire du Congrès de Vienne, par l'auteur de l'histoire de la diplomatie française*, Paris 1829

Flockerzie, Lawrence J., *Saxony, Austria, and the German Question after the Congress of Vienna, 1815–1816,* International History Review, Vol. 12, 1990

Forsyth, M., *The Old European States-System: Gentz versus Hauterive*, Historical Journal, 23, Cambridge 1980

Fraser, Flora, *The Unruly Queen. The Life of Queen Caroline*, London 1996

Freeman, Charles, *The Horses of St Mark's*, London 2004

Gallavresi, Giuseppe, *Le Prince de Talleyrand et le Cardinal Consalvi, une page peu connue de l'histoire du Congrès de Vienne*, Paris 1905

Gallenga, A., *History of Piedmont*, Vol. III, London 1855

Garros, Louis, *Quel Roman que ma vie! Itinéraire de Napoléon Bonaparte (1769–1821)*, Paris 1947

Gash, Norman, *Lord Liverpool. The Life and Political Career of Robert Banks Jenkinson, Second Earl of Liverpool, 1770–1828*, London 1984

Gleason, J.H., *The Genesis of Russophobia in Great Britain*, New York 1972

Gooch, G.P., *Germany and the French Revolution*, London 1920

Grab, Alexander, *Napoleon and the Transformation of Europe*, London 2003

Green, J.E.S., *Castlereagh's Instructions for the Conferences at Vienna 1822*, in *Royal Historical Society Transactions*, 3rd Series, Vol. VII, 1913

Grimsted, Patricia Kennedy, *The Foreign Ministers of Alexander I: Political Attitudes and the Conduct of Russian Diplomacy 1801–1825*, Berkeley 1969

Grossmann, Karl, *Metternichs Plan eines italienischen Bundes*, in *Historische Blätter*, Vienna 1931

Grunewald, Constantin de, *Baron Stein. Enemy of Napoleon*, London 1936

Gruyer, Paul, *Napoléon roi de l'Île d'Elbe*, Paris 1906

Haas, A.G., *Metternich, Reorganization and Nationality 1813–1818*, Wiesbaden 1963

Handelsman, Marceli, *Adam Czartoryski*, 3 vols, Warsaw 1948–50

Haussonville, comte O. d', *Deux Episodes Diplomatiques*, in *Revue des Deux Mondes*, Paris, 15 May 1862

Hazen, Charles Downer, *The Congress of Vienna*, in *Three Peace Congresses of the Nineteenth Century*, Harvard 1917

Hearnshaw, F.J.C., *European Coalitions, Alliances and Ententes since 1792*, Foreign Office Handbooks, no. 152, 1920

Heraud, Guy & Beguelin, Roland, *Europe-Jura. 150ème anniversaire du Congrès de Vienne*, Délémont 1965

Hojer, Torvald, *Bernadotte, Maréchal de France*, Paris 1943

Holbraad, C., *The Concert of Europe*, London 1970

Houssaye, Henri, *La Seconde Abdication. La Terreur Blanche*, Paris 1918

Hundt, Michael, *Die Mindermächtigen Deutschen Staaten auf dem Wiener Kongress*, Mainz 1996

Kasser, Paul, *Le Passage des Alliés en Suisse pendant l'hiver 1813/14*, Geneva 1915

Kissinger, Henry A., *A World Restored. Metternich, Castlereagh and the Problems of Peace 1812–22*, London 1957

Kohler, Max J., *Jewish Rights at the Congresses of Vienna (1814–1815), and Aix-la-Chapelle (1818)*, New York 1918

Kraehe, Enno E., *Metternich's German Policy*, 2 vols, Princeton 1963–83

Krog, Ole Villumsen (ed.), *Danmark og Den Dansende Wienerkongres*, Copenhagen 2002

Kukiel, Marian, *Czartoryski and European Unity 1770–1861*, Princeton 1955

Langslet, Lars Roar, *Christian Frederik Del I*, Oslo 1998

Levey, Michael, *Sir Thomas Lawrence*, London 2005

Ley, Francis, *Madame de Krudener et son Temps*, Paris 1962

— *Alexandre Ier et sa Sainte Alliance*, Paris 1975

Macunn, F.J., *The Contemporary English View of Napoleon*, London 1914

Madelin, Louis, *Fouché 1759–1820*, Paris 1979

Mann, Golo, *Secretary of Europe. The Life of Friedrich Gentz, Enemy of Napoleon*, trs. William H. Woglom, Yale 1946

Mansel, Philip, *Louis XVIII*, London 1981

— *Prince of Europe. The Life of Charles-Joseph de Ligne*, London 2003

Martin, Alexander M., *Romantics, Reformers, Reactionaries. Russian Conservative Thought and Politics in the Reign of Alexander I*, DeKalb 1997

Martineau, Gilbert, *Caroline Bonaparte, Princesse Murat, Reine de Naples*, Paris 1991

McGuigan, Dorothy Gies, *Metternich and the Duchess*, New York 1975

Milne, Andrew, *Metternich*, London 1975

Montbas, vicomte de, *Caulaincourt à Châtillon*, in *La Revue de Paris*, June & July 1928

Montlosier, Reynaud, Comte de, *De la monarchie française*, 7 vols, Paris 1814–24

Naeff, Werner, *Zur Geschichte der Heiligen Allianz*, Bern 1928

Nicolson, Harold, *The Congress of Vienna. A Study in Allied Unity: 1812–1822*, London 1946

Noel, Léon, *Énigmatique Talleyrand, avec des inédits des archives du Vatican et d'ailleurs*, Paris 1975

Nørregard, G., *Danmark og Wienerkongressen 1814–1815*, Copenhagen 1948

O'Dwyer, M.M., *The Papacy in the Age of Napoleon and the Restoration: Pius VII 1800–1823*, Lanham 1985

Oman, Carola, *Britain against Napoleon*, London 1942

Ordioni, Pierre, *Pozzo di Borgo. Diplomate de l'Europe Fançaise*, Paris 1935

Orieux, J., *Talleyrand, ou le Sphinx incompris*, Paris 1970

Parissien, Steven, *George IV. The Grand Entertainment*, London 2001

Perey, Lucien, *Histoire d'une Grande Dame au XVIIIe siècle. La Comtesse Hélène Potocka*, Paris 1888

Phillips, W. Alison, *The Confederation of Europe. A Study of the European Alliance 1813–1823 as an Experiment in the International Organization of Peace*, London 1920

Pingaud, Albert, *Le Congrès de Vienne et la Politique de Talleyrand*, Paris 1899

Pollock, John, *Wilberforce*, London 1977

Raeder, Jac, *Paa Kongsvinger I 1814*, in *Historisk Tidsskrift*, Vol. 3, 1916

Rain, Pierre, *L'Europe et la Restauration des Bourbons 1814–1818*, Paris 1908

Ramm, D., *Le Congrès de Vienne 1814 et 1815. Histoire de l'Origine, de l'action et de l'anéantissement des traités de 1815*, Paris 1866

Rappard, William E., *L'Individu et l'État dans l'évolution constitutionelle de la Suisse*, Zürich 1936

Rath, R.J., *The Fall of the Napoleonic Kingdom of Italy*, New York 1941

— *The Habsburgs and Public Opinion in Lombardy-Venetia, 1814–1815*, in E.M. Earle, ed., *Nationalism & Internationalism*, New York 1950

— *The Provisional Austrian Regime in Lombardy-Venetia, 1814–1815*, Austin 1969

Reinerman, A.J., *Metternich, Alexander I and the Russian Challenge in Italy, 1815–1820, Journal of Modern History*, Vol. 46, 1974

Renier, C.J., *Great Britain and the Establishment of the Kingdom of the Netherlands, 1813–1815*, London 1930

Resnick, Daniel P., *The White Terror and the Political Reaction after Waterloo*, Cambridge, Mass., 1966

Rie, Robert, *Das legitimitätsprinzip des Wiener kongresses, Archiv des Volkerrechts*, 5, 1955–56

Rinieri, Ilario, *La Diplomazia Pontificia nel secolo XIX*, 2 vols, Rome 1902

— *Il Congresso di Vienna e la S. Sede (1813–1815)*, Rome 1904

Roberts, Andrew, *Waterloo. Napoleon's Last Gamble*, London 2005

Robertson, Charles Grant, *The Evolution of Prussia*, Oxford 1946

Robinet de Cléry, Adrien, *Un diplomate d'il y a cent ans. Frédéric de Gents*, Paris 1917

Roveri, Alessandro, *La Missione Consalvi e il Congresso di Viena*, 3 vols, Rome 1970–73

Rowe, Michael, *From Reich to State. The Rhineland in the Revolutionary Age, 1780–1830*, Cambridge 2003

Ryan, Alan, *Indefeasible State Sovereignty, the international community and attempts to abrogate war, from the Congress of Vienna to the establishment of the League of Nations*, doctoral thesis, Cambridge 1991

Schenk, H.G., *The Aftermath of the Napoleonic Wars. The Concert of Europe – an Experiment*, London 1946

Schroeder, Paul W., *An Unnatural 'Natural Alliance': Castlereagh, Metternich and*

Aberdeen in 1813, in *International History Review*, Vol. X No. 4, November 1988

— *Napoleon's Foreign Policy. A Criminal Enterprise?*, in *Journal of Military History*, no. 54, 1990

— *The Transformation of European Politics, 1763–1848*, Oxford 1994

Scott, F.D., *Bernadotte and the Throne of France, 1814*, *Journal of Modern History*, Vol. 5, 1933

Sédouy, Jacques-Alain de, *Le Congrès de Vienne. L'Europe Contre la France, 1812–1815*, Paris 2003

Seeber, Edward Derbyshire, *Anti-Slavery Opinion in France during the Second half of the eighteenth century*, Baltimore, London, Paris 1937

Sherwig, J.M., *Guineas and Gunpowder: British Foreign Aid in the Wars with France, 1793–1815*, Cambridge, Mass., 1969

Shilder, N.K., *Imperator Aleksandr Pervii. Evo Zhizn i Tsarstvovanie*, Vol. III, St Petersburg 1905

Sked, A. (ed.), *Europe's Balance of Power 1815–1848*, New York 1979

Skowronek, Jerzy, *Antynapoleońskie Koncepcje Czartoryskiego*, Warsaw 1969

Sorel, Albert, *Essais d'Histoire et de Critique*, Paris 1894

— *L'Europe et la Révolution Française*, 8 vols, Paris 1904

Sparrow, Elisabeth, *Secret Service. British Agents in France, 1792–1815*, Woodbridge 1999

Spitzer, Alan B., *Old Hatreds and Young Hopes. The French Carbonari against Bourbon Restoration*, Harvard 1971

Srbik, Heinrich von, *Deutsche Einheit*, Vol. I, Munich 1936

Stanislavskaia, A.M., *Russko-angliiskie otnoshenia i problemy Sredizemnomoria 1797–1807*, Moscow 1962

Stenger, Gilbert, *Le Retour des Bourbons*, Paris 1908

Straus, Hannah Alice, *The Attitude of the Congress of Vienna toward Nationalism in Germany, Italy and Poland*, New York 1949

Sweet, Paul R, *Erich Bollman at Vienna in 1815*, in *American Historical Review*, 46, 1941

— *Wilhelm von Humboldt. A Biography*, 2 vols, Columbus, Ohio 1978

Temperley, H.W.V., *Attempts at International Government in Europe; the Period of the Congress of Vienna (1814–25); and the period since the Treaty of Versailles (1919–22)*, Historical Association Leaflet, Brussels 1923

Thaden, Edward C., *Interpreting History: Collective Essays on Russia's relations with Europe*, Boulder 1990

Thomas, Hugh, *The Slave Trade*, London 1997

Thorsøe, A., *Den Danske Stats Historie fra 1814–1848*, Copenhagen 1979

Treitschke, H. von, *History of Germany*, 2 vols, London 1915–16

Verga, E., *La Deputazione dei Collegi Elettorali del Regno d'Italia a Parigi nel 1814*, in *Archivio Storico Lombardo*, Milan 1904, ser. 4, Anno XXXI

Bibliography

Villa-Urrutia, Marqués de, *España en el Congreso de Viena segun la correspondenza Oficial de D. Pedro Gomez Labrador, Marqués de Labrador*, Madrid 1928

Vogler, Werner, *Abt Pankraz Vorster von St. Gallen un der Wiener Kongress 1814/15*, n.p., 1982

Wandycz, Piotr, *The Lands of Partitioned Poland 1795–1918*, Seattle 1974

Ward, Adolphus, *The Period of Congresses*, 2 vols, London 1919

Ward, A.W. & Gooch, G.P., eds.,*The Cambridge History of British Foreign Policy, 1783–1919*, 3 vols, Cambridge 1922

Waresquiel, Émmanuel de, *Le Duc de Richelieu*, Paris 1990

— *Talleyrand. Le Prince Immobile*, Paris 2003

Waresquiel, Émmanuel de, & Yvert, Benoît, *Histoire de la Restauration*, Paris 1996

Wawrzkowicz, Eugeniusz, *Anglia a Sprawa Polska 1813–1815*, Kraków 1919

Webster, C.K., *Some Aspects of Castlereagh's Foreign Policy*, in *Transactions of the Royal Historical Society*, 3rd series, Vol. VI, London 1912

— *England and the Polish-Saxon Problem at the Congress of Vienna*, in *Transactions of the Royal Historical Society*, 3rd series, Vol. VII, London 1913

— *The Congress of Vienna 1814–1815 and the Conference of Paris 1919*, Historical Association leaflet, Brussels 1923

— *The Foreign Policy of Castlereagh 1812–1815. Britain and the Reconstruction of Europe*, London 1931

— *The Congress of Vienna 1814–1815*, London 1934

Weil, Maurice-Henri, *Le Prince Eugène et Murat, 1813–1814. Opérations Militaires et Négociations Diplomatiques*, 4 vols, Paris 1902

— *Joachim Murat, roi de Naples. La dernière année du règne*, 5 vols, Paris 1909–10

Welschinger, Henri, *Les Coulisses du Congrès de Vienne*, Paris 1910

Woolf, S., *Napoleon's Integration of Europe*, London 1991

Zawadzki, W.H., *Adam Czartoryski: an Advocate of Slavonic Solidarity at the Congress of Vienna*, in *Oxford Slavonic Papers*, new series, Vol. X, Oxford 1977

— *A Man of Honour. Adam Czartoryski as a Statesman of Russia and Poland 1795–1831*, Oxford 1993

Ziegler, Philip, *The Duchess of Dino*, London 1962

Zorin, Andrei, *Karmia Dvuglavovo Orla*, Moscow 2004

Index

Page numbers in *italics* denote maps

Aberdeen, George Gordon, Earl of
98–100, 103, 106, 107, 115, 125, 127–30,
131, 136, 157
Abrantès, Laure Junot, duchesse d' 190–1
Aix-la-Chapelle, congress (1818) 543–4
Alexander of Russia, Tsar 11, 15–20, 56–7,
67, 273–7; and abolition of slave trade
411; alliance with Napoleon (1807) 19,
20, 45; and Anglo-French-Austrian
treaty against 464–5; and army 532;
arrival at Congress 276; attitude
towards Britain 19; and Austria 65; and
Baroness Krüdener 491–2, 509, 522; and
Bernadotte 44, 114, 104, 145, 146, 298;
and Bourbons 146, 153, 170, 472; and
Castlereagh 146, 153–4, 544; and
Castlereagh's 'grand design' proposal
129, 130; character and changes in 16,
146, 274, 316, 492–3, 509–10, 532; and
Châtillon congress 158, 159; behaviour
410–11; composing of 'Holy Alliance'
520–2; dealings with and animosity
between Metternich and 277, 278, 320,
326, 330–1, 334, 362–3, 401; dealings
with Talleyrand 283- 5, 324–6, 367;
death 533, 565; departure from Congress
483; enters Paris after defeat of
Napoleon (1814) 179; enters Paris after
defeat of Napoleon (1815) 491; and fate
of Napoleon 182; flirtations and affairs
313, 337, 351–3; and Frederick William
29, 30–1, 292; and Germany 27, 28,
32–3, 37, 97, 110, 112; and Greek
independence 547, 548, 549;
humiliations at Austerlitz and
Friedland 19; ill-health 356; Italy
question 431; and London visit/talks
204, 208–9, 211–12, 213–14; and Louis
XVIII 180, 188, 472, 519; love of
uniforms 350; making contingency
plans in case of war 367; marriage 273,
350–1, 353, 411, 483; and Metternich 98,
117, 132, 135, 148, 154, 163, 216, 320; and
mysticism 32, 491–2, 509, 522, 532–3,
537; and Napoleon 17, 32; Napoleon's
escape and campaign against 446–7,
461, 462–3; and Ottoman Empire issue
415; Polish issue 277–8, 314–17, 325, 326,
329–30, 334–7, 360, 362, 363–4, 416–18,
483; Polish plans 19, 20, 160, 162–3,
195–7, 196, 212, 240, 274–5, 276, 277,
531–2; objectives 275–6; popularity in
London 211–12; and Prince Eugène 468;
and Quadruple Alliance 544, 545;

Alexander of Russia – *cont.*
ratification of Treaty of Kiel 298, 387–8;
reform of Russian state 16; and Russian
western frontier issue 359–60; and
Saxony-Prussia issue 348, 377–8, 391,
396; sense of spiritual destiny xiii, 16,
32, 67, 68, 103–4, 116, 147, 196, 273, 274;
social distractions and activities 350–1,
374; stay at Paris 509–11; and Sweden
44; and Swiss question 424, 427; and
Switzerland 134–5; talks with
Metternich over proposed negotiations
with Napoleon 74; talks with Talleyrand
over post-war political arrangement of
France 179–80; treaty with Frederick
William (Kalisch) (1813) 31–2; and
Treaty of Paris negotiations (1815)
504–5, 518–19, 523; universal respect for
15; and war against Napoleon 27, 52–3,
67, 68, 83, 90, 94–5, 125–6, 147–8, 153,
155; and Wellington 405; and
Wilhelmina 327, 330–1;

Angoulême, Louis Antoine de Bourbon,
duc d' 170, 173

Anker, Carsten 227

Anna Pavlovna, Grand Duchess of Russia
248, 505

Anstett, Jean 85, 126, 334, 484

Apsley, Lord 392

Arakcheyev, General Aleksey Andreevich
532

Arndt, Ernst Moritz 25

Arnstein, Baroness Fanny von 304

Artois, Charles Philippe de Bourbon,
comte d' (Monsieur), later King
Charles X of France 170, 171, 173, 249,
452

Arvaangue, Baron Müller d' 304, 424, 551

Auersperg, Princess Gabrielle 313, 352, 483,
531

Auerstadt, Battle of 26

Augereau, Marshal Pierre François 62, 186

Austerlitz, Battle of 19, 45

Austria 7, 11, 17, 21, 35–7, 55, 225, 567;
alliance with Bavaria (1813) 113; alliance
with France 13, 35, 38–9, 50–1, 58, 76;
army 40; and Britain 41; ceding of

provinces to France 35; and Congress of
Vienna *see* Metternich; and Germany
239; growth of police machine and
surveillance 559–60; and Italy 232, 234,
429–30, 538–9; joins Russian/Prussian
alliance against France 74, 75, 88–9, 91;
Metternich's talks with allies over
negotiations with Napoleon 39–40, 50,
53–4, 59–60, 64–6, 72–5; Napoleon's
escape and campaign against 461, 462;
and prospects of war (1814) 368;
resentment against rule in Italy 539–40;
and Sardinia 539; secret treaty with
Naples (1815) 545–6; treaties with
Britain (1813) 100, 129; treaties signed
with Russia and Prussia at Toeplitz
(1813) 95–6; treaty of alliance with
Britain and France (1815) 392–3; treaty
with King of Württemberg (1813) 124–5;
and Treaty of Paris (1814) 201;
vulnerability of 36; war against France
to liberate Germany (1809) 57; *see also*
Metternich, Count

Baader, Franz von 533

Baden 21, 238, 239, 247, 433

Baden, Karl Ludwig, Grand Duke of 125,
311–12, 385, 401, 404–5, 439–40, 446,
476–7, 536

Bagration, Princess Catherine 258–9, 283,
304, 309–10, 320, 327, 351, 477, 484, 565

Balashov, Aleksandr 67

Bâle, Treaty of (1795) 25, 55

Balkans 20, 415

Banka 208

Barclay de Tolly, Field Marshal Prince
Mikhail Bogdanovich 90, 107, 191

Bathurst, Henry, 3rd Earl 262, 272, 403

Battle of the Nations (Leipzig) (1813)
113–14, 115, 118

Bautzen, defeat of allied forces by
Napoleon at 61, 64, 67

Bavaria 6, 35, 242, 369, 433, 434, 479, 480,
542; alliance with Austria (1813) 113; and
British-Austro-French alliance 392, 402;
compensation for territory returned to
Austria 526; dispute with Austria over

compensation 467–8; gaining of territories though Mediatisation Act (1803) 21, 112–13; and Mainz 267, 439, 468; and Metternich 109, 113; Napoleon's escape and campaign against 462

Bavaria, Ludwig, Crown Prince of 308

Beauharnais, Stephanie de 249

Beethoven, Ludwig van 356–7, 376

Belgium 6, 140, 194, 207, 215, 556, 564

Bellegarde, Marshal Heinrich Josef von, 232, 234

Belliard, General 177

Benevento, principality of 527, 528

Benkendorff, General Alexander 156

Bentham, Jeremy 212; *Principles of Morals and Legislation* 220

Bentinck, Lieutenant-General Lord William 230–1, 233

Berbice 207, 208

Bernadotte, Marshal Jean-Baptiste 42, 131, 192, 298; and Alexander 44, 104, 114, 145, 146, 298; hedging of bets 104–5, 171–2; and Norway 227; ruler of France proposal 44, 104, 145, 146; and Swedish Pomerania 388; war against Napoleon 90, 93, 104, 113, 153

Berne 422, 423, 425, 426, 427, 551

Bernstorff, Countess 307

Berry, Charles Ferdinand de Bourbon, duc de 170, 180, 248; assassination 545

Berthier, Marshal Louis Alexandre 12, 82, 256

Bertuch, Carl 344, 365, 370, 477–8

Bertuch, Friedrich Justin 258

Bessières, Marshal Jean-Baptiste 62–3

Bethmann, Simon Moritz 122

Beugnot, Claude, comte 190

Bignon, Édouard 561

Bigottini, Émilie 310

Bismarck, Prince Otto von 568

Blacas, Pierre, comte de 432, 452, 489

Blücher, General Gebhard 25, 51, 52, 90, 92, 114, 126, 153, 155, 169, 209–10, 470, 471, 488, 490–1, 508, 535

Bonaparte, Jérôme, King of Westphalia 110, 118, 249, 475–6, 552

Bonaparte, Joseph, King of Spain 6, 82, 151, 175

Borghese, Prince Camillo 552–3

Borghese, Pauline Bonaparte, Princess 191

Borodino, Battle of 3, 27

Bouillon 427

Bourbons 144–5, 146, 153, 170, 171, 172, 174, 179, 471–3

Boyen, Leopold von 25

Brentano, Clemens von 56

Brignole-Sale, Marchese de 256, 564

Brionne, Louise de Rohan, comtesse de 484

Britain 17, 40–1, 46–7, 71, 541–2, 567; alliance with Russia (1812) 44; army 366; attitude towards of Alexander 19; and Austria 41; blamed for Napoleon's escape 446; and Bourbons 144, 472; colonies 541–2; and Congress of Vienna *see* Castlereagh; criticism of behaviour of representatives at Congress 344–5; and Denmark 102; economic problems 546; and 'Frankfurt proposals' 128; and Ionian islands 524; and Italy 229–32, 233; left out of talks between Metternich and allies 75; and Malta 428; maritime rights 128, 342; Napoleon's escape and campaign against 461, 462; Napoleon's view of 12, 40; and Netherlands 207; and Norway 227; peace reached with United States (1814) 392; perception of France 41; prepared to enter into negotiations with Napoleon 89–90; and prospects of war (1814) 368–9; and Prussia 41, 42; and Russia 17–18, 41–2, 71; seeking of rapprochement with France (1814) 372–3; seen as chief culprit in removing works of art from France 513, 514; and Six Acts 546; and slave trade 200; and Spain 6, 228, 228–9; and Sweden 41, 42; tariff war with France 45–6; treaties with Austria (1813) 100, 129; treaty of alliance with France and Austria (1815) 392–3; and Treaty of Paris (1814) 201; and Treaty of Paris negotiations (1815) 505, 523–4; treaty with Prussia and

Britain – *cont.*
  Russia (1813) 72; treaty with Sweden
  (1813) 44- 5, 227; view of Napoleon 144;
  war with United States 46, 342, 366;
  wars with France 136; *see also*
  Castlereagh
British Guinea 208
Brougham, Henry, Lord 163
Brune, Marshal Guillaume 495
Bubna, General Count Ferdinand 11, 40,
  59–60, 65
Buchholz, Carl August 379
Bulletins de la Grande Armée 2, 4
Burghersh, Lady Priscilla 122, 123, 153, 158,
  159
Burghersh, Lord 192
Butyagin, Pavel 460–1
Byron, George Gordon, Lord 553

Cambacérès, Jean Jacques de 4, 12
Cambronne, General Pierre-Jean-Étienne
  455
Campo Chiaro, Duke of 257
Canning, George 43, 212, 548
Canning, Stratford 424
Canova, Antonio 511, 513
Capodistrias, Count Ioannis 107, 332, 333,
  429, 500, 521, 524–5; assassination of
  565
Caracciolo, Prince Lucio 257
Carême, Antonin 271
Cariati, Prince 257
Carynthia 58
Castlereagh, Lady Emily 137, 189, 262, 344–5
Castlereagh, Robert Stewart, Viscount,
  later 2nd Marquess of Londonderry xiv,
  42–3, 45, 46, 98, 268–9, 292–3, 300–1,
  542, 563; and abolition of slave trade
  issue 346, 411–14; agrees to join
  negotiations between allies and
  Napoleon 75–6; and Alexander 146,
  153–4, 544; and Alexander's 'Holy
  Alliance' 521–2; arrival at Congress
  260–3; background and career 42–3;
  becomes Foreign Secretary 43–4; and
  Belgium 564; and Bourbon issue 144,
  145, 154, 171, 472–3; character and

attributes 43, 44; concern over state of
  Coalition 98, 105–6, 163, 164; conditions
  for peace 143–4, 149–50, 166; criticism
  of policy of 346, 347- 8, 370, 541, 561;
  death 548, 565; departs for Germany
  and peace talks 136, 137–42; departure
  from Congress 411, 418–19, 420;
  enthusiasm for concept of great single
  act to bind various settlements 415–16,
  418; 'grand design' proposal and signing
  of Treaty of Chaumont 106, 129–31, 164,
  166–7; and Ionian islands issue 524–5;
  and Italy 233, 234, 235, 432; lodgings
  262; and London talks 214; meeting
  with Frederick William 405; meetings
  and dealings with Alexander 406,
  414–16; and Metternich 48, 98, 103,
  142–3, 246; Napoleon's escape and
  allied campaign against 445, 472–3; and
  Netherlands 139, 140, 206–8; and new
  campaign against Napoleon 472–3;
  plenipotentiaries chosen 261–2; and
  Polish issue 163, 262, 277–8, 293, 314–15,
  317, 329, 334–7, 342, 343–4, 364, 389,
  416–17; and Pope 237; and precedence
  issue 421; and procedure issue 264–5,
  282; on prospects of war 370; and
  Prussia's territorial demands 293; and
  Quadruple Alliance 529, 532, 544–5; role
  of Congress seen by 261; and Saxony-
  Prussia issue 361, 377, 380, 390, 391,
  394–5, 396, 410; seeking rapprochement
  with France 373; sees France as
  potential junior partner in new *entente*
  261, 264; and Statistical Committee
  386–7; and Swiss issue 424; and
  Talleyrand 261, 379–80, 387; and treaty
  of alliance between Britain, France and
  Austria 392, 393, 401–2; and Treaty of
  Paris (1814) 199–200, 201; and Treaty of
  Paris negotiations (1815) 505–6, 508–9,
  511, 512, 523; view of plundered works of
  art in France being returned to allies
  512
Catalonia 6
Cathcart, General Charles Murray, Earl
  48, 71, 72, 100, 129, 130, 164, 262, 421

Catherine Pavlovna, Grand Duchess of
Russia 131, 204–5, 206, 208, 212–13,
247–8, 367
Catherine II, Empress of Russia ('the
Great') 18
Catholic Church 224, 436–7
Catholics 236–7
Cato Street conspiracy 546
Caulaincourt, General Armand de, duc de
Vicence 1–4, 12, 60, 61, 64, 85, 86–9,
156, 157–8, 159–60, 460
Charles, Archduke of Austria 131, 247,
468
Charlotte, Princess of England 140, 205–6,
247
Châtillon congress (1814) 144–5, 150, 152,
153, 156–60, 170, 194
Chaumont, Treaty of (1814) 166–8, 202,
241, 462
Christian of Denmark, Prince 102, 227
Clam-Martinitz, Count von 321, 484, 515,
566
Clancarty, Richard Trench, Earl of 206,
262, 443, 485, 502
Cochin 208
Committee on Diplomatic Precedence
(Congress of Vienna) 420–1
Committee on the Free Navigation of
International Rivers (Congress of
Vienna) 427
Confederation of the Rhine *see*
Rheinbund
CONGRESS OF VIENNA (1814–15):
abolition of slave trade issue 346, 347,
411–14; animosity between Metternich
and Alexander 320, 326, 330–1, 334,
362–3, 401; balls 285–6, 287, 304, 307,
322–3, 326, 337–8, 339–40, 374, 398–9,
401; Carrousel 353–5; categories of
business to the addressed 264;
circulation of gossip and rumour
307–8; Committee on Diplomatic
Precedence 420–1; Committee on the
Free Navigation of International Rivers
427; contemporary assessment of 553–4;
counting of 'souls' 386, 467, 561–2;
criticism of 331–3, 550–1, 553, 561–2,

564; criticism of social graces of the
British 344–5; crowned heads attending
255; dealing with claims to lands or
rights 427; decline of respect for
sovereigns and royalty 312–13, 398;
delegates and participants 255–8;
demolishing of elements of by later
events 554–8; Denmark's objectives
297–8; departure of participants and
visitors 480–4; destruction of
Razumovsky Palace by fire 383–4;
disenchantment with 297–301, 331–3,
551–2; disillusionment with of ordinary
people 398; Easter rites 463–4;
entertainments and festivities 288–9,
293–5, 296–7, 303–4, 305- 7, 327,
339–40, 353–7, 374–6, 381–2, 398–401,
440; Festival of Peace 321–2; Final Act
484–6, 528, 537; first official meeting of
Five great powers 395–7; fixing of
frontiers of Holland and Hanover 414;
French objectives 270; German issue
317–18, 386, 432–41, 467–9, 478–80;
gifts handed out 480–3; hopes of
dispossessed petitioners for 219;
housing of guests 253–4; impact of xiii,
566–9; inclusion of France in formal
conferences of great powers issue 395;
incorporation of Genoa into Sardinia
issue 341–2, 430; interplay between the
serious and frivolous 385; Italy question
429–32, 467, 538; joint declaration
issued declaring Napoleon an outlaw
448; meetings between ministers of the
Four powers 260–9; and Napoleon's
escape 442–8, 465; Order of Malta issue
428–9; Polish issue 277–8, 314–17, 324,
325, 326, 329–30, 334–7, 360, 362, 363–4,
389–90, 416–18, 483; Polish settlement
408; postponement of 216, 218;
precedence issue 379, 420–1;
preparations for 214, 252–4; procedure
issue 264–6, 268–9, 273, 279, 281–2,
283, 285, 286–7, 288, 290, 327; Prussia's
territorial claims and agreement on
267–8, 414; public opinion on
convening of and views on future of

CONGRESS OF VIENNA – *cont.*
Europe 219–20; question of France and Spain's inclusion 264, 265, 268–9; ratification of Treaty of Kiel by Alexander 298, 387–8; reconstruction of Europe xiii; Russian western frontier proposal 359–60; salons 304–5; Saxony-Prussia deal 405–10, *408*; Saxony-Prussia issue 296, 360–2, 364–5, 371–2, 376–8, 379–80, 391, 394- 5, 396–7, 402–3; sexual activity at 308–12; signing of Bavaria, Hanover and Holland to British-Austro-French alliance 402; signing of treaty of alliance between Britain, France and Austria (1815) 392–3, 409–10; Spanish priorities 280; Statistical Committee 386–7, 397, 420; surveillance system 250–2, 278–9, 296, 301–3, 475–7; and Swiss question 386, 421–8; tensions between allies and prospect of war 365–70, 378, 391, 402; verdicts on 550–1; and Viennese 254, 312

conquêtes consommées 96

Consalvi, Cardinal Ercole 236, 257, 258, 409, 436, 438, 439, 485–6, 527

Constant, Benjamin 458

Constantine, Grand Duke of Russia 190, 196, 309, 310, 311, 313, 340, 369, 531

Constantinople 19

Continental System 45–6, 101, 172, 532

Cooke, Edward 262

Cotta, Johann Georg von 258

Courland, Duchess of 66, 271, 474

Courland, Duke of 66

Craonne, Battle of (1814) 169

Creevey, Thomas 210

Crimean War 555

Curaçao 208

Czartoryski, Prince Adam Jerzy 160, 353, 410; blueprint for a supranational security system 16, 17; and Congress of Vienna 317, 335–6, 376–7, 416; downfall of 18–19; hanged in effigy 557; and London talks 212; and Poland 163, 212, 416, 531, 556; relationship with Empress Elizabeth 19, 410, 411, 483

Dalberg, Emerich von, duc de 174–5, 272, 425, 438, 477

Davout, Marshal Louis-Nicholas 453

Demerara 207, 208

Denmark 6, 44, 101, 225–7, 387–9, 414, 468, 481; and Britain 102; declaration of war on Sweden 148; joins Coalition 148, 225; map 226; objectives at Congress 297–8; signs new alliance with Napoleon and declares war on Russia (1813) 101–2, 103; treaty with France (1813) 82; and Treaty of Kiel 148, 225, 227, 387–8; *see also* Frederick VI of Denmark, King

Denon, baron Dominique Vivant 192, 193, 490, 513

Dijon 171, 183

Dresden 59, 92, 94, 113

Dresden, Battle of 92, 95

Dupont, General 453

Duroc, Marshal Géraud Christophe 63

Edgcumbe, Lady Emma Sophia 137, 206

Elba 427, 449; Napoleon's exile to 182, 183, 186–7

Elgin Marbles 99

Elizabeth, Empress of Russia 19, 273, 350–1, 353, 410, 483

Engestrom, Lars von 227

Erlon, General Drouet d' 459

Essequibo 207, 208

Esterhazy, Countess Marie 375

Esterhazy, Prince 276, 279

Esterhazy-Roisin, Princess 352

Etruria, Maria Luisa of Spain, Queen of 256–7, 268, 280, 431, 467

Eugène, marquis, then prince, de Beauharnais, Viceroy of Italy 49, 52, 91, 112, 119, 132, 185, 189–90, 232, 233, 248–9, 299–300, 311, 350, 380, 431, 468, 475, 552

Eynard, Anna 312, 313, 321, 338, 354, 380

Eynard, Jean-Gabriel 332, 339, 344, 357, 370, 380, 393–4, 398

family trees 111

Federal Act (1815) 480

Ferdinand IV, King of Naples 120, 230, 257, 270, 457, 466, 527–8
Ferdinand VII, King of Spain 121, 228–9, 248, 436–7, 545
Fichte, Johann Gottlieb 26, 31
Final Act (1815) 484–6, 528, 529, 537
Finland 20, 44, 101, 225, 276
Fismes 169
Fontainebleau, Treaty of (1814) 182, 183–4, 185, 189, 256, 430, 449, 450
Fouché, Joseph, duc d'Otrante 119, 458–60, 472, 489, 494, 520
France: admitted to the Quadruple Alliance 543–4; alliance with Austria 13, 35, 38–9, 50–1, 58, 76; alliance with Prussia 13, 30; alliance with Russia (1807) 19, 45, 47; alliances with Denmark (1813) 82, 101–2, 103; allied troops in 543; armistice signed with allies (1814) 185–6; border with Switzerland issue 525; Bourbons swept from power (1830) 555; Britain's perception of 41; coalitions against 45; and Congress of Vienna *see* Talleyrand; declaration of war on by Prussia (1813) 31, 50; demands for return of works of art by allies 511–14; entering of Prussians into Paris and wreaking of revenge after defeat of Napoleon 490–1, 494; fall of Richelieu's government and replacement of by *ultras* 547; formation of provisional government under Talleyrand after deposition of Napoleon 180–2; lack of success of Bourbon rule and discontent with 451–4; Louis XVIII becomes new ruler 187–8; map 127; objectives of at Congress 270; reinstallation of Louis XVIII after defeat of Napoleon 489; and return of Bourbons issue 144–5, 146, 153, 170, 171, 172, 174, 179; revenge desired by Royalists after Waterloo 494–5; and Saxony 270; treatment of military by Bourbon regime 453; treaty of alliance with Austria and Britain (1815) 392–3; and Treaty of Paris (1814) 197–9, *198*; Treaty of Paris discussions and signing

of 499–511, 516–18, 523–4; war with Russia (1790s) 17; *see also* Napoleon I; Talleyrand
Francis I of Austria, Emperor 57, 74, 126, 186, 216, 234, 368, 403, 437; and Alexander 329; alliance with France 13, 35–6; and Bourbon issue 145; character 57; and Congress of Vienna 276, 303, 313, 362, 389; death 566; and Italy 539, 540; and Napoleon 13, 152, 449; and Poland 418; popularity of 313
Franco-Prussian war (1870) 555
Frankfurt 122–3
'Frankfurt proposals' 126–8, 135, 149, 157
Frederick Augustus of Saxony, King 51–2, 53, 113–15, 536
Frederick II, King of Prussia ('the Great') 24, 28
Frederick VI of Denmark, King 101–3, 255, 297–9, 309, 387–8, 481–2
Frederick William III of Prussia, King 6–7, 26, 28–31, 69–70, 126, 163, 534, 535; affair with Countess Zichy 313; and Alexander 29, 30–1, 292; and Alexander's Polish plans 278; alliance with Napoleon 13, 28, 30; character 28; and Congress of Vienna 276, 297, 313, 334, 405, 482; death 535, 566; and London talks 208–9; in Paris 191; signs Treaty of Kalisch with Alexander (1813) 31–2; and Stein 26, 27, 28, 29
French Empire 6
French Revolution 36, 39, 436
Friedland, Russian defeat at (1806) 19, 45

Gagern, Hans Christoph von 268, 370
Galitzine, Prince Aleksandr 16, 533
Gardes d'Honneur 10
Gartner, Baron von 246
Geneva 300, 424, 426, 427, 525–6
Genoa 235, 300, 551, 564; incorporation of into Sardinia 341–2, 430
Gentz, Friedrich von 39, 41, 66, 80, 142, 337, 550–1; background 55–6; and Congress of Vienna 269, 282–3, 288, 304–6, 366, 370, 382–3, 385, 481, 484–5; death 565; in Paris 507, 526; and Prague

Gentz, Friedrich von – *cont.*
congress 87; on Talleyrand 68; verdict
on Congress 550–1; view of peace
settlement terms offered to France
523–4
George IV of Great Britain, King 561; as
Prince Regent 144, 145–6, 154, 205, 209,
211, 213, 215, 369, 414, 505, 511–12, 521,
522
Germany 6, 20–1, 97, 108–12, 195, 237,
241–6, 540–1, 558, 568; and Breslau
convention (1813) 33–4; call for separate
state 25–6, 27, 31, 109, 563; Catholic
Church in 436, 438–9; clamouring of
rights from various parties 243–4,
246–7, 257–8, 318; collapse of
Napoleon's power-structure in 118–19;
Confederation 527; constitutional issue
241–6; disappointment over Congress
534; discussions on at Congress 317–18,
386, 432–41, 467–9, 478–80; and Final
Act of Congress 537; Hardenberg's plan
for 245–6, 318; Karlsbad Decrees 540–1;
'liberating' of by Russians/Prussians 33,
37, 116–17, 118–19, 122–3; and
'mediatised' princes 243, 245, 247, 257;
and Metternich 97, 109–10, 112, 239,
242–3, 246, 540–1; Metternich's
negotiations to persuade German
princes to become Austrian allies
112–13, 117; and Napoleon 20–1, 118;
plan for new Bund 241, 243; post-
Congress 533–7; and Prussia 21, 24, 216,
239, 534–5; and Prussia-Saxony issue
348- 9, 402, 440; putting case forward
by princes after liberation of 123–4;
scramble between Russia, Prussia and
Austria for influence in 110; signing of
Federal Act at Congress (1815) 480; and
Standesherren issue 243- 4, 245, 257;
status of Jews 560–1; territorial
arrangements for 239–40
Gitschin, castle at 64, 66
Gneisenau, General August Wilhelm 25,
26, 126, 535
Goethe, Johann Wolfgang 117
Görres, Joseph von 245, 536–7, 538

Grassini, Giuseppina 404
Greece 547–8, 549
Grenoble 456
Grey, Charles, 2nd Earl 212
Grolmann, General Karl von 406–7
Grossbeeren, Battle of 92
Grotius, Hugo: *De Iure Belli et Pacis*
220
Grouchy, General Émmanuel de 488
Guadeloupe 45, 143–4, 208, 225, 389
Guizot, François 172

Habsburg, house of 35, 36, *36*
Hager, Baron 251, 252, 278, 301, 301–2, 476,
559
Hague, The 138, 141, 189, 206, 262
Hamburg 73
Hamilton, Sir William 513
Hanau, Battle of 118
Hanover 42, 55, 76, 222, 239, 392, 402, 414
Hardenberg, Baron, later Prince, Karl
August von 33–4, 54–5, 69, 71, 126, 183,
195, 241, 265, 266, 290, 334, 336, 358,
469, 493; attempt to prise apart Austro-
Franco-British front 394–5; background
and career 54–5; character 263; and
claim for Mainz 318, 323–4; German
issue 318, 435; death 565; and German
issue 109, 244, 245–6; and London talks
210–11, 214; and Metternich 55, 58; in
Paris 191; and Poland 195; and Prague
congress 85; proposal of conditions for
negotiations with Napoleon 72–3; and
Prussia's territorial demands 263, 267,
292–3; and restoration of Bourbons
issue 473; and Russian western frontier
issue 359–60, 361; and Saxony-Prussia
issue 260- 2, 267–8, 364–5, 389–90, 391,
394, 406–7; and Treaty of Paris (1814)
202; and Treaty of Paris negotiations
(1815) 501–2; under strain 390
Hatzfeldt, Prince 13, 30
Hazlitt, William 559
Hegel, Georg Wilhelm Friedrich 56
Hertford, Lady 213
Hesse-Darmstadt, Prince of 378, 476
Hobbes, Thomas 220

Hogendorp, Gijsbert van 140

Holland 6, 138–40, 392; and Castlereagh's conditions for peace 143, 144, 166; fixing of frontiers of at Congress 414; incorporation of Belgium into 215; joins British-Austro-French alliance 402; and Napoleon 138; and Prussia 502; *see also* Netherlands

Holland, Henry Vassal Fox, Lord 212, 449–50

Holy Roman Empire: dissolution of by Napoleon (1806) 35, 39, 243

Howden, Lord 565

Humboldt, Alexander von 69

Humboldt, Wilhelm von 25, 26, 69, 107–8, 124; and Châtillon congress 158–9; and Congress of Vienna 266, 310, 332–3, 358, 480–1; and German issue 244–5, 441, 479; and Hardenberg 390; and London talks 215; on Louvre 514; post-Congress career 536; and Prague congress 85, 87

'Hundred Days, the' 455–69

Illyria 6, 58, 60, 73, 88, 232, 538, 539

Ionian islands 429, 524–5, 542

Isabey, Jean-Baptiste 375

Italy 6, 229–37, 257, 563, 568–9; and Austria 232, 234, 429–30, 538–9; and Britain 229–30, 231–2, 233; and Castlereagh's conditions for peace 143, 166; discussion of at Congress 429–32, 466–7, 538; French rule 233, 539; independence issue 160, 230- 2, 233; map 231; post-Congress 538–9; resentment of Austrian rule 539–40

Ivernois, Sir Francis d' 300

Jackson, George 70, 95, 166, 172

Jahn, Friedrich 25

Jena, Battle of 26, 45, 126

Jews 258, 379, 560–1, 568

John, Archduke of Austria 58

Jomini, General Antoine Henri 94

Joseph II, Holy Roman Emperor 57, 436

Josephine, Empress of France 188, 189

Jung Stilling, Johann Heinrich 274, 351, 491

Kalisch, Treaty of (1813) 31–2, 35, 45, 51, 112, 221, 224

Kant, Immanuel: *On Perpetual Peace* 220

Karamzin, Nikolay Mikhailovich 533

Karlsbad Decrees 540–1

Katzbach 94

Kiel, Treaty of (1814) 148, 225, 227, 297–8, 387–8

Kissinger, Henry 553–4, 558

Kleist, Heinrich von 25, 90

Knesebeck, Colonel 30–1

Körner, Theodor 25

Kościuszko, Tadeusz 196

Kotzebue, August von 540

Kraków 359, 360, 361, 363, 391, 532, 557

Krüdener, Baroness Julie von 491–2, 509, 510, 520, 522, 538

Kulm, Battle of 92, 93, 94, 103

Kutuzov, Field Marshal Prince Mikhail Iliaronovich 27, 33

La Besnardère, comte de 272, 484, 485

La Harpe, Frédéric César de 105, 134, 275, 424

La Rothière, defeat of Napoleon at 153

La Tour du Pin, comte de 272

Labedoyère, General de 456, 498

Labrador, Don Pedro Gomez Havela, Marqués de 280–1, 282, 341–2; background 280; and Order of Malta 428; and precedence issue 421; priorities at Congress 280; refuses to sign Final Act 485; and slave trade issue 412, 413; view of Talleyrand 290

Lafayette, Marie Jospeh Motier, marquis de 451

Laibach (Ljubljana) congress (1821) 547

Lamb, Frederick 239, 477

Lambert, Seraphine 311

Landsturm 28

Landwehr 28

Langeron, General comte de 61, 90

Lauenburg, ceded to Prussia by Hanover 414, 485

Lavalette, General de 457, 458, 498

Lawrence, Sir Thomas 543

Lebzeltern, Count Louis-Joseph 56

Leibniz, Gottfried Wilhelm 220
Leipzig 93; Battle of 113–14, 115, 118, 321;
　Prussia's claim to 405, 406, 407
Leopold of Sicily, Prince 482
Lewin, Rahel 56
Lieven, Christoph Heinrich von, Count,
　later Prince 154, 204
Lieven, Dorothea, Countess, later Princess
　211, 213, 543, 548–9, 559
Ligne, prince de 306, 337, 375–6
Liguria 6
Lithuania 11
Liverpool, Robert Banks Jenkinson, 2nd
　Earl of 75, 157, 170, 205–6, 227, 262, 342,
　343, 346–7, 367–8, 372–3, 403, 506, 512,
　521–2
London talks 204–17
Louis XVI of France, King 36, 399
Louis XVIII of France, King 194, 246, 248,
　444, 471, 473, 489, 501, 505; and
　Alexander 180, 188, 472, 518–19;
　character 452; deposed by Napoleon
　456–7; in exile 187; lack of success of
　rule 451–4; reinstallation of after
　Napoleon's defeat (1814) 187–8;
　reinstallation of after Napoleon's defeat
　(1815) 489; and reinstatement of
　Bourbons issue 144, 145, 153, 179, 180;
　and terms offered by Treaty of Paris
　(1815) 518–19; and Wellington 347
Louisiana 229, 280
Louvre 192–3, 511, 512, 513–14
Löwenhielm, Count Charles Axel 388, 477
Löwenstern, Count Otto von 400, 404
Lübeck 73
Lützen, Battle of (1813) 52, 53, 62
Lützow, Adolf von 31
Luxembourg 394, 414, 511
Lyon 169

Macdonald, Marshal Jacques Étienne 10,
　91, 92
Madison, President James 496
Maievsky, Colonel 533
Mainz 197, 267, 318, 323, 360, 439, 467–8,
　485
Maistre, Joseph de 256

Malet, General Claude François de 4–5
Malta 230, 428, 541
Malta, Order of 428
Marches, Papal province of 430, 467
Maret 76, 89, 169–70
Maria Carolina, Queen 230
Marie-Louise, Empress of France 13, 151,
　249–50, 268, 303, 474; evacuation from
　Paris 176; invention of plot to escape
　from Vienna 475; marriage to Napoleon
　35, 39, 50, 58; and Napoleon's escape
　474–5; and Parma 256, 257, 430–1, 432,
　467; separated from Napoleon on exile
　of 186–7
Marmont, Marshal Auguste de 169, 180–1
Marseille 495
Martineau, Harriet 561; *History of the
　Thirty Years' Peace* 559
Maximilian of Bavaria, King 112–13, 119,
　120, 255, 299, 536, 552
Mediatisation, Act of (1803) 21, 426
Metternich, Count, later Prince, Klemens
　Lothar von xiii, 13, 35, 37–8, 55, 64,
　537–8, 564–5; affair with Countess
　Lieven 543, 559–60; and Alexander 98,
　117, 132, 135, 148, 154, 163, 216, 320; and
　Archduke John's conspiracy against
　French rule 58; attempt to get Denmark
　to join Allies 102; attempt to reimpose
　ancien régime by force 559, 560;
　background and career 38–9; and
　Bavaria 468; and Bourbon cause 145;
　and Britain 71, 100–1; and Castlereagh
　48, 98, 103, 142–3, 246; and
　Castlereagh's 'grand design' proposal
　130; character and attributes 37–8;
　conditions for peace 59–60, 72–3, 88,
　126–8; ; dealings and animosity
　between Alexander and 277, 278, 320,
　326, 330–1, 334, 362–3, 401; declaration
　of war on France 88–9; on discomforts
　of war 108; distracted by Wilhelmina
　affair 319–21, 323, 349, 383, 410; and
　'Frankfurt proposals' 126–8, 135; and
　German issue 318, 386, 432, 434, 467,
　479; and Germany 97, 109–10, 112, 239,
　242–3, 246, 540–1; intelligence network

83–5, 250–2; and Italy 429, 430, 564, 538–9, 540, 563; and London visit/talks 203, 211, 215–16; loss of popularity 348; love affair with Wilhelmina 79–80, 87, 89, 95, 116, 166, 189, 215, 239, 283, 319, 507, 543; love affairs 38; low spirits and strain felt 349, 356; made Prince 115; marriage 238–9; on mysticism 537, 537–8; and Naples 546; and Napoleon 39, 58; and Napoleon's escape 442–3, 448, 460; organising of balls 287, 337; in Paris 191, 506–7; and Polish issue 162, 364; and Prague congress 83, 86–9, 96; and Prince Regent 215; procedure issue 264, 265–6, 282, 290; and Prussia-Saxony issue 318–19, 323, 325, 348, 360–1, 402–3; and Quadruple Alliance 545; and Russian western frontier issue 361; secret negotiations to persuade German princes to become Austrian allies 112–13, 117; State Chancellery of 83–4, 250; and Switzerland 134, 134–5, 154, 422; talks with Napoleon over proposed peace negotiations and agreement 76–8, 80–1; travels through Italy 538–9; and treaty with Bavaria 113, 116; and Treaty of Paris (1814) 201; unpopularity 58, 403; view of treatment of France after Waterloo 504; view of war 166; wanting to mediate peace between France and Russia and negotiations with allies over 39–40, 50, 53–4, 59–60, 64- 6, 72–5

Metternich, Leonore (wife) 38, 238–9

Mincio, Battle of (1814) 232

monasteries 436

Montagu, William 138

Montesquiou, comtesse 475

Montesquiou-Fézensac, Anatole de 475

Moreau, General Jean Victor 94

Morel, Josephine 311, 337

Müller, Adam 242

Münster, Count Ernst von 110, 164, 246, 376, 402, 406, 444, 480, 500

Murat, Caroline, Queen of Naples 38, 120

Murat, Joachim, King of Naples 91, 527–9; alliance with Austria (1814) 232; and Congress of Vienna 257; declaration of as an outlaw and defeat of by Austrian forces 466; and escape of Napoleon 466; France and Britain want removed from Naples 270, 289, 431–2; and Italy 232, 233; and Naples 430, 431; and Napoleon 3, 119, 528; secret negotiations with Austria 100, 119–20; seen as dangerous threat by allies 235–6; trial and execution (1815) 529; war against Russia 10, 11, 49

Musée Napoléon (Paris) 192–3

mysticism 537

Naples 6, 119–20, 232, 430, 431, 547; revolution (1820) 545–6; secret treaty with Austria (1815) 545–6; *see also* Murat, Joachim

Napoleon I, Emperor xiii; abdication after Waterloo 488; abolishing of Holy Roman Empire 35, 39, 243; alliance with Prussia 13, 28, 30; alliance with Russia (1807) 19, 20, 45; armistice 69, 71; army of 91; attempt to represent return to power as internal French matter 460; attempted coup against by Malet 4–5; attitude towards of Alexander 17; and Britain 40, 90, 144; capture of after Waterloo and exile to St Helena 496–7; changes brought about by 458; collapse of power-structure in Germany 118–19; death 561; defeat at Battle of Nations 114, 115, 118; defeat at Waterloo 487–8; deposition of 180–1; escape from Elba 442–51; exile of to Elba 182, 183, 186–7; fate of outlined in Treaty of Fontainebleau 182, 185, 450; and 'Frankfurt proposals' 128, 135; gathering of support during march to Paris 455–7; and Germany 20–1, 118; and Holland 138; Hundred Days 455–69; leaves Russian campaign for Paris 1–2, 3–5; Metternich's view of 39; power of before Russian campaign 6; and Prague congress 86, 90; preparation for war against by allies 461–3, 464, 470–2; and Prussia 13, 24–5, 26–7, 28- 9, 30;

Napoleon I, Emperor – *cont.*
  resumption of power 457; road to
  Waterloo 470–86; rumours of plots to
  remove from Elba and to assassinate
  449–50; and Russian campaign 2–3, 4,
  6, 7, 10–11, 12, 20, 27, 35–6, 44, 49–50,
  532; sense of insecurity 5; and
  Switzerland 133; and Talleyrand 474;
  views of peace with Russia and
  Metternich's peace proposals 11–12, 14,
  49, 59–61, 64, 76–9, 80–1, 82–3, 128;
  and war against allies 51, 52, 59, 61–3,
  82, 90–4, 118–21, 151–3, 155–6, 169–70,
  173
Napoleon III, Emperor 558
Narbonne, Louis, comte de 13, 50, 59,
  64–5, 85, 86, 119
Naryshkina, Maria Antonovna 351
nations, rights of 224
Neipperg, Count Adam Adalbert von 187,
  249
Nenadovic, Mateja 379
Nesselrode, Count Charles von 55, 56, 58,
  60, 65, 67–8, 85, 132, 177–8, 192, 263,
  266, 316
Nesselrode, Countess 211
Netherlands 131, 138–9, 206–8; map *139*;
  see also Holland
Ney, Marshal Michel 92–3, 456, 498
Nicholas, Tsar 556
Noailles, comte Alexis de 272
Norway 44, 45, 102, 103, 148, 225, 227,
  565
Nostitz, Karl von 351, 397–8
Novosiltsov, Count Nikolai 17

Oldenburg, George, Duke of 468–9
Orange, Hereditary Prince of (later King
  William II of Holland) 139–40, 205–6,
  247, 505
Orange, Sovereign Prince of (later King
  William I of Holland) 138–9, 140, 206,
  370, 414
Order of Malta 428–9, 551
Orléans, duc d' (later Louis Phillipe, King
  of the French) 472, 555–6
Orlov, Count 177

Orthez 169
Otto, Count 13
Ottoman Empire 415, 547
Oudinot, Marshal Nicolas Charles 92
Oźarowski, General Adam 362

Palffy, Count 398
Palmella, Conde de 281, 411–12, 421
Papal provinces 6, 14, 235, 236, 257, 268,
  409
Paris 188–92, 499; entry into by Louis
  XVIII 188; evacuation of Marie-Louise
  and Regency Council 175; Musée
  Napoléon 192–3; reconvening of
  Congress at 499; Russian advance on
  and capitulation of 175–9
Paris Commune 555
Paris, Treaty of (1814) 197- 203, 241, 261,
  265, 270, 300, 409, 423, 460, 513
Paris, Treaty of (1815) *503*, 529 negotiations
  on 516–29
Parma 256, 268, 303, 432, 467
Paul I of Russia, Tsar 16
Penn, William 220; *Essay towards the
  Present and Future Peace of Europe* 220
Périgord, Dorothée, comtesse de 271–2,
  321, 336, 447, 474, 484, 515, 566
Peterloo Massacre (1817) 546
Pichler, Caroline 31, 304
Pictet, Edmond 300, 313, 502, 504, 525
Piedmont 6, 235
Pilat, Josef von 242
Piombino, Prince of 256, 427
Pitt, William (the Younger) 17, 43, 45, 167
Pius VII, Pope 14, 236–7, 409, 430, 437,
  467, 511
Planta, Joseph 138, 262
Platov, General Matviei Ivanovich 210
Plesswitz, armistice of 63, 65, 67, 69, 75, 85
Poland 7, 54, 212, 240, 266, 563;
  Alexander's plan to create kingdom of
  under his rule and discussion of at
  Congress 18, 19, 20, 160, 162–3, 240,
  274- 5, 277–8, 314–17, 324, 325, 329–30,
  334–7, 360, 362, 363–4, 389–90, 416–18,
  483; constitution of new kingdom of
  (1815) 531–2; and Convention of

Reichenbach 160; Hardenberg's plan for 195–6; map *161*; nationalism 563; and Russia 18, 531, 564–5; settlement of at Congress *408*; secession from Russia and incorporation back into (1830) 556

Poniatowski, Prince Jozef Anton 11, 50, 54, 65

Portugal 45, 281, 413, 543

Posen, grand duchy of 557–8

Potyomkin, Prince Grigory Aleksandrovich 258–9

Pozzo di Borgo, Carl'Andrea 68, 105, 113, 126, 135, 136, 138, 248, 275, 315–16, 317

Pradt, Dominique de 175, 562

Prague, congress of 83, 85–90

Prussia 6–7, 21, 24, 162, 194, 216, 222, 225, 534–5, 567; acquisitions 534; advance on by Russia 27–8, 29, 31; agreement on territorial possessions and frontiers at Congress 414; alliance with France 13, 30; and armistice 69; and Battle of Waterloo 489, 491, 493; and Britain 41, 42; ceding of Swedish Pomerania to 388, 534; and Congress of Vienna *see* Hardenberg, Baron; declaration of war on France (1813) 31, 50, 57; defeat by Napoleon in Saxony 52–3; defection of Yorck from French ranks and signing of alliance with Russia 13, 28–9, 55; entering of Paris after Napoleon's defeat and wrecking of revenge 490–1, 494; and French reparations issue 194, 202; and Germany 21, 24, 216, 239, 534–5; growth of 24; and Holland 502; insecurity and fragility of 24, 241, 263; map *22–3*, *535*; and Napoleon 13, 24–5, 26–7, 28–9, 30; Napoleon's escape and campaign against 369, 461, 462, 470–1; and Polish issue 195; and prospects of war (1814) 369; reforms 25, 26; and Saxony issue 240–1, 267- 8, 323–4, 348, 360–2, 364–5, 371–2, 376–8, 377, 379–80, 391, 394–5, 396–7, 402–3, 542; solving of Saxony issue at Congress 405–10, *408*; treaty with Britain (1813) 72; and Treaty of Paris (1814) 202; and Treaty of Paris discussions (1815) 508–9,

523; treaty with Russia (1805) 221; treaty with Russia (Kalisch) (1813) 31–2, 35, 45, 51, 112; wants France punished after Waterloo 501–2

Pufendorf, Samuel 220

Quadruple Alliance (1814) 529–30, 541, 542, 543–5, 567

Radziwiłł, Prince Antoni 483

Ramel, General 495

Razumovsky, Count Andrei Kirilovich 147, 156, 304, 321, 384, 389

Razumovsky Palace, fire 383–4

Rechberg, Count 434

Regency Council 175

Reichenbach, Convention of (1813) 74, 75, 96, 160, 334, 336

Reinhard, Landamann 121, 134, 424, 425

restitution, principle of 222, 224

Rheims 169

Rheinbund (Confederation of the Rhine) 6, 21, 39, 73, 88, 108, 109, *242*, 243

Rheinische Merkur 535, 537

Rhineland 6, 21

Richelieu, Armand du Plessis, duc de 519, 520, 523, 543, 547

Richter, Jean Paul 56, 357

Ried, Treaty of (1813) 113, 267, 434, 439

Robinson, Frederick (later Lord Goderich) 138

Rosenkrantz, Baron Niels 102, 346, 368

Rousseau, Jean-Jacques 220

Rügen 225, 298, 414

Rumiantsev, Prince Nikolay Petrovich 67

Russia 225, 532–3, 567; advance into Prussia 27–8, 29, 31; alliance with Britain (1812) 44; alliance with France (1807) 19, 45, 47; army 532, 542; and Britain 17–18, 41–2, 71; and Congress of Vienna *see* Alexander, Tsar; economic crisis 532; invasion of by France and war with 2–3, 4, 6, 7, 10–11, 12, 20, 27, 35–6, 44, 49–50, 61, 532; and Ionian islands 524; and Napoleon's escape and campaign against 461, 462; and Netherlands 207; and Poland 531,

Russia – *cont.*
564–5; and prospects of war (1814) 367, 368, 369; and Sweden 44; treaty with Britain (1813) 72; treaty with Prussia (1805) 221; treaty with Prussia (Kalisch) (1813) 31–2, 35, 45, 51; war with France (1790s) 17; western frontier proposal at Congress of Vienna 359; *see also* Alexander, Tsar

Rzewuska, Countess Rozalia 79

Sagan, Wilhelmina, Duchess of 66, 189, 258, 319, 383, 410; affair with Stewart 482; affair with Windischgraetz 80, 89, 319; and Alexander 327, 330–1; background and character 79; death 565; ending of affair with Metternich 319–20; and Lamb 477; Metternich's love affair with 79–80, 87, 89, 95, 116, 166, 189, 215, 239, 283, 319–21, 323, 349, 383, 410, 507, 543; in Vienna 258, 304, 355

Saint-Aignan, baron de 126, 128
St Gallen 300
Saint-Marsan, comte de 13, 30
St Pierre, Abbé de 220
Saint-Priest, General 169
Sand, Karl 540
Sardinia 256, 341–2, 539, 564
Saxe-Coburg, Duke of 299, 311, 394, 468
Saxe-Coburg-Saalfeld, Duchess of 383
Saxe-Weimar, Duke of 195, 428, 468
Saxony 6, 51–2, 113–14, 160, 162, 293, 318–19; British public opinion on issue of 343; and France 270; handing over of to Prussia by Russians 340, 348–9; invasion of by Russia/Prussia 51–2; and Polish issue 195, 240; and Prussia issue 239, 240–1, 267–8, 296, 360–2, 364–5, 371–2, 379–80, 391, 394–5, 396–7, 402–3; solving of Prussia issue at Congress 405–10, *408*
Saxony, King of 270
Scharnhorst, General Gerhard Johann 25, 53
Schlegel, Friedrich 56, 242
Schleiermacher, Friedrich 56

Schoeler, General 292
Schönbrunn, Treaty of (1809) 40
Schönholz, Count Friedrich von 254, 286
Schroeder, Paul W.: *The Transformation of European Politics* 554
Schulenburg, Count Friedrich von der 240
Schwarz, Madame 302
Schwarzenberg, Field Marshal Karl Philipp, Prince von 11, 36, 50–1, 54, 60, 64, 90, 94, 132, 155, 169, 171, 405, 471
Serbs 379
Seufert, Caroline Petronelle 309, 482
Shelley, Frances, Lady 214
Shishkov, Admiral Aleksandr Semionovich 27, 67, 107, 122, 125, 202
Sicily 230, 236
Silber, Police Chief 251
Silesia 24, 50, 534
Six Acts (1819) 546
slave trade 199–201, 208, 211–12, 237, 523, 568; discussion of at Congress 346, 347, 411–14; and Treaty of Paris 199–200
Smith, Sir Sydney 381–2
'souls' 386, 467, 561–2
Soult, Marshal Nicolas Jean 169, 185
Spain 6, 545–6, 549; abolishing of constitution by Ferdinand 228–9; and Britain 6, 228–9; Catholic Church 436–7; defeat of French army by British 82; dispute with Portugal 543; *guerrilla* 224; military mutiny (1820) 545; priorities at Congress 280; and slave trade issue 412, 413
Stackelberg, Count 56, 268, 356
Stadion, Count Johann Philipp 57, 58, 59, 156, 157, 330
Staël, Anne Louise Germaine de 105, 188
Statistical Committee (Congress of Vienna) 397, 420
status quo ante (of 1792): returning to 222–3
Stein, Karl Heinrich vom 25–8, 31, 124, 126, 500, 536; background 25; on Castlereagh 347–8; and Congress of Vienna 349; establishing of society for study of German history 536; and Metternich 135; in Paris 192; plans

for a unified German state 25–6, 27, 28, 29, 97, 108–9, 113, 116, 244, 245, 433–4, 435–6; verdict on Congress 551

Stettin 105

Stewart, Sir Charles, later Lord 48, 61, 70, 72, 75, 93, 100, 122, 125–6, 135–6, 164–5, 190, 261, 345, 400, 425, 482–3

Stockholm, Treaty of (1813) 44–5

Stuart, Sir Charles 261, 506, 559

Sturdza, Roksandra, Countess Edling 274, 344, 345, 351, 355, 411, 491

Sully, duc de: *Grand Dessein* 220

Surinam 208

Sweden 6; and Britain 41, 42; declaration of war on by Denmark (1813) 103; and Guadeloupe 208; joins coalition against Napoleon (1812) 225; and Norway 103, 225, 227, 565; and Russia 44; and Treaty of Kiel 388–9; Treaty of Stockholm with Britain (1813) 44–5, 227

Swedish Pomerania 14, 225, 298, 388, 485, 534

Swiss Confederation 133, 424, 425

Switzerland 6, 133–5, 502, 504; border between France and 525; discussion of at Congress 386, 421–8; map *422*; and Napoleon 133; and neutrality 121, 134, 524; popular risings in (1847) 555; and Treaty of Paris 201, 423

Talleyrand-Périgord, Charles-Maurice de, prince de Bénévent xiii–xiv, 12, 68, 173–81, 189, 221, 261, 269–71, 280–2, 289–92, 320–1, 473–4, 483–4, 489, 500; and abolition of slave trade issue 413; background 173; and Bourbon issue 174, 175, 179, 180, 182; character and qualities 173- 4, 290; builds up following among minor German princes 291; and Castlereagh 379–80, 387; dealings with Alexander 283–5, 324–6, 367; death 566; focus on legitimacy principle and international law 270–1, 290, 291, 329–30, 372, 399, 409; forms provisional government after deposition of Napoleon 180–2; household at

Congress 271–2; and Italy 431; measures introduced at Congress 516; motives for attending Congress 269; and Napoleon's escape 447–8, 473–4, 484; objectives 270, 291; and Polish issue 317, 325, 329–30; and principality of Benevento 527, 528; and procedure issue 282, 283, 286, 288, 290; and proposed terms of Treaty of Paris (1815) 515, 517–18; relationship with Dorothée 484, 515–16, 566; resignation and life after Congress 518, 520, 566; and Saxony-Prussia issue 371- 2, 379–80, 399, 409; and Swiss question 425, 426; talks with Alexander over post-war political arrangement of France 179- 80; *toilette* 178; and treaty of alliance between France, Britain and Austria 392–3; and Treaty of Paris (1814) 197, 199; weakening of position 516

Tatishchev, Count 205

Thorn 266, 275, 360, 361, 391, 406

Toeplitz 93–4, 95, 98, 99, 100, 103, 107, 540

Toeplitz, Treaties of 93–6, 100, 112, 160, 334, 336

Tolentino, Treaty of (1797) 96, 513

Trafalgar, Battle of (1805) 45

Trautmannsdorff, Count Ferdinand von 251, 252

Troppau protocol 546–7, 558

Troyes 155

Tugendbund 25, 402, 563

Turkey 44

Tuscany 6

Tyrol 58

United States: peace with Britain (1814) 392; war with Britain 46, 342, 366

Vandamme, General Dominique Joseph 92

Vattel, Emeric de 220

Verona, congress (1822) 548–9

Victor Emmanuel of Savoy, King of Sardinia 235, 430, 525, 563

Vienna 13

Vilna, defeat of French by Russians at (1812) 11, 15
Vitrolles, baron de 170–1, 174, 175
Volkonskaya, Princess Zinaida 70–1, 116, 122
Volkonsky, Prince 309
Voltaire, François Marie Arouet de 220
Vorster, Abbot 300, 424, 427

Wales, Princess of 248
Walmoden, General von 94
Warsaw, grand duchy of 6, 20, 24, 54, 60, 73, 96, 160, 266, 276, 335
Waterloo, Battle of (1815) 487–9, 493, 499; road to 470–86
Waterloo Despatch 488–9, 491
Wellesley, General Arthur *see* Wellington, Duke of
Wellesley, Sir Henry 228
Wellington, Arthur Wellesley, Duke of xiv, 6, 43, 82, 171, 185, 228, 261, 347, 366, 464; ambassador in Paris 347; and Congress of Vienna 403, 404–5; defeats Napoleon at Waterloo 487–8, 489; and Louis XVIII 347, 489; and Napoleon's escape 448; in Paris 506; preparations for campaign against Napoleon 461, 470–1; and return of works of art issue 513; and slave trade issue 200–1, 347; and Spain 228–9; view of Alexander 461;

view of future of France after Waterloo 501
Werner, Zacharias 400–1
Wessenberg, Johann Philipp, Baron von 40, 41, 165, 425
Westphalia 6
Westphalia, Treaty of (1648) 133, 220–1
Wilberforce, William 200, 211
Wilson, General Robert 232–3, 248–9
Wilson, President Woodrow 553
Windischgraetz, Alfred von 80, 89, 189, 319, 340
Winzingerode, Count 52, 434
Wolters, Josephine 309
Wrede, Prince 369, 434, 467
Württemberg 6, 21, 242, 318, 433, 434, 462, 536
Württemberg, King Frederick I of 124–5, 243, 246, 255, 310, 313, 381, 434–5, 536, 552
Württemberg, Prince Royal of (later King William I of) 247–8, 308, 367, 477

Yorck von Wartemburg, General Hans David 13, 28–9, 55, 90
Ypsilantis, Count Alexandros 547

Zajaçzek, General Jósef 531
Zichy, Countess Julie 308, 313, 331
Zichy, Countess Molly 304, 483